THE RULE OF ST. BENEDICT
In Latin and English with Notes

THE RULE OF ST. BENEDICT
In Latin and English with Notes

Editor
Timothy Fry, O.S.B.

Associate Editors
Imogene Baker, O.S.B.

Timothy Horner, O.S.B.

Augusta Raabe, O.S.B.

Mark Sheridan, O.S.B.

 THE LITURGICAL PRESS
Collegeville, Minnesota

THE LITURGICAL PRESS
Collegeville, Minnesota 56321

Nihil obstat: Joseph C. Kremer, S.T.L., *Censor deputatus.*
Imprimatur: ✠ George H. Speltz, D.D., Bishop of St. Cloud. February 9, 1981.

Printed in the United States of America.

Library of Congress Cataloging in Publication Data

Benedict, Saint, Abbot of Monte Cassino.
  RB 1980: the rule of St. Benedict in Latin and
English with notes.

    Translation of: Regula.
    Bibliography: p.
    Includes indexes.
    1. Benedictines—Rules. I. Fry, Timothy, 1915–
II. Title. III. Title: Rule of St. Benedict.
BX3004.E6 1981   255′.106   81-1013
ISBN 0-8146-1211-3   AACR2
ISBN 0-8146-1220-2 (pbk.)

FOREWORD

In the fall of 1974, presidents of Benedictine federations whose convents and monasteries are located for the most part in Central and North America came together to discuss appropriate ways of marking the fifteen hundredth anniversary of the birth date traditionally ascribed to St. Benedict of Nursia, A.D. 480. Although a variety of ideas surfaced in the course of the meeting, unanimous agreement prevailed concerning the need for a fresh translation into English of the Rule of Benedict.

The renewal of monastic and religious life called for by the Fathers of the Second Vatican Council emphasized "both a constant return to the sources of the whole of the Christian life and to the primitive inspiration of the institutes, and their adaptation to the changed conditions of our time" (*Perfectae Caritatis*, n.2). What better way for Benedictines to return to the sources than through a careful study of the Rule of St. Benedict?

A number of Benedictine scholars were therefore invited to a meeting held at the Convent of St. Benedict, St. Joseph, Minnesota, in August, 1976, under the chairmanship of Rev. Ambrose Wathen, O.S.B. The group concluded that a new edition of the Rule for English readers could be produced, and when it met again in St. Joseph a year later, some of the work was well underway, with various tasks apportioned. An editorial board was chosen, consisting of Rev. Timothy Fry, O.S.B., editor, and Sister Imogene Baker, O.S.B., Rev. Timothy Horner, O.S.B., Sister Augusta Raabe, O.S.B., and Very Rev. Mark Sheridan, O.S.B., as associate editors.

Early in the project, the entire group agreed that far more than simply a translation was needed. If Benedictines were to move into the twenty-first century with a keen awareness of their tradition, if serious study of the Rule of Benedict was to be undertaken in the years ahead, the proposed edition of the Rule would have to contain those scholarly helps that could lead to a deepened understanding of what Benedict taught.

The Benedictine presidents were completely in accord with this kind of thinking. Monasticism in America is a little more than a hundred years of age, and during the early decades much of the energy of the daughters and sons of Benedict was expended on apostolic endeavors. Scholarship was in evidence in certain quarters, but did not penetrate to a study of the Rule of Benedict. Further, the renewed interest in monasticism that arose in the late nineteenth century took time to make itself felt in America, and the pertinent studies that appeared in European languages were not easily available to Benedictines on this side of the Atlantic.

But a new age is upon us, and if ever there was a need for clear understanding of the monastic ethos, the time is now. This edition of the Rule can be a valuable tool if it is well employed, and one can foresee an awakening of interest in the rich monastic tradition represented by St. Benedict and St. Scholastica, given the serious study of the Rule that this volume makes possible.

The presidents are most grateful for the scholarship and dedication of those who undertook the present work. They thank, too, the communities that have generously donated the services of their confreres and sisters to accomplish the task. This volume is dedicated to all who follow the Rule of St. Benedict, with the hope that renewed study of the Rule will lead to a recovery of the riches of the tradition transmitted to us by the Patriarch of Western Monasticism.

RT. REV. MARTIN BURNE, O.S.B.
Chairman, Council of Presidents of Federations
St. Mary's Abbey
Morristown, New Jersey

PREFACE

The progress of Benedictine studies in the past forty to fifty years is in many ways almost as phenomenal as the knowledge explosion that marks this century. Studies of manuscripts, literary sources and relationships, the origin and development of monasticism — all these and other aspects have made possible a fuller understanding of the Rule of St. Benedict. Most of this work has been accessible only to specialists. Our purpose in this volume is to make these developments available to English-speaking monks and nuns for the enrichment of their lives, and to give the general reader a better understanding of the monastic tradition. We do not present a commentary on the Rule, but offer readers a volume that includes a new translation together with the basic tools needed for serious study and analysis of the Rule.

The principal aim of the translation is to present a faithful rendering of the Latin into contemporary English. St. Benedict wrote in the popular Latin of his time, a mixture of classical and later usages. He borrowed frequently from contemporary monastic authors, and sometimes from other sources, and reflects their varying styles. We have tried to show, in the translation and the notes, some awareness of this. St. Benedict liked to use key words both in particular chapters and throughout the Rule. We recognize the significance of these words and have attempted to reflect this in the translation, without, however, following the principle intransigently. For the scriptural passages the Vulgate numbering of chapters is followed; for the psalms the Hebrew numbers are also given. Chapter titles of the Rule have not been translated literally.

The initial translation was made by the group of translators and was then submitted to the stylists. After considerable interaction between them, a version was sent to the editorial board, who, with the help of comments from many others, forged the final version.

The scope of this book

This book is made up of four major divisions: Part I — The Introduction is a history of monasticism, with special attention to its origin in the East and its establishment in the West. This survey enables the reader to see the many elements of the monastic tradition with which St. Benedict was working when he wrote his Rule. There are cross references to the Introduction throughout the volume.

Part II — The text is the core of the book, with the Latin text and English translation on facing pages. (Patristic and Ancient sources are indicated immediately after the Latin text; explanatory notes are given at the bottom of the pages of the translation.) The Latin text is presented with each chapter versified, following the practice established by Anselm Lentini in 1947. This is the first English translation that follows the Lentini versification. Scriptural loci for explicit citations are given only in the English translation; many Scripture allusions can be found with the help of the Scripture Index. Frequent cross references from the explanatory notes to the Introduction, the Appendix, the Thematic Index and the Selected Latin Concordance provide access to more extensive information.

Part III — The Appendix contains longer, expository essays on topics that could not be considered in the explanatory notes. The nature of the subject matter, it was thought, warranted presentation in synthetic form rather than in references at various places in the notes. Again, cross references are made to other parts of the volume.

Part IV contains further study aids, especially in the Thematic Index and the Selected Latin Concordance. Patristic and Scripture indexes and a General Index (proper names and subjects) close the volume. The Thematic Index is a feature unique to this book. On first glance, it appears to be no more than a gathering of pertinent chapter and verse references for ideas or themes in the Rule. But close and purposeful attention to the relationships of concepts will reveal the depth of St. Benedict's spirituality of the monastic life. The Thematic Index, then, provides a skeletal guide; of itself, it is no more than that, but with reflective use it will provide an enrichment seldom realized through any other study aid. For the Latin student, and also for the reader not too familiar with Latin, the Thematic Index and the Selected Latin Concordance can be helpful guides to clusters of words and concepts in the Rule and thereby provide a means of forming a synthesis of St. Benedict's teaching.

Areas of responsibility

In a collaborative work of this kind, it is difficult to say exactly where responsibility for some parts of this volume lies. This is particularly true of the translation. The essays are more readily identifiable, although here again many changes were made at the suggestions of readers in the project. Generally, the procedure was to seek the comments and suggestions of all the members of the project on all parts of the volume. For the record, it should be made clear that the final responsibility for all decisions rests with the board of editors.

The areas of responsibility and the collaborators in the project are as follows:

1. Introduction, Notes, Bibliography, Appendix, Scriptural and Patristic Indexes: Very Rev. Mark Sheridan, O.S.B., St. Anselm's Abbey, Washington, D.C., with Rev. Kenneth Hein, O.S.B., Holy Cross Abbey, Canon City, Colorado; Rev. Timothy Horner, O.S.B., St. Louis Priory, St. Louis, Missouri; Rev. David Hurst, O.S.B., Portsmouth Abbey, Portsmouth, Rhode Island; Rev. Ansgar Kristensen, O.S.B., Mount Saviour Monastery, Pine City, New York; Brother John Leinenweber, O.S.B., Monastery of Christ in the Desert, Abiquiu, New Mexico; Rev. Nathan Mitchell, O.S.B., St. Meinrad Archabbey, St. Meinrad, Indiana; Rev. Claude Peifer, O.S.B., St. Bede Abbey, Peru, Illinois; Rev. Ambrose Wathen, O.S.B., St. Joseph Abbey, St. Benedict, Louisiana.

2. Translators: Rev. Timothy Horner, O.S.B., St. Louis Priory, St. Louis, Missouri, with Rev. Marian Larmann, O.S.B., St. Joseph Abbey, St. Benedict, Louisiana; Very Rev. Matthew Martin, O.S.B., Esquipulas, Guatemala; Rev. Nathan Mitchell, O.S.B., St. Meinrad Archabbey, St. Meinrad, Indiana; Rt. Rev. Jerome Theisen, O.S.B., St. John's Abbey, Collegeville, Minnesota.

3. Stylists: Sister Imogene Baker, O.S.B., Mount St. Scholastica Convent, Atchison, Kansas, with Rev. Timothy Fry, O.S.B., St. Benedict's Abbey, Atchison, Kansas; Sister Raphael Joseph, O.S.B., Immaculate Conception Convent, Ferdinand, Indiana; Sister Elizabeth Mason, O.S.B., Annunciation Priory, Bismarck, North Dakota.

4. Thematic Index, Selected Latin Concordance and General Index: Sister Augusta Raabe, O.S.B., House of Bread, Nanaimo, British Columbia, Canada, with Sister Angelo Haspert, O.S.B., St. Benedict's Convent, St. Joseph, Minnesota; Sister Joan Taylor, O.S.B., Mount St. Scholastica Convent, Atchison, Kansas; Rev. Odo Zimmermann, O.S.B., Monasterio Benedictino del Tepeyac, Tlalnepantla, Mexico.

Specific authors of various parts of the volume are identified by their initials as follows:

Introduction —
The Origins of Monasticism in the Eastern Church, pp. 3–41: MS

Pre-Benedictine Monasticism in the Western Church, pp. 42–64:
CP

The Rule of St. Benedict, pp. 65–112: CP

The Rule in History, pp. 113–141: CP

The Relevance of the Rule Today, pp. 141–151: MS

Patristic Sources and Notes to text of the Rule, pp. 156–297: MS, TH,
JT, CP

Appendix — 1. MS; 2. CP; 3. NM; 4. KH; 5. CP; 6. AK and MS; 7.
MS

Acknowledgments

In the first place, the associate editors and I wish to express our
appreciation to Les Éditions du Cerf, Paris, for permission to use the
text of the Rule established by Dom Jean Neufville for the monumental commentary of Dom Adalbert de Vogüé in the *Sources Chrétiennes*
edition, 181–186 (1971–72). The work of de Vogüé was an invaluable
guide for us in preparing this volume.

There is an endless list of people to whom our group owes a great
debt of gratitude. We regret that we cannot name each one of them.
However, we must mention Rev. Quentin Schaut, O.S.B., St. Vincent
Archabbey, Latrobe, Pennsylvania, and Miss Dorothy Schmanke,
Topeka, Kansas. We want to express our thanks to two communities
for their hospitality to our group in the various stages of the work:
Mother Evin Rademacher, O.S.B., St. Benedict's Convent, St. Joseph,
Minnesota, and Rt. Rev. David Melancon, O.S.B., St. Joseph Abbey,
St. Benedict, Louisiana. Without the inspiring leadership of Rt. Rev.
Martin J. Burne, O.S.B., St. Mary's Abbey, Morristown, New Jersey,
this collaborative undertaking would never have been completed. To
the four associate editors I owe a great debt of appreciation. Their
generous expenditure of time and energy has made it possible to bring
this book to publication. To John Schneider, editor at The Liturgical
Press, it is a pleasure to record my gratitude for his keen sense of the
language and for his many helpful suggestions. To Sister Imogene Baker,
O.S.B., the coordinator of the project, I wish to express personal thanks
for her constant support and prudent judgments. Finally, to Volkmuth
Printers, Inc., St. Cloud, Minnesota, grateful recognition is given for their
generous grant toward the production of this book.

REV. TIMOTHY FRY, O.S.B.
St. Benedict's Abbey
Atchison, Kansas

TABLE OF CONTENTS

Part Two

REGULA SANCTI BENEDICTI

Latin and English with Patristic Sources and Notes

Part Three

APPENDIX

Longer Expositions of Monastic Topics

   The term "monk" (301–311) —The term *monachus*
   in Latin use (311–313) —The tradition of kinds of

Part Four

CLASSIFIED REFERENCE RESOURCES

Guides to Investigation

ABBREVIATIONS

ABR	The American Benedictine Review
ActSS	Acta Sanctorum
ACW	Ancient Christian Writers
ANF	Ante-Nicene Fathers
BAC	Biblioteca de Autores Cristianos
BM	Benediktinische Monatschrift
CCL	Corpus Christianorum, Series Latina
CollCist	Collectanea Cisterciensia
CS	Cistercian Studies
CSCO	Corpus Scriptorum Christianorum Orientalium
CSEL	Corpus Scriptorum Ecclesiasticorum Latinorum
DACL	Dictionnaire d'Archéologie Chrétienne et de Liturgie
DR	Downside Review
DS	Dictionnaire de Spiritualité, Ascétique et Mystique
EA	Erbe und Auftrag
FC	Fathers of the Church
GCS	Die Griechischen Christlichen Schriftsteller der ersten Jahrhunderte
ICC	International Critical Commentary
LCL	Loeb Classical Library
MGH	Monumenta Germaniae Historica
MS	Monastic Studies
NPNF	Nicene and Post-Nicene Fathers
PG	Patrologiae Cursus Completus, Series Graeca
PL	Patrologiae Cursus Completus, Series Latina
PLS	Patrologiae Cursus Completus, Supplementum
PO	Patrologia Orientalis
RAM	Revue d'Ascétique et de Mystique
RBén	Revue Bénédictine
RBS	Regulae Benedicti Studia
RechSR	Recherches de Science Religieuse

RHE	Revue d'Histoire Ecclésiastique
SC	Sources Chrétiennes
SM	Studia Monastica
SMGBO	Studien und Mitteilungen zur Geschichte des Benediktinerordens und seiner Zweige
StA	Studia Anselmiana
TU	Texte und Untersuchungen zur Geschichte der altchristlichen Literatur
ZKG	Zeitschrift für Kirchengeschichte
ZThK	Zeitschrift für Theologie und Kirche
de Vogüé 1–7	*La Règle de saint Benoît*, ed. and comment. Adalbert de Vogüé and Jean Neufville, Sources Chrétiennes 181–186 (Paris: Les Éditions du Cerf 1971–72); vol. 7(Paris: Les Éditions du Cerf 1977), not included in the Sources Chrétiennes series.
de Vogüé, *La communauté*	Adalbert de Vogüé, *La communauté et l'abbé dans la Règle de saint Benoît* (Paris: Desclée de Brouwer 1961).

SHORT TITLES OF PATRISTIC
AND ANCIENT WORKS

This list of Short Titles gives the full bibliographical entry for each Patristic and Ancient work referred to in this volume. English translations are indicated, if available. For the sake of consistency, all works are given their Latin titles and abbreviations, no matter what their original language. Authors' names, however, are given in an English form for the sake of those unfamiliar with the Latin form.

Act.Anastasiae=Acta SS. Anastasiae, Chrysogoni, Chioniae, Irenes et Agapes, Theodotae:ActSS Apr. and H. Delehaye, *Étude sur le légendier romain* (Brussels: Société des Bollandistes 1936).
Act.S.Sebast.=Passio S. Sebastiani (Ps-Ambrosius):*PL* 17.1021; *ActSS* Jan.
*Act.Thomae=Acta Thomae:*M. Bonnet, *Acta apostolorum apocrypha* (Leipzig: Hermannum Mendelssohn 1903) 2 (Greek); Eng.:*ANF* 8; E. Hennecke, *New Testament Apocrypha* (London: Lutterworth 1965) 2.
*Alc. vita Will.=*Alcuin, *Vita S. Willibrordi:PL* 101.693; *MGH* SSRM 7; Eng.:C. H. Talbot, *The Anglo-Saxon Missionaries in Germany* (New York: Sheed and Ward 1954); C. Albertson, *Anglo-Saxon Saints and Heroes* (New York: Fordham Univ. Press 1967).
*Ambr. apol.Dav.=*Ambrose, *De apologia prophetae David:PL* 14.851; CSEL 32,2.
*Ambr. epist.=*Ambrose, *Epistulae:PL* 16.876; Eng.:FC 26.
*Ambr. exhort.virg.=*Ambrose, *Exhortatio virginitatis:PL* 16.335.
*Ambr. explan.ps.=*Ambrose, *Explanatio super psalmos xii:PL* 14.921; CSEL 64.
*Ambr. expos. de psalm.=*Ambrose, *Expositio de psalmo cxviii:PL* 15.1197; CSEL 42.
*Ambr. fid. ad Grat.=*Ambrose, *De fide ad Gratianum:PL* 16.527; CSEL 78; Eng.:*NPNF* ser.2,10.
*Ambr. hex.=*Ambrose, *Hexaemeron:PL* 14.123; CSEL 32,1; Eng.:FC 42.
*Ambr. in Luc.=*Ambrose, *Expositio Evangelii secundum Lucam:PL* 15.1527; CCL 14.
*Ambr. off.=*Ambrose, *De officiis ministrorum:PL* 16.23; G. Banterle (Milano: Biblioteca Ambrosiana 1977).
*Ambr. paenit.=*Ambrose, *De paenitentia:PL* 16.465; CSEL 73.
*Ambr. virg.=*Ambrose, *De virginibus:PL* 16.187; E. Cazzaniga (Turin: I. B. Paravia 1948).

Ammon. *epist.*=Ammonius, *Epistula ad Theophilum de Pachomio et Theodoro:*F. Halkin, *S. Pachomii Vitae graecae*, Subsidia Hag. 19 (Brussels: Société des Bollandistes 1932).

Anon. *hist.abb.*=*Historia abbatum anonyma (Vita Ceolfridi):*C. Plummer, *Baedae opera historica* (Oxford: The Clarendon Press 1896) 1; Eng.:Albertson (see Alc. *vita Will.* above).

Apoph.=*Apophthegmata patrum:PG* 65.71; J.-C. Guy, *Recherches sur la tradition grecque des Apophthegmata Patrum* (Brussels: Société des Bollandistes 1962); Eng.:B. Ward, *The Sayings of the Desert Fathers* (Kalamazoo, Mich.: Cist. Publ. 1975). See *Vitae patr., Verb.senior.*

Arist. *apol.*=Aristides, *Apologia:*J. R. Harris and J. A. Robinson, *The Apology of Aristides on Behalf of the Christians*, Texts and Studies 1,1 (Cambridge 1893); E. Hennecke, *Die Apologie des Aristides*, TU 4.3 (Leipzig 1893); Eng.:Harris-Robinson, as above; *ANF* 9.

Arnob. *ad Greg.*=Arnobius the Younger, *Liber ad Gregoriam:PLS* 3.221; G. Morin, *Études, textes, découvertes* (Maredsous: Éditions de l'Abbaye 1913) 1.

Ath. *epist. ad mon.*=Athanasius, *Epistula ad monachos:PG* 26. 1185.

Ath. *epist. i ad Orsisium*=Athanasius, *Epistula i ad Orsisium:PG* 26.977; see *Vita prima* 150.

Ath. *narr.Ammon.*=Athanasius, *Narratio ad Ammonium episcopum de fuga sua:PG* 26.980; also found in Ammon. *epist.*

Ath. *vita Anton.*=see *Vita Anton.*

Aug. *c.Cresc.*=Augustine, *Contra Cresconium:PL* 43.445; CSEL 52.

Aug. *c.Faust.*=Augustine, *Contra Faustum Manichaeum:PL* 42.207; CSEL 25,1; Eng.:*NPNF* ser.1,4.

Aug. *c.Parm.*=Augustine, *Contra epistulam Parmeniani:PL* 43.33; CSEL 51.

Aug. *civ.*=Augustine, *De civitate Dei:PL* 41.13; CCL 47 and 48; Eng.:Innumerable editions; useful are those by Dutton Co., in the Everyman series, and Doubleday, in Image Books.

Aug. *conf.*=Augustine, *Confessiones:PL* 32.659; CSEL 33,1; Eng.:Innumerable editions, of which the best is F. J. Sheed (London: Sheed and Ward 1943), regularly reprinted.

Aug. *cons.evang.*=Augustine, *De consensu Evangelistarum:PL* 34.1041; CSEL 43; Eng.:*NPNF* ser.1,6.

Aug. *de mend.*=Augustine, *De mendacio:PL* 40.487; CSEL 41; Eng.:FC 16.

Aug. *epist.*=Augustine, *Epistulae:PL* 33.61; *PLS* 2.359; CSEL 34,44,57,58; Eng.:*NPNF* ser.1,1 (fairly complete); FC 12,18,20,30,32.

Aug. *in Ioan.*=Augustine, *In Ioannis Evangelium tractatus* 124:*PL* 35.1379; CCL 36; Eng.:*NPNF* ser.1,7.

Aug. *in psalm.*=Augustine, *Enarrationes in psalmos:PL* 36.67; CCL 38,39,40; Eng.:*NPNF* ser.1,8; also ACW 29–30.

Aug. *mor.eccl.*=Augustine, *De moribus Ecclesiae catholicae et de moribus Manichaeorum:PL* 32.1309; Eng.:FC 56.

Aug. *nat. et grat.*=Augustine, *De natura et gratia:PL* 44.247; CSEL 60; Eng.:*NPNF* ser.1,5; also *Basic Writings* (New York: Random House 1948) 1.

Aug. *obiur.*=Augustine, *Obiurgatio* (= *epist.* 211,1-4):*PL* 33.958; CSEL 57; L.

Verheijen, *La règle de saint Augustin*, 2 vols. (Paris: Études Augustini-ennes 1967) 1; Eng.:FC 32.

Aug. *op.mon.*=Augustine, *De opere monachorum:PL* 40.547; CSEL 51; Eng.:FC 16.

Aug. *ord.mon.*=see Ps-Aug. *ord.mon.*

Aug. *quaest. in Hept.*=Augustine, *Quaestiones in Heptateuchum:PL* 34.547; CSEL 28,2,3; CCL 33.

Aug. *reg.serv.*=Augustine, *Regula ad servos Dei* (also called *Praeceptum):PL* 32.1377; D. de Bruyne "La première règle de saint Benoît" *RBén* 42 (1930) 316–342 (text 320–326); Verheijen, 1 (see Aug. *obiur.* above); Eng.:FC 32 (=Letter 211).

Aug. *serm.*=Augustine, *Sermones:PL* 38–39; *PLS* 2.742; Eng.:selected sermons in *NPNF* ser.1,6; FC 11,38; ACW 5,15.

Aug. *serm. Morin Guelf.*=Augustine, *Sermones codicis Guelferbytani:PLS* 2.593; G. Morin, *Miscellanea Agostiniana* (Roma: Tipografia Poliglotta Vaticana 1930) 1.

Aug. *tract. in Ioan.*=Augustine, *In Ioannis epistulam ad Parthos, tractatus x:PL* 35.1977; Eng.:*NPNF* ser.1,7; also: *Augustine, Later Works*, Library of Christian Classics (London: SCM 1954).

Baedae *hist.abb.*=Bede, *Vita beatorum abbatum Benedicti, Ceolfridi, Eos-terwini, Sigfridi atque Hwaetberhti:PL* 94.713; C. Plummer, *Baedae opera historica* (Oxford: The Clarendon Press 1896) 1; Eng.:LCL.

Baedae *in 1 Ioan.*=Bede, *Super epistulam 1 Sancti Ioannis:PL* 93.85.

Basil. *ad fil.*=Basil(?), *Admonitio ad filium spiritalem* (tr. Rufin.):*PL* 103.683; P. Lehmann, *Die Admonitio S. Basilii ad filium spiritalem*, in Sitz-ungsber. der Bay. Akad. der Wissensch. Philolog.-histor. Klasse 7 (1955–57); Eng.:H. W. Norman, *The Anglo-Saxon Version of the Hexam-eron of St. Basil and the Saxon Remains of St. Basil's Admonitio ad Filium Spiritalem, with a Translation* (London 1848).

Basil. *ad mon.*=Basil, *Admonitio ad monachos:PG* 31.648; A. Wilmart "Le discours de Saint Basile sur l'ascèse et latin" *RBén* 27 (1910) 228–231; Eng.:W.K.L. Clarke, *The Ascetical Works of St. Basil* (London: SPCK 1925).

Basil. *epist.*=Basil, *Epistulae:PG* 32.220; Y. Courtonne, *Saint Basile: Lettres* (Paris: Société d'édition Les Belles Lettres 1957, 1961, 1966); Eng.:FC 13 and 28; LCL.

Basil. *in psalm.*=Basil, *Homiliae super psalmos:PG* 29.209; tr. Rufin. *in psalm. I et LIX:PG* 31.1723,1790; G. Morin, *Anecdota Maredsolana*, 4 vols. (Maredsous: Monastery of St. Benedict 1893–1932) 3.2.

Basil. *reg.*=Basil, *Asceticon parvum* (tr. Rufin.):*PL* 103.483; Eng.:Clarke, as above.

Basil. *reg.fus.*=Basil, *Regulae fusius tractatae:PG* 31.889; Eng.:Clarke.

Caes.Arel. *epist. ad virg.*=Caesarius of Arles, *Epistula hortatoria ad virginem Deo dicatam:PL* 67.1135; G. Morin, *S. Caesarii opera omnia* (Maredsous: Éditions de l'Abbaye 1942) 2.

Caes.Arel. *recapit.*=Caesarius of Arles, *Recapitulatio statutorum sanctarum virginum:*Morin, 2.

Caes.Arel. *reg.mon.*=Caesarius of Arles, *Regula monachorum:PL* 67.1099; Morin, 2.

Caes.Arel. *reg.virg.*=Caesarius of Arles, *Statuta sanctarum virginum:PL* 67.1105; Morin, 2.

Cassian. *conl.*=Cassian, *Conlationes:PL* 49.477; CSEL 13; SC 42,54,64; Eng.:*NPNF* ser.2,2.

Cassian. *inst.*=Cassian, *De institutis coenobiorum:PL* 49.53; CSEL 17; SC 109; Eng.:*NPNF* ser.2,11.

Chrom.Aquil. *serm.* = Chromatius of Aquileia, *Sermo de octo beatitudinibus:PL* 20.323; CCL 9.

Clem. *ad Cor.*=Pope Clement I, *Epistula ad Corinthios:PG* 5.661; F. X. Funk and K. Bihlmeyer, *Die apostolischen Väter*, 2nd ed. (Tübingen: Mohr 1956); Eng.:ACW 1; FC 5; LCL. See Ps-Clem. *ad Cor.* 2.

Clem. *paed.*=Clement of Alexandria, *Paedagogus:PG* 8.247; GCS 12; Eng.: ANF 2; FC 23.

Clem. *strom.*=Clement of Alexandria, *Stromata:PG* 8.685–9.9; GCS 15 (Books 1–6); 17 (Books 7–8); SC 30; Eng.:*ANF* 2.

Concil.Agathense a. 506=Concilium Agathense anno 506:Morin, S. Caesarii opera omnia, 2.

Concil.Gerund. a. 517=Concilium Gerundense anno 517:Mansi, Concil. ampliss. coll. 8.549.

Cypr. *ad Demet.*=Cyprian, *Ad Demetrianum:PL* 4.544; CSEL 3,1; Eng.:*ANF* 5.

Cypr. *ad Don.*=Cyprian, *Ad Donatum:PL* 4.192; CSEL 3,1; Eng.:ACW 20.

Cypr. *ad Fort.*=Cyprian, *Ad Fortunatum (De exhortatione martyrii):PL* 4.651; CSEL 3,1; Eng.:*ANF* 5.

Cypr. *de laps.*=Cyprian, *De lapsis:PL* 4.465; CSEL 3,1; Eng.:*ANF* 5.

Cypr. *de mort.*=Cyprian, *De mortalitate:PL* 4.583; CSEL 3,1; Eng.:*ANF* 5.

Cypr. *de op. et el.*=Cyprian, *De opere et eleemosynis:PL* 4.601; CSEL 3,1; Eng.:*ANF* 5.

Cypr. *de pat.*=Cyprian, *De bono patientiae:PL* 4.622; CSEL 3,1; Eng.:ACW 20.

Cypr. *domin.orat.*=Cyprian, *De dominica oratione:PL* 4.520; 47.1113; CSEL 3,1; Eng.:ACW 20.

Cypr. *eccl.unit.*=Cyprian, *De catholicae ecclesiae unitate:PL* 4.465; PLS 1.45; CSEL 3,1; Eng.:*ANF* 5.

Cypr. *epist.*=Cyprian, *Epistulae:PL* 4.224; CSEL 3,2; Eng.:*ANF* 5 (with different numbering); FC 51.

Cypr. *hab.virg.*=Cyprian, *De habitu virginum:PL* 4.440; CSEL 3,1; Eng.:ACW 20.

Cypr. *quod idola*=Cyprian, *Quod idola dii non sint:PL* 4.564; CSEL 3,1; Eng.:*ANF* 5.

Cypr. *testim.*=Cyprian, *Ad Quirinum (Testimoniorum* 1.3):PL 4.675; CSEL 3,1; Eng.:*ANF* 5.

Cypr. *zel. et liv.*=Cyprian, *De zelo et livore:PL* 4.638; CSEL 3,1; Eng.:*ANF* 5.

Decret.Gelasianum=Decretum Gelasianum de libris recipiendis et non recipiendis:PL 59.157; 62.537; E. von Dobschütz, in TU 38 (1912).

Diad. *cap.gnost.* = Diadochus of Photike, *Capita centum gnostica:PG* 65.1167; SC 5*bis*

Didache = *Didache:PG* 5.661; Funk-Bihlmeyer (see Clem. *ad Cor.* above); Eng.:ACW 1; FC 5; LCL.

Didasc.apost. = *Didascalia apostolorum:* F. X. Funk, *Didascalia et constitutiones Apostolorum* (Paderborn: Ferdinand Schoeningh 1905) 1; Eng.: R. H. Connolly, *Didascalia Apostolorum: The Syriac Version translated and accompanied by the Verona Latin fragments* (Oxford: The Clarendon Press 1929).

Digesta = Justinian, *Corpus Iuris Civilis:Digesta (Pandectae) anno 533* (in part *PL* 72.921) ed. Th. Mommsen, P. Krüger, R. Schoell, W. Kroll (Berlin: Weidmann 1908–12) 1–3.

Donat. *reg. ad virg.* = Donatus, *Regula ad virgines:PL* 87.273.

Edd.Steph. *vita Wilf.* = Eddius Stephanus, *Vita Wilfridi:* B. Colgrave, *The Life of Bishop Wilfrid by Eddius Stephanus* (Cambridge Univ. Press 1927); Eng.:Colgrave and Albertson (see Alc. *vita Will.* above).

Egeriae peregr. = Egeria, *Itinerarium seu Peregrinatio ad loca sancta:PLS* 1.1047; CSEL 39; CCL 175; SC 21; Eng.:ACW 38.

Epiph. *pan.* = Epiphanius, *Panarion:PG* 41.174–42.832; GCS 25,31,37.

Epist.apost. = *Epistula Apostolorum*, Ethiopic version:*PO* 9.3; Eng.:Hennecke, 1 (see *Act.Thomae* above).

Euch. *laud.erem.* = Eucherius of Lyon, *De laude eremi:PL* 50.701; CSEL 31. Also S. Pricoco, *Eucherii de laude eremi* (Catania: Centro di studi sull'antico cristianesimo 1965): offprint from *Miscellanea di studi di litteratura cristiana antica* 15 (1965) 1–117.

Eus. *hist.eccles.* = Eusebius, *Historia ecclesiae:PG* 20.45; GCS 9,1-3; Eng.:LCL; *NPNF* ser.2,1; FC 19 and 29.

Eus. *in psalm.* = Eusebius, *Commentarii in psalmos:PG* 23.441.

Eus. *praep.evang.* = Eusebius, *Praeparatio evangelica:PG* 22.13; GCS 43,1-2.

Evagr. *de orat.* = Evagrius of Pontus, *De oratione:PG* 79.1165; Eng.:J. Bamberger, *Evagrius Ponticus: The Praktikos; Chapters on Prayer* (Spencer, Mass.: Cist. Publ. 1970).

Evagr. *epist.* = Evagrius of Pontus, *Epistulae:W.* Frankenberg, *Evagrius Ponticus*, Abhandlungen der königlichen Gesellschaft der Wissenschaften zu Göttingen, Phil.-hist. Klasse, Neue Folge 13,2 (Berlin: Weidmann 1912).

Evagr. *keph.gnos.* = Evagrius of Pontus, *Kephalaia gnostica:PO* 28.1.

Evagr. *pract.* = Evagrius of Pontus, *Practicus (Epistula ad Anatolium et Liber practicus):PG* 40.1220,1244,1272; SC 170–171; Eng.: See Evagr. *de orat.*

Evagr. *sent.mon.* = Evagrius of Pontus, *Epistula Evagrii ad virgines directa:PL* 20.1181; *PG* 40.1277; A. Wilmart "Les versions latines des sentences d'Évagre pour les vierges" *RBén* (1911) 143–153.

Fulg.Rusp. *epist.* = Fulgentius of Ruspe, *Epistulae xviii:PL* 65.303; 45.1779; CCL 91.

Greg. *dial.* = Gregory the Great, *Dialogorum Libri IV:PL* 77.149; U. Moricca, *Gregorii Magni Dialogi Libri IV* (Roma: Tipografia del Senato 1924); SC 251,260,265; Eng.: FC 39.

Greg. *epist.*=Gregory the Great, *Registrum epistularum:PL* 77.441; 84.831; Ewald and Hartmann in *MGH Epist.* 1–2.

Greg. *libr. I Reg.*=Gregory the Great, *In librum primum Regum expositio:PL* 79.17; CCL 144.

Greg. *past.*=Gregory the Great, *Regula pastoralis:PL* 77.13; Eng.:ACW 11.

Greg.Naz. *orat.*=Gregory of Nazianzen, *Orationes:PG* 35.12–36.664; F. Boulenger, *Grégoire de Nazianze. Discours funèbres en l'honneur de son frère Césaire et de Basile de Césarée* (Paris: A. Picard 1908); Eng.:FC 22 (Orations 7 and 43).

Greg.Nys. *adv.Apoll.*=Gregory of Nyssa, *Adversus Apollinarem:PG* 45.1123; W. Jaeger *et al.*, *Gregorii Nysseni opera* (Leiden: Brill 1958–67) 3.

Greg.Nys. *cont.Eun.*=Gregory of Nyssa, *Contra Eunomium:PG* 45.248; Jaeger 1; Eng.:NPNF ser.2,5.

Greg.Nys. *in Eccl.*=Gregory of Nyssa, *In Ecclesiasten homiliae:PG* 44.615; Jaeger 5.

Greg.Nys. *inst.christ.*=Gregory of Nyssa, *De instituto Christiano:PG* 46.288; Jaeger 8; Eng.:FC 58.

Greg.Nys. *virg.*=Gregory of Nyssa, *De virginitate:PG* 46.317; Jaeger 8; Eng.: FC 58.

Herm. *past.*=Hermas of Rome, *Pastor:PG* 2.891; SC 53*bis*; Eng.:FC 5.

Hier. *apol.adv.libr.Ruf.*=Jerome, *Apologia adversus libros Rufini:PL* 23.397; Eng.:NPNF ser.2,3.

Hier. *de viris illus.*=Jerome, *De viris illustribus:PL* 23.603.

Hier. *epist.*=Jerome, *Epistulae:PL* 22.325; PLS 2.20; CSEL 54,55,56; Eng.:ACW 33 (letters 1–22).

Hier. *in Ezech.*=Jerome, *Commentarii in Ezechielem:PL* 25.15.

Hier. *in Gal.*=Jerome, *Commentarius in epistulam ad Galatas:PL* 26.307.

Hier. *in Matt.*=Jerome, *Commentarius in Matthaeum:PL* 26.15; CCL 77.

Hier. *in psalm.*=Jerome, *Commentarioli in psalmos:PLS* 2.29; CCL 72; Morin, *Anec. Maredsol.* 3 (see Basil. in psalm. above).

Hier. *in Zach.*=Jerome, *Commentarius in Zachariam:PL* 25.1415; CCL 76A.

Hier. *Orsies.doctr.*=See Orsiesii *lib.*

Hier. *reg.Pachom.*=See Pachom. *reg.*

Hier. *vita Hil.*=Jerome, *Vita Hilarionis:PL* 23.29; ActSS Oct.; Eng.:FC 15.

Hier. *vita Mal.*=Jerome, *Vita Malchi:PL* 23.55; C. C. Mierow in *Classical Essays Presented to J. A. Kleist*, ed. R. E. Arnold (St. Louis Univ. 1946); Eng.:NPNF ser.2,6; FC 15.

Hier. *vita Pauli*=Jerome, *Vita Pauli:PL* 23.17; Eng.:FC 15.

Hil. *in Matt.*=Hilary of Poitiers, *In Matthaeum:PL* 9.917; SC 255 and 258.

Hil. *in psalm.*=Hilary of Poitiers, *Tractatus super psalmos:PL* 9.231; CSEL 22.

Hil. *vita Hon.*=Hilary of Arles, *Vita Honorati:PL* 50.1249; SC 235; Eng.:FC 15.

Hild. *exp.reg.*=Hildemar, *Expositio Regulae ab Hildemaro tradita:R.* Mittermüller, *Vita et Regula SS. P. Benedicti una cum Expositione Regulae a Hildemaro Tradita* (Regensburg: Pustet 1880).

Hippol. *trad.apost.*=Hippolytus, *Traditio apostolica:B.* Botte, *La tradition apostolique de saint Hippolyte*, Liturgiewissenschaftliche Quellen und Forschungen 39 (Münster: Aschendorff 1963); Eng.:B. S. Easton, *The Apostolic Tradition of Hippolytus* (Cambridge Univ. Press 1924); G. Dix, *The Treatise on the Apostolic Tradition of St. Hippolytus of Rome* (London: SPCK 1937).

Hist.mon.=*Historia monachorum in Aegypto* (tr. Rufin.):*PL* 21.387; see A.-M. J. Festugière, *Édition critique du texte grec*, Subsidia Hagiographica 34 (Brussels: Société des Bollandistes 1961).

Ign. *Magn.*=Ignatius of Antioch, *Epistula ad Magnesios:PG* 5.661; Funk-Bihlmeyer (see Clem. *ad Cor.* above); Eng.:ACW 1; FC 5; LCL.

Ign. *Smyr.*=Ignatius of Antioch, *Epistula ad Smyrnos:PG* 5.707; Funk-Bihlmeyer; Eng.:ACW 1; FC 5; LCL.

Ign. *Trall.*=Ignatius of Antioch, *Epistula ad Trallianos:PG* 5.673; Funk-Bihlmeyer; Eng.:ACW 1; FC 5; LCL.

Ios. *de bello Iud.*=Flavius Josephus, *De bello Iudaico:*Eng.:LCL.

Iren. *adv.haer.*=Irenaeus, *Adversus haereses:PG* 7.433; SC 100,152,153,210, 211; Eng.:ANF 1.

Iren. *demonstr.apost.praed.*=Irenaeus, *Demonstratio apostolicae praedicationis:PO* 12.5; Eng.: the above edition has English and French translations.

Iust. *apol.*=Justin Martyr, *Apologia pro Christianis:PG* 6.327; L. Pontigny, *Justin: Apologies* (Paris: A. Picard 1904); Eng.:ANF 1.

Iust. *dial.*=Justin Martyr, *Dialogus cum Tryphone:PG* 6.471; G. Archambault, *Justin: Dialogue avec Tryphon*, 2 vols. (Paris: A. Picard 1909); Eng.: *ANF* 1.

Leo.M. *tract.*=Leo the Great, *Tractatus septem et nonaginta:PL* 54.141; CCL 138,138A.

Leo.Ost. *chron.Cas.*=Leo of Ostia, *Chronicon Casinense:PL* 173.440.

Lib.diurn.=*Liber diurnus:PL* 105.9; H. Förster (Bern: Francke 1958).

Lib.grad.=*Liber graduum:Patrologia Syriaca* 3.

Liban. *orat.*=Libanius, *Orationes:*R. Foerster, *Libanii Opera* (Stuttgart: Teubner 1903); Eng.:LCL.

Max.Tur. *sermo.*=Maximus of Turin, *Sermones:PL* 57.221; CCL 23.

Melit. *pasch.*=Melito of Sardis, *Homilia paschalis* (or *Chronicon paschale*):C. Bonner, *The Homily on the Passion by Melito, Bishop of Sardis* (Philadelphia: Univ. of Pennsylvania Press 1940); M. Testuz, *Méliton de Sardes: Homélie sur la Pâque. Papyrus Bodmer xiii* (Geneva: Bibl. Bodmer 1960); SC 123.

Meth. *conviv.*=Methodius, *Convivium:PG* 18.221; GCS 27; SC 95; Eng.:ACW 6; *ANF* 6.

Optat.=Optatus, *Contra Parmenianum Donatistam:PL* 11.883; CSEL 26.

Orat.Manassae=*Oratio Manassae:Biblia sacra iuxta vulgatam versionem*, editio altera emendata, ed. R. Weber (Stuttgart: Württembergische Bibelanstalt 1969) 2; Eng.:R. H. Charles, *The Apocrypha and Pseudepigrapha of the Old Testament in English* (Oxford: The Clarendon Press 1913) 1.

Orig. *c.Cels.*=Origen, *Contra Celsum:PG* 11.641; GCS 2–3; Eng.:*ANF* 4; also H. Chadwick, *Contra Celsum* (Cambridge Univ. Press 1953).

Orig. *hom. in Iesu Nave*=Origen, *Homiliae in Iesu Nave* (tr. Rufin.):*PG* 12.825; GCS 7; Eng.:R. B. Tollington, *Selections from the Commentaries and Homilies of Origen* (London: SPCK 1929).

Orig. *hom.cant.*=Origen, *Homiliae in Canticum canticorum:PG* 13.37; GCS 33.

Orig. *hom. in Ex.*=Origen, *Homiliae in Exodum* (tr. Rufin.):*PG* 12.297; GCS 29.

Orig. *in Ioan.*=Origen, *Commentarii in Ioannem:PG* 14.21; GCS 10; Eng.:*ANF* 9.

Orig. *in Luc.*=Origen, *Homiliae in Lucam* (tr. Hier.):*PL* 26.229; GCS 35.

Orig. *in Matt.*=Origen, *Commentarii in Matthaeum:PG* 13.829; GCS 38,40,41; Eng.:*ANF* 9.

Orig. *in Prov.*=Origen, *Expositio in Proverbia:PG* 17.161.

Orig. *prin.*=Origen, *De Principiis:PG* 11.115; GCS 22; Eng.:*ANF* 4; G. W. Butterworth, *Origen on First Principles* (New York: Harper Torchbook 1966).

Orsiesii *lib.*=Horsiesius, *Liber* (tr. Hier.):*PL* 103.453; A. Boon, *Pachomiana latina*, Bibliothèque de la Revue d'Histoire Ecclésiastique 7 (Louvain: Bureaux de la Revue 1932).

Pachom. *reg.*=Pachomius, *Regula coenobiorum:PL* 23.65; Boon, as above.

Pallad. *dial.*=Palladius, *Dialogus de vita sancti Johannis Chrysostomi:PG* 47.5; P. R. Coleman-Norton, *Palladii Dialogus de vita sancti Joannis Chrysostomi* (Harvard Univ. Press 1928); Eng.:H. Moore, *The Dialogue of Palladius Concerning the Life of Chrysostom* (London: SPCK 1921).

Pallad. *hist.laus.*=Palladius, *Historia Lausiaca:PG* 34.995; *PL* 74.249; C. Butler, *The Lausiac History of Palladius*, 2 vols., Texts and Studies 6,1-2 (Cambridge Univ. Press 1898 and 1904); Eng.:ACW 34.

Passio Iulian. et Bas.=*Passio Iuliani et Basilissae:ActSS* Ian. et Iun.

Passio Iust.=*Passio Iustini et sociorum:*H. Musurillo, *The Acts of the Christian Martyrs* (Oxford: The Clarendon Press 1972); Eng.:*Ibid.*

Passio Perp. Fel.=*Passio Sanctarum Perpetuae et Felicitatis:PL* 3.17; Musurillo; Eng.:*Ibid.*

Paul.diac. *gest.Lang.*=Paul the Deacon, *De gestis Langobardorum:PL* 95.433; Eng.:Paul the Deacon, *History of the Lombards*, tr. W. D. Foulke (1907; rpt. Univ. of Pennsylvania Press 1974).

Paulin.Nol. *epist.*=Paulinus of Nola, *Epistulae:PL* 61.153; CSEL 29; Eng.:ACW 35–36.

Paulin. *vit.Ambr.*=Paulinus, *Vita Ambrosii:PL* 14.29; Eng.:FC 15.

Phil. *cher.*=Philo Iudaeus, *De Cherubim:* L. Cohn et al., *Philonis Alexandrini Opera quae supersunt*, 7 vols. (Berlin: G. Reimer 1896–1930) 1; Eng.:LCL.

Philox. *ad Pat.*=Philoxenus of Mabbug, *Epistula ad Patricium:PO* 30.

Plin. *nat.hist.*=Pliny, *Naturalis historia:*C. Mayhoff, *C. Plini Naturalis historiae libri xxxvii* (Leipzig: Teubner 1870); Eng.:LCL.

Porcar. *mon.*=Porcarius of Lerins, *Monita:PLS* 3.737; A. Wilmart in *RBén* 26 (1909) 475–480.

Porphyr. *ad Marcell.*=Porphyry, *Ad Marcellum*:A. Nauck, *Porphyrii opera* (1886).

Porphyr. *de abstin.*=Porphyry, *De abstinentia*:J. Bouffortique and M. Patillon, *De l'abstinence Porphyre* (Paris: Société d'édition Les Belles Lettres 1977); Eng.:*Porphyry on abstinence from animal food*, tr. Thomas Taylor, ed. Esme Wynn-Tyson (New York: Barnes and Noble 1965).

Possid. *vit.Aug.*=Possidius, *Vita Augustini*:*PL* 32.33; Eng.:FC 15.

Ps-Aug. *ord.mon.*=Pseudo-Augustine, *De ordine monasterii*:*PL* 32.1449; 66.995; De Bruyne (see Aug. *reg.serv.* above); Verheijen, 1 (see Aug. *obiur.* above).

Ps-Clem. *ad Cor. II*=Pseudo-Clement of Rome, *Epistula secunda ad Corinthios*:*PG* 1.329; Funk-Bihlmeyer (see Clem. *ad Cor.* above); Eng.:FC 5; LCL.

Ps-Cypr. *adv.Iud.*=Pseudo-Cyprian, *Adversus Iudaeos*:*PL* 4.705; CCL 4; Eng.:*ANF* 5.

Ps-Dion. *eccl.hier.*=Pseudo-Dionysius, *De ecclesiastica hierarchia*:*PG* 3.369; Eng.:J. Parker, *The Works of Dionysius the Areopagite* (London 1897); D. Rutledge, *Cosmic Theology* (Staten Island, N.Y.: Alba House 1965).

Ps-Macar. *reg.*=Pseudo-Macarius, *Regula monachorum*:*PL* 103.447; *PG* 34.967.

Reg. ii Patr.=*Regula ii SS. Patrum*:*PL* 103.441; *PG* 34.977.

Reg. iv Patr.=*Regula iv Patrum*:J. Neufville "Règle des iv Pères et seconde règle des Pères" *RBén* 77 (1967) 47–106.

Ruf. *hist.eccles.*=Rufinus, *Historia ecclesiae*:*PL* 21.461; *MGH* auct. ant. 9,11,13.

Sacr.Gelasianum=*Sacramentarium Gelasianum Vetus*:*PL* 74.1055; L. Eizenhöfer, P. Siffrin and L. C. Mohlberg, *Liber Sacramentorum Romanae Aeclesiae ordinis anni circuli*, Rer. Eccl. Doc., ser. maior, Fontes iv (Roma: Herder 1960).

Sacr.Leon.=*Sacramentarium Leonianum*:*PL* 55.21; L. Eizenhöfer, P. Siffrin and L. C. Mohlberg, *Sacramentarium Veronese*, Rer. Eccl. Doc., ser. maior, Fontes i (Roma: Herder 1956).

Sext.Pythag. *enchirid.*=Sextus Pythagoricus, *Enchiridion* (tr. Rufin.):H. Chadwick, *The Sentences of Sextus* (Cambridge Univ. Press 1959).

Smarag. *expos. in reg.*=Smaragdus, *Expositio in Regulam S. Benedicti*:*PL* 102.689; *Corpus Consuetudinum Monasticarum* 8.

Soc. *hist.eccles.*=Socrates, *Historia ecclesiae*:*PG* 67.29; Eng.:*NPNF* ser.2,2.

Soz. *hist.eccles.*=Sozomen, *Historia ecclesiastica*:*PG* 67.843; GCS 50; Eng.:*NPNF* ser.2,2.

Stob. *flor.*=John Stobaeus, *Florilegium: Joannis Stobaei Anthologium*, ed. C. Wacksmuth and O. Hense, 5 vols. (Berlin: Weidmann 1884–1912) 3–4.

Sulpic.Sever. *dial.*=Sulpicius Severus, *Dialogorum*:*PL* 20.183; CSEL 1; Eng.:FC 7.

Sulpic.Sever. *epist.*=Sulpicius Severus, *Epistulae*:*PL* 20.175; CSEL 1; Eng.:*NPNF* ser.2,11; FC 7.

Sulpic.Sever. *Mart.*=Sulpicius Severus, *Vita Martini Turonensis*:*PL* 20.159; CSEL 1; SC 133–135; Eng.:FC 7.

Ter. *Andr.*=Terence, *Andria*:P. Terenti Afri Comoediae: *The Comedies of*

Terence, ed. Sidney G. Ashmore, 2nd ed. (New York: Oxford Univ. Press 1965); Eng.:LCL.

Tert. *apol.* = Tertullian, *Apologeticum:PL* 1.559; CSEL 20; CCL 1; Eng.:FC 10.

Tert. *de orat.* = Tertullian, *De oratione:PL* 1.1149; CSEL 20; CCL 1; Eng.:FC 40.

Tert. *de paen.* = Tertullian, *De paenitentia:PL* 1.1223; CSEL 76; CCL 1; Eng.:ACW 28.

Tert. *exhor.cast.* = Tertullian, *De exhortatione castitatis:PL* 2.963; CCL 2; Eng.:ACW 13.

Tert. *pud.* = Tertullian, *De pudicitia:PL* 2.1029; CCL 2; Eng.:ACW 28.

Theod.Cant. *can.* = Theodore of Canterbury, *Canones:PL* 99.927.

Theod. *catech.* = Theodore of Tabennesi, *Catechesis:*CSCO 159–160 (Coptic text and French translation).

Vict.Vit. *hist.pers.* = Victor of Vita, *Historia persecutionis Africanae provinciae:PL* 58.179; CSEL 7.

Vigil. *reg.(orient.)* = Vigilius the Deacon, *Regula orientalis:PL* 50.373; 103.477; PG 34.983.

Visio Pauli = *Visio Sancti Pauli*, or *The Apocalypse of Paul:*T. Silverstein, *Visio Sancti Pauli* (London: Christophers 1935); Eng.:E. Hennecke, 2 (see *Act.Thomae* above).

Vita Anton. = *Vita Antonii:PG* 26.835; *PL* 73.127; see H. Hoppenbrouwers, *La plus ancienne version latine de la vie de S. Antoine par S. Athanase: Étude de critique textuelle* (Nijmegen: Dekker & Van de Vegt 1960); Eng.: ACW 10.

Vita bo = *Vita Pachomii bohairice scripta:*CSCO 89; section numbers from L. Th. Lefort, *Les vie coptes de s. Pachôme et de ses premiers successeurs* (Louvain: Bureaux de Muséon 1943).

Vita Macar. Rom. = *Vita Macarii Romani:PL* 73.415.

Vita Pachom. = *S. Pachomii vita:*tr. Dionysius Exiguus, *PL* 73.231; see H. van Cranenburgh, *La Vie latine de saint Pachôme traduite du grec par Denys le Petit*, Subsidia Hagiographica 46 (Brussels: Société des Bollandistes 1961).

Vita pat. iuren. = *Vita Patrum Iurensium:*SC 142.

Vita prima = *Vita prima graeca Pachomii:*F. Halkin, *Sancti Pachomii Vitae Graecae*, Subsidia Hagiographica 19 (Brussels: Société des Bollandistes 1932); Eng.:A. N. Athanassakis, *The Life of Pachomius* (Missoula, Mont.: Scholars Press 1975).

Vita sa = *Vita Pachomii sahidice scripta:*CSCO 99,100 (the various Sahidic Lives are designated *sa* [1], *sa* [2], etc.); French tr. Lefort, *Les vies coptes.* . . .

Vita tertia = *Vita tertia graeca Pachomii:*Halkin, as above.

Vitae patr., Verb.senior. = *Vitae Patrum, Verba Seniorum:PL* 73.855; J.-C. Guy, *Recherches sur la tradition grecque des Apophthegmata Patrum*, Subsidia Hagiographica 36 (Brussels: Société des Bollandistes 1962); Eng.:O. Chadwick, *Western Asceticism*, Library of Christian Classics (Philadelphia: Westminster Press 1958). See *Apoph.*

Will. *vit.Bon.* = Willibald, *Vita Bonifacii:PL* 89.603; W. Levison, *Scriptores*

Rerum Germanicarum in usum scholarum . . . editi (Hannover: Hahn 1905); Eng.:C. H. Talbot, *The Anglo-Saxon Missionaries in Germany* (New York: Sheed and Ward 1954).

A SELECTED BIBLIOGRAPHY

This Selected Bibliography contains references only to basic works that can be recommended as preliminary to the study of the Rule of St. Benedict. Some guides to the Notes with more complete information are provided; the frequent cross references throughout this volume will facilitate the use of bibliographical entries for various subjects.

Bibliographical Resources

Books—

Albareda, A. *Bibliografia de la Regla benedictina*. Montserrat: Imprenta del Monestir de Montserrat 1933. Limited to editions of the Rule.

Constable, G. *Medieval Monasticism: A Select Bibliography*. Toronto Univ. Press 1976. Intended as a guide for graduate students, this book is the best of its kind; reference chiefly to European studies.

Kapsner, O. *A Benedictine Bibliography*. 2 vols. Collegeville: St. John's Abbey Press 1962. A listing of holdings in American Benedictine libraries of Benedictine authors and subjects.

Louf, A., et al. *The Message of Monastic Spirituality*, tr. L. Stevens. New York: Desclée 1964. A translation of the "Bulletin de Spiritualité Monastique" from *Collectanea Cisterciensia* 1962, and articles in 1960–61. See below under *CS*.

Peifer, C. *Monastic Spirituality*. New York: Sheed and Ward 1966. Some 640 entries.

Turbessi, G. *Ascetismo e monachesimo in S. Benedetto*. Roma: Editrice Studium 1965. Some 745 entries.

Periodicals—
CURRENT SURVEYS:

Bibliographia patristica, ed. W. Schneemelcher. Berlin: DeGruyter 1956–. See entries on individual Fathers for scholarship in relation to monasticism.

CollCist — "Bulletin de Spiritualité Monastique." See Louf above.

CS — "Bulletin of Monastic Spirituality." A supplement that began with 2 (1967). See Louf above.

RBén — "Bulletin d'Histoire Bénédictine." Since 1893.

RHE — "Bibliographie" (Louvain). For works on monasticism, see Part III, 3,D: "Histoire de l'ascétisme" and 4: "Histoire des corporations religieuses."

Revue Mabillon — "Bulletin d'Histoire Monastique." Since 1926.
RBS — Since 1972, intermittently.

COMPLETED SURVEYS:

Bauerreis, R. "Bibliographia Benedictina" *SMGBO* 57 (1939) (1)–(28); 64 (1952) (29–(127).
———— "Bibliographie der Benediktinerregel" *SMGBO* 58 (1940) 3–20.
Rousseau, O. "Chronique des publications monastiques" *Irénikon* 36 (1963) 110–129.

Editions of the Rule

Butler, C. *Sancti Benedicti Regula Monachorum: Editio Critico-Practica.* Freiburg im Breisgau: Herder 1912. One of the first attempts at a critical edition; valuable for its indication of sources.
Hanslik, R. *Benedicti Regula*, CSEL 75. Vienna: Hölder-Pichler-Tempsky 1960, 1977[2]. A major critical edition notable for its use of available manuscripts.
Morin, G. *Regulae Sancti Benedicti traditio codicum Mss. Casinensium a praestantissimo teste usque repetita codice Sangallensi 914.* Montecassino 1900. A diplomatic edition.
de Vogüé, A. See Abbreviations for full entry.

See also Introduction, "Text and Editions of the Rule," pp. 102–109, nn. 39–64.

Concordances

See the editions of Hanslik and de Vogüé 2 for complete concordances.
Clément, J.-M. *Lexique des anciennes règles monastiques occidentales.* 2 vols. Steenbrugge: St. Peter's Abbey 1978. Not a concordance, strictly speaking, but lists principal words in rules other than RB and RM.

Text with Translation and Commentary

Colombás, G., Sansegundo, L., Cunill, O. *San Benito, su vida y su regla*, BAC 115. Madrid: La Editorial Católica 1954, 1968[2].
Lentini, A. *S. Benedetto, La Regola, testo, versione e commento.* Montecassino 1947.
McCann, J. *The Rule of Saint Benedict in Latin and English.* London: Burns Oates 1952. Contains a widely used translation.
Penco, G. *S. Benedicti Regula: introduzione, testo, apparati, traduzione e commento.* Florence: Editrice "la nuova Italia" 1958.
Steidle, B. *Die Benediktusregel: Lateinisch-Deutsch.* Beuron: Kunstverlag 1977[2].

Translation with Commentary

Delatte, P. *The Rule of St. Benedict, A Commentary*, tr. J. McCann. London: Burns Oates 1921. A once widely used commentary that provided background information on monastic practices.

Herwegen, I. *Sinn und Geist der Benediktinerregel.* Einsiedeln: Benziger 1944. Commentary only; interpretation based on charismatic approach.

Steidle, B. *Die Regel St. Benedikts. Eingeleitet, übersetzt und aus dem alten Mönchtum erklärt.* Beuron: Kunstverlag 1952. Ancient monastic practice forms the basis of interpretation. For an English translation of this work, see *The Rule of St. Benedict,* tr. U. Schnitzhofer. Canon City, Colo.: Holy Cross Abbey 1967. Unfortunately this translation is not entirely reliable.

Van Zeller, H. *The Holy Rule. Notes on St. Benedict's Legislation for Monks.* New York: Sheed and Ward 1958. A valuable interpretation, now somewhat dated.

English Translation Only

Listed below are English translations that are representative of relatively successful versions of the Rule in the twentieth century. Some are better known because they were made for specific monastic audiences; others have gained attention by the merit of the translations themselves. Two of the versions listed were made by laymen (Doyle and Chadwick); the others by monks. For further information see Introduction, "Text and Editions of the Rule," p. 112, nn. 68–70.

Bolton, B. *The Rule of St. Benedict for Monasteries.* London: Ealing Abbey 1970.

Chadwick, O. *The Rule of St. Benedict* in *Western Asceticism,* The Library of Christian Classics. Philadelphia: Westminster 1958.

[DeJean, H.] *The Holy Rule of Our Most Holy Father Benedict.* Edited by the monks of St. Meinrad Archabbey. St. Meinrad, Ind.: Abbey Press 1937. Translated by a monk of the Swiss-American Federation.

Doyle, L. *St. Benedict's Rule for Monasteries.* Collegeville: St. John's Abbey Press 1948.

Verheyen, B. *The Holy Rule of Our Most Holy Father St. Benedict in Latin and English.* Atchison, Kans.: The Abbey Student Print 1902. With the third edition (1910) and in many subsequent printings, the English alone was published. The 1949 printing contained the official publication of the Declarations and Constitution of the American Cassinese Congregation.

Lives of St. Benedict

Herwegen, I. *St. Benedict: A Character Study,* tr. P. Nugent. St. Louis: Herder 1924.

Lindsay, T. *Saint Benedict: His Life and Work.* London: Burns Oates 1949.

Maynard, T. *Saint Benedict and His Monks.* New York: P. J. Kenedy 1954.

McCann, J. *Saint Benedict.* New York: Sheed and Ward 1937; rpt. rev. ed. New York: Doubleday Image Books 1958. A widely accepted, objective study of the life of St. Benedict.

Schuster, I. *Saint Benedict and His Times,* tr. G. Roettger. St. Louis: Herder 1951.

For additional materials, see Introduction, "St. Benedict of Nursia," pp. 73–79, and nn. 13f.

Monastic History

Chapman, J. St. Benedict and the Sixth Century. London: Longmans, Green and Co. 1929; rpt. Westport, Conn.: Greenwood Press 1972. Emphasizes the legal background of Benedict.

Colombás, G. El monacato primitivo, BAC 351,376. Madrid: La Editorial Católica 1974–75. Invaluable for information on the early stages of monasticism.

Cousin, P. Précis d'histoire monastique. Paris: Bloud & Gay 1956. A broad survey, with inaccurate bibliography.

Daly, L. Benedictine Monasticism: Its Formation and Development through the 12th Century. New York: Sheed and Ward 1965.

Hilpisch, S. History of Benedictine Nuns, tr. Sister M. J. Muggli, ed. L. Doyle. Collegeville: St. John's Abbey Press 1958. One of the few attempts to write a history of nuns.

Knowles, D. The Monastic Order in England. Cambridge Univ. Press 1940, 1963².

——— The Religious Orders in England. 3 vols. Cambridge Univ. Press 1948, 1955, 1959.

——— Christian Monasticism. New York: McGraw-Hill 1967. A brief survey in paperback.

Schmitz, P. Histoire de l'Ordre de Saint-Benoît. 7 vols. Maredsous: Éditions de l'Abbaye 1942–56. The most complete modern history of Benedictines; vol. 7 treats the history of nuns.

Southern, R. Western Society and the Church in the Middle Ages. Harmondsworth, Eng.: Penguin Books 1970. See especially the section on religious orders, pp. 214–299.

Workman, H. The Evolution of the Monastic Ideal from the Earliest Times down to the Coming of the Friars. London: C. H. Kelly 1913; rpt. Boston: Beacon Press 1962, with introduction by D. Knowles. A standard work on the growth of monasticism.

For specific topics, refer to the General Index and the Introduction and accompanying notes.

Studies in Monastic Spirituality

Bouyer, L. The History of Christian Spirituality, vol. 1, Spirituality of the New Testament and the Fathers, tr. M. P. Ryan. New York: Desclée 1963. Includes a consideration of St. Benedict.

Butler, C. Benedictine Monachism: Studies in Benedictine Life and Rule. London: Longmans, Green and Co. 1919. A statement on Benedict as an innovator of great originality.

Leclercq, J., Vandenbroucke, F., and Bouyer, L. The History of Christian Spirituality, vol. 2, The Spirituality of the Middle Ages. London: Burns Oates 1968. St. Gregory the Great to the Counter Reformation.

Leclercq, J. The Love of Learning and the Desire for God, tr. C. Misrahi. New York: Fordham Univ. Press 1961. A basic study of the importance of lectio in monastic life.

Marmion, C. *Christ the Ideal of the Monk.* St. Louis: Herder 1922. A theological presentation of the spiritual foundation of monastic life.

Merton, T. *Contemplation in a World of Action.* New York: Doubleday Image Books 1973. A well-known Trappist's analysis of the tension between the contemplative life and the demands of the active apostolate.

Morin, G. *The Ideal of the Monastic Life Found in the Apostolic Age,* tr. C. Gunning. New York: Benziger 1914. An early exploration of the foundations of monastic life.

Peifer, C. *Monastic Spirituality.* New York: Sheed and Ward 1966. A compendium of essential elements found in traditional monastic teaching.

Rees, D. (ed.) *Consider Your Call.* London: SPCK 1978. A statement of the English Benedictines on monastic renewal after Vatican II.

Van Zeller, H. *Approach to Monasticism.* New York: Sheed and Ward 1960. Perceptive insights into monastic ideals previous to Vatican II.

Wathen, A. *Silence: The Meaning of Silence in the Rule of St. Benedict.* Washington, D.C.: Cistercian Publications 1973. A model for the thorough study of topics in the Rule.

For particular aspects and topics, see Introduction, Notes to the Rule, the Appendix and the General Index.

Part One

INTRODUCTION

Historical Orientation

INTRODUCTION

The Origins of Monasticism in the Eastern Church

1. INTRODUCTION*

By the time St. Benedict wrote his rule for monasteries in the sixth century, the monastic movement had existed within Christianity for over two centuries, a period fully as long as the United States has existed as a nation. In the course of two centuries a nation or movement can accumulate both a body of traditions and a collection of heroic figures in whom those traditions are seen to be embodied. Such was certainly the case with the monastic movement by the sixth century. In what follows, no attempt will be made to write a full history of the monastic movement but only to indicate its origins, principal forms and heroic figures in the East that contributed to the monastic tradition as it passed into the West and formed the background to the Rule of St. Benedict.

It is difficult to pinpoint the precise beginnings of the monastic movement. Some writers, both ancient and modern, have pushed it back as far as the Decian persecution in the mid-third century or even earlier. However, the great Church historian Eusebius of Caesarea makes no mention of it in his history, whereas he probably would have done so if he had known of it or had regarded it of any importance

* On the origins of Christian monasticism in the East, the following works are particularly worthy of note: D. J. Chitty, *The Desert a City* (Oxford: Basil Blackwell 1966); G. Colombás, *El monacato primitivo*, BAC 351, 376 (Madrid: La Editorial Católica 1974–75); K. Heussi, *Der Ursprung des Mönchtums* (Tübingen: J.C.B. Mohr 1936); P. Labriolle "Les débuts du monachisme" in A. Fliche and V. Martin, *Histoire de l'église*, Vol. 3 (Paris: Bloud & Gay 1950); H. Leclercq "Cénobitisme" *DACL*, 2; "Monachisme" *DACL*, 11; "Nonnes" *DACL*, 12; B. Lohse, *Askese und Mönchtum in der Antike und in der alten Kirche*, Religion und Kultur der alten Mittelmeerwelt in Parallelforschungen 1 (Munich: R. Oldenbourg 1969); S. Schiwietz, *Das morgenländische Mönchtum*, 3 vols. (Mainz: Verlag von Kirchheim 1904–38); G. Turbessi, *Ascetismo e monachesimo prebenedettino* (Rome: Editrice Studium 1961).

4   INTRODUCTION: HISTORICAL ORIENTATION

before A.D. 330. By the time Athanasius died in A.D. 373, the movement had witnessed extraordinary growth and had attracted international attention. It is unlikely that monasticism existed as a recogniz-
able movement before the early part of the fourth century. Its beginnings would then coincide with the end of the age of the martyrs and
the inauguration of the triumph of the Church, a fact which, as we
shall see, may have had considerable influence on its development.

The ascetic tradition in Christianity, on which the monastic movement is built, can of course be traced back to the New Testament.[1] Of
particular importance was the tradition of virginity and celibacy that
was grounded in the example and teaching of Jesus (Matt 19:12) as
well as in the writings of St. Paul (1 Cor 7). The writings of various
Church Fathers, such as Ignatius, Clement, Tertullian, Origen and
Cyprian, testify to the increasing importance of this aspect of asceticism in the life of the Church.[2] What distinguishes the monastic
movement from the earlier tradition of asceticism within Christianity
is the practice of withdrawal from society. The early ascetics had led
their lives in the midst of the society of the Church and often with
their families. The monastic movement, however, was characterized
from the beginning by a certain withdrawal from the ordinary
framework of society and the creation of a special culture, whether
this was in a colony of hermits or in a cenobitic monastery.[3]

[1] The term askēsis has a pre-Christian usage in which it refers to practice or training,
especially that of athletes. The term does not occur in the New Testament. It acquires a
spiritual meaning in non-Christian writers such as Philo. In early Patristic usage it
comes to mean: study, the practice of piety, spiritual exercise or training, an austere life,
and eventually becomes a technical term for the eremitical and monastic life and its
practices. See G.W.H. Lampe, A Greek Patristic Lexicon (Oxford: The Clarendon Press
1961) s.v. askēsis. For a discussion of ascetic tendencies in the New Testament, see H.
von Campenhausen "Early Christian Asceticism" in Tradition and Life in the Church
(Philadelphia: Fortress Press 1968) pp. 90–122; H. Chadwick "Enkrateia" RAC 5 (1962)
349; G. Kretschmar "Ein Beitrag zur Frage nach dem Ursprung frühchristlicher Askese" ZThK 61 (1963) 27. This has been reprinted in: Askese und Mönchtum in der
alten Kirche, ed. K. Suso Frank (Darmstadt: Wissenschaftliche Buchgesellschaft 1975)
pp. 129–182.
[2] Cf. T. Camelot "Virgines Christi" La Vie Spirituelle 70 (1944) 30–43, and especially
F. de B. Vizmanos, Las vírgenes cristianas de la Iglesia primitiva; estudio histórico-
ideológico sequido de una antología de tratados patrísticos sobre la virginidad, BAC
(Madrid: La Editorial Católica 1949). A useful collection of ancient and Patristic texts on
the subject may be found in H. Koch, Quellen zur Geschichte der Askese und des
Mönchtums in der alten Kirche (Tübingen: J.C.B. Mohr 1933).
[3] This distinction is taken from Heussi, Ursprung, p. 53. Although it is not accepted
by all, it provides virtually the only way of distinguishing the monastic movement from
the earlier period. It is not actually a modern distinction. Athanasius himself considered
that Antony's innovation consisted in his withdrawal into the desert (Vita Anton. 11).

2. PRE-CHRISTIAN MONASTICISM[4]

Many historians have sought to find parallels with, and even the origins of, Christian monasticism in institutions and movements in the ancient world outside of Christianity. Weingarten, for example, thought the origin of monasticism could be found in the institution of the *katachoi*. This theory he based on papyrus texts found in the precincts of the Temple of Serapis at Memphis. These were people who lived in cells within the temple enclosure, a custom that can be traced from the second century B.C. until the fourth century A.D. Weingarten assumed that these *katachoi* had an ascetic motive and that the custom was practiced in all temples of the Serapis cult. From this he concluded that Antony would have had contact with them at Memphis, and Pachomius a similar contact at the Temple of Philae. This is based on considerable speculation, especially since the function of the *katachoi* remains a mystery and has given rise to the most diverse theories. These range from the notion that they were prisoners or possessed persons to the idea that they were people who had sought asylum in the temple. At any rate, the custom of living in a temple precinct does not connect them with the practices of the early Christian monks.[5]

The discovery of the Dead Sea Scrolls and the excavation of Khirbet Qumran on the northern shore of the Dead Sea have raised considerable speculation in the last thirty years about the "monastic" character of the Essenes and their relationship with the origins of Christian monasticism.[6] It has been suggested that the Essenes lived a celibate community life at the "monastery" of Qumran (and perhaps elsewhere), withdrawn from the world. The documents found in the environs of Qumran, especially the Rule of the Community (also known as the "Manual of Discipline"), which contains provisions for admission to the community, for its governance and discipline, have added to the comparisons with Christian monastic communities.

The geography of Egypt contributed to make spatial separation a marked feature of northern Egyptian monasticism, but the notion of the necessity of withdrawal can also be found, *mutatis mutandis*, in Basil and Augustine. For further discussion of the role of withdrawal from society in early monasticism, see the discussion of *anachōrēsis* below.

[4] For a discussion of the origin and the use of the term "monk," see Appendix 1, pp. 301–313.

[5] Cf. H. Weingarten "Der Ursprung des Mönchtums im nachconstantinischen Zeitalter" *ZKG* 1 (1877) 1–35; Heussi, *Ursprung*, pp. 283–287; Lohse, *Askese*, pp. 38–39.

[6] See E. F. Sutcliffe, *The Monks of Qumran* (Westminster, Md.: Newman Press 1960) passim; J. A. Mohler, *The Heresy of Monasticism* (Staten Island, N.Y.: Alba House 1971) pp. 15–27.

It is far from clear, however, that the Essenes lived a life of permanent celibacy or that the site of Qumran served as a monastery. The evidence for the practice of celibacy among them comes from the ancient writers Philo, Josephus and Pliny.[7] The Dead Sea documents themselves seem to suggest that the practice of celibacy was at most temporary and that it was undertaken from traditional Jewish notions of ritual purity.[8] The evidence from the cemetery suggests that women and children were also present at Qumran. The practice of perpetual celibacy would certainly have been contrary to traditional Jewish theology, which regarded the injunction of Gen 1:28 to increase and multiply as the first command of the law. And the Essenes, though a separatist group, were certainly traditional in their beliefs. Indeed, it seems to have been their devotion to the observance of the law that led them to become a separatist group.[9]

In regard to the monastic character of the site at Qumran, it is true that certain things, such as the kiln, the scriptorium and the elaborate system of cisterns, might suggest long-term occupation. The documents, however, do not presuppose a community of any appreciable size nor indicate that permanent residence was normal for the members of the Essene sect. Moreover, the lack of any continuous fresh water supply at the site and the intense heat at certain times of the year make it quite improbable that a group of any size could have maintained a community life the year round at Qumran. It seems rather that the site served as a seasonal gathering place for the Essene sect. Therefore, it is rather misleading to refer to the Essenes as monks or to the site of Qumran as a monastery.[10] Since the Essenes do not appear to have occupied Qumran after its destruction during the war of A.D. 66–70 or even to have survived as a distinct group within Judaism after this time, there is no evidence of any historical connection between them and the early Christian monks more than two centuries later.[11]

[7] Philo, *Quod omnis probus liber sit* XII–XIII (75–91) quoted by Eusebius, *praep. evang.* 8,12; *Hypothetica (Apologia pro Iudeis)* quoted by Eusebius, *praep.evang.* 8,11; Jos. *de bello Iud.* 2, 119–161; Pliny, *nat.hist.* 5,15,73.

[8] See J. van der Ploeg "Les Esséniens et les origines du monachisme chrétien" *Orientalia Christiana Analecta* 153 (1958) 327–328; Hans Hubner "Zölibat in Qumran?" *New Testament Studies* 17 (1970/71) 153–167.

[9] See F. L. Cross, Jr., *The Ancient Library of Qumran* (Garden City, N.Y.: Doubleday-Anchor 1961) pp. 127–160.

[10] *Ibid.*, p. 100.

[11] A. Vööbus, *History of Asceticism in the Syrian Orient*, CSCO 184,197 (Louvain: Secrétariat du CSCO 1958, 1960) 1.29, suggests that early Christianity in Syria may

Another group that has fascinated both ancient and modern writers by its apparent resemblance to Christian monasticism is that of the Therapeutae.[12] Our sole source of information about this group is the Hellenistic Jewish writer Philo of Alexandria, who compares them with both the Greek philosophers and the Essenes. According to Philo, the Therapeutae were to be found in many regions even outside of Egypt, but their center was on a hill outside of Alexandria near Lake Mareotis. They pursued the *bios theorētikos* (a term derived from Greek philosophy), which means 'contemplative life,' and acquired their name (*therapeutae* means 'healers') from the fact that they sought healing for the soul from all sorts of passions. The sect included both men and women who, however, lived apart and were separated by a wall even when they came together for instruction. Those who joined the sect left behind family, property and fatherland to give themselves over wholly to their high calling. They also sought to leave behind the noise and cares of the cities by living in a lonely place.

Each member of the sect had a separate house, which contained a holy place called the *semneion* or *monastērion*. This room served as a place for study of the Law and the Prophets, the psalms and other writings. It was not used for bodily needs, which seem to have been held in some contempt. The entire day was spent in spiritual *askēsis*, the study of the Scriptures, in which the higher allegorical meaning was sought (a preoccupation of Philo himself), and at night bodily needs were cared for. On the Sabbath the members assembled, sitting in strict seniority, while the eldest gave a talk. Every seven weeks they held a special feast, for which they wore white clothing (as did the Essenes). They began with prayer and ate in silence. They drank no wine, but took water and ate bread with salt and hyssop. Philo says that the reason for not drinking wine was the command in the law to the priests not to drink wine on the occasion of the sacrifice. Most of the women who belonged to the group were virgins, though a previous marriage was not an obstacle to joining the group. The members preserved chastity out of a desire for wisdom.

Since Philo is our sole source of information about this group, it is difficult to assess the reliability of his report. He probably exaggerates the extent of the group. Some practices of the Therapeutae, such as the

---

have received its ascetic character through Jewish groups that adopted Christianity, such as the Essenes. This is pure speculation for which there is no historical evidence.

[12] Cf. Mohler, *Heresy*, pp. 27–30; Lohse, *Askese*, pp. 95–101.

abstention from wine because of the command to the priests in the Old Testament and the study of Scripture, suggest obvious ties with Judaism, but there also appear to be present strong influences from the philosophic traditions of the Hellenistic world. This would have been particularly strong at Alexandria, which was the intellectual center of the Hellenistic world in the first century A.D. Philo himself was the principal representative of the attempt to make Judaism respectable in terms of Hellenistic culture and therefore was not at all representative of the mainstream of Jewish culture.

About the origins and later history of the Therapeutae, only speculation is possible. This has not been wanting even in antiquity. The Church historian Eusebius of Caesarea decided that Philo had really misunderstood the nature of this group. Because some of their features, such as common ownership, resembled those of the early Christians, as portrayed in the Acts of the Apostles, they appeared to Eusebius to be the early Christian community in Egypt. St. Jerome noted the similarity between this description by Eusebius of the first Christians in Egypt and the monks of his day. Writing almost a century after Eusebius, at a time when the monastic movement was fully developed, Cassian went further and affirmed that the first Christians of Egypt were obviously monks, and thus monastic life was given an apostolic origin.[13] This, of course, appears to the modern historian to be without foundation. There is no evidence of any connection between the Therapeutae and the origins of Christian monasticism other than this literary one.

In the pagan world of antiquity, the movement most frequently compared with Christian monasticism is that of Pythagoras and the later neo-Pythagoreans.[14] Pythagoras himself was a sixth-century (B.C.) philosopher and religious reformer who left no writings and of whom little is known with certainty.[15] It is difficult to distinguish the original Pythagorean teaching from the later, more elaborate pictures given by Philostratus and Iamblichus.[16] According to Iamblichus, admission into the Pythagorean community involved an extensive

[13] Philo, *De vita contemplativa*; Eus. *hist.eccles.* 2,17; Hier. *de viris illus.* 8; Cassian. *inst.* 2,5.

[14] Lohse, *Askese*, pp. 45–46; P. Jordan "Pythagoras and Monachism" *Traditio* 17 (1961) 432–441. Heussi, *Ursprung*, pp. 19–20, suggests that the author of Acts was influenced by a description of the Pythagorean community in his description of the early Christian community. This suggestion has not found much favor with exegetes.

[15] K. Prümm, *Religiongeschichtliches Handbuch für den Raum der altchristlichen Umwelt* (Rome: Biblical Institute Press 1954) pp. 123–128.

[16] Philostratus, *The Life of Apollonius of Tyana*, ed. F. C. Conybeare, 2 vols. (Lon-

examination, a kind of postulancy and novitiate lasting several years. Those fully initiated wore a distinctive dress and followed a regular schedule. Goods were held in common. The goal of this ascetic life was to free the soul from the bonds of the body.[17] Despite certain similarities and the presence of some of the terminology found in early Christian monasticism (askēsis, anachōrēsis, koinobion), there is no evidence of any direct influence of neo-Pythagoreanism upon early Christian monasticism. Indirect influences are possible. Works such as the *Life of Apollonius of Tyana* by Philostratus were widely circulated, and it is not impossible that Athanasius in his *Life of Antony* was deliberately attempting to portray a Christian ascetic motivated by a spirit quite different from that of the neo-Pythagoreans or other philosophical ascetics.[18]

The term "monastic" has also often been used by Western writers to describe the ascetic style of life found among the Hindus and Buddhists, and it is generally agreed that this style of life antedates the origins of Christian monasticism by several centuries at least. There is evidence of considerable contact between India and Alexandria, the most cosmopolitan city of the Hellenistic world.[19] Hindu merchants formed a permanent colony at Alexandria, which is mentioned by ancient historians, and excavations there have turned up Buddhist emblems. The Buddha is mentioned by Clement of Alexandria, and the Brahmans are mentioned by various Greek writers, including Hippolytus of Rome.[20] It has been suggested that some of the gnostic teachers, such as Basilides and Valentinian, were influenced by Buddhist doctrine.[21] Bardesanes († A.D. 222) told of meeting an Indian ambassador in Edessa, from whom he learned about the Buddhist monasteries. This passage is quoted at length by Porphyry in a work with which Athanasius was probably familiar.[22]

In the early fifth century, Palladius composed a letter about the

---

don: Heinemann 1912); Iamblichus, *De vita pythagorica liber*, ed. A. Nauck (1884; rpt. Amsterdam: A. Hakkert 1965); Michael von Albrecht, *Pythagoras; Legenda, Lehre, Lebensgestaltung* (Zürich: Artemis 1963).

[17] Jordan "Pythagoras and Monachism" p. 437.

[18] B. Steidle "Homo Dei Antonius" *Antonius Magnus, Eremita 356–1956*, StA 38 (Rome: Herder 1956) pp. 176–183.

[19] M. Roncaglia, *Histoire de l'église copte IV* (Beirut: Dar Al-Kalima 1973) pp. 191–205.

[20] Clem. *strom.* I,15,71,6. Cf. B. Berg "Dandamis: An Early Christian Portrait of Indian Asceticism" *Classica et Mediaevalia* 31 (1970) 277.

[21] Roncaglia, *Histoire*, pp. 200–207; Berg "Dandamis" p. 279.

[22] Berg "Dandamis" p. 280; Porph. *de abstin.* 4,17.

Brahmans in which he tells how, during his travels in Upper Egypt (and possibly Ethiopia), he met a lawyer from Thebes, who told him of spending six years of captivity in India, where he had learned of the Brahmans and their ascetic practices.[23] This letter formed part of a treatise known as *On the Races of India and the Brahmans*, which circulated widely in the East and also in the West in Latin translation.[24] It served to provide a pagan precedent for the new institution of monasticism and as such was apparently of interest to Christian monks. However, despite these numerous references to, and descriptions (often highly inaccurate) of, Eastern religious practices, there is no direct evidence that the latter inspired the origins of the Christian monastic movement.

It has also been argued that the Manichaean religion was an important influence in the development of Christian monasticism, especially in Syria and Mesopotamia.[25] Mani had an explicitly syncretistic intention in founding his sect, and he may have borrowed extensively from Buddhist practices and ideals.[26] Vööbus has argued that the "monastic" character of Manichaeism is derived from Buddhism and that this in turn heavily influenced the formation of Christian monasticism. The question of the extent of Manichaean influence in the development of Christian monasticism remains a disputed point.[27] It is particularly questionable whether the "elect" of the Manichaean system can properly be described as monks at all.[28]

Another figure often mentioned in connection with the origins of Christian monasticism (although he is not properly classified as a non-Christian) is Hierakas, a Copt born about A.D. 275 in Leontopolis. Early in the fourth century, he assembled a circle to which only virgins, the continent and widowed persons could belong. His group included both men and women. He thought, among other things, that marriage was allowed in the Old Testament but that the new revelation of the Logos consisted in the prohibition of sex and marriage. Without complete abstinence one could not reach the kingdom of heaven. Hierakas' teaching has a resemblance to the tendencies in

[23] B. Berg "The Letter of Palladius on India" *Byzantion* 44 (1974) 5–16.

[24] A. Wilmart "Les textes latins de la lettre de Palladius sur les moeurs des Brahmanes" *RBén* 45 (1933) 29–42.

[25] Vööbus, *History*, 1.109f.

[26] *Ibid.*, p. 112.

[27] *Ibid.*, pp. 164f. Cf. Heussi, *Ursprung*, pp. 287f.

[28] A. Adam, review of Vööbus in *Göttingische Gelehrte Anzeigen* 214 (1960) 127–145. Reprinted in Frank, *Askese*, pp. 230–254.

Syria and Asia Minor that made celibacy a requirement for all Christians.[29] Hierakas has been held up as an example of a widespread ascetic ideal or tendency in Egypt, suggesting a common background from which the other prominent figures of early Christian monasticism also sprang.[30] This is perhaps a dubious generalization on the basis of one example. Our only knowledge of Hierakas and his group comes from Epiphanius, who includes him in his great collection of heresies (Epiph. pan. 67). Hierakas is perhaps more significant in that he provides an instance, as do others elsewhere, of the sharp distinction that could be made in the Church between ascetics who were orthodox and those who had deviated too far from the traditional teaching.

Although we have pointed out that there is no evidence of any direct connection between the various religious movements that have been mentioned and the rise of Christian monasticism, there may be numerous connections to be found in the general stock of popular ideas current in the late Hellenistic world, to which these movements had contributed and from which they were partially derived. This common fund of popular ideas was shared by early monastic writers. This is particularly true of the ideas lying behind various ascetical practices such as fasting.[31] To illustrate this possibility by an analogy, one need only consider how the mental world of a modern Christian can be influenced, often unconsciously, by such diverse teachings as those of Marx, Darwin and Freud.

3. THE LITERATURE OF EARLY CHRISTIAN MONASTICISM

The principal source of our knowledge of the origin of Christian monasticism lies in the literature that the movement produced. This literature includes biographies, collections of sayings, letters and homilies of various monks, *ex professo* treatments of the ascetic and monastic life, such as those of Basil, Evagrius and Cassian, and finally the works of historians.

The most important of the biographies is the *Life of Antony*, generally accepted as the work of Athanasius, who was bishop of Alexandria

---

[29] Lohse, *Askese*, pp. 211f.

[30] *Ibid.*, p. 179; Heussi, *Ursprung*, pp. 58–59.

[31] Studies of the motifs involved in the practice of fasting have been made by R. Arbesmann "Fasting and Prophecy in Pagan and Christian Antiquity" *Traditio* 7 (1949–51) 1–71 and H. Musurillo "The Problem of Ascetical Fasting in the Greek Patristic Writers" *Traditio* 12 (1956) 1–64. An interesting study of the cosmological speculation and demonology present in the ancient world may be found in J. Daniélou "Les démons de l'air dans la Vie d'Antoine" *Antonius Magnus*, pp. 136–147.

and therefore head of the Church in Egypt for almost fifty years in the middle of the fourth century. It was written soon after the death of Antony and was early translated into Latin. It quickly became the most important piece of propaganda for the monastic movement throughout the Christian world. The literary form of this document and the models Athanasius used remain a matter of discussion, but it is generally accepted as the first great work of Christian hagiography.[32] More will be said of it below. A number of letters attributed to Antony also survive in ancient translations and are generally accepted as genuine.[33] Sayings attributed to him may be found in the *Apophthegmata Patrum*, which are anonymous collections of sayings and anecdotes of famous monks compiled in the fifth and sixth centuries A.D. These collections have come down to us in a number of ancient versions, which differ considerably among themselves. Of these, the most important in the West is the Latin collection known as the *Verba Seniorum*.[34]

Another category of monastic literature is composed of Pachomian materials. These include a number of lives of Pachomius and his successors in Greek, Coptic and Arabic. There is disagreement over which are the most important.[35] There have also survived many writings of Pachomius himself and his immediate successors, Horsiesius and Theodore, in Coptic and partially in Latin. Knowledge of Pachomian monasticism passed into the West, however, primarily through St. Jerome's translation of his rule from a Greek version. This rule influenced a number of pre-Benedictine rules in the West and the Rule of St. Benedict itself. Some additional information about the Pachomians may be found in the *Lausiac History* by Palladius. This work, originally written in Greek, was early translated into Latin and was very influential in spreading knowledge of Egyptian monasticism to the West. Its author had spent much time in Egypt, first as a monk

---

[32] For a discussion of the literary form, see R. T. Meyer, *St. Athanasius: The Life of Antony*, ACW 10 (Westminster, Md.: Newman Press 1950) Introduction, pp. 11–14.

[33] D. J. Chitty, *The Letters of St. Antony the Great* (Oxford: SLG Press 1975). Cf. G. Couilleau "La liberté d'Antoine" *Commandements du Seigneur et Libération Évangélique*, StA 70 (Rome: Editrice Anselmiana 1977) pp. 13–40, and "L'alliance aux origines du monachisme égyptien" *CollCist* 39 (1977) 170–193.

[34] For studies on the relationship of these various collections, see W. Bousset, *Apophthegmata: Studien zur Geschichte des ältesten Mönchtums* (Tübingen: J.C.B. Mohr 1923); J. C. Guy, *Recherches sur la tradition Grecque des Apophthegmata Patrum*, Subsidia Hagiographica 36 (Brussels: Société des Bollandistes 1962) and J. Quasten, *Patrology*, 3 vols. (Westminster, Md.: Newman Press 1950–60) 3.187–189.

[35] See note 69 below.

and then as a bishop, where he gathered the stories that make up the collection. A similar work, known as the *Historia monachorum in Aegypto*, was written originally in Greek, but has survived also in a longer Latin version attributed to Rufinus of Aquileia, a contemporary of Jerome and Cassian. It purports to be the record of a journey up the Nile at the end of the fourth century by a group of pilgrims interested in witnessing the phenomenon of Egyptian monasticism.

The extensive works of St. Basil himself provide the best source of knowledge about the form of monasticism he instituted in Asia Minor. The most important of these is the collection known as the *Asceticon*, which includes the longer and shorter rules.[36] These were early translated into Latin (perhaps by Rufinus) and exercised considerable influence on Western monasticism. The works of Evagrius of Pontus and John Cassian also provide an important witness to the spirituality of Egyptian monasticism, especially at the end of the fourth century. The extent of Evagrius' influence in the West, as well as the amount of his work translated into Latin, remains a much disputed point.[37] The work of Cassian, originally written in Latin in southern Gaul, testifies perhaps as much to the adaptation of Egyptian monasticism in the West as it does to the original movement.[38]

There are also the works of the historians Socrates, Sozomen and Theodoret of Cyrrhus. Socrates and Sozomen both wrote in the first half of the fifth century with the express intention of bringing the work of Eusebius up to date. The monastic movement is prominent in their histories, for which they used as sources the works mentioned above as well as others that have been lost. Theodoret, a contemporary of theirs in Syria, wrote a *History of the Monks*, which covers chiefly the area around Antioch.[39]

4. THE DEVELOPMENT OF MONASTICISM
IN RELATION TO THE CHURCH

The more obvious roots of Christian monasticism are to be found in the teachings of the New Testament, with which the early monks

[36] See note 85 below.

[37] For a brief discussion of his influence, see the Preface by Jean Leclercq in *Evagrius Ponticus: The Praktikos, Chapters on Prayer*, tr. J. E. Bamberger (Spencer, Mass.: Cistercian Publications 1970) pp. vii–xxii and A. Wathen "Methodological Considerations of the Sources of the Regula Benedicti as Instruments of Historical Interpretations" *RBS* 5 (1976) 101–117.

[38] On Cassian, see pp. 57–59 below.

[39] See note 66 below.

showed exceptional familiarity,[40] and in the changed relationship of the Church to society that developed in the fourth century. One aspect of this change was the cessation of the persecutions and the consequent acceptance of Christianity by the Roman empire. It should be mentioned, however, that the persecutions themselves have also been invoked as one cause of the rise of monasticism. The last persecutions — those of Decius in A.D. 240 and of Diocletian in 304 and following years — were particularly severe in Egypt. Many Christians fled to avoid martyrdom, and some of these would have formed a nucleus of desert ascetics. The hardships inevitably encountered by such fugitives would have contributed to the ascetic practices they then adopted.[41] This is a difficult conjecture to assess, since we have no certain knowledge of any particular figures who adopted the anchoritic life as a result of flight from martyrdom. Indeed, according to his biographer, the first major figure in the monastic movement, Antony, went to Alexandria during the last persecution in the hope of achieving martyrdom (*Vita Anton.* 46).

The cessation of the persecutions, on the other hand, has also been cited as one of the factors that gave an impetus to the monastic movement. The monk came to replace the martyr as the hero of the early Church in its new triumphal condition. When the triumph of the Church drove the demons from the cities, the new heroes of the faith pursued them to the desert, there to engage in single-handed combat.[42] This rather complex theme can be traced through several stages in the Patristic writings.[43] The martyrs undoubtedly held first rank as the heroes of the early Church. They had made the ultimate sacrifice; like Jesus himself, they had laid down their lives. In the third century, we find the virgins placed in the same company as the martyrs by Origen, who interpreted the thirtyfold, sixtyfold and one hundredfold of the parable of the sower (Mark 4:8) to refer to the widows, virgins and martyrs (Orig. *hom. in Iesu Nave* 2,1). At the end of the third century, Methodius of Olympus calls the virgins martyrs (Meth. *conviv.* 7,3). Athanasius, in a speech placed in the mouth of Antony, cites the

[40] See C. Peifer "The Biblical Foundations of Monasticism" *CS* 1 (1966) 7–31; H. Dörries "Die Bibel im ältesten Mönchtum" *Theologische Literaturzeitung* 72 (1947) 215–222.

[41] Musurillo "The Problem" p. 26. Musurillo quotes a letter of Dionysius, bishop of Alexandria at the time, which he construes to suggest this.

[42] H. I. Bell, *Egypt, from Alexander the Great to the Arab Conquest* (Oxford: The Clarendon Press 1948) pp. 109–110.

[43] See E. E. Malone, *The Monk and the Martyr* (Washington: Catholic Univ. Press 1950).

virgins and the martyrs as testimony to the faith and teaching of Christ (*Vita Anton.* 79).

This equation of the virgins with the martyrs led eventually to a new equation — that of monastic profession with baptism, or rather a second baptism.[44] Martyrdom had earlier been seen as a substitute for baptism or, for those already baptized, as a second baptism. When the monastic life came to be equated with or placed on the same level as martyrdom, it was but a short step to compare monastic profession to baptism, as St. Jerome did in a famous letter to Paula concerning her daughter: "Only four months ago Blesilla, by the grace of Christ, was washed by a kind of second baptism, that of profession" (Hier. *epist.* 39,3-4). Just as baptism was held to forgive sins, so monastic profession came to be held to forgive sins. This idea seems to occur already in Athanasius' *Life of Antony*, though without an explicit reference to monastic profession as a second baptism (*Vita Anton.* 65). There are innumerable references to this complex of ideas in later monastic literature, and it undoubtedly had some role in raising the monastic life to a level of high esteem and providing motivation for following it. To what extent the idea of monastic life as a replacement for martyrdom served to provide the original impetus for the monastic movement is, however, difficult to evaluate.

This idea is related, perhaps, to what we may call the reforming aspect of early Christian monasticism. The steady growth of the Church, especially in the periods of relative peace before and after the Decian persecution, had led to what contemporaries regarded as laxity in discipline. This view is evident already in the writings of Tertullian and particularly in the dispute that arose at the end of the Decian persecution over the reconciliation of the *lapsi*.[45] When the persecutions ceased altogether in the early fourth century and Christianity became the object of imperial favor, the problem became more acute. In the course of the fourth century, the Church ceased to be a persecuted minority and became the state religion of the empire. Whereas formerly the Church had identified itself as a minority group often in opposition to the state, it now came to be identified with the state.[46] By the end of the fourth century, the identification of Christian and

[44] E. E. Malone "Martyrdom and Monastic Profession as a Second Baptism" *Vom Christlichen Mysterium: Gesammelte Arbeiten zum Gedächtnis von Odo Casel, O.S.B.,* ed. A. Mayer, J. Quasten and B. Neunheuser (Düsseldorf: Patmos 1951) pp. 115–134.

[45] Cf. K. Bihlmeyer and H. Tüchle, *Church History* (Westminster, Md.: Newman Press 1958) 1.128–129.

[46] A. Mirgeler, *Mutations of Western Christianity* (New York: Herder and Herder 1964) pp. 27–43.

citizen was virtually complete, and no non-Christian could hope for advancement in the imperial service.

Such a radical change of social position could not but influence the internal operation of the Church. Indeed, the emperors, beginning with Constantine himself, took a very active role in Church affairs, and the imperial family showered the Church with favors such as buildings and endowments. Even before the Council of Nicaea in 325, which Constantine called to settle matters of Church doctrine and discipline, privileges and exemptions from civil burdens had been conferred on all grades of the Christian clergy.[47] In addition, bishops had been given jurisdiction in many instances.[48] In A.D. 321, Sunday had been declared a public holiday. The Christian liturgy also began to show signs of that imperial pomp and splendor that Constantine himself loved to display.[49] All this meant that there were now many additional reasons for becoming a Christian and even for seeking office in the Church other than simple faith in Jesus Christ.

While the identification of the Church with society led to a superficial dominance of society by the forms of Christianity, it also led to an invasion of the Church by the values of secular society (or the "world," as the monastic literature called it), something perceived even by contemporaries.[50] Since the opportunity for martyrdom no longer existed for those who wished to respond fully to the teaching and example of Christ, the development of monasticism may well have been in compensation for this, to provide an outlet for those who were not satisfied with a mediocre Christianity. Monasticism appears, then, against the background of the changes in the Church of the fourth century as a reform movement, or rather as a new form for the older Christian idea of reformation in Christ.[51] This may be one of the principal reasons for the rapid development of monasticism.

[47] A.H.M. Jones, *The Later Roman Empire 284–602: A Social, Economic, and Administrative Survey* (Norman: Univ. of Oklahoma Press 1964) 2.912.

[48] See T. Klauser, *A Short History of the Western Liturgy* (London: Oxford University Press 1969) pp. 33–34 and J. Vogt, *The Decline of Rome: The Metamorphosis of Ancient Civilization* (New York: Praeger 1956) p. 94.

[49] *Ibid.*, pp. 101–106.

[50] *Ibid.*, p. 117.

[51] For a discussion of the role of the idea of reform in early Christianity, see G. B. Ladner, *The Idea of Reform* (Cambridge: Harvard Univ. Press 1959). The explanation of the rise of monasticism as a reform movement was given its classic expression by the German historian Adolf Harnack, *Monasticism: Its Ideals and History* (New York 1895), who regarded monasticism favorably but felt, of course, that the right answer to the problem was only the constant reform of the whole Church. The idea has been adopted by numerous historians since Harnack. Cf. Vogt, *Decline*, p. 123; Mohler, *Heresy*, p. 41.

5. ANACHŌRĒSIS AND THE EREMITICAL MOVEMENT

The term *anachōrēsis*, meaning 'retirement' or 'withdrawal,' has a pre-Christian history of usage in the sense of withdrawal into oneself. This idea can be found in numerous pagan philosophical writings of various schools.[52] A tendency to retreat or withdraw from the world for the sake of contemplation and peace of mind can be found in such varied writers as Cicero, Seneca, Dio Chrysostom, Marcus Aurelius and Plotinus. The notion of flight from the world and detachment from all things is quite explicit in the last. The idea is present also in Jewish and Christian writers such as Philo and Origen. In his life of Plotinus, Porphyry portrayed his master as loving to withdraw from the city. It has been suggested that Athanasius had this work in mind when he composed his *Life of Antony*. Certainly he portrayed Antony as the archetypical anchorite.[53] But by this time *anachōrēsis* may have been almost a technical term for withdrawal from the world.

For the Christian who sought this retirement, however, there were other precedents. In Matt 14:13, it is said of Jesus that "he withdrew . . . into a desert place by himself." The words used here are *anachōrein* and *erēmos topos*, which of course give rise in the monastic vocabulary to 'anchorite' and 'hermit.' In John 6:15, it is said that Jesus "withdrew again to the mountain by himself." There was also the example Jesus had given by spending forty days in the desert engaged in fasting, prayer and spiritual combat (Matt 4:2-10). For the early Christian anchorites, it was this example that was primary, rather than that of the pagan philosophers, of whom most had probably not even heard.[54]

The question of who the first Christians were who took up this life of retirement or *anachōrēsis* was disputed in antiquity and remains surrounded by obscurity today. The earliest example of a Christian hermit known by name is provided by Eusebius, who tells the story of a bishop of Jerusalem named Narcissus. The latter lived at the beginning of the third century. He became so upset because of the slander

[52] A. J. Festugière, *Personal Religion Among the Greeks* (Berkeley: Univ. of California Press 1954) pp. 53–67.

[53] *Ibid.*, p. 67. In Egypt, the word *anachōrēsis* was also used to refer to the case of those who fled to avoid taxes. See M. Rostovtsev, *Social and Economic History of the Roman Empire* (Oxford: The Clarendon Press 1941) pp. 578–579, 599. Later emperors would find it necessary to enact legislation against those who took up monastic life in order to avoid legal obligations. See Jones, *The Later Roman Empire*, 2.931. For a more thorough discussion of the literary form and background of Athanasius' *Life of Antony*, see Heussi, *Ursprung*, pp. 78–100.

[54] Festugière, *Personal Religion*, p. 67.

he suffered on account of his virtuous conduct that he withdrew and lived many years in the deserts and remote regions. He returned during the rule of his third successor and, according to Eusebius, caused great amazement on account of his *anachōrēsis* and his "philosophic" conduct of life (Eus. *hist.eccles.* 6,10).[55] Whether or not this qualifies as an example of the later withdrawal for ascetic motives is dubious. Eusebius does not cite it as an example of a movement.

St. Jerome reports that in his time it was disputed who the first hermit had been. Some said it was Antony. He himself, on information from some disciples of Antony, claimed that it was a certain Paul of Thebes, who had taken up the eremitical life at the time of the Decian persecution (Hier. *vita Pauli* 1).[56] Athanasius claimed that Antony was the first to take up the desert *anachōrēsis*. However, he mentions that before this time, each one who wished to live the ascetic life would practice it not far from his own village. It was to one of these that Antony went to learn about the ascetic life (*Vita Anton.* 3-4). A similar situation is suggested in the Lives of Pachomius, who attached himself to an old man named Palamon to learn the ascetic life (*Vita prima* 6). How this practice came to exist and how widespread it was remains obscure.

Whether or not Antony was the first hermit, there is no doubt that his example and his fame, particularly as spread by Athanasius, gave a great impetus to the eremitical movement in northern Egypt and eventually far beyond the borders of Egypt. Our principal source of knowledge about Antony is the *Life* written by Athanasius. In evaluating the picture given by Athanasius, several things must be kept in mind. Although Athanasius had known Antony personally and is supposed to have written his *Life* soon after the saint's death in 356, his motivation in writing (which he says was at the request of monks in foreign parts) was to spread monasticism. Gregory of Nazianzen, in his own eulogy of Athanasius, says that "the learned bishop in writing this life was really promulgating the precepts of the ideal monastic life in the guise of a story" (Greg.Naz. *orat.* 21,5).[57] In addition to this,

---

[55] "Philosophic" is used by Eusebius as a technical term more or less synonymous with "ascetic." He uses it of other Christian figures, such as Origen, and this usage is continued in later monastic writings. See G. Penco "La vita ascetica come 'Filosofia' nell' antica tradizione monastica" *SM* 2 (1960) 79–93.

[56] Doubt has been cast on the existence of this figure by modern scholars as well as by Jerome's contemporaries. See J.N.D. Kelly, *Jerome* (New York: Harper & Row 1975) pp. 60–61.

[57] The translation is by Musurillo "The Problem of Ascetical Fasting" p. 27.

Athanasius, the greatest champion of orthodoxy in the fourth century, probably wanted to enlist the aid of the saint against Arianism: Antony would now play the role of intercessor from heaven, as he had previously been defender of the faith on earth. He may also have had an eye on the pagan world and wished to show that the Christian was also an initiate of mysteries, also sought and attained perfection, and that Christian wisdom was superior to that of the pagans (*Vita Anton.* 14,72).[58]

According to Athanasius, Antony was born about A.D. 251 in Middle Egypt of well-to-do parents. The early death of his parents left him as guardian of his only sister. One day, when he was about twenty years old, he entered the church and heard the reading "If you wish to be perfect, go, sell all that you have . . . ." (Matt 19:21). So he went home, distributed his farm of two hundred acres to the townspeople, sold his other belongings and gave the money to the poor, retaining only a small sum for his sister. Once again he went to church and heard the exhortation not to be solicitous about tomorrow (Matt 6:34). So he distributed his remaining money to the poor, put his sister in the care of a community of pious women and began to practice the ascetic life near his home by seeking to imitate an old man who had practiced asceticism since his youth (*Vita Anton.* 3). Later he went to live in some tombs much farther from the village and remained there until he was thirty-five, fighting off the temptations of the flesh and demons. Then he decided to go to the desert. This was regarded as an innovation, since there was as yet no such custom (*Vita Anton.* 11). He crossed to the eastern side of the Nile and shut himself up in a deserted fort on the edge of the desert at Pispir, which became known as his "outer mountain." This would have been at about the beginning of the reign of Diocletian. After twenty years, Antony was visited by friends who wished to copy his holy life. They broke down the door, and Antony emerged "as one initiated into sacred mysteries and filled with the Spirit of God" (*Vita Anton.* 14). This sentence is often taken as evidence that Athanasius had his eye on the mystery cults and quest for perfection of the pagan world.

Antony then performed miracles and preached the love of Christ to all who came to see him. In a famous passage, Athanasius ties the development of the monastic life to Antony's preaching: "He induced many to take up the monastic life. And so now monasteries also sprang

[58] Cf. Chitty, *The Desert a City*, p. 4.

up in the mountains, and the desert was populated with monks who left their own people and registered themselves for citizenship in heaven" (Vita Anton. 14). This picture appears to be historically premature, but the aim of Athanasius may have been to show that monasticism was an institution before the peace of the Church.[59]

At the end of the persecution of Maximin Daia in 311, Antony appeared in Alexandria to encourage the martyrs, while even hoping for martyrdom for himself. He was not martyred and returned to his cell "a daily martyr to his conscience, ever fighting the battles of the faith" (Vita Anton. 47). The end of the persecutions meant more visitors for Antony, and so to recover his solitude he decided to move to a location closer to the Red Sea that was reached by traveling several days with a caravan through the desert. This new retreat became known as his "inner mountain." He did not, however, remain there continuously, and on one occasion at least, he went to Alexandria (about A.D. 338) to denounce the Arians and show support for Athanasius. According to Athanasius, Antony's fame was so great that even Constantine and his sons wrote to him (Vita Anton. 81). Finally, when he felt his end approaching (Athanasius claims that he was 105 years old), Antony took two companions with him to his inner mountain, where he died in A.D. 356, leaving to Athanasius his sheepskin and a cloak.

Soon after his death, if not before, Antony came to be regarded as the founder and father of monasticism. He was not of course a founder in the sense of later figures such as Dominic or Ignatius, but was rather, due especially to the influence of Athanasius' writing, an archetype or model for the orthodox hermit. His original settlement at Pispir, where he was succeeded by his disciple Ammonas, became a center of the solitary life in Egypt. His disciples or imitators were instrumental in spreading monasticism elsewhere, even outside of Egypt, and later on monastic settlements sought to find a connection with Antony even when there had been none originally.[60]

Of particular importance for the course of later monastic history are the settlements at Nitria, Cellia (or the Cells) and Scetis. According to Palladius, the colony of hermits at Nitria had been founded by Amoun (Pallad. hist.laus. 8). The latter had been forced to marry at about age twenty-two, but on his wedding night persuaded his bride that they

---

[59] Ibid., p. 5.

[60] Vööbus, 1.137–147, has argued that Syrian monasticism arose independently of Egyptian monasticism and that links with Egyptian figures come later.

should both live a celibate life. This they did, living in the same house for eighteen years until she consented to allow him to leave her for the desert. Amoun then built himself two domed cells on the mountain of Nitria, where he lived for twenty-two years, attracting many disciples and imitators. This would have been about A.D. 330. According to Athanasius (*Vita Anton.* 60), Amoun was well known to Antony, having often come to see him, and when he died, Antony had a vision of his soul being taken to heaven. Rufinus tells us that when he visited Nitria (about A.D. 373), there were about three thousand monks living there (Ruf. *hist.eccles.* 2,3). Palladius says that when he visited the place (about A.D. 390), there were almost five thousand monks at Nitria and about six hundred living in the Great Desert (Pallad. *hist.laus.* 7,2).

This group of monks living farther out in the desert formed what was known as Cellia. Its foundation was said to have occurred in connection with a visit of Antony to see Amoun at Nitria. Apparently Amoun was concerned that because of the increase of numbers at Nitria, there was insufficient solitude, and he asked Antony's advice. Antony suggested they take a walk after their meal in the afternoon. They walked until sunset, when Antony pointed out that those who desired greater solitude could build at that spot, which was said to be twelve miles from Nitria. Other sources give a lesser distance.

About forty miles to the south in the Wadi-el-Natrun, in what was known as the desert of Scetis, another monastic settlement was started about the same time as Nitria by Macarius the Egyptian. He too was soon joined by others; he too is recorded as having visited Antony. Originally there was no priest at Scetis, and Macarius is said to have traveled forty miles to attend Mass at Nitria. By the time of Cassian, there were four congregations or churches at Scetis (Cassian. *conl.* 10,2). Monastic life has continued there to this day.[61]

Our knowledge of the monastic life at Nitria and Scetis comes chiefly from Palladius and the *Historia monachorum*. According to the former, there were some fifty monasteries at Nitria; the monks dwelt singly, in small groups or in groups as large as 210 (Pallad. *dial.* 17). Recent excavations as well as ancient writers suggest that some of the dwellings among the Cells, especially those of the more famous hermits, were comparatively elaborate, consisting of several rooms and an

---

[61] Un moine de Saint-Macaire "La monastère de Saint-Macaire au Désert de Scété (Wâdi el Natrun)" *Irenikon* 51 (1978) 203–215.

enclosed courtyard, including within it a well.[62] According to Palladius, all the monks of both Nitria and the Cells were supplied with bread by seven bakeries (Pallad. *hist.laus.* 7). A great church was built at Nitria, which was used only on Saturdays and Sundays, and near it stood a guesthouse. Guests were allowed a week of leisure and were then put to work in the garden, bakery or kitchen. Palladius says that there were also doctors and pastry cooks at Nitria, and that wine was sold there. The monks all worked at making linen to earn their living. At Scetis the monks produced rope and baskets, which they sold to passing caravans, but they would also hire themselves out at harvest time to work in the fields.

From an early date, the settlements at Nitria and the Cells had their own priests, who came under the jurisdiction of the bishop of Hermopolis Parva. Palladius says that when he stayed at Nitria, there were eight priests, but only the senior priest celebrated the liturgy and preached. These seem to have formed a kind of governing body. However, the government must have been fairly loose, for Palladius also says that the monks of Nitria followed "different ways of life, each as he can or will" (Pallad. *hist.laus.* 7). There was no formal novitiate or profession of vows. A newcomer sought out an older monk whom he might serve as a kind of apprentice and thus learn from him and imitate him. The styles of life ranged from quasi-cenobitic at Nitria itself to the completely eremitical of the Cells. Such a system was open to the abuse of ascetic rivalry and the other aberrations to which the literature bears witness. The eremitic style of monastic life has had severe critics in the ancient world as well as in the modern world. Of the former, the most eloquent, as we shall see, was St. Basil.

The early development of monasticism in Palestine and Syria is shrouded in somewhat greater obscurity than that in Egypt, but it seems to have developed along basically eremitical lines.[63] According to Jerome, monasticism in Palestine owed its origin to Hilarion, a native of the area, who studied at Alexandria and spent a few months with Antony (Hier. *vita Hil.* 10). Returning home at age fifteen, he took up the eremitical life about the year 307 near Gaza, where he spent twenty-two years in solitude. Then others began to join him and imitate him, establishing monasteries throughout the land. One of his

---

[62] C. C. Walters, *Monastic Archaeology in Egypt* (Warminster, England: Aris and Phillips 1974) p. 104.

[63] For an account of the somewhat different form that Latin monasticism took in Palestine, see pp. 48–50 below.

disciples was Epiphanius, whose monastery was located at Eleutheropolis, between Gaza and Jerusalem. It is possible that Jerome obtained the historical core of his account of Hilarion from him.[64] Another figure alleged to have founded monasticism in Palestine even before the time of Antony in Egypt is St. Chariton. Little is known of him, and his biography seems to have been composed out of a desire to make the origins of Palestinian monasticism independent of Egypt.[65] The characteristic form of monasticism in the Judaean wilderness was the "laura," a cluster of hermitages around a church and other common facilities. Lauras were often located on the sides of cliffs, as for example at Douka above Jericho and Mar Saba on the Wadi Kedron.

It seems impossible to pinpoint the origins of monasticism in Syria. By the time Jerome came to the desert of Chalcis in 375, numerous colonies of hermits existed in the desert east of Antioch.[66] To what extent this development had been influenced by the earlier movement in Egypt is a disputed matter.[67] The most important figure of the ascetic movement of the fourth century in Syria was unquestionably Ephraim, a deacon and poet, who lived at Nisibis and later at Edessa, where he died in 373. In his poetry he celebrated the lives of other famous ascetics, such as Abraham Kidunaja and Julian Saba. In Ephraim, however, the ascetical movement was still closely aligned with pastoral considerations. For this reason some would prefer to term his style of life "pre-monastic."[68]

[64] Kelly, *Jerome*, p. 173.

[65] Chitty, *The Desert a City*, pp. 15–16.

[66] Kelly, *Jerome*, pp. 46–47. The material to be found in the *Historia religiosa* of Theodoret of Cyrrhus (†c. 466) does not provide a reliable picture. See E. Beck "Ein Beitrag zur Terminologie des ältesten syrischen Mönchtums" *Antonius Magnus*, p. 254; A. J. Festugière, *Antioche païenne et chrétienne: Libanius, Chrysostome, et les moines de Syrie* (Paris: E. de Boccard 1959); P. Canivet, *Le monachisme syrien selon Théodoret de Cyr*, Théologie Historique 42 (Paris: Beauchesne 1977) and *Théodoret de Cyr: Histoire des moines de Syrie*, SC 234, 257 (Paris: Les Éditions du Cerf 1977–78).

[67] The attempt of Vööbus (see note 11 above) to explain the origin of asceticism and monasticism in Syria in complete independence from that in Egypt and as having originated from Essene, gnostic, Manichaean and other influences has not found wide acceptance. For a critique of his methods and sources, see J. Gribomont "Le monachisme au sein de l'église" *SM* 7 (1965) 7–24. Gribomont also points out that the introduction of the discipline of the common life into Syrian monasticism is due to the influence of St. Basil.

[68] See L. Leloir "Saint Ephrem, moine et pasteur" *Théologie de la vie monastique*, Théologie 49 (Paris: Aubier 1961), and Beck "Ein Beitrag" pp. 254–267.

6. PACHOMIUS AND CENOBITIC MONASTICISM[69]

The warnings against the dangers of the solitary life and the insistence on the cenobitic life as a preparation for the eremitical life by writers such as Cassian and St. Benedict have led many writers to conclude that the cenobitic life was a development from, or adaptation of, the original eremitic inspiration.[70] The precise relationship between the eremitic and cenobitic movements remains a matter of much discussion.[71] It is clear, however, that in the fourth century Pachomius was regarded as the founder of a distinct movement with its own inspiration and goal, which was not merely to prepare for the eremitic life. This is the significance of an often quoted passage in which Theodore, one of Pachomius' early disciples and successors, recalls Pachomius as saying:

> At the moment in our generation in Egypt, I see three principal things which are prospering with the aid of God and men. The first is the blessed athlete, the holy Apa Athanasius, the archbishop of Alexandria, who is fighting even to death for the faith. The second is our holy father Antony, who is the perfect model of the anchoritic life. The third is this

[69] Lives of Pachomius and his successors have survived in Coptic, Greek and Arabic. The Arabic materials remain inadequately edited. The Greek lives have been edited by F. Halkin, *Sancti Pachomii Vitae Graecae*, Subsidia Hagiographica 19 (Brussels: Société des Bollandistes 1932). A French translation of the *Vita Prima Graeca* has been published by A. J. Festugière, *Les Moines d'Orient IV/2, La première vie grecque de saint Pachôme* (Paris: Les Éditions du Cerf 1965). An English translation of the same has been made by A. N. Athanassakis, *The Life of Pachomius* (Missoula, Mont.: Scholars Press 1975). The Coptic lives have been published by L. Th. Lefort, *S. Pachomii Vita, Bohairice Scripta*, CSCO 89 (Paris: Respublica 1925) and *S. Pachomii Vitae Sahidice Scriptae*, CSCO 99 (Paris: Respublica 1933). Lefort also published a French translation of all the Coptic materials, *Les vies coptes de saint Pachôme et de ses premiers successeurs*, Bibliothèque du Muséon 16 (Louvain: Bureaux du Muséon 1943). Extensive discussion of the relationship of the Greek, Coptic and Arabic materials may be found in the latter work as well as in the work by Festugière and in the following works: D. J. Chitty "Pachomian Sources Once More" *Studia Patristica* 10, TU 107 (Berlin: Akademie-Verlag 1970) 54–64; A. Veilleux, *La liturgie dans le cénobitisme pachômien au quatrième siècle*, StA 57 (Rome: Herder 1968). Veilleux and Lefort favor the priority of the Coptic sources, but Chitty and Festugière favor the priority of the Greek works.

[70] E.g., P. Brown, *The World of Late Antiquity: AD 150–750* (New York: Harcourt Brace Jovanovich 1971) p. 99. This generalization is perhaps more applicable to monasticism in northern Egypt. See W. Bousset "Das Mönchtum der sketischen Wüste" *ZKG* 42 (1923) 1–41, and H. G. Evelyn White, *The Monasteries of the Wadi 'n Natrun, Part II: The History of the Monasteries of Nitria and Scetis* (1926; rpt. New York: Arno Press 1973).

[71] See H. Bacht "Antonius und Pachomius: Von der Anachorese zum Cönobitentum" *Antonius Magnus*, and especially Veilleux, *La liturgie*, pp. 167–181.

koinōnia, which is the model for everyone who wishes to gather souls together for God's sake in order to help them become perfect (*Vita sa* [5]).[72]

The juxtaposition in this passage between Antony and koinōnia is quite significant for understanding the spirit of Pachomian monasticism. Disciples were drawn to Antony and other famous ascetics because they recognized in them the gift of the Spirit and wished to become like them.[73] This was probably true in the case of Pachomius as well, but he succeeded in shifting attention, to a certain extent, away from himself and to the community as the locus of the Spirit. The Pachomian community is not just a grouping of individuals around a spiritual father, but a fellowship of brothers, a koinōnia.[74]

The term koinōnia is undoubtedly the key concept of Pachomian monasticism.[75] Here it refers to the congregation or union of monasteries that had developed under Pachomius' guidance. A New Testament term, it has often been translated into English as 'fellowship,' 'communion' or 'sharing.' In 1 Cor 10:16, it is used to refer to the communion in the body and blood of Christ in the Eucharist, and in 1 John 1:3, it refers to the participation Christians have with one another in the life of the Trinity. Most important, however, is the text in Acts 2:42, where Luke uses it to describe the early Christian community. The ideal of imitating the life of the earliest Christian community pervades the Pachomian literature.

Although the basic inspiration of Pachomian monasticism is clear, the stages by which this distinctive ideal developed are not quite so clear. The various lives of Pachomius and his successors have been influenced, at least in part, by Athanasius' *Life of Antony* and have acquired much material of a legendary and edifying character.[76] However, the main lines of the traditional story of Pachomius are the fol-

---

[72] A similar passage occurs in the *Vita prima* 136.

[73] On the notion of the monk as "pneumatophoros" or bearer of the Spirit, see Heussi, *Ursprung*, pp. 164–186.

[74] Veilleux, *La liturgie*, p. 176.

[75] Chitty, *The Desert a City*, p. 24, holds that the term koinōnia is a substitution in the Coptic Lives of Pachomius for the Greek word koinobion, which is used in the *Vita prima* to refer to the whole congregation. The reverse would seem to be more likely. In the Coptic New Testament, the term koinōnia is not translated but simply taken over into Coptic, as are a great many Greek words. As a matter of fact, in this key passage from the *Vita prima* 136, the term used to refer to the whole congregation is not koinobion but koinōnia.

[76] Both the Bohairic Life and the *Vita prima* make explicit mention of Athanasius' *Life of Antony*. Cf. Lefort, *Les vies coptes*, p. 79 and *Vita prima* 2 and 22.

lowing.[77] Pachomius was born of pagan parents in the Thebaid in Upper Egypt in the last years of the third century. During the civil war between Licinius and Maximin, he was drafted into the army at the age of twenty. While the recruits were being taken north, they were shut up in a prison for the night. The people of the town brought them food, and when Pachomius inquired who these kind people were, he was told they were Christians. Because of this incident, the young man resolved to serve the human race his whole life (*Vita prima* 5; *Vita bo* 8).

After a short time, the war ended and the draftees were released. Pachomius found his way to the village of Šeneset (the Greek says Chenoboskeia), where he was soon baptized as a Christian. After he had spent three years ministering to the needs of the people in this area, he decided to become an anchorite. He sought out an old man named Palamon and asked him to teach him this way of life. The old man agreed reluctantly. Pachomius spent several years learning from and imitating this anchorite. While he was walking one day at some distance, he came to the abandoned village of Tabennesi. There, while praying, he heard the voice of an angel telling him to remain there and build a house because many would come to him to become monks. This he did, and he was soon joined by a number of disciples, including his brother John. Another day Pachomius was downcast and puzzling over the will of God for him. An angel appeared to him and told him that the will of God was that he should serve the human race in order to reconcile it to God. Pachomius responded, "I am seeking the will of God and you tell me to serve men!" Then the angel repeated three times, "The will of God is that you serve men in order to call them to him" (*Vita sa* [3]). Whatever may be the historical reliability of these incidents, they certainly illustrate the spirit of Pachomian monasticism, a spirit very different from that of the anchoritic life in which Pachomius supposedly began.

Monastic life at Tabennesi probably began about A.D. 320. It is difficult to trace the development of the structure of Pachomian monasticism.[78] However, the fully developed monastery was a fairly

---

[77] For more detailed accounts, see Chitty, *The Desert a City*, pp. 20–38 and H. Bacht, "Pachôme et ses disciples" *Théologie de la vie monastique*, pp. 39–72.

[78] A plausible attempt to do this has been made by M. M. van Molle in two articles: "Essai de classement chronologique des premières règles de vie commune connue en chrétienté" *La Vie Spirituelle Supplément* 84 (1968) 108–127, and "Confrontation entre les règles et la littérature pachômienne postérieure" *La Vie Spirituelle Supplément* 86 (1968) 394–424. The author attempts to distinguish the different groups of rules and

elaborate affair, capable of accommodating several hundred monks. It contained a number of residence houses, each with its own housemaster and deputy, and was surrounded by a wall.[79] In addition to the living quarters for the monks, there was also a gatehouse, a guesthouse, an infirmary, a kitchen, a refectory and an assembly hall (*synaxis*) used for common prayer. Various tasks were rotated among the different houses. A "steward" or "superior" was appointed to care for the management of the whole establishment. Outside the walls the monks raised their own food, and they used the old tombs on the edge of the desert as their cemetery.

In addition to raising their own food, the monks engaged in various handicrafts, the products of which were sent down to Alexandria to be sold. With the money thus obtained, other things such as cloth for clothing would be purchased. Eventually the community came to own a number of boats for this purpose. The monks also cared, when necessary, for people in the surrounding area. They took in old people and orphans. In time of plague they would care for the sick, feed the hungry and bury the dead.

Before long the number of monks grew too large for one location, so Pachomius formed another community a few miles away at the deserted village of Pbow. We are told that two groups of monks at Chenoboskeia and Monchosis asked to be admitted to the *koinōnia*. Pachomius imposed on them the regulations he had made for his own monasteries and appointed some of his own monks as supervisors (*Vita prima* 54). About A.D. 337, Pachomius moved his own residence from Tabennesi to Pbow and appointed Theodore as the head of

---

regulations in the Pachomian corpus and relate them to stages of development from a single house to the whole congregation, and to relate them as well to Pachomius and especially his successor Theodore. This view has been challenged by A. de Vogüé "Les pièces latines du dossier pachômien. Remarques sur quelques publications récentes" *RHE* 67 (1972) 22–67 and "Saint Pachôme et son oeuvre d'après plusiers études récentes" *RHE* 69 (1974) 425–453.

[79] This seems to be the earliest example of the monastic enclosure. It has been suggested that the enclosure wall, as well as the layout of the monastery in general, derived from Pachomius' experience of a military camp: Chitty, *The Desert a City*, p. 22; or that it is based on the layout of Egyptian temples with which Pachomius was familiar: P. Nagel, *Die Motivierung der Askese in der alten Kirche und der Ursprung des Mönchtums*, TU 95 (Berlin: Akademie-Verlag 1966) pp. 103–104. Both suggestions are highly speculative. It could also have been practical necessity that gave rise to the enclosure wall. This was certainly the case with the monasteries of Scetis. See White, *The Monasteries*, pp. 262, 327–328. H. Bacht sees the enclosure wall as theologically significant, as a means of creating the "common life" of the cenobite. See "Antonius und Pachomius: Von der Anachorese zum Cönobitentum" *Antonius Magnus*, pp. 70–72.

Tabennesi. Pachomius himself remained the spiritual father of the whole congregation and spent much time traveling back and forth among the communities, giving instruction and encouragement.

When Pachomius died in 346 from the plague endemic to the area, there were already eleven monasteries in the "holy *koinōnia*," of which two were for women. The letter of Ammon says there were about six hundred monks at Pbow in A.D. 352 (Ammon. *epist.* 2).[80] The other monasteries were smaller, with a few hundred each. Palladius says that in his time (end of the fourth century), there were seven thousand monks living under the Pachomian rule. Most of these were in southern Egypt in the Thebaid, but there was later at least one monastery in the north at Canopus, near Alexandria, known as the Metanoia, which Jerome knew about and may have visited when he was in northern Egypt (Pachom. *reg.* praef.). Later on he made a Latin translation of the Pachomian materials, from a Greek version, for the benefit of Latin-speaking recruits. These materials must have been translated into Greek by that time.

After the death of Pachomius, there occurred the kind of crisis in the congregation that is not uncommon after the death of a founder. Pachomius had appointed as his successor Petronius, a well-to-do landowner, who had brought his wealth to the community some time earlier and who had been head of several monasteries in the area of Tismenae, even though he did not belong to the first generation of Pachomius' disciples. However, Petronius survived Pachomius by only a few months. He in turn designated Horsiesius, the superior of the monastery at Chenoboskeia, to be his successor. Apparently Horsiesius was unable to control the independent spirit of the other superiors who, led by a certain Apollonius, were threatening to break up the congregation. Horsiesius then called upon Theodore, one of Pachomius' earliest disciples, to act as coadjutor. Theodore had earlier been deposed from a position of authority because of factions that had developed. At any rate, he now took over the active administration of the congregation with a firm hand, disciplined the rebellious superiors, expelled unruly elements and established or re-established rules and regulations for the sake of order in the whole congregation (*Vita bo* 165-67; *Vita sa*[6]). One of those rules was that superiors of monasteries must be transferred to other monasteries every year at the annual general chapter. Theodore continued to govern the *koinōnia*

---

[80] On the nature and authenticity of this document, see Lefort, *Les vies coptes*, pp. LI–LXII and Veilleux, *La liturgie*, pp. 108–111.

until his death in A.D. 368. Thereupon Horsiesius, who had remained the titular head of the congregation, returned to its active leadership, in which he continued for many years (*Vita prima* 149).[81]

The rule of the Pachomian monasteries has survived in the Latin translation of St. Jerome and in a number of Coptic and Greek fragments.[82] In fact, the material that Jerome translated comprises several collections of rules and regulations, which are divided under these Latin headings: *Praecepta*, *Praecepta et Instituta*, *Praecepta atque Iudicia*, and *Praecepta ac Leges*. There seems to be little doubt that the regulations which suppose earlier stages of development go back to Pachomius himself, while those relating to the fully developed congregation probably owe much to Theodore.[83] In general, these are compilations of regulations made as the situations requiring them arose. Most of them relate to the good order to be preserved in everyday affairs, such as food, drink, use of books, care of the sick, coming late to prayer, etc., matters that would also be dealt with in the Rule of St. Benedict. There is, however, none of the more theoretical treatment of the monastic life such as is to be found in the Prologue and first seven chapters of the Rule of St. Benedict.

Because the rule of the Pachomian monasteries is a compilation of regulations, it is necessary to read the Lives of Pachomius and the Catecheses to get a more complete picture of Pachomian monasticism. In these works we can discover the theoretical basis of the life, a basis to be found above all, as noted above, in the term *koinōnia*, which is constantly used in the Coptic lives of Pachomius and his successors to describe the whole congregation. There is also the frequent suggestion that this form of monastic life is an imitation of that of the apostles. Theodore describes the work Pachomius accomplished as that of "making this multitude become one spirit and one body" (*Vita bo* 194). The homilies of Pachomius, Theodore and Horsiesius recorded in the Pachomian literature bear eloquent testimony to the central role of Scripture in the lives of these monks.[84]

The Pachomian monks always maintained cordial relations with An-

---

[81] See W. E. Crum, *Der Papyruscodex saec. vi–vii der Phillipsbibliothek in Cheltenham* (Strassburg: Trübner 1915) pp. 132–145.

[82] These have all been collected and edited by A. Boon and L. Th. Lefort, *Pachomiana Latina* (Louvain: Bureaux de la Revue 1932).

[83] See van Molle "Confrontation entre les règles et la littérature pachômienne postérieure" pp. 394–424.

[84] See P. Deseille, *L'esprit du monachisme pachômien*, Spiritualité Orientale 2 (Nantes: Abbaye de Bellefontaine 1968).

tony and others in the anchoritic tradition, but it is not surprising that, considering their way of life to be an imitation of that of the apostles as they did, unfavorable comparisons were eventually made with the eremitic style of life. A story about an encounter between some of Pachomius' disciples and the great Antony illustrates this. Antony is pictured consoling some of the brothers after the death of Pachomius and is made to say, "the work he did in gathering souls about him to present them holy to the Lord reveals him to be superior to us and the path of the apostles in which he walked is the *koinōnia*." Apa Zachaeus, a Pachomian monk, then asks Antony why, if the *koinōnia* is the superior way of the apostles, he had not lived this way himself. Antony then explains that when he became a monk, there was as yet no *koinōnia* but only a few anchorites who lived a little way from the villages. This is what he did. "Then when the path of the apostles was revealed on the earth, which is the work our able Apa Pachomius undertook, he became the entrance way for everyone who is in danger from the one who has done evil from the beginning." Antony goes on to explain that he was then too old to take up the cenobitic life (*Vita sa*[5]). This and other passages leave no doubt that the Pachomian monks came to consider their form of monastic life preferable to the eremitic ideal.

7. ST. BASIL AND MONASTICISM IN ASIA MINOR[85]

Our knowledge of monasticism in Asia Minor before the time of St. Basil (330–379) is very limited and consists chiefly of what we can deduce from the acts of a regional council held at Gangres about A.D. 340.[86] This council, which did not retain its moral authority later on because many of the bishops involved were Arians, was directed against various errors being propagated in the ascetic movement. The acts of the council condemned those who rejected marriage and who taught that married persons could not achieve beatitude. The council

---

[85] The most extensive treatment of Basil's ascetical works is by David Amand, *L'Ascèse monastique de saint Basile* (Maredsous: Éditions de l'Abbaye 1948). However, this must be read in the light of the later writings by Jean Gribomont, especially *Histoire du texte des Ascétiques de saint Basile*, Bibliothèque du Muséon 32 (Louvain: Publications Universitaires 1953), and the articles listed in the following notes. In addition, the following may be mentioned: W. Clarke, *Saint Basil the Great, A Study in Monasticism* (Cambridge Univ. Press 1913); M. Murphy, *St. Basil and Monasticism* (Washington: Catholic Univ. Press 1930).

[86] J. Gribomont "Le monachisme en Asie-Mineur au IVe siècle, de Gangres au Messalianisme" *Studia Patristica* 2, TU 64 (Berlin: Akademie-Verlag 1957) 2.400–415.

claimed that these people alienated slaves from their masters, made up their own fasting calendar, held married priests in contempt, and that the sacraments administered by married priests were invalid. Apparently they also preached radical renunciation of possessions. The council condemned all these positions as strange to the Church and also censured the use of special ascetic clothing. If the acts of the council are reliable, it is clear that we have here not simply a monastic movement alongside the Church, as in Egypt, but an attempt at reform of the Church as such. A central, though more moderate, figure in this movement was Eustathius of Sebaste, who, according to the historian Sozomen, was the founder of monasticism in Armenia, Paphlagonia and Pontus (Soz. *hist.eccles.* 3,14).[87] Eustathius was himself a priest, the son of a bishop, and eventually became a bishop himself. Basil was to be strongly influenced by Eustathius, although he later broke with him over doctrinal questions.

Basil was born into a wealthy Christian family at Caesarea in Cappadocia about 330. His grandmother, Macrina the Elder, had been a convert of Gregory Thaumaturgus, who had been a pupil of Origen. Basil received an excellent classical education at Caesarea, Constantinople and finally for several years at Athens. About 358 he decided, along with his friend Gregory Nazianzen, to abandon secular studies in favor of a "philosophic" way of life, as fourth-century writers often refer to an ascetic style of life. He returned home to Caesarea and received baptism. This conversion was due in part at least to the influence of Eustathius, who had already influenced Basil's grandmother Macrina to adopt the ascetic way of life. Seeking to join Eustathius, who had left Caesarea on a tour of the monastic East, Basil set out on a lengthy journey that gave him firsthand knowledge of ascetic and monastic practices in Syria, Palestine and northern Egypt.[88]

When he returned home, Basil withdrew from the ordinary affairs of society, took up the ascetic life and devoted himself to an intensive study of Scripture, apparently with the aim of establishing a sound theological basis for the practice of the ascetic life. He wished to avoid the extremist tendencies such as had been manifested in those groups condemned by the Council of Gangres as well as, perhaps, some of the

[87] See J. Gribomont "Eustathe de Sébaste" *DS* 4.1708–1712.

[88] See J. Gribomont "Eustathe le Philosophe et les voyages du jeune Basile de Césarée" *RHE* 54 (1959) 115–124, who interprets the Eustathius of Basil's Letter 1 to refer to Eustathius of Sebaste.

aberrations he had observed in his travels. The result of his study was his first work, *The Moral Rules*, which he composed about 360. This work consists of principles for living the Christian life, which are then supported by quotations from the New Testament (1542 verses, in fact). The basic orientation found in Basil's later ascetical works can be found already in *The Moral Rules*.[89] For Basil, the monastic life is essentially the Christian life, lived as fully as it should be rather than a particular institution in the Church.[90]

Basil, despite his withdrawal from the life of society, remained involved in the life of the Church at Caesarea and before long was ordained a priest. In 370 he became bishop of Caesarea. With his excellent education, wide experience of the world and the Church, as well as his intimate knowledge of Scripture and other Christian writings (he and Gregory Nazianzen had produced an anthology of the writings of Origen, known as the *Philocalia*), he was well qualified to give the monastic movement in the Greek-speaking world a sound theological foundation. This he did in a series of responses to questions put to him concerning various aspects of the ascetic and Christian life. The collection of these became known as the *Asceticon*. An earlier edition was translated into Latin by Rufinus and is now known as the small *Asceticon*, and a later, enlarged edition is known as the large *Asceticon*. These works have also become known mistakenly as the Long and Short Rules.[91] They are not in fact rules at all, at least not in the sense of the Pachomian rules or the other later collections of rules and regulations. For Basil, the only possible rule or norm for Christian conduct was Scripture.

Basil saw clearly that the Christian life can be understood only in terms of response to the double commandment of love. Therefore, he begins his treatment of the principles of the ascetic life with an exposition of the love of God and neighbor (Basil. *reg.* 1-2; *reg.fus.* 1-6). He then goes on to point out the necessity of avoiding distraction in the pursuit of this goal and concludes that it is better to live in retirement, withdrawn from a society that does not share the same goals. The corollary to this is that it is necessary to live in the company of those who are striving for the same goal.

---

[89] J. Gribomont "Les Règles Morales de saint Basile et le Nouveau Testament" *Studia Patristica* 2, TU 64 (Berlin: Akademie-Verlag 1957) 2.417.

[90] J. Gribomont "Saint Basile" *Théologie de la vie monastique*, p. 104.

[91] *Ibid.* The terms "long" and "short" rules are properly used of the divisions within the large *Asceticon*.

Basil is severely critical of the eremitical life. He points out that a person who lives alone does not come to recognize his own defects, does not develop humility, is self-centered, and lacks the opportunity to practice charity. The solitary cannot really fulfill the exhortations of St. Paul to live as members of the body of Christ. On the other hand, he says, "community life offers more blessings than can be fully and easily enumerated." It helps to develop all the virtues, and it is really in accord with the teachings of the New Testament (to support his position Basil cites 1 Cor 12; Rom 12:6; Matt 18:16; John 13:5 and others). In a concluding peroration on the common life, he says, "it is an arena for combat, a good path of progress, continual discipline, and a practicing of the Lord's commandments, when brethren dwell together in community. . . . It maintains also the practice characteristic of the saints, of whom it is recorded in the Acts: 'And all they that believed were together and had all things in common'" (Basil. *reg. fus.* 7).

The monastic life is, then, for Basil as for Pachomius, an imitation of the life of the earliest Christian community as idealized by Luke. There is no reason to believe that Basil derived this idea from any contact with Pachomian monasteries or literature;[92] rather, he seems to have derived it from his own meditation upon the Scripture. In practice, however, Basil does not seem to have been as rigidly opposed to the solitary life as the passage quoted above might lead us to believe. In a passage from his funeral oration for Basil, Gregory Nazianzen tells us that Basil had found a way to reconcile these forms of life. When Basil started out, he explains, the eremitic and cenobitic forms of life were in conflict, and neither possessed all the advantages. "Basil reconciled and united the two in the most excellent way. He had hermitages and monasteries built not far from his cenobites and his communities of ascetics. He did not divide and separate them by an intervening wall, as it were. He brought them close together, yet kept them distinct, that the life of contemplation might not be divorced from community life or the active life from contemplation. . . ." (Greg.Naz. *orat.* 43,62).[93] To what extent this represents the views of Gregory as distinct from those of Basil is difficult to tell.

Basil certainly insisted, following St. Paul (1 Thess 5:17 and 2 Thess

[92] See J. Gribomont "Eustathe le Philosophe" p. 122.

[93] *Funeral Orations by Saint Gregory Nazianzen and Saint Ambrose*, tr. L. P. McCauley, FC 23 (New York: Fathers of the Church, Inc. 1953) p. 79. The word here translated as 'monasteries' is the Greek *monastēria*. It might have been better translated here as 'cells,' its basic meaning.

3:8) on the necessity of both prayer and work. He counseled that those trades should be chosen that allow the tranquil and undisturbed pursuit of the Christian life. Necessity must of course be taken into account, but in the manufacture of articles, simplicity and frugality rather than luxury should be sought. He seems to envisage quite a wide range of trades and arts as well as farming being carried out in the monastic community.

In the large *Asceticon* (Basil. *reg.fus.* 22), Basil discusses the type of clothing fitting for a Christian. It is significant that he does not say "for a monk." As we have noted above, the original impulse of the ascetic movement surrounding Eustathius was not to found distinct communities but to reform the Church. This was Basil's spiritual inheritance as well. However, Basil's program for living the Christian life, basically a program for the reform of the Church, ended up by becoming the rule for particular societies within the Church, cenobitic monastic communities.[94] This tendency is more pronounced in the later edition of the *Asceticon*, which treats many questions that would arise only in the context of a monastic community. These include: how and at what age applicants are to be received, what to do with regard to those who leave the brotherhood, how superiors should behave, how guests are to be received, how to deal with the disobedient, on silence and laughter. In fact, many if not most of the topics that will be treated in the Rule of Benedict are touched on in one way or another by Basil. And this is no mere codification of regulations, such as the Pachomian rule, but provides a well-thought-out rationale for all aspects of monastic life.

8. ORIGEN AND THE SPIRITUALITY OF NORTHERN EGYPTIAN MONASTICISM AT THE END OF THE FOURTH CENTURY[95]

In the last decades of the fourth century, a controversy developed over the use of the works of Origen (c. A.D. 186–255) by the monks of Palestine and Egypt, which was to have far-reaching consequences for the whole history of Christian spirituality. The primary reading matter

[94] J. Gribomont "Sainte Basile" *Théologie*, p. 106.
[95] For more extensive treatments of Origen and his works, see J. Daniélou, *Origen* (New York: Sheed and Ward 1955); R. Cadiou, *Origen: His Life at Alexandria* (St. Louis: Herder 1944); H. Crouzel "Origène, Précurseur du Monachisme" *Théologie de la vie monastique*, pp. 15–38. A useful collection of Origen's ascetical writings with a helpful introduction and bibliography may be found in R. A. Greer, *Origen* (New York: Paulist Press 1979).

for the monks had always been Scripture. It was inevitable, however, that they would become interested in other literature, particularly that which would be useful in the interpretation of Scripture. For those who could read Greek, there was nothing in this area to compare with the works of Origen, the greatest Christian theologian and Scripture scholar up to that time, the first to attempt a synthesis of Greek ideas with Christian revelation on an extensive scale and the first to plot out the development of the spiritual life in a detailed way. It has often been remarked that the direct and indirect influence of Origen on later Christian theology has been pervasive.[96]

It is Origen's theory of the spiritual life that is of particular interest in this development. For Origen, the spiritual life begins when a person comes to realize that he is made in the image of God and that the true world is the world inside him. This is the initial conversion. Origen thus brought together the biblical notion of man's creation in the image and likeness of God (Gen 1:25) and the Platonic notion that the true essence of the soul is divine. Sin has distorted this divine likeness and made man like the devil. The spiritual life is, then, essentially the recovery of the divine image in man.[97]

This recovery is plotted out by Origen through his exegesis of the Exodus from Egypt and the journey of the Israelites through the desert to the promised land. The idea that the departure from Egypt and the crossing of the Red Sea represented man's deliverance from the devil through baptism was already traditional, and indeed was grounded in the New Testament (e.g., 1 Cor 10:6; 1 Pet 1:13–2:10). And Israel itself was of course seen as a figure of the Church. When the Old Testament is interpreted to refer to the Church, we have what is later called allegorical exegesis. A different type of exegesis of the Old Testament, however, can be found in the writings of Philo of Alexandria, a Hellenistic Jew of the first century A.D., who had interpreted certain details of the Exodus story to refer to the spiritual life of the individual person. This type of exegesis is later called tropology. Origen united these two types of exegesis and developed a whole theory of the spiritual life from its beginning in baptism, as represented by the crossing of the Red Sea, until its full development, as represented by the arrival in the promised land.[98]

[96] Daniélou, *Origen*, p. vii.
[97] *Ibid.*, p. 295; Crouzel "Origène" p. 25.
[98] Daniélou, *Origen*, p. 297. For a further discussion of these types of exegesis, see Appendix 6, pp. 473–477.

In developing this theory, Origen introduced certain key distinctions that have colored the whole history of spiritual writing ever since. The first of these is the distinction between action (*praxis*) and contemplation (*theōria*). This is a distinction that can be found already in Aristotle's division of the virtues into the categories of moral and intellectual (*Nicomachean Ethics* I, 13). It has nothing to do with the comparatively modern distinction (and opposition) between the apostolic life and the contemplative life, a distinction Origen would not have understood. The distinction refers rather to two aspects of a person's spiritual life that are by definition overlapping and complementary. For Origen, the active life is the ascetic combat through which vices are conquered and virtues acquired; the contemplative life refers to the intellectual assimilation of truth.

It seems better to refer to action and contemplation in Origen's thought as "aspects" rather than "stages" of the spiritual life, because for him they are not rigidly distinct and successive. Yet Origen certainly envisions progress in the spiritual life, as is evident from his use of the "journey" metaphor. One can, then, speak of stages in the spiritual life as one can of stages in a journey, but these are stages in both the acquisition of virtue and the assimilation of truth. In the earlier stages of the spiritual journey, the struggle against vice may predominate over contemplation, but as the soul becomes proficient in the practice of the moral virtues, its attention is turned more toward the assimilation of truth. However, the practice of the moral virtues is not abandoned as one progresses in the spiritual life. On the other hand, if one compares action and contemplation with one another, the assimilation of truth appears to be a higher activity than the struggle against vice. Origen seems to have been the first to interpret the Martha-Mary story of Luke's Gospel as referring to the higher value of contemplation.[99]

The second important distinction that Origen contributed to the history of Christian spiritual thought is the threefold division of the spiritual life that he develops in his commentary on the Song of Songs. He says that there are three sciences that Solomon treated in three different books in accordance with the degree of knowledge with which each is concerned. Proverbs teaches morals and the rules for a

---

[99] Ladner, *The Idea of Reform*, p. 330; D. Csanyi "'Optima Pars': Die Auslegungsgeschichte von Lk 10, 38-42 bei den Kirchenvätern der ersten vier Jahrhunderte" *SM* 2 (1960) 5–78; A. Kemmer "Maria und Martha. Zur Deutungsgeschichte im alten Mönchtum" *EA* 40 (1964) 355–367.

good life. Ecclesiastes is really physics — the causes of things are set forth as well as their transient nature. Anyone who studies this science comes to realize the transitory nature of the physical world and is moved to turn to that invisible and eternal world of which Solomon spoke in the Song of Songs: "Thus, when the soul has been purified morally and has attained some proficiency in searching into the things of nature, she is fit to pass on to the things that form the object of contemplation and mysticism" (Orig. *hom.cant.* 78).[100] These three stages would later become known as the purgative, illuminative and unitive ways, and this distinction formed the basis of most later Christian theory of the spiritual life until very recent times.

With these distinctions in mind, we can follow Origen's interpretation of Israel's early history as referring to the life of the soul. As the Israelites were pursued by the Egyptians, so the soul is pursued by temptations and evil spirits. The journey through the desert corresponds to the gradual stripping away of the natural life and the discovery of the spiritual life. The fact that the people were led by both Moses and Aaron signifies the need for both action and contemplation. Eventually the purified soul enters the more mystical region and reaches spiritual ecstasy. This, Origen says, "occurs when in knowing things great and wonderful the mind is suspended in astonishment" (Orig. *hom. in num.* 27,12).[101] For Origen, there is no opposition between the contemplative life and apostolic activity such as may be found in later writers; rather, both aspects of the spiritual life, action and contemplation (i.e., the practice of moral virtue and the assimilation of truth), equip a person for the difficult tasks of preaching and teaching.

Among the many monks of the fourth century who studied, developed and applied Origen's theories to the monastic life, the most influential was certainly Evagrius of Pontus (A.D. 345–399).[102] Evagrius had been a disciple of St. Basil the Great, who ordained him a lector. After Basil's death in 379, he had gone to Constantinople, where Basil's friend Gregory Nazianzen had ordained him a deacon.

[100] The translation is from Daniélou, *Origen*, p. 305.

[101] The translation is from *ibid.*, p. 302.

[102] On Evagrius, see *Evagrius Ponticus: The Praktikos, Chapters on Prayer*, tr. J. Bamberger (Spencer, Mass.: Cistercian Publications 1970); O. Chadwick, *John Cassian* (Cambridge Univ. Press 1968²); A. Guillaumont, *Les 'Kephalia gnostica' d'Évagre le Pontique et l'histoire de l'Origénisme chez les grecs et chez les syriens*, Patristica Sorbonensia 5 (Paris: Éditions du Seuil 1962); A. and C. Guillaumont, *Traité Pratique ou le Moine*, SC 170, 171 (Paris: Les Éditions du Cerf 1971).

Following an unhappy love affair (we are told by Palladius), Evagrius left Constantinople and went to Palestine, where he stayed on the Mount of Olives with Melania the Elder. She persuaded him to go to Egypt and take up the monastic life there. This he did, living at Nitria for two years and then at the Cells for fourteen years, until his death in A.D. 399 at the age of fifty-four (Pallad. *hist.laus.* 38).

Evagrius borrowed freely from Origen and built upon his ideas, especially in the area of cosmological speculation. Some of Origen's ideas in this area seem to derive from the middle Platonists, and some from his attempts to wrestle with the perennial theological problem of the evils and inequalities that exist among men. If everything is created by a just God, how can such inequities be just? In order to maintain the justice of God, Origen adopted the theory that before the creation of the world, all spirits were equal and free; but they grew lazy and gave up pursuing the good. Then they were swept away toward the contrary of the good, evil. This happened to all of them, except the soul of Christ, in varying degrees, and the degree to which they fell away from the good determined their status as angels, souls and demons as well as the variations to be found in these three divisions. Matter was then created for the spirits in the intermediate category, and Jesus became man in order to lead souls back to their original state. Since Origen had explained matter as secondary to man's basic nature, he inevitably came to the conclusion that bodiliness would one day come to an end, and so he interpreted the resurrection as one stage along the way. These two points — the pre-existence of souls and the interpretation of the resurrection — as well as others, were to cause great controversy in succeeding centuries and eventually led to the condemnation of his works at the Second Council of Constantinople in 543.[103]

It was with the help of these ideas, however, that Evagrius developed his theories of prayer and contemplation. In his version of Origen's cosmology, he posited in the beginning God, who is essentially unity or a Monad, and a created Henead of rational pure intellects. Through negligence, these latter fell away from their contemplation of the essential knowledge. This resulted in the disruption of unity among themselves and the introduction of inequalities. Evagrius defined the soul as "an intellect which by negligence fell from unity" (Evagr. *keph.gnos.* 3,28). God then created bodies as a means

---

[103] Daniélou, *Origen*, p. viii.

through which souls could gradually regain the essential knowledge. This is the work of contemplation.

The different fallen intellects receive a kind of knowledge for their contemplation appropriate to the degree of their fall. Thus, there are different types of contemplation: that of demons and wicked men; that proper to souls for which the body is needed as an instrument; that of angels; and finally the knowledge of the essential Unity, which is reserved for the completely purified intellects. A soul may pass in stages through these types of contemplation and arrive at salvation by becoming progressively more and more spiritual. The function of Christ in this schema is that he voluntarily took a body like that of the fallen spirits in order to aid in their salvation by revealing the essential knowledge.

Evagrius also took over from Origen the distinction of action and contemplation, but for him they became two distinct and successive phases of the spiritual life. The goal of the active life is to purify the passionate part of the soul and achieve the state of *apatheia*, or passionlessness. This involves a struggle against the demons, which fight against the monk by causing evil thoughts. In analyzing the passions, Evagrius developed a theory of the eight principal thoughts, which passed into the Western ascetic tradition through Cassian and eventually became known as the seven capital sins. The elimination of these thoughts results in the state of passionlessness, a state that Evagrius thought he had attained, according to Palladius (Pallad. *hist.laus.* 38). With characteristic acerbity, Jerome accused Evagrius of using the word *apatheia* to imply that the soul must become either a stone or a god. Evagrius, however, seemed to imply that although temptations do not cease, the soul could achieve a God-given state in which it becomes impervious to evil.[104]

The state of passionlessness results, according to Evagrius, in charity. This is not, however, the goal of the spiritual life, as one might gather from St. Paul, but only a prelude to its higher stages, which are to be achieved through contemplation. The latter he divides into several stages, as mentioned above. The final or "theological" stage of contemplation is achieved in the vision by the intellect of itself. Evagrius does not seem to admit a direct vision of God by the intellect as possible for a soul still in the body. What the intellect can see is "the place of God," of "light without form" or "the light of the intellect."

[104] See A. and C. Guillaumont "Évagre le Pontique" *DS* 4.1739–1740.

This is the condition of "pure prayer," perhaps Evagrius' most characteristic and controversial idea. For him, the purity of prayer was to be judged not merely from its moral quality but from its intellectual qualities as well. Since God is simple and one, the mind cannot approach him as long as it remains complex, that is, filled with wandering thoughts, spiritual images and intellectual concepts. Evagrius was thus able to define prayer as "the lifting up of the mind to God" and as "the expulsion of thoughts." This meant all thoughts and images. Then the mind could be filled with the light of the Holy Trinity, losing self-consciousness and attaining a state of spiritual ecstasy which Evagrius called *anaesthesia* (Evagr. *de orat.* 120).[105]

Theological critics, both ancient and modern, have found serious difficulties with such a theory of contemplation.[106] It is little wonder that many of the uneducated Coptic monks found it confusing and disturbing. They were accustomed to think of God in terms of mental images and to hold conversations with these images. Those who tried to propagate the teaching of Evagrius appeared to them as threatening and even heretical. The more intellectual Greek monks, in turn, regarded their less sophisticated counterparts somewhat contemptuously as "anthropomorphists," because they pictured God in human form. There was, inevitably, the suggestion that this was heretical.

In the last years of the fourth century, this Origenist-anthropomorphist dispute came to involve most of the principal ecclesiastical figures of the time.[107] It became further complicated by the rivalries among the principal episcopal sees and also, perhaps, by the developing nationalism of the Copts. In 386 a certain John became bishop of Jerusalem.[108] He was quite favorable toward the study of Origen, as were the ascetics on the Mount of Olives, among whom were Rufinus and Melania the Elder. Epiphanius, bishop of Famagusta (Salamis) in Cyprus, to whom we are indebted for much of our knowledge of ancient heresies, was a confirmed heresy-hunter and suspected Origenist errors among the intellectuals of Jerusalem. In 393 he came to Palestine in an effort to get others to anathematize Origen. Rufinus refused to do this, but Jerome consented. Epiphanius

---

[105] Chadwick, *John Cassian*, p. 89.

[106] Cf. Hier. *epist.* 133: *PL* 22.1151a, and Hans Urs von Balthasar "The Metaphysics and Mystical Theology of Evagrius" *MS* 3 (1965) 183–196.

[107] For fuller accounts of these events, see Chitty, *The Desert a City*, ch. 3 and especially White, *The Monasteries*, ch. 6, pp. 84–144.

[108] Known to later writers as John of Jerusalem, he succeeded Cyril of Jerusalem and remained bishop of Jerusalem more than thirty years.

did not succeed in persuading John of Jerusalem to condemn Origen. At one point Epiphanius preached a sermon against Origen in Jerusalem, and John replied with one against anthropomorphism. On another visit Epiphanius caused severe offense to John by illicitly ordaining Jerome's brother, Paulinian, and by calling on the monks to break off communion with John, whom he called an Origenist. John appealed to the archbishop of Alexandria, Theophilus, to mediate the dispute. This was done successfully, if only temporarily, by an emissary from Theophilus named Isidore. At this time there seems to be no doubt that Theophilus was sympathetic to the Origenist cause.

It was the custom of the archbishop of Alexandria to publish a paschal letter each year. Shortly after the death of Evagrius in 399, Theophilus published a letter that strongly denounced anthropomorphism. This was naturally welcomed by the Greek-speaking intellectuals of Nitria, but apparently was not even permitted to be read in many other monastic communities. Then, according to the historian Socrates, an angry mob of monks came to Alexandria with the intention of burning down Theophilus' house (Soz. *hist.eccles.* 6,7). Theophilus, hearing that they were on the way, went out to pacify them. He addressed them in such a way as to imply anthropomorphist sympathies: "So I have seen you as the face of God." The monks then demanded that he anathematize the books of Origen, which, in an opportunistic about-face, he did. Rioting took place in Alexandria and Nitria against the Origenists, and in 400 Theophilus called a synod at Alexandria, which condemned Origen. Theophilus himself began to persecute his former Origenist friends. With such a hostile climate prevailing, as many as three hundred of the Greek-speaking monks, including Dioscurus, the bishop of the diocese in which Nitria lay, departed from Egypt. Most went to settle in various parts of Palestine, but many went on to Constantinople to appeal to the patriarch, John Chrysostom. Among these were John Cassian and his friend Germanus. With them the intellectual tradition of Egyptian monasticism was to pass eventually into the West. The further ramifications of the dispute and the deposition of John Chrysostom lie beyond the scope of this narrative. These events, however, mark the end of the first creative period of Egyptian monasticism. After this time Egypt ceased to be an international center of monasticism and became increasingly cut off from the rest of the movement.

Pre-Benedictine Monasticism in the Western Church

1. THE ORIGINS OF WESTERN MONASTICISM

It has often been asserted that the monastic life in the Western Church was simply imported from the East.[1] We have, in fact, little documentary proof of the existence of monasticism in the Western Church before the middle of the fourth century. By that time the movement was widespread in the East, and news of it must have entered the West, especially Rome. Egypt was a Roman colony, and there was constant traffic between Rome and Alexandria. Athanasius, the enthusiastic propagator of monasticism, spent some time at Trier during his first exile in 336–338 and was at Rome in 340, during his second exile. His laudatory description of the Egyptian monks made a profound impression, and later his *Life of Antony*, written expressly for admirers across the sea, was quickly translated into Latin and became popular in the West.[2]

There appears to be no question that the development of Eastern monasticism had a profound effect in the West. But monastic origins in the West were unquestionably more complex than appears at first sight. On the one hand, communication with Egypt was so commonplace that the news of monastic developments did not have to await the visit of Athanasius before reaching Rome. On the other hand, the conditions for the flowering of monastic life were as much present in the West as in the East. It is not unlikely that its first

---

[1] The best treatment of monastic origins in the West is R. Lorenz "Die Anfänge des abendländischen Mönchtums im 4. Jahrhundert" *ZKG* 77 (1966) 1–61. See also G. Colombás, *El monacato primitivo*, BAC 351, 376 (Madrid: La Editorial Católica 1974–75) 1.211–215 and J. Gribomont "L'influence du monachisme oriental sur le monachisme latin à ses débuts" *L'Oriente cristiano nella storia della civiltà* (Rome: Accademia Nazionale dei Lincei 1964) pp. 119–128.

[2] An anonymous translation existed even before the more polished version of Evagrius of Antioch appeared in 374. See H. Hoppenbrouwers, *La plus ancienne version latine de la vie de S. Antoine par S. Athanase. Étude de critique textuelle*, Latinitas Christianorum Primaeva 14 (Nijmegen: Dekker & Van de Vegt 1960); and L. Lorié, *Spiritual Terminology in the Latin Translations of the Vita Antonii with References to Fourth and Fifth Century Literature*, Latinitas Christianorum Primaeva 11 (Nijmegen: Dekker & Van de Vegt 1960).

appearance was an indigenous development quite independent of Eastern influence.

There is no doubt that the ground had been prepared in the Western Church by the practice of asceticism. Western writers of the second century already attest to the presence of virgins, widows and others living an ascetic life (Herm. *past.simil.* 9,10-11; Iust. *apol.* 1,15; Eus. *hist.eccles.* 5,3; Tert. *exhor.cast.* 13,4). We even hear of an ascetic living in seclusion in a cell in the middle of the third century (Eus. *hist.eccles.* 6,43,16). The criterion for distinguishing monastic life in the strict sense from these pre-monastic forms of asceticism can only be that of living separately from the rest of the Christian community, as was observed above in regard to the East. We can discern this transition taking place gradually in the course of the fourth century. Quite apart from the Eastern influence, the developing monastic forms are in continuity with the earlier stages of asceticism. Hence, to a certain extent the origin of monastic life in the West was a native growth, independent of the East.

The scarcity of documentation does not permit us to trace this development in detail. We have evidence from different times and places that shows monastic forms of life springing up in all the principal regions of the Western empire: Italy, North Africa, Gaul, Spain, the British Isles. While Eastern influence is often discernible, there are also differences in the West that seem to point to an independent origin. More significant than the differences, however, is the fundamental unity among all the forms of expression of the monastic phenomenon. Conditions throughout the civilized world in the fourth century evoked a similar response from Christians of the most varied regions, cultures and social classes.

2. MONASTIC ORIGINS IN ITALY

St. Jerome's reference to the adoption of monastic ways of life by noble Roman ladies due to the influence of Athanasius (Hier. *epist.* 127,5) has often been taken to mean that monasticism was unknown in Rome before the patriarch's visit in 340. But in this same letter (Hier. *epist.* 127,8), Jerome says that before this time the name *monachus* was held in scorn and contempt. Therefore, monks must have been known in the vicinity. Elsewhere he speaks of both male and female ascetics in Italy who were comparable to the "hippie" type of charismatic monks in the East, and it is probably these to whom he applies the Coptic term *remnuoth* (Hier. *epist*. 22,27-28; 34). These were the most numerous type of monks in Italy, Jerome observed in the 380s; so it is likely that they had sprung up spontaneously and already existed in the first half of the century.

The ascetic life of the noble Roman ladies was a more disciplined phenomenon. It also developed, however, out of pre-existing ascetical practice within the home and only gradually took on more strictly monastic forms in the second half of the fourth century. Thus Marcella, when widowed at an early age, began to live an ascetic life in her home, probably in the 350s. Jerome says that she was influenced by Athanasius and his successor (and blood brother) Peter, who came to Rome in 373 (Hier. *epist*. 127,5). Marcella's home became the meeting place for a group of noble women with similar interests, who studied the Bible together. When Jerome arrived in 381, he became the spiritual father of these virgins and widows.

The case of Asella is even clearer. According to Jerome, she was consecrated as a virgin at the age of ten. This could not have been later than about 344. Shortly afterward she began to adopt other ascetical practices; in the 380s she was still living in solitude, apparently in her own home (Hier. *epist*. 24).[3] Palladius, who was in Rome in 405, reports that she was then living with a community (Pallad. *hist.laus*. 41). Her career, then, seems to mark by stages the transition from early Christian forms of asceticism to a fully developed cenobitic life.

Jerome was the great promoter of this type of asceticism. He himself had lived the ascetical life with a group of friends at Aquileia in the early 370s, and then, in 375, spent a year as a hermit in the desert of Chalcis near Antioch in Syria. During his stay in Rome from 381 to 384, he propagated Oriental ascetical ideals, especially among the noble ladies who looked to him for direction. There was considerable opposition in the Christian community of Rome to the growing interest in asceticism, but it was favored by Jerome's friend and patron, Pope Damasus.[4] Through his writings Jerome was extremely influential in Western monasticism, but the rest of his career belongs rather to the story of Latin monasticism in the Holy Land.

St. Ambrose was also a promoter of monastic life in Italy. His own sister, Marcellina, lived an ascetic life from 353 onward, first with a companion in the family home at Rome,[5] and later outside of Milan

---

[3] We learn from Hier. *epist*. 45,7 that she was Marcella's sister.

[4] On Jerome, see J.N.D. Kelly, *Jerome* (New York: Harper & Row 1975).

[5] We are told of her consecration by Paulinus, the secretary and biographer of Ambrose, who was personally acquainted with Marcellina and with the sister of her com-

(Ambr. *virg.* 3,7,37). We find here the same evolution toward withdrawal from ordinary society as can be discerned in the case of Asella, of Lea, whose community seems to have been located near Ostia, and of Paula and Melania, who withdrew to Palestine. Augustine discovered functioning monasteries of both sexes when he came to Rome in 387 (Aug. *mor.eccl.* 1,70-71).

Ambrose, upon becoming bishop of Milan in 374, renounced his not inconsiderable property in favor of the Church and the poor, and adopted an ascetical style in his personal life (Paulin. *vit.Ambr.* 38). His writings contain frequent encouragement of virginity and other ascetical practices. He consecrated virgins and maintained contacts with communities of ascetics, and he was himself the patron and apparently the spiritual father of a monastery of men just outside the walls of Milan.[6] It was at Milan that Augustine first heard of the monastic life from Pontitianus, who told him of the Egyptians, of the monastery directed by Ambrose, and the fascinating story of two young men at Trier and their fiancées, who were converted to the monastic life by reading the *Life of Antony* (Aug. *conf.* 8,6). The experience clearly made a profound impression on Augustine.

Other places in northern Italy show knowledge of monastic practices, but our information is fragmentary. It is often affirmed that Eusebius, bishop of Vercelli from about 344 until his death in 371, was the first to introduce a monastic observance for his clergy, thereby anticipating the type of clerical monastery later popularized by Augustine. Eusebius, a native of Sardinia, had served as a lector in the Church of Rome. He became a prominent figure in the anti-Arian struggle that marked the reign of Pope Liberius. Upon his refusal to sign the condemnation of Athanasius voted by a synod at Milan in 355, he was exiled to the East and spent the following years in Palestine, Cappadocia and the Thebaid, until his return to Vercelli in 363.

Eusebius' personal asceticism and the existence of an ascetical community of clerics at Vercelli some twenty-five years after his death are attested by a letter of Ambrose written to urge the choice of a worthy bishop for the church of Vercelli (Ambr. *epist.* 63, probably written in 396). Several anonymous homilies preached at Vercelli a generation or more after Eusebius' death indicate that the bishop him-

---

panion. See Paulin. *vita Ambr.*, prol. and ch. 4. Ambrose gives the discourse of Pope Liberius at her consecration in Ambr. *virg.* 3,1.

[6] See Aug. *conf.* 8,6; Aug. *mor.eccl.* 1,70. On Ambrose, see A. Paredi, *Ambrose: His Life and Times* (Notre Dame: Univ. of Notre Dame Press 1964); A. Roberti "S. Ambrogio e il monachesimo" *Scuola Cattolica* 68 (1942) 140–159; 231–252.

self was responsible for establishing this clerical monastery,[7] but we do not know when he did this. If the monastery was founded in the early days of his episcopate, in the 340s, it would perhaps be the earliest known example of an organized ascetical community in the West. But it is more likely that he took this step only in the 360s after his return from exile, and that he was influenced by the knowledge that he had acquired of the ascetical movement in Cappadocia and the cenobitic monasteries of the Thebaid.

The eremitical life flourished in Italy in the late fourth century, especially in the islands off the Italian Riviera. The first of these solitaries of whom we hear is Martin of Tours; after his release from military service in 356, he came to Milan and lived as a hermit until expelled by the Arian bishop. He then moved with a priest-companion to the island of Gallinaria, opposite Albenga, and there lived an ascetical life (Sulpic.Sever. *Mart.* 6). Martin apparently remained here until 360, when, after a trip to Rome, he followed St. Hilary to Poitiers and established himself at Ligugé. A little later, around 375, Jerome testifies that his friend Bonosus is living the monastic life on an island, but it is more likely that this was in the Adriatic, as he had gone there upon the breakup of the ascetic community in Aquileia (Hier. *epist.* 3,4-5). Jerome and Ambrose refer vaguely to the existence of numerous monks on the islands surrounding Italy (Hier. *epist.* 77,6; Ambr. *hex.* 3,5,23).

Aquileia was the scene of Jerome's own introduction to the ascetic life, and the little we know of the community there is due chiefly to scattered references in his letters. He and his friend Bonosus, after completion of their studies in Rome and a subsequent visit to Trier, where they probably first felt the attraction of asceticism, settled in Aquileia. Rufinus seems to have been there already, and it appears that by 370 there was a fervent group in existence. The bishop, Valerian, was favorable to the ascetic life, but its real animator was Chromatius, a priest, who lived an ascetical life in his home with his mother, his sisters, his brother Eusebius, who was a deacon, and the archdeacon Jovinus.

Little is known about their manner of life, but there is information about a number of Jerome's friends who became associated with the group.[8] There was also a community of virgins nearby at Haemona,

---

[7] J. Lienhard "Patristic Sermons of Eusebius of Vercelli and Their Relation to His Monasticism" *RBén* 87 (1977) 164–172.

[8] Hier. *epist.* 6–10 are addressed to members of the group after his departure from Aquileia; likewise *epist.* 1 to Innocent and *epist.* 3 to Rufinus.

with whom Jerome was in contact (Hier. *epist.* 11). Also associated with the Aquileian group was Evagrius of Antioch, an influential person who had come from the East with Eusebius of Vercelli and who seems to have been a mediator of Eastern monastic influences. It was he who had translated the *Life of Antony* into Latin a few years earlier; and it was with him that Jerome stayed in Antioch after his departure from Aquileia. Athanasius had stayed at Aquileia for two years or more around 345, and it may have been his visit that stirred up the local enthusiasm for the ascetic life. But it hardly seems necessary to seek such a cause, in view of the widespread popularity of asceticism throughout the West in the latter half of the fourth century.

At the end of the century there is another example in Paulinus of Nola and his circle. Like Ambrose, Paulinus was from a wealthy and prominent family. Born in Bordeaux, probably about 353, he received an excellent education under the famous rhetorician Ausonius, who became his friend. In 379 he was governor of Campania, after which he returned to Aquitaine. About 385 he married the noble Therasia, a Spanish lady and fervent Christian. After their only son died in infancy, they resolved to devote themselves to a life of asceticism, continence and prayer. After several years at Barcelona, during which Paulinus distributed his enormous fortune among the poor, they settled at Nola, near Naples, around 395. There they organized an ascetical community, which Paulinus calls *monasterium* and *fraternitas monacha* (Paulin.Nol. *epist.* 5,15; 23,8). It seems to have been quite informally structured, consisting of relatives and friends, all members of the aristocracy and all desirous of living the Christian life in an austere though not extreme fashion.

Paulinus had been ordained a priest, probably in Spain shortly before coming to Nola. After Therasia died in 408, he became bishop of Nola and lived on until 431. He was in correspondence and often personal contact with the principal churchmen of his time, and especially with the leaders of the ascetical movement: Ambrose in Milan; Jerome in Palestine; Rufinus and Melania and their circle in Italy and Jerusalem; Martin of Tours and his biographer Sulpicius Severus in Gaul; Eucherius of Lyons and Honoratus, the founder of Lerins; and Augustine and Alypius in Africa. Living not far from Rome, he was in a position to maintain contacts with monastic developments in the City and with the many visitors from all parts of the Christian world.[9]

[9] On Paulinus of Nola, see J. Lienhard, *Paulinus of Nola and Early Western Monasticism*, Theophaneia 28 (Cologne: Hanstein 1977).

3. LATIN MONASTICISM IN THE HOLY LAND

By the end of the fourth century, the monastic ideal, though it did not go unopposed, had spread throughout Italy. Of all its propagators, Jerome was doubtless the most influential, because of the authority his scholarship had earned for him. During his stay in Rome, however, his sharp attack upon his real or fancied enemies brought him such unpopularity that he was obliged to leave the City upon the death of Damasus, his protector, in 384. Together with his younger brother Paulinian, he sailed for Palestine and spent the rest of his life there, though always remaining in close contact with Western ascetical circles. He was followed to the East by Paula, his most faithful disciple among the noble ladies of the City, and her daughter Eustochium. In Bethlehem, Paula established two monasteries — one for women, which she governed herself, and one for men, ruled by Jerome. We are ill informed about the observance of these houses, but the life appears to have been fully cenobitic.

Before finally settling in Bethlehem, Jerome and Paula had made a tour of the holy places and had gone to Egypt to visit the famous monks. The Latin monasteries of Palestine were always marked with this high regard for Oriental asceticism and for the sacredness of the biblical lands. Jerome's interest in the Scriptures (it was in Bethlehem that he wrote his biblical commentaries and translated the Old Testament from Hebrew) also left a strong imprint of biblical study upon the life of the Bethlehem communities.

These monasteries, however, were not the first examples of Latin monasticism in the Holy Land. The earliest was the work of another noblewoman, Melania the Elder. Widowed at the age of twenty-two, she resolved upon a life of asceticism and in 372 set out with a group of like-minded women for Egypt, where she spent a year visiting the monks. It was probably there that she met Rufinus, the boyhood friend of Jerome, who had shared the latter's ascetical initiation in Aquileia and had gone to Egypt when Jerome directed his steps toward Antioch. Melania went on to Jerusalem in 374 and there established a monastery for women. When Rufinus followed in 380, a monastery for men was added. Again, there are few recorded details about the life practiced in these houses.[10]

---

[10] On Rufinus and Melania, see F. X. Murphy, *Rufinus of Aquileia (345–411): His Life and Works* (Washington: Catholic Univ. Press 1945); "Melania the Elder: A Biographical Note" *Traditio* 5 (1947) 59–77.

The friendship of Rufinus and Jerome was unfortunately shattered by the Origenist controversy, and the monastic establishments of Jerusalem and Bethlehem found themselves divided by bitterness. The first decades of the fifth century were marred by polemic and tragedy: Pelagianism became a danger both in the West and in Palestine, and Italy was invaded by the Goths, who sacked Rome in 410. Paula died in 404, Eustochium around 418, and Jerome a year or two later. The Bethlehem monasteries do not seem to have survived much longer amid the civil and religious tumults of the times and the unfriendliness of the Oriental Christians, who regarded the Latins as intruders.

The Jerusalem monasteries suffered a similar fate. Rufinus returned to Italy in 397 and died in Sicily in 411, unreconciled with Jerome. After an extended visit to Italy, beginning probably in 400, Melania returned to Jerusalem and died sometime before 410. Her influence had, however, inspired her granddaughter, Melania the Younger, to imitate her ideals. Married at fourteen to her distant cousin Pinianus, Melania the Younger persuaded him six years later, after the death of their two infants, to embrace virginity and asceticism. Disposing of their vast fortune, they spent seven years in Tagaste, in close contact with Alypius, the intimate friend of Augustine, and there formed both male and female communities.

Eventually Melania, with Pinianus and her mother, Albina, settled in Jerusalem around 417 and lived the ascetical life there. After Melania and Pinianus had made a pilgrimage to the monastic sites of Egypt, she lived as a recluse on the Mount of Olives for fourteen years. The monasteries founded by her grandmother and Rufinus seem no longer to have existed. After the death of her mother in 431, Melania founded a monastery for women. A year later her husband also died. After another four years in reclusion, Melania established a monastery for men. After her death in 439, the monasteries were governed by her successor and biographer, Gerontius, but in 452, after Chalcedon, he passed over to monophysite allegiance. After this nothing more is known of Latin monasteries in the East until the Crusades.[11]

The enduring effect of these monastic ventures, however, was the literature they bequeathed to the Western Church. Jerome in particu-

[11] On Melania the Younger, see D. Gorce, *Vie de Sainte Mélanie*, SC 90 (Paris: Les Éditions du Cerf 1962).

lar exercised an important influence in the West through his writings. Encouragement to asceticism, often enlivened by hyperbole and invective, appears in all his writings, even the biblical commentaries, and especially in his polemical works against Helvidius, Jovinian and Vigilantius, who were rather cool toward the fast-growing ascetical movement. The monastic teaching of Jerome is more positively expressed in his letters, particularly in two lengthy epistles that are really treatises: *Letter 22*, to Eustochium, written at Rome about 384 in the flush of his enthusiasm over the fervor of the noble ladies of the City; and *Letter 130*, to Demetrias, a more sober statement of his old age, written about 414.

One of the earliest works of Jerome's youth was the *Life of Paul the First Hermit*, written during his attempt at the solitary life in the desert of Chalcis about 375. The fanciful story of a supposed predecessor of Antony in Egypt, it is probably simply a romance without any historical foundation. Later, in his early years at Bethlehem around 390, he also wrote a *Life of St. Hilarion* and a *Life of Malchus the Captive Monk*, extravagant tales reflecting Jerome's preoccupations and his monastic ideals, but, at least in the case of Hilarion, based upon a historical core.

Of great importance, too, were Latin translations of Eastern monastic literature. The Latin monks of Palestine always looked to Egypt as their ideal. Jerome, in 404, translated a collection of Pachomian writings from Greek into Latin: the Rule, the *Monita* and eleven letters of Pachomius, a letter of Theodore, and the instruction of Horsiesius. The knowledge of Pachomian monasticism in the West was due entirely to these translations, and even today we still depend upon them, for the Coptic originals and Jerome's Greek sources exist only in fragmentary form.

Rufinus, too, made translations that were of great significance in the West. In 397 he translated the Rule of St. Basil for Ursacius, abbot of Pinetum in Italy. The Latin text, much shorter than the Greek and lacking the division into "Long and Short Rules," has been shown to be a translation of the first edition of Basil's *Asceticon*, which he later expanded into its fuller Greek form. It is in this earlier and briefer version that Basil became known to Western monks. Rufinus also translated, probably in 404, the *Historia Monachorum in Aegypto*, an account of a journey of seven monks from the Mount of Olives to visit the famous monks of Egypt in 394. While the authorship of the parallel Greek version is disputed, there can be no doubt of Rufinus' responsibility for the Latin.

4. MONASTICISM IN GAUL

St. Martin of Tours has been traditionally regarded as the first monk in the West. While this is an exaggeration, in view of the prevalence of ascetical patterns of life that were springing up everywhere in the fourth century, it is true that Martin was the first great propagator of monasticism in Gaul. The influence of Martin and his disciples, however, seems to have been confined, up to the end of the fifth century, to the western part of Gaul. In the eastern part of the province, and especially in the valley of the Rhone, the monastic movement owed its origins to the monastery of Lerins. These two forms of the ascetic life, then, which radiated from Tours and from Lerins, respectively, constitute the twofold source of ancient Gallic monasticism. In each of the two regions, it was principally due to zealous bishops that monasticism was propagated. In Aquitaine, a number of Martin's disciples who were raised to episcopal sees promoted the cult of Martin and the type of monasticism he had practiced. In eastern Gaul, numerous bishops who had been monks of Lerins or had otherwise been influenced by this monastery spread the monastic ideal through their territory. For more than a century, these two spheres of influence seem to have been mutually exclusive. Under Clovis, however, the cult of Martin was adopted by the Merovingian dynasty, and from this time on his popularity spread throughout the kingdom.[12]

There were, then, two original currents of Gallic monasticism: the Martinian type and that which stemmed from Lerins.

In Western literature and devotion, Martin of Tours is the typical monk-hero, in much the same way as Antony was in the East. This exemplary role of Martin was due to the publicity he received through the popularity and rapid spread of his *Life*, written by Sulpicius Severus just before and shortly after the death of the saint in 397. In addition to the *Life of Martin* itself, Sulpicius published three letters and three dialogues concerning Martin. This biographical collection became immediately popular throughout Western Christendom, rivaling the *Life of Antony* and influencing all subsequent Latin hagiography.[13]

---

[12] The thesis that early Gallic monasticism grew out of two principal sources originally confined to separate regions has been persuasively argued by F. Prinz, *Frühes Mönchtum im Frankenreich* (Munich: Oldenbourg 1965) pp. 19–117. Prinz has assembled extensive evidence to show that the cult of Martin was unknown in eastern Gaul up to the time of Clovis, but was extensively propagated by the saint's disciples in Aquitaine. The Lerins tradition, on the contrary, spread through the Rhone valley owing to the influence of bishops who had been in contact with that monastery.

[13] On Martin of Tours, see the collective volume *Saint Martin et son temps*, StA 46

Sulpicius Severus was a contemporary and devoted friend of Paulinus of Nola. Like him, he came from a prominent family in Aquitaine, enjoyed a first-class education, and became a prominent lawyer. He married into a noble and wealthy family, but his wife died while still young, an event that probably had an influence upon his decision to renounce his wealth and fame and retire into a life of asceticism and study. He did this soon after the similar move of Paulinus. Sulpicius' retreat was at a place in southern Gaul called Primuliacum, whose exact location is uncertain. He kept up a lively correspondence with Paulinus, with whom he shared his double enthusiasm for the ascetic life and for the literary culture of late antiquity. Both of them knew Martin personally. Sulpicius, using Martin as the ideal monk-figure, wanted to propagate monasticism in the West, defend it against its opponents, especially some of the Gallic bishops, and show that its fruits were in no way inferior to those of the East.[14]

The chronology of Martin's life is problematic, but its principal stages are certain. He was born of a pagan family in Sabaria, modern Hungary, probably about 316, and, like his father, followed a military career. During his military service he became a Christian. It is during his catechumenate that Sulpicius places the famous scene at the gate of Amiens, where Martin gave half his cloak to a shivering beggar, only to receive a vision that night in which Christ himself appeared clothed in the severed garment. When released from the army, probably in 356, he attached himself to Hilary of Poitiers, a supporter of the ascetic movement in Gaul, who ordained him an exorcist. After a visit to his native province, which must have coincided with Hilary's exile, he began to live as a hermit at Milan, and then on the island of Gallinaria, as we have seen.

When Hilary returned from exile in 360, Martin left his solitude and, after failing to meet him in Rome, followed him to Poitiers. No doubt he benefited from the bishop's recent contacts with Eastern monasticism. He took up residence in 361 at Ligugé, near Poitiers, to live the solitary life. Disciples were soon attracted, however, and he gradually became the spiritual father of a group of monks who formed a kind of "laura," or loosely knit group of semi-anchorites, rather than

---

(Rome: Herder 1961) and the edition of his *Life*, with extensive introduction and commentary, by J. Fontaine, *Vie de Saint Martin*, SC 133–134–135 (Paris: Les Éditions du Cerf 1967–69).

[14] On Sulpicius Severus, see N. Chadwick, *Poetry and Letters in Early Christian Gaul* (London: Bowes and Bowes 1955).

a real *coenobium*. His popularity grew to such an extent that in 371 he was obliged by popular will to become bishop of Tours, despite his reluctance to leave his solitude. He thus became the first of the great monk-bishops of the Western Church, governing the church of Tours and exercising a remarkable pastoral and charitable activity until his death in 397. At Tours, Martin established a place of solitary retreat outside the city, on the banks of the Loire. Here, too, disciples followed, and another monastic colony was formed that became the monastery of Marmoutier, a source of bishops who contributed a more ascetical quality to the Gallic Church.

Martin propagated the monastic life in his diocese. Sulpicius says that he established hermitages in place of pagan shrines (Sulpic.Sever. *Mart.* 13) and claims that more than two thousand monks were present for his funeral (Sulpic.Sever. *epist.* 3). Those of his disciples who became bishops did the same. The best known of these who promoted the ascetic life in northern Gaul in the late fourth century was Victricius of Rouen, the apostle of Normandy. Like Martin, he had been in military service before becoming a bishop about 380. An energetic promoter of the ascetical life, he had contacts with Paulinus of Nola, a fervent admirer of Martin, and also with Ambrose. Like Martin, he worked for the eradication of paganism in the countryside. He certainly considered the virgins and ascetics to constitute the elite ranks of the Church, but there is not much information about the precise nature of the ascetic life at Rouen at this period.[15]

Martin's reputation as monastic founder was such that more than a century later, when St. Benedict destroyed the temple and grove of Apollo he found on Montecassino, he dedicated to St. Martin of Tours one of the shrines he built to replace it (Greg. *dial.* 2,8).

The second early monastic tradition, which dominated the eastern part of Gaul, sprang from the monastery of Lerins, located on an island just opposite Cannes. It was founded by St. Honoratus, probably between 400 and 410. Information about Honoratus, who left no writings, comes from the commemorative oration delivered by St. Hilary, who had been his disciple at Lerins and later succeeded him as bishop of Arles.[16] Honoratus, born probably around 360, was from a family of consular rank in Gaul. As a youth he yearned for the desert and con-

---

[15] On Victricius, see P. Andrieu-Guitrancourt "La vie ascétique à Rouen au temps de saint Victrice" *Ricerche di storia religiosa* 40 (1952) 90–106.

[16] Hil. *vita Hon.* The edition of M.-D. Valentin in SC contains extensive introductory material. See also A. de Vogüé "Sur la patrie d'Honorat de Lérins, évêque d'Arles" *RBén* 88 (1978) 290–291.

verted his brother Venantius to the ascetic ideal. Together they set out for Greece with an elderly anchorite named Caprasius. After Venantius' death there, Honoratus and Caprasius returned to the West and settled on the island of Lerina, the smaller of the two islands that constitute the Lerins Group, upon the recommendation of Leontius, bishop of Fréjus, their ordinary and adviser. It is not far from Gallinaria, where Martin had lived for a time. Disciples came, and it seems that by 410 Honoratus was directing a community, probably a rather loosely knit one, living in the manner of an Eastern "laura."

It seems certain that Honoratus gave a rule to his monks, which must have existed in written form at least in later times, but it has not survived, and little is known in detail about the life at Lerins. In later centuries the Benedictine Rule was adopted there, and even today there is a Cistercian monastery on the island. It is certain that the leaders of ecclesiastical life in southern Gaul had close contacts with Lerins throughout the fifth century, and that the monastery exported monk-bishops to many dioceses. Honoratus himself spent the last two years of his life as bishop of Arles, and his disciple and panegyrist, Hilary, ruled the see from 430 to 449.[17]

These bishops were the agents who spread the influence of Lerins up and down the valley of the Rhone. Many of them seem to have been members of the Gallo-Roman nobility, fleeing from the incursions of the barbarians farther north; at this time Provence was an island of safety in a world that seemed to be crumbling. Well educated in the classical tradition, these men were naturally suited to be leaders, and the episcopacy provided an arena for leadership in the power vacuum that developed with the collapse of Roman authority. They shared an enthusiasm for the monastic ideal derived from their association with Lerins and left behind a body of literature that contains all that is known of the life and tradition of that monastery. These monastic writings, especially the rules written by the later Lerinians, form a part of the Western monastic context, which, as we shall see later, is indispensable for understanding St. Benedict. Only the principal representatives of this tradition will be considered.

Eucherius of Lyons was an aristocrat who married a devout Christian woman named Galla. Like other couples of the time, they were attracted by the ascetic ideal, placed their two sons in the monastery at Lerins (both later became bishops), and withdrew into retirement on

---

[17] For a study of the fifth-century circle associated with Lerins, see Chadwick, *Poetry and Letters in Early Christian Gaul.*

the neighboring island of Lero. They were in contact with Paulinus and Therasia at Nola in 412. Eucherius seems also to have lived in the community of Lerins, perhaps after his wife's death. He became the bishop of Lyons, probably around 424, and left a number of letters and treatises, most notably his *Praise of the Desert*, in which he salutes Lerins, "who, in her motherly arms, welcomes the sailors cast up from the shipwrecks of the world " (Euch. *laud.erem.*).

The community of Lerins furnished two bishops for the see of Riez: Maximus, who followed Hilary as abbot in 430 and served as bishop of Riez from 433 until his death in 452; and Faustus, who followed him first as abbot (433–452) and then as bishop of Riez (460–495). Faustus, who was originally a Briton or Breton, was one of the greatest thinkers and writers of his time and the principal spokesman for the anti-Augustinian theological viewpoint after the death of Cassian. Even when bishop, he frequently withdrew into ascetic retreat and returned to Lerins to live the monastic life again for certain periods of time. On these occasions he probably preached to the community the sermons on the monastic life that still survive. Another of the great Lerinian bishops was Lupus of Troyes. He was married to Hilary's sister, Pimeniola, but after seven years of marriage they separated by mutual agreement, and he went to Lerins. After a year in the monastery, when he had gone to Mâcon to dispose of his goods, he was seized and made bishop of Troyes. This seems to have taken place about 427. He lived until 479.

The most notable theological work to issue from Lerins was the *Commonitorium* of the monk Vincent of Lerins. There is meager information about him, and it is not even certain whether he was the brother of Lupus, whose name was also Vincent and who seems to have been a monk at Lerins. The *Commonitorium*, written about 434, is famous for its definition of sound catholic tradition. Salvian of Marseilles was another literary figure associated with the Lerins community. Though he was the tutor of Eucherius' sons, he does not seem to have been a monk. We know that he came from the region of Trier, was married to Palladia, daughter of pagan parents, and had a daughter Auspiciola. He and his wife agreed to embrace the ascetic life. They apparently fled to the south when Trier was sacked by barbarians and took up residence in Marseilles. Salvian was a priest and was in close contact with monastic circles of southern Gaul.

The connection between Lerins and so many of the principal literary and ecclesiastical leaders of fifth-century Gaul has led some to believe that the monastery was a center of culture. In fact, however, the known literary works were never published by monks, with the sole exception of Vincent, but by former monks who had become bishops and who wrote to meet pastoral needs. Moreover, they had acquired their learning, not at Lerins, but before their entry into monastic life. Although some teaching went on at Lerins, the monastery was a school of asceticism rather than of literary culture or of theology. Contemporary writers invariably speak of discipline, psalmody and fasting at Lerins, not of study and literary production.

From allusions to the life at Lerins, only a general idea of the observance can be reconstructed. It appears that it was primarily cenobitic, but that experienced monks lived in separate cells as hermits, though under the authority of the abbot. They attended, at least on occasion, the common prayer and instruction by the abbot. Discipline was quite severe. The cenobitic monks lived in strict poverty and apportioned their time to work, reading and prayer. Young monks were subject to an elder, and new recruits went through a kind of novitiate of unknown length. Eastern cenobitism seems to have served as the model, but the solitary life was also held in high esteem.

Lerins maintained its discipline and its influence all through the fifth century and was still producing saints in the sixth. The greatest of its alumni, St. Caesarius of Arles, entered Lerins as a young cleric around the year 490. In 503 he became bishop of Arles, where he distinguished himself as a theologian, administrator and shepherd until his death in 542. As bishop, he wrote two monastic rules, one for virgins and another for monks, to regulate monasteries in his diocese. In his monastic teaching, he combined the tradition of Lerins with the teachings of Augustine. His successor, Aurelian of Arles, likewise wrote a rule for monks and another for nuns. These rules will be considered in connection with the Rule of St. Benedict in a later section.

Elsewhere in Gaul, other monasteries existed within the Lerinian sphere of influence. A type of monasticism similar to that of Lerins developed in the middle of the fifth century in the region of the Jura mountains, just west of Lake Geneva. This is better known to us than most of the monasteries of the fifth and sixth centuries, because the history of its founders was written by a monk of the abbey in the sixth century.[18] The founders were two brothers, Romanus and Lupicinus.

---

[18] *Vita pat. iuren.* The SC edition contains useful introductory material.

The former, captivated by the ascetic ideal, began to live the solitary life in the Jura forest, at a place called Condadisco, around the year 435. There he was joined by his brother, and soon by an increasing number of disciples, who were attracted by the founders' reputation for holiness. Thus there grew up the monastery of Condat; at first a grouping of anchorites, it gradually became more cenobitic. So many monks came that a number of foundations were made, notably Laucone, two miles away, and Baume, a women's monastery built for the founders' sister.

Romanus and Lupicinus jointly governed this family of ascetics during the lifetime of both; Lupicinus was sole superior after the death of Romanus about 460 until his own death about twenty years later. The anonymous author says little of the next abbot, Minasius, but is expansive in regard to his successor, Eugendus, of whom he claims to be a disciple. Eugendus was born about the middle of the fifth century and was brought to the monastery at the age of six. He grew rapidly in holiness and was chosen to govern the community after the death of Minasius. He lived until 510. It does not appear that there was a written rule during the lifetime of the founders, but probably there was one by the sixth century.[19] The reign of St. Eugendus marked a definite evolution toward a more thoroughgoing cenobitism.

The most influential of all the monastic founders of Gaul was John Cassian. Not too much is known about his monastery at Marseilles nor about some aspects of his personal history, but his monastic writings became universally known in the West and have been more influential in the spirituality of Western monasticism than any other, except the Benedictine Rule.[20] Cassian was probably not a native of Gaul, but seems to have been born in the Balkan region, a part of the empire where Latin was spoken but the urban population was almost equally at home with Greek. Accordingly, he was admirably suited for the role of mediator between Eastern and Western monasticism. He must have been born about 360. His family was presumably prosperous, and he received a good education. As a youth he aspired to undertake the

[19] There appears to be a lacuna between paragraphs 174 and 175 in the *Life of St. Eugendus*, which F. Martine, *Vie des Pères du Jura*, SC 142 (Paris: Les Éditions du Cerf 1968), following Tillemont, thinks once contained the rule, since the title of the entire work is *Vita vel Regula Sanctorum Patrum*. Others believe the "rule" is contained in paragraphs 169–174. Thus A. de Vogüé "La Vie des Pères du Jura et la datation de la Regula Orientalis" *RAM* 47 (1971) 121–127.

[20] The best study of Cassian is O. Chadwick, *John Cassian* (Cambridge Univ. Press 1950, 1968²).

ascetic life and with his friend Germanus went off to enter a monastery in Bethlehem. Certainly this was not Jerome's monastery, but we know little about it. It is not even certain when Cassian came, nor at what age, nor how long he stayed, nor why he was so far from home.

After spending some time there (he later realized that his initiation had been too brief), Cassian made a pilgrimage to Egypt with Germanus to drink in the wisdom of the desert monks. They visited the monastic colonies of the delta region, of Scete, and of Nitria and the Cells. Later, in the *Conferences*, Cassian would record the teaching of the great solitaries. The travelers returned to Bethlehem after seven years (unless this number is symbolic) and subsequently made a second visit to Egypt, of unknown duration. Cassian never mentions Evagrius of Pontus, but he has clearly adopted his whole ascetical system. Since he visited the Cells, where Evagrius was then living until his death in 399, he must have known him and absorbed his teaching.

In 400 Cassian and Germanus were in Constantinople; it is certain that they fled from Egypt in connection with the Origenist controversy of 399 and took refuge with Chrysostom, who ordained Cassian a deacon. But Chrysostom was sent into exile, and in 405 the two friends were in Rome to plead his case before the Pope. It is not known whether Cassian returned to the East after this mission, stayed in Rome, or went on immediately to Gaul. At any rate, he was in Provence around 415, and by then he had been ordained priest.

Cassian became an important figure in the ascetical circles of Provence. Monasteries had sprung up everywhere since the days of Martin, but there was no system, no rule, no agreed observance to regulate the life. Who could be better qualified than a man who had had vast experience as both a cenobite and a hermit in the fabled deserts of Egypt and Palestine, and had absorbed the accumulated wisdom of the monastic founders? Cassian was looked to as an authority. From the dedications of his works, it is clear that he was in contact with monks and bishops of the Lerins group and other monastic circles, sometimes responding to their appeals for advice. Cassian himself established two monasteries at Marseilles — one for men, which must have been the monastery of St. Victor, and one for women.

His monastic writings date from the period 420 to 430. The first of these is the *Institutes*, of which the first four books treat of the monastic customs of Egypt: dress, prayer and psalmody, poverty, food, obedience, discipline, and an exhortation on renunciation. These are followed by eight books, each devoted to one of the eight principal vices. The content of this section is taken over from the Evagrian system. After completing the *Institutes*, Cassian proceeded to compose twenty-four books of *Conferences* in three stages of ten, seven, and seven, respectively, each section with a separate preface. These *Conferences* purport to reproduce the instructions he and Germanus received from various Egyptian elders whom they interviewed in the course of their tour of the deserts. They treat of ascetical topics, though the famous *Conference 13* is a discourse on the theology of grace, in which Cassian adopts an anti-Augustinian position that was later declared unorthodox.

About 430 Cassian wrote his seven books on the Incarnation, a refutation of the incipient Nestorian heresy, at the request of Leo the Great, whom he had met at Rome. The fact that Leo turned to Cassian for such an important theological task indicates the stature of his reputation. He must have died soon after this. Of all Western monastic writers before St. Benedict, he was by far the most influential. His teaching was first preserved by the Lerins circle, who shared his views on monastic observance as well as on the theology of grace. The first four books of the *Institutes* were codified into a monastic rule by an unknown author. Cassian was read by the monks of Condat and by Caesarius of Arles, though the latter gave pride of place to Augustine. In the sixth century, the *Rule of the Master* is heavily dependent upon Cassian, and Cassiodorus recommended him. Above all, the Benedictine Rule referred its readers to the *Collationes Patrum et Instituta* and thus ensured the continued reading of Cassian (RB 73.5).[21] The number of extant manuscripts testifies to the popularity of Cassian in the Middle Ages, and his effect upon Western spirituality is incalculable.

5. MONASTICISM IN ROMAN AFRICA

Like every other aspect of the Church's life and thought in North Africa, the development of monasticism there was dominated by the genius and sanctity of St. Augustine. It is not likely, however, that monastic life in Roman Africa began only with the efforts of Augustine.[22] The ascetic tradition in this region had a long history, as well as

---

[21] See A. de Vogüé "Les mentions des oeuvres de Cassien chez Benoît et ses contemporains" *SM* 20 (1978) 275–285.

[22] J. Gavigan, *De vita monastica in Africa Septentrionali inde a temporibus S. Augustini usque ad invasiones Arabum* (Turin: Marietti 1962); G. Folliet "Aux origines de

the support of such prestigious leaders as Tertullian and Cyprian, and there is evidence that it continued through the fourth century. It appears that communities of ascetics had been formed by the latter part of the century, for the Council of Hippo in 393 prescribed the common life for virgins who had no parents. Monastic influences from the East must also have penetrated to Africa, for the monks at Carthage, whose disdain for work prompted Augustine to write his *De opere monachorum* in 400, seem to have been affected by Messalian views.[23]

Augustine, as we have seen, first became acquainted with monasticism at Milan, when the narrative of Pontitianus impressed him so deeply. In 386 he withdrew with some friends to the country estate of Cassiciacum, the first of his quasi-monastic retreats. This first attempt at the common life seems to have been more like a society of Christian philosophers than a monastery. In 387 Augustine began to make his way back to Africa, staying for some time at Rome, where he took a great interest in the monasteries that had grown up there. The following year he arrived in Tagaste and there began to live the common life with his friends in much the same manner as at Cassiciacum.[24] In 391 he was ordained priest by the bishop of Hippo Regius, Valerius, in response to a popular request during a visit of Augustine. Valerius gave him the use of a garden that belonged to the church, and there Augustine established his first real monastery, whose principal characteristic was the common ownership of all goods. The members of the community, laymen whom Augustine called *servi Dei*, totally renounced individual ownership.

For five years Augustine enjoyed an authentic monastic peace in this community. But when he became bishop in 396, he moved to the episcopal residence in order to prevent the frequent disturbance of the *servi Dei*, who continued to occupy the garden monastery. Augustine then turned his own household of clerics into a quasi-monastery by insisting on the *vita apostolica*, the common life and common ownership of property. This custom, which was to become widespread in the West through his influence, would eventually lead to the development of orders of canons regular. Augustine was unwilling to

l'ascétisme et du cénobitisme africain" *Saint Martin et son temps*, StA 46 (Rome: Herder 1961) pp. 25–44; A. Manrique "San Agustino y el monaquismo africano" *Ciudad de Dios* 173 (1960) 118–143.

[23] G. Folliet "Des moines Euchites à Carthage en 400–401" *Studia Patristica* 2, TU 64 (Berlin: Akademie-Verlag 1957) 386–399.

[24] R. Halliburton "The Inclination to Retirement. The Retreat of Cassiciacum and the 'Monastery' of Tagaste" *Studia Patristica* 5, TU 80 (Berlin: Akademie-Verlag 1962) 329–340.

ordain a priest for his diocese unless he agreed to accept poverty and the common life. The idea was not universally popular with his clergy, however, and in his last years he was obliged to mitigate this discipline somewhat. Certainly his monastic ideal was best realized in the garden monastery.

Several works of monastic legislation have come down to us under the name of Augustine. Three separate pieces, known as the *Obiurgatio*, the *Ordo monasterii*, and the *Praeceptum*, appear in the manuscripts in various combinations and in both masculine and feminine forms, constituting an intricate labyrinth of literary problems. The effort to determine the origin and authenticity of these documents has been one of the most complex investigations in the modern study of Patristic literature. Though there is not yet complete agreement, it is now widely held that the *Praeceptum* or *Regula ad servos Dei*, the masculine form of the rule, is an authentic work of Augustine. It was written perhaps about 397 for the garden monastery at Hippo. The *Obiurgatio*, probably also authentic, was addressed to a community of virgins at Hippo formerly ruled by Augustine's sister. To it was later appended a feminine version of the *Praeceptum*, constituting Letter 211 as it now stands. The *Ordo monasterii*, on the other hand, does not appear to be the work of Augustine, though it probably comes from his circle; it has been conjectured to be the work of Alypius.[25] The "Rule of St. Augustine," which is commonly circulated today among the many religious who follow it, consists of the opening sentence of the *Ordo monasterii* followed by the complete *Praeceptum*.

Augustine's rule is brief and was no doubt intended to be merely a summary and a reminder of the fuller teaching he had given orally. For his complete monastic teaching, it is necessary to look further into his enormous literary production. He never wrote a unified theoretical exposition of his concept of the monastic life, and only two of his smaller works deal explicitly with monastic subjects, the *De opere monachorum* and the *De sancta virginitate*. His views on particular aspects of the subject are frequently expressed in brief passages of his letters and sermons, especially Letters 210 and 211, Sermons 355 and 356, and the *Enarratio* on Psalm 132.[26]

[25] See L. Verheijen, *La Règle de Saint Augustin*, 2 vols. (Paris: Études Augustiniennes 1967).

[26] See A. Zumkeller, *Das Mönchtum des heiligen Augustinus*, Cassiciacum 11 (Würzburg: Augustinus Verlag 1969²); A. Manrique, *La vida monástica en San Agustin* (Salamanca: Studia Patristica 1959); *Teología augustiniana de la vida religiosa* (Madrid: El Escorial 1964); L. Verheijen "Saint Augustin" *Théologie de la vie monastique*,

Despite his admiration for the Egyptian anchorites, Augustine's understanding of Christianity led him in a quite different direction. He was incurably cenobitic, and his whole concept of the monastery centered around the value we today call "community." The key to his rule is the description of the primitive Christian community of Jerusalem as given in Acts 4:32-35. The ideal of the monastic community was to reproduce the close union of purpose, thought and action depicted in the Scriptures: a real *unanimitas* activated by charity. Hence, a fully common life was required, including common ownership of all goods, that there might truly be "one heart and one soul."

The essentials of Augustine's ideal are presented in the opening paragraph of the *Regula ad servos Dei*:

> In the first place, live together in harmony and be of one mind and heart in God; for this is the purpose of your coming together. Do not call anything your own, but hold all that you have in common; and let distribution of food and clothing be made by your superior, not to all alike, because all have not the same health, but to each according to his need. For thus you read in the Acts of the Apostles, that they had all things in common, and distribution was made to each, according as anyone had need.

The remaining precepts of the rule are but practical applications of this ideal of "apostolic life."

So dominant in the thinking of Augustine was the ideal of total harmony of brothers united in heart and mind that he even interpreted the word "monk" to conform to this concept. He provides an etymology for the term *monachus* that scarcely corresponds to its original meaning. Whereas the Greek term *monachos* was derived from *monos*, 'one,' and hence was taken by Jerome and others to mean 'a solitary,' Augustine explains in his characteristic fashion:

> Since the Psalm says, "Behold how good and how pleasant it is that brothers should dwell together in unity," why then should we not call monks by this name? For *monos* is 'one.' Not one in just any way, for an individual in a crowd is 'one,' but, though he can be called one when he is with others, he cannot be *monos*, that is 'alone,' for *monos* means 'one alone.' Hence those who live together so as to form one person, so that they really possess, as the Scripture says, "one mind and one heart," who have many bodies but not many minds, many bodies but not many

---

Théologie 49 (Paris: Aubier 1961) pp. 201–212; A. Sage, *La Règle de Saint Augustin commentée par ses écrits* (Paris: La Vie Augustinienne 1961), reproduced in *La vie religieuse selon saint Augustin* (Paris: La Vie Augustinienne 1972); G. Ladner, *The Idea of Reform* (Cambridge: Harvard Univ. Press 1959).

hearts, can properly be called *monos*, that is, 'one alone' (Aug. *in psalm.* 132,6).

While the life of Augustine's monastery is dominated by the demands of fraternal charity, the observances themselves are the traditional monastic practices: humility, psalmody, private prayer, *lectio*, fasting, silence, simplicity of food and clothing, obedience, manual labor, renunciation of property, strict chastity. In general, the regime is quite mild compared to Egyptian austerity, though Augustine can be severe in matters of principle, such as private property and unsuitable relationships with women. The monks slept in individual cells, but meals were taken in common to the accompaniment of table reading. The majority of the African monks were ex-slaves or at least from the poorer classes. Communities were presided over by a *presbyter*, probably a priest appointed by the bishop, and a *praepositus*, who was second in command. If the basic observances were the same as in the East or in Europe, there was nevertheless a difference of tone in the monasticism of Augustine. His concern with the value of community led to an emphasis upon the relationships of brothers to one another, whereas the Egyptian tradition was more concerned with the relationship of each individual to God via the spiritual father.

Augustine's enthusiasm for monastic life promoted its rapid growth in his own diocese, but his preponderant influence in the African Church ensured it a still wider extension. As his friends and disciples came to fill the sees of Africa, they likewise established communities of monks, virgins and clerics in other places. His biographer, Possidius, tells us that monasticism was flourishing at his death (Possid. *vit.Aug.* 31). The invasion of the Arian Vandals, who were already at the gates of Hippo Regius as Augustine lay dying in 430, destroyed many churches and monasteries, and numerous monks and virgins suffered martyrdom. But monasticism did not disappear even during the worst period of persecution. During the century that followed the death of Augustine, the most outstanding figure in African monasticism was Fulgentius of Ruspe, whose devotion to the monastic ideal inspired him to persevere through countless setbacks and sufferings. Both theologically and monastically he was a disciple of Augustine, and the monastic life that he and others promoted during this period remained essentially Augustinian in inspiration.[27]

Augustine's influence, however, spread even farther than Africa be-

[27] On Fulgentius, see J. Gavigan "Fulgenzio di Ruspe" *Dizionario degli Istituti di Perfezione* 4.998–1002.

cause of his enormous prestige as a theologian and the extensive diffusion of his writings. In both Gaul and Italy, his influence upon monastic writers became so massive in the first half of the sixth century that it has been spoken of as an "Augustinian invasion."[28] In southern Gaul, Caesarius of Arles broke with the "semi-Pelagian" teaching of Cassian and of his own predecessors at Lerins, and adopted the Augustinian position on grace at the Council of Orange in 529. Likewise, his *Rule for Virgins* shows the literary influence of Augustine's rule, which it follows quite closely, even if his thought is still largely determined by the Egyptian tradition, which he seems to have derived more from his Lerinian background than from dependence upon Cassian.[29] Augustine continued to influence the Gallic successors of Caesarius, such as Aurelian and the *Regula Tarnantensis*, as well as Isidore of Seville in Spain at the end of the sixth century.

A little later than Caesarius we find a similar wave of Augustinianism in Italy. While the *Regula Magistri* shows very little if any knowledge of Augustine, the florilegium E, which has been identified with the rule of Eugippius, abbot of Lucullanum, near Naples,[30] and which consists entirely of extracts from existing works, takes more from the *Praeceptum* and *Ordo Monasterii* than from any other source, though it also draws extensively upon the *Regula Magistri*, Basil and Cassian. Later the Rule of St. Benedict was likewise influenced by Augustine; though here the actual quantity of literary borrowing is rather discreet, the qualitative influence of Augustine's thought, derived not only from his rule but from numerous other works as well, is extremely significant. While the RB remains primarily in the tradition of Egypt as mediated by Cassian and the RM, the second most important influence upon it is that of Augustine, whose humaneness and concern for fraternal relationships have contributed to the RB some of its best known and most admired qualities. It has rightly been said that "with the Rule of Augustine western monasticism entered upon the road which led to Benedict."[31]

[28] The expression is that of A. de Vogüé "Saint Benoît et son temps: Règles italiennes et règles provençales au VIᵉ siècle" *RBS* 1 (1972) 169–193, with discussion, 219–221; see also "The Cenobitic Rules of the West" *CS* 12 (1977) 175–183.

[29] L. de Seilhac, *L'utilisation par S. Césaire d'Arles de la Règle de S. Augustin*, StA 62 (Rome: Herder 1974).

[30] A. de Vogüé "La Règle d'Eugippe retrouvée?" *RAM* 47 (1971) 233–265. The identification had been independently made by L. Verheijen and previously suggested by Cardinal Schuster. Critical edition by F. Villegas and A. de Vogüé, *Eugippii Regula*, CSEL 87 (Vienna: Hölder-Pichler-Tempsky 1976).

[31] R. Lorenz, article cited above in note 1.

The Rule of St. Benedict

The foregoing summary of monasticism in the West brings this account to sixth-century Italy, the time and place that brought forth the Benedictine Rule, the most influential document in the entire history of Western monasticism. The study and investigation of this Rule, and the complex questions surrounding its origin and relationship to previous monastic literature, will be facilitated by an examination of the immediate historical background, in order to gain an understanding of the circumstances that shaped the development of ecclesiastical institutions at that period.

1. THE SIXTH CENTURY

At this time, the collapse of Roman civilization was at hand in Gaul, where, for a time, Provence provided an island of safety while the northern provinces were being sacked by barbarian invaders; and in Africa, where the Vandals spread pillage and terror everywhere. Italy, too, became prey to the Goths in the early fifth century. The fall of Rome before the onslaught of Alaric in 410 was a traumatic shock to the whole civilized world, and expressions of horror at the news came from Jerome in far-off Bethlehem (Hier. *epist.* 123,16)[1] and from Augustine across the sea in Africa.[2] Rufinus, together with Melania the Younger and Pinianus, fled to Sicily before the advancing barbarians; there Rufinus died, and the others went on to Africa. Paulinus was imprisoned for a short time, but was later allowed to return to Nola.

The barbarian tribes began to dismember an empire already seriously weakened from within by misgovernment and oppressive taxation, and scourged by famine and pestilence. By mid-century the Huns were ravaging northern Italy, and Rome was sacked a second time by the Vandals in 455. The official end of the Western empire

[1] See J. Palanque "St. Jerome and the Barbarians" *A Monument to St. Jerome*, ed. F. X. Murphy (New York: Sheed and Ward 1952).

[2] P. Brown, *Augustine of Hippo* (Berkeley: Univ. of California 1969) pp. 287–298.

came in 476 with the deposition of Romulus, the last emperor, by the barbarian leader Odoacer, who ruled until displaced in 493 by Theodoric, king of the Ostrogoths. Under Theodoric's long rule, there was peace until his death in 526. Soon after this, however, the Eastern emperor Justinian determined to regain the West, and war raged up and down the Italian peninsula almost unceasingly from the coming of the Byzantine armies in 535 until the final defeat of the Ostrogoths in 553. Rome was besieged three times during the Gothic War. The reconquest was short-lived, for in 568 the Lombards arrived to pillage Italy anew and settle in the north. At the end of the sixth century, in the time of Gregory the Great, there was practically no effective political order in Italy, and the Christian world began to look more and more toward the Holy See as the only stable authority.

During this whole period, from the beginnings of monasticism through the sixth century, ecclesiastical society was almost as troubled as its civil counterpart. While the great theological controversies centered for the most part in the East, they had ramifications in the West as well. The fourth century was dominated by the Arian controversy, the fifth by the Christological controversies following the condemnation of Nestorianism at Ephesus in 431. After the Council of Chalcedon in 451, large sections of the East refused to accept the condemnation of monophysitism and went into schism. These heresies had no following in the West, but the Roman See was constantly preoccupied with the preservation of orthodoxy and with countering the political moves of the Eastern emperors, especially their repeated attempts to reconcile the monophysites at the expense of orthodoxy, endeavors that lasted until the Moslem invasions of the seventh century.

The West was troubled by the Pelagian problem and the subsequent controversies about grace, which lasted through the fifth century and into the sixth. This was particularly a problem for monastic circles, which often favored the semi-Pelagian position because the Augustinian views on grace seemed to negate the value of asceticism. The most troubling heresy in the West, however, was Arianism, which survived there long after it had been settled in the East. While the doctrine had little appeal to Western Christians, it became the faith of most of the barbarian invaders. Living on the fringes of the empire, they had first come into contact with Christianity through missionaries whose allegiance was Arian at a time when Arianism had triumphed throughout the Eastern empire. The Vandals were fiercely anti-Catholic, the Goths usually more tolerant, but Arianism remained a powerful force in Italy throughout the fifth and sixth centuries, and survived in some places until the eighth.

These developments in political, social and ecclesiastical life left their mark upon Western monasticism. The breakdown of order in society and the widespread pillage and destruction did not destroy monastic life, but tended to draw monks out of isolation and favored their banding together in communities. Both civil and ecclesiastical authorities became more inclined to regulate the monastic life to combat the anarchy and unorthodox excesses into which it easily degenerated when totally unchecked. Accordingly, monasticism gradually became more organized and institutionalized. While there were still hermits in abundance, a more organized cenobitic life grew in popularity. In the early sixth century, we find a noticeable tightening up of discipline and increasing regimentation in the *coenobia*, a necessity that bears witness to the moral decline that accompanied the decay of ancient culture. Institutions differ from one monastery to another, but on the whole the similarities are more striking than the divergences.

One reason for this is that all the monks drew upon the same sources. The Latin literature — Jerome, Ambrose, Augustine, Sulpicius Severus, Cassian, the Lerins school — became known almost everywhere. In the course of the fifth and sixth centuries, a considerable body of Eastern literature was translated into Latin, so that the monastic practice of Egypt and Cappadocia became the foundation of the Western traditions. We have already spoken of the translation of the *Life of Antony*, the Pachomian literature, the *Small Asceticon* of Basil, and the *History of the Monks in Egypt*. In addition to these, a Latin version of Palladius' *Lausiac History* seems to have been made in the fifth century.[3]

In the first half of the sixth century, Dionysius Exiguus translated the Greek *Life of Pachomius*,[4] and the Roman deacon Pelagius, about the same time, began a Latin version of the *Verba Seniorum*, which was completed about 550 by the subdeacon John.[5] The most important source of Eastern monastic teaching, however, was John Cassian. This

[3] C. Butler, *The Lausiac History of Palladius* (1898; rpt. Hildesheim: G. Ohms Verlag 1967) 1. 58–69.

[4] H. van Cranenburgh, *La vie latine de saint Pachôme traduite du grec par Denys le Petit*, Subsidia Hagiographica 46 (Brussels: Société des Bollandistes 1969).

[5] C. Battle, *Die "Adhortationes Sanctorum Patrum" im lateinischen Mittelalter*, Beiträge zur Geschichte des alten Mönchtums und des Benediktinerordens 31 (Münster: Aschendorff 1972).

whole body of literature constituted a tradition that was the culmination of some two hundred years of monastic experience and became the common inheritance of sixth-century Western monasticism.

In Gaul at this time, the major influence in the south was still the monastery of Lerins, though Arles became, under Caesarius and Aurelian, a center of monastic legislation. The type of life that flourished at Condat and its foundations was becoming increasingly organized in a strictly cenobitic fashion, and a similar evolution can be traced elsewhere in Gaul, which had some two hundred monasteries by the end of the sixth century, in addition to numerous solitaries. In Italy, too, monasticism flourished despite the evils of the time — even because of them, to some extent, for the collapse of Roman civilization led many to reflect upon the transitoriness of the things of this life. Salvian's *De gubernatione Dei*, written in the middle of the fifth century, presents an eloquent case for the barbarian invasions as God's just punishment upon the sins of pagans and Christians alike.[6] At the end of the sixth century, Gregory the Great believed that the end of the world was approaching; and he is our best witness to the flourishing character of monasticism in the preceding century. The monks and virgins, hermits and cenobites who populate the pages of his *Dialogues* clearly demonstrate the variety of monastic forms in sixth-century Italy.

Of all the monasteries that must have flourished in Italy in the first half of the sixth century, aside from the foundations of St. Benedict, only two stand out somewhat from the darkness in which history has shrouded this period. One is the monastery of Eugippius, of which little is known. Born in Africa, he became a disciple and later biographer of the Roman monk St. Severin, apostle of Noricum, who died in 482.[7] Later, about 512, he was abbot of the monastery of Lucullanum, just outside of Naples, built at the tomb of St. Severin. Although information about the life at Lucullanum is sketchy, contemporary accounts indicate that the monastery was a seat of learning. Eugippius was in contact with Dionysius Exiguus, Fulgentius of Ruspe, the latter's disciple and biographer Ferrandus, and Cassiodorus, all of whom had similar interests. That he shared Fulgentius' admiration for Augustine is shown by the fact that he composed for his monks a book of *excerpta* from Augustine, which was popular in the Middle Ages. The

[6] J. O'Sullivan, *The Writings of Salvian the Presbyter*, FC 4 (New York: Cima 1947).
[7] L. Bieler, *Eugippius: Life of St. Severin*, FC 55 (Washington: Catholic Univ. Press 1965).

influence of Augustine on the monastic rule that is probably the work of Eugippius has been noted, and shows how the monks of this period drew upon various sources, both Eastern and Western, for their monastic teaching.

The other monastery is that of Vivarium, the foundation of Cassiodorus in Calabria. Born about 485 of a noble family, Cassiodorus rose to high positions in civic life and was the principal minister of Theodoric and his successors. Amid the disasters of the times, he aspired to save Christian culture for posterity. His plan to found a Christian university at Rome was nullified by the outbreak of the Gothic War and the death of Pope Agapitus. He then retired from public life about 540 and founded a monastery on his estate at Vivarium, though he himself did not make monastic profession. Here he assembled a noteworthy library, wrote his *Institutiones divinarum et saecularium litterarum*,[8] and founded a scriptorium that produced manuscripts that later found their way to numerous libraries of Europe. The monastery does not seem to have long survived its founder, who died about 585 at a very advanced age. Although little is known of the observance of Vivarium, its importance consists less in its monastic influence than in its cultural impact, which was due to the intellectual program of Cassiodorus himself and which he bequeathed to the Middle Ages.[9]

2. ST. BENEDICT AND HIS RULE: THE STATE OF THE QUESTION

It is at this point that we must consider St. Benedict, who was a contemporary of Eugippius and Cassiodorus. A generation ago the entire question of Benedict and his Rule seemed perfectly clear, even though there were many areas about which we knew less than we would have liked. The accepted view may be summarized as follows. The life of Benedict is known to us through a biography written less than a half century after his death by his disciple St. Gregory the Great, the first Benedictine Pope, and based upon testimony provided by men who had known Benedict personally. In this *Life*, Gregory relates that Benedict wrote a rule for monks, which could be none

[8] L. Jones, *An Introduction to Divine and Human Readings by Cassiodorus Senator* (1946; New York: Norton paperback 1969).

[9] P. Riché, *Education and Culture in the Barbarian West, 6th through 8th Centuries* (Columbia: Univ. of South Carolina Press 1976); E. S. Duckett, *Gateway to the Middle Ages: Italy* (1938; Ann Arbor paperback 1961); P. Courcelle, *Late Latin Writers and Their Greek Sources* (Cambridge: Harvard Univ. Press 1969).

other than the Rule known throughout the Western Church under Benedict's name and handed down from earliest times in countless manuscripts. It was believed that this Rule, brought to the Lateran by Benedict's monks when their monastery was destroyed by the Lombards about 570, was followed by Gregory himself in his monastery on the Coelian Hill in Rome, that it was taken to England by Augustine and his companions when sent by Gregory to evangelize the Angles and was subsequently carried back to the continent by the English missionaries.

The Rule, a document whose brevity and simplicity belie its wisdom, was thought to be an original work that forcefully reveals the personality and genius of its author. While he was aware of the forms of monastic life that had preceded him in both East and West and drew copiously upon their literature, he saw that a new beginning had to be made to meet the needs of the times. His moderation, his emphasis upon a stable community life in opposition to individualism, and his encouragement of civilizing work ensured that the institute he founded would become a powerful force in fashioning a Christian Europe out of the ruins of the barbarian invasions. He may even have been commissioned by the Pope to reform Western monasticism; in any case, his work was a contribution of extraordinary originality and foresight that makes him tower above his predecessors and contemporaries.

In the past thirty-five years, some significant changes have been made in this appraisal. It is not a question of totally changing our view of Benedict and his Rule, but of nuancing our judgments in some areas, modifying some positions that went beyond the facts, and abandoning maximalist positions in favor of more sober historical probabilities.[10] But there is no reason for skepticism: the irresponsible rumors occasionally heard that unidentified "scholars" have disproved St. Benedict's existence or found that he never wrote a rule may serve to shock the uninformed and delight the iconoclast, but are nonetheless utterly without foundation. What has happened is that an extraordinary and extremely beneficial renewal of studies in the Rule of St. Benedict and related monastic literature has provided new insights that to some extent alter but, more important, clarify and deepen our understanding.

What has brought about this renewal is the study of a related document, the *Regula Magistri*. A Latin monastic rule of unknown author-

[10] See J. Leclercq "Monasticism and St. Benedict" *MS* 1 (1963) 9–23.

ship, about three times the length of the RB, it has been known from ancient times, since Benedict of Aniane included it in his *Codex Regularum*, or collection of ancient rules,[11] in the early ninth century. Although all these rules were similar insofar as they drew upon the same tradition and did not hesitate to borrow from one another, the RM manifests particularly close contacts with the RB. Large sections of the texts of these two rules are identical, or nearly so; thus practically the entire prologue and first seven chapters of the RB can also be found in the RM, mingled with other material. This had always been explained on the supposition that the RM was a later work, of the seventh or eighth century, and that its anonymous author, whose lack of originality, it was thought, was equaled only by his long-windedness, had simply borrowed large sections from the RB.

This hypothesis was in itself perfectly reasonable, for such procedure was not uncommon in ancient times. The *Rule of Donatus* for virgins, for example, which belongs to seventh-century Gaul, consists almost entirely of extracts from Benedict, Columban and Caesarius. This view of the RM appeared satisfactory to the erudite Maurist scholars of the seventeenth and eighteenth centuries; Dom Hugh Ménard, who edited the *Concordia Regularum* in 1638, conjectured that it might be the work of Benedict Biscop, the Northumbrian admirer of all things Roman and monastic, who founded Wearmouth and Jarrow in the late seventh century. In the meantime, no one had undertaken a thorough study of this rule, which seemed to have little to offer.

This situation changed abruptly, however, in the late 1930s, with the sudden appearance of the contrary hypothesis, namely, that the RM was the earlier of the two rules and that the RB had borrowed from it. This proposal was first made by Father Augustine Genestout, a monk of Solesmes, though it was made public by others before his own studies were published. The initial reaction was one of shock, disbelief and reluctance to accept a view that seemed at first sight to rob St. Benedict of all originality and reduce him to an unimportant imitator. Some scholars reacted with a vigorous defense of the tradi-

---

[11] Critical edition with extensive introduction, notes and verbal concordance, the latter by J.-M. Clément, J. Neufville and D. Demeslay, in A. de Vogüé, *La Règle du Maître*, SC 105–106–107 (Paris: Les Éditions du Cerf 1964–65). Diplomatic edition of the two Paris manuscripts in H. Vanderhoven and F. Masai, *La Règle du Maître* (Brussels: Éditions "Érasme" 1953). English translation of the rule and an abridged version of de Vogüé's introduction in L. Eberle and C. Philippi, *The Rule of the Master* (Kalamazoo, Mich.: Cistercian Publications 1977).

tional view, while others proposed a mediating position. Only after the publication of a reliable text of the RM could the controversy advance on firmer ground. Now, after a generation has passed and innumerable studies have been devoted to the problem, the question can be viewed in a calmer and more objective fashion.[12]

A close literary relationship between two documents poses a complex problem that usually cannot be resolved by any single argument, since individual pieces of evidence can point in opposite directions. The interrelationship of the Synoptic Gospels, for instance, is again being hotly debated, although the majority of New Testament scholars once thought it had been definitively solved. Likewise, the RM-RB question cannot be said to have reached a solution that fully accounts for all the evidence and completely satisfies everyone. Nevertheless, the weight of the evidence is definitely in favor of the priority of the RM, and there is no longer any prominent expert in the field who holds that the RB is earlier than its sister rule. To put it another way, the working hypothesis of the priority of the RM offers an adequate explanation of the composition of the RB in the majority of cases, whereas the contrary hypothesis is unable to account for many features of the RM. The genesis and development of the RM itself, however, and the stage of its development that was known to the author of the RB, are still matters for vigorous dispute.

The view now held by all serious students of the RB that it is dependent upon the RM does not entirely change our appreciation of St. Benedict and his Rule nor diminish his importance. It does, however, alter our approach to him and his work, for we cannot abstract from the present state of the question regarding the RM controversy. The dispute has, in fact, been of enormous value to anyone interested in the life and Rule of St. Benedict, for it has shed light upon previously obscure areas in Western monastic development and more accurately delineated his real contribution to this evolution. The truth is always a

---

[12] The best account in English of the early stages of the controversy is that of D. Knowles "The Regula Magistri and the Rule of St. Benedict" *Great Historical Enterprises and Problems in Monastic History* (London: Nelson 1963) pp. 137–195. See also G. Penco "Origine e sviluppi della questione della 'Regula Magistri'" *Antonius Magnus Eremita 356–1956*, StA 38 (Rome: Herder 1956) pp. 283–306; and B. Jaspert, *Die Regula Benedicti-Regula Magistri Kontroverse*, RBS Supplementa 3 (Hildesheim: Gerstenberg 1975). A complete bibliography of the question up to 1970 was published by B. Jaspert, *Regula Magistri, Regula Benedicti: Bibliographie ihrer Erforschung 1938–1970*, Subsidia Monastica 1 (Publicaciones de l'Abadia de Montserrat 1971), excerpted from *SM* 13 (1971) 129–171. From 1971 on, the current bibliography is listed regularly in the annual publication *Regulae Benedicti Studia*.

gain. It is against the background of these recent studies, then, that we shall attempt to reconstruct an account of St. Benedict and of the Rule that has played such an important role in the Western Church for more than a thousand years.

3. ST. BENEDICT OF NURSIA

Unlike Caesarius, Cassiodorus and other monastic figures of the period, St. Benedict is not mentioned by any of his contemporaries nor in any literature that can be dated earlier than the end of the sixth century. He does not even identify himself in the Rule, and hence it cannot be used as a source of information about him until his authorship can be otherwise established. Nor has he left any other writings. For our knowledge of him, we are entirely dependent upon a single source, the *Dialogues* of Pope Gregory the Great. Of the four books composing this work, written in 593–594, the second is entirely devoted to Benedict, and he is mentioned once again in Book 3, and twice in Book 4.

Gregory, one of the most important personages ever to occupy the papal throne, was a vital link between the Patristic period and the Middle Ages. Born about 540 of a patrician family, he received an excellent education and became prefect of Rome in 570. Five years later, however, after his father's death, he converted the family home on the Coelian into a monastery and established six other monasteries on his estates in Sicily. Nothing is known of the observance followed in his Roman monastery of St. Andrew. The monastic life was congenial to him, but about 579 the Pope called him from it to serve as *apocrisiarius*, or nuncio, to the Byzantine court at Constantinople. Accompanied there by monks, he continued to live the monastic life in the capital, and returned to St. Andrew's when his mission was completed in 586. But he was then chosen deacon to Pope Pelagius II, and when the Pontiff died in 590, was constrained to succeed him despite his unwillingness. He never ceased to mourn the loss of his contemplative peace during the fourteen years of his extremely active pontificate.[13]

Gregory's writings, while displaying a high degree of culture, have an essentially pastoral and practical character. At a time when the

[13] The best overall study of Gregory is still, despite its age, the work of F. Homes Dudden, *Gregory the Great: His Place in History and Thought*, 2 vols. (1905; rpt. New York: Russell and Russell 1967). See also C. Dagens, *Saint Grégoire le Grand. Culture et expérience chrétienne* (Paris: Études Augustiniennes 1977).

institutions of society were collapsing and men believed that the world was coming to an end, he strove to maintain peace and order, and to provide encouragement for all classes of the faithful suffering from the evils of the times. Gregory had a marked mystical bent, yet at the same time, everything he wrote is pedagogically oriented. He says often that the best way to teach is not by explanation but by concrete example. Abstraction and speculation were foreign to his manner; he was always the moralizing teacher. Of all his works, the *Dialogues* are doubtless the most characteristic of this genre. Adopting the ancient form of the dialogue, which goes back at least as far as Plato, he presents his deacon, Peter, as the eager listener who asks naïve and sometimes rather obtuse questions to elicit the pontiff's teaching. The real purpose of the work is to convey Gregory's spiritual and moral instruction; but this is done by telling stories about the saints of Italy, particularly those of the vicinity of Rome. Their example was meant to assure his contemporaries that the gifts of God are still poured forth in their own times, evil as they seem, as much as in previous ages.[14]

Of all these saints adduced as witnesses, St. Benedict holds the most important place. Recent studies have disclosed the careful construction of the work.[15] The stories about him in Book 2 are framed by 12 lesser personages in Book 1, and 37 others in Book 3, making 50 all together, but in such a fashion that Benedict holds the central place. Book 4 corresponds to Book 2 in that it also develops a single theme, that of life after death, a question frequently posed in the earlier books, especially in their concluding episodes. It is especially linked to Book 2 by its opening reference to Germanus of Capua, and its 62 chapters, with the 38 of Book 2, make 100 in all; the addition of Book 3, also with 38, and Book 1, with 12, gives a grand total of 150.

There is a similar organization within the account of Benedict in Book 2 itself. While Gregory follows the principal stages of Benedict's career, he is primarily interested in the gift of prophecy and the power of working miracles. These charisms frequently reproduce biblical

---

[14] English translation by O. Zimmermann, *St. Gregory the Great: Dialogues*, FC 39 (New York: FC Inc. 1959). The best edition of the *Dialogues*, with abundant annotation and indices and an extensive introduction, is the recent work of A. de Vogüé, with French translation by P. Antin, *Grégoire le Grand: Dialogues*, SC 251,260,265 (Paris: Les Éditions du Cerf 1978, 1979, 1980).

[15] A. de Vogüé "Benoît, modèle de vie spirituelle d'après le Deuxième Livre des Dialogues de saint Grégoire" *CollCist* 38 (1976) 147–157; M. Doucet "Pédagogie et théologie dans la 'Vie de saint Benoît' par saint Grégoire le Grand" *CollCist* 38 (1976) 158–173.

models, so that Benedict is shown to be the *Vir Dei*, filled with the spirit of all the just. The account of his early experience depicts his progress toward holiness. There is a discernible sequence of temptation, followed by victory, followed in turn by the increasing radiation of his holiness for the benefit of others. Four times this sequence is repeated, with growing intensity, until Benedict has won the spiritual combat within himself and is ready to be set like a light upon a still higher candlestick, the mountain of Cassino. There he joins battle with the demon outside himself, manifested in the paganism that still survives in the countryside, which he combats by destroying the idols and preaching the faith. Four encounters with the demon then serve to display the power of God in the Man of God. His career at Montecassino is then depicted by two series of twelve miracles each, the first displaying powers of knowledge; the second, powers of action. These are followed by four accounts of visions and miracles concerning the afterlife, forming a pendant to the four demonic assaults that preceded the miracle series.

Clearly, this "Life" is not a biography in any modern sense of the term. The author's purpose is not primarily to tell us what really happened nor to set events in their chronological order. The entire development of his account is ruled by quite different preoccupations. Benedict is an example who shows forth the working of God in man's life. He illustrates the law of paradox: genuine fruitfulness comes from what at first sight seems sterile; life comes forth from death; the man who concentrates upon his own sanctification becomes an apostle, an instrument of God for the good of others. Through Benedict, Gregory teaches his readers the stages through which a man advances toward God.

The pedagogical purpose is so apparent in all this that one may wonder about the reality of the events narrated. Certainly the stories have a symbolic intent; recently a number of attempts have been made by scholars to elucidate the meaning behind some of Gregory's narratives.[16] Symbolism, however, does not exclude historicity, and

---

[16] J. H. Wansbrough "St. Gregory's Intention in the Story of St. Scholastica and St. Benedict" *RBén* 75 (1965) 145–151; P. Courcelle "'Habitare secum' selon Perse et saint Grégoire le Grand" *Revue des études anciennes* 69 (1967) 266–279; C. Dagens "La 'conversion' de saint Benoît selon saint Grégoire le Grand" *Revista di storia e letteratura religiosa* 5 (1969) 384–391; V. Recchia "La visione di San Benedetto e la 'compositio' del secondo libro dei Dialoghi di Gregorio Magno" *RBén* 82 (1972) 148–149; A. de Vogüé "La rencontre de Benoît et de Scholastique. Essai d'interprétation" *RHS* 48 (1972) 257–273; A. Maehler "Évocations bibliques et hagiographiques dans la vie de

the basic facts of Benedict's career in Gregory's account are too well founded to be inventions for some symbolic purpose. He tells us the sources of his information: Constantine and Simplicius, the second and third abbots of Montecassino, who probably knew Benedict in his old age and certainly knew the community's traditions about him; Valentinian, abbot of the Lateran monastery; and Honoratus, who was abbot of Subiaco when Gregory was writing. It is unlikely that the latter could have known Benedict, but Gregory does not say that all these men knew him personally nor that he got his information from them directly. But he surely drew upon sources close to reliable traditions. Moreover, the narrative mentions nearby places such as Enfide, Subiaco, Cassino, Terracina, and historical personages such as Germanus and Sabinus. It is not plausible that a fictitious person could be passed off as real when mingled with known places and people who were still living or only recently deceased. A well-documented and early cult of St. Benedict also testifies to the historical reality of his life.

Consequently, there can be no question that Gregory gives us genuine facts about the life of St. Benedict, even if it is not easy to separate them from what is purely symbolic and imaginative. The *Dialogues* testify that Benedict was born in the region of Nursia, northeast of Rome, in the mountains; the traditional date of 480 cannot be far from the truth. He was sent to Rome for school and there experienced the religious conversion that led him to renounce the world. He is depicted as first living with what seems to have been a group of ascetics at Enfide (now Affile), east of Rome, then in utter solitude for three years at Subiaco. After a bitter experience as head of a group of false monks (probably the "sarabaites" of the Rule or the "remnuoth" of Jerome), he returned to Subiaco, where he was joined by numerous disciples, for whom he established twelve monasteries of twelve

saint Benoît par saint Grégoire" *RBén* 83 (1973) 398–429; P. A. Cusack "St. Scholastica: Myth or Real Person?" *DR* 92 (1974) 145–159; M. Doucet "La tentation de saint Benoît. Relation ou création par saint Grégoire le Grand?" *CollCist* 37 (1975) 63–71; K. Gross "Der Tod des hl. Benedictus. Ein Beitrag zu Greg. d. Gr., *Dial.* 2,37" *RBén* 85 (1975) 164–176; P. A. Cusack "Some Literary Antecedents of the Totila Encounter in the Second Dialogue of Pope Gregory I" *Studia Patristica* 12, TU 115 (Berlin: Akademie-Verlag 1975) 87–90; "The Temptation of St. Benedict: An Essay at Interpretation through the Literary Sources" *ABR* 27 (1976) 143–163. For St. Gregory's concept of the monastic life, see R. Gillet "Spiritualité et place du moine dans l'Église selon saint Grégoire le Grand" in *Théologie de la vie monastique* (Paris: Aubier 1961) pp. 322–351; A. de Vogüé "Les vues de Grégoire le Grand sur la vie réligieuse dans son Commentaire des Rois" *SM* 20 (1978) 17–63.

monks each and appointed deans over them. Some have seen in this a reproduction of the Pachomian system, but the parallel is by no means compelling.

After these monasteries had been firmly established, Benedict left this region with a few disciples and founded a fully cenobitic monastery on top of the mountain rising above Cassino, some eighty miles south of Rome on the way to Naples. Here he acquired a widespread reputation as a holy man invested with divine charisms (his annual visit with his sister, St. Scholastica, and his vision of her death, for example), sent a delegation to found another monastery at Terracina, and died around the middle of the sixth century. A quarter of a century later his monastery was destroyed by the invading Lombards, but the community escaped without loss of life.[17]

Not everything in this sketch is equally certain, and many questions are left unanswered; most modern readers would be happy to trade some of Gregory's miracle stories for a few more hard facts, but his interests were different from ours. Nevertheless, Benedict's activity in the area around Rome and his role as a monastic founder are beyond question. There is one other point Gregory regarded as important, though again he is less specific than we would like: he testifies that Benedict wrote a monastic rule "notable for its discernment (*discretione praecipuam*) and its clarity of language (*sermone luculentam*)."[18] The *Dialogues* describe his *activity*; for his *teaching*, the reader is referred to his Rule, which is a mirror of his own virtuous life.[19]

Presumably Gregory had a personal acquaintance with this Rule

[17] The first "life" of St. Benedict in modern times was that of Abbot L. Tosti of Montecassino, *Saint Benedict: An Historical Discourse on His Life* (London: Kegan Paul 1896). The principal lives that have appeared since then are: F. Cabrol, *Saint Benedict* (London: Burns Oates 1934); J. McCann, *Saint Benedict* (New York: Sheed and Ward 1937; Image paperback 1958); J. Chapman, *Saint Benedict and the Sixth Century* (1929; rpt. Westport, Conn.: Greenwood Press 1972); T. F. Lindsay, *St. Benedict: His Life and Work* (London: Burns Oates 1949); I. Schuster, *Saint Benedict and His Times* (St. Louis: B. Herder 1951); T. Maynard, *Saint Benedict and His Monks* (New York: Kenedy 1954). Of somewhat different character are: I. Herwegen, *St. Benedict: A Character Study* (London: Sands 1924); I. Ryelandt, *Saint Benedict the Man* (St. Meinrad, Ind.: Grail Press 1950).

[18] See A. de Vogüé "'Discretione praecipuam': à quoi Grégoire pensait-il?" *Benedictina* 22 (1975) 325–327, who argues that the phrase refers especially to RB 58, in which Gregory has recognized this quality of "discernment," which he then uses to characterize the whole Rule.

[19] A. de Vogüé "La mention de la 'regula monachorum' à la fin de la 'Vie de Benoît'. Sa fonction littéraire et spirituelle" *RBS* 5 (1977) 289–298.

written by Benedict; surely he could have had access to it through his sources. In the past it has often been supposed that Gregory himself was a "Benedictine," that he followed what we know as the Rule of St. Benedict in his own monastery on the Coelian, and that the monks he sent to England were likewise "Benedictines." Now, however, the increased complexity surrounding the origin of the RB requires a re-examination of these assumptions.[20] Surely it is an anachronism to speak of Gregory and his monks as "Benedictine" in the later sense of that term, for in the sixth century a rule did not serve as a detailed code regulating the life except in the monastery for which it was written. Monasteries frequently made use of several rules, taking from each what they found suitable. There is no evidence that the RB regulated the life at St. Andrew's nor that it was taken to Canterbury in 596; its first clear attestation in England is much later in the seventh century, and in the north rather than at Canterbury.

Attempts have been made to show that the monastic customs mentioned by Gregory in the *Dialogues* and elsewhere do or do not agree with the RB, as a means of establishing whether or not the rule of which Gregory speaks is the one we know as St. Benedict's. In fact, the evidence points in both directions—if in fact it can be called evidence, since the literary form of the *Dialogues* hardly lends itself to such precision. Although it is impossible to show that Gregory regarded the RB as normative, however, there cannot be any reasonable doubt that he was acquainted with it. In the *Commentary on 1 Kings*, now accepted as authentically Gregorian even if given its present form by a disciple, Gregory cites RB 58 (and perhaps alludes to other passages), though he identifies the author only as *arctissimae vitae magister optimus*. It is the earliest known citation of the RB. Indeed, Gregory does not here explicitly say that he is citing the Rule of Benedict mentioned in the *Dialogues*, and we have no clear historical proof that what Gregory thought to be the Rule of Benedict was really the work of the Patriarch of Cassino. But the chain of evidence seems continuous enough to resist all but the most demanding skepticism.

To this can be added the evidence of the manuscript tradition. In

---

[20] Gregory's acquaintance with the RB is denied by K. Hallinger "Pabst Gregor der Grosse und der hl. Benedikt" *Commentationes in Regulam S. Benedicti*, StA 42 (Rome: Herder 1957) pp. 231–319. For the opposite view, see O. Porcel, *San Gregorio Magno y el monacato. Cuestiones controvertidas*, Scripta et Documenta 12 (Montserrat: Abadia 1960) and his earlier work *La doctrina monástica de San Gregorio Magno y la "regula monachorum,"* Catholic Univ. Studies in Sacred Theology 60 (Washington: Catholic Univ. Press 1951).

none of the hundreds of existing manuscripts is the RB ever attributed to anyone else. Not all of them mention the author, but those that do, among which are some of the best and most ancient, attribute it to Benedict. Others do so equivalently by associating it with other literature about him, e.g., Book 2 of the *Dialogues*. It is true that this fact alone is not compelling; the oldest manuscripts do not antedate the middle or, at the earliest, the opening years of the eighth century, some two centuries after Benedict's death. By that time a universal tradition of authorship could have been established even without historical basis. But the witness of Gregory takes it back quite reliably to the sixth century. It is, if not capable of apodictic proof, at least of the highest probability that the Benedict of Nursia of whom St. Gregory wrote is in fact responsible for the Rule attributed to him for more than a thousand years.[21]

4. RELATIONSHIP OF THE RULE TO THE REGULA MAGISTRI

The RM, as we have seen, is now known to be a work of the sixth century. Aside from all hypotheses, this dating is certain from the manuscript tradition alone. The RM probably was not often copied because of its length and because it was not followed in many monasteries after the time of its author. Therefore, we have but few manuscripts—only three complete and several fragmentary copies. Two of these, however, are older than any manuscript of the RB. The Paris Codex P, which contains the entire rule, dates from the early seventh century, and Codex E, the only surviving copy of the florilegium attributed to Eugippius, which contains sixteen extracts from the RM, is probably even earlier, from the end of the sixth century. The composition of the rule, therefore, must belong to the sixth century at the very latest, and internal evidence points to the opening decades of the century. This puts it quite close in time to the RB, assigned to the early or middle part of the sixth century both by the testimony of Gregory and by internal evidence. Only a close comparison of the two rules can show which is earlier; it is now generally agreed that the RM came first. The reasons for this judgment are as follows.[22]

First, the vocabulary of the two rules favors the precedence of the

[21] A. Mundó "L'authenticité de la Regula Sancti Benedicti" in *Commentationes*, pp. 105–158 (cited in previous note); de Vogüé, 1.149–172.

[22] The fullest demonstration of the priority of the RM is that of A. de Vogüé, 1.245–314.

RM. A number of words in the passages common to the two rules are also used in sections proper to the RM, but rarely or never in passages proper to the RB. Conversely, some words belonging to the vocabulary of the RB rarely or never occur in the common passages or in those proper to the RM. One of the striking cases noted early in the dispute is that of *autem:* a favorite word of St. Benedict, it occurs 82 times in the parts proper to the RB, only 8 times in the RM, and never in the passages they have in common. Likewise, St. Benedict writes *omnino* 18 times, but the RM and the common passages do not use it at all. On the other hand, there are no less than 163 words that occur both in the RM and in the common parts but are never used by St. Benedict, while only 12 words absent from the RM appear in both the common parts and in the RB, some of them only once in each. The unity of vocabulary between the common part and the RM suggests that these two are by the same author, but that the RB, which has a different vocabulary in the sections proper to itself, also has a different author, who has taken over the common passages from the RM.

Among other items that could be cited, the words used to designate monastic superiors are significant. The term *doctor* occurs once in the common passages and 12 times in the RM, never in the RB. *Maior* occurs 4 times in the common passages and 28 times in the RM, never in the RB. On the other hand, the RB uses the term *prior* 11 times to mean 'superior,' whereas it never occurs with this meaning either in the common passages or in the RM. Likewise, *senior* appears 13 times in the RB, never in the common parts, and only once in the RM. *Prior* in the sense of 'the older' and *iunior* in the sense of 'the younger' occur 8 and 11 times, respectively, in the RB, never in the RM or the common parts. A member of the community is usually called *discipulus* or *frater* by the RM, and the common parts generally prefer this usage, while avoiding *monachus*. The RB likewise uses all these terms, but in inverse proportion: the word *monachus* occurs 31 times, compared to 7 in the RM and only 2 in the common parts.

A second argument is drawn from the sources utilized by the two rules. The argument runs as follows. In the passages common to both, there are citations from earlier works. The form in which these citations appear in the RM is more faithful to the original than their form in the RB. Thus in several places in the Prologue and chapter 1, the RB contains citations from Cassian. These same citations occur in the parallels in the RM, but in every case the RM reproduces the citation more exactly than the RB. It looks, therefore, as if the Master is following the text of Cassian, while the RB is following the RM and introducing slight changes, perhaps unaware that the passages are citations. The alternative hypothesis would require us to suppose that the Master, following the RB, checked each citation (or knew it by heart) and corrected it according to the original text of Cassian. Though not impossible, this is less likely, unless there is question of citations extremely well known, such as texts from Scripture.

Some of the citations, moreover, are from apocryphal books such as the *Passion of Sebastian* and the *Sentences of Sextus*. Now, it appears certain that these books were used by the Master, because he cites them elsewhere in his rule, in passages that do not occur in the RB. On the other hand, there is no evidence that the author of the RB had independent access to them (as he certainly did to Cassian), since he never cites them in those portions of his rule not paralleled by the RM. It looks, therefore, as if he derived these citations from the RM. The contrary hypothesis, though not totally excluded, is highly improbable. Indeed, the precedence of the RM has been argued precisely from its more liberal attitude toward, and usage of, apocryphal books, in contrast to the RB. The so-called *Gelasian Decree*, which purports to express the Roman clergy's disapproval of certain books such as the *Sentences of Sextus*, seems to have been issued in the early sixth century, and it has been suggested that the RM, with its liberal attitude toward the apocrypha, preceded this decree, while the RB, from a somewhat later period, shares the *Decree's* reservations about the use of these books.

A third argument is drawn from the state of the institutions in the two rules. The Master is much more precise and goes into the smallest details at every opportunity. But at the same time, the organization of his monastery is much more primitive than that of St. Benedict, in whose rule we find a more developed complex of monastic institutions. The Master, for example, does not have a prior in his monastery, nor does he seem to know of such an official. St. Benedict tolerates the practice of having a prior, though he is not very favorable toward it. By the time of St. Gregory the office of prior seems to be taken for granted. It looks, therefore, as if St. Benedict is the middle term between the RM, which represents an earlier stage of development, and St. Gregory, whom we know to be later than the RM and the RB. It is true, of course, that the evolution of institutions does not always proceed in unilinear fashion nor progress at the same pace in different places. The argument has greater force if it is admitted that both rules come from the vicinity of Rome. Although there is considerable evidence for this, some scholars continue to locate the RM in southern Gaul.

The case of the prior is by no means the only instance of a more developed institutional structure in the RB. The Master also has no novice master, no infirmarian, no permanent guest master, no special cooks for guests, no *scrutatores* to check on the monks' application to their *lectio divina*, no monk appointed to give the signal for the divine office. The RB has all these officials. In addition to the monastic chapter, it also introduces the council of seniors, unknown to the RM. In his monastery, the Master, unlike the RB, provides no special place for the novices or for the sick, and no special kitchen for the guests. The more probable interpretation of these differences is that the legislation of the RM is earlier, whereas that of the RB represents a further stage in the evolution of monastic practice and provides for a larger community.

The plan of the two rules and the sequence of subject matter constitute a fourth argument for the priority of the RM. Commentators on the RB have always found it difficult to construct a satisfactory outline of the Rule.[23] There are many places where it is difficult to follow the sequence of thought. Moreover, there are several blocks of material, such as the liturgical section, the disciplinary measures, and the last seven chapters, which look like independent collections of material inserted into the Rule in such a way as to break the continuity. The RM, on the contrary, is a much more unified work; each chapter follows logically from the preceding, often with explicit links. In spite of the fact that the complete RM, in the form in which it appears in Codex P, has probably already been subject to interpolation, the overall plan of the rule is quite clear.

On the hypothesis that the RM is the later work, it would be difficult to imagine the Master creating such a unity and composing such links to weld the disparate sections of the RB together with the additional material that the RM contains. On the other hand, it is easy to understand the process undertaken by St. Benedict if he had the text of the RM before him when he wrote. Given the extent to which he abbreviated the Master's text, it would have been impossible for his redactional activity not to have severely dislocated the order of the RM by displacing certain sections, and particularly by omitting many of the connecting links.

[23] See A. Wathen, *Silence: The Meaning of Silence in the Rule of St. Benedict* (Washington, D.C.: Cistercian Publications 1973) pp. 7–12.

These are not the only arguments that can be adduced. Scholars have also observed that a comparison of the liturgical practices prescribed by the two rules seems to indicate the priority of the RM. The manner of introducing Scriptural citations suggests that the common parts are homogeneous with the passages proper to the RM rather than with those proper to the RB. The Prologue of the RB seems clearly secondary to that of the RM: only the latter develops the argument completely, and the passages proper to the RB that now begin and end its Prologue are not homogeneous with the common parts, since they are in the second person singular, whereas the rest is in the first person plural. Indeed, every parallel passage must, in the end, be examined on its own merits. While no single argument settles the matter, and there remains some evidence that seems to favor the priority of the RB in certain passages, the cumulative effect is impressively in favor of the precedence of the RM.

If this point is now generally agreed upon, there is, however, no unanimity concerning the origin and development of the RM. One school of thought holds that it originated near Rome in the first few decades of the sixth century, and that the form St. Benedict knew and used toward the middle of the century was substantially the same as that we know in Codex P.[24] Another view maintains, on the contrary, that the RM developed in stages: that the florilegium in Codex E represents a very early stage, that St. Benedict used an intermediate form no longer extant, and that the long form in Codex P is a more developed version unknown to him. Hence the RM and RB really are two forms of a single monastic rule, but reflect different stages in its evolution.[25]

Both the author and the place of origin of the RM are objects of dispute. It has been suggested that the RM may be, in fact, an earlier composition of St. Benedict, perhaps dating from his Subiaco period.[26] Though not impossible chronologically, this view is difficult to reconcile with the profound differences in both form and content between the two rules.

[24] This view has been consistently maintained by A. de Vogüé in his editions of the RM and RB and his numerous other writings.
[25] This position is defended by the late F. Masai and E. Manning. While their projected volume setting forth the thesis in detail has not yet appeared, it is sketched in their "Recherches sur les manuscrits et les états de la Regula Monasteriorum" *Scriptorium* 20 (1966) 193–214; 21 (1967) 205–226; 22 (1968) 3–19; 23 (1969) 393–433.
[26] Proposed early in the controversy by O. Zimmermann "The Regula Magistri: The Primitive Rule of St. Benedict" *ABR* 1 (1950) 11–36, this view was re-examined by A. de Vogüé "La Règle du Maître et les Dialogues de S. Grégoire" *RHE* 61 (1966) 44–76.

5. THE CONTEXT OF THE RULE

The priority of the RM involves the admission that St. Benedict derived the teaching of some of the most important parts of his Rule directly from another monastic work. This discussion has obliged us to alter what had become a popular image of him as a solitary genius, detached from his time and locality, handing down from his lofty mountain an atemporal legislation of universal application. Rather, he was a great monastic teacher, taking his place in the ranks of his predecessors and followers, and blending harmoniously into his environment. To see a great historical figure as a man of his time is not to demean him or lessen his greatness but to understand him and his contribution more realistically. His borrowing from the RM is only an outstanding instance of a procedure already recognized in him and other monastic legislators. They had a profound sense of tradition. Like the other great monastic founders of the West, St. Benedict did not envisage himself as a reformer or founder of a new "religious order" but as the father of a community, who handed on to his sons the traditional monastic wisdom he had received from others.

Some modern writers have spoken of St. Benedict as an innovator and a genius of great originality,[27] but in fact this is not how he was perceived in ancient times. His Rule was appreciated not because it was original, but precisely because it was so traditional: it was seen to be a masterful summary of the whole preceding monastic experience. The Western monastic fathers were profoundly conscious of being heirs of a past, of a tradition. Their aim was not to produce something new but to collect, assimilate and propagate the monastic wisdom accumulated by their Eastern and Western predecessors. That wisdom was common property; there was no sense of literary authorship. Each legislator was welcome to borrow anything he found useful in any other monastic writing. Our understanding of the Rule of St. Benedict, therefore, is enhanced by seeing it in context. To the extent that we can reconstruct the development of monastic teaching, terminology, institutions and discipline from their beginnings in the West down to the time of Gregory the Great, we can appreciate the role that the Rule played in this evolution.

While deservedly the most renowned, the Rule of St. Benedict is only one of a whole series of rules that enriched Latin monastic literature during this period. More than two dozen are still extant. The term

---

[27] Particularly influential in this sense was C. Butler, *Benedictine Monachism: Studies in Benedictine Life and Rule* (London: Longmans Green 1919).

"rule" does not designate a well-defined literary form, but has been used to cover a number of works differing substantially from one another. What they have in common is their intent to regulate the life of monks living in a *coenobium*. This legislation normally includes, on the one hand, theoretical spiritual teaching and, on the other, practical regulations to govern the daily life of the monastery by determining the time and measure of food, sleep and liturgical prayer, relationships with the outside, authority structures, etc. These two elements may be combined in quite different proportions. Some rules contain chiefly spiritual doctrine; some consist almost exclusively of practical regulations; others combine both. Their length can vary from a few hundred words to the more than fifty thousand words of the *Regula Magistri*.

Despite the diversity of these rules, the life actually lived in Western monasteries from the end of the fourth century up to the sixth seems to have been basically the same. Both the theory and the practice are more remarkable for their overall homogeneity than for the innumerable differences of detail from one monastery to another. The reason for this is the persistence of a common tradition, which was the determinant of monastic life much more than the rule was. The various rules were merely so many individual expressions of the tradition. All the ancient monks considered their real rule, in the sense of the ultimate determinant of their lives, to be not some product of human effort but the Word of God himself as contained in the Scriptures. Monasticism was simply a form of the Christian life itself, and hence it drew its inspiration from divine revelation. Eastern legislators such as Pachomius and Basil always spoke of the Scriptures as the rule of the monk and diligently searched them for a clear expression of God's will for their communities.[28]

As monasticism grew and gained experience, a traditional interpretation of the Bible gradually accumulated, together with a complex of doctrine and observances forming a deposit, universally accepted, that was handed down in both oral and written tradition. The West inherited this tradition largely from the East, while adapting it to the different local circumstances of climate and culture. A monastic legislator was concerned, not to produce something new, but to draw from the traditional deposit of monastic teaching what was needed in his own circumstances and to apply it to the concrete conditions present in a given community. These contingencies are never precisely the

[28] See C. Peifer "The Biblical Inspiration of Monasticism" *CS* 1 (1966) 7–31.

same, and so the details may vary from one rule to the other, though all draw upon the common fund of tradition. A rule, therefore, was generally intended for a single community; the doctrine might be of wider application, but the concrete observances were laid down in view of local conditions. It is true, however, that some legislators envisaged the possibility of their rule being used in other places. They eagerly studied the work of their predecessors, for each new rule became another link in the chain of monastic tradition that led back to the pure sources of monastic origins and thus to the Word of God.

St. Benedict's indebtedness to earlier monastic fathers has long been known. Modern editions of the Rule have noted his citations from such sources as Pachomius, Basil, Cassian and Augustine, and have often pointed out parallels that may sometimes indicate allusions to other works, but often merely represent a similarity of approach common to the whole tradition. While there is no certain evidence of his having knowledge of Greek sources (most likely he could not read Greek), it has been concluded that he was quite well read in the Latin Fathers, especially but not exclusively in monastic writers, including those Eastern sources translated into Latin by his time. This judgment is undoubtedly correct.

Benedict's knowledge of the tradition is profound. It should be specified, however, that it is not an academic type of knowledge but the thorough assimilation of truth that comes from long application to *lectio divina*, a total immersion of oneself in the Word of God and its exposition by those whom he calls "holy catholic Fathers" and "reputable and orthodox catholic Fathers" (RB 73.4; 9.8). His dependence on the RM, however, shows that some of this contact with sources was not direct but at second or third hand, though the sections proper to the RB also manifest an extensive acquaintance with the earlier tradition. The fact is that monastic writers borrowed so much from one another that it is sometimes impossible to tell whether a particular parallel is due to direct dependence or came to the writer through one or more intermediaries. They were interested in the truth and intrinsic value of the tradition, not in knowing who had first formulated it in a particular way.

An examination of the entire spectrum of the Latin rules shows the lifeblood of this tradition coursing through the body of Western monasticism from the fourth century down to the Middle Ages. It is difficult to perceive all the intricacies of their mutual relationships, so pervasive was their authors' propensity for reading and borrowing from one another.[29] The earliest, which are decisive influences upon the subsequent tradition, are the proto-rules of Pachomius, Basil and Augustine. Of these, only the last is of Western origin and originally in Latin, but the other two, in the Latin versions of Jerome and Rufinus, respectively, made their appearance in the West about the same time as Augustine's, around the year 400. None of them is dependent upon either of the others; they represent the separate interpretations of biblical teaching, as applied to cenobitic life, of three exceptionally perceptive and saintly Christian thinkers, each of whom translated his own teaching into practice or, to put it perhaps more correctly, recorded the fruit of his experience. They were very different personalities and lived in very different circumstances, cultures and ecclesiastical situations. The three forms of monastic life which they conceived, therefore, are also different and lay their stress somewhat diversely upon various Christian values. Yet, they are profoundly at one in their most basic intentionality and achievement, for they flow from the same pure biblical source, and their diversity confers a splendid richness upon the monastic phenomenon.

The first half of the fifth century saw the work of Cassian, which, as we have seen, although not cast in the form of a "rule" (an unknown writer later put together a "Regula Cassiani" out of prescriptions from the *Institutes*), nevertheless was an important link in the chain. Cassian shows no knowledge of the work of Augustine, is acquainted with Basil and occasionally refers to him, but depends chiefly upon Egypt. Though his knowledge of Pachomian cenobitism seems to be quite indirect, suggesting that he had not visited any Pachomian monasteries and was not acquainted with the Rule, he nevertheless was familiar with the wider Egyptian tradition that Pachomius shared. Both the theory and the institutions that he propagates are of Egyptian origin, though they reflect the intellectual sophistication of the Evagrian system rather than the primitive simplicity of the Coptic founders. To this period probably belongs also the *Rule of the Four Fathers*, a mysterious document that appears at the beginning of Codex P with the *Regula Magistri* and is still the object of controversy.

Few monastic rules appeared in the second half of the fifth century. About the only one that can reasonably be placed in this period is the *Second Rule of the Fathers*, a brief work that seems to show no direct dependence on any of its predecessors except the *Rule of the Four*

---

[29] What follows is largely dependent upon A. de Vogüé "The Cenobitic Rules of the West" *CS* 12 (1977) 175–183.

Fathers. These short rules purport to be the minutes of meetings of monastic superiors to discuss problems of monastic life and discipline. It is known that such synods of abbots were in fact held in the fifth century, though the names are a literary fiction. The *Second Rule,* which is concerned with correcting abuses in regard to guests, obedience, humility and the prayer life of the community, is echoed in a surprising number of later rules, and seems to be the immediate inspiration of the RB's famous dictum "nothing is to be preferred to the Work of God."

The opening decades of the sixth century saw the appearance of two rules of major importance: the *Regula Magistri* and the *Rule for Virgins* of St. Caesarius of Arles. The latter, which appears to be earlier than his brief *Rule for Monks,*[30] became the predominant influence upon a series of Gallic rules stretching into the seventh century. Caesarius, although he was a former monk of Lerins, drew primarily upon Augustine and owed but little to Cassian and the Egyptian tradition. No doubt this was due in large part to his abandonment of the Gallic position on the question of nature and grace, and his adoption of Augustinianism. This was the period of the "Augustinian invasion." The tradition of Caesarius continued in his followers: first with the *Rule for Monks* and *Rule for Virgins* of his successor Aurelian of Arles; then with the nearly contemporary *Regula Tarnantensis* and the somewhat later *Rule of Ferreolus,* also Gallic productions of the sixth century.[31]

---

[30] A. de Vogüé "La Règle de Césaire pour les moniales" *RAM* 47 (1971) 369–406. The Rule of Caesarius has been translated into English by M. C. McCarthy, *The Rule for Nuns of St. Caesarius of Arles* (Washington: Catholic Univ. Press 1960).

[31] The extant monastic rules in Latin were collected by Benedict of Aniane in the early ninth century into his *Codex Regularum,* which was printed by L. Holstenius (Rome 1661) and subsequently by M. Brockie (Augsburg 1759; rpt. Graz 1957). It is included in *PL* 103, but for certain rules the reader is sent to other volumes of the *PL,* where they have been printed with the other works of the author in question. Some of these rules have recently appeared in more critical editions. In addition to the critical editions of the RM, the RB and Eugippius already noted, these are: J. Vilanova, *Regula Pauli et Stephani* (Montserrat: Abadia 1959); J. Neufville "Règle des IV Pères et Seconde Règle des Pères. Texte critique" *RBén* 77 (1967) 47–106; F. Villegas *"La Regula Monasterii Tarnantensis.* Textes, sources, et datation" *RBén* 84 (1974) 7–65; A. de Vogüé "La 'Regula Orientalis.' Texte critique et synopse des sources" *Benedictina* 23 (1976) 241–271. See also M. E. Bouillet "Le vrai *Codex Regularum* de saint Benoît d'Aniane" *RBén* 75 (1965) 345–349; J. Neufville "Sur le texte de la Règle des IV Pères" *ibid.* 307–312; "Les éditeurs des *Regulae Patrum:* saint Benoît d'Aniane et Lukas Holste" *RBén* 76 (1966) 327–343; F. Villegas "La *Regula cuiusdam Patris ad Monachos.* Ses sources littéraires et ses rapports avec la *Regula Monachorum* de Columban" *Revue d'histoire de la spiritualité* 49 (1973) 3–36, 135–144.

A similar introduction of Augustinian influence occurs in Italy, but a little later. The RM, contemporary with Caesarius, seems not to know Augustine at all, or at least to have used him very sparingly. It resembles Caesarius, however, in that it produced a progeny in Italy as his work did in Gaul. This fact, plus its similarity to rules of known Italian provenance in features that distinguish them from the rules of Gallic origin, constitutes a forceful argument for the Italian origin of the RM. Its first descendant is the cento-rule found in Codex E (if we suppose that this florilegium is derivative from a longer form of the rule substantially identical with Codex P), which has with great probability been identified as the *Rule of Eugippius*. This latter rule already signals the "Augustinian invasion" of Italy: it opens with the text of the *Ordo Monasterii* and the *Praeceptum*, which occupy a place of honor. But nearly half of its text is drawn from the RM, with substantial passages also from Cassian and Basil, and lesser borrowings from Pachomius, Jerome and the *Rule of the Four Fathers*. There is no attempt to draw these disparate sources together into a unity; passages are simply extracted from the sources and strung together, with only minor changes. But it is important that Eugippius opened his horizons wide to predecessors of such different tendencies; he is the first who depends simultaneously upon Augustine, Basil and the Egyptian tradition, as represented both by the RM and by Cassian and Pachomius.

The RB seems to have made its appearance shortly thereafter. It is like Eugippius in its catholic tendency to admit all previous strands of tradition, whether known directly or only mediately. If its closest dependence is upon the RM, it has nevertheless made generous use of Augustine and has apparently been influenced by his emphasis upon fraternal relationships even more than the textual parallels alone would lead one to suspect. Like Eugippius, it also shows knowledge of the Egyptian tradition from direct acquaintance with Pachomius and Cassian, as well as through the Master. Like him, too, the RB has used Basil, though not so extensively as Augustine, and is moreover acquainted with both the *Four Fathers* and the *Second Rule of the Fathers*.

In another way, however, the RB is most unlike Eugippius. If its sources are nearly the same, the way in which it has used them is totally different. While the earlier work is merely a string of citations arranged in logical order, the RB has made a masterful synthesis of the materials it uses. In it the various rivulets flowing from Gaul, Africa, Egypt, Cappadocia and Italy itself merge to form a powerful stream.

The forceful synthesis of Egyptian tradition enunciated by the RM is taken over, but only after being purified and simplified, and then softened and completed by its merger with the traditions of Basil and Augustine. The disparate branches of the monastic tradition are brought together and harmonized, correcting and completing one another, so that the richness of the whole deposit may be preserved without loss. Diverse elements are not merely juxtaposed but fully assimilated, so that they find their rightful place in a larger unity. This could have been accomplished only by a person of clear vision and liberal attitude of mind, who had for a long time pondered the Word of God in its numerous expressions through the various strands of monastic tradition; who had come to perceive their harmony on a deeper level; and who had arrived at an experiential knowledge of the unity of monastic tradition through his living of it. Is this perhaps an aspect of what is signified by his vision of all creation gathered into a single ray of light (Greg. *dial.* 2,35)?

It is this broadness of vision and synthetic quality that sets the RB apart from the other Latin rules. The stream of tradition continued after St. Benedict, and rules continued to be produced through the seventh century. But his work was not surpassed. Eventually the RB was recognized as the finest expression of monastic tradition the Western experience had produced, and it gradually came to supplant all the others. Not only did it constitute the most complete and masterful synthesis of monastic tradition in its most catholic sense, but it did so in an enduring fashion, free from the narrowness of partial viewpoints and passing over ephemeral details of observance bound to particular circumstances, to bring out the essential evangelical principles of monasticism. The fuller our knowledge of the tradition from which the RB emerged, the clearer becomes our vision of its real greatness.

6. THE CONTENT OF THE RULE

Despite the traditional character of monastic rules, each legislator made a personal contribution. Even if he did not add anything to the tradition he received, his assimilation of it was unique. Both what he included and what he omitted tell us something of his own understanding. So long as the RB was considered an original work, the whole of both the theory and the practical regulations was deemed to be legitimate evidence of St. Benedict's personal contribution to Western monasticism. His probable dependence upon the RM, however, now demands that this methodology be nuanced. His contribution must be sought primarily in the passages proper to the RB, and especially where he corrects or changes the prescriptions of the RM. Elements that he has taken over more or less intact from the RM cannot be considered a contribution of the RB; but here, too, the minor alterations, the omissions and additions, the changed perspective introduced here and there, all help to reconstruct the mentality of its author in contrast to the legislator from whom he is borrowing. To know the mind of St. Benedict has become a more subtle undertaking, requiring confrontation with his predecessors at every step.[32]

One of the most notable features of the RB is its brevity. It has reduced the huge bulk of the RM by more than two thirds. It is true that this has been done at the expense of the grandeur of the Master's structural concept and sometimes with a loss of clarity, but with an enormous gain in intelligibility and simplicity. The RB remains a complete treatment of all the essentials required for cenobitic life: both the spiritual doctrine and the practical ordering of the life are provided in quite a full manner. But simplification has been achieved by omitting the innumerable details of observance, which soon rendered the RM anachronistic, and the endless casuistic treatment of every conceivable possibility so characteristic of the Master's mentality. St. Benedict had the clear vision of a man who instinctively perceives what is important and isolates it from the mass of secondary detail. On occasion, he replaces pages of fussy casuistry with a single sentence summing up the whole issue, clearly states the principle involved in a supremely memorable fashion, and leaves everything else to the abbot's discretion.

The overall pattern of the RB is clear enough, even though the connections between parts are sometimes loose or unclear, and less logical than in the RM. The latter is divided quite clearly into two main portions, which the RM itself calls *actus militiae cordis* and *ordo monasterii*, respectively. (The proponents of a gradually evolving *Regula Monasteriorum* regard these as two originally separate compositions, combined to form an embryonic rule.)[33] The RB maintains this arrangement: the spiritual doctrine is given first (Prol. and chs. 1–7), followed by the regulations (chs. 8–73). The first part follows the RM

---

[32] What follows is partially dependent upon A. de Vogüé "The Rule of St. Benedict" CS 12 (1977) 243–249.

[33] For a sketch of this hypothesis, see F. Masai "Les documents de base de la Règle" RBS 1 (1972) 111–151.

quite closely, and most of its text is derived from the other rule, though large sections are shortened or omitted. After the Prologue and the opening chapter on the kinds of monks, the ascetical program is laid down in three successive articulations: the abbot and his advisers (2–3); a catalogue of good works (4); and the three capital virtues of the monk: obedience, silence and humility (5–7).

In this section the RB largely adopts the teaching of the RM, which is in the tradition of Cassian and Egypt. It harks back to the desert origins of semi-anchoritism and its fundamental constitutive element, the relationship of disciple to master that a monk has to a spiritual father. The latter is the charismatic of proven virtue and experience who is able to guide the disciple, through discernment of spirits, along the same path of self-renunciation he himself has followed. Though the number of his disciples is increased in the *coenobium*, the basic principle remains intact: the abbot is primarily a spiritual father to each monk; the monastery is a *schola*, or place where training is given; the purpose is to lead men to future salvation through the practice of the ascetic life. Hence the importance of the abbot and of the three virtues; these are the monk's primary means of salvation, according to Cassian's interpretation of the Scriptures. While accepting this basic program, the RB makes some discreet modifications of emphasis. To the futurist eschatology of the RM it adds a certain dimension of realized eschatology. This goes along with a greater stress on charity, not merely as a goal to strive for, but as an already present reality — elements giving a foretaste of concerns that will emerge more clearly later in the Rule.

The second part of the RB prescribes the necessary elements of institutional structure and discipline. Some sections have a character of their own and are easily isolated: thus the liturgical code (8–20) regulates the divine office; the penitential code (23–30) sets forth the manner of dealing with delinquents; the code of satisfaction (43–46) prescribes the measure of satisfaction for various faults; chapters 58–63 deal with acceptance of new members and the order of the community. In between these groupings are chapters treating of deans and the dormitory (21–22), material goods (31–34), food and sleep (35–42), work, prayer and exterior relationships (47–52), guests and related subjects (53–57), selection of the abbot and prior (64–65), the porter (66), and finally an appendix (67–73), which has no parallel in the RM and deals largely with fraternal relationships, one of the special emphases of the RB. In this second part of the Rule, both the order and the content are often closely related to the RM, but St. Benedict has here dealt much more freely with his source. Consequently, his own contribution stands out more clearly in this second major division of the Rule.

The RB manifests a certain liberalism and humanism, in the pristine sense of those terms. The author understands human nature, both its grandeur and its weakness, respects it and wants to facilitate its organic growth. He knows that human persons and their actions are of infinite variety and complexity, and that individual problems require individual solutions. Unlike the Master, he does not attempt to regulate everything in advance, to foresee every possible case. He trusts the abbot to make prudent decisions as the need arises; it is enough for the Rule to enunciate the principles. The abbot must exercise discretion, that "mother of virtues" lauded by Cassian, which enables one to select, out of all possible choices, the one that best fits present circumstances. The abbot bears a heavy responsibility, but he is not expected to be omniscient or impeccable; his weakness is also recognized. It is this quality of the RB that, more than anything else, rendered it adaptable to so many different situations. The author himself sometimes explicitly provides for varying circumstances.

Respect for persons appears also in Benedict's sense of community. He has modified the almost exclusively vertical vision of the RM by emphasizing the relationships of the monks to one another. It is here that the influence of Augustine is most apparent. St. Benedict's monks are indeed disciples under a master, come to the *schola* to be trained, but they are also brothers to one another, bound together by ties of mutual charity and support. That this understanding of the monastery as a fraternal communion in love is profoundly evangelical is clear from the fact that Benedict several times cites Augustine's favorite text from Acts 4:32-35. Chapter 72 of RB on good zeal is perhaps the most eloquent expression of this insight.

It is respect for persons and for the mystery of freedom, once again, that lies behind St. Benedict's concern for inner dispositions of the heart. Indeed, a rule must legislate for exterior behavior, and St. Benedict has little tolerance for outward observance that is careless, singular or perfunctory. But he knows that conformity alone is not enough and that legislation cannot solve all problems. Whereas the Master is concerned that the law make provision for every conceivable case, St. Benedict often contents himself with general statements that leave all kinds of details at loose ends. He is more concerned with why things are done and how they are done than with precise regula-tions. The motivation behind the observance is the object of his inter-est — the individual's submission to the action of grace within him. Thereby the whole tone of monastic asceticism is elevated to a lofty spiritual plane.

This does not mean that the standards of monastic observance have been lowered in the RB. Though it is noted for moderation, there is no significant difference between the RB and other Western monastic literature in the role assigned to austerity. In some areas, such as food and drink and the length of the common prayer, the RB is less de-manding than the RM and other earlier rules; but this is because the monks have heavier work to do, probably a result of the economic difficulties brought on by the Gothic War and the ensuing civil chaos. St. Benedict is not anxious to make concessions in regard to observ-ance, and does so only with reluctance. In some cases, which he re-gards as matters of principle, such as private ownership, he is even more severe than the Master, and he sometimes closes a chapter leav-ing a violent threat ringing in the reader's ear. He seems much im-pressed by the evils of the time, which no doubt had a deleterious effect upon the general level of morality, with repercussions upon the life of monasteries as well.

This no doubt explains Benedict's pessimism about the level of the monastic life of his own time in comparison with the giants of the past. The RB makes no extravagant claims for itself; it is only a "little rule for beginners." The monk is sent to the Fathers for further instruction and for acquaintance with an ideal that seems unattainable in the evil times that have befallen Italy. The heroic period of monastic origins is looked back upon as a golden age. The author seems to have had more than his share of experience in attempting to lead and inspire men in an age when everything seems to be getting worse. This gives him a healthy sense of realism; he does not expect heroic performances be-yond the possibilities of human nature, though the ideal is to be kept high. St. Benedict shows an extraordinary understanding of weakness, a compassion for those who fail or are troubled or distressed, a delicate patience even with the hard of heart. In this respect, too, his Rule is deeply human and evangelical.

The monasticism of the Rule, like that of other cenobitic institutes, institutionalizes to some degree, though in a relatively uncomplicated way, what was in its origins purely charismatic. St. Benedict intends his Rule to provide a manual of discipline for the individual cenobite and at the same time to ensure an environment in which the ascetical life may be fruitfully pursued. Indeed, the *coenobium* was the place for only the first phase of the monastic experience, which Cassian calls the *vita activa*, and it was only this that monastic rules presumed to regulate. A monk who has successfully reached the goal of the ascetical life, which is charity or purity of heart, the state in which his own inner turmoil is quieted so that he can listen to the Spirit within him, is ready for the solitary life. In the desert there is no rule but that of the Spirit.

Such at least is the dominant Egyptian tradition, outside Pachomian circles, and Cassian favored it, though he is curiously ambivalent on the role of the *coenobium*. Like the RM, St. Benedict appears to espouse this same view; no doubt he regarded the cenobitic life as safer for the majority of men, but he retains the idea that it is a training school for the desert, and so he must have envisaged the possibility that at least some monks would go on to the solitary life.

The exercises prescribed by the Rule, however, like those of other cenobitic legislation, are those of the "active" life, which are intended to conduct the monk through the ascetical combat so that he may reach the goal of union with God through prayer. The Rule offers no theories about the life of prayer, but it is nevertheless understood to be the objective. The monk's time was divided among three activities: common prayer, *lectio* and work. Several hours each day were devoted to the divine office, or "Work of God." This is more developed than among the solitaries or cenobites of Egypt, for Benedict was influenced by the urban monks of the West. Besides the traditional night office, there were seven prayer-times during the day, consisting of psalms and short readings from the Bible. While the Rule places great emphasis upon the office, there are no overtones of a liturgical theology of the community. The monks pray together because they live together, and thereby form a quasi-local church.

About four additional hours each day were devoted to *lectio*, which included reading, private prayer and *meditatio*, the memorization, repetition and "rumination" of biblical texts. This prayerful reflection upon Scripture and its interpretation by the Fathers and monastic writers kept the monk's mind constantly filled with the Word of God and helped to shape the whole of his inner psychology and outward activity (see Appendix 6, pp. 471–477). The silence and relative solitude maintained by reducing contact with the world outside to a minimum created an atmosphere that favored recollection.

St. Benedict looks upon work in a highly traditional way: its purposes are to provide a means of subsistence for the monks themselves, to be an ascetical discipline in harmony with the rest of their life, and to produce a surplus for almsgiving to the poor. There was a great concern for the unfortunate, for travelers and guests, who were to be received as Christ. There is no mention of work for apostolic ends; the only apostolic activity enunciated, besides the sanctification of the monks themselves, is to show charity to those who come to the monastery. Benedict is reluctant to have monks go out; through enclosure the monastery creates its own desert. Nor is there any academic or cultural purpose expressed in the Rule, as was explicit in the intention of Cassiodorus. The learning acquired through constant reading was purely religious and ascetical in character, though it could well be profound. Those who entered, however, were taught whatever grammar and rhetoric they needed to perform *lectio* and the *opus Dei*.

There was no clerical apostolate, as in later times, for most of the monks were laymen like St. Benedict himself. He shares the misgivings of the Egyptians about the dangers of a monk's receiving holy orders, but he is more open than the Master. He allows priests to enter the community, and even provides that a monk may be ordained priest or deacon if necessary. But the sole purpose of clerics in the monastery was to care for the sacramental needs of the community (and guests), and they were in no way to be exalted over the other monks. The primary concern is always that of the supernatural welfare of the monks themselves, for whom the monastery exists: "that souls may be saved."

7. THE LANGUAGE OF THE RULE

St. Benedict was a man of the mid-sixth century who wrote in the language of his time. But by his time the linguistic situation in the West was becoming quite complex. Latin was already entering upon the process of breakdown that would eventually lead to the formation of the Romance languages. The canons of classical Latinity were still taught in the schools (to the extent that the schools were still functioning amid the chaos of the times) and were followed by cultivated writers of the period, such as Cassiodorus and Boethius. Gregory the Great, though disclaiming any concern for style, could still write good Latin at the end of the sixth century, whereas his contemporary Gregory of Tours, in Gaul, already displays many popular features. In Italy a vulgar tongue, spoken largely by the lower classes, had long coexisted with the literary language; fragments of it have been preserved in some inscriptions and graffiti. Somewhere between these extremes was the living, colloquial language spoken by the middle and upper classes in ordinary day-to-day intercourse. This is the language which St. Benedict commonly used and in which he wrote the Rule. The Master uses the same language, and the RM manuscripts provide an earlier witness to it.[34]

The first task in studying the language of St. Benedict, however, is to recover it. Since the colloquial Latin of his time departed in many respects from the established rules of Latin vocabulary, grammar and syntax, it has always seemed offensive to the cultivated ears of purists. In the next century there was a renaissance of Latin studies in England (where Latin was a rather artificial language of an educated elite, imported by Christian missionaries), and then in the Lombard kingdom of Italy and the Frankish kingdom of Gaul, culminating in the Carolingian renaissance of the eighth century. The scribes trained in the revived norms of the schools were shocked at the "irregularities" of earlier texts and did not hesitate to "correct" them to make them conform to their standards. This process, called normalization, is well known to anyone who studies ancient texts. It is the task of textual criticism to restore the earliest ascertainable form of the text, based upon the evidence of the manuscripts. Textual criticism will be discussed in the following section; here we presuppose its results, which can be found in critical editions of the Latin text.

Perhaps the most obvious difference to one acquainted with classical Latin is in the vocabulary. There are new words like *biberes* (35.12), *synaxis* (17.7) and *contagiare* (28.8); words used in a new and technical sense like *proicere* (58.28), to 'kick out' of the monastery, or *erigere* (57.3), to 'fire' or dismiss someone from a position; new expressions such as *si fuerit unde* (39.3), 'if there are any'; and strange adjectival forms such as *digesti* (8.2), 'having finished digesting.' Best known of all the variations is the opening word of the Prologue: where the normalized version has the classical form *ausculta*, the original text used the popular *obsculta*.

[34] On the language of the RB, see C. Mohrmann "La latinité de saint Benoît. Étude linguistique sur la tradition manuscrite de la règle" *RBén* 62 (1952) 108–139, rpt. in *Études sur le latin des chrétiens*, Storia e letteratura 65 (Rome: Edizioni di Storia e Letteratura 1958) 1.403–435; "La langue de saint Benoît" in P. Schmitz, *Sancti Benedicti Regula Monachorum* (Maredsous: Éditions de l'Abbaye 1955²) pp. 9–39. A valuable analysis of the linguistic features of the RB is contained in the Index Grammaticus of the critical edition by R. Hanslik, *Benedicti Regula*, CSEL 75 (Vienna: Hölder-Pichler-Tempsky 1960; 1977²). See also B. Linderbauer, *S.B. Regula Monachorum, herausgegeben und philologisch erklärt* (Metten: Abtei Verlag 1922).

The spellings occurring in manuscripts and sometimes reproduced in critical editions are a shock to those unacquainted with medieval orthography, which often reflects pronunciation variants and can sometimes be used to suggest the geographical provenance of a codex. In the Rule we find such variants as *obis* for *ovis*, *praecium* for *pretium*, *sepe* for *saepe*, *ortus* for *hortus*, *quirie* for *kyrie*, *promtus* for *promptus*, *clusura* for *clausura*, and *vini* for *bini*. Most editors regularize these forms as in this edition, because it is in any case impossible to reconstruct the orthography of the original; but they will be found in facsimile and diplomatic editions, and sometimes in critical editions, at least in the apparatus. The use of *i* in place of *j*, however, and of *u* in place of *v*, is commonly adopted in many critical editions, because the use of different characters to distinguish the vocalic forms from the consonantal forms of these letters was adopted only in the Middle Ages.

The breakdown of the inflectional system of classical Latin can be observed in St. Benedict's use of cases. The most flagrant examples occur in the liturgical code, which perhaps reflects a more popular usage than the other parts of the Rule. We find examples of the use of the accusative with prepositions that normally take the ablative, and vice versa, such as *de sedilia sua* (9.7), *in lecta sua* (48.5), *post quibus* (11.4) and *usque hora qua sexta* (48.3). Relative pronouns do not agree with their antecedents, as in *tria cantica quas* (11.21); nor verbs with their subjects, as in *canticum unumquemque . . . dicantur* (13.10). Prepositions are freely introduced into constructions where classical Latin uses the ablative alone: *ab* for comparison, as in *meliores ab aliis* (2.21) or *a Christo carius* (5.2); *in* with ablative of time, as in *hieme* (55.5); *cum* with ablative of instrument, as in *lintea cum quibus . . . tergunt* (35.8).

The use of phrases that appear to be dangling is very common in low Latin: these are legitimate nominative absolutes, such as *memor semper abbas* (2.6), *hortans nos de hac re scriptura dicens* (7.45), *noviter veniens quis* (58.1). There is one case of the accusative absolute: *dispositionem uniformem . . . servatam* (18.10). The so-called sympathetic dative occurs in *mihi sermo dirigitur* (Prol.3) and in *pedes . . . omnibus lavent* (35.9); and the epexegetical genitive or genitive of identity in phrases like *supplicatio litaniae* (9.10) and *sapientiae doctrina* (64.2). It is also characteristic of the language to use periphrases instead of a simple verb, as in *taciturnitatem habens* (7.56), *absque murmurationibus sint* (40.9), *munditias faciat* (35.7).

We also find nouns that are treated indeclinably because they had become standard terms, especially in the cases of titles of parts of the Bible: *lectionem de Evangelia* (11.9), *canticum Deuteronomium, qui* [!] *dividatur in duas glorias* (13.9), *a sanctum Pascha* (15.1), *a Pentecosten* (15.2), *Heptateuchum aut Regum* (42.4).

Many of these features are derived simply from the living language of the period. But some aspects of the Latin of the RB (and the RM) depend rather upon traditional Christian and monastic usage. The fact that St. Benedict wrote in the vernacular rather than in the studied Latin of the schools does not tell us anything about his literary culture. Monastic writers often deliberately chose the popular language as more suited to their intended audience and to the simplicity they cultivated. If Cassian and Sulpicius Severus were skilled stylists, the Western rules were generally composed in a more popular style; even Jerome restrained his rhetorical impulses when he translated the Pachomian rule. Christianity, however, had developed its own vocabulary, both by taking over Greek words, such as *scandalum* or *diacon*, and by giving new meanings to existing Latin words, such as *sacramentum* and *missa*. To these the monastic literature added an additional specialized vocabulary.

Therefore, it is not surprising to find terms that designate Christian and especially liturgical subjects: *angelus, antiphona, apocalypsis, apostolus, chorus, diabolus, dioecesis, hebdomada, eleemosyna, episcopus, evangelium, eulogia, hymnus, presbyter, psalmodia, zelus.* Some of the specific monastic terms, largely imported from the East, are: *abbas, acediosus, anachorita, coenobium, decania, eremita, gyrovagus, monachus, monasterium, sarabaita, senpecta, zelotypus.* Other words, like *frater, servire* and *servitium, militia* and *militare*, and *schola* have taken on specifically monastic connotations. The RB also shows the influence of the canonical and liturgical language of the time,[35] particularly of Roman usage, in the use of terms like *si quis, nisi forte, dignari* and *mereamur. Missae* is an interesting case of a word used both in the normal Christian sense, meaning 'Mass' (38.2), and with a specialized monastic meaning, 'concluding formula' (17. passim).

Though St. Benedict did not evidently make a particular point of cultivating style, his language nevertheless is not entirely devoid of literary elegance. Studies of the prose rhythm of the RB have shown

---

[35] See E. Kasch, *Das liturgische Vokabular der frühen lateinischen Mönchsregeln,* RBS Supplementa 1 (Hildesheim: Gerstenberg 1974).

that its author was conscious of the *cursus*.[36] Both Greek and Roman authors had sought to vary the pattern of sentence endings, or *clausulae*, in a way pleasing to the ear. Classical writers based these patterns on quantity.[37] Thus, Cicero's ear was pleased by such endings as

- a. nēglĕgēbāntŭr (cretic ⁻ ⁻ ⁻ + trochee ⁻ ˘)
- b. orātĭōnī lŏcūm (two cretics)
- c. silēntĭūm pōllĭcēntŭr (cretic + two trochees)

As quantity weakened and accent strengthened, writers sought the coincidence of the accent with the quantitative ictus on the first syllable of the foot, e.g., *ēssĕ dēbétĭs*. This tendency is especially noticeable in Pope St. Leo. Eventually accent prevailed, elisions were ignored, and three forms of what became known as the *cursus* achieved a virtual monopoly. These correspond to a, b and c above, and are:

- a. cursus planus (dactyl ´ ˘ ˘ + trochee)   ríght are your júdgments
- b. cursus tardus (two dactyls)   thóse are my coúnselors
- c. cursus velox (dactyl + two trochees) cóme and revére the státutes

An example of the RB's sense of rhythm can be found in chapter 20, on reverence in prayer, if it is divided into sense lines and the clausulae analyzed:

Brevis debet esse et púra orátio	(cursus tardus)
nisi forte ex affectu inspirationis divinae	
grátiae prótendátur.	(cursus velox)
In conventu tamen omnino breviétur orátio,	(cursus tardus)
et facto signo a priore omnes páriter súrgant.	(cursus planus)

A similar case is the beautiful passage of chapter 27 on the abbot's concern for the lost:

Pastoris boni pium imitétur exémplum,	(cursus planus)
qui . . . abiit unam ovem quae erráverat quaérere;	(cursus tardus)
cuius infirmitati tántum compássus est,	(cursus tardus)
ut eam in sacris humeris suis dignarétur impónere	(cursus tardus)
et sic reportáre ad grégem.	(cursus planus)

This passage also shows the influence of biblical and liturgical language upon the author: the words of the Gospel are here paraphrased and put into rhythmic form, and the phrase *ut . . . dignaretur . . .*

---

[36] This has been studied in the RB by A. Lentini, *Il ritmo prosaico nella Regola di San Benedetto* (Montecassino 1942).

[37] See N.G.L. Hammond and H. H. Scullard, eds., *The Oxford Classical Dictionary* (Oxford: The Clarendon Press 1970²) *s.v.* Prose-rhythm, for a good succinct account.

imponere is reminiscent of the liturgical formulas of the Roman sacramentaries. This kind of artful prose is not so much the product of conscious effort as the overflow of a sensibility thoroughly saturated in a tradition, to the extent that the esthetic unity of form and content has become second nature.

The RB also uses a number of rhetorical devices that were cultivated in antiquity.[38] There are cases of repetition for rhetorical effect (*anaphora*), such as the following:

promittant sub iureiurando quia
> *numquam* per se
> *numquam* per suffectam personam . . . . (59.3)

non sit turbulentus et anxius,
non sit nimius et obstinatus,
non sit zelotypus et nimis suspiciosus . . . . (64.16)

Ordines suos in monasterio ita conservent
> *ut* conversationis tempus,
> *ut* vitae meritum discernit
> *utque* abbas constituerit. (63.1)

There are some striking cases of alliteration in the Rule, in which the repetition of similar sounds seems to have been deliberately cultivated to produce an effect:

admoneatur *s*emel et *s*ecundo *s*ecrete a *s*enioribus *s*uis (23.2).
si veniens *p*erseveraverit *p*ulsans et . . . visus fuerit
> *p*atienter *p*ortare et *p*ersistere *p*etitioni suae . . . . (58.3).

*p*rohibent *p*ravorum *p*raevalere consensum, sed *d*omui *D*ei *d*ignum
> constituant *d*ispensatorem (64.5).

Particularly noticeable is a case where the techniques of repetition, anaphora, asyndeton and alliteration combine to produce a memorable phrase:

et *s*ollicitudo *s*it
> *si* revera Deum quaerit,
> *si* *s*ollicitus est
>> *ad* *op*us Dei,
>> *ad* *ob*oedientiam,
>> *ad* *op*probria (58.7).

There are also a few instances of chiastic arrangement of phrases, a figure in which the first element corresponds to the last, the second to

---

[38] See G. Widhalm, *Die rhetorische Elemente in der Regula Benedicti*, RBS Supplementa 2 (Hildesheim: Gerstenberg 1974).

the next-to-the-last, etc., in an A-B-B-A pattern (called *chiasmus* because the pattern forms the Greek letter *chi* [χ]). Some examples are:

accipientes   *nova,*
vetera   semper *reddant* (55.9).
altiori consilio   abbas   *praetulerit*   vel
degradaverit   *certis ex causis* . . . . (63.7).

These few examples provide only an illustration of the rhetorical character of the Rule. They have been chosen solely from the sections proper to the RB, though similar elements can be found in the RM and in the common passages as well. The Prologue, chiefly the work of the Master, has long been recognized as having striking rhetorical qualities, such as the alliterative conclusion: ad *m*ortem in *m*onasterio *per*severantes, *p*assionibus Christi *per p*atientiam *p*articipemur, based on 1 Pet 4:13, but with added rhetorical effect. This feature should not be exaggerated, as it was perhaps often unconscious, but it lends a degree of elegance to the Rule that helps to enforce its message without prejudice to its simplicity.

8. TEXT AND EDITIONS OF THE RULE

Except for the biblical literature, probably no other text from antiquity was copied in the Middle Ages as often as the RB. Hundreds of manuscripts are still extant. Since the first printing at Venice in 1489, more than a thousand editions have appeared, including either the Latin text or translations into numerous vernacular languages, or both together in bilingual editions.[39] As in the case of the New Testament, however, the printed editions invariably reproduced a *textus receptus*, a text that had been normalized and standardized as early as the ninth century, correcting the Latin and smoothing out any difficulties in the text. It was not until the late nineteenth century that the modern critical study of the text began.

The pioneer in this work was a Benedictine scholar, Daniel Haneberg of Munich, monk and then abbot of St. Boniface, and sub-

[39] The fundamental bibliography of printed editions of the RB is A. Albareda, *Bibliografia de la Regla Benedictina* (Montserrat: Abadia 1933). Father J. D. Broekaert of St. André has been working to correct and complete the repertory of Albareda; see his notice "Bibliographie des éditions imprimées de la Règle de saint Benoît de 1489 à 1929" *RBS* 1 (1972) 167. For editions since 1930, see B. Jaspert "Neuere französische Ausgaben der Benedictusregel. Eine Statistik" *SMGBO* 79 (1968) 435–438; "Regula S. Benedicti. Die deutschen Ausgaben (1930–1965)" *ibid.* 80 (1969) 225–230; "Regula S. Benedicti. International Bibliography. A Work-Report" *ABR* 20 (1969) 157–160.

sequently bishop of Speyer. He collated a number of manuscripts himself and then, when prevented by other duties from continuing, turned over his materials to Father Edmund Schmidt of Metten, encouraging him to complete the project. Schmidt published the first critical edition in 1880.[40] He already observed that the manuscripts fall into two principal groups, often called the *ausculta* and *obsculta* texts, respectively, from the form of the opening word. The former is represented chiefly by the Oxford Codex Hatton 48; the latter by the Codex Sangallensis 914.[41] Schmidt attributed both forms to St. Benedict himself, believing that he had issued two editions of the Rule.

The next critical edition was that of Eduard Wölfflin, an authority on Low Latin, who was interested in the RB chiefly from a linguistic viewpoint.[42] His edition of 1895 was based on only four manuscripts (Schmidt had used fifteen), and he considered the *ausculta* text to be superior, though he later confessed that his judgment had been premature.

In 1898 Wölfflin's contention was reversed in a brilliant demonstration by the German philologist Ludwig Traube, who reconstructed the history of the text of the Rule in a fashion that has determined all subsequent study of it.[43] Traube showed that the *ausculta* text was widely diffused throughout Italy, Gaul, Germany and England in the seventh and eighth centuries. The *obsculta* text was introduced into the Frankish kingdom in the late eighth or early ninth century under the influence of the Carolingian revival. One would normally suspect, therefore, as Wölfflin did, that the text of the older codices is the more authentic, and the Carolingian text a normalizing revision. Traube's contention was that, in this case, exactly the opposite is true, and to support it he offered historical arguments as well as those drawn from the internal evidence of the manuscripts.

Traube's historical reconstruction is based upon several documents: some statements about the Rule made by Paul the Deacon, a late eighth-century monk of Montecassino, in his *History of the Lom-*

---

[40] E. Schmidt, *Regula Sancti Patris Benedicti* (Ratisbon: Pustet 1880).

[41] The Oxford codex has been published in a facsimile edition by H. Farmer, *The Rule of St. Benedict*, Early English Manuscripts in Facsimile 15 (Copenhagen: Rosenkilde and Bagger 1968). A diplomatic edition of the St. Gall codex was published by G. Morin, *Regulae Sancti Benedicti traditio codicum Mss. Casinensium a praestantissimo teste usque repetita codice Sangallensi 914* (Montecassino 1900).

[42] E. Wölfflin, *Benedicti Regula Monachorum* (Leipzig: Teubner 1895).

[43] L. Traube, *Textgeschichte der Regula S. Benedicti* (Munich: Verlag der Königlichen Akademie 1898, 1910[2]).

bards; a passage in the *Cassinese Chronicle*, by the twelfth-century chronicler Leo of Ostia; a letter from Theodomar, abbot of Montecassino (really the work, it would seem, of Paul the Deacon), to the Emperor Charlemagne, which survives in a number of manuscripts; and a letter from two monks of the abbey of Reichenau (located on an island in the Lake of Constance) to the librarian of their abbey; this letter is bound into the same codex as the St. Gall copy of the RB and has probably been there since the tenth century.

We know from St. Gregory that Montecassino was destroyed by the Lombards after their invasion of Italy in 568 (the exact date of the destruction is uncertain), but that all the monks escaped with their lives (Greg. *dial.* 2,17).[44] The monastery then lay in ruins for a century and a half, until its restoration about 717 by Petronax of Brescia, who was joined by some monks, probably hermits, already living there (Paul. diac. *gest. Lang.* 6,40). The abbey probably began to follow the Benedictine Rule once more only upon the arrival of the Anglo-Saxon Willibald in 729. He was accustomed to the RB from its use in England, and he remained at Montecassino for about a decade, until sent by Pope Gregory III to assist St. Boniface in Germany.[45]

In 774 Frankish rule replaced that of the Lombards in Italy. At this time, under its first Frankish abbot, Theodomar, Montecassino enjoyed an intellectual renaissance. The greatest light of this movement was Paul the Deacon, a Lombard of noble extraction who had been educated by the grammarian Flavianus and who became a monk at Montecassino around 775. In the 780s he spent several years at the court of Charlemagne, where he was highly esteemed along with other intellectuals such as Alcuin and Theodulph, and he is probably the chief reason for the ties between Montecassino and the Frankish monarchy at this time. Toward the end of his life, he wrote his *History of the Lombards*, an important source for the period.

Paul says that when the monks of Cassino fled from the Lombard destruction in the late sixth century, they took refuge in Rome, taking with them a copy of the Rule Benedict had written (Paul. diac. *gest. Lang.* 4,17). Traube interpreted this to mean the autograph, though this is hardly explicit in the text nor intrinsically probable. The much

---

[44] On the date, see H. Brechter "Monte Cassinos erste Zerstörung: Kritische Versuch einer zeitlichen Fixierung" *SMGBO* 56 (1938) 109–150.

[45] Willibald's life, *The Hodoeporicon of St. Willibald*, was written by Huneberc, an Anglo-Saxon nun of Heidenheim. The text can be found in *MGH SS* 15,1,80–117. It has been translated by C. H. Talbot, *The Anglo-Saxon Missionaries in Germany* (New York: Sheed and Ward 1954) pp. 151–177.

later Leo of Ostia says that they went to the monastery of the Lateran, whose abbot is mentioned in the *Dialogues*. We know little about this monastery, but it seems to have passed out of existence in the seventh century (Leo.Ost. *chron.Cas.*). In the middle of the eighth century, however, after the restoration of Cassino, Paul the Deacon tells us that Pope Zachary (741–752) sent to Petronax, among other things, "the rule that the blessed Father Benedict wrote with his own holy hands" (Paul. diac. *gest. Lang.* 6,40). Traube suggested that the autograph had passed from the Lateran monastery to the papal library, from which it was returned to Montecassino.

We are next told, by Leo of Ostia, that Montecassino was again destroyed by the Saracens, in 883, and that the monks fled to the monastery of Teano near Capua, taking the precious manuscript with them. This monastery burned to the ground, however, and the codex with it, probably in 886 (Leo.Ost. *chron.Cas.* 1,48). Until the end of the eighteenth century, Montecassino possessed a single leaf (containing RB 72–73), which was traditionally held to be a surviving page of the autograph, but, in the judgment of Mabillon, who examined it, was not old enough to be authentic.[46] It appears that the Cassinese monks had other copies, however, for the manuscripts that modern editors classify as "Cassinese" seem to have derived their text-form at least in part from the destroyed "autograph" or a related manuscript.

The best witness to this "autograph," however, has been otherwise preserved. Fortunately, it was copied a century before its destruction. This came about because Charlemagne, on his visit to Montecassino in 787, had apparently seen the famous codex. The emperor was interested in obtaining authentic copies of texts, as he did in other instances, and he asked that an exact copy be made and sent to him. The letter from Theodomar, actually written by Paul the Deacon, is the covering letter sent with the manuscript, which was probably copied under the supervision of Paul. It repeats that the copy was made from the codex "which he [Benedict] wrote with his own holy hands."[47]

This copy sent to Aachen became the standard text of the Rule (*Normalexemplar*) for purposes of the Carolingian monastic reform,

[46] P. Meyvaert "Problems Concerning the 'Autograph' Manuscript of Saint Benedict's Rule" *RBén* 69 (1959) 3–21.

[47] A critical edition of the letter of Theodomar to Charlemagne has been published by K. Hallinger and W. Wegener in *Corpus Consuetudinum Monasticarum* (Siegburg: F. Schmitt Respublica Verlag 1963) 1.137–175. See J. Neufville "L'authenticité de l'"Epistula ad regem Carolum de monasterio sancti Benedicti directa et a Paulo dictata'" *SM* 13 (1971) 295–309.

which involved adoption of the Rule of St. Benedict and observance of the statutes promulgated by Benedict of Aniane during the reign of Charlemagne's son, Louis the Pious, at the Synod of Aachen in 817. The abbot of Reichenau sent two of his monks, Grimalt and Tatto, to Aachen to be instructed in the principles of the reform at the royal monastery, probably around 820. At the request of their librarian, Reginbert, they made an exact copy of the normative codex kept at Aachen, as they explain in their letter to him: "It has been copied from that exemplar which was copied from the very codex that the blessed Father took care to write with his own sacred hands."[48] The copy the two monks made is thought to be the codex into which their letter is bound, the famous manuscript Sangallensis 914, or Codex A, the principal representative of the *obsculta* text.

Grimalt and Tatto took their copy back to Reichenau with them. Tatto subsequently became abbot of Reichenau, and Grimalt became abbot of St. Gall in 840. It is believed, therefore, that Codex A, which is still at St. Gall and paleographically is of early ninth-century origin, was brought there by Grimalt when he became abbot. Others, however, believe that the copy remained at Reichenau and later perished, and that Sangallensis 914 is a copy of it that Grimalt had made for St. Gall.[49]

In any case, Sangallensis 914 is only two, or at most three, steps removed from the Cassinese manuscript that Montecassino got from the Pope around 750 and that was then believed to be St. Benedict's autograph. Internal evidence confirms this: it is in Carolingian script of the early ninth century, and Traube produced abundant evidence to support his contention that it contained the "pure" text, whereas the *ausculta* text, despite the greater antiquity of its witnesses, shows signs of extensive correction and normalization. Traube accordingly called it the "interpolated" text (commonly referred to as the "revised" text).

The thesis of Traube that the *obsculta* text-type is the oldest and has the best claim to represent the original has won the assent of almost all subsequent scholars. Attempts to weaken the authority of Sangallensis 914[50] have been refuted both by further paleographical studies and by

---

[48] Text of the letter in Traube, *Textgeschichte*, pp. 692–693.

[49] This is the view of Hanslik, *Benedicti Regula*, pp. xxiv–xxv; "Die Benediktiner-regel im Wiener Kirchenvätercorpus" *Commentationes*, pp. 159–169.

[50] The most notable was that of B. Paringer "Le manuscrit de Saint-Gall 914 représente-t-il le latin original de la Règle de saint Benoît?" *RBén* 61 (1951) 81–140.

philological analysis of the type of Latin the manuscript represents: it correctly preserves forms that were current in the sixth century but not acceptable in the ninth. The scribes were therefore faithful in copying what lay before them, even though it did not conform to their own tastes.[51]

On the other hand, Traube's historical reconstruction is open to more serious questioning, and in fact was never accepted in its entirety by everyone. Some of the steps in his reasoning are really surmises for which there is no clear historical evidence. It is by no means certain that the codex saved from the Lombard invasion was really the autograph, or that this manuscript was taken to Rome, or that it is identical with the one Pope Zachary sent to Petronax. The supposition that the Lateran monastery constituted a link between the community of Benedict and the Montecassino of the eighth century is only a conjecture that cannot be substantiated by any historical evidence. It is not mentioned by Paul the Deacon; it first appears with Leo of Ostia in the twelfth century. Some have also questioned the authenticity of the letter to Charlemagne, but there seems to be no compelling reason to deny this.[52] The letter of Grimalt and Tatto also appears to be authentic, though it has been questioned whether the copy to which it refers is actually the manuscript in which it is now bound.[53]

What is beyond any doubt is that Montecassino, in the eighth century, possessed a codex (the *Urexemplar*) that was believed to be the autograph and that was known to have come from Pope Zachary. We do not know where the papal library got it. If it was brought to Rome by the refugees from Cassino in the late sixth century, as has been conjectured but cannot be proved, this still does not mean that it was the autograph. But the codex must have been of early date and must have represented a text-tradition stemming from central Italy. We are certain that the St. Gall codex gives us a faithful image of the *Urexemplar*, for the chain of evidence that links it through Charlemagne's Aachen copy is firm and direct; we can therefore reconstruct with reasonable assurance the text of Pope Zachary's manuscript, allowing for some inevitable errors in copying. The same text-

---

[51] This has been established especially by C. Mohrmann "La latinité de saint Benoît" cited above in note 34, who explicitly refutes the contentions of Paringer, and also by A. Mundó "L'authenticité" cited in note 21.

[52] See J. Neufville "L'authenticité de l'"Epistula ad regem Carolum'" cited in note 47.

[53] E. Manning "Problèmes de la transmission du texte de la Regula Benedicti" *RBS* 5 (1977) 75–84.

type can be recognized to some extent in other manuscripts of the Cassinese tradition, which must have descended from ancestors with a similar text, though much contamination from other traditions has occurred.

The internal analysis of Sangallensis 914 shows that the type of text it represents has the best claim among all surviving witnesses to represent the earliest ascertainable form of the text; in a whole series of cases it can be shown convincingly that the reading of Sangallensis, supported by other codices of the same tradition, is authentic, while that of Oxoniensis and other representatives of the interpolated text is secondary. The marginal readings of Codex A, which present variants from other text traditions and were copied directly from the Aachen *Normalexemplar*, are almost certainly derived from the Italian *Urexemplar* and are most probably the work of Paul the Deacon. Moreover, linguistic analysis of the Latinity of Codex A has established that its language is that of sixth-century Italy, whereas the *ausculta* tradition is the result of normalization.[54]

The critical editions of the twentieth century have followed Traube's principles. First among them was that of Cuthbert Butler, monk and later abbot of Downside, which appeared in 1912.[55] Because it was intended for practical use, Butler normalized the grammatical irregularities, but provided a text based on sound textual criticism and did valuable pioneer work in the investigation of the sources of the RB. Bruno Linderbauer, a monk of Metten, provided a more accurate text, accompanied by a philological commentary, in 1922,[56] and added a fuller apparatus than Butler's in a 1928 edition.[57] Other useful Latin editions were published by Anselmo Lentini of Montecassino in 1947, with Italian translation and commentary;[58] by Justin McCann of Ampleforth in 1952,[59] with English translation and notes; and by Gregorio Penco of Finalpia in 1958, the first to indicate the RM parallels and include the readings of RM manuscripts in the

[54] See C. Mohrmann "La latinité" cited in note 34.

[55] C. Butler, *Sancti Benedicti Regula Monachorum: Editio Critico-Practica* (Freiburg im Breisgau: Herder 1912).

[56] B. Linderbauer, *S. Benedicti Regula, herausgegeben und philologisch erklärt* (Metten: Abtei Verlag 1922).

[57] B. Linderbauer, *S. Benedicti Regula Monasteriorum*, Florilegium Patristicum 17 (Bonn: Peter Hanstein 1928).

[58] A. Lentini, *S. Benedetto, La regola: testo, versione e commento* (Montecassino 1947).

[59] J. McCann, *The Rule of Saint Benedict in Latin and English* (London: Burns and Oates 1952).

apparatus, together with an Italian translation and a commentary on the common and parallel passages.[60]

The task of preparing the definitive edition of the RB, which was to reconstruct the original text as well as trace the entire history of the text tradition, was entrusted by the Vienna Academy to Heribert Plenkers, a pupil of Traube's. After thirty years of work, in which he came increasingly to see the complexity of the problems, Plenkers died in 1931 without completing it.[61] Subsequently, in 1951, the assignment was undertaken by Rudolph Hanslik, who produced his Vienna Corpus edition in 1960.[62] Hanslik collated some three hundred manuscripts and retained sixty-three for his edition. Though criticized for its methodology and its many errors[63] (some of which have been corrected in the second edition of 1977), this edition contains the fullest apparatus so far assembled and provides excellent tools for study in its carefully constructed indices.

The most recent edition is that of Jean Neufville of Pierre-qui-Vire, which appeared in 1972. This edition has limited the apparatus to the readings of codices A and O, with their corrections and marginal notations, but a separate volume provides the complete text of the three principal manuscripts of the RM and some twenty-five manuscripts of the RB for all of RB Prol. and chapters 1–7; for selected passages of RB 8–73, the text from the same twenty-five manuscripts is given. The edition is the first to adopt the priority of the RM as a working principle for the establishment of the text. It is furnished with a French translation, notes and extensive commentary based on the same working hypothesis, all by Adalbert de Vogüé of Pierre-qui-Vire.[64]

---

[60] G. Penco, S. Benedicti Regula: introduzione, testo, apparati, traduzione e commento (Florence: Editrice "la nuova Italia" 1958).

[61] Some of his early studies are incorporated in H. Plenkers, Untersuchungen zur Überlieferungsgeschichte der ältesten lateinischen Mönchsregeln (Munich: Oskar Beck 1906). Plenkers also edited the second edition of Traube's Textgeschichte in 1910.

[62] Hanslik, Benedicti Regula.

[63] See A. Mundó "La nouvelle édition critique de la Règle de saint Benoît" RBén 71 (1961) 381–399; and especially P. Meyvaert "Towards a History of the Textual Transmission of the 'Regula S. Benedicti'" Scriptorium 17 (1963) 83–110.

[64] A. de Vogüé and J. Neufville, La Règle de saint Benoît, 1–6. The first volume contains the introduction and the Prologue and first seven chapters of RB, with critical text, translation and notes. The remainder of the Rule is contained in the second volume. The third volume provides the complete text of some twenty-five important manuscripts for the Prologue and first seven chapters, and other significant passages. Volumes 4 to 6 provide historical and critical commentary. A seventh volume, Commentaire doctrinal et spirituel (1977), has exactly the same format and is called Tome vii, though it is not

The definitive edition has not yet appeared, and no one today believes that it is imminent. Though it is relatively easy, thanks to the excellence of Codex A, to construct an accurate text (the texts of modern critical editions differ in relatively few places), the task of reconstructing the history of the text's transmission is enormously complex. The abundance of the manuscript tradition and the amount of contamination that has taken place are almost unique. The origin of the interpolated or *ausculta* text remains a mystery. Do the manuscripts of this class, which have a short version of the Prologue, ending at verse 39, go back to a common archetype, as Traube thought, or did they result from gradual normalization and corruption in the course of transmission? Traube attributed this text-form to a recension made by Simplicius, the third abbot of Montecassino; Hanslik seeks its origins at Rome. In any case, the interpolated text was circulating at a very early date in the seventh century and probably began in Italy. The manuscript tradition has not yet been sufficiently studied to clarify this and other obscure points.

In recent times a new objection has arisen to the pre-eminence given the *obsculta* text.[65] In Codex E of the RM, the passage parallel to the RB's Prologue 40-50 occurs at the end of chapter 1, on the kinds of monks. Now this happens to be the same section that is missing in the short form of the RB's prologue, which occurs in the *ausculta* text-form. Those who believe that Codex E represents an early form of the RM have therefore seen this as a vestige of a primitive form of the Rule. Hence the *ausculta* text, with its short prologue, would have descended from a primitive state of the rule and would have priority over the *obsculta* or "pure" text, which would be the descendant of a later recension. This view does not attempt to destroy the value of the A-text as witness to the final redaction of the RB nor to contend that the O-text is superior to it, but would seek the origin of the O-text in an earlier recension, thereby proposing a new solution to the problem of the origin of the *ausculta* text—a solution that is in some ways a return to the position of Schmidt. This would of course involve a rehabilitation of some of the "interpolated" readings. The problem is also con-

---

enumerated in the *Sources Chétiennes* series (it is listed as *hors série*). An earlier volume, *La communauté et l'abbé dans la Règle de saint Benoît* (Paris: Desclée 1961) contains de Vogüé's commentary on eighteen chapters of the RB and must be used along with the other volumes, as this material is not repeated in the other seven volumes.

[65] F. Masai and E. Manning "Les états du chapitre premier du Maître et la fin du Prologue de la Règle bénédictine" *Scriptorium* 23 (1969) 393–433.

nected to the long-debated question whether there was an earlier recension of the RB that lacked chapters 67–73.

The recent debate about the RB, therefore, has further increased the complexity of the problem of the textual transmission and made it clear that the time has not yet come for a definitive edition.

A significant achievement in recent editions of the RB is the general agreement reached on the division of the text into verses. The chapter divisions, whether or not they go back to the author of the Rule, appear in all the manuscripts as far back as we can penetrate. The introduction of verse divisions analogous to those of the Bible, however, seems to date only from the seventeenth century, and no standard system was established until very recent times. In 1947 Anselmo Lentini's edition of the RB included a verse division that he had carefully worked out on the basis of sound principles. An authority on the prose rhythm of the RB, Lentini used the natural rhythm of the clausulae as his principal criterion for versification, along with the meaning of the phrases, and the principle that more than one biblical citation should never be included in a single verse. His system was adopted in the Latin editions of Montserrat (1954; 1968[2]),[66] Penco (1958), Hanslik (1960), Steidle (1964; 1977[2]),[67] and Neufville-de Vogüé (1972), and in numerous vernacular editions. In his 1964 critical edition of the RM, de Vogüé provided an analogous versification of the RM based upon, and conforming to, Lentini's division of the RB.

This system is extraordinarily useful, especially for making references to particular passages, and it is fortunate that its adoption by the major critical editions has ensured its standardization and permanency. Anyone who has attempted to track down citations by page and line number of a particular edition (especially if it is an edition to which one does not have access!) will appreciate this contribution. It is also helpful in bringing out the rhythmic pattern of the text, thereby facilitating its public reading and enhancing its intelligibility. In view of these obvious advantages, it is astonishing that so far not a single English version of the RB, even those published in the past few years, has included the verse numbers. The present translation is the first to employ them in the English-speaking world.

The first translation of the RB made in England, so far as we know,

---

[66] G. Colombás, L. Sansegundo and O. Cunill, *San Benito: Su vida y su regla*, BAC 115 (Madrid: La Editorial Católica 1954, 1968[2]).

[67] B. Steidle, *Die Benedictus-Regel lateinisch-deutsch* (Beuron: Kunstverlag 1964, 1977[2]).

was produced by St. Ethelwold, one of the leaders of the tenth-century reform, at Abingdon about 960.[68] The Anglo-Saxon text is preserved in a tenth-century bilingual codex of Corpus Christi College, Oxford, formerly at Bury St. Edmunds, in which the translation of each chapter is appended to the Latin text, as well as in other manuscripts, sometimes in interlinear form. Since the invention of printing, there have been countless English translations and editions. Until recently, however, the available editions were invariably translated from the *textus receptus* and are therefore full of incorrect readings. They were generally also done in an archaizing kind of "Bible English," which often had all the defects of this kind of language with little of its beauty.

Two modern translations have succeeded to some extent in producing a more contemporary English: one by Leonard Doyle, an American, published in 1948;[69] the other by Basil Bolton of Ealing Abbey, London, in 1970.[70] Both translated from Butler's text. From a scholarly viewpoint, the most satisfactory text is the Latin-English edition by Justin McCann of Ampleforth in 1952; the introduction and notes are well-informed, though now somewhat dated, and the Latin text is constructed with an understanding of the textual problems, but the translation, while careful and intelligent, adopts an archaism that is stultifying. As noted above, none of these editions contains the verse numbers. The present Latin text and translation are therefore intended to satisfy a pressing need in the English-speaking world.

[68] M. Gretsch, *Die* Regula Sancti Benedicti *in England und Ihre Altenglische Übersetzung,* Texte und Untersuchungen zur Englischen Philologie 2 (Munich: W. Fink 1973); J. Oetgen "The Old English *Rule* of St. Benedict" *ABR* 26 (1975) 38–53.

[69] L. Doyle, *St. Benedict's Rule for Monasteries* (Collegeville, Minn.: The Liturgical Press 1948). The original hardcover edition has the text arranged in sense lines; this format has not been preserved in the popular paperback edition.

[70] B. Bolton, *The Rule of St. Benedict for Monasteries* (London: Ealing Abbey 1970). The most recent American translation is that of A. C. Meisel and M. L. del Mastro, *The Rule of St. Benedict Translated, with Introduction and Notes* (Garden City: Doubleday Image Books 1975). Unfortunately this edition cannot be recommended; the translation is inaccurate and misleading, and some of the information provided is erroneous.

The Rule in History

The Rule of St. Benedict was one of many Latin rules written by monastic founders between the fifth and seventh centuries to provide a basic framework of spirituality and discipline for a particular monastery. Like the others, it was meant to reflect the universally received tradition, though its own scope was severely limited: St. Benedict did not intend to establish an "order" or to legislate for monks of future centuries. Unlike the others, however, with the sole exception of St. Augustine's, his Rule was gradually adopted throughout the Western Church and eventually became almost the sole norm of Western monasticism. This development was the result of a long and gradual historical process involving many factors. It is the purpose of this section of the Introduction to offer a brief sketch of this process, which may enable the reader to see the connection between the historical document that is here introduced and the Benedictine life that is today implanted in almost every part of the world.

1. THE EARLY DIFFUSION OF THE RB

The earliest period is the most obscure.[1] During St. Benedict's lifetime, the Rule was written for his monastery of Montecassino; there is no record that it was followed anywhere else, except perhaps at the foundation St. Gregory says he made at Terracina, about which nothing is known except what is contained in the *Dialogues* (Greg. *dial.* 2,22). Montecassino was destroyed sometime between the Lombard invasion in 568 and the composition of the *Dialogues* in 593; St. Gregory says that the monks escaped with their lives (Greg. *dial.* 2,17). Two centuries later Paul the Deacon reports the tradition that the community took refuge in Rome, taking the Rule with them (Paul. diac. *gest.Lang.* 4,17). There is no reliable evidence of what subsequently became of the community, though this copy of the Rule was

---

[1] On this period, see G. Penco "La prima diffusione della Regola di S. Benedetto" *Commentationes in Regulam S. Benedicti*, StA 42 (Rome: Herder 1957) pp. 321–345.

probably the same one that was still in Rome around 750, when Pope Zachary sent it to the restored Montecassino.

St. Gregory knew the Rule, which he praises in the *Dialogues* (Greg. *dial*. 2,36) and cites once in the *Commentary on Kings* (Greg. *lib. 1 Reg.* 4,70), though not by name. This does not mean that his monastery of St. Andrew on the Coelian was governed by the RB; monasteries at this period usually drew upon a number of rules. Subsequently, there is no clear evidence of a Roman monastery governed exclusively by the RB until the tenth century, under Cluniac influence.[2] The monasteries of Italy were practically all destroyed during the Lombard period. It was not until the end of the seventh century that a renewal took place, leading to the foundation of Farfa in 705 and of St. Vincent on the Volturno soon after, as well as to the restoration of Montecassino around 720. This renewal was due chiefly to outside influences, principally from Gaul and England, but also from Byzantine refugees fleeing to the West from the iconoclasts and the Moslems.

In the late sixth and early seventh centuries, another powerful monastic influence invaded the continent — the Irish. The ascetical life flourished among the Celts of Ireland from the late fifth century onward, following St. Patrick's missionary activity. The Celtic peoples developed their own form of the monastic life, both solitary and cenobitic, which had some features in common with Eastern monasticism, perhaps by way of Lerins. In Ireland, which had never known Roman occupation and therefore had no towns, an unusual form of Church organization developed along tribal lines. The local church coincided with the clan, which took on a monastic character, with the abbot as chieftain. Though he might also be bishop, in many cases the bishop was a subject of the abbot. The Celtic monks also developed a great love of learning, and their monasteries became centers of an extraordinary culture. Their liturgical practice included some peculiarities that later brought them into conflict with the Roman tradition. They promoted a harsh discipline with severe penitential practices.[3]

Full-fledged monastic life probably developed among the Celts of England even earlier than in Ireland, for the British Church was in

[2] See G. Ferrari, *Early Roman Monasteries*, Studi di antichità cristiana 23 (Rome: Pontificio Istituto di Archeologia Cristiana 1957).

[3] On Celtic monasticism, see J. Ryan, *Irish Monasticism: Origins and Early Development* (Dublin: Talbot Press 1931).

close contact with Gaul, especially with St. Germain of Auxerre, in the fifth century. The withdrawal of Roman troops in 407 had left the Island undefended before the pagan Angles, Saxons and Jutes, and the native Britons were gradually pushed back into Cornwall and Wales. There the monastic life was propagated in the early sixth century by St. Illtud, who established a monastery on the island later called Caldey, as well as the abbey of Llantwit in southern Wales. His principal disciples were St. Gildas, who migrated to Brittany and founded monasteries there, and St. David, the patron of Wales. Both seem to have promoted the monastic life in the middle of the sixth century, contemporary with St. Benedict.

The earliest of the sixth-century founders in Ireland was apparently St. Enda, founder of Killeany in the Aran Islands off the coast of Galway, of whom little is known. More famous is St. Finnian, founder of Clonard in central Ireland, for it was principally his disciples who established the other great monastic houses around the middle of the century: St. Ciarán founded Clonmacnois; St. Brendan, the abbey of Clonfert; and St. Columcille, better known as Columba, the monastery of Derry. Columba subsequently crossed to Scotland about 583 and established Iona on a solitary island just off the west coast; it was from here that St. Aidan later founded Lindisfarne on the coast of Northumbria. These two monasteries spread Christianity in its Celtic form in Scotland and the north of England. Meanwhile, St. Comgall founded Bangor in Ulster, which was to send out the greatest of the Irish missionary monks, St. Columban,[4] often confused with the St. Columba mentioned above.

The Celtic monks were intrepid travelers; their exploits inspired the *Navigatio Brendani*, so popular in the Middle Ages. They were motivated not only by their native restlessness and a desire to bring the faith to pagan peoples but also by the ascetical ideal of seeking exile from home and family for the sake of Christ: *peregrinatio pro Christo*. Columban, born around 530 or 540, became a monk at Bangor, where he absorbed a remarkable degree of literary culture. Probably around 590, though perhaps earlier, he led a band of monks to the continent and established successively the monasteries of Annegray, Fontaine and Luxeuil in the Vosges mountains, just on the edge of Burgundy. These Celtic abbeys became centers of culture and evangelization in Gaul. Severe and uncompromising, Columban was

---

[4] See B. Lehane, *The Quest of Three Abbots* (New York: Viking Press 1968).

expelled from the Merovingian domains in 610 for his stubborn independence (Irish abbots were not used to being subject to bishops) and his open criticism of the Gallic episcopate and the royal family. He crossed the Alps to Switzerland and eventually to Italy. There, in the territory now ruled by the Lombards, he founded the abbey of Bobbio, where he died in 615.[5]

While the Celtic monasteries were often governed solely by oral teaching and tradition, Columban wrote two monastic rules, the *Regula monachorum* and the *Regula coenobialis*.[6] The latter is rather misnamed, for it is simply a penal code, to which many subsequent additions have been made. The former, however, is a genuine rule, showing knowledge of Cassian, Jerome and Basil. It was followed by the Celtic monasteries on the continent, which continued to multiply after Columban's death through the work of his disciples and admirers. The most prominent of these were St. Amandus, apostle of northern France and Belgium; St. Wandrille, founder of Fontenelle; St. Philibert, founder of Jumièges; St. Owen, bishop of Rouen and founder of Rebais; and St. Riquier, founder of Centula. They spread the Irish form of monastic life throughout Gaul and propagated the Rule of Columban.[7]

Columban's stubborn attachment to Celtic usages, however, provoked violent opposition in Gaul and stirred up dissension even within his communities. His followers gradually abandoned both the particularities of Celtic liturgical practice and the extreme severity of the Irish monastic customs. Without abandoning his Rule, they increasingly combined its observance with that of another monastic code. In the course of the seventh and eighth centuries, we find an

[5] Our knowledge of Columban is derived from his own writings and from the *Vita S. Columbani* written by Jonas of Bobbio around 640. Jonas did not know Columban personally, as he came to Bobbio some three years after the saint's death, but he wrote the *Life* at the request of Bertulf, third abbot of Bobbio, and of Waldebert, abbot of Luxeuil, and consulted eyewitnesses who were still living at both monasteries. Critical text by E. Krusch in *MGH* SSRM 4 (1902); separate edition 1905. See J. Laporte "Columbano",*Dizionario degli Istituti di Perfezione* 2.1228–1236, with good bibliography. See also G. Metlake, *The Life and Writings of St. Columban* (Philadelphia: Dolphin Press 1914); T. Concannon, *The Life of St. Columban: A Study of Ancient Irish Monastic Life* (St. Louis: B. Herder 1915); M. M. Dubois, *Un pionnier de la civilisation Occidentale: Saint Columban (c.540–615)* (Paris: Alsatia 1950); J. Wilson, *Life of St. Columban* (London: Burns Oates 1952); F. MacManus, *Saint Columban* (New York: Sheed and Ward 1952).

[6] Critical edition and translation by G. Walker, *S. Columbani Opera*, Scriptores Latini Hiberniae 2 (Dublin: Institute for Advanced Studies 1957).

[7] See F. Prinz, *Frühes Mönchtum im Frankenreich* (Munich: Oldenbourg Verlag 1965) pp. 121–151.

ever-growing tendency to observe the Benedictine Rule conjointly
with that of Columban, at Luxeuil itself and in the numerous houses of
its progeny. The RB was found suitable especially for two reasons: its
moderation provided a welcome counterbalance to Columban's austerity, and its liturgical provisions reflected a "Roman" practice that
these monasteries were increasingly adopting.

How and when did the RB come to Gaul? It is certain that it was
known there in the early seventh century, but there is no clear indication how it was transmitted. There is no evidence that the Gregorian
mission to England in 596 brought along the RB and communicated it
to monastic centers in Gaul, though this is not impossible. Our earliest
indication of it comes from southern Gaul about 620–630, in a letter
written by Venerandus, founder of the monastery of Altaripa, to
Bishop Constantius of Albi (northeast of Toulouse), the diocese in
which the monastery was located.[8] The founder says that he is sending
the bishop a copy of the RB (regula sancti Benedicti abbatis romensis)
and asks that its observance be imposed upon the abbot and monks.
Shortly after this, a disciple of Columban named Donatus, who became bishop of Besançon, wrote a rule for a convent founded by his
mother. This Regula Donati consists solely of extracts from the rules
of Benedict, Caesarius and Columban, the majority of which are derived from the RB.[9] Waldebert, Columban's second successor at
Luxeuil (629–670), introduced the RB into monastic foundations and
probably at Luxeuil itself.[10] To him is ascribed the Regula cuiusdam
Patris ad virgines, which seems to have been followed at Faremou-
tiers, a convent that Waldebert established before he became abbot.[11]

During the rest of the seventh century, it was through the network
of Columbanian foundations in northern and eastern Gaul that the RB
was propagated. Numerous documents of the period specify that the
observance is to be that of the regula mixta.[12] We are certain, therefore, that the RB was known both at Albi and at Luxeuil in the first
third of the seventh century, and that the followers of Columban
were a significant influence upon its gradual penetration thereafter.

[8] Text in L. Traube, Textgeschichte der Regula S. Benedicti (Munich: Verlag der k.
Akademie 1898) pp. 92–93.

[9] PL 87.274–298.

[10] Vita Sadalbergae 8: MGH SSRM 5,54.

[11] PL 88.1051. See Prinz, Frühes Mönchtum, pp. 286–287.

[12] We find such phrases as sub regula sanctorum patrum, maxime beati Benedicti et
sancti Columbani abbatum; secundum normam patrum domni Benedicti et domni
Columbani; sub regula beati Benedicti et ad modum Luxoviensis monasterii; secundum regulam sancti Benedicti vel domni Columbani, etc. See Prinz, pp. 268–284.

Indeed, it is not unlikely that the RB was known to Columban himself. While this is not admitted by all, there are a few places in his *Regula monachorum* that seem to echo the RB, both in order and in phraseology. One case in particular seems clear enough to qualify as an indication of literary dependence.[13] Columban could easily enough have come into contact with the RB, since he corresponded with Gregory while still at Luxeuil, and he ended his career in Italy. Even if he came to know it only at Bobbio (it is not known at what stage of his career the rule was written), it would have been transmitted to Luxeuil by the efficient monastic grapevine that kept the Columbanian foundations in close contact with one another. If the founder himself had used and recommended the RB, this would more easily explain his followers' readiness to adopt it so soon after his death. The regime of the *regula mixta* thus introduced would eventually lead to the exclusive acceptance of the RB at the expense of the Rule of Columban.

Another factor was at work in furthering this process by the end of the seventh century: the influence of the Anglo-Saxons. It was characteristic of the remarkable foresight of Gregory the Great that in a time when everything seemed to be collapsing around him, he took the bold step of extending the preaching of the faith to the world's farthest corner. In 596 he sent Augustine, the *praepositus* of his monastery on the Coelian, together with some forty companions, to evangelize England.[14] King Aethelbert of Kent, who had a Christian wife from Gaul, allowed the monks to settle at Canterbury and eventually became a Christian himself. Within a generation the faith had spread throughout Kent and into neighboring Essex and East Anglia, and by the end of the seventh century, despite some setbacks and pagan reactions, the Anglo-Saxon heptarchy had been Christianized. Meanwhile, the Celtic monks from Iona and Lindisfarne had been evangelizing in Northumbria, where their influence was mingled with that of the Roman mission. Conflict between Celtic and Roman usages persisted, even after King Oswiu decided in favor of the Roman practice at the Synod of Whitby in 664, but eventually England became firmly allied with the Roman See.

The Canterbury missionaries were monks, but we are not told that they followed the Benedictine Rule. We are sure that by the second

[13] De Vogüé, 1.162–169.

[14] M. Deanesly, *Augustine of Canterbury* (Palo Alto, Calif.: Stanford Univ. Press 1964). There is a good account of the Gregorian mission and its aftermath in P. Hunter Blair, *The World of Bede* (New York: St. Martin's Press 1970).

half of the seventh century the RB was known both in Northumbria and in the south, but there is no clear evidence revealing how it came to England. It may have been brought by the Gregorian missionaries, but there is no support for this assumption. In fact, its presence in Northumbria is attested earlier than its presence in Kent, and it may be that it came first to the north. If such is the case, the probable agent would be Wilfrid of York, whose biographer, Eddius, attributes to him the introduction of the RB into his monasteries at Ripon and Hexham (Edd.Steph. *vita Wilf.* 14 and 17). Born in 634, Wilfrid was abbot of Ripon already about 660, it seems, after a journey to Rome that involved a lengthy stay at Lyons. On the continent he became enamored of all things Roman and was the champion of Roman usages at the Council of Whitby in 664. In the 680s Wilfrid spent one of his several exiles preaching in Sussex, where he founded the monastery of Salsey, and may thus have been instrumental in propagating the RB in the south of England also.

Another champion of Roman observance in England was Benedict Biscop, a Northumbrian noble who accompanied Wilfrid on his journey to Rome in 653. On a second trip he spent two years at Lerins (665–667), where he took the name Benedict; was it there that he came into contact with the RB?[15] He returned to England with Theodore, a Greek monk whom Pope Vitalian had appointed archbishop of Canterbury (668), and Hadrian, an African who had been abbot of a monastery near Naples and who now became head of the monastery at Canterbury. Benedict established Wearmouth in 673 and its sister monastery of Jarrow in 682. Here the religious and cultural renaissance marking the high point of the Anglo-Saxon period produced its finest fruit in the life and work of Venerable Bede (673–735). The RB was used and revered at Wearmouth and Jarrow, though not exclusively.[16] It is noteworthy that our oldest copy of the RB, Codex Hatton 48 of the Bodleian Library at Oxford, was copied in England at the time of Bede, the first half of the eighth century, at an undetermined place, possibly Worcester.[17]

[15] It is not certain when Lerins adopted the RB, but it was already known at Albi, not very far distant, a generation earlier. Benedict and Wilfrid may also have become acquainted with it in Italy.

[16] Bede says that the observance of Wearmouth and Jarrow was based upon the practices of seventeen monasteries Benedict had visited. See Baedae *hist.abb.* 7 and 11; also Anon. *hist.abb.* 16 and 25.

[17] Facsimile edition by H. Farmer, *The Rule of St. Benedict*, Early English Manuscripts in Facsimile 15 (Copenhagen: Rosenkilde and Bagger 1968). See P. Engelbert "Paläographische Bemerkungen zur Faksimileausgabe der ältesten Handschrift der

By the end of the seventh century, the Anglo-Saxon monks from both the north and south of England were undertaking missionary enterprises on the continent. Already begun by Wilfrid (Edd.Steph. *vita Wilf.* 26), the evangelization of the Low Countries was accomplished by Willibrord, a Northumbrian who had been trained at Ripon under Wilfrid and later in Ireland (Alc. *vita Will.*). The greatest of the monk-missionaries, however, was Boniface, a native of Wessex, who was trained at the monasteries of Exeter and Nursling, worked under Willibrord, and then was commissioned by the Holy See to evangelize Germany. From 718 until his martyrdom in 754, Boniface, with the help of many monks, nuns and clerics from England as well as natives trained in the monasteries he founded on the continent, worked untiringly to organize the Church in the German territories and to reform the Frankish Church, collaborating with the Holy See and the Carolingian monarchs.[18] Boniface and his companions spread the RB throughout their sphere of influence, making it the basis of monastic reform in the Frankish empire, and his successors were to carry it as far as Scandinavia and Hungary. In the literature that has come down to us from Boniface and his disciples, there is no longer any mention of other rules; the RB is called simply "the Rule" and "the Holy Rule." Thus, in the course of the eighth century, while the RB was gradually ousting the Rule of Columban in the monasteries where the regime of the *regula mixta* had prevailed, the Anglo-Saxon missionary movement likewise contributed to bringing it into even greater prominence.[19]

Regula Benedicti" *RBén* 79 (1969) 399–413. This codex represents the "interpolated text." Did this recension originate in Rome? It is noteworthy that the Verona codex, which also belongs to this text tradition, entitles the RB "regula a sancto Benedicto romense edita," just as the letter of Venerandus calls it "regula sancti Benedicti abbatis romensis." Both in England and in Gaul the RB was received as a *Roman* rule, a quality that especially recommended it to the Anglo-Saxons and the Carolingians.

[18] Boniface's life (Will. *vita Bon.*) was written soon after his death by the priest Willibald. Boniface's surviving letters are also a valuable source for his life. See E. Emerton, *The Letters of St. Boniface*, Records of Civilization 31 (New York: Columbia Univ. Press 1940).

[19] The Anglo-Saxons also influenced the renewal of monastic life at Montecassino after its restoration by Petronax. St. Willibald spent some ten years there before joining Boniface and seems to have been influential in restoring the observance of the RB. Later on, Boniface maintained contact with Montecassino, sending disciples there and to other Italian monasteries to learn more of monastic observance. See Eigil of Fulda, *Vita Sturmii* 14: *MGH SS* 2,371; translation in C. H. Talbot, *The Anglo-Saxon Missionaries in Germany* (New York: Sheed and Ward 1954) pp. 181–202; and Rudolph of Fulda, *Vita Leobae: MGH SS* 15,125; translation also in Talbot, pp. 205–226.

2. THE TRIUMPH OF THE RB: THE BENEDICTINE CENTURIES

In spite of the growing influence of the RB during the eighth century, Western monasticism was far from being totally Benedictine by the year 800. That it should become so, however, was part of the policy of the Carolingian reform movement pursued during the long reign of Charlemagne (768–814). Charles wished to establish a single empire uniting the Roman and Germanic peoples on the basis of his own God-given power and the universal authority of the Holy See. The corruptions of the Merovingian age would be removed by a return to the culture of the Roman empire, thoroughly Christianized. The monasteries played a significant role in this grand design, and it was important that they become centers of genuine spirituality and culture. This was to be achieved by securing uniformity of observance, and the basis for such uniformity was to be the "Roman rule" of St. Benedict, whose excellence was being increasingly recognized.

Charles himself moved in this direction, but the decisive step was taken after his death, with the work of St. Benedict of Aniane (c. 750–821).[20] Originally named Witiza, he had served at court, but became a monk at Saint-Seine in Burgundy around 774. Later he founded his own monastery on the family estate at Aniane, near the Pyrenees, and instituted an austere life that owed much to Eastern monastic inspiration. He became convinced, however, that the RB was more suitable for the Western mentality, and his monastery grew into a large feudal institution with some three hundred monks. His interest in reform attracted the attention of Louis the Pious, Charlemagne's son, who wished to reorganize the monasteries in his kingdom of Aquitaine. Benedict sent groups of his monks to other houses to institute reform according to the RB and soon formed a congregation of monasteries that remained subject to him.

When Louis became emperor in 814, this plan was extended to the entire realm. A royal monastery called Inde was built near the palace at Aachen, and there Benedict presided over a community whose ob-

---

[20] His life was written by his disciple Ardo: critical edition by G. Waitz in *MGH* SS 15,200–220. See also J. Narberhaus, *Benedikt von Aniane: Werk und Persönlichkeit*, Beiträge zur Geschichte des alten Mönchtums und des Benediktinerordens 16 (Münster: Aschendorff 1930); J. Winandy "L'oeuvre monastique de saint Benoît d'Aniane" *Mélanges Bénédictines* (S. Wandrille: Éd. de Fontenelle 1947) pp. 237–258; Ph. Schmitz "L'influence de saint Benoît d' Aniane dans l'histoire de l'Ordre de saint Benoît" *Il monachesimo nell' alto Medioevo e la formazione della civiltà occidentale*, Centro Italiano di Studi sull' alto Medioevo, Settimane di Studio 4 (Spoleto: Presso la Sede del Centro 1957) pp. 401–415.

servance was to be a model for the whole empire. Benedict was authorized to enforce a standard observance in the monasteries of France and Germany (the plan was never extended to Italy). For this purpose he drew up a capitulary that was promulgated at two synods of abbots held at Aachen in 816 and 817.[21] Monks were to be sent to Inde from every monastery to learn the observance, and inspectors could visit monasteries to secure compliance. The authentic copy of the RB that Charlemagne had obtained from Montecassino (the *Normalexemplar*) was kept at Inde, where it could be copied; we have seen that the Codex 914 of St. Gall is the happy result of this provision. Benedict also left two important works: the *Codex Regularum*, in which he collected the existing Latin rules,[22] and the *Concordia Regularum*, a kind of commentary on the RB consisting of extracts from the other rules arranged in parallel to the RB to show the continuity of the latter with tradition.[23]

In fact, this reform was short-lived. Benedict died in 821, and the empire was soon torn apart by internecine strife among Louis' sons.[24] For the rest of the ninth century, the continent was inundated by waves of invaders, both Northmen and Saracens, and many monasteries were unable even to survive. Consequently, the great Carolingian project was never brought to completion. But when it became possible to build once more, both on the continent and in England, it was on Benedict's foundations that the structure was raised. He is one of the most important figures in Benedictine history; what he envisaged, or something very like it, became the pattern of Benedictine life for most of the Middle Ages.

The cardinal point of the Carolingian monastic policy was the exclusive use of the RB. While other observances survived for a long time in some places (Spain, for instance, lay largely outside the Carolingian sphere of influence, and the RB did not take firm root there until the tenth and eleventh centuries),[25] eventually the other Latin rules all fell into disuse. This does not mean that a Benedictine monastery according to the conception of Benedict of Aniane was

---

[21] The relevant documents, edited by J. Semmler, can be found in *Corpus Consuetudinum Monasticarum* (Siegburg: F. Schmitt 1963) 1.423–582.

[22] See above, p. 88, n. 31.

[23] *PL* 103.701–1380.

[24] On Louis the Pious, see E. S. Duckett, *Carolingian Portraits* (Ann Arbor: Univ. of Michigan Press 1962) pp. 20–57; on his monastic concepts, see T. Noble "The Monastic Ideal as a Model for Empire: The Case of Louis the Pious" *RBén* 86 (1976) 235–250.

[25] See A. Linage Conde, *Los orígenes del monacato benedictino en la península Ibérica*, 3 vols. (Leon: Centro de Estudios e Investigación "San Isidoro" 1973).

exactly like Montecassino of the sixth century. The introduction of the RB did not displace the numerous layers of tradition that had already accumulated in Gaul. The Gallic monasteries still bore the imprint of the old Martinian monasticism, of the tradition of Lerins, of the Celtic and Anglo-Saxon contributions, and especially of the vastly changed social and economic situation of the feudal period.

A great Carolingian abbey was a vast establishment that might have several hundred monks and a number of boys to be instructed in the monastery school. It might be surrounded by a town whose life was dominated by the monastery. The abbey was supported by large tracts of land worked by serfs and had to fulfill obligations toward its feudal overlord. The life of the monks was highly ritualized: many additional psalms and prayers were added to the Benedictine *opus Dei;* churches, altars and private Masses were multiplied; there were daily processions for the veneration of altars and relics. A monastery was an image in miniature of the empire itself, the earthly kingdom of God in which law and culture produced the order and peace that were a foretaste of the heavenly realm. The life of the monks was indeed a continual seeking of God through prayer, asceticism and liturgical service. But the monastery was conceived of as an organ of the Christian state: the abbot became an important political functionary, the abbey was a powerful economic force, and the state assured control by reserving the right to appoint the abbot in most cases. This factor was to have disastrous consequences. The camel's nose was already under the tent-flap.

Western monasticism, like that of the East, had heretofore managed to maintain a basic unity of doctrine and purpose in the midst of a bewildering, chaotic welter of observances. Now uniformity had become the ideal. The RB, that most flexible of all rules, scarcely furnished such a program; it habitually leaves practical decisions to the abbot's discretion. Therefore, it had to be supplemented by documents that would specify details of discipline and liturgical practice. The eighth and ninth centuries, consequently, saw the introduction of "customaries" or "statutes." [26] An important step was thus taken, leading eventually to the concept of a centralized "religious order" and of the "constitutions" that serve as its legislative framework.[27]

---

[26] The earliest ones are published in Volume I of *Corpus Consuetudinum Monasticarum,* which is appropriately subtitled: *Initia Consuetudinis Benedictinae: Consuetudines Saeculi Octavi et Noni.* See note 21 above.

[27] On the question of making profession according to a particular customary, see J. Leclercq "Profession according to the Rule of St. Benedict" *Rule and Life,* ed. M. B.

Political considerations indeed played a part in the triumph of the RB over other rules. It was the "Roman rule" that best served the Carolingian design for an empire based upon the Roman-German axis. But its success, in the last analysis, was due not solely to political expediency but to a recognition of its own innate qualities. Paradoxically, its very flexibility recommended it, for by not legislating in matters of ephemeral detail, it still proved usable at a time when profound social and economic changes had taken place in the West. Many other rules, too much bound to the situations of other times and places, were patently obsolete. Subsequent history has vindicated this judgment of the adaptability of the RB. Moreover, when the RB was followed in conjunction with other rules, it was increasingly perceived that it had given superior expression to the essentials of monastic tradition. No other text summed up so trenchantly and yet so fully the "deposit" of monastic doctrine and practice. The *Concordia Regularum* is a testimony to Benedict of Aniane's recognition of this. However his work may appear in hindsight, he did not intend to innovate; he wanted to restore the purity that monastic life had had in its origins, and he saw the RB as the best means to achieve this goal.

The Benedictine Rule, therefore, was to be the channel through which contemporary monasticism might keep in touch with its origins. A monk was to be defined by the Rule of Benedict as a canon could be defined by the Rule of Augustine. It is not surprising, then, that we find the RB to be the object of study at this period: it is the time of the first commentaries. Aside from the work of Benedict of Aniane, which is not a commentary in the strict sense, the earliest[28] is that of Smaragdus, abbot of St. Mihiel in Lorraine, in the first decades of the ninth century.[29] He was present at the Synod of Aachen and probably wrote his *Expositio* on the RB shortly after. The commentary shows considerable acquaintance with Latin Patristic and monastic literature. Another commentary seems to date from around the middle of the

---

Pennington, Cistercian Studies 12 (Spencer, Mass.: Cistercian Publications 1971) pp. 117–150.

[28] Recently a fragment of a still earlier commentary was discovered, which may come from Corbie. See K. Hallinger "Das Kommentarfragment zu Regula Benedicti IV aus der ersten Hälfte des 8. Jahrhunderts" *Wiener Studien* 82 (1969) 211–232. This shows that the tendencies that appear in the time of Benedict of Aniane had been developing for some time; Smaragdus was working out of an already existing tradition of interpreting the Rule, though perhaps it was more often oral than written.

[29] Critical text in A. Spannagel and P. Engelbert, *Smaragdi Abbatis Expositio in Regulam S. Benedicti*, Corpus Consuetudinum Monasticarum 8 (Siegburg: F. Schmitt 1974).

ninth century. It is preserved in several recensions, one of which is attributed to Paul the Deacon in some manuscripts.[30] It seems, however, that the work cannot be older than the mid-ninth century; hence the authorship of Paul, who died before 800, is out of the question.[31] More likely it is the work of Hildemar, who may have been a monk of Corbie.[32] Both of these commentaries are of considerable interest in reflecting the concerns of the period, and they are the beginning of a form of literature that has continued to accumulate around the RB to the present day.[33]

The decline that followed the abortive reform of Benedict of Aniane led to a reaction with the foundation of new centers of reform in the tenth century. The first and most prominent of these was Cluny, founded in 910, but there were numerous lesser centers that, like Cluny, formed groupings of monasteries, following the RB through the observance of the same statutes. The formation of such "orders," centralized in varying degrees, was necessary to counter the influence of lay and episcopal overlords, from whom "exemption" was achieved, in some cases, by submission of the abbey to the Roman See. Some of these centers were Brogne in Belgium, founded by St. Gerard in 923; Gorze, reformed by John of Vandières in 933; Fleury, reformed by Odo of Cluny in 931 but remaining outside the Cluniac organization; and St. Benignus of Dijon, reformed by William of Volpiano in 989. In the eleventh century there were added such centers as Verdun, reformed under Richard of St. Vanne in 1005, and Bec in Normandy, founded by Herluin in 1035, the monastery that produced Lanfranc and St. Anselm. These reforming houses differed consid-

[30] Published as *Pauli Warnefridi Diaconi Casinensis Commentarium in regulam S.P.N. Benedicti*, Bibliotheca Casinensis 4 (Montecassino 1880).

[31] Thus W. Hafner "Paulus Diaconus und der ihm zugeschriebene Kommentar zur Regula S. Benedicti" *Commentationes in Regulam S. Benedicti*, StA 42 (Rome: Herder 1957) pp. 347–358; *Der Basiliuskommentar zur Regula S. Benedicti: Ein Beitrag zur Autorenfrage karolingischer Regelkommentare*, Beiträge zur Geschichte des alten Mönchtums und des Benediktinerordens 23 (Münster: Aschendorff 1959).

[32] R. Mittermüller, *Expositio Regulae ab Hildemaro tradita et nunc primum typis mandata* (Ratisbon: Pustet 1880). For a study of this commentary, see A. Schroll, *Benedictine Monasticism as Reflected in the Warnefrid-Hildemar Commentaries on the Rule* (New York: Columbia Univ. Press 1941).

[33] See the general bibliography for the principal commentaries on the RB; a discussion of their merits can be found in C. Butler, *Benedictine Monachism* (London: Longmans Green 1919) pp. 177–183. See also the "Catalogus alphabeticus auctorum qui in Regulam S. Benedicti scripserunt" in A. Calmet, *Commentarius litteralis, historico-moralis in Regulam S.P. Benedicti* (Liège 1750) pp. liii–lxxviii, and the appendix of the work of Schroll, pp. 197–205, cited in the previous note.

erably in details of observance and in structure, but all unquestion-
ingly accepted the RB as the basis of their life, interpreted according
to a conception fundamentally that of the Carolingian reform.

The same development occurred in other countries. In Italy the
reforming activity of Odo of Cluny brought the RB to the monasteries
of Rome and implanted the Cluniac ideal, which flourished in the
eleventh century in the congregation of Cava. In England the destruction wrought by the Danish invasions was followed in the tenth century by a restoration under SS. Dunstan, Ethelwold and Oswald on the
basis of the *Regularis Concordia*, statutes that borrowed from conti-
nental models.[34] In Spain the Cluniacs introduced the Benedictine
Rule in the eleventh century and established a network of monasteries
along the pilgrimage route to Compostella. In Germany, William of
Hirsau introduced a modified Cluniac observance in 1079 and formed
a union of over a hundred monasteries, which resolutely supported
Gregory VII in the investiture struggle.

Characteristic of this form of Benedictine monasticism was a certain
centralization and uniformity of observance, an enormous development of ritual, a refined monastic culture based upon intensive study
of the Bible and the Fathers, a genuinely contemplative orientation, a
far-reaching charitable activity, serious though limited work, especially that of the scriptorium, and a discreet practice of the eremitical
life alongside and subject to the *coenobium*.[35] Its most impressive
realization was that of Cluny, which grew into a monastic empire of
almost incredible proportions and yet for more than two centuries,
under a series of abbots whose sanctity was equal to their discretion
and administrative ability, maintained a disciplined and fruitful
monastic life that constituted the most powerful reforming influence
in the Church.[36]

[34] See D. Knowles, *The Monastic Order in England* (Cambridge Univ. Press 1963[2]);
J. Robinson, *The Times of St. Dunstan* (Oxford: The Clarendon Press 1923; rpt. 1969);
Tenth-Century Studies, ed. D. Parsons (London: Phillimore 1975).

[35] See J. Leclercq, *The Love of Learning and the Desire for God: A Study of Monastic
Culture* (New York: Fordham Univ. Press 1961).

[36] On Cluny, see especially G. de Valous, *Le monachisme clunisien des origines au
XVe siècle*, 2 vols. (Paris: Picard 1970[2]); J. Evans, *Monastic Life at Cluny, 910–1157*
(1931; rpt. Hamden, Conn.: Archon Books 1968); N. Hunt, *Cluny under St. Hugh, 1049–
1109* (London: Edw. Arnold 1967); *Cluniac Monasticism in the Central Middle Ages*,
ed. N. Hunt (Hamden, Conn.: Archon Books 1971); K. Hallinger, *Gorze-Kluny: Studien
zu den monastischen Lebensformen und Gegensätzen im Hochmittelalter*, StA 22–23
(Rome: Herder 1950–51; rpt. Graz: Akademische Druck- und Verlagsanstalt 1971); H.
Cowdrey, *The Cluniacs and the Gregorian Reform* (Oxford: The Clarendon Press 1970).

In the eleventh century and well into the twelfth, while these monasteries were still prosperous and fervent, a reaction was nevertheless developing. They had become the Establishment; they had not changed with the times, whereas society was beginning to undergo profound transformations. For this reason, there developed a fervent and widespread desire for a life that would be more simple, less institutionalized, more solitary, less involved in the political and economic fabric of society — in short, a return to monastic origins. It is not surprising, then, that it often led to a reintroduction of the eremitical life. This movement, which sprang up spontaneously all over Europe, brought about a revolution in the monastic world and produced a whole variety of new "orders" and observances alongside the established houses. Though it was often chaotic and sometimes deviated into excess and heresy, under the direction of its most worthy representatives it produced remarkable fruits of holiness in the Church and enriched monasticism with forms of life that in many cases endure to the present day.[37]

Almost all these movements remained under the patronage of the RB. The Rule had become so entrenched that while it was desirable to go beyond it to seek out the deepest monastic roots, few wished to dispense with it. It remained the most direct approach to the ancient monastic tradition, and its flexibility was again demonstrated as it became combined with the particular emphases of the "new orders." The earliest of these was Camaldoli, founded in 1010 by St. Romuald, who combined the RB with the practice of the solitary life; the same formula, with greater emphasis on austerity, was followed by his disciple Peter Damian at Fonte Avellana. John Gualbert, on the other hand, instituted a fully cenobitic life, but one marked by austere simplicity, at Vallombrosa in 1022. Robert of Arbrissel combined the austere life of a hermit with itinerant preaching; then, to provide for his many followers, he established in 1099 the double monastery of Fontevrault under the RB, with large numbers of monks and nuns governed by an abbess who exercised complete jurisdiction. The congregation eventually grew to over a hundred houses. St. Bruno went to the desert of Chartreuse in 1084 to lead the solitary life with a few companions; after six years he was summoned to Rome to serve as adviser to Pope Urban II. Only later were the *Consuetudines* adopted

---

[37] See J. Leclercq "La crise du monachisme aux XIe et XIIe siècles" *Aux sources de la spiritualité occidentale: Étapes et constantes* (Paris: Les Éditions du Cerf 1964) pp. 175–199; C. Peifer "Monastic Renewal in Historical Perspective" *ABR* 19 (1968) 1–23.

and the various hermitages that grew up united into an order. The Carthusians have never followed the RB, though their life stresses many of the same values.

The most successful of the new orders was that of Cîteaux, founded in a Burgundian swamp in 1098 by Robert of Molesmes and twenty-one companions. Robert himself had founded Molesmes, an observant though traditional monastery, but the Cistercian pioneers wanted greater solitude and poverty and the "literal" observance of the Rule of St. Benedict. Robert was ordered back to Molesmes by the Pope, but the rest remained at Cîteaux, living in great austerity under Alberic and then Stephen Harding. In 1112 St. Bernard arrived with thirty companions, inaugurating a deluge of vocations that continued for a century and filled all Europe with Cistercian abbeys, from Scandinavia to the Balkans and from Ireland to the Holy Land. When Stephen died in 1134, there were 19 monasteries; at Bernard's death in 1153, there were 343; at the end of the twelfth century, 525. While there was a strict uniformity of observance, the rigid centralization of authority characteristic of Cluny was abandoned in favor of a looser structure defined in Stephen Harding's *Carta Caritatis* (1114): each abbey was autonomous, but was subject to some control by the annual general chapter and by visitations from the abbot of its motherhouse. Cîteaux's phenomenal success soon brought it prominence, wealth, power and the very involvement in temporal affairs that the first white monks had sought to escape.[38]

During the Middle Ages the Benedictine community became a quite different reality from that outlined in the RB. For a long time the monks had been more and more assimilated to clerics insofar as their life demanded a level of education that separated them from the laity. As vernacular development made Latin the language of an educated minority, the people became less active in the liturgy, which was more and more identified as the work of clerics and monks. In the course of the Middle Ages, there was a gradual increase in the number of monks admitted to sacred orders. The ritual development in the monasteries meant that the monks were occupied chiefly with sacred duties and did less of the common work. The new orders developed the institution of the *conversi* to take care of the work. They seem to

[38] On Cîteaux, see L. Lekai, *The White Monks* (Okauchee, Wis.: Our Lady of Spring Bank 1953); *The Cistercians: Ideals and Realities* (Kent, Ohio: Kent State Univ. Press 1977); B. Lackner, *The Eleventh Century Background of Cîteaux* (Washington, D.C.: Cistercian Publications 1972).

have appeared first at Vallombrosa; later we find them at Hirsau and especially at Cîteaux, where they were very numerous. The *conversi* were not lay brothers in the modern sense, but laymen who were admitted to a religious life different from that of the monks. Their vocation was not to a life of liturgical and private prayer and *lectio*, but to a life of service for the monastery; they were often illiterate and were generally occupied with work.[39] In the Cistercian abbeys they spent most of the week at distant granges and came to the monastery only for Sunday. It was only much later that they were considered a kind of second-class monks. Many of them became extremely holy men, but this new development harbored an ambiguity whose effects remain to the present day.

In every period of monastic history, women as well as men fully lived the monastic life. The life of the nuns was unfortunately one of the neglected areas of monastic history until fairly recently. From its very beginnings, in the East, women played an important role in monasticism. The *Apophthegmata* mentions female solitaries in the desert; Pachomius established a monastery for virgins, and Basil legislated for them. Paula and Melania and the other associates of Jerome and Rufinus were among the most enthusiastic propagators of the monastic life in the Latin world. St. Gregory speaks of nuns in the entourage of St. Benedict and has left us an unforgettable portrait of St. Scholastica's power of prayer. A number of Latin rules were written especially for women. In the Anglo-Saxon world they were of special importance: one thinks of Hilda presiding over the double monastery of Whitby, and of Lioba and the other female collaborators who contributed so much to the work of Boniface and who appear so frequently in his letters.

Throughout the high Middle Ages, the dowries required for entrance to monasteries usually limited admission to women of the aristocratic and middle classes. The law in Western Europe severely restricted the status of women, but in fact they often exercised a great deal of actual power. Many abbesses ruled large establishments with complicated economic, political, and sometimes military problems. Some abbesses in England, for example, played an important role in the wool trade, since their monasteries possessed large flocks, and in the late thirteenth and throughout the fourteenth century several

---

[39] J. Dubois "The Laybrothers' Life in the 12th Century: A Form of Lay Monasticism" *CS* 7 (1972) 161–213; K. Hallinger "Woher kommen die Laienbrüder?" *Analecta Sacri Ordinis Cisterciensis* 12 (1956) 1–104.

abbesses were summoned to parliament, because kings wanted to tax their wealth. While many were involved in secular affairs, there were also such inspiring figures as SS. Hildegard, Mechtild and Gertrude, who illustrate the high degree of culture and spirituality that flourished in women's monasteries. Hrosthwitha (tenth century) of the Saxon abbey of Gandersheim achieved in her times a considerable fame as author, poet and translator of the plays of Terence; many of her poems had as their theme opposition to the classical view of the frailty of women. The abbess Hildegard (1098–1179) of Rupertsberg in Hesse, Germany, served as physician to Emperor Frederick Barbarossa, and her book *On the Physical Elements* shows a rare degree of careful scientific observation; she was one of the most famous physicians of the twelfth century. Although attempts were made for a stricter enclosure, the life of nuns was fundamentally the same as that of monks. Throughout history, nuns have often lived the Rule in a more authentic and fruitful manner than the monks, and have constituted an eloquent testimony to its ability to lead Christians to sanctity.[40]

The climax of the Benedictine centuries was reached in the unique flowering of religious culture that came to fruition in the eleventh and twelfth centuries. The fruits of monastic *lectio* then appeared, enriched with new insights gained from an acquaintance with the Greek Fathers, in the religious literature produced by monks of this period. There are no really essential differences among monastic authors of different schools: Bernard of Clairvaux, William of St. Thierry, Aelred of Rievaulx and the lesser Cistercians; John of Fécamp, Peter of Celle and Peter the Venerable among the black monks; and Carthusian writers like Guy I and Guy II. They share the same basic approach to religious reality, one that grew out of a life of self-discipline and inner conversion, nourished by silence and prayer, a contemplative orientation less concerned to analyze than to rest peacefully in grateful admiration of the mystery of God and his works. The unity of this "monastic theology" is more striking than the divergences among its various

[40] See Ph. Schmitz, *Histoire de l'Ordre de saint Benoît*, vol. 7: *Les moniales* (Maredsous: Éditions de l'Abbaye 1956); Eileen Power, *English Medieval Nunneries*, rev. ed. (Cambridge Univ. Press 1940), which is the standard work; there is an interesting, if short chapter on nuns in her *Medieval Women* (Cambridge Univ. Press 1976); S. Hilpisch, *A History of Benedictine Nuns* (Collegeville, Minn.: Liturgical Press 1958); N. Hunt "Notes on the History of Benedictine and Cistercian Nuns in Britain" *CS* 8 (1973) 157–177; M. Connor "The First Cistercian Nuns and Renewal Today" *CS* 5 (1970) 131–168; J. McNamara and S. F. Wemple "Sanctity and Power: The Dual Pursuit of Medieval Women" *Becoming Visible: Women in European History*, ed. R. Bridenthal and C. Koonz (Boston: Houghton Mifflin 1977).

representatives. It is an eloquent testimony to the latent ability of the RB to stimulate a productive spiritual growth in the lives of those who assimilate its doctrine and submit to its discipline.

3. DECLINE AND RENEWAL: THE RB FROM THE THIRTEENTH CENTURY TO MODERN TIMES

If it is true that the practice of the RB reached its high point in the achievement of the Benedictine centuries, this does not mean that all that has happened since is but an anachronistic survival of a golden age. Profound changes in society led to the establishment of new forms of religious life from the thirteenth century onward; these new forms have contributed immensely to the life of the Church. The monastic life, which in the West had become identified with the Benedictine Rule, thus lost its monopoly. But it continued during the following centuries to play a role, even though a less conspicuous one. The RB has continued to provide the principal framework for the monastic life and to put monks into contact with their origins. Since the constitutive period of Western monasticism was completed by the twelfth century, however, we can summarize more briefly the role that the RB has played in the monastic order down to modern times.

In the late Middle Ages both the black and the white monks fell quite rapidly into decadence. There were many causes for this, some of them external to the monasteries: the shift from feudalism to urban life ruined the economic base of the monasteries; ecclesiastical and secular princes impoverished them by exacting revenues and interfered in their internal affairs; the Black Death and the Hundred Years' War severely depopulated many houses; and the great schism of the West divided orders and communities into conflicting allegiances. One of the worst abuses was the *commendam* system, hardly new but much more generally extended, especially by the Avignon popes in the fourteenth century: an outsider, not himself a monk, was appointed abbot of a monastery so that he could collect its revenues, though he did not live as a monk himself and did not perform the traditional role of an abbot.

There were also, however, internal causes of decadence. Too many monasteries had been established, and not all of them could be maintained at a level of fervor when the number of monastic vocations sharply declined in the thirteenth century. The monks often seemed incapable of adapting to the development of society around them and seemed intent solely upon preserving the past. Much of the leadership, the vitality and the supply of fervent vocations passed to the new mendicant orders, which responded so well to the needs and the spirit of the times. Inertia often became an occupational hazard of large monasteries, and many seemed unable to meet the challenge of the new learning, the new economy, the new aspirations of the rising generation. Sometimes they sank into a comfortable mediocrity, satisfied with drawing their revenues and perpetuating their privileges.

The abbot, when he was still a monk, often functioned as a powerful prince, enjoying the rights and insignia of bishops. He drew his own revenues, which had to be separated from the community's income to protect the monks from total impoverishment. He became more and more separated from the community, with separate dwelling, and concerned himself with administration, defending the rights of his abbey and playing the role of a great lord. If he was a *commendam* abbot, he made no pretense of even living at the monastery. Some held title to several abbeys at the same time, and some monasteries were given *in commendam* to boys of tender age. In these circumstances, the concept of the abbot's spiritual fatherhood, a foundation stone of the spirituality of the RB, deteriorated beyond repair. The monks usually did not do manual labor to provide for their own subsistence, but lived from benefices. They still performed the divine office, but the liturgy was also in a serious state of decadence at this period, and they easily became influenced by sentimental and anthropocentric currents of spirituality.

Consequently, the contemplative orientation of the Benedictine life deteriorated, and candidates were sometimes accepted who came to seek an easy life rather than to seek God. The splendid religious culture of the twelfth century degenerated into mediocrity and sometimes ignorance. The ever-increasing clericalism led to large-scale ordination of monks, and they became more and more assimilated to regular clerics, so that monasticism was no longer recognized as a distinct form of life with a value of its own. Clericalism, in turn, sometimes led to the assumption of activities that removed monks from the life of the community. There were abuses of poverty, for the various officials, who were virtually irremovable, received revenues they came to use as they saw fit; and monks received "pittances" in memory of deceased benefactors who had provided for them in their wills.

Indeed, the decay of the monasteries should not be overgeneralized, for not all houses were reduced to this state. There is no period in history at which there were not some fervent and disciplined abbeys. Even in the worst of times there were valiant reforming efforts, and new forms of Benedictine life continued to spring up. In the thirteenth century, St. Sylvester Gozzolini founded Monte Fano, from which the Sylvestrine Congregation grew;[41] and the hermit St. Peter Morrone, the future Pope Celestine V, organized his disciples into the abbey of Monte Majella, which grew into the Celestine Order. A century later St. Bernard Tolomei, after living the solitary life in a harsh desert near Siena, gave the RB to his disciples and founded the Olivetans. These branches of the Benedictine family all flourished, bringing forth fruits of holiness in an unfavorable time, and, except for the Celestines, still exist today.

The Holy See also attempted to bring about the reform of the monasteries. Already in 1215 the Fourth Lateran Council, convoked by Innocent III, prescribed that monasteries should meet in general chapter every three years on a national basis and appoint visitators to ensure the maintenance of discipline. Except in England, these provisions were never consistently carried out, and in fact they were not entirely clear nor free from internal contradiction. Again, in 1336 a much more detailed program of reform was promulgated by the Cistercian Pope Benedict XII in the bull *Summi Magistri*, but it too proved ineffectual in the long run. For many complex reasons it was not possible to reverse the general trend toward decline. Not all these reasons were the fault of the monks, who were often at the mercy of the civil and ecclesiastical power.

The fifteenth century saw a great flowering of reform movements. The prototype in the Latin countries was the reform brought about by Louis Barbo at the abbey of St. Justina in Padua. After restoring poverty, stability and the common life in his own monastery, he extended the reform to several other houses. As the movement progressed, some radical measures were taken to prevent its being undone by the *commendam* system: the autonomy of the monasteries and the traditional abbatial office were suppressed; all monks were professed for the congregation; and supreme authority resided in the annual general chapter, which appointed all the superiors and could move monks as well as abbots from one house to another. Originally called the Congregatio de Unitate, it became the Cassinese Congregation after Mon-

---

[41] His *Life* by Andrew Jacobi is translated in F. Fattorini, *The Saints of the Benedictine Order of Montefano* (Clifton, N.J.: Holy Face Monastery 1972).

tecassino entered it in 1504. It eventually reformed practically all the Benedictine monasteries of Italy, though at the price of rather notable departures from the Rule.

In Spain a similar though somewhat less radical system was followed in the Congregation of Valladolid. These measures were not necessary in the German countries, where the *commendam* system had never become firmly established. Hence, a more traditional approach prevailed in the reforms of Melk in Austria and Bursfeld in Germany, which grew out of the reform efforts of the Councils of Constance and Basel. The former was simply an observance without real congregational structures, but the Bursfeld Union, which eventually embraced about 180 monasteries, was a clearly structured juridical entity. In France political conditions defeated all efforts to overcome the *commendam*, and no general reform was possible, though limited success was achieved in some monasteries.

In the countries affected by the Reformation, about half the monasteries disappeared in the sixteenth century. In England they were totally suppressed,[42] though the English Benedictines later organized several houses in exile on the continent that devoted their efforts to the English mission and continued to prosper in France until they were allowed to return to England in the eighteenth century. In the Scandinavian countries, monasticism disappeared completely. In the Low Countries, Switzerland and the German regions, the situation was more complex: in the regions that became Protestant, all the monasteries eventually ceased to exist; elsewhere they survived, but often under conditions of great hardship because of the religious wars. In Italy, Spain and Portugal, many houses continued to prosper.

During the Counter Reformation the surviving monasteries were grouped into national congregations, and generally the state of discipline was quite good. In France there was a remarkable revival in the Congregations of St. Vanne and especially St. Maur, both founded in the early seventeenth century with a structure modeled on that of the Cassinese, deemed necessary to combat the *commendam*. St. Maur, which came to embrace nearly two hundred fervent monasteries, devoted the talents of its most gifted members to ecclesiastical studies. The Abbey of Saint-Germain des Prés in Paris became the center of European scholarship. The Maurists did pioneer work in paleography and historical criticism, and produced editions of the Fathers that

[42] See D. Knowles, *The Religious Orders in England*, Vol. 3 (Cambridge Univ. Press 1959).

have, in some cases, not yet been surpassed. At the same time, a remarkable Cistercian reform was undertaken at the Abbey of La Trappe by the famous Armand-Jean de Rancé, founder of what became the Trappist observance.[43]

In the eighteenth century, however, widespread relaxation developed, even though many monasteries throughout Europe remained observant. Monks became unpopular in an age dominated by rationalism, and they were themselves infected by the spirit of the times. They were considered tolerable only if they contributed something "useful" to society; thus, the Austrian monasteries in the time of Joseph II were obliged to undertake parish and school work in order to avoid suppression. Increasingly, secular princes began to cast envious eyes upon monastic property and were delighted to be provided with justifications for confiscating it. In France the Revolution wiped out all the monasteries, and in the confused decades that followed, the mania of suppression swept across Europe. Promoted by liberal governments, it continued to appear sporadically through the nineteenth century. By the end of the Napoleonic period, there were scarcely thirty monasteries left of the hundreds that had for so long played a major role in the life of Europe.

The nineteenth century brought the monasteries back. In some cases it was a question of continued existence of houses that had survived, as in Austria, or the restoration of pre-revolutionary Benedictine life along the same lines, as in Bavaria. In other cases there was a complete break with the past and a new beginning based upon a rethinking. The pioneer of this new type of Benedictine life was Prosper Guéranger, who in 1833 re-established the monastic life at Solesmes. He deliberately decided against the restoration of pre-revolutionary monasticism in favor of an older model, the style of the high Middle Ages. If the effort was strongly colored by the romanticism of the times and failed to go far enough in its return to sources, it was nevertheless a fruitful beginning that held rich potentialities for the future. A similar program led to the establishment of the Beuronese Congregation in Germany by Maurus and Placid Wolter in the 1860s.

Most of the Benedictine and Cistercian monasteries existing today owe their origin to the efforts of their nineteenth-century forefathers, who ensured that the RB would continue to be influential in shaping

[43] A. Krailsheimer, *Armand-Jean de Rancé, Abbot of La Trappe* (Oxford: The Clarendon Press 1974).

monastic life. By the end of the century, it seemed desirable to Pope Leo XIII to create a structure uniting all the black-monk monasteries, in order to promote communication and concerted action among them. His initiative led to the formation of the Benedictine Confederation, a loose international union of congregations and unaffiliated monasteries, presided over by an abbot primate, who periodically assembles all the abbots and priors for discussion of questions of mutual concern. A similar unification was effected for the Cistercians of both the strict and common observances. In recent times the smaller branches of the Benedictine family—Camaldolese, Vallombrosans and Sylvestrines— have entered the Benedictine Confederation.

4. THE RULE IN THE NEW WORLD

Long before any permanent colony was established in North America, the RB was already being followed elsewhere in the New World. The earliest monasteries of both monks and nuns are said to have been implanted in Greenland by Scandinavians already in the thirteenth century.[44] In the sixteenth century, the reformed Portuguese houses, erected into a new congregation in 1566, sent a colony of monks to Brazil, where they founded the abbey of Bahia in 1581. Before the end of the century, three other monasteries had been established in Rio de Janeiro, Olinda and São Paolo. They were erected into a separate Brazilian congregation in 1827. Although almost annihilated by an anti-clerical government, they were revived in 1895 by Beuronese monks.[45] All four of these sixteenth-century abbeys exist today. Peru and Mexico also possessed monasteries in colonial times.

In the eighteenth century, several Americans from the Maryland colony became Benedictines in English monasteries in exile on the continent. Richard Chandler of Charles County made his profession for the Douai community in 1705, after having been sent there for study. Seven Maryland women, including three sisters from the Semmes family, went to Europe in the eighteenth century for schooling and subsequently joined the English communities of Benedictine nuns at Paris, Ghent, Brussels and Pontoise.[46]

---

[44] See B. Danzer, *Die Benediktinerregel in der Übersee* (St. Ottilien: Missionsverlag 1929) pp. 95–96. There seems to be no satisfactory documentary proof of this tradition.

[45] O. Kapsner "The Benedictines in Brazil" *ABR* 28 (1977) 113–132.

[46] M. Hall "Colonial American Benedictines" St. Anselm's Abbey Newsletter (Washington, D.C. Spring 1980).

The first Benedictine in the United States is thought to have been Pierre-Joseph Didier, a monk of St. Denis in Paris, who came to America in 1790 when the French monasteries were suppressed and spent the rest of his life doing pastoral work in Ohio and St. Louis.[47] Trappist refugees from the Revolution came in 1803 and for many years underwent extraordinary hardships in an unsuccessful attempt to establish a foundation; a later effort finally resulted, in 1848, in the foundation of a permanent monastery at Gethsemani, Kentucky.[48]

Before this, however, the first Benedictine monastery, St. Vincent, was established at Latrobe, Pennsylvania, by Boniface Wimmer. Wimmer was a young diocesan priest when in 1832 he entered the newly re-established abbey of Metten in Bavaria. He conceived a great interest in doing missionary work in America among the German immigrants, who were in danger of losing their faith because of the lack of German-speaking priests. Although his superiors did not share his enthusiasm, having problems enough of their own in re-establishing the monastic life in Bavaria, he was finally permitted to set out in 1846 with a group of eighteen candidates who were not yet monks.[49]

Wimmer's foundation prospered, in spite of the many hardships and obstacles he encountered. Vocations were numerous and expansion rapid. Generous financial support was provided by King Ludwig I of Bavaria and by the German missionary society he had founded in Munich, the Ludwig-Missionsverein. After ten years Wimmer was already making foundations in other parts of the country. In 1856 he sent monks to far-off Minnesota to found what was to become St. John's Abbey.[50] The following year other foundations were made in Atchison, Kansas,[51] and in Newark, New Jersey. Wimmer also sent monks, in the years that followed, to North Carolina, Georgia, Florida, Alabama, Illinois and Colorado. When he died in 1887, there were five abbeys and one conventual priory, and four of his other foundations

[47] T. O'Connor "A Benedictine in Frontier America" DR 53 (1935) 471–479; A. Plaisance "Dom Pierre Joseph Didier, Pioneer Benedictine in the United States" ABR 3 (1952) 23–26.

[48] The story of the Trappists in America is told by T. Merton, The Waters of Siloe (New York: Harcourt Brace 1949).

[49] J. Oetgen, An American Abbot: Boniface Wimmer, O.S.B. (Latrobe, Pa.: The Archabbey Press 1976).

[50] C. Barry, Worship and Work (1956; rpt. Collegeville, Minn.: The Liturgical Press 1980).

[51] P. Beckman, Kansas Monks (Atchison, Kans.: Abbey Student Press 1957).

were later raised to abbatial status. The American-Cassinese Congregation had been established already in 1855.

On his very first return to Bavaria in 1851, Wimmer appealed to the Benedictine community of St. Walburga's Convent at Eichstätt to send nuns to Pennsylvania. The following year Sister Benedicta Riepp and two other nuns arrived and established a convent at St. Mary's, Pennsylvania.[52] This convent was the original source from which the Benedictine life for women eventually spread throughout the United States. The first foundation was made in Erie, Pennsylvania, already in 1856;[53] the following year sisters were sent also to Newark and to Minnesota.[54] Although the Eichstätt community, which had been sending more nuns in the meantime, wished to retain the American mission as a dependency, Father Wimmer succeeded in obtaining its separation from Bavaria in 1859. The Roman decree specified that the sisters in America could make only simple vows, since they could not maintain strict enclosure, and would be subject to the diocesan ordinary. The sisters further expanded to Kentucky in 1859, Illinois in 1861, Kansas in 1863,[55] and Indiana in 1867.[56]

Meanwhile, monks from Switzerland had arrived in the United States with their tradition of the observance of the Rule. The Swiss abbeys were being hard pressed by anti-clerical governments in the mid-nineteenth century and were also attracted by the needs of the American Church. Monks from Einsiedeln arrived in 1854 and settled in southern Indiana. This foundation, named for St. Meinrad, which became an abbey in 1870, was the first Swiss-American monastery.[57] In 1873 the abbey of Engelberg also sent monks, who established Conception Abbey in Missouri (1873; abbey, 1881)[58] and Mount Angel in Oregon (1882; abbey, 1904). St. Meinrad founded daughter houses in Arkansas (New Subiaco, 1878)[59] and Louisiana (St. Joseph,

[52] R. Baska, *The Benedictine Congregation of St. Scholastica: Its Foundation and Development* (Washington: Catholic Univ. Press 1935).
[53] L. Morkin and T. Seigel, *Wind in the Wheat* (Erie, Pa.: St. Benedict's Convent 1956).
[54] G. McDonald, *With Lamps Burning* (1957; rpt. St. Joseph, Minn.: St. Benedict's Convent 1979); S. Campbell, *Chosen for Peace* (Paterson, N.J.: St. Anthony Guild Press 1968).
[55] M. F. Schuster, *The Meaning of the Mountain* (Baltimore: Helicon 1953).
[56] F. Dudine, *The Castle on the Hill* (Milwaukee: Bruce 1967).
[57] A. Kleber, *History of St. Meinrad Archabbey 1854–1954* (St. Meinrad, Ind.: Grail Press 1954).
[58] E. Malone, *Conception* (Omaha: Interstate Printing Co. 1971).
[59] H. Assenmacher, *A Place Called Subiaco* (Little Rock: Rose Publ. Co. 1977).

1888), and sent monks to work for the conversion of the American Indians in the Dakotas, an apostolate in which Conception Abbey also cooperated.

Benedictine sisters also came from Switzerland after the founding of Conception Abbey. They were from the recently founded convent of Maria Rickenbach, which was closely associated with the monks of Engelberg. Five sisters arrived in Missouri in 1874; they settled first at Maryville, but moved to Clyde the following year. Within a few years contingents had gone out to Yankton, South Dakota; Mount Angel, Oregon, and Pocahontas, Arkansas. Maria Rickenbach continued to send nuns, and two other Swiss convents also made American foundations: Sarnen at Cottonwood, Idaho, in 1882, and Melchthal at Sturgis, South Dakota (later moved to Rapid City), in 1889. These sisters, like those from Bavaria, experienced a rapid and fruitful growth, and, while suffering severe hardships under the rough conditions of frontier life, contributed generously to the apostolate in the rapidly expanding American Church.

By the end of the nineteenth century, the Rule of St. Benedict was guiding the lives of men and women throughout the United States. The growth continued in the first part of the twentieth century, though more slowly. The majority of Benedictine monasteries of monks now belong to one of the two large federations that reflect their national origin. The American-Cassinese Federation groups together twenty-two independent monasteries descended from Boniface Wimmer's foundation of 1846.[60] The Swiss-American Federation, established in 1881, is composed of the monasteries founded from Einsiedeln and Engelberg and their descendants, now fifteen in all. Each federation has one abbey in Canada, and the American-Cassinese also has one in Mexico. Several of the monasteries in each federation have dependencies, both in the United States and in other parts of the world, notably Latin America.

Other Benedictine congregations are also represented in the United States. The English Congregation has three monasteries. The Ottilien

---

[60] There are two exceptions. St. Gregory's Abbey, Shawnee, Oklahoma, was founded (at a different location) in 1875 by French monks from Pierre-qui-Vire and belonged to the Primitive Observance Congregation until 1924: see J. Murphy, *Tenacious Monks: The Oklahoma Benedictines, 1875–1975* (Shawnee, Okla.: St. Gregory's Abbey 1974). Assumption Abbey at Richardton, North Dakota, founded in 1893 and originally located at Devil's Lake, belonged to the Swiss-American Federation until its transfer in 1932. See V. Odermann "Abbot Placid Hoenerbach and the Bankruptcy of St. Mary's Abbey, Richardton" *ABR* 29 (1978) 101–133.

and Belgian Congregations, the two Camaldolese Congregations, the Sylvestrines and the Olivetans have one each, and the French Congregation has an abbey in Quebec. There are also two independent monasteries that are not affiliated with a congregation but belong to the Benedictine Confederation. St. Gregory's Abbey at Three Rivers, Michigan, is a Benedictine monastery belonging to the Episcopal Church. The Cistercians of the Common Observance have three monasteries, and the Cistercians of the Strict Observance, who experienced an enormous growth after World War II, have twelve.

The formation of congregations for the nuns was a slow and arduous task. The convents remained subject to the bishops until the second quarter of the twentieth century. Most of them now belong to one of four principal federations. Having been formed much later than the founding era, they do not always reflect precisely the historical origin of each convent. The oldest and largest is that of St. Scholastica, established in 1922 after the failure of earlier efforts dating back as far as 1879. It consists of twenty-three convents, all descended from the Bavarian foundation at St. Mary's.[61] The Federation of St. Gertrude the Great, formed in 1937, includes fifteen communities of chiefly but not exclusively Swiss origin. The Clyde convent, however, and several houses founded from it constitute the Congregation of the Benedictine Sisters of Perpetual Adoration. Another federation was formed in 1956 by St. Benedict's Convent, St. Joseph, Minnesota, together with six other houses. All of them except one are daughter houses of St. Benedict's.[62]

There are a few communities of nuns outside these federations. The community of Jonesboro, Arkansas, founded by Swiss nuns from Maria Rickenbach, via Maryville, in 1887 (originally at Pocahontas, Arkansas), has been affiliated with the Olivetans since 1893.[63] Regina Laudis at Bethlehem, Connecticut, is a foundation of Jouarre in France, made in 1947. The convent at Norfolk, Nebraska, belongs to the Benedictine Missionary Congregation of Tutzing in Bavaria. The nuns of Eichstätt have two American dependencies at Greensburg, Pennsylvania, and Boulder, Colorado.[64] The Trappistines, who came

---

[61] Baska, *The Benedictine Congregation*, in note 52 above.

[62] The exception is St. Mary's Priory in Nauvoo, Illinois, which was founded from St. Scholastica's in Chicago in 1874. On the history of this convent, see R. Gallivan, *Shades in the Fabric* (Nauvoo, Ill.: St. Mary's Priory 1970).

[63] A. Voth, *Green Olive Branch* (Chicago: Franciscan Herald Press 1973).

[64] See the informative summary by C. Meyer "Communities of Benedictine Women 1852–1970" *Benedictines* 28 (1973) 79–83.

to America only after World War II, have already grown to four convents, and there is one of Cistercian nuns of the Common Observance.

The Rule of St. Benedict has proved its flexibility over the centuries as it has been lived in many different ways in a bewildering variety of social and cultural situations. The American experience of it—or rather, the variety of American experiences, for there have been and continue to be many different forms of life according to the Rule in America—has had its own unique contribution to make.[65] However the American monastic phenomenon may be judged eventually by history, it is clear that even in the changed circumstances of the New World, the RB has retained its viability to teach men and women.[66]

5. THE RELEVANCE OF THE RULE TODAY

The purpose of this section is not to propose a particular interpretation of the Rule for our time nor to resolve the question of this or that particular monastic practice, but rather to point out the contexts in which the question of relevance has arisen and to suggest a framework in which the discussion of its relevance can be pursued.

The question of whether or not and to what extent the Rule of St. Benedict is relevant to the lives of Benedictines in the twentieth century arises in the first instance because it is obvious to even a casual observer that a great many of the concrete provisions of the Rule are not observed today. Indeed, there is no monastery in the world in which all of the provisions of the Rule are observed. This has, of course, been the case for well over a thousand years. In the past, the perception of the discrepancy between the letter of the Rule and monastic practice has often troubled the consciences of those who had made their profession to live "according to the Rule of St. Benedict," and has led to various reform movements aimed at restoring the observance of the Rule more or less in its full integrity. It is doubtful, as most historians will grant, whether any of these movements ever succeeded in that goal. What they usually produced was a new, and often fruitful, observance and adaptation of the Rule for their own time.

In the second place, since the Second Vatican Council the question

---

[65] See the well-informed and carefully documented study of B. Doppelfeld, *Mönchtum und kirchlicher Heilsdienst* (Münsterschwarzach: Vier-Türme Verlag 1974).

[66] An excellent set of maps showing the location of Benedictine monasteries can be found in J. Müller, *Atlas O.S.B.*, Vol. II: *Tabulae Geographicae* (Rome: Editiones Anselmianae 1973). These maps, however, do not include Benedictine sisters. There are more detailed, though now somewhat dated, maps of the United States in *The Scriptorium* (St. John's Abbey) 19 (1960) between pp. 60 and 61.

of relevance has been made more complex because of the directives for reform that the Council gave to religious communities. The Council stated: "The up-to-date renewal of the religious life comprises both a constant return to the sources of the whole of the Christian life and to the primitive inspiration of the institutes, and their adaptation to the changed conditions of our time."[67] For better or worse, these directions for renewal have led during the past fifteen years to the abandonment of even more of the concrete provisions of the Rule in many communities that profess to live according to the Rule. For example, many of the provisions of the liturgical code that were observed until the recent liturgical reform have now fallen into desuetude in the face of innumerable and diverse "experiments." Indeed, to many people the efforts at returning to the "primitive inspiration" and at "adaptation" seem to lead in opposite directions. In view of this apparently increasing discrepancy between the provisions of the Rule and life as it is actually lived in Benedictine communities, can modern monks and nuns claim with any plausibility to be living "according to the Rule of St. Benedict" as they continue to profess to do?

In the third place, there is the more generalized question of whether or not a document written in sixth-century Italy, in a relatively primitive social and economic context, can actually be relevant to people living in the complex technological culture of the late twentieth century. This of course involves the a priori assumption that the situation of modern man really is substantially different from that of people in late antiquity or the early medieval period. It usually involves also the assumption that there has been so much progress since the sixth century that there is not much point in wasting one's time looking for solutions to modern problems in a sixth-century document. It is often pointed out that modern man has been conditioned not only by progress in the area of technology but by the vast expansion of knowledge in historical consciousness, natural science, the social sciences, and even in theology. All this has even led some to abandon or avoid the use of the words "monastic" and "monk" as containing in themselves connotations of "medieval" and "outmoded."

These three aspects of the question of relevance will be discussed in the order in which they have been raised. The solutions proposed have been many and varied.[68] They range from the observation, on the

---

[67] *Perfectae Caritatis* n.2.

[68] For more extensive discussion of the question of the relevance of the Rule, the following may be consulted: C. Peifer "What does it mean to live 'According to the

one hand, that the Rule should be treated as a distant historical ancestor without much bearing on real life to the insistence, on the other
hand, that as many of the concrete provisions of the Rule that can
possibly be observed should be observed. There have been others
who try to sift out from the Rule those elements that are supposedly
"time-conditioned," and others who try to translate the Rule into the
language of modern philosophers and psychologists. Few if any would
advocate today that we should attempt to restore the observance of all
the concrete provisions of the Rule. We shall not attempt to discuss all
of these points of view here in detail.

1. *"Observance" of the Rule*

It is doubtful whether the question of the Rule's relevance can be
adequately resolved as long as the discussion remains focused on the
comparatively narrow question of the observance of the precise directives of the Rule. This is not to assert that individual observances or
regulations are unimportant, or that a "spirit" of the Rule can be dis-
tilled and preserved apart from the actual text (a question that will be
discussed below), but rather that the question of the Rule's relevance
is a much more complex one, involving the historical relationship of
the Rule to the previous monastic tradition and to subsequent monastic history. The Rule has not, in fact, provided an adequate and
sufficiently detailed organizational basis for monastic life for well over
a thousand years, and perhaps never did outside of St. Benedict's own
monastery. This has been supplied by declarations, constitutions and
written as well as unwritten sets of customs. Yet, the Rule has always
formed an important part of the tradition that has governed and inspired monastic life in the West.

Much of the modern study of the Rule has been inspired by and has
followed the historical-critical methodology developed from the time

---

Rule'?" *MS* 5 (1968) 19–44; A. Wathen "Relevance of the Rule Today" *ABR* 19 (1968)
234–253; A. Veilleux "The Interpretation of a Monastic Rule" *The Cistercian Spirit*, ed.
M. B. Pennington (Shannon: Irish Univ. Press 1970) pp. 48–65; O. du Roy, *Moines
Aujourd'hui* (Paris: EPI 1972); A. de Vogüé "Sub regula vel abbate: A Study of the
Theological Significance of the Ancient Monastic Rules" *Rule and Life: An Interdisciplinary Symposium,*. ed. M. B. Pennington (Spencer, Mass.: Cistercian Publications 1971) pp. 21–63; "Saint Benedict Today: The Monastic Life and Its Aggioma-
mento" *CS* 14 (1979) 205–218; D. Rees, *Consider Your Call* (London: SPCK 1978)
pp. 43–56; A. Zegveld "Que veut dire 'selon la Règle'?" *CollCist* 41 (1979) 155–176;
J. Leclercq "Qu'est-ce que vivre selon une règle?" *CollCist* 32 (1970) 155–163; also in
Moines et moniales ont-ils un avenir? (Brussels: Lumen Vitae 1971) pp. 131–142.

of the Renaissance onward and particularly refined in the study of Scripture. It is axiomatic to this method that before one can determine the question of a text's relevance, one must first determine its meaning; and to determine its meaning, it must be situated in its historical and literary context.[69] It has been the purpose of this lengthy Introduction to do just that for the Rule of St. Benedict.[70] It should be emphasized, however, that this is only an introduction and does not pretend to provide an adequate description of the historical and literary context of the Rule. To provide such would be the work of a commentary, which this volume does not pretend to be.

As was noted at the beginning of this Introduction, there were in existence when the Rule was written a monastic tradition well over two hundred years old and a large body of literature reflecting and transmitting that tradition. At this point we do not wish to recapitulate what has already been said but merely to add a few observations about the relationship of the Rule to that tradition, both from the point of view of the Rule's author and from our point of view. St. Benedict viewed his Rule as a modest addition to the previously existing body of monastic literature (RB 73). His point of view should be taken seriously. He did not intend to replace the previous literature, but to provide a modest compendium and adaptation of it to serve as an introduction for those who wished to take up the practice of the monastic life in his time. The Rule can be fully appreciated only when it is viewed as an addition to this previous literature.

Part of the problem, however, in understanding the literary context of the Rule derives from the term itself (*regula*) and the connotations it has acquired. It has been demonstrated that in the tradition prior to RM, the term "rule" has a much broader meaning than simply a set of written regulations, and indeed in its usage in RB 73 it retains something of this broader meaning. In the writings of Jerome, Sulpicius Severus and others, it designates not a law distinct from the abbot but the authority of the abbot himself. In Cassian's writings it designates the whole prior monastic tradition, the practices and observances of all the monasteries which Cassian sees as dating back to apostolic times, and which is for him a living tradition preserved above all in Egypt. In RM 2 and RB 2, the phrase *sub regula* has come to mean a

---

[69] Some would prefer to distinguish the question of relevance, the question of meaning for today, as the hermeneutical question and to describe the quest for the meaning of the text in its historical and literary context as the exegetical task.

[70] See especially: The Context of the Rule, pp. 84–90 above.

written rule that complements the authority of the abbot.[71] But in the last analysis, the function of both rule and abbot is similar: to pass on, adapt and concretize the previous monastic tradition. And this tradition in turn derives, according to RB 73.3, from Scripture itself, which provides the ultimate norm for human life (*norma vitae humanae*).

This last phrase is of particular importance for appreciating the literary genre of the Rule. It has been customary to regard the Rule of St. Benedict as belonging to the genre of legal literature or law codes, and the author as a great lawgiver. As we have noted, however, he sees his work as belonging to a body of literature that includes Scripture, the earlier Patristic literature and especially the writings of Cassian and Basil. "Law" is hardly an adequate classification for such a body of literature. Yet the author of RB sees all this literature as having something in common, namely, that it provides a practical guide for living and for the cultivation of virtue. The whole body of early monastic literature resembles rather that body of literature in the Old Testament that today is called "wisdom literature." It has this in common with Old Testament wisdom literature, that although it contains certain theological principles, it is derived primarily from, and reflects experience of, life. It is intended to be a guide to wise living in the practical situations of life.

What is suggested here is not that there is direct continuity between Old Testament wisdom literature and early monastic literature, or that they are exactly the same genres. The body of early monastic literature is unthinkable without the intervention of the teaching of Jesus and the whole New Testament on which it depends far more than on the Old Testament wisdom literature. And early monastic literature is far more restricted in scope than Old Testament wisdom literature. It is concerned, not with the wide variety of life-situations of the latter, but only with living the monastic life wisely. All the early monastic literature has this in common: it stems from the lived experience of the monastic life and represents an effort to preserve and pass on the wisdom gained from that experience. This wisdom was first passed on by living teachers who had gained it through their own experience. It was in many cases their disciples or admirers who sought to preserve their wisdom in written form to pass on to future generations. In cenobitic monastic settings where the community survived the death of the founder and where succeeding superiors were chosen from

---

[71] For more detailed discussion of the usage of *regula* in antiquity, see de Vogüé "Sub regula vel abbate" pp. 24–35, cited above in note 68.

among the community, it became particularly important to have the wisdom of earlier generations available to guide both the superior and his subjects. It is of comparatively little importance whether this was passed on in the form of biographies, collections of sayings and anecdotes, compilations of regulations, or even more systematic efforts to set forth the spiritual life, such as the *Institutes* of Cassian. All served the same function — that of transmitting a wisdom tradition.

It is, then, to this broad genre of literature that the Rule of St. Benedict belongs and this wisdom tradition that it sought to transmit and adapt to the local conditions of sixth-century Italy. How this modest work came to occupy such a dominant position in Western monastic tradition has already been explained earlier in this Introduction. If one were to view the Rule simply as legislation for organizing the daily routine of a monastery, one would miss its essential character almost entirely. Nor is it merely the Prologue and first seven chapters that should be regarded as transmitting this wisdom tradition; in the rest of the Rule as well, the author sought to transmit and regulate those practices that experience of the monastic life had shown to be fruitful. Regulations are in fact one way of transmitting practical wisdom or the fruit of experience.

One aspect of wisdom literature, and indeed of law, is that it must be taught or inculcated without the expectation of immediate comprehension. Unlike more speculative knowledge, which can be assimilated through study, through simply following the thought process of the original author, practical wisdom is essentially related to experience. The insights of past generations provide a kind of matrix within which new experiences of life can be organized and assimilated. Proverbial insights from the past remain empty unless they are filled with fresh experiences of life. If this is true of wisdom in general, it is especially true of the spiritual life. Practice is essential to the assimilation of spiritual wisdom. One does not expect the novice to appreciate the wisdom of many provisions of the Rule, such as silence, obedience, the pursuit of humility, until he or she has actually practiced them. Nor can anyone who has not lived in the context of monastic life and experienced the situations that arise there be expected to appreciate many other provisions of the Rule, such as the need for the rule of seniority, the need to regulate the reception of guests, and the hesitancy of the Rule's author over the appointment of a prior. Before one decides, then, that this or that provision of the Rule is "time-conditioned" and therefore to be discarded, one should consider the possible wisdom, the experience of human life and perennial human situations for which the provision has been developed. To adapt institutions, as will be argued below, is by no means the same thing as simply to discard or abandon them.

2. *Renewal and adaptation*

As was noted above, the Second Vatican Council suggested that two principles are involved in the renewal of religious life: a return to the sources and their adaptation to the changed conditions of our time. It suggested a "constant return to the sources of the whole of the Christian life and to the primitive inspiration of the institutes." In attempting to spell this out further, the Council stated that "the spirit and aims of each founder should be faithfully accepted and retained, as indeed should each institute's sound traditions."[72] Anyone who has read this Introduction thus far cannot but be aware that for those in the Western monastic tradition this is no simple task. Nor is it surprising that such an enormous task has been carried out in such a desultory fashion in the last fifteen years. St. Benedict is not a founder in the same sense as St. Dominic or St. Ignatius was. Nor is it very easy to determine his spirit and aims, since we know virtually nothing of him apart from the Rule itself. And it is very difficult to try to disengage the "spirit" of a text from the actual text itself. Some would deny that it is possible.

It is possible to learn something of the spirit of the author of the Rule by a careful comparison of the provisions and words of the Rule with its sources in the monastic tradition, particularly with the *Rule of the Master*, from which St. Benedict borrowed so much and yet whose text he so often altered significantly. This method, parallel to that used in the study of the Synoptic Gospels, can lead to considerable insight into the mind of the author. The "spirit of the founder," however, can hardly be restricted to the results obtained in this way if one takes seriously St. Benedict's own attitude toward the prior monastic tradition to which he consciously attaches himself in RB 73. The spirit of the founder is to be found in the main teachings of the monastic tradition that the author of the Rule intended to transmit as well as in the changes and adaptations he made in that tradition. In fact, the "spirit of the founder" for men and women in the Western monastic tradition is to be sought not only in the Rule of St. Benedict but in the whole monastic tradition, especially in its formative period preceding the time of St. Benedict. And in this tradition, despite many variations,

[72] *Perfectae Caritatis* n.2.

local adaptations and occasional contradictions, there is a remarkable unanimity of teaching about the principal aspects of the monastic life: the practice of renunciation involving celibacy, sharing of goods, the need for self-discipline, the pursuit of humility, obedience, the centrality of prayer.

It is perhaps symptomatic of the present state of affairs (which, it is hoped, this volume may help to remedy) that many people today, even when they are acquainted with the Rule of St. Benedict, have not the slightest understanding of what is meant by the "monastic tradition." Even those who profess to live according to the Rule are often unaware of the rich store of wisdom to be found in this whole body of literature. A major obstacle, then, to renewal has been ignorance, and much of this has been due to the inaccessibility of most of this literature to the non-scholar. This is being gradually remedied. One practical way in which the Rule can be relevant to the "constant" process of renewal is that it can provide a doorway, for those who study it carefully, to this whole body of wisdom concerning the spiritual life.

An additional and by no means inconsiderable role of the Rule in the past and the present is that it provides a common source and a common language for those seeking to live in the monastic tradition. These are aspects of the larger question of identity. Without a history a person has no identity, and without a history a social institution also will have a very difficult time maintaining an identity. Just as a family's identity depends upon common ancestors, a common language and a common fund of memories, so does that of an institution such as monasticism. The weaker the knowledge of the past, the weaker the identity will be.

The second principle offered by the Council to guide the process of renewal was "adaptation to the changed conditions of our times." This is a deceptively simple formulation of a very complex process. It presupposes a thorough familiarity with, and appreciation of, that which is to be adapted. It presupposes also an understanding of the relationship between monasticism and society, especially in the formative period of the monastic tradition. And finally, it presupposes the ability to single out those things that really are significantly changed conditions, that really do make our society different from that of antiquity or the Middle Ages and that therefore should impinge upon the monastic way of life.

As has already been indicated, the first of these conditions has been in large part missing from much of the discussion in recent times. A wisdom tradition is in constant need of being rethought and re-experienced if it is to remain alive. It needs to be expressed anew in contemporary language, contemporary situations and contemporary behavior. But to do this, one must first be thoroughly steeped in the wisdom tradition. It is precisely this depth, however, that has been lacking. Without it, we run the risk of simply abandoning the tradition and substituting modern ideas and behavior as the norm. This is not adaptation; it is accommodation, or even surrender, to the values of the world.

Second, there has often been the presupposition that in antiquity monasticism somehow blended more peacefully into the social scene than it does today. This was hardly the case. The rise of the monastic movement represented in antiquity a notable rejection of what were then regarded as contemporary values and a deliberate choice of a way of life at sharp variance with accepted mores. The monastic movement represented an alternative to the normal social structure and to normal social behavior. This antithetical relationship to society and its mores is an essential aspect of the "spirit of the founder" as that can be discovered in the ancient monastic tradition. Therefore, the rule for adaptation cannot be simply what people do today; this will produce accommodation with the "world," the ancient enemy of monasticism, rather than adaptation. A monasticism that is authentic must offer a way of life that provides an alternative to the values of contemporary society, not an echo of them.[73]

Third, it is not a simple matter to sort out the significantly changed conditions that make our time different from earlier ages of monastic history. Clearly, when people no longer speak or understand Latin, then it is time to use a language people can understand. When one lives and works in an agricultural environment, a certain schedule is appropriate; in a city a different one may be needed. But it would be naïve to imagine that people in antiquity had less difficulty with silence or obedience and that because conditions today are different, these practices should be abandoned. Likewise, the discovery that there are alternative ways of doing something does not imply that one should immediately abandon the traditional way of doing it. Change for its own sake is of no benefit to a society or institution. Stability and continuity are important values in any society.

[73] For a description of the relationship of monasticism to society in antiquity, see p. 16 of this Introduction and P. Brown "The Rise and Function of the Holy Man in Late Antiquity" *Journal of Roman Studies* 61 (1971) 80–101.

3. Has the human condition changed fundamentally?

It remains to consider the third ground mentioned earlier for questioning the relevance of the Rule, namely, that life and people today are so different from life and people in late antiquity that a document written then can hardly be of much use now.

It seems to be a perennial temptation in all ages to imagine that contemporary culture represents the apogee of human development. Certainly, the rapidity of change in our culture has engendered a belief both in progress itself and in progress as a solution to human problems. Rooted in the Renaissance and strengthened by the Industrial Revolution, this belief has received added energy from popularizations of Hegel, Marx, Darwin and others. It underlies and underpins the view that reading the documents of the past is like reading the books of our nursery days. That this belief in progress is very widespread needs no documentation; that it is sound is, on many grounds, questionable.

First, it rests on a number of insecure assumptions. There is reason to question the assumption of the perfectibility of fallen man, and to ask whether the idea of constant progress is compatible with a realistic view of the evil and sin present in the world. Equally questionable is the assumption that rapid change is necessarily a motion of constant upward progress. Might not the motion be circular, or wavelike as in alternating current, or even downward, or now one, now another?

Second, do the observable facts really support such a trust in progress? Undoubtedly, in the last few centuries there has been an enormous expansion in human knowledge and in man's ability to control and utilize the material world. Ever more rapidly accelerating technological progress has brought many present benefits and countless possibilities for improving the quality of human life in the future. Nor is such progress limited to the obvious material benefits of a higher standard of living (at least for those who share in it). To cite but a few examples: the progress in medicine has greatly alleviated human suffering; psychiatry and other social sciences continue to shed new light on mental illness and human behavior generally; vast amounts of research have given us a greater knowledge of human history than ever before.

But a less optimistic observer could point out that all this progress has produced greater and greater disparity between the few rich and the many poor of the world. The last hundred years have witnessed human atrocities on a scale unknown before; Dachau, Hiroshima and

Vietnam are not milestones of progress. And technology is answerable for our capacity to destroy on a scale scarcely imaginable even now. Then there are the numerous ecological problems that continue to arise.

Adding up the balance sheet on the human race is a precarious and possibly futile exercise at any point in history, but it is difficult to feel wholly confident that the bottom line today shows a larger profit than ever before.

And so one need not deny that there has been progress, or that further progress is both possible and desirable, in order to see that an uncritical trust in progress may be mistaken.

We believe, in fact, that it is incorrect to belittle the past and to lose a sense of what is perennial in the affairs of the human spirit. When individuals and societies come to regard their problems as unique, then no help can be sought from others and a sense of shared humanity is lost. But it is a liberating experience when individuals discover that the difficulties and troubles they experience link them with, rather than separate them from, the rest of humanity. So too is it with nations and societies.

Anyone who is acquainted with the writings of Alexis de Tocqueville, published long before either the Communist Manifesto or the Russian Revolution, knows that the present rivalry of the two most powerful nations on earth is hardly due to the clash of rival ideologies alone. Likewise, anyone who has read Thucydides is hardly surprised to observe the shifting alliances in the United Nations or the role that jealousy seems to play in international affairs.

By the same token, in the realm of the Spirit (where Christians have always had grounds for being most optimistic about the possibilities of progress), a discovery of the wisdom in the monastic tradition, even in this "little rule for beginners," can help to put us in touch with what is perennial and human, thereby broadening and deepening our humanity and our life in the Spirit. Perhaps if the ancient monastic wisdom were more widely known in our time, so many thousands of Westerners would not be seeking spiritual peace in non-Western and non-Christian settings. The great challenge to monasticism in our society, which should also be the challenge of monasticism to our time, is to show by a life of renunciation and self-discipline that it is possible to achieve spiritual peace and simplicity of heart in the midst of the technological complexity of contemporary culture, to show that it is still possible for brothers to "dwell together in unity" (Ps 132[133]).

Part Two

REGULA SANCTI BENEDICTI

Latin and English with
Patristic Sources and Notes

Notes to the Text and Translation of the RB

The notes to the text and translation are intended to provide a justification or explanation for the translators' choices, to explain obscurities and to provide the reader with leads for further investigation. In this edition, no critical apparatus has been supplied for the Latin text. For that, the now standard editions of Hanslik and de Vogüé should be consulted (see Bibliography).

The Latin text printed here is based, by kind permission of Les Éditions du Cerf, who hold the copyright, on that in the edition of the Rule by de Vogüé. That text, established by J. Neufville, is based on the venerable MS 914 of Saint Gall, which, though not the oldest extant manuscript of RB, may well be the closest we have to St. Benedict's autograph. We have not attempted a new critical edition. For additional discussion of the Latin text, see the Introduction, pp. 102f.

Believing that the majority of those who read our Latin text will not be palaeographers, but rather people with a memory of Latin of varying degrees of clarity, we have made a few changes of orthography in order to present the Latin in a form with which most of our readers will be familiar. Neufville himself indulged in a certain amount of *normalization* (de Vogüé 1.399–401). For this we have used *The Oxford Latin Dictionary* and C. T. Lewis and C. Short, *A Latin Dictionary* (Oxford: The Clarendon Press 1933), but we have distinguished the consonantal from the vocalic *u* (e.g., *novus*, not *nouus*) although *The Oxford Latin Dictionary* does not. Otherwise, we have attempted to follow the recommendations of St. Benedict's contemporary Cassiodorus (*Institutiones* 1,9) and made the changes that affect the assimilation of prefixes (*acc-* for *adc-*, and similarly before *l, p, q, s* and *t; coll-* and *comp-* for *conl-* and *conp-*; *exsisto* for *existo*, and *exsp-* and *exst-* for *exp-* and *ext-* when the stem starts with *s; imb-* for *inb-* and similarly before *l, m, p* and *r;* and *surr-* for *subr-*) and Greek derivatives, where we have given the standard Latin transliteration (e.g., *Kyrie* for *quirie, eremita* for *heremita, hemina* for *emina*). We have retained the unexpected case-endings of *ipsud, cogitatos* and *cibūs* as unlikely to confuse the reader, whose convenience has been our criterion. We have not attempted to normalize the grammar and syntax.

The references to Patristic and Ancient Works in boldface may be considered quotations. This does not necessarily imply that the author of RB was quoting directly from the work in question. The rest of the references include possible sources and allusions as well as passages containing similar ideas or language. Although many of the latter may not be immediate sources for RB, they nevertheless bear witness to its cultural and linguistic background. See pp. xxi–xxxi for a complete list of short titles.

REGULA SANCTI BENEDICTI

[1]Obsculta, o fili, praecepta magistri, et inclina aurem cordis tui, et admonitionem pii patris libenter excipe et efficaciter comple, [2]ut ad eum per oboedientiae laborem redeas, a quo per inoboedientiae desidiam recesseras. [3]Ad te ergo nunc mihi sermo dirigitur, quisquis abrenuntians propriis voluntatibus, Domino Christo vero regi militaturus, oboedientiae fortissima atque praeclara arma sumis.

Prol.1 **Basil.** ad fil. 1; Hier. *epist.* 22,1.
Prol.2 Aug. *civ.* 11,28; *Vitae patr.*, *Verb.senior.* 5,14,15; Aug. *nat. et grat.* 20,22; Cypr. *epist.* 65,5.
Prol.2 Leo.M. *tract.* 90,2.
Prol.3 **Basil.** ad fil. 1.
Prol.3 **Hier.** epist. 22,15; *Vitae patr.*, *Verb.senior.* 5,1,9; *Hist.mon.* 31; Cypr. *hab.virg.* 3.

Title: "The Rule of Saint Benedict" (*Regula Sancti Benedicti*): The original or proper title of the RB remains uncertain. H. Brechter "Zum authentischen Titel der Regel des heiligen Benedikt" *SMGBO* 55 (1937) 157–229, argued for *Regula Benedicti* or *Sancti Benedicti sancta regula*. Numerous variations occur in the manuscripts. Codex Sangallensis 914 gives: *In nomine Domini nostri Iesu Christi incipit prologus regulae patris eximii beati Benedicti*, which can hardly have been original. The commonly used title, *Regula Monachorum*, probably derives from Gregory the Great (Greg. *dial.* 2,36). J. McCann, *The Rule of Saint Benedict* (1929; rpt. Westwood, Conn.: Greenwood Press 1972) n.1, considers this evidence for its originality.

Prologue: Most of the Prologue (vv.5-45,50) is taken almost word for word from the fourth section of the Introduction to RM, specifically RM's commentary on Pss 33(34) and 14(15). (On the possible origin of this material in baptismal catechesis, see de Vogüé 4.42–48.) This is likewise true of the major portion of RB 1-7, which is taken from RM 1-10. This fact accounts for the unity of style and content that has often been observed in RB Prologue through ch. 7. In both rules, these sections deal with fundamental aspects of the spiritual life such as obedience and humility, in contrast to the more detailed directions for the organization of daily life that follow. For a more extended discussion of the relationship of RB and RM, see the Introduction, pp. 79–96.

Prol.1 "Listen" (*Obsculta*): *Ausculta* is the spelling of the oldest extant manuscript of RB, Oxford Hatton 48, while *obsculta* is the spelling of Codex Sangallensis 914. Most modern editors have preferred *obsculta* as more authentic. For a more extended discussion of the text types represented by these two manuscripts, see the Introduction, pp. 102–111.

The mode of address represented by the opening words of RB, "Listen carefully, my son," no doubt intentionally echoes that to be found in the wisdom tradi-

THE RULE OF SAINT BENEDICT

PROLOGUE

¹Listen carefully, my son, to the master's instructions, and attend to them with the ear of your heart. This is advice from a father who loves you; welcome it, and faithfully put it into practice. ²The labor of obedience will bring you back to him from whom you had drifted through the sloth of disobedience. ³This message of mine is for you, then, if you are ready to give up your own will, once and for all, and armed with the strong and noble weapons of obedience to do battle for the true King, Christ the Lord.

---

tion of the Old Testament (cf. Prov 1:8; 4:1,10,20; 6:20). These opening words, which set the "wisdom" tone of RB, seem to be related to the key notion of the monastery as a "school for the Lord's service" (see note on Prol.45 below). The RB can certainly be viewed as a compendium of practical wisdom for living the monastic life. On the RB as "wisdom literature," see the Introduction, pp. 145–147. The opening words also bear a strong resemblance to Ps 44(45):11, which is used as the beginning of Hier. *epist.* 22. See Thematic Index: LISTENING.

"my son" (*o fili*): Although the Latin text does not contain the personal pronoun, the sense of intimacy evoked here has led most translators to write: "my son." This may be due to the influence of Proverbs as well. At any rate, it has become a solidly established convention of modern-language translations of RB. While the number of addressees (one or many) varies in the Prologue, especially in quotations from RM and Scripture, the verses proper to RB (1-4, 46-49) are directed to only one person.

"the master's instructions" (*praecepta magistri*): Although some commentators have thought the "master" here to be Christ or the Holy Spirit rather than the author of the RB, there seems to be no compelling reason to interpret it this way. Elsewhere in RB (2.24; 3.6; 5.9; 6.6) the term is applied to the abbot or superiors generally. It is also possible, though not provable, that the word contains an allusion to RM, from which so much of this portion of RB is derived. The RM regularly begins each chapter with: *Respondit Dominus per magistrum* (the Lord has replied through the Master). Thus the author of RB would not be guilty of innovation in applying the title to himself. Both RB (2.2; 63.13) and RM (2.2) regard the abbot as holding the place of Christ.

Prol.2 "obedience. . .disobedience" (*oboedientiae. . .inoboedientiae*): There seems to be an allusion here to the Adam-Christ typology of Rom 5:19. See also Phil 2:8. See B. Steidle "Per oboedientiae laborem. . .per inoboedientiae desidiam. Zu Prolog 2 der Regel St. Benedikts" *EA* 53 (1977) 428–435; 54 (1978) 200–216; 280–285.

Prol.3 "own will" (*propriis voluntatibus*): When used in the plural, as here, this phrase refers to the particular promptings or suggestions of will. The human will is not considered evil in itself, but the renunciation of one's own particular

⁴In primis, ut quicquid agendum inchoas bonum, ab eo perfici instantissima oratione deposcas, ⁵ut qui nos iam in filiorum dignatus est numero computare non debet aliquando de malis actibus nostris contristari. ⁶Ita enim ei omni tempore de bonis suis in nobis parendum est ut non solum iratus pater suos non aliquando filios exheredet, ⁷sed nec, ut metuendus dominus irritatus a malis nostris, ut nequissimos servos perpetuam tradat ad poenam qui eum sequi noluerint ad gloriam.

⁸Exsurgamus ergo tandem aliquando excitante nos scriptura ac dicente: *Hora est iam nos de somno surgere,* ⁹et apertis oculis nostris ad deificum lumen, attonitis auribus audiamus divina cotidie clamans quid nos admonet vox dicens: ¹⁰*Hodie si vocem eius audieritis, nolite obdurare corda vestra.* ¹¹Et iterum: *Qui habet aures audiendi audiat quid spiritus dicat ecclesiis.* ¹²Et quid dicit? *Venite, filii, audite me; timorem Domini docebo vos.* ¹³*Currite dum lumen* vitae *habetis, ne tenebrae* mortis *vos comprehendant.*

Prol.4 Basil. *ad fil.* 11; *Vitae patr., Verb.senior.* 5,7,18 (cf. 11,29).
Prol.9-18 Aug. *in psalm.* 33,9; 33,16-18; 143,9.

---

desires is undertaken in imitation of Jesus, as multiple citations in RB 5.13 and 7.12-32 make clear. A given desire can be good, as is evident from 61.5. See note on 5.7 and Thematic Index: WILL.

"to do battle. . .for" (*militaturus*): The words *militia* and *militare* by this time refer to both military and civil service; see de Vogüé 7.53–59, especially note 63, and C. Mohrmann in Philibert Schmitz, *Sancti Benedicti Regula Monachorum* (Maredsous: Éditions de l'Abbaye 1955) pp. 30–31 and E. Manning "La signification de 'militare-militia-miles' dans la Règle de Saint Benoît" *RBén* 72 (1962) 135–138. Military metaphors for the spiritual life recur throughout RB, both in borrowings from RM and in original passages, and are indeed a commonplace already in the New Testament (see Eph 6:10-17; 1 Thess 5:8; 1 Tim 1:18; 6:12; 2 Tim 2:3-4) and in Hellenistic philosophy: see H. Emonds "Geistlicher Kriegsdienst. Der Topos der militia spiritualis in der antiken Philosophie" *Heilige Überlieferung: Festgabe I. Herwegen,* ed. O. Casel (Münster: Aschendorff 1938) pp. 21–50. RB uses the image to depict the monastic life as service of Christ, the present Lord and King. See Thematic Index: CHRIST and SERVICE, as spiritual combat.

Prol.4 "you begin a good work" (*inchoas bonum*): The semi-Pelagians of the fifth and sixth centuries (Faustus of Riez in particular) overstressed personal initiative in the economy of salvation. St. Benedict carefully joins work and prayer at the beginning of monastic life. However, it has been argued that here, as well as in Prol.21,35 and 41, the RB may be open to a semi-Pelagian interpretation. For further discussion see Cipriano Vagaggini "La posizione di S. Benedetto nella questione Semipelagiana" *StA* 18–19 (1947) 17–83 and Basilius

⁴First of all, every time you begin a good work, you must pray to him most earnestly to bring it to perfection. ⁵In his goodness, he has already counted us as his sons, and therefore we should never grieve him by our evil actions. ⁶With his good gifts which are in us, we must obey him at all times that he may never become the angry father who disinherits his sons, ⁷nor the dread lord, enraged by our sins, who punishes us forever as worthless servants for refusing to follow him to glory.

⁸Let us get up then, at long last, for the Scriptures rouse us when they say: *It is high time for us to arise from sleep* (Rom 13:11). ⁹Let us open our eyes to the light that comes from God, and our ears to the voice from heaven that every day calls out this charge: ¹⁰*If you hear his voice today, do not harden your hearts* (Ps 94 [95]:8). ¹¹And again: *You that have ears to hear, listen to what the Spirit says to the churches* (Rev 2:7). ¹²And what does he say? *Come and listen to me, sons; I will teach you the fear of the Lord* (Ps 33[34]:12). ¹³*Run while you have the light* of life, *that the darkness* of death *may not overtake you* (John 12:35).

Steidle, *Die Regel St. Benedikts* (Beuron: Beuroner Kunstverlag 1952) pp. 54, n. 4; 55, n. 6; 58, n. 12; 59, n. 13 and 144–145.

Prol.5 "grieve" (*contristari*): RB uses this word mostly of the relationships of the brothers among themselves. See Thematic Index: JOY, *Antithesis*: Grief.

Prol.9 "the light that comes from God" (*deificum lumen*): The light is Sacred Scripture (see de Vogüé 2.415, n. 9). The Latin words *deificum* and *attonitis*, as McCann notes (*The Rule of Saint Benedict*, n.3), are strong words which, as is common enough in informal usage, have lost much of their original strength.

"every day calls out" (*cotidie clamans*): There is reference here to the daily use of Ps 94(95) as the Invitatory (see RB 9.3). This phrase is taken from RM, which also uses Ps 94 as the Invitatory.

Prol.12 "Come and listen to me, sons" (*Venite, filii, audite me*): Prol.12-18 cites and comments upon Ps 33(34):12-16. The psalm is understood to mean that Christ is calling out and inviting men. This supposes that the "Lord" of the psalm is Christ, and that the psalm is prayed to him as God. This view, which is frequent in the RB, is often found in the early Church; the earliest example of it, which also concerns Ps 33:12, can be found in Clem. *ad Cor.* 22,1-8. This usage derives from the conviction that Christ is the fulfillment of the Old Testament: since the title *Kyrios* is conferred upon him, the *Kyrios* of the Old Testament can be understood as Christ already present. This view was propagated by Origen, in whose exegesis Christ is discovered speaking through the Old Testament under the veil of symbols. His exegesis was particularly influential in monastic circles, where the practice of praying to Christ was very common. See B. Fischer "Le Christ dans les Psaumes. La dévotion aux Psaumes dans l'Église des Martyrs" *La Maison-Dieu* 27 (1951) 86–113; F. Vandenbroucke, *Les Psaumes, le Christ et Nous*, 2nd ed. (Louvain: Mont-César 1965); also Appendix 2, pp. 360–363.

Prol.13 "life" (*vitae*): See Thematic Index: LIFE.

¹⁴Et quaerens Dominus in multitudine populi cui haec clamat operarium suum, iterum dicit: ¹⁵*Quis est homo qui vult vitam et cupit videre dies bonos?* ¹⁶Quod si tu audiens respondeas: Ego, dicit tibi Deus: ¹⁷*Si vis habere veram et perpetuam vitam, prohibe linguam tuam a malo et labia tua ne loquantur dolum; deverte a malo et fac bonum, inquire pacem et sequere eam.* ¹⁸Et cum haec feceritis, *oculi* mei *super* vos *et aures* meas ad *preces* vestras, *et antequam me invocetis dicam* vobis: *Ecce adsum.* ¹⁹Quid dulcius nobis ab hac voce Domini invitantis nos, fratres carissimi? ²⁰Ecce pietate sua demonstrat nobis Dominus viam vitae. ²¹Succinctis ergo fide vel observantia bonorum actuum lumbis nostris, per ducatum evangelii pergamus itinera eius, ut mereamur eum *qui* nos *vocavit in regnum suum* videre.

²²In cuius regni tabernaculo si volumus habitare, nisi illuc bonis actibus curritur, minime pervenitur. ²³Sed interrogemus cum propheta Dominum dicentes ei: *Domine, quis habitabit in tabernaculo tuo, aut quis requiescet in monte sancto tuo?* ²⁴Post hanc interrogationem, fratres, audiamus Dominum respondentem et ostendentem nobis viam ipsius tabernaculi, ²⁵dicens: *Qui ingreditur sine macula et operatur iustitiam;* ²⁶*qui loquitur*

Prol.18 *Passio Iulian. et Bas.* 12.
Prol.20 Cypr. *testim.* pr.

Prol.14 "to him" (*cui*): The antecedent could be either *multitudine populi* or *operarium*.

Prol.16 "you" (*tu*): English conceals that the pronoun is singular here but plural in v.18. Though no doubt the shift is partly due to the quotation, it may also suggest that to God's individual call each must first make an individual response, and then our individual responses bind us together as a community of those seeking God.

"God" (*Deus*): The word *Deus* in the context of vv.14-17 appears to refer to Christ. The RB uses the words *Dominus* and *Deus* sometimes to refer to Christ, sometimes to God in general. For more extended discussion of this, see A. Borias "Dominus et Deus dans la Règle de Saint Benoît" *RBén* 79 (1969) 414–423. See Thematic Index: GOD.

Prol.17 "*peace*" (pacem): Peace is one of the goals of monastic life. See Thematic Index: PEACE.

Prol.21 "Clothed" (*Succinctis...lumbis*): The words here rendered as "clothed" have been traditionally and more literally translated as "with our loins girded." They probably are an allusion to Eph 6:14-16, where the words "faith" and "gospel" are also to be found. For the notion of the Gospel as our guide, see A. de Vogüé "Per ducatum Evangelii" *CollCist* 35 (1973) 186–198.

"to see him" (*eum...videre*): In the context of the preceding verse, the pronoun *eum* would seem to refer to Christ (see note on "God" in v.16 above).

¹⁴Seeking his workman in a multitude of people, the Lord calls out to him and lifts his voice again: ¹⁵*Is there anyone here who yearns for life and desires to see good days?* (Ps 33[34]:13) ¹⁶If you hear this and your answer is "I do," God then directs these words to you: ¹⁷If you desire true and eternal life, *keep your tongue free from vicious talk and your lips from all deceit; turn away from evil and do good; let peace be your quest and aim* (Ps 33[34]:14-15). ¹⁸Once you have done this, my *eyes will be upon you and my ears will listen* for your *prayers; and even before you ask me, I will say* to you: *Here I am* (Isa 58:9). ¹⁹What, dear brothers, is more delightful than this voice of the Lord calling to us? ²⁰See how the Lord in his love shows us the way of life. ²¹Clothed then with faith and the performance of good works, let us set out on this way, with the Gospel for our guide, that we may deserve to see him *who has called* us *to his kingdom* (1 Thess 2:12).

²²If we wish to dwell in the tent of this kingdom, we will never arrive unless we run there by doing good deeds. ²³But let us ask the Lord with the Prophet: *Who will dwell in your tent, Lord; who will find rest upon your holy mountain?* (Ps 14[15]:1) ²⁴After this question, brothers, let us listen well to what the Lord says in reply, for he shows us the way to his tent. ²⁵*One who walks without blemish*, he says, *and is just in all his dealings;* ²⁶*who speaks the truth from his heart and has not practiced deceit with*

However, in the context of the quotation from 1 Thess 2:12 that follows, it would refer to God generally or to the Father, since *theos* in the New Testament usage usually designates the Father. Moreover, the phrase "to see God" inevitably evokes Matt 5:8 and the monastic quest for purity of heart as well as the speculation on the goal of contemplation in earlier monastic literature. See Introduction, pp. 34–40.

Prol.22 "tent" (*tabernaculo*): In RB this word, taken from Ps 14(15):1, occurs only in the Prologue in this verse and in vv.23,24, and 39. The word evokes Israel's years of camping in the desert, the feast of Tabernacles (Lev 23:33) and especially (in the Vulgate) the solemn formulation of the covenant in Lev 26:11.

Prol.25 "he says" (*dicens*): The present participle is used not infrequently in RB in a way that disregards the structure of the sentence.

"*just*" (iustitiam): *iustitia* (for Hebrew *sedek*) has a wide range of meanings in Scripture: justice, observance of the law, holiness, God's just ways or decrees. Its translation poses a problem, since "justice" is not used in normal English in the sense of doing what is right, and the other traditional translation, "righteousness," now sounds archaic as well as having unpleasant connotations. Yet *iustitia* and its translation as "justice" or "just" has a long history and many resonances. It recurs in 2.5,9,14,19,35; 4.33; 16.5 and in the title of ch. 73. See Thematic Index: JUSTICE.

veritatem in corde suo, qui non egit dolum in lingua sua; [27]*qui non fecit proximo suo malum, qui opprobrium non accepit adversus proximum suum;* [28]qui *malignum* diabolum aliqua suadentem sibi, cum ipsa suasione sua a *conspectibus* cordis sui respuens, *deduxit ad nihilum,* et *parvulos* cogitatos eius *tenuit et allisit ad* Christum; [29]qui, *timentes Dominum,* de bona observantia sua non se reddunt elatos, sed ipsa in se bona non a se posse sed a Domino fieri existimantes, [30]operantem in se Dominum *magnificant,* illud cum propheta dicentes: *Non nobis, Domine, non nobis, sed nomini tuo da gloriam;* [31]sicut nec Paulus apostolus de praedicatione sua sibi aliquid imputavit, dicens: *Gratia Dei sum id quod sum;* [32]et iterum ipse dicit: *Qui gloriatur, in Domino glorietur.* [33]Unde et Dominus in evangelio ait: *Qui audit verba mea haec et facit ea, similabo eum viro sapienti qui aedificavit domum suam super petram;* [34]*venerunt flumina, flaverunt venti, et impegerunt in domum illam, et non cecidit, quia fundata erat super petram.*

[35]Haec complens Dominus exspectat nos cotidie his suis sanctis monitis factis nos respondere debere. [36]Ideo nobis propter emendationem malorum huius vitae dies ad indutias relaxantur, [37]dicente apostolo: *An nescis quia patientia Dei ad paenitentiam te adducit?* [38]Nam pius Dominus dicit: *Nolo mortem peccatoris, sed convertatur et vivat.*

Prol.28 Orig. *hom. in Num.* 20,22; Orig. *c.Cels.* 7,22; Hil. *in psalm.* 136,14; Ambr. *paenit.* 2,106; Hier. *epist.* 22,6; Hier. *in psalm.*; Aug. *in psalm.* 136,21; Aug. *conf.* 8,12,28; Cassian. *inst.* 6,13.

Prol.29 Cassian. *inst.* 12,17; Cypr. *ad Don.* 4.

Prol.32 Clem. *ad Cor.* 13.

Prol.33-34 Cypr. *eccl.unit.* 2.

Prol.35-38 Cypr. *de pat.* 4.

Prol.28 "He has *foiled* the *evil one* . . ." (qui *malignum* diabolum aliqua suadentem sibi, cum ipsa suasione sua a *conspectibus* cordis sui respuens, *deduxit ad nihilum*): It is clear from a comparison with the Latin of Ps 14(15):4 (*ad nihilum deductus est in conspectu eius malignus*) that the first half of Prol.28 is ingeniously built upon the latter, thus continuing the citations of Ps 14 begun in Prol.23 and continued in 25-27. For the use of Ps 14 here, see B. Egli, *Die vierzehnte Psalm im Prolog der Regel des heiligen Benedikt: Eine patrologisch-monastische Studie* (Sarnen: Buchdruckerei Louis Ehrli & Cie 1962).

"*dashed them against* Christ" (allisit ad *Christum*): For an explanation of the chain of associations involved in this allegorical interpretation of Ps 136(137):9, see Appendix 6, p. 475. The interpretation may be found in the allusion to the same verse in RB 4.50.

his tongue; [27] *who has not wronged a fellowman in any way, nor listened to slanders against his neighbor* (Ps 14[15]:2-3). [28] He has *foiled* the *evil one,* the devil, at every turn, flinging both him and his promptings far *from the sight* of his heart. While these temptations were still *young, he caught hold of them and dashed them against* Christ (Ps 14[15]:4; 136[137]:9). [29] These people *fear the Lord,* and do not become elated over their good deeds; they judge it is the Lord's power, not their own, that brings about the good in them. [30] *They praise* (Ps 14[15]:4) the Lord working in them, and say with the Prophet: *Not to us, Lord, not to us give the glory, but to your name alone* (Ps 113[115:1]:9). [31] In just this way Paul the Apostle refused to take credit for the power of his preaching. He declared: *By God's grace I am what I am* (1 Cor 15:10). [32] And again he said: *He who boasts should make his boast in the Lord* (2 Cor 10:17). [33] That is why the Lord says in the Gospel: *Whoever hears these words of mine and does them is like a wise man who built his house upon rock;* [34] *the floods came and the winds blew and beat against the house, but it did not fall: it was founded on rock* (Matt 7:24-25).

[35] With this conclusion, the Lord waits for us daily to translate into action, as we should, his holy teachings. [36] Therefore our life span has been lengthened by way of a truce, that we may amend our misdeeds. [37] As the Apostle says: *Do you not know that the patience of God is leading you to repent* (Rom 2:4)? [38] And indeed the Lord assures us in his love: *I do not wish the death of the sinner, but that he turn back to me and live* (Ezek 33:11).

Prol.31 *"grace"* (Gratia): See Thematic Index: GRACE.

Prol.35 "With this conclusion" *(Haec complens): Haec* could be interpreted as an external accusative referring to the whole series of admonitions drawn from Scripture thus far in the Prologue. It seems more likely, however, that it is to be taken as an internal accusative: "with this conclusion." The "conclusion" alluded to would then be the preceding verses, which form part of the conclusion of the Sermon on the Mount (Matt 7:24-25) and which in the context of the Prologue are the last of the series of admonitions drawn from Scripture. These words *(haec complens)* are, however, taken from RM, where they conclude a much longer prologue (and the *Thema*), including a lengthy commentary on the Lord's Prayer, which is, of course, also to be found in the Sermon on the Mount.

Prol.37 *"patience"* (patientia): This is the only place in RB where *patientia* is used of God. Elsewhere (e.g., Prol.50) it, as well as *patiens* and *patienter*, applies to us. Here it is contained in the quotation from Rom 2:4. See Thematic Index: PASCHAL MYSTERY.

[39]Cum ergo interrogassemus Dominum, fratres, de habitatore tabernaculi eius, audivimus habitandi praeceptum, sed si compleamus habitatoris officium. [40]Ergo praeparanda sunt corda nostra et corpora sanctae praeceptorum oboedientiae militanda, [41]et quod minus habet in nos natura possibile, rogemus Dominum ut gratiae suae iubeat nobis adiutorium ministrare. [42]Et si, fugientes gehennae poenas, ad vitam volumus pervenire perpetuam, [43]dum adhuc vacat et in hoc corpore sumus et haec omnia per hanc lucis vitam vacat implere, [44]currendum et agendum est modo quod in perpetuo nobis expediat.

[45]Constituenda est ergo nobis dominici schola servitii. [46]In qua institutione nihil asperum, nihil grave, nos constituturos speramus; [47]sed et si quid paululum restrictius, dictante aequitatis ratione, propter emendationem vitiorum vel conservationem caritatis processerit, [48]non ilico pavore perterritus refugias viam salutis quae non est nisi angusto initio incipienda. [49]Processu vero conversationis et fidei, dilatato corde inenarra-

---

Prol.41 Fulg.Rusp. *epist.* 17,47.
Prol.46 Leo.M. *tract.* 88,5.
Prol.48 *Hist.mon.* 9; Cypr. *de op. et el.* 1; Cypr. *epist.* 13,3.
Prol.48-49 Cassian. *conl.* 3,15; Pachom. *reg.* 190; *Vitae patr., Verb.senior.* 5,11,29.
Prol.49 *Sacr.Gelasianum* 3,25,1322.
Prol.49-50 Cypr. *epist.* 65,10.

Prol.39 "but only if we fulfill the obligations of those who live there" (*sed si compleamus habitatoris officium*): The Latin here is elliptical. The sense seems to be, "we have heard the instruction for living there (and now have a chance of making our home where the Lord lives), but only if we fulfill the obligations of those who live there." Many manuscripts of RB do in fact interpolate a phrase to this effect. See Hanslik, *ad loc.*

Prol.40 "for the battle of holy obedience" (*sanctae. . .oboedientiae militanda*): The form of the verb is equivalent to *militatura*. See C. Mohrmann "La Latinité de Saint Benoît" *Études sur le Latin des Chrétiens,* I (Rome: Edizioni di Storia e Letteratura 1958) p. 419, and McCann, *The Rule of Saint Benedict,* n. 10. As in Prol.3, the image of military and civil service refers to the labor of obedience. See note to Prol.3 above. The "battle of holy obedience" means the "battle for holy obedience," i.e., the struggle to achieve obedience. One might compare this with the phrase "civil rights struggle," which means, of course, "struggle for civil rights." Other interpreters, however, understand it to mean that obedience itself is the battle for which we must prepare.

Prol.41 "to us" (*in nos*): The use of the accusative (instead of: *in nobis*) provides a very clear example of the tendency of the accusative to take over the functions of the other cases.

"let us ask. . ." (*rogemus Dominum ut gratiae suae iubeat. . .*): Another possible translation would be: "let us ask the Lord to command the help of his grace to

[39]Brothers, now that we have asked the Lord who will dwell in his tent, we have heard the instruction for dwelling in it, but only if we fulfill the obligations of those who live there. [40]We must, then, prepare our hearts and bodies for the battle of holy obedience to his instructions. [41]What is not possible to us by nature, let us ask the Lord to supply by the help of his grace. [42]If we wish to reach eternal life, even as we avoid the torments of hell, [43]then — while there is still time, while we are in this body and have time to accomplish all these things by the light of life — [44]we must run and do now what will profit us forever.

[45]Therefore we intend to establish a school for the Lord's service. [46]In drawing up its regulations, we hope to set down nothing harsh, nothing burdensome. [47]The good of all concerned, however, may prompt us to a little strictness in order to amend faults and to safeguard love. [48]Do not be daunted immediately by fear and run away from the road that leads to salvation. It is bound to be narrow at the outset. [49]But as we progress in this way of life and in faith, we shall run on the path of God's commandments, our hearts overflowing with the inexpressible delight of love.

---

supply it." See de Vogüé, 1.423, n.41 and *La Règle du Maître*, 1.325, n.41.

Prol.44 "run" (*currendum*): This verb is used four times in the Prologue, in vv.13,22,44, and 49. All usages, except the last, are taken from RM. In vv.13 and 44, there is an allusion to John 12:35, where the verb in the Vulgate is *ambulate* (walk). The image of "running" may derive from elsewhere in the New Testament, e.g., 2 Tim 4:7.

Prol.45 "a school for the Lord's service" (*dominici schola servitii*): In this noble and often quoted phrase, a school "for" rather than "of" seems best to catch the idea that the monastery is a place where the monks both learn how to serve the Lord and actually do so. In the Latin of this period, *schola* could mean not only a place where instruction was received but the group receiving instruction as well as, more generally, a vocational corporation (such as a guild) of people devoted to a common craft or service. A similar usage can be seen in the English "school of painters" or "school of porpoises." See Appendix 2, p. 365. The "school for the Lord's service" may certainly be regarded as the central idea of the Prologue (see de Vogüé 7.27–74). It implies that the monastery (the school) is the place where Christ continues to teach his disciples the baptismal renunciation of sin and the ways that lead to the repose of eternal life. It implies that life in the monastery is a service of Christ, the Lord. It implies, finally, that service calls for strenuous obedience and suffering with Christ but that such service leads even now to a joyful and loving observance of the commandments of God. See Thematic Index: DISCIPLINE, as divine teaching.

Prol.49 "But as we progress in this way of life" (*Processu...conversationis*): *Conversatio* means generally a way of life, here the monastic way of life. The monk is the Christian who turns to the monastic life (58.1), who makes a beginning (73.1), who is exhorted to progress in the monastic way of life (Prol.49), who

bili dilectionis dulcedine curritur via mandatorum Dei, [50]ut ab ipsius numquam magisterio discedentes, in eius doctrinam usque ad mortem in monasterio perseverantes, passionibus Christi per patientiam participemur, ut et regno eius mereamur esse consortes. Amen.

Prol.50 Caes.Arel. *reg.mon.* 1; Cypr. *hab.virg.* 21; Cypr. *ad Fort.* 11; Cypr. *de op. et el.* 13; Cypr. *epist.* 57,1-3.

⁵⁰Never swerving from his instructions, then, but faithfully observing his teaching in the monastery until death, we shall through patience share in the sufferings of Christ that we may deserve also to share in his kingdom. Amen.

---

promises to live the monastic life (58.17), and who is hurrying toward the perfection of the monastic life (73.2). For further discussion of this term, see Appendix 5, pp. 459–463. See Thematic Index: CONVERSATIO; LIFE, as journey.

Prol.50 "faithfully observing his teaching" (*in eius doctrinam. . .perseverantes*): There is an allusion here to the picture of the early Christian community drawn by Luke in Acts 2:42 (*perseverantes in doctrina apostolorum*). References to these texts from Acts describing the life of the Jerusalem community abound in early monastic literature, for monastic authors saw in the practices of the Jerusalem community a justification for the practices of cenobitic monasticism. Cassian develops the theme most extensively and sees in the Jerusalem community both the prototype and origin of cenobitic monasticism. See A. de Vogüé "Monasticism and the Church in the Writings of Cassian" *MS* 3 (1965) 19–51 and Pier Cesare Bori, *Chiesa Primitiva: L'immagine della comunità delle origini—Atti 2,42-47; 4,32-37—nella storia della chiesa antica*, Testi e ricerche di Scienze religiose 10 (Brescia: Paideia Editrice 1974). On the notion of perseverance contained in this phrase, see also Appendix 5, pp. 464–466. See Thematic Index: PASCHAL MYSTERY.

"patience. . .sufferings" (*passionibus. . .patientiam*): The two Latin words are from the same root, something that could not be indicated neatly in the translation. See Col 1:24.

[INCIPIT TEXTUS REGULAE]
[Regula appellatur ab hoc quod oboedientum dirigat mores]

I. DE GENERIBUS MONACHORUM

[1]Monachorum quattuor esse genera manifestum est. [2]Primum coenobitarum, hoc est monasteriale, militans sub regula vel abbate.

[3]Deinde secundum genus est anachoritarum, id est eremitarum, horum qui non conversationis fervore novicio, sed monasterii probatione diuturna, [4]qui didicerunt contra diabolum multorum solacio iam docti pugnare, [5]et bene exstructi fraterna ex acie ad singularem pugnam eremi, securi iam sine consolatione alterius, sola manu vel brachio contra vitia carnis vel cogitationum, Deo auxiliante, pugnare sufficiunt.

[6]Tertium vero monachorum taeterrimum genus est sarabaitarum, qui nulla regula approbati, experientia magistra,

---

1.1-8 Cassian. conl. 18,4-8; Hier. epist. 22,34; Cypr. *epist.* 57,1-3; Cypr. *de mort.* 12.

1.3-5 Cassian. *inst.* 5,36; Hier. *epist.* 125,9.

1.4-5 Leo.M. *tract.* 18,2; 88,3-4; 89,2; Cassian. *conl.* 18,6.

1.5 Leo.M. *tract.* 39,4; 40,1.

1.6 Cassian. *conl.* 18,4; 19,7 (cf. 12,4 et 16); 18,7.

["It is called a rule. . ." (*Regula appellatur. . .*)]: Not all MSS have this phrase, and of those that do, not all have it before ch. 1. There is reason to doubt that this statement goes back to St. Benedict. However, there is no denying that *regula*, meaning literally a 'straight edge,' is a derivative of *rego*. *Dirigo*, meaning 'rule' (set in separate straight lines) or 'keep straight,' is a compound of *rego*. *Rectus*, meaning 'straight' (or 'true' in the carpenter's sense), is the past participle of *rego*, used as an adjective (see 7.21; 73.3,4).

A similar attempt to explain the derivation of *regula* can be found in RM Prol.23-27. The meaning of words, however, depends as much on usage and context as upon etymology, even when that is correctly given. For discussion of the usage of *regula* prior to RM, see the Introduction, pp. 84–88.

1.1 "monks" (*Monachorum*): For the literary background of this chapter and additional discussion of the terms "monk," "cenobite," etc., see Appendix 1, pp. 301–321. Except for vv. 11-13, the wording of RB 1 is identical with that of RM 1. However, RB omits much material in RM. See Thematic Index: MONK.

1.2 "cenobites" (*coenobitarum*): The Latin word is derived from the Greek *koinos bios*, which means literally: 'common life.'

"serve" (*militans*): See notes to Prol.3 and 40.

"a rule and an abbot" (*regula vel abbate*): In later Latin *vel* often, as here, means 'and.' In earlier Western monastic tradition, *regula* does not necessarily refer to a written rule distinct from the authority of the abbot. It is the innovation of RM to complement the authority of the latter with a written document. See A.

[HERE BEGINS THE TEXT OF THE RULE]
[It is called a rule because it regulates the lives of those who obey it]

CHAPTER 1. THE KINDS OF MONKS

¹There are clearly four kinds of monks. ²First, there are the cenobites, that is to say, those who belong to a monastery, where they serve under a rule and an abbot.

³Second, there are the anchorites or hermits, who have come through the test of living in a monastery for a long time, and have passed beyond the first fervor of monastic life. ⁴Thanks to the help and guidance of many, they are now trained to fight against the devil. ⁵They have built up their strength and go from the battle line in the ranks of their brothers to the single combat of the desert. Self-reliant now, without the support of another, they are ready with God's help to grapple single-handed with the vices of body and mind.

⁶Third, there are the sarabaites, the most detestable kind of monks, who with no experience to guide them, no rule to try them *as gold is tried in a furnace* (Prov 27:21), have a character

---

de Vogüé "*Sub regula vel abbate*: A Study of the Theological Significance of the Ancient Monastic Rules" *Rule and Life: An Interdisciplinary Symposium*, ed. M. B. Pennington (Spencer, Mass.: Cistercian Publications 1971) pp. 21–63. See Thematic Index: RULE.

1.3 "anchorites" (*anachoritarum*): The Latin word is a transliteration of the Greek *anachōrētēs*, which means: one who withdraws or retires. See Introduction, pp. 17–18.

"hermits" (*eremitarum*): The Latin word comes from the Greek *erēmitēs*, meaning: one who lives in the desert (*erēmos*). In RB, RM and Cassian, the cenobitic life is viewed as the necessary preparation for the life of a hermit.

"monastic life" (*conversationis*): The term *conversio* in RM has been replaced here by *conversatio*. For a discussion of the meaning of the terms, see Appendix 5, pp. 459–463.

1.5 "of body and mind" (*carnis vel cogitationum*): The phrase may be rendered more literally: "of the flesh and of the thoughts." It does not derive from a Greek body-soul anthropology, nor does it represent two mutually distinct categories of vices. Both terms derive ultimately from New Testament usage, where both are used to cover a wide variety of vices. For the reference of "flesh," see Gal 5:19, and for "thoughts" (*dialogismoi* in Greek), see Mark 7:21 (Matt 15:19). Evagrius of Pontus had developed a theory of the eight principal "thoughts" (*logismoi*), which was transmitted to the West as the eight principal vices (Cassian. *inst.* 5,1) and became eventually better known as the seven capital sins. See Introduction, p. 39.

1.6 "sarabaites" (*sarabaitarum*): The term is of Coptic origin, where it did not originally have a pejorative connotation. See Appendix 1, p. 318, n. 39.

sicut aurum fornacis, sed in plumbi natura molliti, [7]adhuc operibus servantes saeculo fidem, mentiri Deo per tonsuram noscuntur. [8]Qui bini aut terni aut certe singuli sine pastore, non dominicis sed suis inclusi ovilibus, pro lege eis est desideriorum voluntas, [9]cum quicquid putaverint vel elegerint, hoc dicunt sanctum, et quod noluerint, hoc putant non licere.

[10]Quartum vero genus est monachorum quod nominatur gyrovagum, qui tota vita sua per diversas provincias ternis aut quaternis diebus per diversorum cellas hospitantur, [11]semper vagi et numquam stabiles, et propriis voluntatibus et gulae illecebris servientes, et per omnia deteriores sarabaitis.

[12]De quorum omnium horum miserrima conversatione melius est silere quam loqui. [13]His ergo omissis, ad coenobitarum fortissimum genus disponendum, adiuvante Domino, veniamus.

II. QUALIS DEBEAT ESSE ABBAS

[1]Abbas qui praeesse dignus est monasterio semper meminere

1.9 Aug. *c.Parm.* 2,13,31; Aug. *c.Cresc.* 4,37.
1.10-11 Aug. *op.mon.* 36; Aug. *in psalm.* 132,3.
1.11 Leo.M. *tract.* 39,1; 42,4; Cassian. *inst.* 10,6; *Vitae patr.*, *Verb.senior.* 5, 14,10.
1.12 Cypr. *ad Demet.* 1; *Hist.mon.* 7; Hier. *epist.* 58,8 (cf. 77, 17).
1.13 Hier. *epist.* 22,35.
2.1-2 Cypr. *zel. et liv.* 12.

"no experience to guide them" (*experientia magistra*): The juxtaposition of "rule" and "experience" suggests that the experience by which the monk should be taught is not only his own but that of teachers as well. The sarabaites lack a rule and a teacher, while the cenobites have both (RB 1.2). The quotation "as gold is tried in a furnace" can be found in Prov 27:21, Sir 2:5 and Wis 3:6.

1.7 "tonsure" (*tonsuram*): Although it has been suggested that the origin of the tonsure is to be found in the Eastern custom of cutting the hair of slaves and that the monks did this to identify themselves as slaves of Christ, the evidence is uncertain and the origins of the custom remain obscure. It does not seem to belong to the earliest monastic tradition. Cassian does not mention it as an Egyptian practice or when describing the sarabaites. It seems to have been of rather recent origin in the time of RM and RB. The Roman practice, to which this is presumably an allusion, was, at this period, not to shave the head but simply to cut the hair short. Given the role that hair has always played in the fashions of society, it may reasonably be conjectured that a motive for the development of the practice lay in the desire to combat vanity. The recurrent aversion, on ascetical grounds, to bathing (RB 36.8) may also have provided hygienic reasons. The most thorough treatment of the evidence is by H. Leclercq "Tonsure" *DACL* 15.2430–43, who also provides the best information on the related area of facial hair, "Barbe" *DACL* 2.478–493.

as soft as lead. [7]Still loyal to the world by their actions, they clearly lie to God by their tonsure. [8]Two or three together, or even alone, without a shepherd, they pen themselves up in their own sheepfolds, not the Lord's. Their law is what they like to do, whatever strikes their fancy. [9]Anything they believe in and choose, they call holy; anything they dislike, they consider forbidden.

[10]Fourth and finally, there are the monks called gyrovagues, who spend their entire lives drifting from region to region, staying as guests for three or four days in different monasteries. [11]Always on the move, they never settle down, and are slaves to their own wills and gross appetites. In every way they are worse than sarabaites.

[12]It is better to keep silent than to speak of all these and their disgraceful way of life. [13]Let us pass them by, then, and with the help of the Lord, proceed to draw up a plan for the strong kind, the cenobites.

CHAPTER 2. QUALITIES OF THE ABBOT

[1]To be worthy of the task of governing a monastery, the abbot must always remember what his title signifies and act as a

---

1.10 "gyrovagues" (gyrovagum): This word is a mongrel formation from the Greek gūros (circle) and the Latin vagari (to wander). RM is the first to use this term. Perhaps it is fervor novicius that makes the Master go on for sixty-two verses about these wretched men whom St. Benedict dismisses in two.

1.13 "the strong kind" (fortissimum genus): It seems unlikely, though not altogether impossible, that fortissimum is a true superlative, meaning the 'strongest' of the four. The Latin superlative, even in classical times, could mean no more than 'very strong' and by the sixth century is often no more forceful than the positive forte. It is unlikely, given the context of vv. 3-5 and the authority of the tradition (Cassian. conl. 19, passim), that St. Benedict is expressing a preference for cenobites. The order of the four types is one not of preference but of supposed historical emergence, and this is based on Cassian's theory of the apostolic origins of cenobitism (Cassian. conl. 18). Note further that the use of fortis in RB 18.16, of the longer (fortiores) psalms, and in 70.6 of older (fortiori aetate) men, suggests that the idea "numerically stronger" may also have been at the back of the author's mind here.

2.1 "abbot" (Abbas): The word almost certainly derives from the Aramaic abba, meaning 'father' (Mark 14:36; Rom 8:15; Gal 4:6). For further discussion of the word and of this chapter generally, see Appendix 2, pp. 322f.

debet quod dicitur et nomen maioris factis implere. [2]Christi
enim agere vices in monasterio creditur, quando ipsius vocatur
pronomine, [3]dicente apostolo: *Accepistis spiritum adoptionis
filiorum, in quo clamamus: abba, pater.* [4]Ideoque abbas nihil
extra praeceptum Domini quod sit debet aut docere aut constituere vel iubere, [5]sed iussio eius vel doctrina fermentum divinae iustitiae in discipulorum mentibus conspargatur, [6]memor
semper abbas quia doctrinae suae vel discipulorum oboedientiae, utrarumque rerum, in tremendo iudicio Dei facienda erit
discussio. [7]Sciatque abbas culpae pastoris incumbere quicquid
in ovibus paterfamilias utilitatis minus potuerit invenire. [8]Tan-
tundem iterum erit ut, si inquieto vel inoboedienti gregi pastoris
fuerit omnis diligentia attributa et morbidis earum actibus universa fuerit cura exhibita, [9]pastor eorum in iudicio Domini absolutus dicat cum propheta Domino: *Iustitiam tuam non
abscondi in corde meo, veritatem tuam et salutare tuum dixi;
ipsi autem contemnentes spreverunt me,* [10]et tunc demum inoboedientibus curae suae ovibus poena sit eis praevalens ipsa
mors.

[11]Ergo, cum aliquis suscipit nomen abbatis, duplici debet doctrina suis praeesse discipulis, [12]id est omnia bona et sancta factis
amplius quam verbis ostendat, ut capacibus discipulis mandata
Domini verbis proponere, duris corde vero et simplicioribus factis suis divina praecepta monstrare. [13]Omnia vero quae discipulis
docuerit esse contraria in suis factis indicet non agenda, *ne aliis*

2.4 Basil. *reg.* 15.
2.12 Orsiesii *lib.* 9 et 13; Caes.Arel. *epist. ad virg.* 4.
2.12-13 Cypr. *zel. et liv.* 12.

"superior" (*maioris*): The "title" in question is *maior.* There is a play in Latin,
partly carried over into English, on the comparative form *maior* suggesting that
more exemplary (superior) conduct is demanded of the abbot. In this translation,
maior, when used of the abbot (cf. 5.4,15; 7.34), is rendered "superior," as is also
prior (see note on 6.7).

2.2 "to hold the place of" (*agere vices*): This Latin phrase is possibly a
theatrical metaphor meaning, like *partes agere,* "to take the role of." See Appendix 2, p. 350.

"a title of Christ" (*ipsius. . .pronomine*): The biblical text invoked here does
not actually give the title *abba* to Christ but to God the Father. For a discussion of
how Christ came to be regarded as father, see Appendix 2, pp. 356–363.

2.5 "leaven" (*fermentum*): The image is probably drawn from Matt 13:33 and
identifies the teaching of the abbot with the divine precepts.

2.6 "Let the abbot always remember" (*memor semper abbas*): *Memor* is being
treated here virtually as a present participle. (Cf. note on Prol.25). In RB it is

superior should. [2]He is believed to hold the place of Christ in the monastery, since he is addressed by a title of Christ, [3]as the Apostle indicates: *You have received the spirit of adoption of sons by which we exclaim, abba, father* (Rom 8:15). [4]Therefore, the abbot must never teach or decree or command anything that would deviate from the Lord's instructions. [5]On the contrary, everything he teaches and commands should, like the leaven of divine justice, permeate the minds of his disciples. [6]Let the abbot always remember that at the fearful judgment of God, not only his teaching but also his disciples' obedience will come under scrutiny. [7]The abbot must, therefore, be aware that the shepherd will bear the blame wherever the father of the household finds that the sheep have yielded no profit. [8]Still, if he has faithfully shepherded a restive and disobedient flock, always striving to cure their unhealthy ways, it will be otherwise: [9]the shepherd will be acquitted at the Lord's judgment. Then, like the Prophet, he may say to the Lord: *I have not hidden your justice in my heart; I have proclaimed your truth and your salvation* (Ps 39[40]:11), *but they spurned and rejected me* (Isa 1:2; Ezek 20:27). [10]Then at last the sheep that have rebelled against his care will be punished by the overwhelming power of death.

[11]Furthermore, anyone who receives the name of abbot is to lead his disciples by a twofold teaching: [12]he must point out to them all that is good and holy more by example than by words, proposing the commandments of the Lord to receptive disciples with words, but demonstrating God's instructions to the stubborn and the dull by a living example. [13]Again, if he teaches his disciples that something is not to be done, then neither must he do it, *lest after preaching to others, he himself be found reprobate*

---

sometimes followed by a genitive, as in classical Latin (2.26; 31.16), sometimes by a direct object (4.61; 7.11; 31.8 and probably 19.3).

2.7 "father of the household" (*paterfamilias*): This word occurs only once in RB. While Abbot Herwegen saw comparisons between the Roman *paterfamilias* and the abbot of the monastery, it seems better to understand the term according to biblical and monastic tradition. It is Christ, not the abbot, who is the *paterfamilias*. See Appendix 2, pp. 351–352.

2.8 "to cure" (*cura*): The metaphor is medical, as in RB 28. See Appendix 2, p. 352, and Thematic Index: CARE and CONCERN.

2.13 "reprobate" (reprobus): The Greek word (*adokimos*) translated by *reprobus* in 1 Cor 9:27 can mean "disqualified" and could then be understood as a continuation of the boxing imagery used in 1 Cor 9:26. But the question here, as always in similar passages in RB, is not how modern scholars interpret the phrase but how the ancient writer understood the text.

praedicans ipse reprobus inveniatur, [14]ne quando illi dicat Deus
peccanti: *Quare tu enarras iustitias meas et assumis testamentum meum per os tuum? Tu vero odisti disciplinam et proiecisti
sermones meos post te,* [15]et: *Qui in fratris tui oculo festucam
videbas, in tuo trabem non vidisti.*

[16]Non ab eo persona in monasterio discernatur. [17]Non unus
plus ametur quam alius, nisi quem in bonis actibus aut oboedientia invenerit meliorem. [18]Non convertenti ex servitio praeponatur ingenuus, nisi alia rationabilis causa exsistat. [19]Quod si
ita, iustitia dictante, abbati visum fuerit, et de cuiuslibet ordine
id faciet. Sin alias, propria teneant loca, [20]quia *sive servus sive
liber, omnes in Christo unum sumus* et sub uno Domino
aequalem servitutis militiam baiulamus, quia *non est apud
Deum personarum acceptio.* [21]Solummodo in hac parte apud
ipsum discernimur, si meliores ab aliis in operibus bonis et
humiles inveniamur. [22]Ergo aequalis sit ab eo omnibus caritas,
una praebeatur in omnibus secundum merita disciplina.

[23]In doctrina sua namque abbas apostolicam debet illam
semper formam servare in qua dicit: *Argue, obsecra, increpa,*
[24]id est, miscens temporibus tempora, terroribus blandimenta,
dirum magistri, pium patris ostendat affectum, [25]id est indisciplinatos et inquietos debet durius arguere, oboedientes autem et
mites et patientes ut in melius proficiant obsecrare, neglegentes
et contemnentes ut increpat et corripiat admonemus.

2.16-17 *Reg. iv patr.* 5,11-12; Cassian. *conl.* 16,14,4; Orsiesii *lib.* 9 et 16.
2.16-22 Caes.Arel. *epist. ad virg.* 4.
2.18 *Digesta* 41,2,20.
2.20 Ambr. *epist.* 63,85; Cypr. *domin.orat.* 23.
2.22 Vigil. *reg.(orient.)* 1.
2.23-24 *Reg. iv patr.* 2,5-7.
2.25 Basil. *reg.* 98.

(1 Cor 9:27) [14]and God some day call to him in his sin: *How is it that you repeat my just commands and mouth my covenant when you hate discipline and toss my words behind you* (Ps 49[50]:16-17)? [15]And also this: *How is it that you can see a splinter in your brother's eye, and never notice the plank in your own* (Matt 7:3)?

[16]The abbot should avoid all favoritism in the monastery. [17]He is not to love one more than another unless he finds someone better in good actions and obedience. [18]A man born free is not to be given higher rank than a slave who becomes a monk, except for some other good reason. [19]But the abbot is free, if he sees fit, to change anyone's rank as justice demands. Ordinarily, everyone is to keep to his regular place, [20]because *whether slave or free, we are all one in Christ* (Gal 3:28; Eph 6:8) and share alike in bearing arms in the service of the one Lord, for *God shows no partiality among persons* (Rom 2:11). [21]Only in this are we distinguished in his sight: if we are found better than others in good works and in humility. [22]Therefore, the abbot is to show equal love to everyone and apply the same discipline to all according to their merits.

[23]In his teaching, the abbot should always observe the Apostle's recommendation, in which he says: *Use argument, appeal, reproof* (2 Tim 4:2). [24]This means that he must vary with circumstances, threatening and coaxing by turns, stern as a taskmaster, devoted and tender as only a father can be. [25]With the undisciplined and restless, he will use firm argument; with the obedient and docile and patient, he will appeal for greater virtue; but as for the negligent and disdainful, we charge him to use reproof

---

2.17 "and obedience" (*aut oboedientia*): The rest of vv. 16-17 is borrowed from RM, but these two words are, significantly, original to RB.

2.20 "*whether slave or free. . .*"(sive servus sive liber. . .): The quotation is a conflation of Eph 6:8 and Gal 3:28. Cf. RB 7.65 for another example of this kind of conflation.

"bearing" (*baiulamus*): In the Vulgate this word is used of Jesus carrying the cross in John 19:17.

2.21 "in good works and in humility" (*in operibus bonis et humiles*): These words are an addition of RB to RM.

2.22 "according to their merits" (*secundum merita*): These words are likewise an addition of RB to RM.

"discipline" (*disciplina*): See Appendix 4, pp. 434–435, and Thematic Index: DISCIPLINE.

²⁶Neque dissimulet peccata delinquentium; sed et mox ut coeperint oriri radicitus ea ut praevalet amputet, memor periculi Heli sacerdotis de Silo. ²⁷Et honestiores quidem atque intellegibiles animos prima vel secunda admonitione verbis corripiat, ²⁸improbos autem et duros ac superbos vel inoboedientes verberum vel corporis castigatio in ipso initio peccati coerceat, sciens scriptum: *Stultus verbis non corrigitur*, ²⁹et iterum: *Percute filium tuum virga et liberabis animam eius a morte.*

³⁰Meminere debet semper abbas quod est, meminere quod dicitur, et scire quia cui plus committitur, plus ab eo exigitur.

³¹Sciatque quam difficilem et arduam rem suscipit regere animas et multorum servire moribus, et alium quidem blandimentis, alium vero increpationibus, alium suasionibus; ³²et secundum uniuscuiusque qualitatem vel intellegentiam, ita se omnibus conformet et aptet ut non solum detrimenta gregis sibi commissi non patiatur, verum in augmentatione boni gregis gaudeat. ³³Ante omnia, ne dissimulans aut parvipendens salutem animarum sibi commissarum, ne plus gerat sollicitudinem de rebus transitoriis et terrenis atque caducis, ³⁴sed semper cogitet quia animas suscepit regendas, de quibus et rationem redditurus est. ³⁵Et ne causetur de minori forte substantia, meminerit scriptum: *Primum quaerite regnum Dei et iustitiam eius, et haec omnia adicientur vobis*, ³⁶et iterum: *Nihil deest timentibus eum.*

2.26 Cassian. *conl.* 16,6,4; 16,20.
2.30 Cypr. *zel. et liv.* 12; Ambr. *apol.Dav.* 51; Aug. *quaest. in Hept.* 3,31; Hier. *epist.* 14,9.
2.31 Cypr. *ad Fort.* 11.
2.32 *Sacr.Gelasianum* 38; Orsiesii *lib.* 17.
2.33 Aug. *civ.* 22,2; Aug. *serm.* 113,6; Cassian. *conl.* 9,24; 16,9.
2.34 Aug. *epist.* 211,15.

and rebuke. [26] He should not gloss over the sins of those who err, but cut them out while he can, as soon as they begin to sprout, remembering the fate of Eli, priest of Shiloh (1 Sam 2:11–4:18). [27] For upright and perceptive men, his first and second warnings should be verbal; [28] but those who are evil or stubborn, arrogant or disobedient, he can curb only by blows or some other physical punishment at the first offense. It is written, *The fool cannot be corrected with words* (Prov 29:19); [29] and again, *Strike your son with a rod and you will free his soul from death* (Prov 23:14).

[30] The abbot must always remember what he is and remember what he is called, aware that more will be expected of a man to whom more has been entrusted. [31] He must know what a difficult and demanding burden he has undertaken: directing souls and serving a variety of temperaments, coaxing, reproving and encouraging them as appropriate. [32] He must so accommodate and adapt himself to each one's character and intelligence that he will not only keep the flock entrusted to his care from dwindling, but will rejoice in the increase of a good flock. [33] Above all, he must not show too great concern for the fleeting and temporal things of this world, neglecting or treating lightly the welfare of those entrusted to him. [34] Rather, he should keep in mind that he has undertaken the care of souls for whom he must give an account. [35] That he may not plead lack of resources as an excuse, he is to remember what is written: *Seek first the kingdom of God and his justice, and all these things will be given you as well* (Matt 6:33), [36] and again, *Those who fear him lack nothing* (Ps 33[34]:10).

2.28 "evil" (*improbos*): The root sense of *improbus* seems to be "not up to standard." From this derives a wide range of meanings. In a particular phrase some general term of reprobation, such as "evil," may be the best translation; or it may be necessary to supply from the context the particular tone needed, as in 23.5: "lacking in understanding" (from *intellegit* in 23.4), or "insensitivity" for *improbitate* in 52.3 (from the general tenor of the chapter).

"some other physical punishment" (*vel corporis castigatio*): E.g., fasting.

2.30 "what he is called" (*quod dicitur*): I.e., *abbas*. Cf. v.1 above.

"more will be expected of a man to whom more has been entrusted" (*cui plus committitur, plus ab eo exigitur*): Although the wording in the Vulgate is different (*cui commendaverunt multum, plus petent ab eo*), there is no doubt that this is a free citation of Luke 12:48 and even represents a stylistic improvement over the latter.

2.35 "excuse" (*causetur*): This seems to be the abbatial equivalent of *murmuratio*, and Benedict is severe on both excuses and grumbling.

[37]Sciatque quia qui suscipit animas regendas paret se ad rationem reddendam, [38]et quantum sub cura sua fratrum se habere scierit numerum, agnoscat pro certo quia in die iudicii ipsarum omnium animarum est redditurus Domino rationem, sine dubio addita et suae animae. [39]Et ita, timens semper futuram discussionem pastoris de creditis ovibus, cum de alienis ratiociniis cavet, redditur de suis sollicitus, [40]et cum de monitionibus suis emendationem aliis sumministrat ipse efficitur a vitiis emendatus.

III. DE ADHIBENDIS AD CONSILIUM FRATRIBUS

[1]Quotiens aliqua praecipua agenda sunt in monasterio, convocet abbas omnem congregationem et dicat ipse unde agitur, [2]et audiens consilium fratrum tractet apud se et quod utilius iudicaverit faciat. [3]Ideo autem omnes ad consilium vocari dixi-

---

2.38 Orsiesii *lib.* 11.
2.38-39 Cypr. *epist.* 57,4; Cypr. *ad Fort.* pr. 2.

2.38 "submit a reckoning to the Lord" (*redditurus Domino rationem*): There is a reference here to Heb 13:17, from which several words have been borrowed (*rationem pro animabus vestris reddituri*). See A. de Vogüé "*Semper cogitet quia rationem redditurus est* (RB 2.34 et 64.7). Benoît, le Maître, Augustin et l'Épître aux Hébreux" *Benedictina* 23 (1976) 1–7.

3.1 "the whole community" (*omnem congregationem*): The abbot is assisted by the advice of the community and the seniors. While RM attaches the material on consultation of the monks to chapter 2 (2.41-52), RB makes a separate chapter of it. The former speaks only of assembling the whole community (which is assumed to be small) and restricts the subject matter to questions of the temporal possessions of the monastery. RB, on the contrary, provides for a council of seniors for questions of less importance, so that the whole community need be consulted only on affairs of great importance. While it may be that St. Benedict, like RM, is thinking primarily of temporal administration, this is not evident in RB, and it seems more probable that he wishes to broaden the scope of the consultation. There is precedent in Pachomian and Basilian cenobitism for consultation of the seniors about monastic affairs, but there seems to be no earlier example of seeking the advice of the whole community. The concern of RM and of later rules about property decisions seems to reflect the viewpoint of Justinian's legislation giving communities a voice in matters regarding the ownership of temporalities. See M. Blecker "Roman Law and 'Consilium' in the *Regula Magistri* and the *Rule* of St. Benedict" *Speculum* 47 (1972) 1–28 and A. de Vogüé, *RBS* 2 (1973) 13*–18*.

The outlook of RB is different, therefore, and approaches the question from a more supernatural viewpoint. At first sight it may appear to be an exercise in

[37] The abbot must know that anyone undertaking the charge of souls must be ready to account for them. [38] Whatever the number of brothers he has in his care, let him realize that on judgment day he will surely have to submit a reckoning to the Lord for all their souls — and indeed for his own as well. [39] In this way, while always fearful of the future examination of the shepherd about the sheep entrusted to him and careful about the state of others' accounts, he becomes concerned also about his own, [40] and while helping others to amend by his warnings, he achieves the amendment of his own faults.

CHAPTER 3. SUMMONING THE BROTHERS FOR COUNSEL

[1] As often as anything important is to be done in the monastery, the abbot shall call the whole community together and himself explain what the business is; [2] and after hearing the advice of the brothers, let him ponder it and follow what he judges the wiser course. [3] The reason why we have said all should be called for counsel is that the Lord often reveals what is better to the

---

parliamentary democracy, but the mentality is actually quite different. It is clear that the role of the community or council is purely consultative — the decision remains with the abbot. The purpose of the consultation is not to ascertain the majority view, but to try to discern the will of God. If the abbot ordinarily does this through the Scriptures and the Rule and by the inspiration of the Holy Spirit, he is not the exclusive mediator of wisdom and must recognize that the Spirit may choose to speak to him through other channels. The monks, too, or perhaps only one of them — it may be the youngest of all — may receive an authentic inspiration. The abbot must be open to this possibility. His consultation, then, is not a matter of assembling human opinions, but of listening to all the sources through which the divine will may manifest itself, and then discerning which of these has made known an authentic communication of the Spirit. On the part of both monks and abbot, this process demands, not political techniques designed to ensure the acceptance of one's own view, but a genuine humility and self-effacement, and an opening of one's mind and heart to the mysterious action of God. It does not remove from the abbot the burden of decision, but assists him in discovering "the divine precepts" in regard to a particular decision.

On ch. 3, see de Vogüé, *La communauté*, pp. 187–206; "L'abbé et son conseil: cohérence du chapître second du Maître" *RBS* 3–4 (1974–75) 7–14; B. Steidle "Der Abt und der Rat der Brüder. Zu Kapitel 3 der Regel St. Benedikts" *EA* 52 (1976) 339–353; "Der Rat der Brüder nach der ältesten Regula Benedicti-Kommentaren des Abtes Smaragdus († um 826) und des Magisters Hildemar († um 850)" *ibid.* 53 (1977) 181–192.

See Thematic Index: COMMUNITY, corporate actions.

mus quia saepe iuniori Dominus revelat quod melius est. ⁴Sic autem dent fratres consilium cum omni humilitatis subiectione, et non praesumant procaciter defendere quod eis visum fuerit, ⁵et magis in abbatis pendat arbitrio, ut quod salubrius esse iudicaverit ei cuncti oboediant. ⁶Sed sicut discipulos convenit oboedire magistro, ita et ipsum provide et iuste condecet cuncta disponere.

⁷In omnibus igitur omnes magistram sequantur regulam, neque ab ea temere declinetur a quoquam. ⁸Nullus in monasterio proprii sequatur cordis voluntatem, ⁹neque praesumat quisquam cum abbate suo proterve aut foris monasterium contendere. ¹⁰Quod si praesumpserit, regulari disciplinae subiaceat. ¹¹Ipse tamen abbas cum timore Dei et observatione regulae omnia faciat, sciens se procul dubio de omnibus iudiciis suis aequissimo iudici Deo rationem redditurum.

¹²Si qua vero minora agenda sunt in monasterii utilitatibus, seniorum tantum utatur consilio, ¹³sicut scriptum est: *Omnia fac cum consilio et post factum non paeniteberis.*

IV. QUAE SUNT INSTRUMENTA BONORUM OPERUM

¹In primis *Dominum Deum diligere ex toto corde, tota anima, tota virtute;* ²deinde *proximum tamquam seipsum.* ³Deinde *non occidere,* ⁴*non adulterare,* ⁵*non facere furtum,* ⁶*non concupi-*

3.5 Cassian. *conl.* 24,26,14; Sulpic.Sever. *dial.* 1,10,1.
3.11 Cypr. *epist.* 16,3.
3.12 Cassian. *inst.* 7,9.
4.1 Aug. *ord.mon.* 1.
4.1-2 Cypr. *domin.orat.* 15;28.

3.3 "the younger" (*iuniori*): There may be an allusion here to Matt 11:25 (Luke 10:21). The junior in rank is often, but not necessarily, younger in age. Here the reference is probably to rank; so de Vogüé, *La communauté*, p. 202, n. 2.

3.6 "proper...becoming" (*convenit...condecet*): The same pair of words is used in RB 6.6.

3.9 "defiantly, or outside the monastery" (*proterve aut foris monasterium*): The Latin *proterve aut foris* is a curious phrase, and one that upset the copyists. As it stands, the sense seems to be that respectful disagreement is tolerable inside the monastery, but no sort of disagreement outside. However, the phrase *aut foris monasterium* seems to be better placed after *in monasterio* of v.8. It may have been a marginal note that came to be included in the text; so de Vogüé 1.454, nn.8-9.

3.10 "discipline of the rule" (*regulari disciplinae*): This is the first occurrence of the full phrase. See Appendix 4, pp. 434–435.

younger. ⁴The brothers, for their part, are to express their opinions with all humility, and not presume to defend their own views obstinately. ⁵The decision is rather the abbot's to make, so that when he has determined what is more prudent, all may obey. ⁶Nevertheless, just as it is proper for disciples to obey their master, so it is becoming for the master on his part to settle everything with foresight and fairness.

⁷Accordingly in every instance, all are to follow the teaching of the rule, and no one shall rashly deviate from it. ⁸In the monastery no one is to follow his own heart's desire, ⁹nor shall anyone presume to contend with his abbot defiantly, or outside the monastery. ¹⁰Should anyone presume to do so, let him be subjected to the discipline of the rule. ¹¹Moreover, the abbot himself must fear God and keep the rule in everything he does; he can be sure beyond any doubt that he will have to give an account of all his judgments to God, the most just of judges.

¹²If less important business of the monastery is to be transacted, he shall take counsel with the seniors only, ¹³as it is written: *Do everything with counsel and you will not be sorry afterward* (Sir 32:24).

CHAPTER 4. THE TOOLS FOR GOOD WORKS

¹First of all, *love the Lord God with your whole heart, your whole soul and all your strength,* ²*and love your neighbor as yourself* (Matt 22:37-39; Mark 12:30-31; Luke 10:27). ³Then the following: *You are not to kill,* ⁴*not to commit adultery;* ⁵*you are not to steal* ⁶*nor to covet* (Rom 13:9); ⁷*you are not to bear false*

3.12 "seniors" (*seniorum*): The seniors in rank are probably intended here. See Thematic Index: MONASTIC LEADERS.

4.t "Tools" (*Instrumenta*): It seems likely that this list, which St. Benedict has, with modifications, taken over from RM, has two principal earlier sources: an originally non-monastic catalogue of maxims, which has not been identified, and the *Passio Iuliani.* See de Vogüé 4.131-180. The non-monastic character of the original catalogue is indicated, for example, in the change introduced in RB 4.8 from honoring father and mother (RM 3.8) to honoring everyone. See note on 53.2. Evidently the earlier version was thought less applicable to monks, who are supposed to be withdrawing from the ties of family.

4.2 "*your neighbor as yourself*" (proximum tamquam seipsum): Although these and the following commands are to be found originally in the Pentateuch, it seems likely that the more immediate source of this portion of the list is the New Testament, where they are cited a number of times, especially since the list goes on to include a number of commands found only in the New Testament. See the Indexes of Scripture.

scere, [7]*non falsum testimonium dicere,* [8]*honorare omnes* homines, [9]et *quod sibi quis fieri non vult, alio ne faciat.*

[10]*Abnegare semetipsum* sibi ut *sequatur Christum.* [11]*Corpus castigare,* [12]delicias non amplecti, [13]ieiunium amare. [14]Pauperes recreare, [15]*nudum vestire,* [16]*infirmum visitare,* [17]mortuum sepelire. [18]In tribulatione subvenire, [19]dolentem consolari.

[20]Saeculi actibus se facere alienum, [21]nihil amori Christi praeponere. [22]Iram non perficere, [23]iracundiae tempus non reservare. [24]Dolum in corde non tenere, [25]pacem falsam non dare. [26]Caritatem non derelinquere. [27]Non iurare ne forte periuret, [28]veritatem ex corde et ore proferre.

[29]*Malum pro malo non reddere.* [30]Iniuriam non facere, sed et factas patienter sufferre. [31]*Inimicos diligere.* [32]Maledicentes se non remaledicere, sed magis benedicere. [33]*Persecutionem pro iustitia sustinere.*

[34]*Non esse superbum,* [35]*non vinolentum,* [36]non multum edacem, [37]non somnulentum, [38]*non pigrum,* [39]non murmuriosum, [40]non detractorem.

[41]Spem suam Deo committere. [42]Bonum aliquid in se cum viderit, Deo applicet, non sibi; [43]malum vero semper a se factum sciat et sibi reputet.

[44]Diem iudicii timere, [45]gehennam expavescere, [46]vitam aeternam omni concupiscentia spiritali desiderare, [47]mortem

---

4.9 Cypr. *domin.orat.* 28.

4.10 Ambr. *paenit.* 2,96-97; *Hist.mon.* 31; *Passio Iulian. et Bas.* 46; Cypr. *domin.orat.* 15.

4.13-15 *Passio Iulian. et Bas.* 46.

4.16 Cypr. *de pat.* 24; Cypr. *testim.* 109.

4.17 *Hist.mon.* 9.

4.20-23 *Passio Iulian. et Bas.* 46.

4.21 **Vita Anton.** 14; Cypr. *domin.orat.* 15; Cypr. *testim.* 3,18.

4.22 Hier. *epist.* 79,9; 130,13.

4.25 Cypr. *domin.orat.* 15; Cypr. *epist.* 59,13.

4.26 Cypr. *domin.orat.* 15.

4.27 Cypr. *testim.* 3,12; Ambr. *exhort.virg.* 74; Aug. *epist.* 157,40; Aug. *de mend.* 15,28.

4.29 Hier. *epist.* 81,1; *Passio Iulian. et Bas.* 46; Cypr. *de pat.* 16; Cypr. *testim.* 23.

4.30 Cypr. *testim.* 22; 106; Cypr. *domin.orat.* 15; Ps-Macar. *reg.* 21; Cassian. *inst.* 4,39,2.

4.31 Cypr. *domin.orat.* 17; Cypr. *de pat.* 24; Cypr. *testim.* 49.

4.32 Cypr. *testim.* 13-14.

4.42-43 Porphyr. *ad Marcell.* 12; Aug. *serm.* 96,2; Aug. *serm.* Morin Guelf. 22,5; Aug. *tract. in Ioan.* 43,1; Aug. *in psalm.* 25,11; Sext.Pythag. *enchirid.* 113-114; Cypr. *domin.orat.* 15.

witness (Matt 19:18; Mark 10:19; Luke 18:20). [8]*You must honor everyone* (1 Pet 2:17), [9]and *never do to another what you do not want done to yourself* (Tob 4:16; Matt 7:12; Luke 6:31).

[10]*Renounce yourself in order to follow Christ* (Matt 16:24; Luke 9:23); [11]*discipline your body* (1 Cor 9:27); [12]do not pamper yourself, [13]but love fasting. [14]You must relieve the lot of the poor, [15]*clothe the naked,* [16]*visit the sick* (Matt 25:36), [17]and bury the dead. [18]Go to help the troubled [19]and console the sorrowing.

[20]Your way of acting should be different from the world's way; [21]the love of Christ must come before all else. [22]You are not to act in anger [23]or nurse a grudge. [24]Rid your heart of all deceit. [25]Never give a hollow greeting of peace [26]or turn away when someone needs your love. [27]Bind yourself to no oath lest it prove false, [28]but speak the truth with heart and tongue.

[29]*Do not repay one bad turn with another* (1 Thess 5:15; 1 Pet 3:9). [30]Do not injure anyone, but bear injuries patiently. [31]*Love your enemies* (Matt 5:44; Luke 6:27). [32]If people curse you, do not curse them back but bless them instead. [33]*Endure persecution for the sake of justice* (Matt 5:10).

[34]You must *not be proud,* [35]*nor be given to wine* (Titus 1:7; 1 Tim 3:3). [36]Refrain from too much eating [37]or sleeping, [38]and *from laziness* (Rom 12:11). [39]Do not grumble [40]or speak ill of others.

[41]Place your hope in God alone. [42]If you notice something good in yourself, give credit to God, not to yourself, [43]but be certain that the evil you commit is always your own and yours to acknowledge.

[44]Live in fear of judgment day [45]and have a great horror of hell. [46]Yearn for everlasting life with holy desire. [47]Day by day re-

---

4.17 "bury the dead" (*mortuum sepelire*): The commands of vv.17-28 are for the most part based on a very diverse set of spiritual loci. The same holds true for most of the items that are not direct quotations in the rest of this chapter. See the Indexes of Scripture.

4.21 "the love of Christ" (*amori Christi*): See Thematic Index: CHRIST, love of.

4.32 "but bless them instead" (*sed magis benedicere*): This whole verse, while not an exact quotation of any one, clearly echoes several New Testament loci: Luke 6:28; 1 Cor 4:12; 1 Pet 3:9.

4.42 "give credit to God" (*Deo applicet*): This verse and the following one may be taken as additional evidence of the orthodox position of the RB in comparison with the semi-Pelagian doctrine that attributed some good to man unaided by grace. See note on Prol.4 above.

cotidie ante oculos suspectam habere. [48]Actus vitae suae omni hora custodire, [49]in omni loco Deum se respicere pro certo scire. [50]Cogitationes malas cordi suo advenientes mox ad Christum allidere et seniori spiritali patefacere, [51]os suum a malo vel pravo eloquio custodire, [52]multum loqui non amare, [53]verba vana aut risui apta non loqui, [54]risum multum aut excussum non amare.

[55]Lectiones sanctas libenter audire, [56]orationi frequenter incumbere, [57]mala sua praeterita cum lacrimis vel gemitu cotidie in oratione Deo confiteri, [58]de ipsis malis de cetero emendare.

[59]*Desideria carnis non efficere*, [60]voluntatem propriam odire, [61]praeceptis abbatis in omnibus oboedire, etiam si ipse aliter— quod absit—agat, memores illud dominicum praeceptum: *Quae dicunt facite, quae autem faciunt facere nolite.*

[62]Non velle dici sanctum antequam sit, sed prius esse quod verius dicatur. [63]Praecepta Dei factis cotidie adimplere, [64]castitatem amare, [65]nullum odire, [66]zelum non habere, [67]invidiam non exercere, [68]contentionem non amare, [69]elationem fugere. [70]Et seniores venerare, [71]iuniores diligere. [72]In Christi amore pro inimicis orare; [73]cum discordante ante solis occasum in pacem redire.

[74]Et de Dei misericordia numquam desperare.

4.47 *Vitae patr., Verb.senior.* 3,196; 5,3,5; 7,35,1; Cassian. *inst.* 12,25; Cassian. *conl.* 16,6.

4.49 Cypr. *domin.orat.* 4; Cypr. *zel. et liv.* 18.

4.50 Cassian. inst. 4,9 (cf. 37); Evagr. *sent.mon.* 1,55; *Vitae patr., Verb.senior.* 5,4,25.

4.52 Cypr. *testim.* 103.

4.53 Cypr. *testim.* 41; Cypr. *domin.orat.* 15.

4.54 Basil. *reg.* 17.

4.55 Hier. *epist.* 58,5 et 60,10.

4.55-56 Cypr. *epist.* 11,1,5; 38,2; 60,5; 65,1; Cypr. *domin.orat.* 29; 31; 35; Cypr. *ad Don.* 15; Cypr. *zel. et liv.* 16.

4.56 Cypr. *testim.* 120; Hier. *epist.* 58,6; Cassian. *conl.* 9,36; Cassian. *inst.* 2,10,3.

4.57 Cassian. *conl.* 20,6-7.

4.60 Cypr. *testim.* 19.

4.61 Cypr. *de pat.* 24; Cypr. *epist.* 72,1.

4.62 Sulpic.Sever. *epist. ii ad soror.* 17; *Passio Iulian. et Bas.* 46.

4.62-63 Cypr. *domin.orat.* 15.

4.65 *Didache* 2,7.

4.66-67 Cypr. *zel. et liv.* 10.

4.70 Stob. *flor.* 3,1,173.

4.70-71 Clem. *ad Cor.* 3.

4.72 Cypr. *domin.orat.* 15.

4.74 Cypr. *de laps.* 35; Cypr. *domin.orat.* 15.

mind yourself that you are going to die. [48]Hour by hour keep careful watch over all you do, [49]aware that God's gaze is upon you, wherever you may be. [50]As soon as wrongful thoughts come into your heart, dash them against Christ and disclose them to your spiritual father. [51]Guard your lips from harmful or deceptive speech. [52]Prefer moderation in speech [53]and speak no foolish chatter, nothing just to provoke laughter; [54]do not love immoderate or boisterous laughter.

[55]Listen readily to holy reading, [56]and devote yourself often to prayer. [57]Every day with tears and sighs confess your past sins to God in prayer [58]and change from these evil ways in the future.

[59]*Do not gratify the promptings of the flesh* (Gal 5:16); [60]hate the urgings of self-will. [61]Obey the orders of the abbot unreservedly, even if his own conduct—which God forbid—be at odds with what he says. Remember the teaching of the Lord: *Do what they say, not what they do* (Matt 23:3).

[62]Do not aspire to be called holy before you really are, but first be holy that you may more truly be called so. [63]Live by God's commandments every day; [64]treasure chastity, [65]harbor neither hatred [66]nor jealousy of anyone, [67]and do nothing out of envy. [68]Do not love quarreling; [69]shun arrogance. [70]Respect the elders [71]and love the young. [72]Pray for your enemies out of love for Christ. [73]If you have a dispute with someone, make peace with him before the sun goes down.

[74]And finally, never lose hope in God's mercy.

4.50 "dash them against Christ" (*ad Christum allidere*): See note on Prol.28 above.

4.54 "immoderate or boisterous laughter" (*risum multum aut excussum*): That St. Benedict does not forbid all laughter is clear from this verse and from 49.7, where he recommends giving up some talking and joking during Lent. He seems to forbid laughter that is out of control and over subjects inappropriate in monastic life.

4.56 "prayer" (*orationi*): Actually the ritual action of prostration is suggested by the phrase. See A. de Vogüé "*Orationi frequenter incumbere*. Une invitation à la prière continuelle" *RAM* 41 (1965) 467–472.

4.58 "change" (*emendare*): On the usage of this word in RB, see note on 43.7 and Appendix 4, p. 435.

4.65 "harbor neither hatred. . .of anyone" (*nullum odire*): See A. de Vogüé "'Ne haïr personne.' Jalons pour l'histoire d'une maxime" *RAM* 44 (1968) 3–9.

[75]Ecce haec sunt instrumenta artis spiritalis. [76]Quae cum fuerint a nobis die noctuque incessabiliter adimpleta et in die iudicii reconsignata, illa merces nobis a Domino recompensabitur quam ipse promisit: [77]*Quod oculus non vidit nec auris audivit, quae praeparavit Deus his qui diligunt illum.*

[78]Officina vero ubi haec omnia diligenter operemur claustra sunt monasterii et stabilitas in congregatione.

V. DE OBOEDIENTIA

[1]Primus humilitatis gradus est oboedientia sine mora. [2]Haec convenit his qui nihil sibi a Christo carius aliquid existimant. [3]Propter servitium sanctum quod professi sunt seu propter metum gehennae vel gloriam vitae aeternae, [4]mox aliquid imperatum a maiore fuerit, ac si divinitus imperetur moram pati nesciant in faciendo. [5]De quibus Dominus dicit: *Obauditu auris oboedivit mihi.* [6]Et item dicit doctoribus: *Qui vos audit me audit.* [7]Ergo hi tales, relinquentes statim quae sua sunt et volun-

---

4.75 Cassian. *conl.* 1,7.
5.4 Cassian. *inst.* 4,10; 4,24,4; 12,32, 2; Pachom. *reg.* 30.
5.7 Cassian. *inst.* 4,8.
5.7-10 Cassian. *inst.* 4,12.

4.76 "returned" (*reconsignata*): The metaphor of "tools" is being continued here by analogy with the kitchen utensils. See 35.10, where the same word is used in reference to the latter.

4.78 "enclosure" (*claustra*): See note on 67.7

"stability" (*stabilitas*): For the meaning of this term, see Appendix 5, pp. 463–465. See also Thematic Index: STABILITY.

5.0 "obedience" (*oboedientia*): See Appendix 5, pp. 458–459, and Thematic Index: OBEDIENCE.

5.1 "The first step" (*Primus. . .gradus*): How to reconcile this statement with 7.10, which states that the first step of humility is fear of God, has proved to be a classic difficulty in Benedictine exegesis, as is noted by de Vogüé, *La communauté*, p. 214. The solution suggested by the latter is a redactional one: the Master, when he wrote this chapter (RM 7), had the intention of writing the later chapter (RM 10) on humility, using the image of a ladder suggested by Cassian's use of the word *gradus*, but not developed by him (Cassian. *inst.* 4,38-39). The first several of Cassian's indices of humility involve obedience. When he composed ch. 7 (=RB 5), the Master was thinking of this. However, when he composed ch. 10 (=RB 7) on the basis of ladder imagery, he decided to expand the number of "steps" to twelve (from Cassian's ten indices) in order to include "fear of the Lord," which Cassian had mentioned before the indices as a "principle of our salvation." This the Master did in order to have a certain correspondence between the first step of the ladder and the top step, which is the love that casts

[75]These, then, are the tools of the spiritual craft. [76]When we have used them without ceasing day and night and have returned them on judgment day, our wages will be the reward the Lord has promised: [77]*What the eye has not seen nor the ear heard, God has prepared for those who love him* (1 Cor 2:9).

[78]The workshop where we are to toil faithfully at all these tasks is the enclosure of the monastery and stability in the community.

CHAPTER 5. OBEDIENCE

[1]The first step of humility is unhesitating obedience, [2]which comes naturally to those who cherish Christ above all. [3]Because of the holy service they have professed, or because of dread of hell and for the glory of everlasting life, [4]they carry out the superior's order as promptly as if the command came from God himself. [5]The Lord says of men like this: *No sooner did he hear than he obeyed me* (Ps 17[18]:45); [6]again, he tells teachers: *Whoever listens to you, listens to me* (Luke 10:16). [7]Such people as these immediately put aside their own concerns, abandon

---

out fear. For an otherwise blatant contradiction, this is the most plausible explanation.

5.2 "Christ above all" (*a Christo carius*): This is a curious sentence in Latin, containing as it does the use of *a* with an ablative of comparison (cf. Prol.19; 2.21; 10.3; 18.24; 55.14 and some Indo-Germanic languages such as Urdu), and a pleonastic *aliquid*.

5.3 "holy service" (*servitium sanctum*): Obedience is service of Christ in the school that is the monastery. See note to Prol.45 above. But "service" may implicitly refer to the image of military service as well. See note to Prol.3 above.

5.4 "from God himself" (*divinitus*): The idea that the superior's orders represent a divine command is based on the notion that the abbot holds the place of Christ (*Christi enim agere vices*, RB 2.2). In the following two verses and v.15, which are meant to support this idea, one may observe the tendency of this period to regard Christ simply as "God." See note on Prol.16 above.

5.7 "immediately" (*statim*): Vv. 7-8 clearly suggest the model of the disciples who put aside their nets immediately in order to follow Christ when he called them (Matt 4:22).

"own will" (*voluntatem propriam*): Monastic tradition extols the renunciation of one's own will as a fundamental ascetic practice based on the example of Christ himself (cf. RB 4.10) and as a way of heeding the voice of God through the superior's command. However, there are significant variations in the understanding of this practice. The passage in RM 2.36-37, which allows subjects, at the last judgment, to impute all actions done under obedience to their superior, is omitted in RB. See note on Prol.3 and Thematic Index: WILL.

tatem propriam deserentes, [8]mox exoccupatis manibus et quod agebant imperfectum relinquentes, vicino oboedientiae pede iubentis vocem factis sequuntur, [9]et veluti uno momento praedicta magistri iussio et perfecta discipuli opera, in velocitate timoris Dei, ambae res communiter citius explicantur.

[10]Quibus ad vitam aeternam gradiendi amor incumbit, [11]ideo angustam viam arripiunt—unde Dominus dicit: *Angusta via est quae ducit ad vitam*— [12]ut non suo arbitrio viventes vel desideriis suis et voluptatibus oboedientes, sed ambulantes alieno iudicio et imperio, in coenobiis degentes abbatem sibi praeesse desiderant. [13]Sine dubio hi tales illam Domini imitantur sententiam qua dicit: *Non veni facere voluntatem meam, sed eius qui misit me*.

[14]Sed haec ipsa oboedientia tunc acceptabilis erit Deo et dulcis hominibus, si quod iubetur non trepide, non tarde, non tepide, aut cum murmurio vel cum responso nolentis efficiatur, [15]quia oboedientia quae maioribus praebetur Deo exhibetur — ipse enim dixit: *Qui vos audit me audit*. [16]Et cum bono animo a discipulis praeberi oportet, quia *hilarem datorem diligit Deus*. [17]Nam, cum malo animo si oboedit discipulus et non solum ore sed etiam in corde si murmuraverit, [18]etiam si impleat iussionem, tamen acceptum iam non erit Deo qui cor eius respicit murmurantem, [19]et pro tali facto nullam consequitur gratiam; immo poenam murmurantium incurrit, si non cum satisfactione emendaverit.

5.10-11 Cypr. *epist.* 4-5.
5.12-13 Cassian. *conl.* 24,26,14; Cassian. *inst.* 4,15; Sulpic.Sever. *dial.* 1,10,1.
5.13 Cassian. *conl.* 16,6,4.
5.14 Aug. *cons.evang.* 1,13; Cassian. *conl.* 23,7,2; Cypr. *de mort.* 14; Cypr. *epist.* 63,1.
5.17-19 Aug. *ord.mon.* 5.

their own will, [8]and lay down whatever they have in hand, leaving it unfinished. With the ready step of obedience, they follow the voice of authority in their actions. [9]Almost at the same moment, then, as the master gives the instruction the disciple quickly puts it into practice in the fear of God; and both actions together are swiftly completed as one.

[10]It is love that impels them to pursue everlasting life; [11]therefore, they are eager to take the narrow road of which the Lord says: *Narrow is the road that leads to life* (Matt 7:14). [12]They no longer live by their own judgment, giving in to their whims and appetites; rather they walk according to another's decisions and directions, choosing to live in monasteries and to have an abbot over them. [13]Men of this resolve unquestionably conform to the saying of the Lord: *I have come not to do my own will, but the will of him who sent me* (John 6:38).

[14]This very obedience, however, will be acceptable to God and agreeable to men only if compliance with what is commanded is not cringing or sluggish or half-hearted, but free from any grumbling or any reaction of unwillingness. [15]For the obedience shown to superiors is given to God, as he himself said: *Whoever listens to you, listens to me* (Luke 10:16). [16]Furthermore, the disciples' obedience must be given gladly, for *God loves a cheerful giver* (2 Cor 9:7). [17]If a disciple obeys grudgingly and grumbles, not only aloud but also in his heart, [18]then, even though he carries out the order, his action will not be accepted with favor by God, who sees that he is grumbling in his heart. [19]He will have no reward for service of this kind; on the contrary, he will incur punishment for grumbling, unless he changes for the better and makes amends.

5.12 "their whims" (*desideriis suis*): An allusion here to Jude 16 seems likely.

5.14 "free from any grumbling" (*aut cum murmurio*): Apart from 4.39 in the list of "tools," this is the first occurrence of this key idea in the Rule. It is to be avoided "above all else" (40.9). St. Benedict sees grumbling as a grave danger to order in the community, and as a special threat to obedience and the ideal of mutual service. See Thematic Index: GRUMBLING.

5.16 "gladly" (*cum bono animo*): The words *bono animo* can be found in Sir 35:10 in a similar context. Indeed, the idea of 2 Cor 9:7 may be built on Sir 35:10. *Hilarem* (cheerful) occurs in both.

5.19 "punishment for grumbling" (*poenam murmurantium*): The punishment referred to here is that suffered by the Israelites in the desert. The immediate reference, however, seems to be 1 Cor 10:10, which in turn refers to Num 14:2,36 and 21:5.

VI. DE TACITURNITATE

[1]Faciamus quod ait propheta: *Dixi: Custodiam vias meas, ut non delinquam in lingua mea. Posui ori meo custodiam. Obmutui et humiliatus sum et silui a bonis.* [2]Hic ostendit propheta, si a bonis eloquiis interdum propter taciturnitatem debet taceri, quanto magis a malis verbis propter poenam peccati debet cessari. [3]Ergo, quamvis de bonis et sanctis et aedificationum eloquiis, perfectis discipulis propter taciturnitatis gravitatem rara loquendi concedatur licentia, [4]quia scriptum est: *In multiloquio non effugies peccatum,* [5]et alibi: *Mors et vita in manibus linguae.* [6]Nam loqui et docere magistrum condecet, tacere et audire discipulum convenit.

[7]Et ideo, si qua requirenda sunt a priore, cum omni humilitate et subiectione reverentiae requirantur. [8]Scurrilitates vero vel verba otiosa et risum moventia aeterna clausura in omnibus locis damnamus et ad talia eloquia discipulum aperire os non permittimus.

VII. DE HUMILITATE

[1]Clamat nobis scriptura divina, fratres, dicens: *Omnis qui se exaltat humiliabitur et qui se humiliat exaltabitur.* [2]Cum haec ergo dicit, ostendit nobis omnem exaltationem genus esse superbiae. [3]Quod se cavere propheta indicat dicens: *Domine, non est exaltatum cor meum neque elati sunt oculi mei, neque ambulavi*

6.3 Cassian. *inst.* 11,4.
6.6 Aug. *serm.* 211,5.

6.2 "out of esteem for silence" (*propter taciturnitatem*): There seems to be no significant difference in meaning between *taciturnitas* and *silentium*. St. Benedict urges actual silence and quiet, not just a spirit of silence. For a comprehensive treatment of the role of silence in the monastic tradition, including RB, see A. Wathen, *Silence: The Meaning of Silence in the Rule of St. Benedict* (Washington, D.C.: Cistercian Publications, Inc. 1973).
6.3 "mature disciples" (*perfectis discipulis*): The term *perfectus* as used in monastic circles and applied to a "disciple" probably derives from the New Testament (e.g., 1 Cor 2:6; 14:20), where it denotes maturity in faith, understanding and behavior. The Pauline usage reflects the terminology of moralists and popular profane use in which *perfectus* means 'adult,' in contrast to the *infans* or *parvulus* (cf. 1 Cor 14:20). This holds true also of the Greek *teleios*, of which *perfectus* is the Vulgate rendering. See J. Dupont, *Gnosis* (Bruges: Desclée de Brouwer 1949) p. 151, n. 1.

CHAPTER 6. RESTRAINT OF SPEECH

[1]Let us follow the Prophet's counsel: *I said, I have resolved to keep watch over my ways that I may never sin with my tongue. I have put a guard on my mouth. I was silent and was humbled, and I refrained even from good words* (Ps 38[39]:2-3). [2]Here the Prophet indicates that there are times when good words are to be left unsaid out of esteem for silence. For all the more reason, then, should evil speech be curbed so that punishment for sin may be avoided. [3]Indeed, so important is silence that permission to speak should seldom be granted even to mature disciples, no matter how good or holy or constructive their talk, [4]because it is written: *In a flood of words you will not avoid sin* (Prov 10:19); [5]and elsewhere, *The tongue holds the key to life and death* (Prov 18:21). [6]Speaking and teaching are the master's task; the disciple is to be silent and listen.

[7]Therefore, any requests to a superior should be made with all humility and respectful submission. [8]We absolutely condemn in all places any vulgarity and gossip and talk leading to laughter, and we do not permit a disciple to engage in words of that kind.

CHAPTER 7. HUMILITY

[1]Brothers, divine Scripture calls to us saying: *Whoever exalts himself shall be humbled, and whoever humbles himself shall be exalted* (Luke 14:11; 18:14). [2]In saying this, therefore, it shows us that every exaltation is a kind of pride, [3]which the Prophet indicates he has shunned, saying: *Lord, my heart is not*

The restrictions placed on speech even for the mature monk must be understood in reference to his role as disciple (v.6). This is somewhat clearer in the longer version of RM, where the monks are allowed to converse quietly if the abbot is absent but not if he is present or only with his permission, and then only to ask questions of him (RM 9.41-50). See Wathen, *Silence*, pp. 200–201.

6.7 "a superior" (*priore*): The word *prior* is used twelve times in RB to refer to the abbot. It is never used to designate the monastic official later known as the prior, who in RB is called *praepositus*. See note on 65.1.

6.8 "absolutely" (*aeterna clausura*): The image in Latin is that of enclosure. The mouth is like the door of an inner cloister. St. Benedict wants the door closed to certain kinds of speech. The Master (RM 9.41-51) develops the image more elaborately, allowing for degrees of enclosure.

7.0 See Thematic Index: HUMILITY.

7.2 "exaltation" (*exaltationem*): Throughout this chapter St. Benedict uses images of height and depth. The monk strives for the heights of heaven, but paradoxically they are reached by the opposite of exaltation, the lowliness of humility. See Thematic Index: PRIDE.

in magnis neque in mirabilibus super me. ⁴Sed quid *si non
humiliter sentiebam, si exaltavi animam meam?* — *sicut ablactatum super matrem suam, ita retribues in animam meam.*

⁵Unde, fratres, si summae humilitatis volumus culmen attingere et ad exaltationem illam caelestem ad quam per praesentis vitae humilitatem ascenditur volumus velociter pervenire,
⁶actibus nostris ascendentibus scala illa erigenda est quae in
somnio Iacob apparuit, *per quam ei descendentes et ascendentes
angeli* monstrabantur. ⁷Non aliud sine dubio descensus ille et
ascensus a nobis intellegitur nisi exaltatione descendere et
humilitate ascendere. ⁸Scala vero ipsa erecta nostra est vita in
saeculo, quae humiliato corde a Domino erigatur ad caelum.
⁹Latera enim eius scalae dicimus nostrum esse corpus et
animam, in qua latera diversos gradus humilitatis vel disciplinae
evocatio divina ascendendo inseruit.

¹⁰Primus itaque humilitatis gradus est si, *timorem Dei* sibi
ante oculos semper ponens, oblivionem omnino fugiat ¹¹et
semper sit memor omnia quae praecepit Deus, ut qualiter et
contemnentes Deum gehenna de peccatis incendat et vita
aeterna quae timentibus Deum praeparata est animo suo semper
evolvat. ¹²Et custodiens se omni hora a peccatis et vitiis, id est
cogitationum, linguae, manuum, pedum vel voluntatis propriae

7.5 *Hist.mon.* 31.
7.6-9 Hier. *epist.* 98,3; Basil. *in psalm.* 1,4; Ambr. *explan.ps.* 1,18; Chrom.
Aquil. *serm.* 1,6.
7.9 Cassian. *conl.* 14,2.
7.10 Cassian. *conl.* 11,7,13; Cassian. *inst.* 4,39,1.
7.10-11 Cypr. *epist.* 8,2; 58,11; 67,2; Cypr. *de op. et el.* 22.

7.4 *"a weaned child"* (ablactatum): Ps 130(131) is interpreted by modern
scholars as a picture of comfort and security, whereas in RB the picture is of God
threatening the monk who fails to be humble. Our question is what the psalm
meant to St. Benedict. The phrase *ablactatum super matrem suam* cannot mean
"weaned *from* its mother." It is rendered "sur sa mère" by de Vogüé, which must
be correct. Steidle has "das man [gewaltsam] von der Mutterbrust wegnimmt";
the insertion of "forcibly" is a tacit admission that something has gone wrong.
   Perhaps the picture is this: if the weaned child were humble, it would accept
without fuss the substitute for its mother's breast. If it does not have a humble
spirit, it will reach for the now forbidden breast, and so incur retribution.
7.6 *"ladder"* (*scala*): Christian authors frequently used the image of a ladder to
depict the return to God. The ladder image indicates that monks must work to
climb, that monastic life is an effort, though always pursued with the help of God.
See Thematic Index: PASCHAL MYSTERY, *Images.*
7.9 *"as we ascend"* (*ascendendo*): Some MSS read *ascendendos*, "rungs to be
climbed," which is certainly easier and is what de Vogüé ("pour qu'on les

exalted; my eyes are not lifted up and I have not walked in the ways of the great nor gone after marvels beyond me (Ps 130[131]:1). ⁴And why? *If I had not a humble spirit, but were exalted instead, then you would treat me like a weaned child on its mother's lap* (Ps 130[131]:2).

⁵Accordingly, brothers, if we want to reach the highest summit of humility, if we desire to attain speedily that exaltation in heaven to which we climb by the humility of this present life, ⁶then by our ascending actions we must set up that ladder on which Jacob in a dream saw *angels descending and ascending* (Gen 28:12). ⁷Without doubt, this descent and ascent can signify only that we descend by exaltation and ascend by humility. ⁸Now the ladder erected is our life on earth, and if we humble our hearts the Lord will raise it to heaven. ⁹We may call our body and soul the sides of this ladder, into which our divine vocation has fitted the various steps of humility and discipline as we ascend.

¹⁰The first step of humility, then, is that a man keeps the *fear of God* always *before his eyes* (Ps 35[36]:2) and never forgets it. ¹¹He must constantly remember everything God has commanded, keeping in mind that all who despise God will burn in hell for their sins, and all who fear God have everlasting life awaiting them. ¹²While he guards himself at every moment from sins and vices of thought or tongue, of hand or foot, of self-will or

gravisse") and Steidle ("die wir ersteigen sollen") seem to translate. McCann translates and prints *ascendendos*. On the other hand, the principle of text criticism *lectio difficilior potior* (the more difficult reading is preferable) supports *ascendendo*.

Although Latin does use a so-called dative of purpose and although this does occur with the gerund, none of the examples given by R. Kühner, *Ausführliche Grammatik der Lateinischen Sprache* (Hannover: Hahnsche Buchhandlung 1887–89) II.I, pp. 557–559, is really parallel to what we have here. It seems better to take *ascendendo* as ablative and translate it "as we ascend," even though the Latin is then a little muddled.

Ascendendos has reasonable MSS support and may after all be the true reading.

7.10 "first step" (*Primus. . .gradus*): *Gradus* means both 'step' and 'degree,' but the image of the ladder determines the question here. RM lists twelve steps of humility, while Cassian lists ten indices or signs of humility (Cassian. *inst.* 4,39), to some of which he also refers by the term *gradus*. Although Thomas Aquinas reversed the order (*Summa Theol.* II–II^{ae}, 161,6), the original order in the monastic tradition seems to have been intended to indicate a progression from the internal cultivation of humility to its external manifestations. See note on 5.1.

"before his eyes" (ante oculos): The image of keeping the fear of God before one's eyes may be found in Ps 35(36):2.

sed et desideria carnis, [13]aestimet se homo de caelis a Deo semper respici omni hora et facta sua omni loco ab aspectu divinitatis videri et ab angelis omni hora renuntiari.

[14]Demonstrans nobis hoc propheta, cum in cogitationibus nostris ita Deum semper praesentem ostendit dicens: *Scrutans corda et renes Deus*; [15]et item: *Dominus novit cogitationes hominum*; [16]et item dicit: *Intellexisti cogitationes meas a longe*; [17]et: *Quia cogitatio hominis confitebitur tibi.* [18]Nam ut sollicitus sit circa cogitationes suas perversas, dicat semper utilis frater in corde suo: *Tunc ero immaculatus coram eo* si *observavero me ab iniquitate mea.*

[19]Voluntatem vero propriam ita facere prohibemur cum dicit scriptura nobis: *Et a voluntatibus tuis avertere.* [20]Et item rogamus Deum in oratione ut *fiat illius voluntas in* nobis. [21]Docemur ergo merito nostram non facere voluntatem cum cavemus illud quod dicit sancta scriptura: *Sunt viae quae putantur ab hominibus rectae, quarum finis usque ad profundum inferni demergit,* [22]et cum item pavemus illud quod de neglegentibus dictum est: *Corrupti sunt et abominabiles facti sunt in voluntatibus suis.*

[23]In desideriis vero carnis ita nobis Deum credamus semper esse praesentem cum dicit propheta Domino: *Ante te est omne desiderium meum.* [24]Cavendum ergo ideo malum desiderium quia mors secus introitum delectationis posita est. [25]Unde scriptura praecepit dicens: *Post concupiscentias tuas non eas.*

[26]Ergo si *oculi Domini speculantur bonos et malos* [27]et *Dominus de caelo* semper *respicit super filios hominum, ut videat si est intellegens aut requirens Deum,* [28]et si ab angelis nobis deputatis cotidie die noctuque Domino factorum nostrorum opera nuntiantur, [29]cavendum est ergo omni hora, fratres, sicut dicit in psalmo propheta, ne nos *declinantes* in malo et *inutiles factos* aliqua hora aspiciat Deus [30]et, parcendo nobis in hoc

---

7.13 Cassian. *inst.* 5,9; *Visio Pauli* 7.

7.13-14 Cypr. *epist.* 76,7; Cypr. *zel. et liv.* 18; Cypr. *domin.orat.* 4; Cypr. *de laps.* 27.

7.20 Cypr. *domin.orat.* 14.

7.21 Cassian. *conl.* 20,9.

7.23 Cypr. *domin.orat.* 4.

7.24 Act.S.Sebast. 4,14.

7.26 Cypr. *domin.orat.* 4.

7.28 *Visio Pauli* 7 et 10.

bodily desire, [13]let him recall that he is always seen by God in heaven, that his actions everywhere are in God's sight and are reported by angels at every hour.

[14]The Prophet indicates this to us when he shows that our thoughts are always present to God, saying: *God searches hearts and minds* (Ps 7:10); [15]again he says: *The Lord knows the thoughts of men* (Ps 93[94]:11); [16]likewise, *From afar you know my thoughts* (Ps 138[139]:3); [17]and, *The thought of man shall give you praise* (Ps 75[76]:11). [18]That he may take care to avoid sinful thoughts, the virtuous brother must always say to himself: *I shall be blameless in his sight if I guard myself from my own wickedness* (Ps 17[18]:24).

[19]Truly, we are forbidden to do our own will, for Scripture tells us: *Turn away from your desires* (Sir 18:30). [20]And in the Prayer too we ask God that his *will be done* in us (Matt 6:10). [21]We are rightly taught not to do our own will, since we dread what Scripture says: *There are ways which men call right that in the end plunge into the depths of hell* (Prov 16:25). [22]Moreover, we fear what is said of those who ignore this: *They are corrupt and have become depraved in their desires* (Ps 13[14]:1).

[23]As for the desires of the body, we must believe that God is always with us, for *All my desires are known to you* (Ps 37[38]:10), as the Prophet tells the Lord. [24]We must then be on guard against any base desire, because death is stationed near the gateway of pleasure. [25]For this reason Scripture warns us, *Pursue not your lusts* (Sir 18:30).

[26]Accordingly, if *the eyes of the Lord are watching the good and the wicked* (Prov 15:3), [27]if at all times *the Lord looks down from heaven on the sons of men to see whether any understand and seek God* (Ps 13[14]:2); [28]and if every day the angels assigned to us report our deeds to the Lord day and night, [29]then, brothers, we must be vigilant every hour or, as the Prophet says in the psalm, God may observe us *falling* at some time into evil and *so made worthless* (Ps 13[14]:3). [30]After

---

7.13 "by God in heaven" (*de caelis a Deo*): This image seems to be taken from Ps 13(14):2 (*Dominus de caelo prospexit*).

7.18 "virtuous" (*utilis*): In RM and RB, this is a rather colorless word of approval.

7.21 "*ways*" (viae): This is a somewhat free citation of Prov 16:25, which actually speaks of "a way." The plural here may be due to attraction of the plural in the second half of Prov 14:12, which is the same saying.

tempore quia pius est et exspectat nos converti in melius, ne dicat nobis in futuro: *Haec fecisti et tacui.*

³¹Secundus humilitatis gradus est si propriam quis non amans voluntatem desideria sua non delectetur implere, ³²sed vocem illam Domini factis imitetur dicentis: *Non veni facere voluntatem meam, sed eius qui me misit.* ³³Item dicit scriptura: Voluntas habet poenam et necessitas parit coronam.

³⁴Tertius humilitatis gradus est ut quis pro Dei amore omni oboedientia se subdat maiori, imitans Dominum, de quo dicit apostolus: *Factus oboediens usque ad mortem.*

³⁵Quartus humilitatis gradus est si, in ipsa oboedientia duris et contrariis rebus vel etiam quibuslibet irrogatis iniuriis, tacite conscientia patientiam amplectatur ³⁶et sustinens non lassescat vel discedat, dicente scriptura: *Qui perseveraverit usque in finem, hic salvus erit;* ³⁷item: *Confortetur cor tuum et sustine Dominum.* ³⁸Et ostendens fidelem pro Domino universa etiam contraria sustinere debere, dicit ex persona sufferentium: *Propter te morte afficimur tota die, aestimati sumus ut oves occisionis.* ³⁹Et securi de spe retributionis divinae subsequuntur gaudentes et dicentes: *Sed in his omnibus superamus propter eum qui dilexit nos.* ⁴⁰Et item alio loco scriptura: *Probasti nos, Deus, igne nos examinasti sicut igne examinatur argentum; induxisti nos in laqueum; posuisti tribulationes in dorso nostro.* ⁴¹Et ut ostendat sub priore debere nos esse, subsequitur dicens: *Imposuisti homines super capita nostra.* ⁴²Sed et praeceptum Domini in adversis et iniuriis per patientiam adimplentes, qui

---

7.31-61 Cassian. inst. 4,39.
7.31-32 Basil. *reg.* 12; *Hist.mon.* 31; Cassian. *conl.* 24, 23.
7.32 Cassian. *conl.* 16,6,4; Cypr. *domin.orat.* 14.
7.33 **Acta Anastasiae** 17; Optat. 7,1.
7.34 Basil. *reg.* 65; Cassian. *conl.* 19,6.
7.35 Cassian. *inst.* 4,41; 12,33; Cassian. *conl.* 16,22; 16,26,2; 18,11.
7.42 Cypr. *de pat.* 20.

7.33 "we read" (*scriptura*): The quotation is not from Scripture but from the *Acta Anastasiae* 17, in reference to the martyr Irene († A.D. 304). In RM, from which this comes (10.44), *scriptura* is used for sources other than the Bible, e.g., RM 9.31; 11.31. In the latter, the Master, speaking of St. Eugenia, has *dicente scribtura ipsius,* "as her biography says."
"Consent" (*Voluntas*): Although Hanslik with Codex Sangallensis 914 reads *voluptas,* the principle *lectio difficilior* supports *voluntas,* as do many MSS. In the *Acta,* Irene, threatened with forcible prostitution, replies that, as with those forced to eat meat sacrificed to idols, this would be no guilt to her if done under

sparing us for a while because he is a loving father who waits for us to improve, he may tell us later, *This you did, and I said nothing* (Ps 49[50]:21).

³¹The second step of humility is that a man loves not his own will nor takes pleasure in the satisfaction of his desires; ³²rather he shall imitate by his actions that saying of the Lord: *I have come not to do my own will, but the will of him who sent me* (John 6:38). ³³Similarly we read, "Consent merits punishment; constraint wins a crown."

³⁴The third step of humility is that a man submits to his superior in all obedience for the love of God, imitating the Lord of whom the Apostle says: *He became obedient even to death* (Phil 2:8).

³⁵The fourth step of humility is that in this obedience under difficult, unfavorable, or even unjust conditions, his heart quietly embraces suffering ³⁶and endures it without weakening or seeking escape. For Scripture has it: *Anyone who perseveres to the end will be saved* (Matt 10:22), ³⁷and again, *Be brave of heart and rely on the Lord* (Ps 26[27]:14). ³⁸Another passage shows how the faithful must endure everything, even contradiction, for the Lord's sake, saying in the person of those who suffer, *For your sake we are put to death continually; we are regarded as sheep marked for slaughter* (Rom 8:36; Ps 43[44]:22). ³⁹They are so confident in their expectation of reward from God that they continue joyfully and say, *But in all this we overcome because of him who so greatly loved us* (Rom 8:37). ⁴⁰Elsewhere Scripture says: *God, you have tested us, you have tried us as silver is tried by fire; you have led us into a snare, you have placed afflictions on our backs* (Ps 65[66]:10-11). ⁴¹Then, to show that we ought to be under a superior, it adds: *You have placed men over our heads* (Ps 65[66]:12).

⁴²In truth, those who are patient amid hardships and unjust treatment are fulfilling the Lord's command: *When struck on one*

---

necessitas, but rather would win her a crown. In RM and RB, the meaning of the quotation is changed; the statement is cited to express the idea that there is punishment for self-will but a crown for the pursuit of obligation or necessity. See H. Delehaye, *Étude sur le Légendier Romain* (Brussels: Société des Bollandistes 1936) p. 234.

7.38 "Another passage shows" (*Et ostendens*): Although this refers to the quotation from Ps 43(44):22, the latter has been taken from Rom 8:36, where it is quoted, as the following verse of RB clearly demonstrates.

percussi in maxillam praebent et aliam, auferenti tunicam di-
mittunt et pallium, angariati miliario vadunt duo, [43] cum Paulo
apostolo *falsos fratres* sustinent et *persecutionem sustinent et*
maledicentes se *benedicent.*

[44] Quintus humilitatis gradus est si omnes cogitationes malas
cordi suo advenientes vel mala a se absconse commissa per
humilem confessionem abbatem non celaverit suum. [45] Hortans
nos de hac re scriptura dicens: *Revela ad Dominum viam tuam*
et spera in eum. [46] Et item dicit: *Confitemini Domino quoniam*
bonus, quoniam in saeculum misericordia eius. [47] Et item propheta: *Delictum meum cognitum tibi feci et iniustitias meas*
non operui. [48] *Dixi: Pronuntiabo adversum me iniustitias meas*
Domino, et tu remisisti impietatem cordis mei.

[49] Sextus humilitatis gradus est si omni vilitate vel extremitate
contentus sit monachus, et ad omnia quae sibi iniunguntur velut
operarium malum se iudicet et indignum, [50] dicens sibi cum
propheta: *Ad nihilum redactus sum et nescivi; ut iumentum fac-*
tus sum apud te et ego semper tecum.

[51] Septimus humilitatis gradus est si omnibus se inferiorem et
viliorem non solum sua lingua pronuntiet, sed etiam intimo cordis credat affectu, [52] humilians se et dicens cum propheta: *Ego*
autem sum vermis et non homo, opprobrium hominum et abiec-

7.43 Cypr. *testim.* 39.
7.44 Cassian. *conl.* 2,10,1; *Vitae patr., Verb.senior.* 5,4,25.
7.49 Cypr. *epist.* 2,2.
7.51 Ps-Macar. *reg.* 3; *Vitae patr., Verb.senior.* 3,206; Basil. *reg.* 62; Cassian.
inst. 12,32,1; 12,33; Cassian. *conl.* 12,13; 24,16.

7.42 *"pressed into service"* (angariati): This verse is a free citation of Matt
5:39-41. The word *angariati* has been taken over from Greek but is, in fact, a
Persian loan word and perhaps originally Babylonian. It refers to the practice of
requisitioning people for civil or military service and is used in Matt 27:32 of
Simon of Cyrene, who is pressed into service to carry Jesus' cross.

7.44 "confesses" *(confessionem)*: The manifestation of sins and evil thoughts
to the spiritual father of the monastery is not synonymous with the sacrament of
reconciliation. In the Patristic period the monk who acted as spiritual father was
generally not a priest. However, it was commonly thought that such people had
the power to forgive sins. For example, see *Vita sa*[5] 148 and P. Brown "The Rise
and Function of the Holy Man in Late Antiquity" *Journal of Roman Studies* 61
(1971) 80–101. On the development of the sacrament of reconciliation, see Appendix 4, pp. 416–419. See Thematic Index: ABBOT, *Images.*

7.49 "the lowest and most menial treatment" *(omni vilitate vel extremitate):*
The phrase is derived ultimately from Cassian: *si omni vilitate contentus sit et ad*
omnia se quae sibi praebentur velut operarium malum iudicarit indignum (Cassian. *inst.* 4,39,2). The Master has added *vel extremitate* after *vilitate* (10.66).

cheek, they turn the other; when deprived of their coat, they offer their cloak also; when pressed into service for one mile, they go two (Matt 5:39-41). ⁴³With the Apostle Paul, they bear with *false brothers, endure persecution,* and *bless those who curse them* (2 Cor 11:26; 1 Cor 4:12).

⁴⁴The fifth step of humility is that a man does not conceal from his abbot any sinful thoughts entering his heart, or any wrongs committed in secret, but rather confesses them humbly. ⁴⁵Concerning this, Scripture exhorts us: *Make known your way to the Lord and hope in him* (Ps 36[37]:5). ⁴⁶And again, *Confess to the Lord, for he is good; his mercy is forever* (Ps 105[106]:1; Ps 117 [118]:1). ⁴⁷So too the Prophet: *To you I have acknowledged my offense; my faults I have not concealed.* ⁴⁸*I have said: Against myself I will report my faults to the Lord, and you have forgiven the wickedness of my heart* (Ps 31[32]:5).

⁴⁹The sixth step of humility is that a monk is content with the lowest and most menial treatment, and regards himself as a poor and worthless workman in whatever task he is given, ⁵⁰saying to himself with the Prophet: *I am insignificant and ignorant, no better than a beast before you, yet I am with you always* (Ps 72[73]:22-23).

⁵¹The seventh step of humility is that a man not only admits with his tongue but is also convinced in his heart that he is inferior to all and of less value, ⁵²humbling himself and saying with the Prophet: *I am truly a worm, not a man, scorned by men*

Although there is a tradition of translating this phrase as if it referred to things (cf. de Vogüé: "ce qui est le plus vil et le plus abject"), there is strong lexicographical support for taking it to refer to the status of the workman, as does Gibson: "if he is contented with the lowest possible position. . ." (*NPNF* ser. 2,2.232).

A. Blaise, *Dictionnaire Latin-Français des Auteurs du Moyen-Age* (Turnhout: Brepols 1975) has under *vilitas:* "1. condition inférieure: *servilis enim vilitas clericalem non accipit dignitatem.* Bern. Pap. *Summ.* 1.10 2. lâcheté"; and nothing relevant under *extremitas* and cognates.

J. F. Niermeyer, *Mediae Latinitatis Lexicon Minus* (Leiden: E. J. Brill 1976) has nothing under *extremitas* or *vilitas,* and nothing relevant under *extremus, extrema,* but under *vilipensio:* "harmful or scornful treatment" and under *vilis:* "of servile or dependant [sic] status," with quotations from the eighth and ninth centuries about not admitting *viles quaeque et servili condicione obligatae personae* to the priesthood.

It seems, therefore, that *vilitas* means "being treated like a slave" or some such phrase, much as we talk of a *corpus vile* or "vile body." This also suits the context here, "like a bad workman," much better than the usual translation. We easily forget that slavery was a present reality for St. Benedict (cf. RB 2.18); hence our instinct to translate *servus* as "servant."

tio plebis. [53]*Exaltatus sum et humiliatus et confusus.* [54]Et item: *Bonum mihi quod humiliasti me, ut discam mandata tua.*

[55]Octavus humilitatis gradus est si nihil agat monachus, nisi quod communis monasterii regula vel maiorum cohortantur exempla.

[56]Nonus humilitatis gradus est si linguam ad loquendum prohibeat monachus et, taciturnitatem habens, usque ad interrogationem non loquatur, [57]monstrante scriptura quia *in multiloquio non effugitur peccatum,* [58]et quia *vir linguosus non dirigitur super terram.*

[59]Decimus humilitatis gradus est si non sit facilis ac promptus in risu, quia scriptum est: *Stultus in risu exaltat vocem suam.*

[60]Undecimus humilitatis gradus est si, cum loquitur monachus, leniter et sine risu, humiliter cum gravitate vel pauca verba et rationabilia loquatur, et non sit clamosus in voce, [61]sicut scriptum est: *Sapiens verbis innotescit paucis.*

[62]Duodecimus humilitatis gradus est si non solum corde monachus sed etiam ipso corpore humilitatem videntibus se semper indicet, [63]id est in opere Dei, in oratorio, in monasterio, in horto, in via, in agro vel ubicumque sedens, ambulans vel stans, inclinato sit semper capite, defixis in terram aspectibus, [64]reum se omni hora de peccatis suis aestimans iam se tremendo iudicio repraesentari aestimet, [65]dicens sibi in corde semper illud quod publicanus ille evangelicus fixis in terram oculis dixit: *Domine, non sum dignus, ego peccator, levare oculos meos ad caelos.* [66]Et item cum propheta: *Incurvatus sum et humiliatus sum usquequaque.*

[67]Ergo, his omnibus humilitatis gradibus ascensis, monachus mox *ad caritatem* Dei perveniet illam quae *perfecta foris mittit timorem,* [68]per quam universa quae prius non sine formidine observabat absque ullo labore velut naturaliter ex consuetudine incipiet custodire, [69]non iam timore gehennae, sed amore Christi

---

7.55 Cassian. *conl.* 2,10.
7.56 *Vitae patr., Verb.senior.* 7,32,3.
7.59 Basil. *ad mon.* 1,11.
7.60 Cypr. *ad Demet.* 1.
7.61 Sext.Pythag. enchirid. 145.
7.62-64 Basil. *reg.* 86.
7.63 Basil. *ad mon.* 1,12.
7.65 *Orat.Manassae* 9.
7.67-69 Cassian. inst. 4,39,3; Cassian. *conl.* 11,7,13.
7.69 Cassian. *conl.* 11,6; 11,8,1.

and despised by the people (Ps 21[22]:7). ⁵³*I was exalted, then I was humbled and overwhelmed with confusion* (Ps 87[88]:16). ⁵⁴And again, *It is a blessing that you have humbled me so that I can learn your commandments* (Ps 118[119]:71,73).

⁵⁵The eighth step of humility is that a monk does only what is endorsed by the common rule of the monastery and the example set by his superiors.

⁵⁶The ninth step of humility is that a monk controls his tongue and remains silent, not speaking unless asked a question, ⁵⁷for Scripture warns, *In a flood of words you will not avoid sinning* (Prov 10:19), ⁵⁸and, *A talkative man goes about aimlessly on earth* (Ps 139[140]:12).

⁵⁹The tenth step of humility is that he is not given to ready laughter, for it is written: *Only a fool raises his voice in laughter* (Sir 21:23).

⁶⁰The eleventh step of humility is that a monk speaks gently and without laughter, seriously and with becoming modesty, briefly and reasonably, but without raising his voice, ⁶¹as it is written: "A wise man is known by his few words."

⁶²The twelfth step of humility is that a monk always manifests humility in his bearing no less than in his heart, so that it is evident ⁶³at the Work of God, in the oratory, the monastery or the garden, on a journey or in the field, or anywhere else. Whether he sits, walks or stands, his head must be bowed and his eyes cast down. ⁶⁴Judging himself always guilty on account of his sins, he should consider that he is already at the fearful judgment, ⁶⁵and constantly say in his heart what the publican in the Gospel said with downcast eyes: *Lord, I am a sinner, not worthy to look up to heaven* (Luke 18:13). ⁶⁶And with the Prophet: *I am bowed down and humbled in every way* (Ps 37[38]:7-9; Ps 118[119]: 107).

⁶⁷Now, therefore, after ascending all these steps of humility, the monk will quickly arrive at that *perfect love* of God which *casts out fear* (1 John 4:18). ⁶⁸Through this love, all that he once performed with dread, he will now begin to observe without effort, as though naturally, from habit, ⁶⁹no longer out of fear of

---

7.63 "Work of God" (*opere Dei*): See Appendix 3, pp. 405–406.

7.65 "what the publican...said" (*quod publicanus...dixit*): Since the publican occurs only in Luke's Gospel, the author of RB (RM) must have had in mind Luke 18:13. However, the line attributed to the publican is a free conflation of Matt 8:8 and Luke 18:13-14.

et consuetudine ipsa bona et delectatione virtutum. ⁷⁰Quae
Dominus iam in operarium suum mundum a vitiis et peccatis
Spiritu Sancto dignabitur demonstrare.

VIII. DE OFFICIIS DIVINIS IN NOCTIBUS

¹Hiemis tempore, id est a kalendas Novembres usque in
Pascha, iuxta considerationem rationis, octava hora noctis
surgendum est, ²ut modice amplius de media nocte pausetur et
iam digesti surgant. ³Quod vero restat post vigilias a fratribus qui
psalterii vel lectionum aliquid indigent meditationi inserviatur.

⁴A Pascha autem usque ad supradictas Novembres, sic temperetur hora ut vigiliarum agenda parvissimo intervallo, quo
fratres ad necessaria naturae exeant, mox matutini, qui incipiente
luce agendi sunt, subsequantur.

IX. QUANTI PSALMI DICENDI SUNT NOCTURNIS HORIS

¹Hiemis tempore suprascripto, in primis versu tertio dicen-
dum: *Domine, labia mea aperies, et os meum adnuntiabit
laudem tuam.* ²Cui subiungendus est tertius psalmus et gloria.
³Post hunc, psalmum nonagesimum quartum cum antiphona, aut
certe decantandum. ⁴Inde sequatur ambrosianum, deinde sex
psalmi cum antiphonas.

8.2 Cassian. *conl.* 2,26.
8.4 Cassian. *inst.* 3,4.

8.0 **Chapters 8–20:** See Appendix 3, pp. 379–414, on the liturgical code. See
Thematic Index: MONASTIC RITUALS and PRAYER.

8.1 "the first" (*kalendas*): In the Roman calendar — the word itself is derived
from *kalendae* — each month had three fixed points: the kalends, the nones
(*nonae*) and the ides (*idus*). The kalends always fell on the first of the month. The
nones and ides fell normally on the fifth and thirteenth of the month respectively,
but in March, May, July and October on the seventh and the fifteenth.

The Romans calculated dates as being either one of these fixed points in the
month or so many days before it. Thus March 15 is "the ides of March," March 14
is "the day before (*pridie*) the ides"; March 13 is three (13,14 and 15), not two,
days before the ides; and so on. See E. J. Bickermann, *Chronology of the Ancient
World* (Ithaca, N.Y.: Cornell Univ. Press 1969) pp. 43f.

McCann's suggestion (n. 72) that *kalendae Octobres* means September 14,
has some force, because September 14 was the first day calculated as "before the
kalends" of October. Nonetheless, we disagree with him for reasons given on
pp. 408–411 of Appendix 3.

hell, but out of love for Christ, good habit and delight in virtue. [70]All this the Lord will by the Holy Spirit graciously manifest in his workman now cleansed of vices and sins.

CHAPTER 8. THE DIVINE OFFICE AT NIGHT

[1]During the winter season, that is, from the first of November until Easter, it seems reasonable to arise at the eighth hour of the night. [2]By sleeping until a little past the middle of the night, the brothers can arise with their food fully digested. [3]In the time remaining after Vigils, those who need to learn some of the psalter or readings should study them.

[4]Between Easter and the first of November mentioned above, the time for Vigils should be adjusted so that a very short interval after Vigils will give the monks opportunity to care for nature's needs. Then, at daybreak, Lauds should follow immediately.

CHAPTER 9. THE NUMBER OF PSALMS AT THE NIGHT OFFICE

[1]During the winter season, Vigils begin with the verse: *Lord, open my lips and my mouth shall proclaim your praise* (Ps 50[51]:17). After this has been said three times, [2]the following order is observed: Psalm 3 with "Glory be to the Father"; [3]Psalm 94 with a refrain, or at least chanted; [4]an Ambrosian hymn; then six psalms with refrain.

"it seems reasonable" (*iuxta considerationem rationis*): Another possible translation is "at what they calculate to be the eighth hour." The Roman *hora* was simply the total amount of daylight (or, for the night *horae*, of darkness) divided by twelve. As this varied with the season from about seventy-five to about forty-five minutes — in the summer the day *horae* were long and the night *horae* short — establishing the eighth hour would have needed some calculation. See J. E. Sandys, *A Companion to Latin Studies*, 3rd ed. (Cambridge Univ. Press 1921; rpt. 1963) pp. 200–202.

8.2 "food fully digested" (*iam digesti*): Comparing RB 8.2 with RM 33.19-21, one may conclude that what is at issue is a proper digestion of the meal. The RB is mercifully laconic by comparison with RM.

8.3 "study" (*meditationi*): The study in question is primarily the memorization of the Psalter and Scripture passages. See Appendix 5, pp. 446–447.

"readings" (*lectionum*): See Appendix 3, pp. 404–405.

"Vigils" (*vigilias*): See Appendix 3, pp. 397–400, 407–408.

8.4 "Lauds" (*matutini*): See Appendix 3, p. 405.

9.3 "refrain" (*antiphona*): See Appendix 3, pp. 401–403.

9.4 "an Ambrosian hymn" (*ambrosianum*): See Appendix 3, p. 401.

[5]Quibus dictis, dicto versu, benedicat abbas et, sedentibus omnibus in scamnis, legantur vicissim a fratribus in codice super analogium tres lectiones, inter quas et tria responsoria cantentur: [6]duo responsoria sine gloria dicantur; post tertiam vero lectionem, qui cantat dicat gloriam. [7]Quam dum incipit cantor dicere, mox omnes de sedilia sua surgant, ob honorem et reverentiam sanctae Trinitatis. [8]Codices autem legantur in vigiliis divinae auctoritatis, tam veteris testamenti quam novi, sed et expositiones earum, quae a nominatis et orthodoxis catholicis patribus factae sunt.

[9]Post has vero tres lectiones cum responsoria sua, sequantur reliqui sex psalmi, cum alleluia canendi. [10]Post hos, lectio apostoli sequatur, ex corde recitanda, et versus, et supplicatio litaniae, id est Kyrie eleison. [11]Et sic finiantur vigiliae nocturnae.

X. QUALITER AESTATIS TEMPORE AGATUR NOCTURNA LAUS

[1]A Pascha autem usque ad kalendas Novembres, omnis ut supra dictum est psalmodiae quantitas teneatur, [2]excepto quod lectiones in codice, propter brevitatem noctium, minime legantur, sed pro ipsis tribus lectionibus una de veteri testamento memoriter dicatur, quam brevis responsorius subsequatur. [3]Et reliqua omnia ut dictum est impleantur, id est ut numquam minus a duodecim psalmorum quantitate ad vigilias nocturnas dicantur, exceptis tertio et nonagesimo quarto psalmo.

XI. QUALITER DIEBUS DOMINICIS VIGILIAE AGANTUR

[1]Dominico die temperius surgatur ad vigilias. [2]In quibus vigiliis teneatur mensura, id est, modulatis ut supra disposuimus sex psalmis et versu, residentibus cunctis disposite et per ordinem in subselliis, legantur in codice, ut supra diximus, quattuor lectiones cum responsoriis suis. [3]Ubi tantum in quarto responsorio

---

9.8 *Vitae patr., Verb.senior.* 5,14,13.
9.11 Cassian. *inst.* 2,3; Cassian. *conl.* 2,26.
10.3 Cassian. *inst.* 2,4.

⁵After the psalmody, a versicle is said and the abbot gives a blessing. When all are seated on the benches, the brothers in turn read three selections from the book on the lectern. After each reading a responsory is sung. ⁶"Glory be to the Father" is not sung after the first two responsories, but only after the third reading. ⁷As soon as the cantor begins to sing "Glory be to the Father," let all the monks rise from their seats in honor and reverence for the Holy Trinity. ⁸Besides the inspired books of the Old and New Testaments, the works read at Vigils should include explanations of Scripture by reputable and orthodox catholic Fathers.

⁹When these three readings and their responsories have been finished, the remaining six psalms are sung with an "alleluia" refrain. ¹⁰This ended, there follow a reading from the Apostle recited by heart, a versicle and the litany, that is, "Lord, have mercy." ¹¹And so Vigils are concluded.

CHAPTER 10. THE ARRANGEMENT OF THE NIGHT OFFICE IN SUMMER

¹From Easter until the first of November, the winter arrangement for the number of psalms is followed. ²But because summer nights are shorter, the readings from the book are omitted. In place of the three readings, one from the Old Testament is substituted. This is to be recited by heart, followed by a short responsory. ³In everything else, the winter arrangement for Vigils is kept. Thus, winter and summer, there are never fewer than twelve psalms at Vigils, not counting Psalms 3 and 94.

CHAPTER 11. THE CELEBRATION OF VIGILS ON SUNDAY

¹On Sunday the monks should arise earlier for Vigils. ²In these Vigils, too, there must be moderation in quantity: first, as we have already indicated, six psalms are said, followed by a versicle. Then the monks, seated on the benches and arranged in their proper order, listen to four readings from the book. After each reading a responsory is sung, ³but "Glory be to the Father" is

---

11.2 "there must be moderation in quantity" (*teneatur mensura*): Another possible translation is "they should keep to the amount," i.e., the same number of psalms should be said as on weekdays. That this is not otiose advice is clear both from previous monastic tendencies and from the later Cluniac horarium. See note on RB 18.25 below.

dicatur a cantante gloria; quam dum incipit, mox omnes cum reverentia surgant.

[4] Post quibus lectionibus sequantur ex ordine alii sex psalmi cum antiphonas sicut anteriores, et versu. [5] Post quibus iterum legantur aliae quattuor lectiones cum responsoriis suis, ordine quo supra.

[6] Post quibus dicantur tria cantica de prophetarum, quas instituerit abbas; quae cantica cum alleluia psallantur. [7] Dicto etiam versu et benedicente abbate, legantur aliae quattuor lectiones de novo testamento, ordine quo supra. [8] Post quartum autem responsorium incipiat abbas hymnum Te Deum laudamus. [9] Quo perdicto, legat abbas lectionem de Evangelia, cum honore et timore stantibus omnibus. [10] Qua perlecta, respondeant omnes Amen, et subsequatur mox abbas hymnum Te decet laus, et data benedictione incipiant matutinos.

[11] Qui ordo vigiliarum omni tempore tam aestatis quam hiemis aequaliter in die dominico teneatur. [12] Nisi forte—quod absit— tardius surgant: aliquid de lectionibus breviandum est, aut responsoriis. [13] Quod tamen omnino caveatur ne proveniat. Quod si contigerit, digne inde satisfaciat Deo in oratorio per cuius evenerit neglectum.

XII. QUOMODO MATUTINORUM SOLLEMNITAS AGATUR

[1] In matutinis dominico die, in primis dicatur sexagesimus sextus psalmus, sine antiphona, in directum. [2] Post quem dicatur quinquagesimus cum alleluia. [3] Post quem dicatur centesimus septimus decimus et sexagesimus secundus. [4] Inde benedictiones et laudes, lectionem de Apocalypsis una ex corde, et responsorium, ambrosianum, versu, canticum de Evangelia, litania, et completum est.

XIII. PRIVATIS DIEBUS QUALITER AGANTUR MATUTINI

[1] Diebus autem privatis, matutinorum sollemnitas ita agatur, [2] id est, ut sexagesimus sextus psalmus dicatur sine antiphona,

---

11.12 Caes.Arel. *reg.virg.* 66-69.
13.1 Caes.Arel. *reg.virg.* 66-69; Cassian. *inst.* 3,3.

added only to the fourth. When the cantor begins it, all immediately rise in reverence.

⁴After these readings the same order is repeated: six more psalms with refrain as before, a versicle, ⁵then four more readings and their responsories, as above. ⁶Next, three canticles from the Prophets, chosen by the abbot, are said with an "alleluia" refrain. ⁷After a versicle and the abbot's blessing, four New Testament readings follow with their responsories, as above. ⁸After the fourth responsory, the abbot begins the hymn "We praise you, God." ⁹When that is finished, he reads from the Gospels while all the monks stand with respect and awe. ¹⁰At the conclusion of the Gospel reading, all reply "Amen," and immediately the abbot intones the hymn "To you be praise." After a final blessing, Lauds begin.

¹¹This arrangement for Sunday Vigils should be followed at all times, summer and winter, ¹²unless—God forbid—the monks happen to arise too late. In that case, the readings or responsories will have to be shortened. ¹³Let special care be taken that this not happen, but if it does, the monk at fault is to make due satisfaction to God in the oratory.

CHAPTER 12. THE CELEBRATION OF THE SOLEMNITY OF LAUDS

¹Sunday Lauds begin with Psalm 66, said straight through without a refrain. ²Then Psalm 50 follows with an "alleluia" refrain. ³Lauds continue with Psalms 117 and 62, ⁴the Canticle of the Three Young Men, Psalms 148 through 150, a reading from the Apocalypse recited by heart and followed by a responsory, an Ambrosian hymn, a versicle, the Gospel Canticle, the litany and the conclusion.

CHAPTER 13. THE CELEBRATION OF LAUDS ON ORDINARY DAYS

¹On ordinary weekdays, Lauds are celebrated as follows: ²First, Psalm 66 is said without a refrain and slightly protracted

---

11.6 "canticles from the Prophets" (cantica de prophetarum): See Appendix 3, p. 404.

11.12 "God forbid" (quod absit): This is originally a pagan expression for which a functional equivalent rather than a literal translation has been given.

12.4 "the Canticle of the Three Young Men" (benedictiones): See Appendix 3, pp. 403–404.

"Psalms 148 through 150" (laudes): See Appendix 3, p. 404.

subtrahendo modice, sicut dominica, ut omnes occurrant ad quinquagesimum, qui cum antiphona dicatur. [3]Post quem alii duo psalmi dicantur secundum consuetudinem, id est: [4]secunda feria, quintum et tricesimum quintum; [5]tertia feria, quadragesimum secundum et quinquagesimum sextum; [6]quarta feria, sexagesimum tertium et sexagesimum quartum; [7]quinta feria, octogesimum septimum et octogesimum nonum; [8]sexta feria, septuagesimum quintum et nonagesimum primum; [9]sabbatorum autem, centesimum quadragesimum secundum et canticum Deuteronomium qui dividatur in duas glorias. [10]Nam ceteris diebus canticum unumquemque die suo ex prophetis sicut psallit ecclesia Romana dicantur. [11]Post haec sequantur laudes; deinde lectio una apostoli memoriter recitanda, responsorium, ambrosianum, versu, canticum de Evangelia, litania et completum est.

[12]Plane agenda matutina vel vespertina non transeat aliquando, nisi in ultimo per ordinem oratio dominica, omnibus audientibus, dicatur a priore, propter scandalorum spinas quae oriri solent, [13]ut conventi per ipsius orationis sponsionem qua dicunt: *Dimitte nobis sicut et nos dimittimus*, purgent se ab huiusmodi vitio. [14]Ceteris vero agendis, ultima pars eius orationis dicatur, ut ab omnibus respondeatur: *Sed libera nos a malo.*

XIV. IN NATALICIIS SANCTORUM QUALITER AGANTUR VIGILIAE

[1]In sanctorum vero festivitatibus, vel omnibus sollemnitatibus, sicut diximus dominico die agendum, ita agatur, [2]excepto quod psalmi aut antiphonae vel lectiones ad ipsum diem pertinentes dicantur; modus autem suprascriptus teneatur.

13.12 *Concil.Gerunda* a. 517 canon 10; Cassian. *conl.* 9,33.
13.13 Aug. *serm.* 56,13; Cypr. *domin.orat.* 23.

13.10 "according to the practice of the Roman Church" (*sicut psallit ecclesia Romana*): This is an explicit reference to one of RB's sources for the liturgical code. See Appendix 3, pp. 398–400.
13.12 "Vespers" (*vespertina*): See Appendix 3, p. 406.
"contention" (*scandalorum*): This word comes from *skandalon*, a Hellenistic Greek word for the earlier *skandalē* and *skandalēthron*, which meant originally a "stick in a trap on which the bait is placed and which, when touched by the animal, springs up and shuts the trap" (Liddell, Scott, Jones, s.vv.). In the New Testament the sense of trap or snare or cause of ruin persists, and this last is

as on Sunday so that everyone can be present for Psalm 50, which has a refrain. [3] Next, according to custom, two more psalms are said in the following order: [4] on Monday, Psalms 5 and 35; [5] on Tuesday, Psalms 42 and 56; [6] on Wednesday, Psalms 63 and 64; [7] on Thursday, Psalms 87 and 89; [8] on Friday, Psalms 75 and 91; [9] on Saturday, Psalm 142 and the Canticle from Deuteronomy, divided into two sections, with "Glory be to the Father" after each section. [10] On other days, however, a Canticle from the Prophets is said, according to the practice of the Roman Church. [11] Next follow Psalms 148 through 150, a reading from the Apostle recited by heart, a responsory, an Ambrosian hymn, a versicle, the Gospel Canticle, the litany and the conclusion.

[12] Assuredly, the celebration of Lauds and Vespers must never pass by without the superior's reciting the entire Lord's Prayer at the end for all to hear, because thorns of contention are likely to spring up. [13] Thus warned by the pledge they make to one another in the very words of this prayer: *Forgive us as we forgive* (Matt 6:12), they may cleanse themselves of this kind of vice. [14] At other celebrations, only the final part of the Lord's Prayer is said aloud, that all may reply: *But deliver us from evil* (Matt 6:13).

CHAPTER 14. THE CELEBRATION OF VIGILS ON THE ANNIVERSARIES
OF SAINTS

[1] On the feasts of saints, and indeed on all solemn festivals, the Sunday order of celebration is followed, [2] although the psalms, refrains and readings proper to the day itself are said. The procedure, however, remains the same as indicated above.

---

expanded to include not only bad things but also good, and ultimately is extended to Jesus himself. It is linked with acceptance or rejection of faith in Jesus, and there is a consequent shift from the notion of an external object (over which one trips) to the idea of internal rejection and ruin. See Staehlin, s.v. in *Theological Dictionary of the New Testament*, ed. Gerhard Kittel and tr. and ed. Geoffrey W. Bromiley, 9 vols. (Grand Rapids, Mich.: Eerdmans 1964). The monastic equivalent of this would be the abandonment of a vocation. This would be in line with the thought of passages such as 58.28 or 59.6, but probably, given the contexts of the four occurrences (13.12; 65.1,2; 69.3), some translation such as "resentments," "contention," or "conflict" (favored by de Vogüé and Steidle) is preferable.

14.2 "proper to the day itself" (*ad ipsum diem*): Although there is some ambiguity, the direction seems to be that the psalms, refrains and readings proper to the feast rather than to the ordinary daily office are to be used. There would have been no need to comment on "The Celebration of Vigils on the Anniversaries of Saints" if the ordinary ferial office were envisioned.

XV. ALLELUIA QUIBUS TEMPORIBUS DICATUR

[1]A sanctum Pascha usque Pentecosten, sine intermissione dicatur alleluia, tam in psalmis quam in responsoriis. [2]A Pentecosten autem usque caput quadragesimae, omnibus noctibus, cum sex posterioribus psalmis tantum ad nocturnos dicatur. [3]Omni vero dominica extra quadragesima, cantica, matutinos, prima, tertia, sexta nonaque cum alleluia dicatur, vespera vero iam antiphona. [4]Responsoria vero numquam dicantur cum alleluia, nisi a Pascha usque Pentecosten.

XVI. QUALITER DIVINA OPERA PER DIEM AGANTUR

[1]Ut ait propheta, *septies in die laudem dixi tibi.* [2]Qui septenarius sacratus numerus a nobis sic implebitur, si matutino, primae, tertiae, sextae, nonae, vesperae completoriique tempore nostrae servitutis officia persolvamus, [3]quia de his diurnis horis dixit: *Septies in die laudem dixi tibi.* [4]Nam de nocturnis vigiliis idem ipse propheta ait: *Media nocte surgebam ad confitendum tibi.* [5]Ergo his temporibus referamus *laudes* Creatori nostro *super iudicia iustitiae* suae, id est matutinis, prima, tertia, sexta, nona, vespera, completorios, et *nocte surgamus ad confitendum* ei.

XVII. QUOT PSALMI PER EASDEM HORAS CANENDI SUNT

[1]Iam de nocturnis vel matutinis digessimus ordinem psalmodiae; nunc de sequentibus horis videamus.

[2]Prima hora dicantur psalmi tres singillatim et non sub una

---

16.0 Cypr. *domin.orat.* 35-36.
16.1 Cassian. *inst.* 3-4.
16.2 *Sacr.Gelasianum* 37.
16.3 Cassian. *inst.*3-4.

15.0 "Alleluia" (*Alleluia*): "Alleluia" is a Hebrew phrase meaning: "Praise Yah[weh]." It occurs frequently in the Psalter, e.g., as an introduction to Pss 146–150 and four times in Rev 19, where it occurs in the description of the heavenly liturgy. It was evidently never translated into Greek, but was retained in the liturgy of the early Church, as were other very familiar phrases, such as "Amen" and "Maranatha." Compare also the retention of the Greek phrase *Kyrie eleison* when the liturgy was translated into Latin in the fourth century.

15.2 "beginning of Lent" (*caput quadragesimae*): See Appendix 3, p. 409.

16.1 "The Prophet says" (*ut ait propheta*): Until comparatively recent times, the entire Psalter was thought to have been composed by David, who already in the New Testament period was thought to be a prophet (cf. Acts 2:30). Hence, in the Patristic period also, the Psalter was treated as a prophetic book and interpreted accordingly.

CHAPTER 15. THE TIMES FOR SAYING ALLELUIA

[1]From the holy feast of Easter until Pentecost, "alleluia" is always said with both the psalms and the responsories. [2]Every night from Pentecost until the beginning of Lent, it is said only with the last six psalms of Vigils. [3]Vigils, Lauds, Prime, Terce, Sext and None are said with "alleluia" every Sunday except in Lent; at Vespers, however, a refrain is used. [4]"Alleluia" is never said with responsories except from Easter to Pentecost.

CHAPTER 16. THE CELEBRATION OF THE DIVINE OFFICE
DURING THE DAY

[1]The Prophet says: *Seven times a day have I praised you* (Ps 118[119]:164). [2]We will fulfill this sacred number of seven if we satisfy our obligations of service at Lauds, Prime, Terce, Sext, None, Vespers and Compline, [3]for it was of these hours during the day that he said: *Seven times a day have I praised you* (Ps 118[119]:164). [4]Concerning Vigils, the same Prophet says: *At midnight I arose to give you praise* (Ps 118[119]:62). [5]Therefore, we should *praise* our Creator *for his just judgments* at these times: Lauds, Prime, Terce, Sext, None, Vespers and Compline; and *let us arise at night to give* him *praise* (Ps 118[119]:164,62).

CHAPTER 17. THE NUMBER OF PSALMS TO BE SUNG AT THESE HOURS

[1]We have already established the order for psalmody at Vigils and Lauds. Now let us arrange the remaining hours.

[2]Three psalms are to be said at Prime, each followed by "Glory

---

16.2 "sacred number of seven" (*septenarius sacratus numerus*): Benedict cites Ps 118(119):164 to justify the seven times of prayer during the day, Ps 118(119):62 to justify prayer during the night. While sacred Scripture notes particular times of prayer, no single passage lists the eight prayer hours of this chapter. In Benedict's time the office of Prime was still a subject of contention. Monasteries of some regions (e.g., southern Italy) omitted it; monasteries of other regions (e.g., Rome and RM) included it. RB finds scriptural "proof" to include it. See A. de Vogüé, 5.514–518, and "*Septies in die laudem dixi tibi.* Aux origines de l'interprétation bénédictine d'un texte psalmique" *RBS* 3–4 (1975) 1–5.

16.5 "*for his just judgments*" (super iudicia iustitiae): This phrase forms the second half of Ps 118(119):164. The first half was quoted in the first verse of the chapter. The last part of v.5, "let us arise. . .," is a slight rephrasing of Ps 118(119):62, already quoted in v.4. Thus, in the conclusion of his argument, Benedict includes allusions to both his premises.

gloria, [3]hymnum eiusdem horae post versum *Deus in adiutorium antequam psalmi incipiantur.* [4]Post expletionem vero trium psalmorum recitetur lectio una, versu et Kyrie eleison et missas.

[5]Tertia vero, sexta et nona, item eo ordine celebretur oratio, id est versu, hymnos earundem horarum, ternos psalmos, lectionem et versu, Kyrie eleison et missas. [6]Si maior congregatio fuerit, cum antiphonas, si vero minor, in directum psallantur.

[7]Vespertina autem synaxis quattuor psalmis cum antiphonis terminetur. [8]Post quibus psalmis, lectio recitanda est; inde responsorium, ambrosianum, versu, canticum de Evangelia, litania, et oratione dominica fiant missae.

[9]Completorios autem trium psalmorum dictione terminentur. Qui psalmi directanei sine antiphona dicendi sunt. [10]Post quos hymnum eiusdem horae, lectionem unam, versu, Kyrie eleison, et benedictione missae fiant.

XVIII. QUO ORDINE IPSI PSALMI DICENDI SUNT

[1]In primis dicatur versu *Deus in adiutorium meum intende, Domine ad adiuvandum me festina,* gloria, inde hymnum uniuscuiusque horae.

[2]Deinde, prima hora dominica, dicenda quattuor capitula psalmi centesimi octavi decimi; [3]reliquis vero horis, id est tertia, sexta vel nona, terna capitula suprascripti psalmi centesimi octavi decimi dicantur. [4]Ad primam autem secundae feriae, dicantur tres psalmi, id est primus, secundus et sextus; [5]et ita per singulos dies ad primam usque dominica dicantur per ordinem terni psalmi usque nonum decimum psalmum, ita sane ut nonus psalmus et septimus decimus partiantur in binos. [6]Et sic fit ut ad vigilias dominica semper a vicesimo incipiatur.

[7]Ad tertiam vero, sextam nonamque secundae feriae, novem capitula quae residua sunt de centesimo octavo decimo, ipsa terna per easdem horas dicantur. [8]Expenso ergo psalmo centesimo octavo decimo duobus diebus, id est dominico et secunda feria, [9]tertia feria iam ad tertiam, sextam vel nonam psallantur terni psalmi a centesimo nono decimo usque centesimo vicesimo septimo, id est psalmi novem. [10]Quique psalmi semper usque

---

17.7 Cassian. *inst.* 2,10; Cassian. *conl.* 8,16,1.
17.9 Caes.Arel. *reg.mon.* 21.
18.1 Cassian. *conl.* 10,10,2.

be to the Father." ³The hymn for this hour is sung after the opening versicle, God, come to my assistance (Ps 69[70]:2), before the psalmody begins. ⁴One reading follows the three psalms, and the hour is concluded with a versicle, "Lord, have mercy" and the dismissal.

⁵Prayer is celebrated in the same way at Terce, Sext and None: that is, the opening verse, the hymn appropriate to each hour, three psalms, a reading with a versicle, "Lord, have mercy" and the dismissal. ⁶If the community is rather large, refrains are used with the psalms; if it is smaller, the psalms are said without refrain.

⁷At Vespers the number of psalms should be limited to four, with refrain. ⁸After these psalms there follow: a reading and responsory, an Ambrosian hymn, a versicle, the Gospel Canticle, the litany, and, immediately before the dismissal, the Lord's Prayer.

⁹Compline is limited to three psalms without refrain. ¹⁰After the psalmody comes the hymn for this hour, followed by a reading, a versicle, "Lord, have mercy," a blessing and the dismissal.

CHAPTER 18. THE ORDER OF THE PSALMODY

¹Each of the day hours begins with the verse, God, come to my assistance; Lord, make haste to help me (Ps 69[70]:2), followed by "Glory be to the Father" and the appropriate hymn.

²Then, on Sunday at Prime, four sections of Psalm 118 are said. ³At the other hours, that is, at Terce, Sext and None, three sections of this psalm are said. ⁴On Monday three psalms are said at Prime: Psalms 1, 2 and 6. ⁵At Prime each day thereafter until Sunday, three psalms are said in consecutive order as far as Psalm 19. Psalms 9 and 17 are each divided into two sections. ⁶In this way, Sunday Vigils can always begin with Psalm 20.

⁷On Monday at Terce, Sext and None, the remaining nine sections of Psalm 118 are said, three sections at each hour. ⁸Psalm 118 is thus completed in two days, Sunday and Monday. ⁹On Tuesday, three psalms are said at each of the hours of Terce, Sext and None. These are the nine psalms, 119 through 127. ¹⁰The

---

17.4 "dismissal" (missas): The term refers to the conclusion and dismissal of the prayer assembly, not to the Mass. See note on 35.14 and Appendix 3, pp. 410–412.

17.6 "without refrain" (in directum): See Appendix 3, p. 403.

dominica per easdem horas itidem repetantur, hymnorum nihilominus, lectionum vel versuum dispositionem uniformem cunctis diebus servatam. [11]Et ita scilicet semper dominica a centesimo octavo decimo incipietur.

[12]Vespera autem cotidie quattuor psalmorum modulatione canatur. [13]Qui psalmi incipiantur a centesimo nono usque centesimo quadragesimo septimo, [14]exceptis his qui in diversis horis ex eis sequestrantur, id est a centesimo septimo decimo usque centesimo vicesimo septimo et centesimo tricesimo tertio et centesimo quadragesimo secundo; [15]reliqui omnes in vespera dicendi sunt. [16]Et quia minus veniunt tres psalmi, ideo dividendi sunt qui ex numero suprascripto fortiores inveniuntur, id est centesimum tricesimum octavum et centesimum quadragesimum tertium et centesimum quadragesimum quartum; [17]centesimus vero sextus decimus, quia parvus est, cum centesimo quinto decimo coniungatur. [18]Digesto ergo ordine psalmorum vespertinorum, reliqua, id est lectionem, responsum, hymnum, versum vel canticum, sicut supra taxavimus impleatur.

[19]Ad completorios vero cotidie idem psalmi repetantur, id est quartum, nonagesimum et centesimum tricesimum tertium.

[20]Disposito ordine psalmodiae diurnae, reliqui omnes psalmi qui supersunt aequaliter dividantur in septem noctium vigilias, [21]partiendo scilicet qui inter eos prolixiores sunt psalmi et duodecim per unamquamque constituens noctem.

[22]Hoc praecipue commonentes ut, si cui forte haec distributio psalmorum displicuerit, ordinet si melius aliter iudicaverit, [23]dum omnimodis id attendat ut omni hebdomada psalterium ex integro numero centum quinquaginta psalmorum psallantur, et dominico die semper a caput reprehendatur ad vigilias. [24]Quia nimis inertem devotionis suae servitium ostendunt monachi qui minus a psalterio cum canticis consuetudinariis per septimanae circulum psallunt, [25]dum quando legamus sanctos patres nostros uno die hoc strenue implesse, quod nos tepidi utinam septimana integra persolvamus.

XIX. DE DISCIPLINA PSALLENDI

[1]Ubique credimus divinam esse praesentiam et *oculos Domini*

18.25 *Vitae patr.*, *Verb.senior.* 5,4,57; 3,6.
19.1-6 Cypr. *domin.orat.* 4.

same psalms are repeated at these hours daily up to Sunday. Likewise, the arrangement of hymns, readings and versicles for these days remains the same. [11]In this way, Psalm 118 will always begin on Sunday.

[12]Four psalms are sung each day at Vespers, [13]starting with Psalm 109 and ending with Psalm 147, [14]omitting the psalms in this series already assigned to other hours, namely, Psalms 117 through 127, Psalm 133 and Psalm 142. [15]All the remaining psalms are said at Vespers. [16]Since this leaves three psalms too few, the longer ones in the series should be divided: that is, Psalms 138, 143 and 144. [17]And because Psalm 116 is short, it can be joined to Psalm 115. [18]This is the order of psalms for Vespers; the rest is as arranged above: the reading, responsory, hymn, versicle and canticle.

[19]The same psalms— 4, 90 and 133—are said each day at Compline.

[20]The remaining psalms not accounted for in this arrangement for the day hours are distributed evenly at Vigils over the seven nights of the week. [21]Longer psalms are to be divided so that twelve psalms are said each night.

[22]Above all else we urge that if anyone finds this distribution of the psalms unsatisfactory, he should arrange whatever he judges better, [23]provided that the full complement of one hundred and fifty psalms is by all means carefully maintained every week, and that the series begins anew each Sunday at Vigils. [24]For monks who in a week's time say less than the full psalter with the customary canticles betray extreme indolence and lack of devotion in their service. [25]We read, after all, that our holy Fathers, energetic as they were, did all this in a single day. Let us hope that we, lukewarm as we are, can achieve it in a whole week.

CHAPTER 19. THE DISCIPLINE OF PSALMODY

[1]We believe that the divine presence is everywhere and that

---

18.25 "in a single day" (uno die): See Vitae patr., Verb.senior. 5,4,57. The practice of reciting the 150 psalms daily was more exceptional than common. Benedict incites his monks to fervor while idealizing earlier monasticism.

19.t "discipline" (disciplina): The word disciplina is a key word in the Rule with a variety of meanings, including 'arrangements,' 'discipline,' and here it refers to the interior dispositions the monks should have. See Thematic Index: DISCIPLINE.

in omni loco speculari bonos et malos, [2]maxime tamen hoc sine aliqua dubitatione credamus cum ad opus divinum assistimus.

[3]Ideo semper memores simus quod ait propheta: *Servite Domino in timore*, [4]et iterum: *Psallite sapienter*, [5]et: *In conspectu angelorum psallam tibi*. [6]Ergo consideremus qualiter oporteat in conspectu divinitatis et angelorum eius esse, [7]et sic stemus ad psallendum ut mens nostra concordet voci nostrae.

XX. DE REVERENTIA ORATIONIS

[1]Si, cum hominibus potentibus volumus aliqua suggerere, non praesumimus nisi cum humilitate et reverentia, [2]quanto magis Domino Deo universorum cum omni humilitate et puritatis devotione supplicandum est. [3]Et non in multiloquio, sed in puritate cordis et compunctione lacrimarum nos exaudiri sciamus. [4]Et ideo brevis debet esse et pura oratio, nisi forte ex affectu inspirationis divinae gratiae protendatur. [5]In conventu tamen omnino brevietur oratio, et facto signo a priore omnes pariter surgant.

XXI. DE DECANIS MONASTERII

[1]Si maior fuerit congregatio, eligantur de ipsis fratres boni testimonii et sanctae conversationis, et constituantur decani, [2]qui sollicitudinem gerant super decanias suas in omnibus secundum mandata Dei et praecepta abbatis sui. [3]Qui decani tales

---

19.6-7 Cypr. *domin.orat.* 5; 24; 31.

19.7 Aug. *epist.* 48,3; 211,7.

20.1-2 Basil. *reg.* 108; Cassian. *conl.* 23,6.

20.1-5 Cypr. *domin.orat.* 4; 5; 26.

20.3 Cassian. *conl.* 9,8,1; 9,15; 9,28.

20.3-4 Aug. *epist.* 130,20.

20.4 Cassian. *inst.* 2,10,3; *Hist.mon.* 1; Cassian. *conl.* 2,22; 4,2; 9,3; 9,26; 9,36,1; 10,5.

20.5 Cassian. *conl.* 9,15; Pachom. *reg.* 6; Cassian. *inst.* 2,7,3.

21.1 Aug. *mor.eccl.* 1,67; Hier. *epist.* 22,35.

21.2 Cassian. *inst.* 4,10.

20.3 "not our many words" (*non in multiloquio*): There is certainly an allusion here to the teaching of Jesus on prayer in the Sermon on the Mount, Matt 6:7 (*in multiloquio* in the Vulgate).

20.4 "Prayer" (*oratio*): See Appendix 3, pp. 412–413. For the notion of "pure" prayer, see Introduction, pp. 39–40 and Cassian. *conl.* 10,11.

21.1 "good repute" (*boni testimonii*): This phrase is taken from Acts 6:3. Thus

in every place the eyes of the Lord are watching the good and the wicked (Prov 15:3). [2]But beyond the least doubt we should believe this to be especially true when we celebrate the divine office.

[3]We must always remember, therefore, what the Prophet says: *Serve the Lord with fear* (Ps 2:11), [4]and again, *Sing praise wisely* (Ps 46[47]:8); [5]and, *In the presence of the angels I will sing to you* (Ps 137[138]:1). [6]Let us consider, then, how we ought to behave in the presence of God and his angels, [7]and let us stand to sing the psalms in such a way that our minds are in harmony with our voices.

CHAPTER 20. REVERENCE IN PRAYER

[1]Whenever we want to ask some favor of a powerful man, we do it humbly and respectfully, for fear of presumption. [2]How much more important, then, to lay our petitions before the Lord God of all things with the utmost humility and sincere devotion. [3]We must know that God regards our purity of heart and tears of compunction, not our many words. [4]Prayer should therefore be short and pure, unless perhaps it is prolonged under the inspiration of divine grace. [5]In community, however, prayer should always be brief; and when the superior gives the signal, all should rise together.

CHAPTER 21. THE DEANS OF THE MONASTERY

[1]If the community is rather large, some brothers chosen for their good repute and holy life should be made deans. [2]They will take care of their groups of ten, managing all affairs according to the commandments of God and the orders of their abbot. [3]The

---

there is an implicit comparison between the Lukan concept of deacons and the role of deans. There is no etymological connection; see the following note.

"deans" (*decani*): Literally, a dean (*decanus*) is a person put in charge of a group of ten (*decania*). There is both biblical and monastic precedent for the deanery structure of RB. Moses appointed officials for groups of one thousand, one hundred, fifty and ten (Exod 18:13-17; Deut 1:9-18). According to Jerome (Hier. *epist.* 22,35), Pachomius arranged for leaders of groups of ten. Cassian (Cassian. *inst.* 4,10) and Augustine (Aug. *mor.eccles.* 1,31) also refer to deans. RM 11 prescribes the appointment of two deans (called *praepositi*) for each group of ten; in the event that one dean is occupied elsewhere or that the group is divided into two work details, one dean can remain with the group to supervise the monks and to guard them from vices. See Thematic Index: MONASTIC LEADERS.

eligantur in quibus securus abbas partiat onera sua, ⁴et non eligantur per ordinem, sed secundum vitae meritum et sapientiae doctrinam.

⁵Quique decani, si ex eis aliqua forte quis inflatus superbia repertus fuerit reprehensibilis, correptus semel et iterum atque tertio si emendare noluerit, deiciatur, ⁶et alter in loco eius qui dignus est surrogetur. ⁷Et de praeposito eadem constituimus.

XXII. QUOMODO DORMIANT MONACHI

¹Singuli per singula lecta dormiant. ²Lectisternia pro modo conversationis secundum dispensationem abbatis sui accipiant.

³Si potest fieri omnes in uno loco dormiant; sin autem multitudo non sinit, deni aut viceni cum senioribus qui super eos solliciti sint pausent. ⁴Candela iugiter in eadem cella ardeat usque mane.

⁵Vestiti dormiant et cincti cingellis aut funibus, ut cultellos suos ad latus suum non habeant dum dormiunt, ne forte per somnum vulnerent dormientem; ⁶et ut parati sint monachi semper et, facto signo absque mora surgentes, festinent invicem se praevenire ad opus Dei, cum omni tamen gravitate et modestia. ⁷Adulescentiores fratres iuxta se non habeant lectos, sed permixti cum senioribus. ⁸Surgentes vero ad opus Dei invicem se moderate cohortentur propter somnulentorum excusationes.

21.5 Caes.Arel. *reg.virg.* 10; Aug. *ord.mon.* 10.
22.5-6 Cassian. *inst.* 1,1; 1,11.

21.5 "reproved" (*correptus*): The verb *corripere* means 'to reprimand,' 'to rebuke,' 'to reprove'; so C. Mohrmann "La Langue de Saint Benoît" in *Études sur le Latin des Chrétiens*, Tome II: *Latin Chrétien et Médiéval* (Rome: Edizioni di Storia e Letteratura 1961) p. 331. Except in 64.12, *correptio* is explicitly contrasted with verbal correction.

21.7 "prior" (*praeposito*): The word used in RB for the second in command is *praepositus*, a word used in Cassian. *inst.* 4,10 and 27 and in RM 11 to describe the deans. See notes on RB 6.7 and 65.1.

22.2 "suitable to monastic life" (*pro modo conversationis*): This phrase is understood here to refer to the simple kind of bedding that is in keeping with the monastic life. The words could also indicate the variety of bedding that exists in the same monastery, a variety that accords with the monk's personal level of asceticism and with the regulations of the abbot; so de Vogüé, 5.653–655. McCann, *The Rule of Saint Benedict*, n.44, suggests that *lectisternia* means 'beds' and that *pro modo conversationis* refers to an arrangement of beds in the

deans selected should be the kind of men with whom the abbot can confidently share the burdens of his office. [4]They are to be chosen for virtuous living and wise teaching, not for their rank.

[5]If perhaps one of these deans is found to be puffed up with any pride, and so deserving of censure, he is to be reproved once, twice and even a third time. Should he refuse to amend, he must be removed from office [6]and replaced by another who is worthy. [7]We prescribe the same course of action in regard to the prior.

CHAPTER 22. THE SLEEPING ARRANGEMENTS OF THE MONKS

[1]The monks are to sleep in separate beds. [2]They receive bedding as provided by the abbot, suitable to monastic life.

[3]If possible, all are to sleep in one place, but should the size of the community preclude this, they will sleep in groups of ten or twenty under the watchful care of seniors. [4]A lamp must be kept burning in the room until morning.

[5]They sleep clothed, and girded with belts or cords; but they should remove their knives, lest they accidentally cut themselves in their sleep. [6]Thus the monks will always be ready to arise without delay when the signal is given; each will hasten to arrive at the Work of God before the others, yet with all dignity and decorum. [7]The younger brothers should not have their beds next to each other, but interspersed among those of the seniors. [8]On arising for the Work of God, they will quietly encourage each other, for the sleepy like to make excuses.

---

dormitory according to monks' time of entry into the monastery; so also B. Linderbauer, S. Benedicti Regula Monachorum, herausgegeben und philologisch erklärt (Metten: Verlag des Benediktinerstiftes 1922) p. 266.

"bedding" (Lectisternia): The word lectisternium may mean the same as lectum (bed); so B. Linderbauer, p. 266; G. Widhalm, Die Rhetorischen Elemente in der Regula Benedicti (Hildesheim: Verlag Dr. H. A. Gerstenberg 1974) pp. 112 and 125. See also du Cange, Glossarium Mediae et Infimae Latinitatis, 5.52: "Lectisternium: Lecti apparatus et instrumentum, vel lectus ipse." But in this context it more probably means 'bedding'; so de Vogüé, 5.652–653.

XXIII. DE EXCOMMUNICATIONE CULPARUM

[1]Si quis frater contumax aut inoboediens aut superbus aut murmurans vel in aliquo contrarius exsistens sanctae regulae et praeceptis seniorum suorum contemptor repertus fuerit, [2]hic secundum Domini nostri praeceptum admoneatur semel et secundo secrete a senioribus suis. [3]Si non emendaverit, obiurgetur publice coram omnibus. [4]Si vero neque sic correxerit, si intellegit qualis poena sit, excommunicationi subiaceat; [5]sin autem improbus est, vindictae corporali subdatur.

XXIV. QUALIS DEBET ESSE MODUS EXCOMMUNICATIONIS

[1]Secundum modum culpae, et excommunicationis vel disciplinae mensura debet extendi; [2]qui culparum modus in abbatis pendat iudicio.

[3]Si quis tamen frater in levioribus culpis invenitur, a mensae participatione privetur. [4]Privati autem a mensae consortio ista erit ratio ut in oratorio psalmum aut antiphonam non imponat, neque lectionem recitet, usque ad satisfactionem. [5]Refectionem autem cibi post fratrum refectionem solus accipiat, [6]ut, si verbi gratia fratres reficiunt sexta hora, ille frater nona, si fratres nona, ille vespera, [7]usque dum satisfactione congrua veniam consequatur.

XXV. DE GRAVIORIBUS CULPIS

[1]Is autem frater qui gravioris culpae noxa tenetur suspendatur

23.1 Ps-Macar. *reg.* 12; Pachom. *reg.* 150; 165; Cassian. *inst.* 4,41,2.
23.1-2 Orig. *hom. in Iesu Nave* 7.
23.2-4 Vigil. *reg.(orient.)* 32.
23.5 Ps-Macar. *reg.* 27.
24.1 Ps-Macar. *reg.* 12; *Reg. iv patr.* 5,1.
24.2 Vigil. *reg.(orient.)* 32.
24.4 Caes.Arel. *reg.virg.* 11; Vigil. *reg.(orient.)* 32.
25.1-2 Vigil. *reg.(orient.)* 32; Cassian. *inst.* 2,16.

23.0 Disciplinary measures are found in many chapters of the Rule, but especially in 23–30 and in 43–46, where the norms for satisfaction are set forth. The presence of these measures is a concrete recognition of faults in the monastery. St. Benedict's aim is not primarily satisfaction (the making up for a fault) and punishment of wrongdoing, but the conversion of the wayward monk. See Appendix 4, p. 426 and *passim*.
23.2 "twice" (*semel et secundo*): See Appendix 4, p. 420.

CHAPTER 23. EXCOMMUNICATION FOR FAULTS

[1] If a brother is found to be stubborn or disobedient or proud, if he grumbles or in any way despises the holy rule and defies the orders of his seniors, [2] he should be warned twice privately by the seniors in accord with our Lord's injunction (Matt 18:15-16). [3] If he does not amend, he must be rebuked publicly in the presence of everyone. [4] But if even then he does not reform, let him be excommunicated, provided that he understands the nature of this punishment. [5] If however he lacks understanding, let him undergo corporal punishment.

CHAPTER 24. DEGREES OF EXCOMMUNICATION

[1] There ought to be due proportion between the seriousness of a fault and the measure of excommunication or discipline. [2] The abbot determines the gravity of faults.

[3] If a brother is found guilty of less serious faults, he will not be allowed to share the common table. [4] Anyone excluded from the common table will conduct himself as follows: in the oratory he will not lead a psalm or a refrain nor will he recite a reading until he has made satisfaction, [5] and he will take his meals alone, after the brothers have eaten. [6] For instance, if the brothers eat at noon, he will eat in midafternoon; if the brothers eat in midafternoon, he will eat in the evening, [7] until by proper satisfaction he gains pardon.

CHAPTER 25. SERIOUS FAULTS

[1] A brother guilty of a serious fault is to be excluded from both

---

23.3 "in the presence of everyone" (*coram omnibus*): This direction is based on Matt 18:17; the previous verse refers to Matt 18:15-17. Since the directions in Matthew are for the maintenance of good order in a church (one of the two occasions the word "church" is used in the Gospels), it would appear that the monastic community is, by analogy, understood as "a church" in RB. See note on Prol.50.

23.5 "lacks understanding" (*improbus est*): See note to RB 2.28.

24.3 "less serious faults" (*levioribus culpis*): Literally, minor or lighter faults. The faults that require satisfaction in the monastery are much less serious than those that require public ecclesiastical penance. See de Vogüé 7.263-277, and Appendix 4, pp. 415-420.

25.1 "serious fault" (*gravioris culpae*): Major or weightier faults involve a greater degree of isolation from the community. On the practice of excommunication, see Appendix 4, pp. 421-430.

a mensa, simul ab oratorio. [2]Nullus ei fratrum in nullo iungatur consortio nec in colloquio. [3]Solus sit ad opus sibi iniunctum, persistens in paenitentiae luctu, sciens illam terribilem apostoli sententiam dicentis [4]*traditum eiusmodi hominem in interitum carnis, ut spiritus salvus sit in die Domini.* [5]Cibi autem refectionem solus percipiat, mensura vel hora qua praeviderit abbas ei competere; [6]nec a quoquam benedicatur transeunte nec cibum quod ei datur.

XXVI. DE HIS QUI SINE IUSSIONE IUNGUNT SE EXCOMMUNICATIS

[1]Si quis frater praesumpserit sine iussione abbatis fratri excommunicato quolibet modo se iungere aut loqui cum eo vel mandatum ei dirigere, [2]similem sortiatur excommunicationis vindictam.

XXVII. QUALITER DEBEAT ABBAS SOLLICITUS ESSE CIRCA EXCOMMUNICATOS

[1]Omni sollicitudine curam gerat abbas circa delinquentes fratres, quia *non est opus sanis medicus sed male habentibus.* [2]Et ideo uti debet omni modo ut sapiens medicus, immittere senpectas, id est seniores sapientes fratres, [3]qui quasi secrete consolentur fratrem fluctuantem et provocent ad humilitatis satisfac-

---

25.4 Orig. *hom. in Iesu Nave* 7.
26.1-2 Cassian. *inst.* 2,16; Vigil. *reg.(orient.)* 33.
27.1-9 Cypr. *epist.* 68,4.
27.2 *Vitae patr., Verb.senior.* 5,5,4 (cf. 5,10,85); Orig. *hom. in Iesu Nave* 7.

25.6 "not be blessed" (*nec. . .benedicatur*): Cf. Ps 128(129):8.

26.1 "presumes" (*praesumpserit*): The word *praesumere* means literally 'to take ahead of time' (RB 43.18) and so, 'to arrogate to oneself,' 'to assume or claim presumptuously.' It is used very extensively in the monastic literature of this period (thirty times in RB and the substantive *praesumptio* twice). This frequency of usage seems to be connected with the monastic concern for the development of humility. See Mohrmann "La Langue de Saint Benoît," p. 334, and especially P. Miquel "'Praesumere-Praesumptio' dans l'ancienne littérature monastique" *RBén* 79 (1969) 424–436.

27.2 "a wise physician" (*sapiens medicus*): The metaphor introduced here extends into ch. 28. For the background of the idea of the abbot as a physician, see Appendix 4, n.77. See also Appendix 2, p. 352 and the note on 2.8.

"*senpectas*": This word, which appears nowhere else in Christian literature, is variously interpreted. Some suggest a "mustard paste" (poultice); so E. Molland "Ut sapiens medicus. Medical Vocabulary in St. Benedict's Regula

the table and the oratory. [2]No other brother should associate or converse with him at all. [3]He will work alone at the tasks assigned to him, living continually in sorrow and penance, pondering that fearful judgment of the Apostle: [4]*Such a man is handed over for the destruction of his flesh that his spirit may be saved on the day of the Lord* (1 Cor 5:5). [5]Let him take his food alone in an amount and at a time the abbot considers appropriate for him. [6]He should not be blessed by anyone passing by, nor should the food that is given him be blessed.

CHAPTER 26. UNAUTHORIZED ASSOCIATION WITH THE EXCOMMUNICATED

[1]If a brother, acting without an order from the abbot, presumes to associate in any way with an excommunicated brother, to converse with him or to send him a message, [2]he should receive a like punishment of excommunication.

CHAPTER 27. THE ABBOT'S CONCERN FOR THE EXCOMMUNICATED

[1]The abbot must exercise the utmost care and concern for wayward brothers, because *it is not the healthy who need a physician, but the sick* (Matt 9:12). [2]Therefore, he ought to use every skill of a wise physician and send in *senpectae,* that is, mature and wise brothers [3]who, under the cloak of secrecy, may support the wavering brother, urge him to be humble as a way of making satisfaction, and *console* him *lest he be overwhelmed by excessive sorrow* (2 Cor 2:7). [4]Rather, as the Apostle also says:

Monachorum" *SM* 6 (1964) 273–296; J. Svennung "The Origin and Meaning of the Word Senpecta" *ibid.* 297–298; J. Svennung "S. Benedicti Senpecta = sinapismus. Zur Haplologie in den composita" *Rivista di filologia e d'istruzione classica* 95 (1967) 65–71. B. Steidle suggests a play on words; Benedict hears the word *sen-ior* (elder) in the foreign word *sen-pecta* (Greek: *sumpaiktēs,* meaning 'companion'); see *Die Benediktus-Regel. Lateinisch-Deutsch* (Beuron: Beuroner Kunstverlag 1975) p. 115. De Vogüé, 2.548–549, also thinks it more likely is derived from the Greek word, strengthening his case by a reference to G. Goetz, *Corp. Gloss. Lat.* 4.565, 62; 5.331, 39, where *sunodos* has become *senodus* and is interpreted as *congregatio senum* (a gathering of old men). Because of this remarkable parallel, linguistics supports de Vogüé and Steidle, whereas the context lends weight to the mustard plaster theory. Whatever may be the etymology, what is important is what St. Benedict understands the term to signify and that he has explained.

tionem et *consolentur* eum *ne abundantiori tristitia absorbeatur*, [4]sed, sicut ait item apostolus, *confirmetur in eo caritas* et oretur pro eo ab omnibus.

[5]Magnopere enim debet sollicitudinem gerere abbas et omni sagacitate et industria currere, ne aliquam de ovibus sibi creditis perdat. [6]Noverit enim se infirmarum curam suscepisse animarum, non super sanas tyrannidem; [7]et metuat prophetae comminationem per quam dicit Deus: *Quod crassum videbatis assumebatis et quod debile erat proiciebatis*. [8]Et pastoris boni pium imitetur exemplum, qui, relictis nonaginta novem ovibus in montibus, abiit unam ovem quae erraverat quaerere; [9]cuius infirmitati in tantum compassus est, ut eam *in* sacris *humeris suis* dignaretur *imponere* et sic reportare ad gregem.

XXVIII. DE HIS QUI SAEPIUS CORREPTI EMENDARE NOLUERINT

[1]Si quis frater frequenter correptus pro qualibet culpa, si etiam excommunicatus non emendaverit, acrior ei accedat correptio, id est ut verberum vindicta in eum procedant. [2]Quod si nec ita correxerit, aut forte—quod absit—in superbia elatus etiam defendere voluerit opera sua, tunc abbas faciat quod sapiens medicus: [3]si exhibuit fomenta, si unguenta adhortationum, si medicamina scripturarum divinarum, si ad ultimum ustionem excommunicationis vel plagarum virgae, [4]et iam si viderit nihil suam praevalere industriam, adhibeat etiam—quod maius est— suam et omnium fratrum pro eo orationem, [5]ut Dominus qui omnia potest operetur salutem circa infirmum fratrem. [6]Quod si nec isto modo sanatus fuerit, tunc iam utatur abbas ferro abscisionis, ut ait apostolus: *Auferte malum ex vobis*, [7]et iterum: *Infidelis, si discedit, discedat*, [8]ne una ovis morbida omnem gregem contagiet.

27.4 *Vitae patr., Verb.senior.* 5,13,13.
27.5-9 Cypr. *epist.* 55,15-16.
27.8-9 Orig. *hom. in Iesu Nave* 7.
28.1 Ps-Macar. *reg.* 17; *Concil.Agathense a.506* canon 38.
28.2-3 *Vitae patr., Verb.senior.* 5,10,85 (cf. 5,5,4); Cypr. *epist.* 55,15-16.
28.2-6 Orig. *hom. in Iesu Nave* 7.
28.3-6 Ambr. *off.* 2,135; Cassian. *inst.* 10,7.
28.6 et 8 Cypr. *hab.virg.* 17; Cypr. *eccl.unit.* 9; Cypr. *de mort.* 14.
28.8 Orig. *hom. in Iesu Nave* 7; Cypr. *epist.* 59,15; Aug. *epist.* 211,11; Vigil. *reg.(orient.)* 35; Hier. *epist.* 2,1; 16,1; 130,19.

Let love for him be reaffirmed (2 Cor 2:8), and let all pray for him.

⁵It is the abbot's responsibility to have great concern and to act with all speed, discernment and diligence in order not to lose any of the sheep entrusted to him. ⁶He should realize that he has undertaken care of the sick, not tyranny over the healthy. ⁷Let him also fear the threat of the Prophet in which God says: *What you saw to be fat you claimed for yourselves, and what was weak you cast aside* (Ezek 34:3-4). ⁸He is to imitate the loving example of the Good Shepherd who left the ninety-nine sheep in the mountains and went in search of the one sheep that had strayed. ⁹So great was his compassion for its weakness that *he* mercifully *placed it on his* sacred *shoulders* and so carried it back to the flock (Luke 15:5).

CHAPTER 28. THOSE WHO REFUSE TO AMEND AFTER FREQUENT REPROOFS

¹If a brother has been reproved frequently for any fault, or if he has even been excommunicated, yet does not amend, let him receive a sharper punishment: that is, let him feel the strokes of the rod. ²But if even then he does not reform, or perhaps becomes proud and would actually defend his conduct, which God forbid, the abbot should follow the procedure of a wise physician. ³After he has applied compresses, the ointment of encouragement, the medicine of divine Scripture, and finally the cauterizing iron of excommunication and strokes of the rod, ⁴and if he then perceives that his earnest efforts are unavailing, let him apply an even better remedy: he and all the brothers should pray for him ⁵so that the Lord, who can do all things, may bring about the health of the sick brother. ⁶Yet if even this procedure does not heal him, then finally, the abbot must use the knife and amputate. For the Apostle says: *Banish the evil one from your midst* (1 Cor 5:13); ⁷and again, *If the unbeliever departs, let him depart* (1 Cor 7:15), ⁸lest one diseased sheep infect the whole flock.

28.5 "all things" (*omnia*): This is probably a reference to Matt 18:26.
"health" (*salutem*): See Thematic Index: HEALING.

XXIX. SI DEBEANT FRATRES EXEUNTES DE MONASTERIO ITERUM RECIPI

[1]Frater qui proprio vitio egreditur de monasterio, si reverti voluerit, spondeat prius omnem emendationem pro quo egressus est, [2]et sic in ultimo gradu recipiatur, ut ex hoc eius humilitas comprobetur. [3]Quod si denuo exierit, usque tertio ita recipiatur, iam postea sciens omnem sibi reversionis aditum denegari.

XXX. DE PUERIS MINORI AETATE, QUALITER CORRIPIANTUR

[1]Omnis aetas vel intellectus proprias debet habere mensuras. [2]Ideoque, quotiens pueri vel adulescentiores aetate, aut qui minus intellegere possunt quanta poena sit excommunicationis, [3]hi tales dum delinquunt, aut ieiuniis nimiis affligantur aut acris verberibus coerceantur, ut sanentur.

XXXI. DE CELLARARIO MONASTERII, QUALIS SIT

[1]Cellararius monasterii eligatur de congregatione, sapiens, maturis moribus, sobrius, non multum edax, non elatus, non turbulentus, non iniuriosus, non tardus, non prodigus, [2]sed timens Deum; qui omni congregationi sit sicut pater. [3]Curam gerat de omnibus; [4]sine iussione abbatis nihil faciat. [5]Quae iubentur cu-

---

29.1-2 Pachom. *reg.* 136.
31.1-16 Vigil. *reg.(orient.)* 25.
31.4-5 Cypr. *epist.* 63,1.

29.1 "for leaving" (*pro quo egressus est*): In this translation, *pro quo* is understood as *pro eo quod*, that is, "because" [he left]. See L. Traube, *Textgeschichte der Regula S. Benedicti* (Munich: Verlag der R. Akademie 1898) p. 17 and McCann, *The Rule of Saint Benedict*, n.50. Another interpretation (de Vogüé, 2.554, n.1) understands *pro quo* as *pro vitio pro quo*, i.e., "full amends for the fault for which he left."

30.t "boys" (*pueris minori aetate*): Only young boys are mentioned in the title of the chapter, but v.2 adds two other categories of persons: the younger in age (*adulescentiores aetate*) and those who cannot understand the penalty of excommunication. In the corresponding chapter of RM (14.78-87), whipping is prescribed for boys up to the age of fifteen, a limit also mentioned in RB 70.4. Excommunication, as it is explained at greater length in RM 14, is effective only for those who are sufficiently socialized to appreciate the need for internal change. On the presence of boys in the monastery, see note on RB 59.1. See Thematic Index: MONK, social differentiation, age.

31.0 Chs. 31–42 deal generally with the offices of service to the community:

CHAPTER 29. READMISSION OF BROTHERS WHO LEAVE
THE MONASTERY

[1]If a brother, following his own evil ways, leaves the monastery but then wishes to return, he must first promise to make full amends for leaving. [2]Let him be received back, but as a test of his humility he should be given the last place. [3]If he leaves again, or even a third time, he should be readmitted under the same conditions. After this, however, he must understand that he will be denied all prospect of return.

CHAPTER 30. THE MANNER OF REPROVING BOYS

[1]Every age and level of understanding should receive appropriate treatment. [2]Therefore, as often as boys and the young, or those who cannot understand the seriousness of the penalty of excommunication, [3]are guilty of misdeeds, they should be subjected to severe fasts or checked with sharp strokes so that they may be healed.

CHAPTER 31. QUALIFICATIONS OF THE MONASTERY CELLARER

[1]As cellarer of the monastery, there should be chosen from the community someone who is wise, mature in conduct, temperate, not an excessive eater, not proud, excitable, offensive, dilatory or wasteful, [2]but God-fearing, and like a father to the whole community. [3]He will take care of everything, [4]but will do nothing without an order from the abbot. [5]Let him keep to his orders.

---

mutual service, the renunciation of goods, the community of goods, the amount of food and drink, and fasting.

31.1 "cellarer" (*Cellararius*): The functions of the cellarer (a distinctively monastic term derived from the Latin *cellarium*, meaning 'storeroom') include, in secular terminology, those of 'business manager,' 'treasurer,' 'bursar.' In the Pachomian monasteries, the corresponding official was known as the *oikonomos*, or 'steward.' Because of his many concerns — the care and distribution of the goods of the monastery — the cellarer is like a father (*sicut pater*: 31.2) to the whole community, while the abbot is the father. See Thematic Index: MONASTIC LEADERS and STEWARDSHIP.

"temperate" (*sobrius*): Some of the attributes desired in the cellarer are drawn from the list of qualities to be sought in bishops in 1 Tim 3:2-4. The general tone of the chapter is very like that of chs. 2 and 64 on the abbot. See specifically 2.36 *timentibus eum*, 64.2 *sapientia*, 64.9 *sobrium*, 64.16 *non turbulentus*, besides the striking *sicut pater* referred to in the preceding note.

stodiat; [6]fratres non contristet. [7]Si quis frater ab eo forte aliqua irrationabiliter postulat, non spernendo eum contristet, sed rationabiliter cum humilitate male petenti deneget. [8]Animam suam custodiat, memor semper illud apostolicum quia *qui bene ministraverit gradum bonum sibi acquirit.* [9]Infirmorum, infantum, hospitum pauperumque cum omni sollicitudine curam gerat, sciens sine dubio quia pro his omnibus in die iudicii rationem redditurus est. [10]Omnia vasa monasterii cunctamque substantiam ac si altaris vasa sacrata conspiciat. [11]Nihil ducat neglegendum. [12]Neque avaritiae studeat, neque prodigus sit et stirpator substantiae monasterii, sed omnia mensurate faciat et secundum iussionem abbatis.

[13]Humilitatem ante omnia habeat, et cui substantia non est quod tribuatur, sermo responsionis porrigatur bonus, [14]ut scriptum est: *Sermo* bonus *super datum optimum.* [15]Omnia quae ei iniunxerit abbas, ipsa habeat sub cura sua; a quibus eum prohibuerit, non praesumat. [16]Fratribus constitutam annonam sine aliquo typho vel mora offerat, ut non scandalizentur, memor divini eloquii quid mereatur *qui scandalizaverit unum de pusillis.*

[17]Si congregatio maior fuerit, solacia ei dentur, a quibus adiutus et ipse aequo animo impleat officium sibi commissum. [18]Horis competentibus dentur quae danda sunt et petantur quae petenda sunt, [19]ut nemo perturbetur neque contristetur in domo Dei.

XXXII. DE FERRAMENTIS VEL REBUS MONASTERII

[1]Substantia monasterii in ferramentis vel vestibus seu quibuslibet rebus praevideat abbas fratres de quorum vita et moribus securus sit, [2]et eis singula, ut utile iudicaverit, consignet custodienda atque recolligenda. [3]Ex quibus abbas brevem teneat, ut dum sibi in ipsa assignata fratres vicissim succedunt, sciat quid dat aut quid recipit.

31.6 *Vitae patr., Verb.senior.* 3,170.
31.7 Aug. *in psalm.* 103,1,19.
31.8-10 *Reg. iv patr.* 3,26-27.
31.10 Basil. *reg.* 103 (cf. 104); Cassian. *inst.* 4,19,3-20.
31.16 Aug. *epist.* 22,6; Cypr. *de pat.* 24.
32.3 Pachom. *reg.* 66.

⁶He should not annoy the brothers. ⁷If any brother happens to make an unreasonable demand of him, he should not reject him with disdain and cause him distress, but reasonably and humbly deny the improper request. ⁸Let him keep watch over his own soul, ever mindful of that saying of the Apostle: *He who serves well secures a good standing for himself* (1 Tim 3:13). ⁹He must show every care and concern for the sick, children, guests and the poor, knowing for certain that he will be held accountable for all of them on the day of judgment. ¹⁰He will regard all utensils and goods of the monastery as sacred vessels of the altar, ¹¹aware that nothing is to be neglected. ¹²He should not be prone to greed, nor be wasteful and extravagant with the goods of the monastery, but should do everything with moderation and according to the abbot's orders.

¹³Above all, let him be humble. If goods are not available to meet a request, he will offer a kind word in reply, ¹⁴for it is written: A kind *word is better than the best gift* (Sir 18:17). ¹⁵He should take care of all that the abbot entrusts to him, and not presume to do what the abbot has forbidden. ¹⁶He will provide the brothers their allotted amount of food without any pride or delay, lest they be led astray. For he must remember what the Scripture says that person deserves *who leads one of the little ones astray* (Matt 18:6).

¹⁷If the community is rather large, he should be given helpers, that with their assistance he may calmly perform the duties of his office. ¹⁸Necessary items are to be requested and given at the proper times, ¹⁹so that no one may be disquieted or distressed in the house of God.

CHAPTER 32. THE TOOLS AND GOODS OF THE MONASTERY

¹The goods of the monastery, that is, its tools, clothing or anything else, should be entrusted to brothers whom the abbot appoints and in whose manner of life he has confidence. ²He will, as he sees fit, issue to them the various articles to be cared for and collected after use. ³The abbot will maintain a list of these, so that when the brothers succeed one another in their assigned

---

31.10 "sacred vessels" (*vasa sacrata*): See Zech 14:20-21.
31.19 "the house of God" (*domo Dei*): See Thematic Index: HOUSE OF GOD.
32.3 "what he hands out" (*quid dat*): See Sir 42:7.

⁴Si quis autem sordide aut neglegenter res monasterii tractaverit, corripiatur; ⁵si non emendaverit, disciplinae regulari
subiaceat.

XXXIII. SI QUID DEBEANT MONACHI PROPRIUM HABERE

¹Praecipue hoc vitium radicitus amputandum est de monasterio, ²ne quis praesumat aliquid dare aut accipere sine iussione
abbatis, ³neque aliquid habere proprium, nullam omnino rem,
neque codicem, neque tabulas, neque graphium, sed nihil omnino, ⁴quippe quibus nec corpora sua nec voluntates licet habere
in propria voluntate; ⁵omnia vero necessaria a patre sperare
monasterii, nec quicquam liceat habere quod abbas non dederit
aut permiserit. ⁶*Omniaque omnium sint communia*, ut scriptum
est, *ne quisquam suum aliquid dicat* vel praesumat.

⁷Quod si quisquam huic nequissimo vitio deprehensus fuerit
delectari, admoneatur semel et iterum; ⁸si non emendaverit, correptioni subiaceat.

XXXIV. SI OMNES AEQUALITER DEBEANT NECESSARIA ACCIPERE

¹Sicut scriptum est: *Dividebatur singulis prout cuique opus
erat.* ²Ubi non dicimus ut personarum—quod absit—acceptio
sit, sed infirmitatum consideratio; ³ubi qui minus indiget agat
Deo gratias et non contristetur, ⁴qui vero plus indiget humilietur
pro infirmitate, non extollatur pro misericordia; ⁵et ita omnia
membra erunt in pace. ⁶Ante omnia, ne murmurationis malum
pro qualicumque causa in aliquo qualicumque verbo vel sig-

32.4 Caes.Arel. *reg.virg.* 32; *Reg. iv patr.* 3,29.
33.t Basil. reg. 29.
33.1 Cassian *inst.* 7,21; 7,27; Cassian. *conl.* 16,6,4.
33.2 *Reg. ii patr.* 10; Vigil. *reg.(orient.)* 30-31; Pachom. *reg.* 106.
33.3 *Vita Pachom.* 28; Sulpic.Sever. *Mart.* 10,6; Aug. *ord.mon.* 4.
33.4 Cassian. *inst.* 2,3 (cf. *conl.* 24,23) (cf. RB 58.25); Basil. *reg.* 106 (cf. RB 58.25).
33.5 Caes.Arel. *reg.mon.* 2; 16; Pachom. *reg.* 81.
33.6 Aug. *epist.* 211,5.
33.7 Cassian. *inst.* 7,21.
34.1 Aug. *epist.* 211,5.
34.3-4 Aug. *epist.* 211,9.
34.5 Cypr. *domin.orat.* 23.

32.4 "clean" (*sordide*): The Latin means literally, "if anyone handles the things of the monastery dirtily or carelessly."
33.1 "evil practice" (*vitium*): St. Benedict calls private possession of goods a vice or an evil, for it is a manifestation of one's own will and an act of disobedi-

tasks, he may be aware of what he hands out and what he receives back.

⁴Whoever fails to keep the things belonging to the monastery clean or treats them carelessly should be reproved. ⁵If he does not amend, let him be subjected to the discipline of the rule.

CHAPTER 33. MONKS AND PRIVATE OWNERSHIP

¹Above all, this evil practice must be uprooted and removed from the monastery. ²We mean that without an order from the abbot, no one may presume to give, receive ³or retain anything as his own, nothing at all—not a book, writing tablets or stylus—in short, not a single item, ⁴especially since monks may not have the free disposal even of their own bodies and wills. ⁵For their needs, they are to look to the father of the monastery, and are not allowed anything which the abbot has not given or permitted. ⁶*All things should be the common possession* of all, as it is written, *so that no one* presumes to *call anything his own* (Acts 4:32).

⁷But if anyone is caught indulging in this most evil practice, he should be warned a first and a second time. ⁸If he does not amend, let him be subjected to punishment.

CHAPTER 34. DISTRIBUTION OF GOODS ACCORDING TO NEED

¹It is written: *Distribution was made to each one as he had need* (Acts 4:35). ²By this we do not imply that there should be favoritism—God forbid—but rather consideration for weaknesses. ³Whoever needs less should thank God and not be distressed, ⁴but whoever needs more should feel humble because of his weakness, not self-important because of the kindness shown him. ⁵In this way all the members will be at peace. ⁶First and foremost, there must be no word or sign of the evil of grumbling,

---

ence. The monk looks to the abbot for all his needs. See Thematic Index: COM-MUNITY, sharing all things in common, *Antithesis*: personal ownership.

33.6 "as it is written" (*ut scriptum est*): The slightly adapted quotation from Acts 4:32 indicates that St. Benedict envisions the church of Jerusalem, especially in its free dispossession of property and its sharing of goods according to need, as a model of cenobitic monasticism. This is a common theme of early monastic literature. See note to Prol.50 above and Patristic references.

34.2 "favoritism—God forbid" (*personarum—quod absit—acceptio*): The reference is to Rom 2:11 (*non est acceptio personarum apud Deum* [Vulgate]). Cf. RB 2.20.

34.5 "all the members" (*omnia membra*): See 1 Cor 12:12-30.

nificatione appareat; [7]quod si deprehensus fuerit, districtiori disciplinae subdatur.

XXXV. DE SEPTIMANARIIS COQUINAE

[1]Fratres sibi invicem serviant, ut nullus excusetur a coquinae officio, nisi aut aegritudo, aut in causa gravis utilitatis quis occupatus fuerit, [2]quia exinde maior merces et caritas acquiritur. [3]Imbecillibus autem procurentur solacia, ut non cum tristitia hoc faciant; [4]sed habeant omnes solacia secundum modum congregationis aut positionem loci. [5]Si maior congregatio fuerit, cellararius excusetur a coquina, vel si qui, ut diximus, maioribus utilitatibus occupantur; [6]ceteri sibi sub caritate invicem serviant.

[7]Egressurus de septimana sabbato munditias faciat. [8]Lintea cum quibus sibi fratres manus aut pedes tergunt lavent. [9]Pedes vero tam ipse qui egreditur quam ille qui intraturus est omnibus lavent. [10]Vasa ministerii sui munda et sana cellarario reconsignet; [11]qui cellararius item intranti consignet, ut sciat quod dat aut quod recipit.

[12]Septimanarii autem ante unam horam refectionis accipiant super statutam annonam singulas biberes et panem, [13]ut hora refectionis sine murmuratione et gravi labore serviant fratribus suis. [14]In diebus tamen sollemnibus usque ad missas sustineant.

35.1 Hier. *epist.* 22,35.
35.6-11 Cassian. *inst.* 4,19,1-3.
35.13 Aug. epist. 211,13.

35.8 "He is to wash" (*lavent*): Literally, "they are to wash." The plural seems to come from the succession of weekly servers; the singular seems to follow from the directions given in v.7.

35.12 "An hour before mealtime" (*ante unam horam refectionis*): Despite the interesting suggestion of B. Steidle "Ante unam horam refectionis" StA 42 (1957) 73-104 and "Ante unam horam refectionis. . .Zur neuen Deutung von Kapitel 35, 12-14 der Regel St. Benedikts" EA 41 (1965) 387–394, that the true meaning is "before the single mealtime," a brachylogy for "before the meal on days when there is only one meal," it seems better to keep the traditional translation. *Unus* can mean 'single,' 'unique,' etc., and this yields good sense, but *ante* with an accusative of the time and a genitive of the event is a regular late-Latin idiom for "so much time before so-and-so." There are also limitations on the use of *unus* in Steidle's sense, which in any case is less likely in late-Latin, and no parallel example has been adduced of *unus* in a simple attributive position, as here, being used in the sense required by Steidle. See Lewis and Short, *A Latin Dictionary*, s.vv. *ante* II.B.1.c and *unus* I.B.3; A. Blaise, *Dictionnaire Latin-Français*, s.vv. *ante* II.3 and *unus*; and J. B. Hofmann, *Lateinische Umgangssprache*, 2nd ed. (Heidelberg: Winter 1939) pp. 101–102.

no manifestation of it for any reason at all. [7]If, however, anyone is caught grumbling, let him undergo more severe discipline.

CHAPTER 35. KITCHEN SERVERS OF THE WEEK

[1]The brothers should serve one another. Consequently, no one will be excused from kitchen service unless he is sick or engaged in some important business of the monastery, [2]for such service increases reward and fosters love. [3]Let those who are not strong have help so that they may serve without distress, [4]and let everyone receive help as the size of the community or local conditions warrant. [5]If the community is rather large, the cellarer should be excused from kitchen service, and, as we have said, those should also be excused who are engaged in important business. [6]Let all the rest serve one another in love.

[7]On Saturday the brother who is completing his work will do the washing. [8]He is to wash the towels which the brothers use to wipe their hands and feet. [9]Both the one who is ending his service and the one who is about to begin are to wash the feet of everyone. [10]The utensils required for the kitchen service are to be washed and returned intact to the cellarer, [11]who in turn issues them to the one beginning his week. In this way the cellarer will know what he hands out and what he receives back.

[12]An hour before mealtime, the kitchen workers of the week should each receive a drink and some bread over and above the regular portion, [13]so that at mealtime, they may serve their brothers without grumbling or hardship. [14]On solemn days, however, they should wait until after the dismissal.

The Master does not seem to allow this mitigation at all, for immediately after the servers receive Communion, the abbot is to warn them not to take any food or drink before the common prayer at table (RM 21.8).

35.14 "until after the dismissal" (usque ad missas): It is uncertain whether the dismissal in question is that at the end of Mass or that at the end of the meal. It is quite possible that it refers to Mass here, since it is a question of solemn feasts. See Appendix 3, pp. 410–412. In this case the reason for having the servers wait would be the Eucharistic fast, a practice that was developing at the time. This assumes also that the meal took place immediately after Mass. RM 21-23 prescribes that the meal is to take place after that office which includes a Communion rite. See Appendix 3, pp. 410–411. Steidle holds (see note on 35.12) that missas refers to the end of the meal. The reason would then be that there was no reason for taking food ahead of time, since there would be two meals on feast days, one taken at midday (prandium) and one taken in the evening (cena). On ordinary days there would have been only one meal later in the day.

[15]Intrantes et exeuntes hebdomadarii in oratorio mox matutinis finitis dominica omnibus genibus provolvantur postulantes pro se orari. [16]Egrediens autem de septimana dicat hunc versum: *Benedictus es, Domine Deus*, qui *adiuvasti me et consolatus es me*; [17]quo dicto tertio accepta benedictione egrediens, subsequatur ingrediens et dicat: *Deus in adiutorium meum intende, Domine ad adiuvandum me festina*, [18]et hoc idem tertio repetatur ab omnibus et accepta benedictione ingrediatur.

XXXVI. DE INFIRMIS FRATRIBUS

[1]Infirmorum cura ante omnia et super omnia adhibenda est, ut sicut revera Christo ita eis serviatur, [2]quia ipse dixit: *Infirmus fui et visitastis me*, [3]et: *Quod fecistis uni de his minimis mihi fecistis*. [4]Sed et ipsi infirmi considerent in honorem Dei sibi servire, et non superfluitate sua contristent fratres suos servientes sibi; [5]qui tamen patienter portandi sunt, quia de talibus copiosior merces acquiritur. [6]Ergo cura maxima sit abbati ne aliquam neglegentiam patiantur.

[7]Quibus fratribus infirmis sit cella super se deputata et servitor timens Deum et diligens ac sollicitus. [8]Balnearum usus infirmis quotiens expedit offeratur — sanis autem et maxime iuvenibus tardius concedatur. [9]Sed et carnium esus infirmis omnino debilibus pro reparatione concedatur; at, ubi meliorati fuerunt, a carnibus more solito omnes abstineant.

[10]Curam autem maximam habeat abbas ne a cellarariis aut a servitoribus neglegantur infirmi. Et ipsum respicit quicquid a discipulis delinquitur.

XXXVII. DE SENIBUS VEL INFANTIBUS

[1]Licet ipsa natura humana trahatur ad misericordiam in his

35.15 *Sacr.Gelasianum* 41.
36.1-3 Basil. *reg.* 36.
36.8 Caes.Arel. *reg.virg.* 29
36.9 Caes.Arel. *reg.mon.* 24.

35.15 "a profound bow. . .before all" (*omnibus genibus provolvantur*): The action prescribed seems to be a profound bow to the level of the knees rather than a kneeling down. The Oxford MS reads *omnium*: "to (or at) the knees of all." After the Council of Nicaea (325), it was Church practice not to kneel on Sundays during the formal liturgical services. See A. Mundó "À propos des rituels du Maître et de saint Benoît: La 'Provolutio'" *SM* 4 (1962) 177-191.

¹⁵On Sunday immediately after Lauds, those beginning as well as those completing their week of service should make a profound bow in the oratory before all and ask for their prayers. ¹⁶Let the server completing his week recite this verse: *Blessed are you, Lord God, who have helped me and comforted me* (Dan 3:52; Ps 85[86]:17). ¹⁷After this verse has been said three times, he receives a blessing. Then the one beginning his service follows and says: *God, come to my assistance; Lord, make haste to help me* (Ps 69[70]:2). ¹⁸And all repeat this verse three times. When he has received a blessing, he begins his service.

CHAPTER 36. THE SICK BROTHERS

¹Care of the sick must rank above and before all else, so that they may truly be served as Christ, ²for he said: *I was sick and you visited me* (Matt 25:36), ³and, *What you did for one of these least brothers you did for me* (Matt 25:40). ⁴Let the sick on their part bear in mind that they are served out of honor for God, and let them not by their excessive demands distress their brothers who serve them. ⁵Still, sick brothers must be patiently borne with, because serving them leads to a greater reward. ⁶Consequently, the abbot should be extremely careful that they suffer no neglect.

⁷Let a separate room be designated for the sick, and let them be served by an attendant who is God-fearing, attentive and concerned. ⁸The sick may take baths whenever it is advisable, but the healthy, and especially the young, should receive permission less readily. ⁹Moreover, to regain their strength, the sick who are very weak may eat meat, but when their health improves, they should all abstain from meat as usual.

¹⁰The abbot must take the greatest care that cellarers and those who serve the sick do not neglect them, for the shortcomings of disciples are his responsibility.

CHAPTER 37. THE ELDERLY AND CHILDREN

¹Although human nature itself is inclined to be compassionate

---

37.1 "the young" (*infantum*): Although the term *infans* can be used for anyone under legal age, it seems likely that a lower age is envisioned here. In comparable situations in RM 27.41 and 28.24, the age of twelve is set, but in RM 14.78 and RB 70.4, where it is a question of the kind of punishment to be administered, the differentiating age is set at fifteen.

aetatibus, senum videlicet et infantum, tamen et regulae auctoritas eis prospiciat. [2]Consideretur semper in eis imbecillitas et ullatenus eis districtio regulae teneatur in alimentis, [3]sed sit in eis pia consideratio et praeveniant horas canonicas.

XXXVIII. DE HEBDOMADARIO LECTORE

[1]Mensis fratrum lectio deesse non debet, nec fortuito casu qui arripuerit codicem legere ibi, sed lecturus tota hebdomada dominica ingrediatur. [2]Qui ingrediens post missas et communionem petat ab omnibus pro se orari, ut avertat ab ipso Deus spiritum elationis, [3]et dicatur hic versus in oratorio tertio ab omnibus, ipso tamen incipiente: Domine, labia mea aperies, et os meum adnuntiabit laudem tuam; [4]et sic accepta benedictione ingrediatur ad legendum.

[5]Et summum fiat silentium, ut nullius mussitatio vel vox nisi solius legentis ibi audiatur. [6]Quae vero necessaria sunt comedentibus et bibentibus sic sibi vicissim ministrent fratres ut nullus indigeat petere aliquid; [7]si quid tamen opus fuerit, sonitu cuiuscumque signi potius petatur quam voce. [8]Nec praesumat ibi aliquis de ipsa lectione aut aliunde quicquam requirere, ne detur occasio; [9]nisi forte prior pro aedificatione voluerit aliquid breviter dicere.

[10]Frater autem lector hebdomadarius accipiat mixtum priusquam incipiat legere, propter communionem sanctam, et ne forte grave sit ei ieiunium sustinere. [11]Postea autem cum coquinae hebdomadariis et servitoribus reficiat.

37.2 Hier. epist. 22,35
38.5 Hist.mon. 3.
38.5-7 Cassian. inst. 4,17.
38.6 Cypr. epist. 14,2.
38.7 Caes.Arel. reg.virg. 16; Pachom. reg. 33 (cf. 116).
38.8 Reg. iv patr. 2,42; Cypr. epist. 4,2.
38.9 Ps-Macar. reg. 18.

37.3 "allowed to eat before the regular hours" (praeveniant horas canonicas): See C. Gindele "Praeveniant Horas Canonicas. Die Ordnung der Mahlzeiten für die Kinder und Greise in der Regel St. Benedikts, Kapitel 37,3" StA 44 (1959) 129–135. He maintains that this anticipation of the regular hour of the meals takes place about six hours before the meal and only on fast days, days on which only one meal is eaten.

38.2 "Mass and Communion" (missas et communionem): See Appendix 3, pp. 410–412.

38.8 "lest occasion be given [to the devil]" (ne detur occasio): The bracketed words, though not actually in the Latin text, seem to be required for sense. See

toward the old and the young, the authority of the rule should also provide for them. ²Since their lack of strength must always be taken into account, they should certainly not be required to follow the strictness of the rule with regard to food, ³but should be treated with kindly consideration and allowed to eat before the regular hours.

CHAPTER 38. THE READER FOR THE WEEK

¹Reading will always accompany the meals of the brothers. The reader should not be the one who just happens to pick up the book, but someone who will read for a whole week, beginning on Sunday. ²After Mass and Communion, let the incoming reader ask all to pray for him so that God may shield him from the spirit of vanity. ³Let him begin this verse in the oratory: *Lord, open my lips, and my mouth shall proclaim your praise* (Ps 50[51]:17), and let all say it three times. ⁴When he has received a blessing, he will begin his week of reading.

⁵Let there be complete silence. No whispering, no speaking — only the reader's voice should be heard there. ⁶The brothers should by turn serve one another's needs as they eat and drink, so that no one need ask for anything. ⁷If, however, anything is required, it should be requested by an audible signal of some kind rather than by speech. ⁸No one should presume to ask a question about the reading or about anything else, *lest occasion be given* [to the devil] (Eph 4:27; 1 Tim 5:14). ⁹The superior, however, may wish to say a few words of instruction.

¹⁰Because of holy Communion and because the fast may be too hard for him to bear, the brother who is reader for the week is to receive some diluted wine before he begins to read. ¹¹Afterward he will take his meal with the weekly kitchen servers and the attendants.

---

the similar constructions in 43.8 (*maligno*) and 54.4 (*diabolo*). Despite these parallels, Steidle interprets it to mean "occasion for speaking," an interpretation that may be more complementary than contradictory in view of RB 6.4.

38.10 "Because of holy Communion" (*propter communionem sanctam*): Comparison with RM 24.14 (*propter sputum sacramenti*) indicates that the wine acts as a mouth rinse for the reader, a precaution against spitting out the Sacrament in the act of reading. See Appendix 3, p. 411.

38.11 "the attendants" (*servitoribus*): It is not clear whether these are attendants of the sick (36.7,10) or assistants of kitchen workers (35.3), or both.

¹²Fratres autem non per ordinem legant aut cantent, sed qui aedificant audientes.

XXXIX. DE MENSURA CIBUS

¹Sufficere credimus ad refectionem cotidianam tam sextae quam nonae, omnibus mensis, cocta duo pulmentaria, propter diversorum infirmitatibus, ²ut forte qui ex illo non potuerit edere ex alio reficiatur. ³Ergo duo pulmentaria cocta fratribus omnibus sufficiant et, si fuerit unde poma aut nascentia leguminum, addatur et tertium. ⁴Panis libra una propensa sufficiat in die, sive una sit refectio sive prandii et cenae: ⁵quod si cenaturi sunt, de eadem libra tertia pars a cellarario servetur reddenda cenandis.

⁶Quod si labor forte factus fuerit maior, in arbitrio et potestate abbatis erit, si expediat, aliquid augere, ⁷remota prae omnibus crapula et ut numquam surripiat monacho indigeries, ⁸quia nihil sic contrarium est omni christiano quomodo crapula, ⁹sicut ait Dominus noster: *Videte ne graventur corda vestra crapula.*

¹⁰Pueris vero minori aetate non eadem servetur quantitas, sed minor quam maioribus, servata in omnibus parcitate.

¹¹Carnium vero quadrupedum omnimodo ab omnibus abstineatur comestio, praeter omnino debiles aegrotos.

XL. DE MENSURA POTUS

¹*Unusquisque proprium habet donum ex Deo, alius sic, alius vero sic;* ²et ideo cum aliqua scrupulositate a nobis mensura victus aliorum constituitur. ³Tamen infirmorum contuentes imbecillitatem, credimus heminam vini per singulos sufficere per diem.

39.4 "A generous pound of bread" (*Panis libra una propensa*): The Roman pound in imperial times was twelve ounces.

39.11 "the meat of four-footed animals" (*Carnium. . .quadrupedum*): Although the ancient monastic tradition was unanimously opposed to the use of the meat of four-footed animals, there was some fluctuation on the subject of fish and fowl. St. Jerome was opposed to fowl (Hier. *epist.* 79,7). For additional material on the distinction between *pullos* and *carnes*, see de Vogüé 6.1105–07. On the origin of, and the motives involved in, abstention from meat as well as fasting generally, see H. Musurillo "The Problem of Ascetical Fasting in the Greek Patristic Writers" *Traditio* 12 (1956) 1–64.

40.3 "a half bottle" (*heminam*): Hemina is a Greek word taken into Latin. It was originally a measure used in Sicily, equivalent to the Greek *kotulē*. In classical Rome, the *hemina* was half a *sextarius*, and so contained 0.273 litres, or about half a pint. See *The Oxford Classical Dictionary*, ed. N.G.L. Hammond and H. H. Scullard, 2nd ed. (Oxford: The Clarendon Press 1970) s.v. measures.

Abbot Salvatore Marsili states that in his youth Sabine shepherds used a

¹²Brothers will read and sing, not according to rank, but according to their ability to benefit their hearers.

CHAPTER 39. THE PROPER AMOUNT OF FOOD

¹For the daily meals, whether at noon or in midafternoon, it is enough, we believe, to provide all tables with two kinds of cooked food because of individual weaknesses. ²In this way, the person who may not be able to eat one kind of food may partake of the other. ³Two kinds of cooked food, therefore, should suffice for all the brothers, and if fruit or fresh vegetables are available, a third dish may also be added. ⁴A generous pound of bread is enough for a day whether for only one meal or for both dinner and supper. ⁵In the latter case the cellarer will set aside one third of this pound and give it to the brothers at supper.

⁶Should it happen that the work is heavier than usual, the abbot may decide—and he will have the authority—to grant something additional, provided that it is appropriate, ⁷and that above all overindulgence is avoided, lest a monk experience indigestion. ⁸For nothing is so inconsistent with the life of any Christian as overindulgence. ⁹Our Lord says: *Take care that your hearts are not weighed down with overindulgence* (Luke 21:34).

¹⁰Young boys should not receive the same amount as their elders, but less, since in all matters frugality is the rule. ¹¹Let everyone, except the sick who are very weak, abstain entirely from eating the meat of four-footed animals.

CHAPTER 40. THE PROPER AMOUNT OF DRINK

¹*Everyone has his own gift from God, one this and another that* (1 Cor 7:7). ²It is, therefore, with some uneasiness that we specify the amount of food and drink for others. ³However, with due regard for the infirmities of the sick, we believe that a half

---

measure of about 0.75 litres, which they called a *mina*, but the word seems to have fallen into desuetude: de Vogüé 2.677 and 6.1142–69, esp. notes 431–434 and 490. It is perhaps legitimate to conclude the RB's *hemina* may have been larger than the classical one. For examples of early medieval concern and research in the matter, see J. Mabillon, *Annales ordinis S. Benedicti* (Lucca: L. Venturini 1739) Tome II, Lib. XXV, n. 70, p. 264 and Lib. XXVIII, n. 61, p. 405.

Our translation reflects both the *hemi-* (half) of *hemina* and our ignorance of the exact amount.

[4] Quibus autem donat Deus tolerantiam abstinentiae, propriam se habituros mercedem sciant.

[5] Quod si aut loci necessitas vel labor aut ardor aestatis amplius poposcerit, in arbitrio prioris consistat, considerans in omnibus ne surrepat satietas aut ebrietas. [6] Licet legamus vinum omnino monachorum non esse, sed quia nostris temporibus id monachis persuaderi non potest, saltem vel hoc consentiamus ut non usque ad satietatem bibamus, sed parcius, [7] quia *vinum apostatare facit etiam sapientes.*

[8] Ubi autem necessitas loci exposcit ut nec suprascripta mensura inveniri possit, sed multo minus aut ex toto nihil, benedicant Deum qui ibi habitant et non murmurent. [9] Hoc ante omnia admonentes ut absque murmurationibus sint.

XLI. QUIBUS HORIS OPORTET REFICERE FRATRES

[1] A sancto Pascha usque Pentecosten, ad sextam reficiant fratres et sera cenent.

[2] A Pentecosten autem, tota aestate, si labores agrorum non habent monachi aut nimietas aestatis non perturbat, quarta et sexta feria ieiunent usque ad nonam; [3] reliquis diebus ad sextam prandeant; [4] quam prandii sextam, si operis in agris habuerint aut aestatis fervor nimius fuerit, continuanda erit et in abbatis sit providentia. [5] Et sic omnia temperet atque disponat qualiter et animae salventur et quod faciunt fratres absque iusta murmuratione faciant.

[6] Ab idus autem Septembres usque caput quadragesimae, ad nonam semper reficiant.

[7] In quadragesima vero usque in Pascha, ad vesperam reficiant; [8] ipsa tamen vespera sic agatur ut lumen lucernae non indigeant reficientes, sed luce adhuc diei omnia consummentur. [9] Sed et omni tempore, sive cena sive refectionis hora sic temperetur ut luce fiant omnia.

40.4 Cassian. *conl.* 24,2,3.
40.5 Cypr. *epist.* 2,2.
40.6 **Vitae patr., Verb.senior.** 5,4,31; Basil. *reg.* 9.
40.8 Cypr. *testim.* 3,14; Cypr. *epist.* 2,2.
41.1-4 Pachom. *reg.* praef. 5.

bottle of wine a day is sufficient for each. ⁴But those to whom God gives the strength to abstain must know that they will earn their own reward.

⁵The superior will determine when local conditions, work or the summer heat indicates the need for a greater amount. He must, in any case, take great care lest excess or drunkenness creep in. ⁶We read that monks should not drink wine at all, but since the monks of our day cannot be convinced of this, let us at least agree to drink moderately, and not to the point of excess, ⁷for *wine makes even wise men go astray* (Sir 19:2).

⁸However, where local circumstances dictate an amount much less than what is stipulated above, or even none at all, those who live there should bless God and not grumble. ⁹Above all else we admonish them to refrain from grumbling.

CHAPTER 41. THE TIMES FOR THE BROTHERS' MEALS

¹From holy Easter to Pentecost, the brothers eat at noon and take supper in the evening. ²Beginning with Pentecost and continuing throughout the summer, the monks fast until midafternoon on Wednesday and Friday, unless they are working in the fields or the summer heat is oppressive.

³On the other days they eat dinner at noon. ⁴Indeed, the abbot may decide that they should continue to eat dinner at noon every day if they have work in the fields or if the summer heat remains extreme. ⁵Similarly, he should so regulate and arrange all matters that souls may be saved and the brothers may go about their activities without justifiable grumbling.

⁶From the thirteenth of September to the beginning of Lent, they always take their meal in midafternoon. ⁷Finally, from the beginning of Lent to Easter, they eat towards evening. ⁸Let Vespers be celebrated early enough so that there is no need for a lamp while eating, and that everything can be finished by daylight. ⁹Indeed, at all times let supper or the hour of the fast-day meal be so scheduled that everything can be done by daylight.

40.4 "own reward" (*propriam. . .mercedem*): See 1 Cor 3:8.

40.6 "We read" (*legamus*): The reference seems to be *Vitae patr.* 5,4,31: "Some brothers told Abba Poemen of a brother who did not drink wine. He said, 'Wine is not for monks.'"

41.6 "thirteenth" (*idus. . .Septembres*): See the note on 8.1 above for an explanation of the Roman computation of dates.

XLII. UT POST COMPLETORIUM NEMO LOQUATUR

[1]Omni tempore silentium debent studere monachi, maxime tamen nocturnis horis. [2]Et ideo omni tempore, sive ieiunii sive prandii: [3]si tempus fuerit prandii, mox surrexerint a cena, sedeant omnes in unum et legat unus Collationes vel Vitas Patrum aut certe aliud quod aedificet audientes, [4]non autem Heptateuchum aut Regum, quia infirmis intellectibus non erit utile illa hora hanc scripturam audire, aliis vero horis legantur. [5]Si autem ieiunii dies fuerit, dicta vespera parvo intervallo mox accedant ad lectionem Collationum, ut diximus. [6]Et lectis quattuor aut quinque foliis vel quantum hora permittit, [7]omnibus in unum occurrentibus per hanc moram lectionis, si qui forte in assignato sibi commisso fuit occupatus, [8]omnes ergo in unum positi compleant et, exeuntes a completoriis, nulla sit licentia denuo cuiquam loqui aliquid — [9]quod si inventus fuerit quisquam praevaricare hanc taciturnitatis regulam, gravi vindictae subiaceat— [10]excepto si necessitas hospitum supervenerit aut forte abbas alicui aliquid iusserit, [11]quod tamen et ipsud cum summa gravitate et moderatione honestissima fiat.

XLIII. DE HIS QUI AD OPUS DEI VEL AD MENSAM TARDE OCCURRUNT

[1]Ad horam divini officii, mox auditus fuerit signus, relictis omnibus quaelibet fuerint in manibus, summa cum festinatione curratur, [2]cum gravitate tamen, ut non scurrilitas inveniat fomitem. [3]Ergo nihil operi Dei praeponatur. [4]Quod si quis in nocturnis vigiliis post gloriam psalmi nonagesimi quarti, quem propter hoc omnino subtrahendo et morose volumus dici, occurrerit, non stet in ordine suo in choro, [5]sed ultimus omnium stet aut in loco quem talibus neglegentibus seorsum constituerit abbas, ut videantur ab ipso vel ab omnibus, [6]usque dum completo opere Dei publica satisfactione paeniteat. [7]Ideo autem eos in ultimo aut seorsum iudicavimus debere stare

---

42.2-5 Aug. *ord.mon.* 2.
42.3-8 Aug. *ord.mon.* 2.
43.1-3 **Reg. ii patr.** 31; Cassian. *conl.* 4,12.
43.2 Cypr. *domin.orat.* 4.
43.3 Porcar. *mon.* 12.
43.4 Pachom. *reg.* 10; Cassian. *inst.* 3,7,2.

CHAPTER 42. SILENCE AFTER COMPLINE

¹Monks should diligently cultivate silence at all times, but especially at night. ²Accordingly, this will always be the arrangement whether for fast days or for ordinary days. ³When there are two meals, all the monks will sit together immediately after rising from supper. Someone should read from the *Conferences* or the *Lives* of the Fathers or at any rate something else that will benefit the hearers, ⁴but not the Heptateuch or the Books of Kings, because it will not be good for those of weak understanding to hear these writings at that hour; they should be read at other times.

⁵On fast days there is to be a short interval between Vespers and the reading of the *Conferences*, as we have indicated. ⁶Then let four or five pages be read, or as many as time permits. ⁷This reading period will allow for all to come together, in case any were engaged in assigned tasks. ⁸When all have assembled, they should pray Compline; and on leaving Compline, no one will be permitted to speak further. ⁹If anyone is found to transgress this rule of silence, he must be subjected to severe punishment, ¹⁰except on occasions when guests require attention or the abbot wishes to give someone a command, ¹¹but even this is to be done with the utmost seriousness and proper restraint.

CHAPTER 43. TARDINESS AT THE WORK OF GOD OR AT TABLE

¹On hearing the signal for an hour of the divine office, the monk will immediately set aside what he has in hand and go with utmost speed, ²yet with gravity and without giving occasion for frivolity. ³Indeed, nothing is to be preferred to the Work of God.

⁴If at Vigils anyone comes after the "Glory be to the Father" of Psalm 94, which we wish, therefore, to be said quite deliberately and slowly, he is not to stand in his regular place in choir. ⁵He must take the last place of all, or one set apart by the abbot for such offenders, that they may be seen by him and by all, ⁶until they do penance by public satisfaction at the end of the Work of God. ⁷We have decided, therefore, that they ought to stand either in the last place or apart from the others so that the at-

---

42.2 "fast days or. . .ordinary days" (*ieiunii sive prandii*): On fast days (*ieiunii*) there is only one meal, either in midafternoon or in the evening. On ordinary days (*prandii*) there are both dinner and supper.

ut, visi ab omnibus, vel pro ipsa verecundia sua emendent; [8]nam, si foris oratorium remaneant, erit forte talis qui se aut recollocet et dormit, aut certe sedit sibi foris vel fabulis vacat, et *datur occasio maligno*; [9]sed ingrediantur intus, ut nec totum perdant et de reliquo emendent.

[10]Diurnis autem horis, qui ad opus Dei post versum et gloriam primi psalmi qui post versum dicitur non occurrerit, lege qua supra diximus in ultimo stent, [11]nec praesumant sociari choro psallentium usque ad satisfactionem, nisi forte abbas licentiam dederit remissione sua, [12]ita tamen ut satisfaciat reus ex hoc.

[13]Ad mensam autem qui ante versu non occurrerit, ut simul omnes dicant versu et orent et sub uno omnes accedant ad mensam, [14]qui per neglegentiam suam aut vitio non occurrerit, usque secunda vice pro hoc corripiatur; [15]si denuo non emendaverit, non permittatur ad mensae communis participationem, [16]sed sequestratus a consortio omnium reficiat solus, sublata ei portione sua vinum, usque ad satisfactionem et emendationem. [17]Similiter autem patiatur qui et ad illum versum non fuerit praesens qui post cibum dicitur.

[18]Et ne quis praesumat ante statutam horam vel postea quicquam cibi aut potus praesumere; [19]sed et cui offertur aliquid a priore et accipere renuit, hora qua desideraverit hoc quod prius recusavit aut aliud, omnino nihil percipiat usque ad emendationem congruam.

XLIV. DE HIS QUI EXCOMMUNICANTUR, QUOMODO SATISFACIANT

[1]Qui pro gravibus culpis ab oratorio et a mensa excommunicantur, hora qua opus Dei in oratorio percelebratur, ante fores oratorii prostratus iaceat nihil dicens, [2]nisi tantum posito in terra capite, stratus pronus omnium de oratorio exeuntium pedibus; [3]et hoc tamdiu faciat usque dum abbas iudicaverit satisfactum esse. [4]Qui dum iussus ab abbate venerit, volvat se ipsius

---

43.8 Cypr. *epist.* 4,2.
43.10-11 Pachom. *reg.* 9; Cassian. *inst.* 3,7,1.
43.14-16 Caes.Arel. *reg.virg.* 10-12.
43.18 Cassian. *inst.* 4,18.
43.19 Basil. *reg.* 96.
44.1 Ps-Macar. *reg.* 26.
44.1-3 Cassian. *inst.* 2,16; 4,16,1.

43.13 "the verse" (*versu*): There is no indication in RB what this verse is.
44.1 "serious faults" (*gravibus culpis*): Cf. RB 25.

tention they attract will shame them into amending. [8]Should they remain outside the oratory, there may be those who would return to bed and sleep, or, worse yet, settle down outside and engage in idle talk, thereby *giving occasion to the Evil One* (Eph 4:27; 1 Tim 5:14). [9]They should come inside so that they will not lose everything and may amend in the future.

[10]At the day hours the same rule applies to anyone who comes after the opening verse and the "Glory be to the Father" of the first psalm following it: he is to stand in the last place. [11]Until he has made satisfaction, he is not to presume to join the choir of those praying the psalms, unless perhaps the abbot pardons him and grants an exception. [12]Even in this case, the one at fault is still bound to satisfaction.

[13]But, if anyone does not come to table before the verse so that all may say the verse and pray and sit down at table together, [14]and if this failure happens through the individual's own negligence or fault, he should be reproved up to the second time. [15]If he still does not amend, let him not be permitted to share the common table, [16]but take his meals alone, separated from the company of all. His portion of wine should be taken away until there is satisfaction and amendment. [17]Anyone not present for the verse said after meals is to be treated in the same manner.

[18]No one is to presume to eat or drink before or after the time appointed. [19]Moreover, if anyone is offered something by a superior and refuses it, then, if later he wants what he refused or anything else, he should receive nothing at all until he has made appropriate amends.

CHAPTER 44. SATISFACTION BY THE EXCOMMUNICATED

[1]Anyone excommunicated for serious faults from the oratory and from the table is to prostrate himself in silence at the oratory entrance at the end of the celebration of the Work of God. [2]He should lie face down at the feet of all as they leave the oratory, [3]and let him do this until the abbot judges he has made satisfaction. [4]Next, at the bidding of the abbot, he is to prostrate himself

---

44.3 "satisfaction" (*satisfactum*): For the idea of "satisfaction" in chs. 44–45, see Appendix 4, p. 435. For a comparison of the rites in RM and RB, see C. Gindele "Zum grossen Rekonziliationsritus nach der Magister- und Benediktusregel" *RBén* 80 (1970) 153–156.

abbatis deinde omnium vestigiis ut orent pro ipso, ⁵et tunc, si iusserit abbas, recipiatur in choro vel in ordine quo abbas decreverit; ⁶ita sane ut psalmum aut lectionem vel aliud quid non praesumat in oratorio imponere nisi iterum abbas iubeat; ⁷et omnibus horis, dum percompletur opus Dei, proiciat se in terra in loco quo stat, ⁸et sic satisfaciat usque dum ei iubeat iterum abbas ut quiescat iam ab hac satisfactione.

⁹Qui vero pro levibus culpis excommunicantur tantum a mensa, in oratorio satisfaciant usque ad iussionem abbatis; ¹⁰hoc perficiant usque dum benedicat et dicat: Sufficit.

XLV. DE HIS QUI FALLUNTUR IN ORATORIO

¹Si quis dum pronuntiat psalmum, responsorium, antiphonam vel lectionem fallitus fuerit, nisi satisfactione ibi coram omnibus humiliatus fuerit, maiori vindictae subiaceat, ²quippe qui noluit humilitate corrigere quod neglegentia deliquit. ³Infantes autem pro tali culpa vapulent.

XLVI. DE HIS QUI IN ALIIS QUIBUSLIBET REBUS DELINQUUNT

¹Si quis dum in labore quovis, in coquina, in cellario, in ministerio, in pistrino, in horto, in arte aliqua dum laborat, vel in quocumque loco, aliquid deliquerit, ²aut fregerit quippiam aut perdiderit, vel aliud quid excesserit ubiubi, ³et non veniens continuo ante abbatem vel congregationem ipse ultro satisfecerit et prodiderit delictum suum, ⁴dum per alium cognitum fuerit, maiori subiaceat emendationi.

⁵Si animae vero peccati causa fuerit latens, tantum abbati aut spiritalibus senioribus patefaciat, ⁶qui sciat curare et sua et aliena vulnera, non detegere et publicare.

45.1 Cassian. *inst.* 4,16,2.
45.2 Cassian. *inst.* 3,7,2.
45.3 Aug. *ord.mon.* 10.
46.1-2 Cassian. *inst.* 4,16,1.
46.2 Pachom. *reg.* 125; 131.
46.3-4 Aug. *epist.* 211,11.
46.5 *Vitae patr.*, *Verb.senior.* 5,4,25; 5,5,3.
46.5-6 Cypr. *de op. et el.* 3; Cassian. *inst.* 4,9; Cassian. *conl.* 2,12-13.

44.9 "less serious faults" (*levibus culpis*): Cf. RB 24.3-7.
46.1 "in serving" (*in ministerio*): Some translators have taken this word to refer to a place (e.g., "pantry") as do the other items in the list. Some MSS read *in*

at the abbot's feet, then at the feet of all that they may pray for him. [5]Only then, if the abbot orders, should he be admitted to the choir in the rank the abbot assigns. [6]Even so, he should not presume to lead a psalm or a reading or anything else in the oratory without further instructions from the abbot. [7]In addition, at all the hours, as the Work of God is being completed, he must prostrate himself in the place he occupies. [8]He will continue this form of satisfaction until the abbot again bids him cease.

[9]Those excommunicated for less serious faults from the table only are to make satisfaction in the oratory for as long as the abbot orders. [10]They do so until he gives his blessing and says: "Enough."

CHAPTER 45. MISTAKES IN THE ORATORY

[1]Should anyone make a mistake in a psalm, responsory, refrain or reading, he must make satisfaction there before all. If he does not use this occasion to humble himself, he will be subjected to more severe punishment [2]for failing to correct by humility the wrong committed through negligence. [3]Children, however, are to be whipped for such a fault.

CHAPTER 46. FAULTS COMMITTED IN OTHER MATTERS

[1]If someone commits a fault while at any work—while working in the kitchen, in the storeroom, in serving, in the bakery, in the garden, in any craft or anywhere else— [2]either by breaking or losing something or failing in any other way in any other place, [3]he must at once come before the abbot and community and of his own accord admit his fault and make satisfaction. [4]If it is made known through another, he is to be subjected to a more severe correction.

[5]When the cause of the sin lies hidden in his conscience, he is to reveal it only to the abbot or to one of the spiritual elders, [6]who know how to heal their own wounds as well as those of others, without exposing them and making them public.

---

monasterio, a variation that suggests uncertainty over the meaning of the phrase at an early date.

46.5 "only to the abbot" (*tantum abbati*): Cf. RB 7.44.

46.6 "who know" (*sciat*): Although the verb form is singular, St. Benedict seems to include both abbot and seniors.

248 REGULA SANCTI BENEDICTI

XLVII. DE SIGNIFICANDA HORA OPERIS DEI

[1]Nuntianda hora operis Dei dies noctesque sit cura abbatis: aut ipse nuntiare aut tali sollicito fratri iniungat hanc curam, ut omnia horis competentibus compleantur.

[2]Psalmos autem vel antiphonas post abbatem ordine suo quibus iussum fuerit imponant. [3]Cantare autem et legere non praesumat nisi qui potest ipsud officium implere ut aedificentur audientes; [4]quod cum humilitate et gravitate et tremore fiat, et cui iusserit abbas.

XLVIII. DE OPERA MANUUM COTIDIANA

[1]Otiositas inimica est animae, et ideo certis temporibus occupari debent fratres in labore manuum, certis iterum horis in lectione divina. [2]Ideoque hac dispositione credimus utraque tempore ordinari: [3]id est ut a Pascha usque kalendas Octobres a mane exeuntes a prima usque hora paene quarta laborent quod necessarium fuerit; [4]ab hora autem quarta usque hora qua sextam agent lectioni vacent; [5]post sextam autem surgentes a mensa pausent in lecta sua cum omni silentio, aut forte qui voluerit legere sibi sic legat ut alium non inquietet; [6]et agatur nona temperius mediante octava hora, et iterum quod faciendum est operentur usque ad vesperam. [7]Si autem necessitas loci aut paupertas exegerit ut ad fruges recolligendas per se occupentur, non contristentur, [8]quia

47.3 *Reg. iv patr.* 2,10-11.
48.1 **Basil. reg. 192;** Cypr. *testim.* 3; Cypr. *domin.orat.* 7; Cypr. *ad Fort.* pr. 1; pr. 3; Cypr. *zel. et liv.* 16; Cypr. *epist.* 38,2; Aug. *op.mon.* 37.
48.3 *Vitae patr., Verb.senior.* 5,6,21.

48.t "The Daily Manual Labor" (*De opera manuum cotidiana*): Although only manual labor is mentioned in the title, the chapter also deals with the horarium, the use of time, and reading.
48.1 "prayerful reading" (*lectione divina*): A literal rendering of the phrase *lectio divina* is "divine reading." The adjective "divine" refers in the first instance to the nature or quality of the text being read rather than to the action of reading or the reader. Cf. note to Prol.9. This activity has been understood traditionally as a meditative, reflective reading of the Bible, the Fathers of the Church, or some other spiritual writing. For further discussion, see J. Leclercq, *The Love of Learning and the Desire for God*, pp. 16–22 and *passim*; D. Rees, *Consider Your Call* (London: SPCK 1978) pp. 261–273; and especially D. Gorce, *La Lectio Divina* (Paris: Picard 1925). See Thematic Index: SCRIPTURE, to be read.

CHAPTER 47. ANNOUNCING THE HOURS FOR THE WORK OF GOD

¹It is the abbot's care to announce, day and night, the hour for the Work of God. He may do so personally or delegate the responsibility to a conscientious brother, so that everything may be done at the proper time.

²Only those so authorized are to lead psalms and refrains, after the abbot according to their rank. ³No one should presume to read or sing unless he is able to benefit the hearers; ⁴let this be done with humility, seriousness and reverence, and at the abbot's bidding.

CHAPTER 48. THE DAILY MANUAL LABOR

¹Idleness is the enemy of the soul. Therefore, the brothers should have specified periods for manual labor as well as for prayerful reading.

²We believe that the times for both may be arranged as follows: ³From Easter to the first of October, they will spend their mornings after Prime till about the fourth hour at whatever work needs to be done. ⁴From the fourth hour until the time of Sext, they will devote themselves to reading. ⁵But after Sext and their meal, they may rest on their beds in complete silence; should a brother wish to read privately, let him do so, but without disturbing the others. ⁶They should say None a little early, about midway through the eighth hour, and then until Vespers they are to return to whatever work is necessary. ⁷They must not become distressed if local conditions or their poverty should force them to do the harvesting themselves. ⁸When they live by the labor of

---

48.3 "first" (*kalendas*): See note on RB 8.1 on the Roman computation of time.

"after Prime" (*a prima*): This translation understands *prima* to refer to the office of Prime. It could also be understood to refer to the first hour of the morning: "going out to work at the first hour of the morning."

48.5 "without disturbing the others" (*ut alium non inquietet*): Normally the monks, like the ancients generally, pronounced what they read in an audible fashion. If this reading took place in the common dormitory, the monks who chose to read would disturb the monks who preferred to sleep. Augustine (Aug. *conf.* 6,2) notes with some amazement that Ambrose read silently.

48.7 "poverty" (*paupertas*): The word *paupertas* occurs only once in the Rule. The local conditions mentioned in this verse are precisely those of economic poverty and are not related to a vow (see Appendix 5, pp. 457–458). By contrast, RM 86 forbids work in the fields, since such labor is not compatible with a regular schedule of prayer and fasting.

tunc vere monachi sunt si labore manuum suarum vivunt, sicut et patres nostri et apostoli. [9]Omnia tamen mensurate fiant propter pusillanimes.

[10]A kalendas autem Octobres usque caput quadragesimae, usque in hora secunda plena lectioni vacent; [11]hora secunda agatur tertia, et usque nona omnes in opus suum laborent quod eis iniungitur; [12]facto autem primo signo nonae horae, deiungant ab opera sua singuli et sint parati dum secundum signum pulsaverit. [13]Post refectionem autem vacent lectionibus suis aut psalmis.

[14]In quadragesimae vero diebus, a mane usque tertia plena vacent lectionibus suis, et usque decima hora plena operentur quod eis iniungitur. [15]In quibus diebus quadragesimae accipiant omnes singulos codices de bibliotheca, quos per ordinem ex integro legant; [16]qui codices in caput quadragesimae dandi sunt.

[17]Ante omnia sane deputentur unus aut duo seniores qui circumeant monasterium horis quibus vacant fratres lectioni, [18]et videant ne forte inveniatur frater acediosus qui vacat otio aut fabulis et non est intentus lectioni, et non solum sibi inutilis est, sed etiam alios distollit: [19]hic talis si—quod absit—repertus fuerit, corripiatur semel et secundo; [20]si non emendaverit, correptioni regulari subiaceat taliter ut ceteri timeant. [21]Neque frater ad fratrem iungatur horis incompetentibus.

[22]Dominico item die lectioni vacent omnes, excepto his qui variis officiis deputati sunt.

[23]Si quis vero ita neglegens et desidiosus fuerit ut non velit aut

---

48.8 *Vita Anton.* 25; *Hist.mon.* 1; Aug. *mor.eccl.* 1,70; *Vitae patr.*, *Verb.senior.* 5,1,16; Cassian. *inst.* 2,3; 5,39,3; Cassian. *conl.* 18,11; 24,12,2.

48.10-11 Caes.Arel. *reg.mon.* 14; Ps-Macar. *reg.* 11.

48.22 Hier. *epist.* 22,35.

48.23 Pachom. *reg.* 179.

48.8 "our fathers and the apostles" (*patres nostri et apostoli*): See Ps 127 (128):2; Acts 18:3; 1 Cor 4:12; 2 Thess 3:10-12. By "our fathers" is meant, presumably, the monastic fathers (cf. RB 18.25). For a list of possible references, see the Indexes of Patristic and Ancient Works.

48.13 "to their reading" (*lectionibus suis*): The Latin form is actually plural, as it is in the identical phrase (*vacent lectionibus suis*) in the following verse. In v.13 the use of the plural "readings" in conjunction with the psalms suggests that St. Benedict may have in mind preparation of the readings to be used in the office or even the memorization of some of them. Cf. RB 8.3 for the coupling of psalms and readings, and 10.2 for recitation from memory. See also Appendix 5, p. 446.

their hands, as our fathers and the apostles did, then they are really monks. [9]Yet, all things are to be done with moderation on account of the fainthearted.

[10]From the first of October to the beginning of Lent, the brothers ought to devote themselves to reading until the end of the second hour. [11]At this time Terce is said and they are to work at their assigned tasks until None. [12]At the first signal for the hour of None, all put aside their work to be ready for the second signal. [13]Then after their meal they will devote themselves to their reading or to the psalms.

[14]During the days of Lent, they should be free in the morning to read until the third hour, after which they will work at their assigned tasks until the end of the tenth hour. [15]During this time of Lent each one is to receive a book from the library, and is to read the whole of it straight through. [16]These books are to be distributed at the beginning of Lent.

[17]Above all, one or two seniors must surely be deputed to make the rounds of the monastery while the brothers are reading. [18]Their duty is to see that no brother is so apathetic as to waste time or engage in idle talk to the neglect of his reading, and so not only harm himself but also distract others. [19]If such a monk is found — God forbid — he should be reproved a first and a second time. [20]If he does not amend, he must be subjected to the punishment of the rule as a warning to others. [21]Further, brothers ought not to associate with one another at inappropriate times.

[22]On Sunday all are to be engaged in reading except those who have been assigned various duties. [23]If anyone is so remiss and

---

48.15 "book from the library" (*codices de bibliotheca*): A. Mundó suggests that Benedict has in mind nine sections (*codices*) of the Bible. See "Bibliotheca, Bible et lecture de carême d'après S. Benoît" *RBén* 60 (1950) 65–92. De Vogüé finds the matter unclear (2.602–603, n.15).

48.16 "the beginning of Lent" (*caput quadragesimae*): This might be the first Sunday of Lent. See Appendix 3, p. 409.

48.18 "apathetic" (*acediosus*): This state of mind is not to be confused with the state described by Evagrius of Pontus as *apatheia* (see Introduction, pp. 39–40) but refers rather to one of the eight principal *logismoi* (see note on RB 1.5). Evagrius identified *akēdia* with the "noonday devil" (Evagr. *pract.* 12). Cassian treated of it extensively (Cassian. *inst.* 10). It is essentially lack of interest in spiritual things and boredom with the monastic life. See also G. Bardy "Acedia" *DS* 1.166–169.

48.20 "as a warning to others" (*ut ceteri timeant*): This is an allusion to 1 Tim 5:20 (*ut et ceteri timorem habeant* [Vulgate]), which is also cited explicitly in RB 70.3 (*ut ceteri metum habeant*).

non possit meditare aut legere, iniungatur ei opus quod faciat, ut non vacet. [24]Fratribus infirmis aut delicatis talis opera aut ars iniungatur ut nec otiosi sint nec violentia laboris opprimantur aut effugentur. [25]Quorum imbecillitas ab abbate consideranda est.

XLIX. DE QUADRAGESIMAE OBSERVATIONE

[1]Licet omni tempore vita monachi quadragesimae debet observationem habere, [2]tamen, quia paucorum est ista virtus, ideo suademus istis diebus quadragesimae omni puritate vitam suam custodire omnes pariter, [3]et neglegentias aliorum temporum his diebus sanctis diluere. [4]Quod tunc digne fit si ab omnibus vitiis temperamus, orationi cum fletibus, lectioni et compunctioni cordis atque abstinentiae operam damus. [5]Ergo his diebus augeamus nobis aliquid solito pensu servitutis nostrae, orationes peculiares, ciborum et potus abstinentiam, [6]ut unusquisque super mensuram sibi indictam aliquid propria voluntate *cum gaudio Sancti Spiritus* offerat Deo, [7]id est subtrahat corpori suo de cibo, de potu, de somno, de loquacitate, de scurrilitate, et cum spiritalis desiderii gaudio sanctum Pascha exspectet.

[8]Hoc ipsud tamen quod unusquisque offerit abbati suo suggerat, et cum eius fiat oratione et voluntate, [9]quia quod sine permissione patris spiritalis fit, praesumptioni deputabitur et vanae gloriae, non mercedi. [10]Ergo cum voluntate abbatis omnia agenda sunt.

L. DE FRATRIBUS QUI LONGE AB ORATORIO LABORANT AUT IN VIA SUNT

[1]Fratres qui omnino longe sunt in labore et non possunt oc-

---

49.1-4 **Leo.M. tract. 39,2; 42,1,6.**
49.2 Leo.M. *tract. (de quadragesima)* 5,2.
49.3 Leo.M. *tract.* 89,2; Leo.M. *tract.* 2.2,3.
49.5 Leo.M. *tract.* 40,1; Ambr. *virg.* 3,17.
49.5-7 Pallad. *hist.laus.*: de Macario Alexandrino 1.
49.7 Leo.M. *tract.* 42,2; *Sacr.Gelasianum* 55.
49.10 *Reg. ii patr.* 1.
50.1 Basil. *reg.* 107.

indolent that he is unwilling or unable to study or to read, he is to be given some work in order that he may not be idle.

²⁴Brothers who are sick or weak should be given a type of work or craft that will keep them busy without overwhelming them or driving them away. ²⁵The abbot must take their infirmities into account.

CHAPTER 49. THE OBSERVANCE OF LENT

¹The life of a monk ought to be a continuous Lent. ²Since few, however, have the strength for this, we urge the entire community during these days of Lent to keep its manner of life most pure ³and to wash away in this holy season the negligences of other times. ⁴This we can do in a fitting manner by refusing to indulge evil habits and by devoting ourselves to prayer with tears, to reading, to compunction of heart and self-denial. ⁵During these days, therefore, we will add to the usual measure of our service something by way of private prayer and abstinence from food or drink, ⁶so that each of us will have something above the assigned measure to offer God of his own will *with the joy of the Holy Spirit* (1 Thess 1:6). ⁷In other words, let each one deny himself some food, drink, sleep, needless talking and idle jesting, and look forward to holy Easter with joy and spiritual longing.

⁸Everyone should, however, make known to the abbot what he intends to do, since it ought to be done with his prayer and approval. ⁹Whatever is undertaken without the permission of the spiritual father will be reckoned as presumption and vainglory, not deserving a reward. ¹⁰Therefore, everything must be done with the abbot's approval.

CHAPTER 50. BROTHERS WORKING AT A DISTANCE OR TRAVELING

¹Brothers who work so far away that they cannot return to the

---

49.2 "the entire community" (*omnes pariter*): This phrase occurs in RB 20.5, and *pariter* in 53.4 and 72.12. M. Larmann "The Meaning of *omnes pariter*" *ABR* 29 (1978) 153–165 has argued that the phrase should be construed with *custodire* rather than *neglegentias*, and hence means "as a community." Others place the comma after *custodire* in v.2 and take *omnes* with *neglegentias* (de Vogüé 2.605–606). Advocates of both views acknowledge the influence on this chapter of St. Leo's Sermons 39–50 on Lent. See de Vogüé 6.1217–33. It is significant, too, that RM has a community form of Lenten observance.

49.7 "Easter" (*Pascha*): See Thematic Index: PASCHAL MYSTERY.

currere hora competenti ad oratorium— [2]et abbas hoc perpendet, quia ita est— [3]agant ibidem opus Dei, ubi operantur, cum tremore divino flectentes genua.

[4]Similiter, qui in itinere directi sunt, non eos praetereant horae constitutae, sed ut possunt agant sibi et servitutis pensum non neglegant reddere.

LI. DE FRATRIBUS QUI NON LONGE SATIS PROFICISCUNTUR

[1]Frater qui pro quovis responso dirigitur et ea die speratur reverti ad monasterium, non praesumat foris manducare, etiam si omnino rogetur a quovis, [2]nisi forte ei ab abbate suo praecipiatur. [3]Quod si aliter fecerit, excommunicetur.

LII. DE ORATORIO MONASTERII

[1]Oratorium hoc sit quod dicitur, nec ibi quicquam aliud geratur aut condatur. [2]Expleto opere Dei, omnes cum summo silentio exeant, et habeatur reverentia Deo, [3]ut frater qui forte sibi peculiariter vult orare non impediatur alterius improbitate. [4]Sed et si aliter vult sibi forte secretius orare, simpliciter intret et oret, non in clamosa voce, sed in lacrimis et intentione cordis. [5]Ergo qui simile opus non facit, non permittatur explicito opere Dei remorari in oratorio, sicut dictum est, ne alius impedimentum patiatur.

LIII. DE HOSPITIBUS SUSCIPIENDIS

[1]Omnes supervenientes hospites tamquam Christus suscipiantur, quia ipse dicturus est: *Hospes fui et suscepistis me*; [2]et *om-*

50.4 Pachom. *reg.* 142.
51.1 Aug. *ord.mon.* 8.
52.1-3 Aug. *epist.* 211,7.
52.2-5 Cassian. *inst.* 2,10,2.
52.4 Cypr. *domin.orat.* 4-5; Cassian. *inst.* 2,5,5; 2,10,2; 2,12; 5,34; Cassian. *conl.* 1,7; 2,12; 4,4; 9,6,7,12,35; 10,8; 12,8; 21,22; 23,11.
53.1-13 *Hist.mon.* 1-2; 9; 21.
53.2 Pachom. *reg.* 51.

52.1 "what it is called" (*quod dicitur*): The word "oratory" (*oratorium*) stems from the Latin verb *orare*: 'to pray.' See Thematic Index: HOUSE OF GOD, *Embodied in*: oratory.

oratory at the proper time— ²and the abbot determines that is the case— ³are to perform the Work of God where they are, and kneel out of reverence for God.

⁴So too, those who have been sent on a journey are not to omit the prescribed hours but to observe them as best they can, not neglecting their measure of service.

CHAPTER 51. BROTHERS ON A SHORT JOURNEY

¹If a brother is sent on some errand and expects to return to the monastery that same day, he must not presume to eat outside, even if he receives a pressing invitation, ²unless perhaps the abbot has ordered it. ³Should he act otherwise, he will be excommunicated.

CHAPTER 52. THE ORATORY OF THE MONASTERY

¹The oratory ought to be what it is called, and nothing else is to be done or stored there. ²After the Work of God, all should leave in complete silence and with reverence for God, ³so that a brother who may wish to pray alone will not be disturbed by the insensitivity of another. ⁴Moreover, if at other times someone chooses to pray privately, he may simply go in and pray, not in a loud voice, but with tears and heartfelt devotion. ⁵Accordingly, anyone who does not pray in this manner is not to remain in the oratory after the Work of God, as we have said; then he will not interfere with anyone else.

CHAPTER 53. THE RECEPTION OF GUESTS

¹All guests who present themselves are to be welcomed as Christ, for he himself will say: *I was a stranger and you wel-*

52.3 "insensitivity" (*improbitate*): See note to RB 2.28.

53.0 The first section of the chapter (1-15) advocates a warm and open reception of guests. The second section (16-23) provides practical directions for the accommodation of the guest, directions that prevent the guests from disturbing the common life of the monastery. In RM more extensive directions are given for putting guests to work after two days, or if they are unwilling, suggesting that they depart, and for protecting the goods of the monastery from less spiritually minded guests (RM 78–79). Palladius reports that at Nitria guests were allowed a week of leisure before being put to work in the garden, bakery or kitchen (Pallad. *hist.laus.* 7). See Thematic Index: GUESTS.

nibus congruus honor exhibeatur, *maxime domesticis fidei* et peregrinis.

[3]Ut ergo nuntiatus fuerit hospes, occurratur ei a priore vel a fratribus cum omni officio caritatis, [4]et primitus orent pariter, et sic sibi socientur in pace. [5]Quod pacis osculum non prius offeratur nisi oratione praemissa, propter illusiones diabolicas.

[6]In ipsa autem salutatione omnis exhibeatur humilitas omnibus venientibus sive discedentibus hospitibus: [7]inclinato capite vel prostrato omni corpore in terra, Christus in eis adoretur qui et suscipitur. [8]Suscepti autem hospites ducantur ad orationem et postea sedeat cum eis prior aut cui iusserit ipse. [9]Legatur coram hospite lex divina ut aedificetur, et post haec omnis ei exhibeatur humanitas. [10]Ieiunium a priore frangatur propter hospitem, nisi forte praecipuus sit dies ieiunii qui non possit violari; [11]fratres autem consuetudines ieiuniorum prosequantur. [12]Aquam in manibus abbas hospitibus det; [13]pedes hospitibus omnibus tam abbas quam cuncta congregatio lavet;

53.3-13 Hist.mon. 7; *Hist.mon.* 17.
53.4 Cypr. *domin.orat.* 23.
53.7 *Sacr.Gelasianum* 38; 66; Ambr. *off.* 2,107.
53.9 Cassian. *conl.* 2,25-26.
53.10 Cassian. *inst.* 5,24; Cassian. *conl.* 21,14,3; 24,17.

53.2 *"to all"* (omnibus): Cf. RB 4.8, to which St. Benedict is probably alluding here and therefore to 1 Pet 2:17 as well. RB 4.8 should then be understood as a maxim of hospitality. See note on 4.t and A. de Vogüé "Honorer tous les hommes" *RAM* 40 (1964) 129–138, who argues persuasively that the insistence on "all" in 53.1,2,6,13 reflects the concern that guests be given honor in light of their relationship to Christ rather than in terms of their rank in society. The "proper honor" *(congruus honor)* would mean, then, not that all receive the same honor, but that those in whom Christ is more readily recognized should receive more honor. See also the following notes.

"those who share our faith" (domesticis fidei): The phrase appears at first sight to contrast Christians and non-Christians, and therefore to single out fellow Christians for special treatment, as it certainly does in Gal 6:10. Despite the insistent use of "all" in this chapter (see previous note), the pre-ecumenical temper of the sixth century militates strongly against this interpretation, as was pointed out by Linderbauer, *S. Benedicti Regula Monachorum*, p. 346. It is quite unlikely that heretics (chiefly Arians in sixth-century Italy) and non-Christians would have been received at all (cf. Hier. *apol. adv. libr. Ruf.* 3,17; *Vita Anton.* 68-69; *Vita sa*[5] 123), and orthodox Christians would certainly not have agreed to pray with them as vv.4-5 direct (cf. *Vita bo* 185). The suggestion that the phrase is a scribal error for *domestici Dei* (Eph 2:19), which could more readily be understood as referring specifically to clerics and monks, has no manuscript support. Nevertheless, in view of the probable exclusion of heretics and non-Christians, the phrase probably should be taken in a narrower sense to refer to

comed me (Matt 25:35). ²Proper honor must be shown *to all, especially to those who share our faith* (Gal 6:10) and to pilgrims.

³Once a guest has been announced, the superior and the brothers are to meet him with all the courtesy of love. ⁴First of all, they are to pray together and thus be united in peace, ⁵but prayer must always precede the kiss of peace because of the delusions of the devil.

⁶All humility should be shown in addressing a guest on arrival or departure. ⁷By a bow of the head or by a complete prostration of the body, Christ is to be adored because he is indeed welcomed in them. ⁸After the guests have been received, they should be invited to pray; then the superior or an appointed brother will sit with them. ⁹The divine law is read to the guest for his instruction, and after that every kindness is shown to him. ¹⁰The superior may break his fast for the sake of a guest, unless it is a day of special fast which cannot be broken. ¹¹The brothers, however, observe the usual fast. ¹²The abbot shall pour water on the hands of the guests, ¹³and the abbot with the entire commu-

---

clerics and monks, an interpretation to be found already in Smarag. *expos. in reg.* 53.2. The Rule of Pachomius directs explicitly that clerics and monks are to be received with greater honor (Pachom. *reg.* 51). De Vogüé (*loc. cit.* 135) argues that the phrase includes these and also pious laymen — in fact, all who are connected with the house of God (monastery) "by a certain connaturality with its religious ideal and the type of life led there."

"pilgrims" (*peregrinis*): This term can mean either 'pilgrim' or 'visiting,' 'strange,' 'foreign,' etc. The context seems to favor the more technical meaning of 'pilgrim' in this chapter. The pilgrims could possibly be understood as a subdivision of the *domestici fidei*. See G. Morin *RBén* 34 (1922) 128. In v.15, the fact that people were on a holy journey could single them out for special attention. Although pilgrimage as a form of popular spiritual exercise peaked after St. Benedict's time (see J. Leclercq *et al., The Spirituality of the Middle Ages* [London: Burns and Oates 1968] esp. pp. 42–43, 58–60), there is good evidence before his time for pilgrimage to the tombs of the martyrs and saints, especially at Rome, and to the Holy Places. See M. C. McCarthy "Pilgrimages: Early Christian" *New Catholic Encyclopedia* (1967) 11.364; F. X. Murphy "Pilgrimages, Roman" *ibid.*, 372–373; H. Leclercq "Pélerinage à Rome" *DACL* 14.40–48; and "Pélerinage aux lieux saints" *ibid.* 65–124. De Vogüé (*loc. cit.* 136) points out, however, that in v.15 the *peregrini* are associated with the poor in contrast to the rich. This suggests that they should be considered to be socially disadvantaged by being far from their own land and should therefore be the objects of special concern. Such an interpretation could include pilgrims in the more technical sense. Smaragdus also defines *peregrini* as those far from their own land.

53.9 "every kindness" (*omnis. . .humanitas*): *Humanitas* in the writings of Cassian most frequently denotes a meal, as probably also here. See de Vogüé 2.678.

[14] quibus lotis, hunc versum dicant: *Suscepimus, Deus, misericordiam tuam in medio templi tui.*

[15] Pauperum et peregrinorum maxime susceptioni cura sollicite exhibeatur, quia in ipsis magis Christus suscipitur; nam divitum terror ipse sibi exigit honorem.

[16] Coquina abbatis et hospitum super se sit, ut, incertis horis supervenientes hospites, qui numquam desunt monasterio, non inquietentur fratres. [17] In qua coquina ad annum ingrediantur duo fratres qui ipsud officium bene impleant. [18] Quibus, ut indigent, solacia administrentur, ut absque murmuratione serviant, et iterum, quando occupationem minorem habent, exeant ubi eis imperatur in opera. [19] Et non solum ipsis, sed et in omnibus officiis monasterii ista sit consideratio, [20] ut quando indigent solacia accommodentur eis, et iterum quando vacant oboediant imperatis.

[21] Item et cellam hospitum habeat assignatam frater cuius animam timor Dei possidet; [22] ubi sint lecti strati sufficienter. Et domus Dei a sapientibus et sapienter administretur.

[23] Hospitibus autem cui non praecipitur ullatenus societur neque colloquatur; [24] sed si obviaverit aut viderit, salutatis humiliter, ut diximus, et petita benedictione pertranseat, dicens sibi non licere colloqui cum hospite.

LIV. SI DEBEAT MONACHUS LITTERAS VEL ALIQUID SUSCIPERE

[1] Nullatenus liceat monacho neque a parentibus suis neque a quoquam hominum nec sibi invicem litteras, eulogias vel quaelibet munuscula accipere aut dare sine praecepto abbatis. [2] Quod si etiam a parentibus suis ei quicquam directum fuerit non praesumat suscipere illud, nisi prius indicatum fuerit abbati. [3] Quod si iusserit suscipi, in abbatis sit potestate cui illud iubeat

53.15 Cypr. *epist.* 14,2; Cassian. *inst.* 4,7; Ps-Macar. *reg.* 20.
53.21-24 *Reg. iv patr.* 2,37-38; 2,40.
53.23-24 Basil. *reg.fus.* 32-33; Pachom. *reg.* 50.
54.1 **Aug. epist.** 211,11; Pachom. *reg.* 106; Caes.Arel. *reg.mon.* 15; Caes.Arel. *reg.virg.* 23; Cassian. *inst.* 4,16.
54.2-3 **Aug. epist.** 211,12; Caes.Arel. *reg.mon.* 1; Caes.Arel. *reg.virg.* 40; Pachom. *reg.* 52.

nity shall wash their feet. [14]After the washing they will recite this verse: *God, we have received your mercy in the midst of your temple* (Ps 47[48]:10).

[15]Great care and concern are to be shown in receiving poor people and pilgrims, because in them more particularly Christ is received; our very awe of the rich guarantees them special respect.

[16]The kitchen for the abbot and guests ought to be separate, so that guests—and monasteries are never without them—need not disturb the brothers when they present themselves at unpredictable hours. [17]Each year, two brothers who can do the work competently are to be assigned to this kitchen. [18]Additional help should be available when needed, so that they can perform this service without grumbling. On the other hand, when the work slackens, they are to go wherever other duties are assigned them. [19]This consideration is not for them alone, but applies to all duties in the monastery; [20]the brothers are to be given help when it is needed, and whenever they are free, they work wherever they are assigned.

[21]The guest quarters are to be entrusted to a God-fearing brother. [22]Adequate bedding should be available there. The house of God should be in the care of wise men who will manage it wisely.

[23]No one is to speak or associate with guests unless he is bidden; [24]however, if a brother meets or sees a guest, he is to greet him humbly, as we have said. He asks for a blessing and continues on his way, explaining that he is not allowed to speak with a guest.

CHAPTER 54. LETTERS OR GIFTS FOR MONKS

[1]In no circumstances is a monk allowed, unless the abbot says he may, to exchange letters, blessed tokens or small gifts of any kind, with his parents or anyone else, or with a fellow monk. [2]He must not presume to accept gifts sent him even by his parents without previously telling the abbot. [3]If the abbot orders

---

53.15 "poor people" (*Pauperum*): Giving precedence to the poor reverses the "worldly" order of precedence and is one of the many ways in which monks are urged by their tradition to depart from the values of society.

54.1 "blessed tokens" (*eulogias*): The word seems to refer to blessed objects of some sort, perhaps even relics. In RM 76.2 and Caes.Arel. *reg.virg.* 107,22, it refers to blessed bread sent as a gift.

dari, [4]et non contristetur frater cui forte directum fuerat, *ut non
detur occasio diabolo.* [5]Qui autem aliter praesumpserit, disciplinae regulari subiaceat.

LV.   DE VESTIARIO VEL CALCIARIO FRATRUM

[1]Vestimenta fratribus secundum locorum qualitatem ubi
habitant vel aërum temperiem dentur, [2]quia in frigidis regionibus amplius indigetur, in calidis vero minus. [3]Haec ergo
consideratio penes abbatem est. [4]Nos tamen mediocribus locis
sufficere credimus monachis per singulos cucullam et tunicam—
[5]cucullam in hieme villosam, in aestate puram aut vetustam—

54.4 Cypr. epist. 4,2.
55.1 Cassian. *inst.* 1,10.
55.1-2 Cypr. *epist.* 14,2.

55.1 "The clothing" (*Vestimenta*): The wearing of distinctive garb is attested
from the earliest days of the monastic movement. See H. G. Evelyn White, *The
Monasteries of the Wadi 'N Natrun*, II. *The History of the Monasteries of Nitria
and Scetis* (New York: Metropolitan Museum of Art 1932) pp. 194–197. In Egypt
at least, where it quickly became fairly standard and universal, this consisted of a
tunic, a leather belt, a hood and a cloak. Some other pieces of clothing are mentioned. While undoubtedly influenced by what was then contemporary dress, the
monastic habit (*schēma* in Greek) was by no means identical with it. The desire
of the monks to flee from the "world" (see Introduction, pp. 16f.), to escape
from the tyranny of fashion (cf. Cassian. *inst.* 1,2) and to manifest their rejection of
such values no doubt had much to do with this development. That the desired
effect was achieved is confirmed, for example, by the vehemence with which
Libanius, the pagan rhetorician and friend of the Emperor Julian, berated the
monks for, among other things, their severe dress (Liban. *orat.* 2,32). At an early
stage in the monastic movement, symbolic significance was attributed to the
various pieces that made up the monastic *schēma* (see Evagr. *pract.* prol.2-7 and
Basil. *reg.fus.* 22-23). Basil adds motives for wearing distinctive dress that become standard: it provides a common witness, proclaims the profession of the
devout life, and acts as a pedagogue for those who might be tempted to act
otherwise than in accordance with their profession. For more extended treatment
of the subject, see M. Augé, *L'Abito Religioso: studio storico e psico-sociologico
dell'abbigliamento religioso* (Rome: Istituto di Teologia della Vita Religiosa
[Claretianum] 1977); G. Colombás "Abito Religioso" *Dizionario degli Istituti di
Perfezione* 1.50–56; P. Oppenheim, *Das Mönchskleid im christlichen Altertum*,
Römische Quartalschrift für christliche Altertumskunde und für Kirchengeschichte, Supplementheft 28 (Freiburg: Herder 1931); *Symbolik und religiöse
Wertung des Mönchskleides im christlichen Altertum* (Münster: Aschendorff
1932). On the last two, see, however, P. de Meester in *Ephemerides Liturgicae* 47
(1933) 446–458 and L. Th. Lefort in *RHE* 28 (1932) 851–853. For opinions on the
relationship between ancient practice and modern adaptation, see J.-C. Guy

acceptance, he still has the power to give the gift to whom he will; [4]and the brother for whom it was originally sent must not be distressed, *lest occasion be given to the devil* (Eph 4:27; 1 Tim 5:14). [5]Whoever presumes to act otherwise will be subjected to the discipline of the rule.

CHAPTER 55. THE CLOTHING AND FOOTWEAR OF THE BROTHERS

[1]The clothing distributed to the brothers should vary according to local conditions and climate, [2]because more is needed in cold regions and less in warmer. [3]This is left to the abbot's discretion. [4]We believe that for each monk a cowl and tunic will suffice in temperate regions; [5]in winter a woolen cowl is neces-

---

"Religious Costume, Yesterday and Today" *The Way*, Supplement 4 (Nov. 1967) 66–77; R. Gazeau "Un 'habit monastique'?" *CollCist* 33 (1971) 179–190; and de Vogüé 7.377–388.

"local conditions" (*locorum qualitatem ubi habitant*): In the parallel treatment of RM 81.25-30, the concern is with clothing suited to the different seasons rather than different regions and climates. This is an indication that St. Benedict foresaw somewhat extensive use of his Rule.

55.4 "a cowl" (*cucullam*): The English word is derived from the Latin one, though by a tortuous and uncertain route. See *The Oxford English Dictionary* s.v. The word and the garment appear to be of Celtic origin (see Pauly-Wissowa, *Real-Encyclopädie* IV, 2.1739–1740). In classical Latin the word denoted a mantle with a hood. However, its use in monastic circles is probably dependent on the parallel Greek form *koukoullion*, which is frequently attested in the earliest monastic literature as a typical piece of monks' clothing. See G.W.H. Lampe, *A Greek Patristic Lexicon*, s.v. for numerous examples. Jerome mentions it (*vita Hil.* 44 and 46). Cassian (*inst.* 1,3) describes it as a child's hood and, quoting Ps 130(131):1-2 (cf. RB 7.4), says that monks wear it "in order that they may constantly be moved to preserve the simplicity and innocence of little children by imitating their actual dress." This explanation, without the allusion to Ps 130(131), can be found already in Evagrius (*pract.* prol.2) and is followed by many others (e.g., Pallad. *hist.laus.* 32,3; Soz. *hist.eccles.* 3,14). In RM 81 the tunic and cowl seem to form the *paratura*, or basic monastic ensemble (see de Vogüé 6.911). In the course of the centuries the mantle part of this garment seems to have lengthened, until the word *cuculla* came to denote a long flowing choir robe, often with hood attached. See J. Mabillon, *Annales ordinis S. Benedicti* (Lucca: L. Venturini 1739) Tome 1, Lib. V, pp. 108–109 (with useful illustrations); H. Leclercq "Capuchon" *DACL* 2,2.2127–34 (also with useful illustrations); and S. Reinach "Cucullus..." Daremberg-Saglio, *Dictionnaire des Antiquités Grecques et Romaines* 1.1577–79.

"tunic" (*tunicam*): This is a loose-fitting or gownlike outer garment, with or without sleeves, that falls below the knees. It is usually fastened by a leather belt or "girdle." Although mention of the latter is absent in RB, it is accorded considerable symbolic significance in the earlier monastic tradition, e.g., Cassian. *inst.* 1,1.

[6] et scapulare propter opera, indumenta pedum pedules et caligas.

[7] De quarum rerum omnium colore aut grossitudine non causentur monachi, sed quales inveniri possunt in provincia qua degunt aut quod vilius comparari possit. [8] Abbas autem de mensura provideat ut non sint curta ipsa vestimenta utentibus ea, sed mensurata.

[9] Accipientes nova, vetera semper reddant in praesenti reponenda in vestiario propter pauperes. [10] Sufficit enim monacho duas tunicas et duas cucullas habere propter noctes et propter lavare ipsas res; [11] iam quod supra fuerit superfluum est, amputari debet. [12] Et pedules et quodcumque est vetere reddant dum accipiunt novum.

[13] Femoralia hi qui in via diriguntur de vestiario accipiant, quae revertentes lota ibi restituant. [14] Et cucullae et tunicae sint aliquanto a solito quas habent modice meliores; quas exeuntes in via accipiant de vestiario et revertentes restituant.

[15] Stramenta autem lectorum sufficiant matta, sagum et lena, et capitale.

[16] Quae tamen lecta frequenter ab abbate scrutinanda sunt propter opus peculiare, ne inveniatur; [17] et si cui inventum fuerit quod ab abbate non accepit, gravissimae disciplinae subiaceat. [18] Et ut hoc vitium peculiaris radicitus amputetur, dentur ab ab-

---

55.7 Basil. reg. 9.
55.7-11 Cassian. inst. 1,3.
55.9 Caes.Arel. reg.virg. 40.
55.10 Orsiesii lib. 22.
55.11 Pachom. reg. 81.
55.16 Cassian. inst. 4,14; 4,16,3; 7,7.
55.17-18 Cypr. epist. 2,2.

55.6 "a scapular" (scapulare): This word is found in antiquity only here in RB and in Vita patr. iuren. 3,5, where it appears as a summer garment. De Vogüé 6.916 thinks it is a modified version of the cuculla specially adapted for work. It clearly derives from the Latin scapula, meaning 'shoulders,' and it may reasonably be concluded that it was a sleeveless or short-sleeved garment. Its light or summer character is confirmed by Old English usage; see The Oxford English Dictionary, s.v. scapulary 1.a. However, A. Guillaumont, Évagre le Pontique: Traité Pratique, SC 171 (Paris: Éditions du Cerf 1971) p. 488, suggests that the scapular may be equivalent to the Greek analabos, which Cassian (inst. 1,5) translates uncertainly by three terms: subcinctoria, redimicula and rebracchiatoria, the purpose of which is to fasten the tunic for work.

"sandals and shoes" (pedules et caligas): In RM 81.25 caligas denotes winter footwear for outside, and pedules refers to fur-lined footwear used indoors at the

sary, in summer a thinner or worn one; [6]also a scapular for work, and footwear—both sandals and shoes.

[7]Monks must not complain about the color or coarseness of all these articles, but use what is available in the vicinity at a reasonable cost. [8]However, the abbot ought to be concerned about the measurements of these garments that they not be too short but fitted to the wearers.

[9]Whenever new clothing is received, the old should be returned at once and stored in a wardrobe for the poor. [10]To provide for laundering and night wear, every monk will need two cowls and two tunics, [11]but anything more must be taken away as superfluous. [12]When new articles are received, the worn ones—sandals or anything old—must be returned.

[13]Brothers going on a journey should get underclothing from the wardrobe. On their return they are to wash it and give it back. [14]Their cowls and tunics, too, ought to be somewhat better than those they ordinarily wear. Let them get these from the wardrobe before departing, and on returning put them back.

[15]For bedding the monks will need a mat, a woolen blanket and a light covering as well as a pillow.

[16]The beds are to be inspected frequently by the abbot, lest private possessions be found there. [17]A monk discovered with anything not given him by the abbot must be subjected to very severe punishment. [18]In order that this vice of private ownership may be completely uprooted, the abbot is to provide all things

---

night office (RM 81.30). It is not clear that this distinction is preserved in RB.

55.7 "at a reasonable cost" (*vilius comparari*): *Vilius* is, of course, a comparative of *vilis*, which seems to denote a lower or perhaps "rustic" social condition. See note on 7.49. The suggestion seems to be that the cloth used by a lower class may be cheaper and is to be preferred. Cassian (*inst.* 1,2) also uses the word of the monks' clothing.

55.9 "for the poor" (*propter pauperes*): Some have taken this to mean that monastic dress was no different from that of ordinary people. In view of the long tradition of distinctive monastic clothing prior to RB, this is untenable. What is suggested is not that the poor be dressed up in the monastic ensemble but that individual pieces of clothing (e.g., tunic, shoes) be given them as needed.

55.18 "vice of private ownership" (*vitium peculiaris*): See note on 33.1.

bate omnia quae sunt necessaria, [19]id est cuculla, tunica, pedules, caligas, bracile, cultellum, graphium, acum, mappula, tabulas, ut omnis auferatur necessitatis excusatio.

[20]A quo tamen abbate semper consideretur illa sententia Actuum Apostolorum, quia *dabatur singulis prout cuique opus erat.* [21]Ita ergo et abbas consideret infirmitates indigentium, non malum voluntatem invidentium; [22]in omnibus tamen iudiciis suis Dei retributionem cogitet.

LVI. DE MENSA ABBATIS

[1]Mensa abbatis cum hospitibus et peregrinis sit semper. [2]Quotiens tamen minus sunt hospites, quos vult de fratribus vocare in ipsius sit potestate. [3]Seniore tamen uno aut duo semper cum fratribus dimittendum propter disciplinam.

LVII. DE ARTIFICIBUS MONASTERII

[1]Artifices si sunt in monasterio cum omni humilitate faciant ipsas artes, si permiserit abbas. [2]Quod si aliquis ex eis extollitur pro scientia artis suae, eo quod videatur aliquid conferre monasterio, [3]hic talis erigatur ab ipsa arte et denuo per eam non transeat, nisi forte humiliato ei iterum abbas iubeat.

[4]Si quid vero ex operibus artificum venumdandum est, videant ipsi per quorum manus transigenda sint ne aliquam fraudem praesumant. [5]Memorentur semper Ananiae et Saphirae, ne forte mortem quam illi in corpore pertulerunt, [6]hanc isti vel omnes qui aliquam fraudem de rebus monasterii fecerint in anima patiantur.

55.20 Aug. *epist.* 211,5; Basil. *reg.* 94.
56.1 *Reg. iv patr.* 2,41.
57.2 Aug. *epist.* 211,6.
57.4-7 Aug. *ord.mon.* 8.
57.5-6 Cassian. *inst.* 7,25,1.

55.19 "stylus. . .writing tablets" (*graphium. . .tabulas*): This interesting detail (absent from RM) suggests a rather high rate of literacy in the monastic population. This in turn suggests, given the fact that universal education was an as yet unknown concept in the sixth century, that the social composition of the monasteries in this period (and in antiquity generally) was essentially middle and upper class. Such a generalization is confirmed by other details, e.g., RB 48.7. See note on 59.1. Despite these indications of a relatively high level of literacy in the monasteries, it may be noted that there is abundant evidence of a notable decline in the general level of literary culture from that which prevailed in the time of Augustine. The numerous barbarian invasions of the fifth and sixth centuries had taken a heavy toll. See G. B. Ladner, *The Idea of Reform* (Cambridge: Harvard

necessary: [19]that is, cowl, tunic, sandals, shoes, belt, knife, stylus, needle, handkerchief and writing tablets. In this way every excuse of lacking some necessity will be taken away.

[20]The abbot, however, must always bear in mind what is said in the Acts of the Apostles: *Distribution was made to each one as he had need* (Acts 4:35). [21]In this way the abbot will take into account the weaknesses of the needy, not the evil will of the envious; [22]yet in all his judgments he must bear in mind God's retribution.

CHAPTER 56. THE ABBOT'S TABLE

[1]The abbot's table must always be with guests and travelers. [2]Whenever there are no guests, it is within his right to invite any of the brothers he wishes. [3]However, for the sake of maintaining discipline, one or two seniors must always be left with the brothers.

CHAPTER 57. THE ARTISANS OF THE MONASTERY

[1]If there are artisans in the monastery, they are to practice their craft with all humility, but only with the abbot's permission. [2]If one of them becomes puffed up by his skillfulness in his craft, and feels that he is conferring something on the monastery, [3]he is to be removed from practicing his craft and not allowed to resume it unless, after manifesting his humility, he is so ordered by the abbot.

[4]Whenever products of these artisans are sold, those responsible for the sale must not dare to practice any fraud. [5]Let them always remember Ananias and Sapphira, who incurred bodily death (Acts 5:1-11), [6]lest they and all who perpetrate fraud in monastery affairs suffer spiritual death.

Univ. Press 1959) pp. 421–424, and P. Riché, *Education and Culture in the Barbarian West: Sixth through Eighth Centuries* (Columbia: Univ. of South Carolina Press 1976).

55.20 "what is said in the Acts" (*illa sententia Actuum*): See note on Prol.50.

56.0 This brief chapter, by comparison with RM 84, is an interesting example of the greater flexibility of RB. See Introduction, pp. 93–94. While in RM more exact prescriptions are given regarding those who may dine with the abbot, in RB all is left to the latter's discretion.

56.2 "no guests" (*minus sunt hospites*): The Latin word *minus*, as used in RB, can mean "fewer" or "no." Here it seems to mean the latter.

⁷In ipsis autem pretiis non surripiat avaritiae malum, ⁸sed
semper aliquantulum vilius detur quam ab aliis saecularibus dari
potest, ⁹*ut in omnibus glorificetur Deus*.

LVIII. DE DISCIPLINA SUSCIPIENDORUM FRATRUM

¹Noviter veniens quis ad conversationem, non ei facilis
tribuatur ingressus, ²sed sicut ait apostolus: *Probate spiritus si ex
Deo sunt*. ³Ergo si veniens perseveraverit pulsans et illatas sibi
iniurias et difficultatem ingressus post quattuor aut quinque dies
visus fuerit patienter portare et persistere petitioni suae, ⁴ad-
nuatur ei ingressus et sit in cella hospitum paucis diebus.

⁵Postea autem sit in cella noviciorum ubi meditent et mandu-
cent et dormiant. ⁶Et senior eis talis deputetur qui aptus sit ad
lucrandas animas, qui super eos omnino curiose intendat.

⁷Et sollicitudo sit si revera Deum quaerit, si sollicitus est ad
opus Dei, ad oboedientiam, ad opprobria. ⁸Praedicentur ei
omnia dura et aspera per quae itur ad Deum. ⁹Si promiserit de
stabilitate sua perseverantia, post duorum mensuum circulum
legatur ei haec regula per ordinem ¹⁰et dicatur ei: Ecce lex sub
qua militare vis; si potes observare, ingredere; si vero non potes,

---

57.9 *Vitae patr.*, *Verb.senior.* 5,10,98.
58.1 Pachom. *reg.* 49.
58.1-4 Caes.Arel. *reg.mon.* 1; Caes.Arel. *recapit.* 8; Cassian. *conl.* 20,1; Cassian. *inst.* 4,3.
58.3 *Reg. iv patr.* 2,27.
58.6 **Vita Pachom.** 25; Cassian. *inst.* 4,7.
58.7 Basil. *reg.* 6.
58.8 Cassian. *conl.* 24,25,2; *Reg. iv patr.* 2,26; Cypr. *hab.virg.* 21.
58.9 Caes.Arel. *reg.virg.* 58.
58.9-14 Caes.Arel. *recapit.* 8; Ps-Macar. *reg.* 23; *Decret.Gelasianum* 21.

58.t "procedure" (*disciplina*): See note on 19.t for the term *disciplina*. For a
treatment of the subject matter of this chapter generally, see Appendix 5. RB 58 is
a free reworking of the much longer RM 90 (95 verses).

58.1 "monastic life" (*conversationem*): A full discussion of this much controverted term may be found in Appendix 5, pp. 459–463.

58.3 "if someone comes and keeps knocking" (*si veniens perseveraverit pulsans*): The words *si. . .perseveraverit pulsans* are taken from Luke 11:8.

"harsh treatment and difficulty of entry" (*illatas sibi iniurias et difficultatem ingressus*): For a discussion of the tradition prior to RB of making entry
into monastic life difficult, see Appendix 5, pp. 437–443. *Iniuriae* are, strictly
speaking, instances of injustice. The willingness to suffer personal injustice is
intimately related to the monastic goal of humility (cf. RB 7.35,42, borrowed
from RM), which in turn is based on the imitation of Christ.

58.5 "novitiate" (*cella noviciorum*): The phrase means, literally, "the room

7The evil of avarice must have no part in establishing prices, 8which should, therefore, always be a little lower than people outside the monastery are able to set, 9*so that in all things God may be glorified* (1 Pet 4:11).

CHAPTER 58. THE PROCEDURE FOR RECEIVING BROTHERS

1Do not grant newcomers to the monastic life an easy entry, 2but, as the Apostle says, *Test the spirits to see if they are from God* (1 John 4:1). 3Therefore, if someone comes and keeps knocking at the door, and if at the end of four or five days he has shown himself patient in bearing his harsh treatment and difficulty of entry, and has persisted in his request, 4then he should be allowed to enter and stay in the guest quarters for a few days. 5After that, he should live in the novitiate, where the novices study, eat and sleep.

6A senior chosen for his skill in winning souls should be appointed to look after them with careful attention. 7The concern must be whether the novice truly seeks God and whether he shows eagerness for the Work of God, for obedience and for trials. 8The novice should be clearly told all the hardships and difficulties that will lead him to God.

9If he promises perseverance in his stability, then after two months have elapsed let this rule be read straight through to him, 10and let him be told: "This is the law under which you are choosing to serve. If you can keep it, come in. If not, feel free to

---

for the novices." On the relationship between this verse and v.11 and the question of the length of time spent in the novitiate, see Appendix 5, pp. 443–445.

"study" (*meditent*): Cf. RB 48.3. This study involved memorization of the psalms and Scripture passages used in the Divine Office. For a discussion of the term and related concepts, see Appendix 5, pp. 446–447.

58.6 "winning" (*lucrandas*): The word suggests a possible reference to Matt 18:15-16. It occurs in different form but similar context in 1 Cor 9:20.

58.7 "The concern" (*sollicitudo*): "His concern" would be smoother, but there seems to be a suggestion that this is a concern of the whole community, not simply of the novice master. But see Appendix 5, p. 447.

"seeks God" (*Deum quaerit*): On this theme in Patristic literature, see G. Turbessi "*Quaerere Deum*. Variazioni Patristiche su un tema centrale della *Regula Sancti Benedicti*" *Benedictina* 14 (1967) 14–22; 15 (1968) 181–205.

"the Work of God" (*opus Dei*): In RB this phrase means the Divine Office. See Appendix 3, pp. 405–406.

"trials" (*opprobria*): For a discussion of the content and background of this term, see Appendix 5, pp. 448–449.

liber discede. [11]Si adhuc steterit, tunc ducatur in supradictam cellam noviciorum et iterum probetur in omni patientia. [12]Et post sex mensuum circuitum legatur ei regula, ut sciat ad quod ingreditur. [13]Et si adhuc stat, post quattuor menses iterum relegatur ei eadem regula. [14]Et si habita secum deliberatione promiserit se omnia custodire et cuncta sibi imperata servare, tunc suscipiatur in congregatione, [15]sciens et lege regulae constitutum quod ei ex illa die non liceat egredi de monasterio, [16]nec collum excutere de sub iugo regulae quem sub tam morosam deliberationem licuit aut excusare aut suscipere.

[17]Suscipiendus autem in oratorio coram omnibus promittat de stabilitate sua et conversatione morum suorum et oboedientia, [18]coram Deo et sanctis eius, ut si aliquando aliter fecerit, ab eo se damnandum sciat quem irridit. [19]De qua promissione sua faciat petitionem ad nomen sanctorum quorum reliquiae ibi sunt et abbatis praesentis. [20]Quam petitionem manu sua scribat, aut certe, si non scit litteras, alter ab eo rogatus scribat et ille novicius signum faciat et manu sua eam super altare ponat. [21]Quam dum imposuerit, incipiat ipse novicius mox hunc versum: *Suscipe me*, Domine, *secundum eloquium tuum et vivam, et ne confundas me ab exspectatione mea.* [22]Quem versum omnis congregatio tertio respondeat, adiungentes Gloria Patri. [23]Tunc ille frater novicius prosternatur singulorum pedibus ut orent pro eo, et iam ex illa die in congregatione reputetur.

[24]Res, si quas habet, aut eroget prius pauperibus aut facta sollemniter donatione conferat monasterio, nihil sibi reservans ex omnibus, [25]quippe qui ex illo die nec proprii corporis potestatem se habiturum scit.

58.16 *Vita Macar. Rom.* 2.
58.17 Cassian. *inst.* 7,9.
58.18 Cassian. *inst.* 4,36,2.
58.23 *Vitae patr., Verb.senior.* 5,13,13.
58.24-25 Ps-Macar. reg. 24; Caes.Arel. reg.mon. 1.
58.25 Cassian. *inst.* 2,3,1; 4,20; Cassian. *conl.* 24,23; Basil. *reg.* 106.

58.11 "in all patience" (*in omni patientia*): The phrase occurs in 2 Tim 4:2.
58.17 "promises" (*promittat*): For a discussion of the history and the ceremony of monastic profession, see Appendix 5, pp. 449–457.
"stability. . ." (*stabilitate*): "Stability, fidelity to monastic life, and obedience" are not understood in RB to be three distinct vows, as the vows of religious life later came to be understood. Rather, the phrase describes the content of the monk's promise. See Appendix 5, pp. 457–458; for the reference of the three terms, see pp. 458–466.
58.18 "mocks" (*irridit*): This word occurs in Gal 6:7 also in reference to God.

leave." ¹¹If he still stands firm, he is to be taken back to the
novitiate, and again thoroughly tested in all patience. ¹²After six
months have passed, the rule is to be read to him, so that he may
know what he is entering. ¹³If once more he stands firm, let four
months go by, and then read this rule to him again. ¹⁴If after due
reflection he promises to observe everything and to obey every
command given him, let him then be received into the community. ¹⁵But he must be well aware that, as the law of the rule es-
tablishes, from this day he is no longer free to leave the monastery, ¹⁶nor to shake from his neck the yoke of the rule which, in
the course of so prolonged a period of reflection, he was free either
to reject or to accept.

¹⁷When he is to be received, he comes before the whole community in the oratory and promises stability, fidelity to monastic life, and obedience. ¹⁸This is done in the presence of
God and his saints to impress on the novice that if he ever acts
otherwise, he will surely be condemned by the one he mocks.
¹⁹He states his promise in a document drawn up in the name of
the saints whose relics are there, and of the abbot, who is
present. ²⁰The novice writes out this document himself, or if he
is illiterate, then he asks someone else to write it for him, but
himself puts his mark to it and with his own hand lays it on the
altar. ²¹After he has put it there, the novice himself begins the
verse: *Receive me*, Lord, *as you have promised, and I shall live;
do not disappoint me in my hope* (Ps 118[119]:116). ²²The whole
community repeats the verse three times, and adds "Glory be to
the Father." ²³Then the novice prostrates himself at the feet of
each monk to ask his prayers, and from that very day he is to be
counted as one of the community.

²⁴If he has any possessions, he should either give them to the
poor beforehand, or make a formal donation of them to the
monastery, without keeping back a single thing for himself,
²⁵well aware that from that day he will not have even his own

---

58.24 "formal donation" (*sollemniter donatione*): The donation is apparently
included in the profession document (vv.19-21). See Appendix 5, pp. 456–457
and de Vogüé 6.956. The practice of making a donation of goods to the monastery (forbidden by Cassian. *inst.* 4.4, but allowed by RM and RB) later led, not
surprisingly, to considerable problems and further legal restrictions. See Joseph H. Lynch, *Simoniacal Entry into Religious Life from 1000 to 1260* (Colum-
bus: Ohio State Univ. Press 1976).

²⁶Mox ergo in oratorio exuatur rebus propriis quibus vestitus est et induatur rebus monasterii. ²⁷Illa autem vestimenta quibus exutus est reponantur in vestiario conservanda, ²⁸ut si aliquando suadenti diabolo consenserit ut egrediatur de monasterio—quod absit—tunc exutus rebus monasterii proiciatur. ²⁹Illam tamen petitionem eius, quam desuper altare abbas tulit, non recipiat, sed in monasterio reservetur.

LIX. DE FILIIS NOBILIUM AUT PAUPERUM QUI OFFERUNTUR

¹Si quis forte de nobilibus offerit filium suum Deo in monasterio, si ipse puer minor aetate est, parentes eius faciant petitionem quam supra diximus ²et cum oblatione ipsam petitionem et manum pueri involvant in palla altaris, et sic eum offerant.

³De rebus autem suis, aut in praesenti petitione promittant sub iureiurando quia numquam per se, numquam per suffectam personam nec quolibet modo ei aliquando aliquid dant aut tribuunt

---

58.26 Cassian. inst. 4,5-6; Pachom. *reg.* 49.

58.25 "body at his disposal" (*corporis potestatem*): This phrase seems to be taken from 1 Cor 7:4 (*vir sui corporis potestatem non habet*), thus suggesting an interesting analogy with the marital situation.

58.26 "clothed" (*induatur*): In RB the conferral of the habit is connected with renunciation. See Appendix 5, pp. 456–457. On the origin and nature of the monastic habit, see notes to RB 55.

59.1 "a member of the nobility" (*quis forte de nobilibus*): The contrast of nobles and poor men did not, in the sixth century, cover the whole range of social stations as it might in modern times. Considerable portions of the population were excluded by law from entrance into monastic life, including those who belonged to the slave class and those with various hereditary social obligations. See J. Chapman, *St. Benedict and the Sixth Century* (New York: Longmans, Green and Co. 1929) pp. 147–193. On the social composition of early monasticism, see G. Penco "La composizione sociale delle comunità monastiche nei primi secoli" *SM* 4 (1962) 257–281.

"too young" (*minor aetate*): The Rule treats in a number of places (30.1; 37.1; 39.10; 70.4) of boys in the monastery; this chapter makes clear what they are doing there. It forms a parallel with the preceding one. Together they treat of the two methods of entrance into monastic life. Both involve the renunciation of goods; both are considered permanent and irrevocable. The only difference between profession (ch. 58) and oblation (ch. 59) is that the written document is drawn up and signed by the parents in the case of oblation. That such a decision involving the renunciation not only of goods but also of marriage should be made by the parents may be somewhat shocking to the modern English-speaking reader.

body at his disposal. [26]Then and there in the oratory, he is to be stripped of everything of his own that he is wearing and clothed in what belongs to the monastery. [27]The clothing taken from him is to be put away and kept safely in the wardrobe, [28]so that, should he ever agree to the devil's suggestion and leave the monastery—which God forbid—he can be stripped of the clothing of the monastery before he is cast out. [29]But that document of his which the abbot took from the altar should not be given back to him but kept in the monastery.

CHAPTER 59. THE OFFERING OF SONS BY NOBLES OR BY THE POOR

[1]If a member of the nobility offers his son to God in the monastery, and the boy himself is too young, the parents draw up the document mentioned above; [2]then, at the presentation of the gifts, they wrap the document itself and the boy's hand in the altar cloth. That is how they offer him.

[3]As to their property, they either make a sworn promise in this document that they will never personally, never through an intermediary, nor in any way at all, nor at any time, give the boy

---

However, it should be remembered that in the past, marriages too were arranged by parents. In addition to piety, various social pressures, such as the number of children, the role of primogeniture, etc., entered into the development and perpetuation of this practice. As a matter of fact, RB is one of the earliest witnesses to it. (The parallel place in RM 91 does not deal with underage children.) Although Basil allowed for the presence of children in the monastery, he required that permanent commitment be the result of personal decision made no earlier than sixteen or seventeen years of age (Basil. *epist.* 199,18). Numerous other affirmations of the principle of free choice can be found in the monastic tradition even in the medieval period. See de Vogüé 6.1355–68 and H. Leclercq "Oblat" *DACL* 12.1857–77. The institution of *oblati*, without juridical force, has survived in some non–English-speaking lands into modern times. It may be noted that the *iuniores* of RB 3.3 possibly include those who are *minores aetate* (so Leclercq). Exactly what the age limit for this description was is difficult to determine. In Roman law a child came of age and had the right to marry at puberty (12–14) but, because of the institution of the *paterfamilias*, was not necessarily *sui iuris*. Even if they were *sui iuris*, they were required to have a court-appointed *curator* to sanction contractual obligations up to the age of twenty-five. See J. A. Crook, *Law and Life of Rome* (Ithaca: Cornell Univ. Press 1967) pp. 116–118. In RB, however, the term seems to be used more loosely. See notes on RB 30.2 and 37.1.

59.2 "at the presentation of the gifts" (*cum oblatione*): The ceremony evidently took place during a Eucharistic celebration. See Appendix 5, pp. 451–452.

59.3 "their property" (*rebus. . .suis*): The clearest example in RB of *suus* used non-reflexively is in 68.4, but cf. also Prol.1,6; 9.9; 54.2; 63.16; 72.5; and possibly 59.4.

occasionem habendi; ⁴vel certe si hoc facere noluerint et aliquid
offerre volunt in eleemosynam monasterio pro mercede sua,
⁵faciant ex rebus quas dare volunt monasterio donationem, re-
servato sibi, si ita voluerint, usufructu. ⁶Atque ita omnia
obstruantur ut nulla suspicio remaneat puero per quam deceptus
perire possit—quod absit—quod experimento didicimus.

⁷Similiter autem et pauperiores faciant. ⁸Qui vero ex toto nihil
habent, simpliciter petitionem faciant et cum oblatione offerant
filium suum coram testibus.

LX. DE SACERDOTIBUS QUI FORTE VOLUERINT
IN MONASTERIO HABITARE

¹Si quis de ordine sacerdotum in monasterio se suscipi
rogaverit, non quidem citius ei assentiatur. ²Tamen, si omnino
persteterit in hac supplicatione, sciat se omnem regulae disciplinam servaturum, ³nec aliquid ei relaxabitur, ut sit sicut scriptum est: *Amice, ad quod venisti?* ⁴Concedatur ei tamen post
abbatem stare et benedicere aut missas tenere, si tamen iusserit
ei abbas; ⁵sin alias, ullatenus aliqua praesumat, sciens se disciplinae regulari subditum, et magis humilitatis exempla omnibus
det. ⁶Et si forte ordinationis aut alicuius rei causa fuerit in
monasterio, ⁷illum locum attendat quando ingressus est in

59.6 Cypr. *epist.* 15,2.
59.8 Basil. *reg.* 7.

59.4 "their reward" (*pro mercede sua*): This can mean either "for their advantage" (McCann) or "in reimbursement for him," i.e., to defray the community's
expenses in feeding and clothing him, etc. (Steidle). The former is more natural
Latin, but the latter is possible, and it too is consistent with what we know of the
admission practice. This whole passage becomes clearer after reference to 58.24
and to RM 91, esp. vv.48-57. Cf. also RM 89.17-23 and 31-35. The concern in the
mind of both authors is that if the son has any property outside the monastery that
he can call his own, he may be tempted in later years to leave the monastery,
knowing that he has a ready-made livelihood waiting for him. To ensure that no
such suspicion remains in the son's mind, the Master recommends that the parents either (a) give away their son's share to the poor, or (b) divide it into three
parts, giving one to the abbot for the poor, keeping one for the family and giving
the third to their son as his "journey money" (*viatici sui utilitate* 91.52) to be
given to the monastery, or (c) simply swear on the Gospels that the son is disinherited. St. Benedict here recommends (c) or a form of (b) whereby the whole
sum, not one third of it, is given to the monastery. "The property that they want to
give to the monastery" seems to be either their son's share of the inheritance or a
substitute for it.

anything or afford him the opportunity to possess anything; [4]or else, if they are unwilling to do this and still wish to win their reward for making an offering to the monastery, [5]they make a formal donation of the property that they want to give to the monastery, keeping the revenue for themselves, should they so desire. [6]This ought to leave no way open for the boy to entertain any expectations that could deceive and ruin him. May God forbid this, but we have learned from experience that it can happen.

[7]Poor people do the same, [8]but those who have nothing at all simply write the document and, in the presence of witnesses, offer their son with the gifts.

CHAPTER 60. THE ADMISSION OF PRIESTS TO THE MONASTERY

[1]If any ordained priest asks to be received into the monastery, do not agree too quickly. [2]However, if he is fully persistent in his request, he must recognize that he will have to observe the full discipline of the rule [3]without any mitigation, knowing that it is written: *Friend, what have you come for* (Matt 26:50)? [4]He should, however, be allowed to stand next to the abbot, to give blessings and to celebrate Mass, provided that the abbot bids him. [5]Otherwise, he must recognize that he is subject to the discipline of the rule, and not make any exceptions for himself, but rather give everyone an example of humility. [6]Whenever there is question of an appointment or of any other business in the monastery, [7]he takes the place that corresponds to the date of

60.1 "any ordained priest" (*quis de ordine sacerdotum*): As is clear from RB 61.12 and 62.1, the term *sacerdos* and the phrase *ordo sacerdotum* include both priests and deacons. In 65.3 *sacerdos* refers to the bishop. In allowing priests and deacons to join the community as well as in permitting members of the community to be ordained, St. Benedict departs from the Master (RM 83), who considers them to be "outsiders."

60.3 "*Friend. . .*" (Amice. . .): In Matt 26:50 Jesus says this to Judas. St. Benedict uses the phrase, which had perhaps become a monastic cliché, without regard to its original context. However, it clearly suggests that a priest who does not wish to observe the full discipline of the Rule has, like Judas, come for the wrong reason.

60.4 "to celebrate Mass" (*missas tenere*): It is not certain that this phrase refers to the celebration of the Eucharist. See Appendix 3, pp. 411–412. The corresponding passage of RM (83.5) refers only to prayers and blessings. *Tenere*, however, is one of the regular words used with *missa* in the sense of Mass. It seems preferable, therefore, to keep that meaning.

60.5 "not make any exceptions" (*ullatenus aliqua praesumat*): See note on 26.1.

monasterio, non illum qui ei pro reverentia sacerdotii concessus est.

[8] Clericorum autem si quis eodem desiderio monasterio sociari voluerit, loco mediocri collocentur; [9] et ipsi tamen si promittunt de observatione regulae vel propria stabilitate.

LXI. DE MONACHIS PEREGRINIS, QUALITER SUSCIPIANTUR

[1] Si quis monachus peregrinus de longinquis provinciis supervenerit, si pro hospite voluerit habitare in monasterio [2] et contentus est consuetudinem loci quam invenerit, et non forte superfluitate sua perturbat monasterium, [3] sed simpliciter contentus est quod invenerit, suscipiatur quanto tempore cupit. [4] Si qua sane rationabiliter et cum humilitate caritatis reprehendit aut ostendit, tractet abbas prudenter ne forte pro hoc ipsud eum Dominus direxerit.

[5] Si vero postea voluerit stabilitatem suam firmare, non renuatur talis voluntas, et maxime quia tempore hospitalitatis potuit eius vita dinosci. [6] Quod si superfluus aut vitiosus inventus fuerit tempore hospitalitatis, non solum non debet sociari corpori monasterii, [7] verum etiam dicatur ei honeste ut discedat, ne eius miseria etiam alii vitientur. [8] Quod si non fuerit talis qui mereatur proici, non solum si petierit suscipiatur congregationi sociandus, [9] verum etiam suadeatur ut stet, ut eius exemplo alii erudiantur, [10] et quia in omni loco uni Domino servitur, uni regi militatur. [11] Quem si etiam talem esse perspexerit abbas, liceat eum in superiori aliquantum constituere loco. [12] Non solum autem monachum, sed etiam de suprascriptis gradibus sacerdotum vel clericorum stabilire potest abbas in maiori quam ingrediuntur loco, si eorum talem perspexerit esse vitam.

61.6 Basil. *reg.* 6.

60.8 "Any clerics" (*Clericorum. . .quis*): The order of clerics as distinguished from the *ordo sacerdotum* included at this period: doorkeepers (porters), lectors, exorcists, acolytes and subdeacons.

61.1 "A visiting monk" (*quis monachus peregrinus*): See note on RB 53.2. The context here seems to favor the meaning "foreign" or "visiting" for *peregrinus*. It would hardly be proper to try to persuade (v.9) a genuine pilgrim to abandon his goal or to waylay him on his return journey. The early monastic literature (e.g., Pallad. *hist.laus.*) bears constant witness to the practice of visiting other monasteries or holy monks to learn more about the spiritual life. For some it became a way of life inimical to spiritual progress (cf. RB 1.10-11).

his entry into the community, and not that granted him out of respect for his priesthood.

⁸Any clerics who similarly wish to join the community should be ranked somewhere in the middle, ⁹but only if they, too, promise to keep the rule and observe stability.

CHAPTER 61. THE RECEPTION OF VISITING MONKS

¹A visiting monk from far away will perhaps present himself and wish to stay as a guest in the monastery. ²Provided that he is content with the life as he finds it, and does not make excessive demands that upset the monastery, ³but is simply content with what he finds, he should be received for as long a time as he wishes. ⁴He may, indeed, with all humility and love make some reasonable criticisms or observations, which the abbot should prudently consider; it is possible that the Lord guided him to the monastery for this very purpose.

⁵If after a while he wishes to remain and bind himself to stability, he should not be refused this wish, especially as there was time enough, while he was a guest, to judge his character. ⁶But if during his stay he has been found excessive in his demands or full of faults, he should certainly not be admitted as a member of the community. ⁷Instead, he should be politely told to depart, lest his wretched ways contaminate others.

⁸If, however, he has shown that he is not the kind of man who deserves to be dismissed, let him, on his request, be received as a member of the community. ⁹He should even be urged to stay, so that others may learn from his example, ¹⁰because wherever we may be, we are in the service of the same Lord and doing battle for the same King. ¹¹Further, the abbot may set such a man in a somewhat higher place in the community, if he sees that he deserves it. ¹²In fact, whether it is a monk or someone in the priestly or clerical orders mentioned above, the abbot has the power to set any of them above the place that corresponds to the date of his entry, if he sees that his life warrants it.

61.12 "orders" (*gradibus*): These are the *ordo sacerdotum* and the *ordo clericorum*. See notes to 60.1 and 60.8.

[13]Caveat autem abbas ne aliquando de alio noto monasterio monachum ad habitandum suscipiat sine consensu abbatis eius aut litteras commendaticias, [14]quia scriptum est: *Quod tibi non vis fieri, alio ne feceris.*

LXII. DE SACERDOTIBUS MONASTERII

[1]Si quis abbas sibi presbyterum vel diaconem ordinari petierit, de suis eligat qui dignus sit sacerdotio fungi. [2]Ordinatus autem caveat elationem aut superbiam, [3]nec quicquam praesumat nisi quod ei ab abbate praecipitur, sciens se multo magis disciplinae regulari subdendum. [4]Nec occasione sacerdotii obliviscatur regulae oboedientiam et disciplinam, sed magis ac magis in Deum proficiat. [5]Locum vero illum semper attendat quod ingressus est in monasterio, [6]praeter officium altaris, et si forte electio congregationis et voluntas abbatis pro vitae merito eum promovere voluerint. [7]Qui tamen regulam decanis vel praepositis constitutam sibi servare sciat.

[8]Quod si aliter praesumpserit, non sacerdos sed rebellio iudicetur. [9]Et saepe admonitus si non correxerit, etiam episcopus adhibeatur in testimonio. [10]Quod si nec sic emendaverit, clarescentibus culpis, proiciatur de monasterio, [11]si tamen talis fuerit eius contumacia ut subdi aut oboedire regulae nolit.

61.13 *Reg. iv patr.* 4,3-8.
62.4 Cypr. *epist.* 13,16.
62.10 Vigil. *reg.(orient.)* 35.

61.13 "another known monastery" (*alio noto monasterio*): This rule, which fosters peace between monasteries, seems to apply only to "known" monasteries. Synods of the fourth century required clerics to carry letters of recommendation from their bishop if they resided outside their diocese. The rule began to apply to monks in the second half of the fifth century (see de Vogüé 6.1381–82).

62.1 "Any abbot" (*quis abbas*): This is one of the indications that the Rule was written with more than one monastery in view. Cf. RB 18.22; 73.1.

"priest or deacon" (*presbyterum vel diaconem*): In RB the word *presbyter* (elder) designates the priest as distinguished from the bishop and deacon. The term *sacerdos*, as is clear from the title of this chapter, includes all three. See notes on RB 60.1 and 61.12. This is the only reference in RB to the deacon; no indication is given of his function in the monastery.

"to exercise the priesthood" (*sacerdotio fungi*): The phrase occurs in Sir 45:19 (Vulgate) in reference to Aaron. An example of those not worthy to exercise the priesthood may be found in 1 Sam 3:10-14.

62.4 "more and more progress" (*magis ac magis...proficiat*): Cf. the similar phrase in RB 2.25, *ut in melius proficiant.* The notion of spiritual progress is basic to the monastic life and is evident in many places in RB. It is implicit in the idea

[13] The abbot must, however, take care never to receive into the community a monk from another known monastery, unless the monk's abbot consents and sends a letter of recommendation, [14] since it is written: *Never do to another what you do not want done to yourself* (Tob 4:16).

CHAPTER 62. THE PRIESTS OF THE MONASTERY

[1] Any abbot who asks to have a priest or deacon ordained should choose from his monks one worthy to exercise the priesthood. [2] The monk so ordained must be on guard against conceit or pride, [3] must not presume to do anything except what the abbot commands him, and must recognize that now he will have to subject himself all the more to the discipline of the rule. [4] Just because he is a priest, he may not therefore forget the obedience and discipline of the rule, but must make more and more progress toward God.

[5] He will always take the place that corresponds to the date of his entry into the monastery, [6] except in his duties at the altar, or unless the whole community chooses and the abbot wishes to give him a higher place for the goodness of his life. [7] Yet, he must know how to keep the rule established for deans and priors; [8] should he presume to act otherwise, he must be regarded as a rebel, not as a priest. [9] If after many warnings he does not improve, let the bishop too be brought in as a witness. [10] Should he not amend even then, and his faults become notorious, he is to be dismissed from the monastery, [11] but only if he is so arrogant that he will not submit or obey the rule.

---

of a school for the Lord's service (Prol.45), in the *processu. . .conversationis et fidei* of Prol.49 and above all in the climbing image of RB 7, where spiritual progress is equated with progress in humility. The first great Christian exponent of progress in the spiritual life was Origen, whose influence on all later writers is immeasurable. See Introduction, pp. 34–41.

62.7 "for deans and priors" (*decanis vel praepositis*): This seems to refer to 21.5-7 and possibly to ch. 65. The plural, *praepositis*, apparently refers to the succession of priors. Cf. note on 35.8 for a similar plural.

62.9 "as a witness" (*in testimonio*): In RM 83.18, where there is a question of asking priests to depart if they refuse to work, the abbot is instructed to do this in the presence of a number of "religious," but no mention is made of the bishop. But in RM 87.36, which deals with the candidate who is making a donation of his property to the monastery, it is urged that the bishop be one of the witnesses. On the relationship of monastic communities and bishops, see K. Seasoltz "Monastic Autonomy and Exemption; Charism and Institution" *The Jurist* 34 (1974) 316–355.

LXIII.　DE ORDINE CONGREGATIONIS

[1]Ordines suos in monasterio ita conservent ut conversationis tempus ut vitae meritum discernit utque abbas constituerit. [2]Qui abbas non conturbet gregem sibi commissum nec, quasi libera utens potestate, iniuste disponat aliquid, [3]sed cogitet semper quia de omnibus iudiciis et operibus suis redditurus est Deo rationem. [4]Ergo secundum ordines quos constituerit vel quos habuerint ipsi fratres sic accedant ad pacem, ad communionem, ad psalmum imponendum, in choro standum; [5]et in omnibus omnino locis aetas non discernat ordines nec praeiudicet, [6]quia Samuel et Daniel pueri presbyteros iudicaverunt. [7]Ergo excepto hos quos, ut diximus, altiori consilio abbas praetulerit vel degradaverit certis ex causis, reliqui omnes ut convertuntur ita sint, [8]ut verbi gratia qui secunda hora diei venerit in monasterio iuniorem se noverit illius esse qui prima hora venit diei, cuiuslibet aetatis aut dignitatis sit, [9]pueris per omnia ab omnibus disciplina conservata.

[10]Iuniores igitur priores suos honorent, priores minores suos diligant. [11]In ipsa appellatione nominum nulli liceat alium puro appellare nomine, [12]sed priores iuniores suos fratrum nomine, iuniores autem priores suos nonnos vocent, quod intellegitur paterna reverentia. [13]Abbas autem, quia vices Christi creditur agere, dominus et abbas vocetur, non sua assumptione sed honore et amore Christi; [14]ipse autem cogitet et sic se exhibeat ut dignus sit tali honore.

[15]Ubicumque autem sibi obviant fratres, iunior priorem bene-

---

63.2-3 Cypr. *epist.* 55,21.
63.4 Pachom. *reg.* praef. 3.
63.6 Hier. *epist.* 58,1.
63.7 Sulpic.Sever. *dial.* 1,10,1.
63.12 Hier. *epist.* 117,6.

63.4 "for Communion" (*ad communionem*): See Appendix 3, pp. 410–412.
　　63.10 "The younger monks" (*Iuniores*): In vv. 10-17, *iuniores* and *minores* are used for the younger monks, and *priores*, *maiores* and *seniores* for the older. It is difficult to discern any clear difference in usage or meaning. Cf. de Vogüé, *La communauté*, p. 503. *Iunior* and *senior* refer, etymologically, to age; *maior* and *minor* to size; and *prior* is the comparative of an obsolete preposition, *pri*, of which *primus* (first) is the superlative.
　　63.12 "brother" (*fratrum*): This is the ancient term for Christians (57 times in Acts, 343 in the New Testament) and is used freely in RB as well as the earlier monastic literature as a synonym for "monk." On the respective usage of *frater*,

CHAPTER 63. COMMUNITY RANK

¹The monks keep their rank in the monastery according to the date of their entry, the virtue of their lives, and the decision of the abbot. ²The abbot is not to disturb the flock entrusted to him nor make any unjust arrangements, as though he had the power to do whatever he wished. ³He must constantly reflect that he will have to give God an account of all his decisions and actions. ⁴Therefore, when the monks come for the kiss of peace and for Communion, when they lead psalms or stand in choir, they do so in the order decided by the abbot or already existing among them. ⁵Absolutely nowhere shall age automatically determine rank. ⁶Remember that Samuel and Daniel were still boys when they judged their elders (1 Sam 3; Dan 13:44-62). ⁷Therefore, apart from those mentioned above whom the abbot has for some overriding consideration promoted, or for a specific reason demoted, all the rest should keep to the order of their entry. ⁸For example, someone who came to the monastery at the second hour of the day must recognize that he is junior to someone who came at the first hour, regardless of age or distinction. ⁹Boys, however, are to be disciplined in everything by everyone.

¹⁰The younger monks, then, must respect their seniors, and the seniors must love their juniors. ¹¹When they address one another, no one should be allowed to do so simply by name; ¹²rather, the seniors call the younger monks "brother" and the younger monks call their seniors *nonnus*, which is translated as "venerable father." ¹³But the abbot, because we believe that he holds the place of Christ, is to be called "lord" and "abbot," not for any claim of his own, but out of honor and love for Christ. ¹⁴He, for his part, must reflect on this, and in his behavior show himself worthy of such honor.

¹⁵Wherever brothers meet, the junior asks his senior for a

---

discipulus and *monachus* in RM and RB, see de Vogüé 1.255–256 and Introduction, p. 80. See A Selected Latin Concordance.

"which is translated" (*quod intellegitur*): Cf. the similar phrase (*quod est interpretatum*) in John 1:41. The need to give a translation suggests, of course, that we are dealing with a foreign word that had, however, become part of the common monastic vocabulary. For a discussion of the origin of *nonnus* and its feminine equivalent, *nonna* (nun), see Appendix 1, p. 321.

63.13 "holds the place of Christ" (*vices Christi. . .agere*): See note on 2.2.

dictionem petat. ¹⁶Transeunte maiore minor surgat et det ei
locum sedendi, nec praesumat iunior consedere nisi ei praecipiat
senior suus, ¹⁷ut fiat quod scriptum est: *Honore invicem
praevenientes.*

¹⁸Pueri parvi vel adulescentes in oratorio vel ad mensas cum
disciplina ordines suos consequantur. ¹⁹Foris autem vel ubiubi,
et custodiam habeant et disciplinam, usque dum ad intellegibilem aetatem perveniant.

LXIV. DE ORDINANDO ABBATE

¹In abbatis ordinatione illa semper consideretur ratio ut hic
constituatur quem sive omnis concors congregatio secundum
timorem Dei, sive etiam pars quamvis parva congregationis
saniore consilio elegerit. ²Vitae autem merito et sapientiae doctrina eligatur qui ordinandus est, etiam si ultimus fuerit in ordine
congregationis.

³Quod si etiam omnis congregatio vitiis suis—quod quidem
absit—consentientem personam pari consilio elegerit, ⁴et vitia
ipsa aliquatenus in notitia episcopi ad cuius dioecesim pertinet
locus ipse vel ad abbates aut christianos vicinos claruerint, ⁵pro-
hibeant pravorum praevalere consensum, sed domui Dei dignum
constituant dispensatorem, ⁶scientes pro hoc se recepturos mercedem bonam, si illud caste et zelo Dei faciant, sicut e diverso
peccatum si neglegant.

⁷Ordinatus autem abbas cogitet semper quale onus suscepit et

63.16-17 Cypr. *testim.* 3,85.
64.1-5 Cypr. *epist.* 67, 2-3; Cypr. *domin.orat.* 23.
64.7 Aug. *epist.* 211,15.

63.16 "an older monk" (*maiore*): Cf. Lev 19:32, and see above on 63.10.
"to sit down" (*consedere*): This word can mean "sit down," "settle," or "sit with." If, when the younger monk offers the older a seat, the older sits down, the younger will not sit with him unless bidden; if the older does not sit down, the younger will not settle (sit) down again unless bidden.
63.17 "*respect*" (Honore): In the translation of *honor* and *honorare*, "honor" has been used where the one honored is God, or men in whom Christ is specially present (e.g., the abbot, guests) except in 4.8, where we keep the biblical term (but see note on 53.2).
63.18 "youths" (*adulescentes*): In Roman law one became an *adulescens* at the age of puberty (fourteen for males), but the term *adulescens* is probably used more loosely in RB. See following note.

blessing. [16]When an older monk comes by, the younger rises and offers him a seat, and does not presume to sit down unless the older bids him. [17]In this way, they do what the words of Scripture say: *They should each try to be the first to show respect to the other* (Rom 12:10).

[18]In the oratory and at table, small boys and youths are kept in rank and under discipline. [19]Outside or anywhere else, they should be supervised and controlled until they are old enough to be responsible.

CHAPTER 64. THE ELECTION OF AN ABBOT

[1]In choosing an abbot, the guiding principle should always be that the man placed in office be the one selected either by the whole community acting unanimously in the fear of God, or by some part of the community, no matter how small, which possesses sounder judgment. [2]Goodness of life and wisdom in teaching must be the criteria for choosing the one to be made abbot, even if he is the last in community rank.

[3]May God forbid that a whole community should conspire to elect a man who goes along with its own evil ways. But if it does, [4]and if the bishop of the diocese or the abbots or Christians in the area come to know of these evil ways to any extent, [5]they must block the success of this wicked conspiracy, and set a worthy steward in charge of God's house. [6]They may be sure that they will receive a generous reward for this, if they do it with pure motives and zeal for God's honor. Conversely, they may be equally sure that to neglect to do so is sinful.

[7]Once in office, the abbot must keep constantly in mind the

---

63.19 "old enough to be responsible" (*ad intellegibilem aetatem*): The phrase means literally 'the age of reason' or 'understanding.' See note on 59.1.

64.1 "choosing" (*ordinatione*): The words *ordinatio* and *ordinare* seem to cover the whole action from the choice of an abbot to his installation. On this chapter generally, including the meanings of *ordinare*, *eligere* and *constituere*, see Appendix 2, pp. 370–378.

"sounder judgment" (*saniore consilio*): For the meaning of this phrase and this manner of choice, see Appendix 2, pp. 372–374.

64.5 "God's house" (*domui Dei*): There may be an allusion here to Ps 104 (105):21, where the reference is to Joseph being placed over Pharaoh's house. See also Luke 12:42.

64.7 "Once in office" (*Ordinatus*): No rite of installation, such as that described at length in RM 93–94, is outlined in RB, but the word *ordinatus* may be a passing reference to a ritual. See Appendix 2, p. 375.

cui *redditurus est rationem vilicationis* suae, [8]sciatque sibi oportere prodesse magis quam praeesse. [9]Oportet ergo eum esse doctum lege divina, ut sciat et sit unde *proferat nova et vetera*,
castum, sobrium, misericordem, [10]et semper *superexaltet misericordiam iudicio*, ut idem ipse consequatur. [11]Oderit vitia, di-
ligat fratres. [12]In ipsa autem correptione prudenter agat et ne
quid nimis, ne dum nimis eradere cupit aeruginem frangatur vas;
[13]suamque fragilitatem semper suspectus sit, memineritque
calamum quassatum non conterendum. [14]In quibus non dicimus
ut permittat nutriri vitia, sed prudenter et cum caritate ea amputet, ut viderit cuique expedire sicut iam diximus, [15]et studeat
plus amari quam timeri.

[16]Non sit turbulentus et anxius, non sit nimius et obstinatus,
non sit zelotypus et nimis suspiciosus, quia numquam requiescit;
[17]in ipsis imperiis suis providus et consideratus, et sive secundum Deum sive secundum saeculum sit opera quam iniungit,
discernat et temperet, [18]cogitans discretionem sancti Iacob dicentis: *Si greges* meos *plus in ambulando fecero laborare,
morientur cuncti una die.* [19]Haec ergo aliaque testimonia discretionis matris virtutum sumens, sic omnia temperet ut sit et
fortes quod cupiant et infirmi non refugiant.

64.8 **Aug. serm.** 340,1; Aug. *civ.* 19,19; Aug. *c.Faust.* 25,56.
64.11 **Aug. serm.** 49,5; Aug. *civ.* 14,6; Aug. *epist.* 211,11; Caes.Arel. *reg.virg.* 22.
64.12 Ter.*Andr.* I,i,34; Hier.*epist.* 60,7; 108,20; 130,11; Aug. *in psalm.* 118,4,1.
64.15 **Aug. epist.** 211,15.
64.19 Cassian. *conl.* 2,4,4; Cassian. *inst.* 2,12,2.

64.8 "profit. . .preeminence" (*prodesse. . .praeesse*): This jingle is a commonplace. Cf. Aug. *serm.* 340,1; *civ.* 19,19; *c.Faust.* 22,56; Greg. *past.* 2,6; *Lib.diurn.*
46. It is not easy to reproduce the word-play in English: "profit. . .prominence"
or "profit. . .preside over" (McCann) are less neat than the Latin.

64.9 "chaste, temperate and merciful" (*castum, sobrium, misericordem*): Cf.
the requirements for bishops in 1 Tim 3:2-4; Titus 1:7-9; 2:2-5.

64.10 "win mercy" (*idem ipse consequatur*): This is probably a reference to
Matt 5:7, where the word *consequentur* is used in the same context.

64.12 "punish" (*correptione*): In all its other occurrences in RB (28.1; 33.8;
48.20; 64.19), *correptio* is contrasted with verbal reproof or warning. See note on
21.5.

"avoid extremes" (*ne quid nimis*): The phrase is used in RM 27.25 in a different
context. It translates *mēden agan*, a typical maxim of Greek ethics attributed to
Chilon, Solon and most other Greek sages. Terence, the Roman playwright,
seems to be the first to use the phrase in Latin (*Andr.* I,i,34).

64.12-13 "break. . .frailty" (*frangatur. . .fragilitatem*): The two Latin words are

nature of the burden he has received, and remember to whom he will have *to give an account of his stewardship* (Luke 16:2). [8]Let him recognize that his goal must be profit for the monks, not preeminence for himself. [9]He ought, therefore, to be learned in divine law, so that he has a treasury of knowledge from which he can *bring out what is new and what is old* (Matt 13:52). He must be chaste, temperate and merciful. [10]He should always *let mercy triumph over judgment* (Jas 2:13) so that he too may win mercy. [11]He must hate faults but love the brothers. [12]When he must punish them, he should use prudence and avoid extremes; otherwise, by rubbing too hard to remove the rust, he may break the vessel. [13]He is to distrust his own frailty and remember *not to crush the bruised reed* (Isa 42:3). [14]By this we do not mean that he should allow faults to flourish, but rather, as we have already said, he should prune them away with prudence and love as he sees best for each individual. [15]Let him strive to be loved rather than feared.

[16]Excitable, anxious, extreme, obstinate, jealous or oversuspicious he must not be. Such a man is never at rest. [17]Instead, he must show forethought and consideration in his orders, and whether the task he assigns concerns God or the world, he should be discerning and moderate, [18]bearing in mind the discretion of holy Jacob, who said: *If I drive my flocks too hard, they will all die in a single day* (Gen 33:13). [19]Therefore, drawing on this and other examples of discretion, the mother of virtues, he must so arrange everything that the strong have something to yearn for and the weak nothing to run from.

---

from the same root, underlining that the abbot shares the frailty of the brothers.

64.15 "to be loved rather than feared" (*plus amari quam timeri*): See K. Gross "*Plus amari quam timeri*. Eine antike politische Maxime in der Benediktinerregel" *Vigiliae Christianae* 27 (1973) 218–229.

64.17 "concerns. . .the world" (*secundum saeculum*): O. Chadwick, *Western Asceticism* (Philadelphia: Westminster Press 1958) pp. 332–333 suggests the translation ". . .examine his commands to see whether they are in accordance with God's will or arise from worldly motives. . ." on the grounds that *saeculum* usually has a bad sense in RB, e.g., 1.7; 4.20. Against this, RB 7.8 is probably not pejorative, nor is the adjective *saecularis* in 57.8, and the order of the Latin is perhaps slightly against taking it as an indirect question.

64.19 "discretion" (*discretionis*): It may be recalled that Gregory the Great described the Rule as *discretione praecipuam*. See Introduction, p. 77.

"that. . .to run from" (*ut sit. . .refugiant*): This is "prices are expensive" Latin. The author seems to have two pairs of ideas in mind: *ut sit et fortes quod cupiant*

[20]Et praecipue ut praesentem regulam in omnibus conservet, [21]ut dum bene ministraverit audiat a Domino quod servus bonus qui erogavit triticum conservis suis in tempore suo: [22]*Amen dico vobis*, ait, *super omnia bona sua constituit eum.*

LXV. DE PRAEPOSITO MONASTERII

[1]Saepius quidem contigit ut per ordinationem praepositi scandala gravia in monasteriis oriantur, [2]dum sint aliqui maligno spiritu superbiae inflati et aestimantes se secundos esse abbates, assumentes sibi tyrannidem, scandala nutriunt et dissensiones in congregationes faciunt, [3]et maxime in illis locis ubi ab eodem sacerdote vel ab eis abbatibus qui abbatem ordinant, ab ipsis etiam et praepositus ordinatur. [4]Quod quam sit absurdum facile advertitur, quia ab ipso initio ordinationis materia ei datur superbiendi, [5]dum ei suggeritur a cogitationibus suis exutum eum esse a potestate abbatis sui, [6]quia ab ipsis es et tu ordinatus a quibus et abbas. [7]Hinc suscitantur invidiae, rixae, detractiones, aemulationes, dissensiones, exordinationes, [8]ut dum contraria sibi abbas praepositusque sentiunt, et ipsorum necesse est sub hanc dissensionem animas periclitari, [9]et hi qui sub ipsis sunt, dum adulantur partibus, eunt in perditionem. [10]Cuius periculi malum illos respicit in capite qui talius inordinationis se fecerunt auctores.

[11]Ideo nos vidimus expedire propter pacis caritatisque custodiam in abbatis pendere arbitrio ordinationem monasterii sui; [12]et si potest fieri per decanos ordinetur, ut ante disposuimus, omnis utilitas monasterii, prout abbas disposuerit, [13]ut, dum

---

65.t Caes.Arel. *reg.virg.* 16; Ps-Macar. *reg.* 27.
65.1-2 Cypr. *eccl.unit.* 10; Cypr. *zel. et liv.* 6.
65.11 Cypr. *domin.orat.* 23.
65.12 Cypr. *eccl.unit.* 10; Cassian. *inst.* 7,9.

---

et non sit infirmi quod refugiant and *ut fortes plus cupiant neve infirmi refugiant. Refugio* can be transitive or intransitive, which may have added to the confusion. It is passages like this, not all that rare in the Rule, that make one feel that the author, though certainly capable of powerful writing, is a spiritual, not a literary, giant. See 65.1-3 for an example of sprawling syntax and the Introduction, pp. 96–102 for further discussion of the style of RB.

65.1 "prior" (*praepositi*): The term *praepositus* means, literally, 'one who is placed before' or over a community. It is the term used by Augustine to designate the superior of a community, and from it come the English "provost" and the German "Probst." In RM the *praepositi* are deans or other officials. In RB the

[20] He must, above all, keep this rule in every particular, [21] so that when he has ministered well he will hear from the Lord what that good servant heard who gave his fellow servants grain at the proper time: [22] *I tell you solemnly*, he said, *he sets him over all his possessions* (Matt 24:47).

CHAPTER 65. THE PRIOR OF THE MONASTERY

[1] Too often in the past, the appointment of a prior has been the source of serious contention in monasteries. [2] Some priors, puffed up by the evil spirit of pride and thinking of themselves as second abbots, usurp tyrannical power and foster contention and discord in their communities. [3] This occurs especially in monasteries where the same bishop and the same abbots appoint both abbot and prior. [4] It is easy to see what an absurd arrangement this is, because from the very first moment of his appointment as prior he is given grounds for pride, [5] as his thoughts suggest to him that he is exempt from his abbot's authority. [6] "After all, you were made prior by the same men who made the abbot."

[7] This is an open invitation to envy, quarrels, slander, rivalry, factions and disorders of every kind, [8] with the result that, while abbot and prior pursue conflicting policies, their own souls are inevitably endangered by this discord; [9] and at the same time the monks under them take sides and so go to their ruin. [10] The responsibility for this evil and dangerous situation rests on the heads of those who initiated such a state of confusion.

[11] For the preservation of peace and love we have, therefore, judged it best for the abbot to make all decisions in the conduct of his monastery. [12] If possible, as we have already established, the whole operation of the monastery should be managed through deans under the abbot's direction. [13] Then, so long as it is

latter are called *decani* (ch. 21), and the *praepositus* is definitely the second in command. This office seems to have been of relatively recent origin in the time of St. Benedict (see Introduction, p. 81). The term "prior" has been used for this official since the tenth century. See de Vogüé, *La communauté*, pp. 388–404 and Thematic Index: MONASTIC LEADERS.

"contention" (*scandala*): See note on 13.12.

65.3 "bishop" (*sacerdote*): De Vogüé, *La communauté*, p. 413, holds that the practice of having the same bishop and abbots appoint both abbot and prior was not widespread. See note on RB 60.1.

65.7 "envy, quarrels. . ." (*invidiae, rixae*): Cf. similar lists in 2 Cor 12:20 and Gal 5:20-21.

pluribus committitur, unus non superbiat. [14]Quod si aut locus expetit aut congregatio petierit rationabiliter cum humilitate et abbas iudicaverit expedire, [15]quemcumque elegerit abbas cum consilio fratrum timentium Deum ordinet ipse sibi praepositum. [16]Qui tamen praepositus illa agat cum reverentia quae ab abbate suo ei iniuncta fuerint, nihil contra abbatis voluntatem aut ordinationem faciens, [17]quia quantum praelatus est ceteris, ita eum oportet sollicitius observare praecepta regulae.

[18]Qui praepositus si repertus fuerit vitiosus aut elatione deceptus superbire, aut contemptor sanctae regulae fuerit comprobatus, admoneatur verbis usque quater; [19]si non emendaverit, adhibeatur ei correptio disciplinae regularis. [20]Quod si neque sic correxerit, tunc deiciatur de ordine praepositurae et alius qui dignus est in loco eius surrogetur. [21]Quod si et postea in congregatione quietus et oboediens non fuerit, etiam de monasterio pellatur. [22]Cogitet tamen abbas se de omnibus iudiciis suis Deo reddere rationem, ne forte invidiae aut zeli flamma urat animam.

LXVI. DE OSTIARIIS MONASTERII

[1]Ad portam monasterii ponatur senex sapiens, qui sciat accipere responsum et reddere, et cuius maturitas eum non sinat

---

65.15-22 Cypr. *zel. et liv.* 6.
65.16 Pachom. *reg.* 158.
66.1 Cassian. *inst.* 4,7; *Hist.mon.* 17.

65.18 "the holy rule" (*sanctae regulae*): Although it has been doubted whether St. Benedict, who in 73.8 describes his work as "this little rule. . .for beginners," would himself have applied the epithet "holy" to it, it may be noted that his contemporary Caesarius does the same in regard to his own rule (Caes.Arel. *reg.virg.* 43,62 and 64). In the last instance (64), which is perhaps reminiscent of Rev 22:18-19, Caesarius declares that any abbess or prioress who does anything contrary to the holy rule "which I have written with my own hand" will have to face the tribunal of Christ. The phrase "holy rule" occurs also in RB 23.1 in juxtaposition with the commands of the seniors. The description of the rule as "holy" is an important indication that these authors regarded their work not simply as their own original literary productions but as the adaptation of a common monastic tradition. The written rule is holy because it embodies that tradition, especially as that tradition was itself seen as embodying the tradition of the Gospel. This notion of a normative tradition can be traced especially to Cassian, who speaks of a *monasteriorum regulam*, of the *Aegyptiorum regulam* (*inst.* praef.) and of a *communis usus* (*inst.*11,19). In *inst.* 4,39, Cassian speaks of the observance of a *communis regula* as his sixth indication of humility. The phrase becomes, by way of RM 10.72, the "common rule of the monastery" (*communis monasterii regula*) in St. Benedict's description of the eighth step in humility (RB

entrusted to more than one, no individual will yield to pride.
¹⁴But if local conditions call for it, or the community makes a
reasonable and humble request, and the abbot judges it best,
¹⁵then let him, with the advice of God-fearing brothers, choose
the man he wants and himself make him his prior. ¹⁶The prior for
his part is to carry out respectfully what his abbot assigns to him,
and do nothing contrary to the abbot's wishes or arrangements,
¹⁷because the more he is set above the rest, the more he should
be concerned to keep what the rule commands.

¹⁸If this prior is found to have serious faults, or is led astray by
conceit and grows proud, or shows open contempt for the holy
rule, he is to be warned verbally as many as four times. ¹⁹If he
does not amend, he is to be punished as required by the discipline of the rule. ²⁰Then, if he still does not reform, he is to be
deposed from the rank of prior and replaced by someone worthy.
²¹If after all that, he is not a peaceful and obedient member of the
community, he should even be expelled from the monastery.
²²Yet the abbot should reflect that he must give God an account
of all his judgments, lest the flames of jealousy or rivalry sear his
soul.

CHAPTER 66. THE PORTER OF THE MONASTERY

¹At the door of the monastery, place a sensible old man who
knows how to take a message and deliver a reply, and whose age

---

7.55). This idea is closely related to the notion of the "holy rule." See de Vogüé,
La communauté, pp. 260–262 and the Introduction, pp. 85–86.

65.19 "discipline of the rule" (*disciplinae regularis*): See Appendix 4, pp.
434–435.

66.t "The porter" (*ostiariis*): In spite of the plural in the title, the chapter
legislates for only one doorkeeper. The plural refers to the succession of doorkeepers. Cf. 62.7 and 71.3 on *praepositi*. The English word "porter" has been
retained in this translation because of its hallowed usage in monastic circles,
even though it commonly has a very different meaning. It derives from the Latin
porta, meaning 'door.' In its more common meaning the word 'porter' is derived
from the Latin *portare*, meaning 'to carry.'

66.1 "roaming about" (*vagari*): Although the critical texts read *vacari* (to be
free from, to have leisure for, to be unoccupied), the context requires the meaning
"to wander" (*vagari*). De Vogüé 1.396 regards *vacari* as a variant in spelling. See
the long and enjoyable note in McCann, *The Rule of Saint Benedict*, n. 102.

In RM 95.1-13, two decrepit brothers (*aetate decrepiti*) are to have a cell near
the gate. They open and close the gate, but also attend choir and reading, do what
manual labor they can, feed the dogs and other animals, and keep a lamp lit at the
gate.

vagari. ²Qui portarius cellam debebit habere iuxta portam, ut venientes semper praesentem inveniant a quo responsum accipiant. ³Et mox ut aliquis pulsaverit aut pauper clamaverit, Deo gratias respondeat aut Benedic, ⁴et cum omni mansuetudine timoris Dei reddat responsum festinanter cum fervore caritatis. ⁵Qui portarius si indiget solacio iuniorem fratrem accipiat.

⁶Monasterium autem, si possit fieri, ita debet constitui ut omnia necessaria, id est aqua, molendinum, hortum, vel artes diversas intra monasterium exerceantur, ⁷ut non sit necessitas monachis vagandi foris, quia omnino non expedit animabus eorum.

⁸Hanc autem regulam saepius volumus in congregatione legi, ne quis fratrum se de ignorantia excuset.

LXVII. DE FRATRIBUS IN VIAM DIRECTIS

¹Dirigendi fratres in via omnium fratrum vel abbatis se orationi commendent, ²et semper ad orationem ultimam operis Dei commemoratio omnium absentum fiat. ³Revertentes autem de via fratres ipso die quo redeunt per omnes canonicas horas, dum expletur opus Dei, prostrati solo oratorii ⁴ab omnibus petant orationem propter excessos, ne qui forte surripuerint in via visus aut auditus malae rei aut otiosi sermonis. ⁵Nec praesumat quisquam referre alio quaecumque foris monasterium viderit aut audierit, quia plurima destructio est.

⁶Quod si quis praesumpserit, vindictae regulari subiaceat. ⁷Similiter et qui praesumpserit claustra monasterii egredi vel quocumque ire vel quippiam quamvis parvum sine iussione abbatis facere.

66.6-7 Hist.mon. 17.
66.7 Hist.mon. 2.
67.5 *Vitae patr.*, *Verb.senior.* 5,15,59; Pachom. *reg.* 57; 86.
67.7 Pachom. *reg.* 84; Vigil. *reg.(orient.)* 31; Cassian. *inst.* 4,10.

66.3 "Your blessing, please" (*Benedic*): RM 95.20, in discouraging monks from going outside the enclosure, gives as one reason that people may honor them by asking for their blessing when they are not worthy to give one.

66.4 "gentleness" (*mansuetudine*): The root meaning of the word, which occurs only here and at 68.1, is "accustomed to the hand," and is used literally of training wild animals. It occurs in RM, but in quite different contexts.

66.6 "constructed" (*constitui*): This key and frequently used word in RB has a variety of meanings, depending of course on the context. It can mean 'set up' or 'establish' (e.g., Prol.45), 'designate' (43.5), 'arrange,' 'lay out,' 'lay down,' etc.

keeps him from roaming about. [2]This porter will need a room near the entrance so that visitors will always find him there to answer them. [3]As soon as anyone knocks, or a poor man calls out, he replies, "Thanks be to God" or "Your blessing, please"; [4]then, with all the gentleness that comes from the fear of God, he provides a prompt answer with the warmth of love. [5]Let the porter be given one of the younger brothers if he needs help.

[6]The monastery should, if possible, be so constructed that within it all necessities, such as water, mill and garden are contained, and the various crafts are practiced. [7]Then there will be no need for the monks to roam outside, because this is not at all good for their souls.

[8]We wish this rule to be read often in the community, so that none of the brothers can offer the excuse of ignorance.

CHAPTER 67. BROTHERS SENT ON A JOURNEY

[1]Brothers sent on a journey will ask the abbot and community to pray for them. [2]All absent brothers should always be remembered at the closing prayer of the Work of God. [3]When they come back from a journey, they should, on the very day of their return, lie face down on the floor of the oratory at the conclusion of each of the customary hours of the Work of God. [4]They ask the prayers of all for their faults, in case they may have been caught off guard on the way by seeing some evil thing or hearing some idle talk.

[5]No one should presume to relate to anyone else what he saw or heard outside the monastery, because that causes the greatest harm. [6]If anyone does so presume, he shall be subjected to the punishment of the rule. [7]So too shall anyone who presumes to leave the enclosure of the monastery, or go anywhere, or do anything at all, however small, without the abbot's order.

66.7 "is not at all good" (*non expedit*): Cf. RB 67.4-5 and RM 95.17-23.

66.8 "this rule" (*Hanc autem regulam*): This phrase seems to refer to the entire Rule and appears to be a primitive conclusion of the Rule. RB 66.8 corresponds to the end of RM. However, it seems likely that ch. 73 formed the real conclusion, even if chs. 67-72 are a later addition. See note on 73.t.

67.7 "the enclosure of the monastery" (*claustra monasterii*): The word *claustra* in its ancient pre-monastic usage signified any sort of space set off or closed to access by some sort of a barrier, natural or otherwise. In monastic circles it quickly became a technical term (as here and in 4.78). The enclosure was usually achieved by a wall and gates (cf. RB 66). The idea of enclosure, which can

LXVIII. SI FRATRI IMPOSSIBILIA INIUNGANTUR

[1]Si cui fratri aliqua forte gravia aut impossibilia iniunguntur, suscipiat quidem iubentis imperium cum omni mansuetudine et oboedientia. [2]Quod si omnino virium suarum mensuram viderit pondus oneris excedere, impossibilitatis suae causas ei qui sibi praeest patienter et opportune suggerat, [3]non superbiendo aut resistendo vel contradicendo. [4]Quod si post suggestionem suam in sua sententia prioris imperium perduraverit, sciat iunior ita sibi expedire, [5]et ex caritate, confidens de adiutorio Dei, oboediat.

LXIX. UT IN MONASTERIO NON PRAESUMAT ALTER ALTERUM DEFENDERE

[1]Praecavendum est ne quavis occasione praesumat alter alium defendere monachum in monasterio aut quasi tueri, [2]etiam si qualivis consanguinitatis propinquitate iungantur. [3]Nec quolibet modo id a monachis praesumatur, quia exinde gravissima occasio scandalorum oriri potest. [4]Quod si quis haec transgressus fuerit, acrius coerceatur.

LXX. UT NON PRAESUMAT PASSIM ALIQUIS CAEDERE

[1]Vitetur in monasterio omnis praesumptionis occasio; [2]atque constituimus ut nulli liceat quemquam fratrum suorum excommunicare aut caedere, nisi cui potestas ab abbate data fuerit. [3]*Peccantes* autem *coram omnibus arguantur ut ceteri metum habeant.* [4]Infantum vero usque quindecim annorum aetates disciplinae diligentia ab omnibus et custodia sit; [5]sed et hoc cum omni mensura et ratione.

68.1-3 Basil. *reg.* 69; Basil. *ad fil.* 6.
68.4-5 Cassian. *inst.* 4,10.
69.1 Basil. *reg.* 26; Orsiesii *lib.* 24; Pachom. *reg.* 176.

---

be traced to the earliest period of cenobitic monasticism in Egypt, is obviously related to, and the expression of, the more fundamental notion of separation from the world. See Introduction, p. 27, n. 79; H. Leclercq "Cloître" *DACL* 3.1991–92 and E. Renoir "Clôture monastique" *ibid.*, 2024–34. The typical square or U-shaped "cloister," normally located to the south of the church, seems to be an invention of the Carolingian period. See Walter Horn and Ernest Born, *The Plan of St. Gall: A Study of the Architecture and Economy of, and Life in a Paradigmatic Carolingian Monastery* (Berkeley: Univ. of California Press 1979) 1.245.

CHAPTER 68. ASSIGNMENT OF IMPOSSIBLE TASKS TO A BROTHER

[1]A brother may be assigned a burdensome task or something he cannot do. If so, he should, with complete gentleness and obedience, accept the order given him. [2]Should he see, however, that the weight of the burden is altogether too much for his strength, then he should choose the appropriate moment and explain patiently to his superior the reasons why he cannot perform the task. [3]This he ought to do without pride, obstinacy or refusal. [4]If after the explanation the superior is still determined to hold to his original order, then the junior must recognize that this is best for him. [5]Trusting in God's help, he must in love obey.

CHAPTER 69. THE PRESUMPTION OF DEFENDING ANOTHER
IN THE MONASTERY

[1]Every precaution must be taken that one monk does not presume in any circumstance to defend another in the monastery or to be his champion, [2]even if they are related by the closest ties of blood. [3]In no way whatsoever shall the monks presume to do this, because it can be a most serious source and occasion of contention. [4]Anyone who breaks this rule is to be sharply restrained.

CHAPTER 70. THE PRESUMPTION OF STRIKING ANOTHER MONK
AT WILL

[1]In the monastery every occasion for presumption is to be avoided, [2]and so we decree that no one has the authority to excommunicate or strike any of his brothers unless he has been given this power by the abbot. [3]*Those who sin should be reprimanded in the presence of all, that the rest may fear* (1 Tim 5:20). [4]Boys up to the age of fifteen should, however, be carefully controlled and supervised by everyone, [5]provided that this too is done with moderation and common sense.

68.1 "accept" (*suscipiat*): The Latin verb may mean either 'accept' or 'undertake.' It is tempting to think that the author intends the monk both to accept the order and to undertake the task. The monk would then be in a much stronger position for making his comments in v.2.

70.1 "presumption" (*praesumptionis*): The presumption in question is an encroachment upon the abbot's right to punish. Cf. note on RB 26.1.

⁶Nam in fortiori aetate qui praesumit aliquatenus sine praecepto abbatis vel in ipsis infantibus sine discretione exarserit, disciplinae regulari subiaceat, ⁷quia scriptum est: *Quod tibi non vis fieri, alio ne feceris.*

LXXI. UT OBOEDIENTES SIBI SINT INVICEM

¹Oboedientiae bonum non solum abbati exhibendum est ab omnibus, sed etiam sibi invicem ita oboediant fratres, ²scientes per hanc oboedientiae viam se ituros ad Deum. ³Praemisso ergo abbatis aut praepositorum qui ab eo constituuntur imperio, cui non permittimus privata imperia praeponi, ⁴de cetero omnes iuniores prioribus suis omni caritate et sollicitudine oboediant. ⁵Quod si quis contentiosus reperitur, corripiatur.

⁶Si quis autem frater pro quavis minima causa ab abbate vel a quocumque priore suo corripitur quolibet modo, ⁷vel si leviter senserit animos prioris cuiuscumque contra se iratos vel commotos quamvis modice, ⁸mox sine mora tamdiu prostratus in terra ante pedes eius iaceat satisfaciens, usque dum benedictione sanetur illa commotio. ⁹Quod qui contempserit facere, aut corporali vindictae subiaceat aut, si contumax fuerit, de monasterio expellatur.

LXXII. DE ZELO BONO QUOD DEBENT MONACHI HABERE

¹Sicut est zelus amaritudinis malus qui separat a Deo et ducit ad infernum, ²ita est zelus bonus qui separat a vitia et ducit ad Deum et ad vitam aeternam. ³Hunc ergo zelum ferventissimo

---

71.1 Aug. *civ.* 13,20; Cassian. *inst.* 4,30,1; 12,31.
71.6-8 Cassian. *conl.* 16,15.
71.9 Clem. *ad Cor.* 3.
72.0 Clem. *ad Cor.* 2; 3; 38.
72.1 Cypr. *zel. et liv.* 10-11; Ambr. *expos. de psalm.* 18,10,11,12,13,17; Clem. *ad Cor.* 9; Iren. *demonstr. apost. praedic.* 1; Hier. *in Ezech.* 16,52.
72.3 Ambr. *expos. de psalm.* 18,14.

71.3 "priors" (*praepositorum*): The word is used in the plural in RB only here and at 62.7. Some have taken it to mean "officials," its regular sense in RM. It may equally well, and perhaps better, refer to a succession of priors. See notes on RB 65; 62.7 and 66.0 as well as de Vogüé 2.668, n.3.

71.5 "objecting" (*contentiosus*): See 1 Cor 11:16, where the word is used. In RB 3.9 *contendere* refers to arguing with the abbot. In 4.68 *contentionem* is a general tendency to be contentious. The meaning here is closer to the former.

⁶If a brother, without the abbot's command, assumes any power over those older or, even in regard to boys, flares up and treats them unreasonably, he is to be subjected to the discipline of the rule. ⁷After all, it is written: *Never do to another what you do not want done to yourself* (Tob 4:16).

CHAPTER 71. MUTUAL OBEDIENCE

¹Obedience is a blessing to be shown by all, not only to the abbot but also to one another as brothers, ²since we know that it is by this way of obedience that we go to God. ³Therefore, although orders of the abbot or of the priors appointed by him take precedence, and no unofficial order may supersede them, ⁴in every other instance younger monks should obey their seniors with all love and concern. ⁵Anyone found objecting to this should be reproved.

⁶If a monk is reproved in any way by his abbot or by one of his seniors, even for some very small matter, ⁷or if he gets the impression that one of his seniors is angry or disturbed with him, however slightly, ⁸he must, then and there without delay, cast himself on the ground at the other's feet to make satisfaction, and lie there until the disturbance is calmed by a blessing. ⁹Anyone who refuses to do this should be subjected to corporal punishment or, if he is stubborn, should be expelled from the monastery.

CHAPTER 72. THE GOOD ZEAL OF MONKS

¹Just as there is a wicked zeal of bitterness which separates from God and leads to hell, ²so there is a good zeal which separates from evil and leads to God and everlasting life. ³This, then,

---

72.t "zeal" (*zelo*): The word "zeal" derives from the Greek *zēlos*, which occurs many times in the New Testament, both in a good sense (e.g., John 2:17) and in a bad sense (e.g., 1 Cor 3:3). This no doubt provides the background of the usage in RB, where it likewise occurs in a good sense (e.g., 64.6) and in a bad sense (e.g., 4.66; 64.16; 65.22). The Greek word already had a wide range of meanings in classical times, including jealousy, rivalry, passion, ambition, fervor, etc. See Thematic Index: ZEAL.

72.1 "wicked zeal" (*zelus amaritudinis*): The phrase is taken from Jas 3:14.

72.2 "leads to God" (*ducit ad Deum*): The image of the two paths is derived from Matt 7:13-14. See also Gal 4:17-18. This image is a commonplace of Patristic literature and all later Christian preaching. See Thematic Index: LIFE, *Image*: the two ways.

amore exerceant monachi, [4]id est ut *honore se invicem praeveniant*, [5]infirmitates suas sive corporum sive morum patientissime tolerent, [6]oboedientiam sibi certatim impendant; [7]nullus quod sibi utile iudicat sequatur, sed quod magis alio; [8]caritatem fraternitatis caste impendant, [9]amore Deum timeant, [10]abbatem suum sincera et humili caritate diligant, [11]Christo omnino nihil praeponant, [12]qui nos pariter ad vitam aeternam perducat.

LXXIII. DE HOC QUOD NON OMNIS IUSTITIAE OBSERVATIO IN HAC SIT REGULA CONSTITUTA

[1]Regulam autem hanc descripsimus, ut hanc observantes in monasteriis aliquatenus vel honestatem morum aut initium conversationis nos demonstremus habere. [2]Ceterum ad perfectionem conversationis qui festinat, sunt doctrinae sanctorum patrum, quarum observatio perducat hominem ad celsitudinem perfectionis. [3]Quae enim pagina aut qui sermo divinae auctori-

---

72.5 Cassian. *conl.* 6,3,5; 19,9.

72.7-8 Ambr. *expos. de psalm.* 18,11.

72.9 Cypr. *domin.orat.* 15; *Sacr.Leon.* 30,1104; Ambr. *expos. de psalm.* 18,10.

72.11 **Cypr. domin.orat.** 15; Cypr. *ad Fort.* 6; Aug. *in psalm.* 29,9.

72.11-12 Cypr. *epist.* 76,7; Cypr. *quod idola* 11.

73.t Clem. *ad Cor.* 3.

73.1 Cassian. *conl.* 21,10,1; Cassian. *inst.* 4,39; *Hist.mon.* 31; *Vitae patr., Verb.senior.* 5,11,29.

73.2 Cassian. *inst.* 4,8; Cassian. *conl.* 2,24; 9,2,3; 9,7,4; 10,8; 21,5,4.

72.5 "one another's" (*suas*): This seems the most probable meaning in the context, but *suas* could be a true reflexive (cf. Cassian, *conl.* 6,3,5). No followers of the Rule would deny that their own weaknesses are among their principal trials.

72.7 "better for someone else" (*quod magis alio*): This basic principle of Christian life can be found in a variety of New Testament formulations: 1 Cor 10:24, 33; 1 Cor 13:5; Phil 2:4; Rom 12:10.

72.8 "the pure love of brothers" (*caritatem fraternitatis caste*): "fraternal charity" (brotherly love) is highly recommended in the New Testament; the phrase itself occurs in 1 Thess 4:9, Heb 13:1, 1 Pet 1:22. St. Benedict has added the qualification *caste*. E. Dekkers "'Caritatem caste impendant': Qu'a voulu dire Saint Benoît?" *Ciudad de Dios* 18 (1968) 656–660, provides numerous Latin Patristic texts to show that *caste* often has no sexual connotation but means disinterested, generous, or unselfish. Cf. RB 64.6.

72.9 "to God, loving fear" (*amore Deum timeant*): The juxtaposition of fraternal love and fear of God suggests 1 Pet 2:17. On the punctuation of this sentence by which *amore* is construed with *timeant* (following Sangallensis 914 against most other MSS) rather than with *impendant*, see G. Penco "'Amore Deum

is the good zeal which monks must foster with fervent love: ⁴*They should each try to be the first to show respect to the other* (Rom 12:10), ⁵supporting with the greatest patience one another's weaknesses of body or behavior, ⁶and earnestly competing in obedience to one another. ⁷No one is to pursue what he judges better for himself, but instead, what he judges better for someone else. ⁸To their fellow monks they show the pure love of brothers; ⁹to God, loving fear; ¹⁰to their abbot, unfeigned and humble love. ¹¹Let them prefer nothing whatever to Christ, ¹²and may he bring us all together to everlasting life.

CHAPTER 73. THIS RULE ONLY A BEGINNING OF PERFECTION

¹The reason we have written this rule is that, by observing it in monasteries, we can show that we have some degree of virtue and the beginnings of monastic life. ²But for anyone hastening on to the perfection of monastic life, there are the teachings of the holy Fathers, the observance of which will lead him to the very heights of perfection. ³What page, what passage of the inspired

---

Timeant,' sull'interpunzione di *Regula S. Benedicti* c. 72,12" *RBén* 64 (1954) 273-277.

72.12 "to everlasting life" (*ad vitam aeternam*): If chs. 67–72 are a later insertion, this verse might be their conclusion. See note on RB 73.t.

73.t "a beginning of perfection" (*non omnis iustitiae observatio*): A literal translation of the title would be: "The Full Observance of Justice Is Not Laid Down in This Rule," or "The Observance of Full Justice Is Not Laid Down in This Rule." Although in present context the word *omnis* can, grammatically, modify either *iustitiae* or *observatio*, it should be noted that the phrase *omnem iustitiam* is found in Matt 3:15, where it translates the Greek: *pasan dikaiosunēn*. "Holiness" is perhaps the best modern equivalent to this traditional biblical notion. See note to Prol.25.

The word *constituta*, which has been omitted from the English paraphrase, is used twice in Prol.45-46, to which this usage may allude. On the relationship of this whole chapter to the Prologue, see de Vogüé 4.103–118.

According to G. Penco, ch. 73 followed ch. 66 in an earlier version of the Rule, before the insertion of chs. 67–72. See "Ricerche sul capitolo finale della Regola di S. Benedetto" *Benedictina* 8 (1954) 25–42.

73.1 "in monasteries" (*in monasteriis*): The plural here is another indication that the Rule was intended for more than one monastery. Cf. RB 18.22; 62.1.

"some degree of virtue" (*honestatem morum*): See M. Rothenhäusler "Honestas Morum. Eine Untersuchung zu cap. 73.3 der Regula S. Benedicti" StA 18/19 (1947) 127–156, who finds in this phrase a rich classical and Patristic background and a summary of the whole kind of life at which the Rule aims.

73.2 "for anyone hastening" (*qui festinat*): There is an awkward ellipsis in the Latin.

tatis veteris ac novi testamenti non est rectissima norma vitae humanae? ⁴Aut quis liber sanctorum catholicorum patrum hoc non resonat ut recto cursu perveniamus ad creatorem nostrum? ⁵Necnon et Collationes Patrum et Instituta et Vitas eorum, sed et Regula sancti patris nostri Basilii, ⁶quid aliud sunt nisi bene viventium et oboedientium monachorum instrumenta virtutum? ⁷Nobis autem desidiosis et male viventibus atque neglegentibus rubor confusionis est.

⁸Quisquis ergo ad patriam caelestem festinas, hanc minimam inchoationis regulam descriptam, adiuvante Christo, perfice, ⁹et tunc demum ad maiora quae supra commemoravimus doctrinae virtutumque culmina, Deo protegente, pervenies. Amen.

73.6 Ambr. *expos. de psalm.* 18,17-18; Cassian. *conl.* 6,10.
73.7 Ambr. *expos. de psalm.* 18,11; 18,13; Cassian. *conl.* 12,16,3.
73.8 *Vitae patr.*, *Verb.senior.* 5,11,29; Aug. *ord.mon.* 10.
73.9 Cassian. *conl.* 18,15; 21,34,3; 22,7; Cassian. *inst.* 4,23.

books of the Old and New Testaments is not the truest of guides
for human life? ⁴What book of the holy catholic Fathers does not
resoundingly summon us along the true way to reach the
Creator? ⁵Then, besides the *Conferences* of the Fathers, their
Institutes and their *Lives*, there is also the rule of our holy father
Basil. ⁶For observant and obedient monks, all these are nothing
less than tools for the cultivation of virtues; ⁷but as for us, they
make us blush for shame at being so slothful, so unobservant, so
negligent. ⁸Are you hastening toward your heavenly home?
Then with Christ's help, keep this little rule that we have written for beginners. ⁹After that, you can set out for the loftier sum-
mits of the teaching and virtues we mentioned above, and under
God's protection you will reach them. Amen.

73.5 "the *Conferences* of the Fathers, their *Institutes*" (Collationes *Patrum
et* Instituta): There is little doubt that these titles refer to the widely diffused
works of John Cassian († c. 435). See Introduction, pp. 58–59 and list of Short
Titles of Patristic and Ancient Works. The *Conferences* are also mentioned in
RB 42.5. See A. de Vogüé "Les mentions des oeuvres de Cassien chez Benoît et
ses contemporains" *SM* 20 (1978) 275–285.

"their *Lives*" (Vitas *eorum*): This could refer to the brief lives contained in the
Conferences or to other well-known biographies of monks, such as those of Paul
the Hermit, Hilarion and Malchus by Jerome or that of Antony by Athanasius.
It probably does not refer to the extensive work known as the *Vitae Patrum*,
which was compiled in the course of the sixth century.

"the rule of our holy father Basil" (*Regula sancti patris nostri Basilii*): This
refers to the translation made by Rufinus of Aquileia. See Introduction, p. 50.

73.8 "heavenly home" (*patriam caelestem*): For the image of hurrying toward
the heavenly home, see Heb 4:11 and 11:14-15.

73.9 "you will reach" (*pervenies*): This word occurs twice in ch. 73 and twice
in the Prologue (22,42), thus constituting a kind of "inclusion," a favorite literary
device of ancient authors for tying together a work. See also the observation on
constituta in the note on 73.t. Likewise, the word *conversatio*, which occurs at
the end of the Prologue (49), occurs twice at the beginning of ch. 73. See Thematic Index: LIFE, as journey.

Part Three

APPENDIX

Longer Expositions of Monastic Topics

Appendix 1

Monastic Terminology: Monk, Cenobite, Nun

Chapter 1 of RB on "The Kinds of Monks" contains a number of traditional monastic terms, such as "monk," "cenobite," "sarabaite." Because of the complex philological and literary background of these words, they are conveniently treated together in this section. Other conventional terms are considered elsewhere in this Appendix.

1. The term "monk"

The term "monk" (Greek: *monachos*)[1] has been used in antiquity and even more so in recent times to denote many different forms of religious life.[2] The anachronistic use of the term to describe groups as disparate as the Pythagoreans, Essenes, Therapeutae and Buddhists may be dismissed at once, because none of these people used the term *monachos* to describe themselves. It has been argued in the Introduc-

---

[1] The most recent and thorough treatment of the evidence on this subject is F. E. Morard "Monachos, Moine. Histoire du terme grec jusqu'au 4ᵉ siècle" *Freiburger Zeitschrift für Philosophie und Theologie* 20 (1973) 332–411. A summary presentation of this author's conclusions may be found in F. E. Morard "Monachos: une importation sémitique en Égypte? Quelques aperçus nouveaux" *Studia Patristica*, TU 12 (1975) 242–246. The following treatments of one or another aspect of the subject should also be mentioned: A. Adam "Grundbegriffe des Mönchtums in sprachlicher Sicht" *ZKG* 65 (1953) 209–239; E. Beck "Ein Beitrag zur Terminologie des ältesten syrischen Mönchtums" *Antonius Magnus Eremita*, StA 38 (Rome: Herder 1956) pp. 254–267; L. Lorié, *Spiritual Terminology in the Latin Translations of the Vita Antonii* (Nijmegen: Dekker & Van de Vegt 1955) pp. 25–34; J. Leclercq, *Études sur le vocabulaire monastique du Moyen Age*, StA 48 (Rome: Herder 1961) pp. 7–38; A. Baker "Syriac and the Origins of Monasticism" *DR* 86 (1968) 342–353.

[2] The English word "monk" is derived from the Latin *monachus*, which in turn is simply a transliteration into Latin of the Greek *monachos*; this occurred in the fourth century, as will be demonstrated further on. There is, curiously, no exact feminine equivalent in English to "monk" or *monachus*. The now archaic "monial," based on the Latin *monialis*, is attested in sixteenth-century English. See *The Oxford English Dictionary*, s.v. However, "nun" is the more common English equivalent of "monk." The origin of this term will be discussed later.

tion to this volume that, on the basis of the available historical evidence, the rise of the monastic movement is essentially a Christian phenomenon of the first half of the fourth century. Here it will be argued on philological grounds that the development of the special terminology of the movement, including above all the term "monk," is likewise essentially a Christian phenomenon of the same period.

Even after excluding from consideration this late and anomalous use of the term "monk," there remain considerable difficulties in describing the original content and the development of this terminology. This is due chiefly to the fact that already in antiquity the term "monk" was widely applied, and diverse meanings were given to the term by ancient writers. In fact, it is apparent from the variety of definitions offered that already in the late fourth century there was some uncertainty over the original meaning of the term. It has been commonly supposed, even in the ancient world, that the term *monachos* was originally equivalent to "solitary" or "hermit."[3] In one place Jerome interprets it this way (Hier. *epist.* 14,6,1). But, writing his famous letter to Eustochium in 384, Jerome mentions that in Egypt there are three kinds of monks, and he clearly refers to the cenobites as monks (Hier. *epist.* 22,34). If the term was originally equivalent to solitary or hermit, it is difficult to understand how it could so quickly have come to denote a form of life as different as that of the Pachomian cenobites.

The usual explanation for this has been a historical one. From antiquity until very recent times, a stereotyped picture of monastic origins has been a commonplace in historical writing on the subject.[4] In

---

[3] See *The Oxford English Dictionary*, s.v. Lorié, *Spiritual Terminology*, p. 25, ignoring the evidence presented by Adam, states dogmatically: "The original meaning of *monachos* is a monk living in solitude, which meaning is still clearly preserved in the English 'a solitary' as it is in the German 'Einsiedler.' As monachism developed more and more from eremitic into cenobitic life, the word *monachos* gradually widened its meaning and came to designate any monk whether he lived in a hermitage or a monastery." While showing much greater familiarity with the literature, G. Colombás "El concepto de monje y vida monástica hasta fines del siglo v" *SM* 1 (1959) 260, opts finally for the rather late evidence of Palladas, Jerome and others that suggests the equivalence of monk-solitary. But it is precisely the reliability of this evidence that must be questioned. (An unfortunately truncated English version of this article may be found in *MS* 2 [1964] 66–117.) See also C. Peifer, *Monastic Spirituality* (New York: Sheed and Ward 1966) p. 63.

[4] G. Colombás, *El monacato primitivo*, BAC 351,376 (Madrid: La Editorial Católica 1974–75) 1.40, notes that this picture comes from "the remote origins of Christian monasticism," but states that it must be evaluated in the light of the very complex evidence now available.

this picture monasticism begins when the first hermits retire to the Egyptian desert. Gradually colonies of anchorites develop around them. A little later Pachomius established cenobitic monastic life and later still Basil reformed cenobitic life, giving it the form in which it has survived in the East, while even later Benedict reformed monasticism in the West. It is now generally admitted that this picture hardly does justice to the complexities of the evidence.

A similar stereotype of the philological development of the terminology has served to reinforce this simple historical picture. Or perhaps it would be more accurate to say that the philological picture was developed on the historical model. At any rate, the common and insufficiently questioned assumption has been that the term *monachos* (and related terms) originally referred to the anchorite or hermit and that its extension to the cenobite paralleled the historical development itself. The notion of "kinds of monks" would represent the last stage of this development. Thus history and philology have been repeatedly invoked to reinforce each other. And finally, both history and philology have been invoked in the perennial theological dispute over the relative merits of the hermit and the cenobite. It has been repeatedly argued, either explicitly or implicitly, that because the original meaning of the word "monk" is 'hermit' or 'anchorite,' this must be the original and truest form of monastic life.

The complexities of the historical question have already been dealt with at some length in the Introduction to this volume, and some of the theological positions developed in antiquity have also been indicated. It remains to indicate the complexity of the philological question. But first it is necessary to distinguish and formulate it more precisely. Although the historical, philological and theological questions are inevitably intertwined, it is important, for purposes of analysis, to insist that these are three distinct questions. The historical question belongs to the history of Christian asceticism and relates to the emergence of those forms of life that have traditionally been called "monastic." In its simplest, indeed simplistic, form the question has usually been put: Which came first, the hermit or the cenobite? The philological question is distinct but related: What did *monachos* originally mean (i.e., denote), when did it first come into currency, and did it undergo development and expansion? The theological question is again quite distinct: Which is preferable or more meritorious, the eremitic or the cenobitic form of life? Although history and philology have frequently been invoked to answer this question, it really ought to be dealt with on strictly theological grounds. No attempt will be made to answer this last question here.

The manner in which a question is posed, of course, can greatly affect the outcome of research on the subject. As has already been indicated, the philological question has often been cast in the form: How did the term *monachos*, which originally meant 'hermit' or 'solitary,' come to be used in a wider sense? In other words, the problem has been posed in historical terms, as if the only possibility of accounting for what appear to be disparate uses of the term was one of simple linear development.

A more obvious, non-historically oriented question has generally gone unasked: What do these various forms of life have in common that permitted them to be denoted by the same term? The reason why this more logical question has been generally ignored is not difficult to discover. It seems to be due in large part to the overwhelming influence of Athanasius' *Life of Antony*. This influential work created the archetype and equation of monk-hermit. It has tended ever since to dominate, often unconsciously, the historical, philological and theological questions described above. It has often been cited as primary evidence for the original equivalence of monk-hermit; the question of what contribution this work itself made toward producing that equivalence has gone unasked.[5] In view of these considerations, the following presentation of the evidence has been guided by the logical rather than the historical formulation of the philological question.[6]

Etymology is one factor, though often not the decisive one, in de-

[5] Colombás "El concepto" acknowledges that the term *monachos* came into common usage in large part through the *Vita Antonii* (p. 259) and claims that in this work it is always used in the original strict technical sense, i.e., as "solitary" (p. 261). Lorié, *Spiritual Terminology*, p. 27, admits that there are numerous passages in the work that foreshadow the "new way of life in monachism," i.e., cenobitism. Neither author bothers to question the reliability of this work or to ask what contribution the work itself made in producing the definition of "monk" as "hermit."

[6] K. Heussi, *Der Ursprung des Mönchtums* (Tübingen: J.C.B. Mohr 1936) pp. 39, 53–54, 58, distinguishes the question of the historical development of monasticism from the question of the meaning of the word *monachos*. He also admits that the word could mean 'unmarried' as well as 'living alone.' Nevertheless, the influence of the traditional historical schema of development proves too strong, and he ends up by positing a historical development of the word *monachos* in which it acquires the meaning of 'anchorite' in the course of the third century and comes to refer to cenobites as well in the fourth century. Heussi was not aware of much of the evidence assembled by Morard. This greater array of evidence cannot be made to fit very easily into a simple historical schema of development from the meaning 'anchorite' to that of 'cenobite.' What follows here is in large part a brief summary of the evidence presented by Morard.

termining the meaning of words.[7] The decisive factor is usage, or in literary works, context; if the word is used many times, the context must be considered to include the entire work. *Monachos* is derived from the adjective *monos*, which, though itself of uncertain etymology, is generally understood to involve the idea of 'one,' 'one alone,' 'one only,' or 'single.' It (*monachos*) is a post-Homeric formation and occurs first in classical Greek literature in an adverbial form, *monachē*, for which there are other analogous numerical formations. *Monachē* is used by Xenophon to refer to passage by a single or unique mountain pass, by Plato to refer to a single as opposed to a double way and also in the sense of 'unique.' Aristotle uses the adjective *monachos* in the sense of 'unique,' and the adverb in the sense of 'single' as opposed to several. Epicurus uses both adjective and adverb in the sense of 'single,' 'simple,' and 'unique.'[8]

The word continues to occur in classical texts, generally of a technical nature, over the next several centuries. Morard concludes that it can designate a being that is unique in its genre, individual and singular, such as the sun or moon for Aristotle; a being that is solitary or isolated in relation to others, such as the supreme being for Plotinus; or an island that is separated from the archipelago to which it belongs; or, finally, a being that is simple and unified in opposition to that which is multiple and divided, as in "a single piece of cloth."[9] The extensive Greek papyrus evidence from Egypt leads to essentially the same conclusions.[10]

The evidence for use of the term *monachos* in the Greek Old Testament provides more immediate background for the Christian use of the term. The word does not occur in the Septuagint version (mid-third century B.C. and later), but it is used in the versions by Aquila (c. A.D. 130) and Symmachus (c. A.D. 180). In all cases except Gen 2:18, it is used to render some form of the Hebrew *yāḥîd*. Both Aquila and Symmachus use it to translate *lĕbaddô* in Gen 2:18. This last case is of particular interest because of the context: "the man" is being described as *lĕbaddô* (*monachos*), a situation that is remedied by the subsequent creation of woman. He is alone, single in the sense of not

---

[7] Colombás "El concepto" pp. 259–260 does not advert sufficiently to this in noting the etymology of *monachos*. One can be "alone" in various circumstances, so that the actual meaning of "alone" is different in different situations. One can be alone in a desert, at a bus-stop, and in the sense of being unmarried.

[8] Morard, p. 338.

[9] *Ibid.*, p. 340.

[10] *Ibid.*, p. 346.

yet married, and this is perceived by God to be an unfortunate condition. This principle, that "it is not good for man to be alone," reflects the common view of the Old Testament and Judaism that denies positive meaning to celibacy, voluntary or otherwise. It is a view that, in fact, is contradicted by Paul in 1 Cor 7:1, one of the two principal New Testament texts used to defend or inspire Christian celibacy. It will be necessary to advert to this last text later. Although we may not conclude that the Christian use of *monachos* is derived from the versions of Aquila and Symmachus, it is legitimate to infer that in the second century A.D. the word *monachos* could mean 'alone' or 'single' in the sense of celibate.

In the cases where *monachos* is used to translate *yāḥíd*, the meaning varies somewhat, depending on the context, but includes 'single,' 'alone,' 'solitary,' 'only one,' as does *yāḥíd* itself. One case must be examined in detail because of the exegetical tradition that attaches to it. In Ps 67(68):7, *yĕḥídím* is translated as *monachois* by Symmachus and as *monachous* in a reading attributed to Theodotion. Whatever may have been the meaning of the original or that understood by the translator, there was a strong rabbinic tradition of exegesis in which the word in this verse was understood to refer to those in an unmarried state. It has been conjectured that Symmachus may have had knowledge of the celibate Syrian Christian ascetics known as *īḥídāyā* (the Syriac cognate of the Hebrew *yĕḥídím*). At any rate, the equivalence of this Syriac term with *monachos* is shown by the fact that the Syro-Hexapla employs *īḥídāyā* to render the *monachois* of Symmachus.[11]

Among the ecclesiastical writers, Eusebius of Caesarea is the first to use the word *monachos*. Writing about A.D. 330, he is commenting on this same verse of Ps 68 and is referring to the various translations of *yĕḥídím* that had been assembled by Origen in the Hexapla. The passage is worth quoting in full:

> "He makes the *monotropous* [Septuagint] dwell in a house." According to Symmachus, he gives a house to the *monachois* and, according to Aquila, he makes the *monogeneis* be seated in a house. According to the fifth version, he makes the *monozonous* dwell in a house. This, then, was his first deed, which is also the greatest of those deeds he has done on behalf of the race of men. In fact, the first rank of those who are in progress in Christ is that of the *monachoi*, but they are rare, and that is

---

[11] *Ibid.*, pp. 347–352. In a tradition stemming from Eusebius, Symmachus has been traditionally identified as an Ebionite or Jewish Christian. However, recent research has identified him as a Samaritan convert to orthodox Judaism. See D. Barthélemy "Qui est Symmaque?" *Catholic Biblical Quarterly* 36 (1974) 451–465.

why, according to Aquila, they are called *monogeneis*, for they have become like the unique [*monogenei*] Son of God. According to the Septuagint, they have a single way of life [*monotropous*], not several, nor do they change their way of life but follow one alone that leads to the height of virtue. Thus the fifth version calls them *monozonous*, since they are *monēreis* [living alone, single, unmarried] and are girded up by themselves. These are all those who lead a single and pure life [*monēre kai hagnon bion*], as did the first disciples of our Savior, to whom he said, "Do not keep gold or silver in your belt nor a knapsack, nor two tunics, nor sandals nor walking stick" (Matt 10:9-10) — (Eus. *in psalm.* 67,7).

Eusebius is trying to relate the various translations of *yĕḥîdîm* to a single referent that he calls the *monachoi*. This is in accord with the traditional Christian understanding of the psalter as a prophetic book that finds its fulfillment in Christ and the Church. It is the first Christian use of the word *monachos* to denote a group in the Church. These, he says, are rare. Their distinguishing characteristic is that they are celibate, as the first disciples are understood to have been. In his Church History, Eusebius does not mention the monastic movement, which was of course in 330 A.D. in its earliest stages of development in Egypt and Palestine. It is possible that the passage quoted refers to it, but it seems more likely to be a general reference to celibate Christian ascetics than a reference to those who had started to live the ascetic life in some form of separation from the rest of society. A. Adam regards this passage as the source from which the concept *monachos* came into use in the Greek-speaking Church. This is probably going too far. As we shall see, there is additional evidence which suggests that the word was already in wide use in Egypt at this date. The importance of the passage is that it suggests that the term *monachos* signified 'alone' or 'single' in the sense of 'celibate' rather than in the sense of 'hermit' or 'anchorite.' [12]

The term *bios monērēs*, which Eusebius introduces in this passage to describe the *monachoi*, is also of special interest because it is used by a number of pagan authors as a synonym for 'unmarried.' Philo uses the phrase to describe the situation of Adam before the creation of woman. Athanasius himself uses it as virtually a definition of *monachos*. Morard offers two examples. One is an address of a letter to Horsiesius: "To Horsiesius, the father of monks, and to all those practicing the celibate life [*tōn monēre bion*] with him. . . ."; the other, his letter to monks: "To those everywhere practicing the celibate life

_____

[12] See Adam "Grundbegriffe" p. 215; Morard, pp. 352–353; 379–380.

[tōn monērē bion] who are firmly established in faith in God and sanctified in Christ and who say, 'Behold, we have left everything and have followed you' (Matt 19:27)." In this last passage the term denotes a life of complete renunciation that certainly includes celibacy. It is clear, then, that for Athanasius as well as for Eusebius the term monachos is not equivalent to 'solitary' in the sense of 'hermit,' but refers in the first instance to those who are 'single' in the sense of celibate. Only in this sense could he describe Horsiesius as the "father of monks," for Horsiesius was the successor of Pachomius.[13]

There are also many papyrus documents from Christian Egypt that provide additional evidence that early in the fourth century the term monachos was used to describe cenobites. Of particular interest are two that can be dated to 334 and 335 A.D. and that use the term in reference to a cenobitic community of Melitian monks. A number of others from the fourth to the sixth centuries qualify the term monachos by the terms anachōrētēs or erēmitēs, suggesting clearly that the term by itself did not denote anchorite or hermit.[14]

The earliest occurrences of the word monachos in Coptic literature confirm this. In the Gospel of Thomas, a gnostic document from Nag Hammadi, the word occurs in three sayings attributed to Jesus. Saying 16, which is parallel to Luke 12:51-53, ends with the phrase "they will be standing alone [monachos]." The context is the division within families created by the message of Jesus. In Saying 49, Jesus says: "Blessed are the single [monachos] and the elect, because you will find the kingdom. Because you are from it, you will return there." Here the word seems to denote those who are separated from the world and worldly ties such as marriage. This is certainly suggested by the converse of the statement in Saying 27: "If you do not abstain from the world, you will not find the kingdom." These sayings involve

[13] Ibid., pp. 381–383.

[14] Ibid., pp. 388–389. For the Melitian documents, see H. I. Bell, Jews and Christians in Egypt (Oxford: Oxford Univ. Press 1924) pp. 48, 57. Additional early papyrus evidence has been assembled by E. A. Judge "The Earliest Use of Monachos for 'Monk' (P. Coll. Youtie 77) and the Origins of Monasticism" Jahrbuch für Antike und Christentum 20 (1977) 72–89. Judge dates the earliest occurrence of the term in a non-Christian papyrus referring to a Christian monachos to A.D. 324. The evidence assembled by Judge supports the contention of Morard that the term cannot originally have meant 'hermit' or 'anchorite,' but Judge does not accept Morard's thesis that the word in Christian use originally meant 'celibate.' However, he does not offer sufficient grounds for rejecting this thesis, nor does he evaluate the mass of evidence assembled by Morard.

the typical gnostic motif of a fall into the material world from which the elect are destined to escape through separation or abstention from the ties of the material world. In Saying 75, Jesus says: "Many are standing at the door but it is the single ones [*monachos*] who will enter the nuptial chamber." This last saying seems to equate *monachos* even more clearly with 'celibate,' for it appears to be a summary of the parable of the virgins in Matt 25:1-13.[15]

The Coptic version of the Gospel of Thomas belongs to the fourth century. Although the matter is uncertain, it has been argued with considerable plausibility that behind the Coptic version lies a Syriac original as early as the second century and that the term *monachos* translates the Syriac *īḥīdāyā*, which, as we have already seen above, is the rendering of the Syro-Hexapla for *monachos* in Symmachus' version. There is abundant independent evidence to show that *īḥīdāyā* did in fact refer to celibates in the Syrian Church.[16]

The word *monachos* occurs a number of times in the Pachomian literature, including the Coptic and Greek Lives, the Rules and the Catecheses. Most of this literature is from the fourth century, and some of it (such as portions of the Rules and the Catecheses) is probably from the first half of the century. All these texts show that in the fourth century and even during the lifetime of Pachomius (d. 346), there was no hesitation about using the word to refer to the cenobites of his communities. The term describes one who comes to the monastery "to become a monk" (*Vita bo* 111).[17] Of Pachomius it is said that he became a monk at age twenty-one and spent thirty-nine years as a

---

[15] Morard, pp. 362–377. Morard shows that in the Gospel of Thomas, *monachos* is distinguished from *oua ouōt*, meaning 'a single one' or 'one alone.'

[16] *Ibid.*, p. 375. See also Beck "Ein Beitrag" pp. 258–260. However, A. Adam "Der Monachos-Gedanke innerhalb der Spiritualität der alten Kirche" *Glaube, Geist, Geschichte: Festschrift E. Benz* (Leiden: Brill 1967), p. 262, denies that *īḥīdāyā* and *monachos* refer to the celibate state and insists that the meaning is derived from the notion of "unique" (*monogenēs*) as applied to Christ. The words would then have come to be applied to Christians because of the degree of their union with Christ. Although this interpretation receives some support from the passage from Eusebius quoted above, it seems to be more theological than philological, as is, indeed, the explanation by Eusebius. It is true that Aristotle used the word *monachos* in the sense of "unique," but this does not insure that the word used several centuries later will have the same connotations. Adam did not take into account the mass of evidence later assembled by Morard. On this kind of interpretation, which seems to belong, not to the earliest period of Christian usage of these terms, but to a slightly later one, see below, p. 311.

[17] Although the Bohairic Life in its present form is from a considerably later period, it probably reflects a Sahidic substratum of the fourth century.

monk (*Vita sa* [7]). In one of the "call narratives," a voice from heaven
tells Pachomius that a crowd of men will join him to become monks
(*Vita bo* 17). The term can also refer to an anchorite in this literature,
but in this case it is usually qualified. Thus barbarians are said to have
come across "an anchorite monk" and made him a prisoner (*Vita sa* [10]).
Early in his career, Pachomius is said to have sought to become a
monk and to lead the anchoritic life (*Vita bo* 10). From these instances
it is clear that to the Pachomian monks the term *monachos* did not of
itself signify the solitary life.

The term *monachos* is also used in the Coptic Pachomian literature
as an abstract noun (*m^{e}ntmonachos*) and must be translated as either
'celibacy' or 'monastic life.' In one of his catecheses Pachomius says,
"Since we have promised God purity, since we have promised monastic life, let us act in accord with it, with fasting, unceasing prayer,
purity of body and purity of heart." The wider context, which is an
exhortation to chastity, reinforces the impression that the meaning of
monachos here is basically the celibate life.[18]

The sum of the evidence suggests, then, that in the early fourth
century the term *monachos*, far from denoting in the first instance the
solitary in the sense of hermit or anchorite, was used rather to refer to
those who were solitary or single in the sense of unmarried or celibate. It is impossible to describe the development of the term more
precisely because there is no evidence between the first occurrence of
it with this sense in Symmachus' description of Adam and the evidence of the first part of the fourth century, when it appears to be in
widespread use, at least in Egypt. From its use in the Pachomian and
Melitian documents, it would appear that the term had already acquired a technical sense and that this included a celibate life lived in
some form of separation from society. It could be used of either cenobites or anchorites, but when it referred to the latter it was often
qualified. Athanasius' preface to the *Life of Antony* seems to reflect an
awareness that the name as well as the monastic movement was of
recent origin and that both were still spreading, now outside of Egypt.
Since all the early evidence, with the exception of the passage from
Eusebius, is from Egypt, it seems reasonable to conclude that the use

---

[18] For the text cited, see L. Th. Lefort, *Oeuvres de S. Pachôme et de ses disciples*,
CSCO 159 (Louvain: L. Durbecq 1956) p. 20. This text may in fact originally be from a
catechesis of Athanasius, but this would not alter its value as a witness to the meaning of
monachos. In fact, it would enhance it, since Athanasius is usually cited as the primary
witness to the meaning of *monachos* as 'hermit.' See A. Veilleux, *La liturgie dans le
cénobitisme pachômien*, StA 57 (Rome: Herder 1968) p. 217.

of the term *monachos* for celibate Christian ascetics first became current in Egypt, as indeed Athanasius seems to suggest.

Certain ancient writers from a slightly later period interpreted the term *monachos* to refer basically to unity. Although these interpretations tend to be highly theological in content, they are not unrelated to the original meaning of the word and to its original Christian use. Etymologically, the term was certainly related to the word for 'one' (*monos*), and, as noted above, one of the earliest attested meanings of *monachos* was 'single' in the sense of 'undivided.' This idea was exploited by Pseudo-Dionysius: "That is why our divine masters . . . called them monks . . . because their life, far from being divided, remained perfectly one, because they unified themselves by a holy recollection which excluded all distraction so as to tend toward a unity of conduct conformed to God and toward the perfection of divine love" (Ps-Dion. *hier.eccles.* 6,3).

But even this interpretation may be related to the fact that *monachos* denoted a celibate, for in the text alluded to earlier, one of the values ascribed by Paul to celibacy is precisely that it leaves a person totally "undivided" and at the disposal of God (1 Cor 7:33). Likewise, the interpretation given by Augustine to the word *monachos* is, while highly theological, built upon the same semantic possibility exploited by Pseudo-Dionysius.[19] It is also quite interesting to note that a similar interpretation is given the word *īhīdāyā* in Syriac by Philoxenus of Mabbug, again suggesting a close relation in semantic content between *monachos* and *īhīdāyā*.[20] Nevertheless, the absence of the word *monachos* from many earlier ancient writers who do develop the theme of interior unity (Philo, Clement of Alexandria, Origen) or simply of unity suggests that this nuance was a semantic possibility of *monachos* rather than its original reference in Christian usage.[21]

2. *The term* monachus *in Latin use*

Athanasius states in the preface to his *Life of Antony* that the word "monk" was becoming known outside of Egypt. It is often reasonably presumed that he was thinking of the Latin-speaking West, where he had spent periods of exile many years earlier. Likewise, it has been assumed that Athanasius himself used this time of exile (A.D. 340) to

[19] See the Introduction, pp. 62–63.
[20] Morard, pp. 370–371.
[21] *Ibid.*, pp. 372–373.

promote monasticism in the West. Jerome certainly implies this (Hier. *epist.* 127,5-8).[22] However, the earliest literary occurrences of the term *monachus* in Latin are in fact from the Latin translations of the *Life of Antony*. It is difficult to date the earliest Latin translation of this work, but it must have been after 357 (Antony died in 356) and before 370. The more polished literary translation by Evagrius of Antioch was made before 374.[23] The writings of Jerome also had much to do with the spread of the term in the West in the last part of the fourth century. As late as A.D. 416, however, the hostile Latin writer Rutilius Namatianus regarded the word as a neologism of Greek origin.[24]

The earlier Latin translation of the *Life of Antony* is quite literal and, with few exceptions of no significance, renders the Greek *monachos* by the Latin *monachus*. In a few cases the translator also used a paraphrase such as *locum monachorum* to translate the Greek *monastērion*.[25] Evagrius of Antioch, on the other hand, used the Latin *monachus* to translate not only the Greek *monachos* but the words *philokaloi*, *spoudaioi* and *askētai* as well, all of which are more general terms for those devoted to the ascetic life (*Vita Anton.* 4;7;36). This certainly confirms the Greek and Coptic evidence that the word *monachos* did not in Christian practice designate exclusively the anchorite. Evagrius also rendered the general term *askēsis* by *institutum monachorum*.[26]

Despite the broader usage of the term in the *Life of Antony* and in both Greek and Latin, this work was probably in large part responsible, as has already been suggested, for the creation of the archetype "hermit-monk" and for the perception that the term originally meant solitary in the sense of hermit or anchorite. This mistaken perception can be traced already to the last quarter of the fourth century and is due in part to St. Jerome. Jerome was himself strongly influenced by the *Life of Antony*, as was Sulpicius Severus, and he produced several

---

[22] See the Introduction, pp. 43–44.

[23] See G. Garitte "Le texte grec et les versions anciennes de la vie de saint Antoine" *Antonius Magnus Eremita*, pp. 5–6, and G.J.M. Bartelinck "Einige Bemerkungen über Evagrius' von Antiochien Übersetzung der Vita Antonii" *RBén* 82 (1972) 98–105.

[24] See P. de Labriolle "Rutilius Claudius Namatianus et les moines" *Revue des études latines* 6 (1928) 30–41.

[25] Lorié, *Spiritual Terminology*, p. 28.

[26] Given his presuppositions (see note 3), Lorié naturally assumes that this is evidence of expansion of the word *monachos* and a departure from its original meaning (see pp. 28–29). Against this, however, it should be noted that Evagrius of Antioch was bilingual, a native Greek speaker, and had every reason to know what *monachos* meant to Greek speakers of his day and what *monachus* would mean to Latin readers.

works more or less in imitation of it.[27] It was Jerome also who gave it an etymological interpretation in the sense of solitary: "Translate the word 'monk': that's your proper title. What are you, a 'solitary,' doing in a crowd?" (Hier. *epist.* 14,6.1).[28] His own devotion (theoretical rather than practical) to the eremitic ideal is perhaps revealed also in his translation (in the version *Iuxta Hebraeos*) of *yĕḥîdîm* in Ps 67 (68):7 as *solitarius* where, it will be remembered, Symmachus and Theodotion had used *monachos*. Nevertheless, Jerome himself also used the word in its broader original sense when describing the kinds of monks (Hier. *epist.* 22,34) and in the preface to his translation of the Pachomian Rules (Pachom. *reg.*, praef.).

The evidence surveyed thus far suggests then that the term *monachos* in both Greek and Latin originally designated those living 'alone' in the sense of 'unmarried.' The equation of the term with 'hermit' represents a narrowing rather than a broadening of the original meaning, as has often been supposed. The opposite assumption, namely, that the term originally meant 'hermit' and was extended to include a wide variety of styles of life not only corresponds less well to the available evidence but makes many other questions more difficult to explain. These include: how Evagrius of Antioch could have translated such a variety of words by *monachus*, how Cassian could have portrayed the cenobites as the first kind of monks in the order of historical development, and indeed, how a tradition of "kinds of monks" could have developed at all.

3. *The tradition of kinds of monks*

The oldest literary evidence for the development of the theme of different kinds of monks is found in the *Consultationes Zacchaei et Apollonii*, an anonymous work attributed by some to Firmicus Maternus and dated about A.D. 381.[29] The author distinguishes three styles of life in which monks live. First, there are the hermits or anchorites, said to be the highest grade, who live in deserted places or in caves and follow the most severe ascetical practices in regard to food, clothing, sleep, hours spent in prayer, etc. Then there are those who live

[27] See the Introduction, pp. 43–44, 48–50.

[28] ". . . interpretare vocabulum monachi, hoc est nomen tuum: quid facis in turba qui solus es?"

[29] See G. Morin, *I. Firmici Materni Consultationes Zacchaei et Apollonii*, Florilegium Patristicum 39 (Bonn: P. Hanstein 1935) and G. M. Colombás "Sobre el autor de las Consultationes Zacchaei et Apollonii" *SM* 14 (1972) 7–15. An English translation of III,1-6 may be found in *MS* 12 (1976) 271–287.

apart from society but come together for prayer. Finally, there are those who lead a chaste and religious life but one not otherwise distinct from that of the rest of Christians. This author's distinctions are based on the degree of asceticism pursued and the degree of separation from the rest of the society. The only technical term used to describe these various ways of life is *monachus*; it appears to be applied to these different forms precisely because what they have in common is the practice of the celibate life.[30]

The next literary classification of monks to appear is in St. Jerome's famous letter to Eustochium. This piece is actually a treatise on the ascetic life; it is usually dated to the year 384, when Jerome was living in Rome and seeking to advance the cause of the ascetic life there. Jerome distinguishes three kinds (*genera*) of monks (Hier. *epist.* 22,34). While the author of the *Consultationes* did not locate the kinds of monks he was describing, Jerome is quite specific in naming Egypt as the place where these three kinds are to be found. This may be the first literary instance, apart from the *Life of Antony*, where the institution of monasticism in Egypt has come to be regarded as normative.

The first category of monks Jerome describes are called cenobites. He says they are called *sauhes* in "their foreign tongue," and he defines them as "those who live in a community."[31]

The second category Jerome mentions are the anchorites, who, he says, are called by this name "because they have withdrawn from society."[32] The founder of this manner of life was Paul (the hermit), but Antony was the one who made it illustrious. Actually, Jerome adds, John the Baptist was the first. These survive on bread and salt (Hier. *epist.* 22,36).

The third type of monks are called *remnuoth*.[33] These, Jerome says,

---

[30] See Morin, pp. 100–102, for the text. Colombás, *El monacato primitivo*, 1.41, says this work gives evidence of an extension of the term in a deprecatory sense to those earlier called "continent" or "ascetics." However, one must distinguish the value judgments of the author of the *Consultationes* (he prefers anchorites) from the question of what the term actually meant.

[31] The word *sauhes* comes from the Coptic *soouhᵉs*, meaning a 'congregation,' or 'monastic community.' See W. E. Crum, *A Coptic Dictionary* (Oxford: The Clarendon Press 1939) p. 373b. It can also mean the monastery itself (*Vita sa*⁵ 20). The same holds true of the Greek *koinobion*. The phrase *prôme ᵉntsoouhᵉs* (Pachom. *reg.* 118,119) could mean either the superior of the monastery or of the community. However, the term does not seem to be attested in Coptic with the meaning 'cenobite.' The normal term in the Pachomian literature for referring to the whole institution of cenobitic life is *koinōnia*. See the Introduction, pp. 24–25.

[32] The word *anachōrein* means 'to withdraw.' See the Introduction, pp. 17–18.

[33] For the etymology of this word see note 39 below.

are a very inferior (*determimum*; cf. RB 1.6) and despised kind but are the only ones or the principal kind to be found in "our province." That, presumably, means Rome or Italy. They are characterized as living together by twos or threes according to their own will and independently. In a satirical passage foreshadowing the more lengthy one devoted to the gyrovagues in RM 1, Jerome describes the *remnuoth*: "Among them everything is done for effect. They wear loose sleeves, flapping boots, clumsy clothing. They sigh a great deal, pay visits to virgins, belittle the clergy and, whenever a feast day comes round, eat themselves sick" (Hier. *epist.* 22,34).

Dismissing these as "a plague," Jerome then devotes a lengthy passage to describing the way of life of the cenobites. The first mark of the cenobites is that they live under a superior (*maior*) and are obedient. He goes on to describe how they are divided into tens and hundreds under deans (called *decani* and *praepositi*), how they meet for prayer, their ascetic diet, their edifying discourse, their practice of silence, and their work.

It is clear that Jerome is describing the Pachomian monks of Upper Egypt. We do not know where he obtained his information; at this point in his monastic career he had not yet visited Egypt. Two years after he wrote this, Jerome did visit Egypt in the company of Paula, but he never did travel up the Nile to the principal Pachomian centers. However, he had spent some time in Syria, where he had become acquainted with Eastern monasticism and had many monastic contacts. He may have had access to some Pachomian literature in a Greek version, or he may have received his information from verbal reports about Pachomian practice. Some of his details may also have been drawn from the descriptions of the Essenes given by Philo and Josephus, for Jerome mentions explicitly that they lived a life similar to that of the cenobites (Hier. *epist.* 22,35).

Augustine is the next (c. 387–389) to provide a description of these new Christian styles of life. He does not in fact use the term *monachus* nor any other technical term to describe them. The one factor common to all those he mentions, and in fact the reason why they are invoked at all in a work directed against the Manichaeans, is their practice of celibacy. "Who can be unaware," writes Augustine, "that the multitude of Christians practicing perfect continence increases and spreads day by day, particularly in Egypt and in the East?" (Aug. *mor.eccl.* 65). Again we may note that Egypt has come to be regarded as the home and norm of monasticism from the Latin point of view.

Augustine mentions three ways of living the celibate life. The first is that of the solitaries, who live in desolate places and practice rigorous asceticism (Aug. *mor.eccl.* 66). Next are those who live in common and pass their time in prayer, reading and spiritual conferences (Aug. *mor.eccl.* 67-68). Many features of this description, including the organization in terms of "deans," the manual labor, the role of superiors, the diet, the care of the poor, etc., suggest that Augustine already had and was dependent on Jerome's *Letter* 22 for his description. However, he does not bother to mention the *remnuoth* described by Jerome, but goes on to describe another kind he had heard of that might be termed "urban monasticism" (Aug. *mor.eccl.* 70). He mentions communities at Milan and Rome in which holy men and women live a retired life under a superior. Augustine sees these communities as especially inspired by the injunctions of Paul about manual labor (2 Thess 3:6-12) and about moderation and charity (Rom 14:2-21).

Some thirty years after Augustine, John Cassian took up the theme of the "kinds of monks" and developed it at greater length, adding some new features. It has been suggested that Cassian is dependent for his information on that supplied by Jerome in *Letter* 22.[34] There is every reason to believe that he was acquainted with Jerome's work, but there are several reasons for thinking that he is also a distinct witness to the same Egyptian tradition on which Jerome's report is based. In the first place, Cassian had lived in Egypt for many years, and although it seems he never visited the Thebaid, he was certainly well acquainted with the monasticism of Nitria and Scetis.

Cassian states that there are three kinds of monks in Egypt, but he later describes a fourth kind. The first kind of monks are the cenobites, who live together in a congregation under the direction of an elder. They are the most numerous kind and are found throughout Egypt (Cassian. *conl.* 18,4). According to Cassian, the cenobites were the original kind of monks and can be traced back to the time of the apostles. In fact, he would lead us to believe that they are simply a continuation of that ideal of the Christian life described by Luke (Acts 4:32-35) from which the rest of the Church had fallen away. The more fervent Christians, not content with the careless and lax life of the general body of Christians, gradually separated from them to live a common life apart from the rest. "Because they abstained from marriage and cut themselves off from intercourse with their kinsmen and

[34] See Colombás, *El monacato primitivo*, 1.42 and de Vogüé, *La communauté*, pp. 52–54.

the life of the world, [they] were termed monks (*monachi*) or *monazontes* from the strictness of their lonely and solitary life" (Cassian. *conl.* 18,5). Although this is historically untrue, Cassian's definition of the term "monk" primarily in terms of celibacy is in accord with all the evidence previously mentioned.

In another version of the origin of the cenobites, Cassian traces them back to the early Church at Alexandria founded by St. Mark. Here he combines the picture of the early Church provided by Luke with the information supplied by Philo concerning the Therapeutae, who had already been identified by Eusebius as the early Christians.[35] Cassian then assumes not only that these were the first Christians in Egypt, as his source had done (Eus. *hist.eccles.* 2,15) but that cenobitism in Egypt could be traced back to them (Cassian. *inst.* 2,5).[36] Thus, whatever may have been Cassian's familiarity with Jerome's description of the kinds of monks, he has modified it considerably by omitting, at least at this point, any reference to the Pachomians and by tracing instead the supposed historical origins of the cenobites back to northern Egypt, even to Alexandria.[37] This he no doubt did for the didactic purpose of demonstrating the necessity of training in the cenobitic life before one takes up the anchoritic life.

Cassian's account of anchoritic origins is very similar to that of Jerome, with the exception that he implies that the first hermits, Paul and Antony, had been cenobites originally (Cassian. *conl.* 18,6). They sought the recesses of the desert out of a desire for the loftier heights of perfection and divine contemplation. As Jerome had done, Cassian invokes the example of John the Baptist and then goes on to mention Elijah and Elisha with quotations from Job, Jeremiah and the Psalms in support of the anchorites. Along with the author of the *Consultationes*, Jerome and many others, Cassian shared the by now traditional view that the anchoritic life was a higher form of monastic life, not because the anchorites came first historically, nor because the word *monachus* was originally equivalent to anchorite, but because

---

[35] See the Introduction, p. 7.

[36] See A. de Vogüé "Monasticism and the Church in the Writings of Cassian" *MS* 3 (1965) 19–51.

[37] Far more than his predecessors, Cassian seeks to establish the practices of Egyptian monasticism as a normative tradition. On this point see especially A. de Vogüé "Sub regula vel abbate: A Study of the Theological Significance of the Ancient Monastic Rules" *Rule and Life: An Interdisciplinary Symposium*, ed. M. B. Pennington (Spencer, Mass.: Cistercian Publications 1971) pp. 28–29. Perhaps this is why in many places, especially in the *Institutes*, he does not differentiate between the practices of northern and southern Egyptian monasticism nor between those of cenobites and anchorites.

the anchoritic life was perceived as a higher or more advanced form of asceticism. To Cassian must go credit, however, for the notion that the cenobitic life is a training ground for hermits.[38]

The third kind of monks mentioned by Cassian are the sarabaites (Cassian. *conl.* 18,7). These correspond to the *remnuoth* mentioned by Jerome. The distinct name suggests that Cassian had independent access to the same Egyptian tradition on which Jerome had drawn.[39] Cassian regards this kind as a sort of heresy. They have broken away from the congregations of the cenobites, where the authentic monastic tradition is taught, and live an undisciplined life. They shirk the severity of the monastery and live two or three together in their cells, not satisfied to be under the care and governance (*imperio*) of an abbot (Cassian. *conl.* 18,7). Cassian describes the sarabaites at considerable length, contrasting them unfavorably with the cenobites. He notes that the two kinds are almost equally numerous in southern Gaul. The reason for his exaltation of the cenobites is clear. Cassian is aiming to establish the idea of an authentic and normative monastic tradition that is transmitted in cenobitic monasteries. Those who seek to become anchorites must first be formed in this authentic tradition.

[38] Whether or not Cassian invented this idea or found it in Egypt is uncertain. He is certainly the one chiefly responsible for introducing it into the Western monastic tradition. A somewhat similar but less developed notion may be found in Sulpic. Sever. *dial.* 1, 10, where the traveler Postumian relates that in the monasteries of the Thebaid the monks are not permitted to take up the solitary life without the permission of the abbot.

[39] The names *remnuoth* (var. *remoboth, remeboth,* etc.) and *sarabait* have given rise to numerous etymological speculations. See W. Spiegelberg "Koptische Miscellen" *Recueil de travaux* 28 (1906) 211–212; A. Jacoby "Der Name der Sarabaiten" *Recueil de travaux* 34 (1912) 15–16; Adam "Grundbegriffe" pp. 233–234; Morard, p. 379. Krüger (as reported by Adam), Jacoby and Morard appear to be correct in seeing the Coptic word *auēt* (dialect variants: *abēt, aouēt, aoubēt*) in *sar-abait*. See Crum, *A Coptic Dictionary,* p. 21b. The word means a 'collection' or 'company' and is also a technical word for monastic community or monastery. As Morard has noted, however, the attempt to derive *sar-* from the verb *sōr,* meaning 'to disperse,' will not work, nor is it necessary to read it as *šēre* (so Krüger), meaning 'sons of.' Morard is probably correct in seeing in *sar-abait* the prefix *sa(r)-,* meaning simply 'man of.' See Crum, p. 316a.

Spiegelberg was probably originally correct (according to Jacoby, he later changed his mind) in identifying the same Coptic word (*auēt*) in *remn-uoth.* Some of the Latin variants may in fact reflect variant Coptic pronunciations. The prefix *rem(n)-* also means 'man of' or 'from.' See Crum, p. 295a.

What we may have, then, in these two words, which no one seems to have noticed heretofore, is simply two parallel formations built on the same Coptic word, *auēt,* but with different prefixes meaning the same thing. This is in fact what one would expect, given the fact that the *remnuoth* and the sarabaites are described in the same way by Jerome and Cassian. How these words acquired their pejorative connotations it is not possible to determine. These forms are not attested as such in Coptic literature.

Finally, Cassian mentions a fourth kind of monk, to whom he gives no name. These are false hermits who have spent some time in a *coenobium* but not enough to receive a proper formation. They leave and set out on their own before they have learned to deal with their own vices (Cassian. *conl.* 18,8).

The immediate literary antecedent and source of RB 1 is RM 1. The latter's description of the kinds of monks is in turn drawn largely from Cassian. The Master states that there are four kinds of monks. The first are the cenobites, defined exactly as by RB 1.1-2. The second are the anchorites, again described as in RB 1. The third are the sarabaites. This passage of RM 1.6-10 is reproduced in RB 1.6-9 in slightly abbreviated form. Cassian's fourth, unnamed kind seems to be appended to the description of the sarabaites by the Master (RM 1.11-12). Then the Master introduces his fourth kind, the gyrovagues, about whom he digresses in a lengthy, often amusing satire. This is a new variety in the tradition; evidently these wandering, homeless monks had become quite a problem in early sixth-century Italy. The need to regulate them is reflected also in the directions given for receiving visiting monks (RM 78,87 and RB 61).[40]

This short chapter of the Rule of St. Benedict is, then, the end product of a long and rich literary tradition in which repeated efforts have been made to distinguish the genuine from the false article in monastic life. It is the fruit of a wisdom tradition based on the assumption that monastic life has as a goal, and should be oriented toward, the spiritual progress of the individual person. It reflects the experience that certain forms of monastic life enhance the possibility of progress and certain forms hinder it. In this tradition the cenobitic became the preferred form of monastic life because it was the consensus of the monastic movement that in order to achieve spiritual progress, the person who has chosen voluntary celibacy in imitation of Jesus needs training, a training that aims at absorbing the wisdom and profiting from the experience of many previous generations. This chapter reflects also the traditional idea that this training is best acquired in the company of others under the tutelage of a master, someone who has already combined the spiritual insights of the past with his or her own

---

[40] A. de Vogüé, "Scholies sur la règle du maître" *RAM* 44 (1968) 265, sees the ancestors of the gyrovagues in the writings of Augustine, Cassian, Evagrius and Paulinus of Nola. For the satire on the gyrovagues, as well as the relationship of RB 1 and RM 1 generally, see also A. de Vogüé "Saint Benoît et son temps: règles italiennes et règles provençales au VI⁰ siècle" *RBS* 1 (1972) 176–180 and "Le *De generibus monachorum* du Maître et de Benoît. Sa source — son auteur" *RBS* 2 (1973) 1–26.

experience.[41] This normative monastic tradition embodied in RB 1 grew up in Egypt, but was enriched by the observations and experience of other writers as it passed into, and was handed on in, the West.[42]

4. The monastic terminology for women

There is no single term for religious women with the same connotations and widespread use as the word *monachos* (monk) for men, a term that has remained remarkably constant through many changes of language. Lampe's lexicon offers only one comparatively late instance of the feminine form *monachē*.[43] More common are other formations on the same root, such as *monastria* and *monazousa* (corresponding to the masculine *monazōn*).[44] Far more common for women, however, is the less specifically monastic term *parthenos* (virgin).[45]

In Latin the form *monacha* appears at a relatively early date (A.D. 384; Hier. *epist.* 22,13) in a context that, surprisingly, suggests common or widespread use. It continues in use for several centuries, appearing in diverse writings, such as those of Augustine, Gregory of Tours, Gregory the Great and the Lives of the Jura fathers.[46] Although it has survived as a common term in Italian (*monaca*), it did not become the usual Latin term for monastic women or even remain in common use. The more common terms in Latin are *sanctimonialis* and *virgo sacrata*. *Sanctimonialis* (from which comes also the later short form *monialis*) is found already in pre-Christian use. It is an

[41] It will readily be perceived, then, why chapter 1 had to precede chapter 2 on the abbot. On this role of spiritual paternity in early monasticism, see Appendix 2.

[42] This little chapter provides, then, a good example of the growth of the monastic wisdom tradition as discussed in the Introduction, and of how the Rule of St. Benedict can serve as an entrance to the rediscovery of that tradition.

[43] See G. W. Lampe, *A Greek Patristic Lexicon* (Oxford: The Clarendon Press 1961) s.v.

[44] *Monazontes* appears as an equivalent or alternative to *monachoi* in Cassian. *conl.* 18,5 (*monachi sive monazontes*) and in the travel narrative of Egeria (Eger. *peregr.* 24,1; 25,2; 25,7; 25,12), as well as in numerous Greek authors of the same period. In her account of Jerusalem, Egeria speaks of the *monazontes et parthenae*, which suggests that the feminine form was less common than the masculine. See the following note. For further discussion of the term, see Morard, pp. 404–406.

[45] This is undoubtedly due to the greater emphasis placed on the specific quality of virginity in women in the Patristic period, which is related in turn to the example of the Virgin Mary.

[46] For specific references, see the *Thesaurus Linguae Latinae*, s.v. The *TLL* gives *monastria* as the Greek equivalent of *monacha*, but Gregory the Great (Greg. *epist.* 23) defines *monastria* as 'handmaids of God' (*ancillis Dei, quas vos [Constantinopolitani] Graeca lingua monastrias dicitis*).

adjectival formation from *sanctimonia*, designating an existence consecrated to the practice of a holy life.[47] In Christian literature it occurs first in Augustine (Aug. *epist.* 169; *retract.* 1,2,22; *serm.* 22,1). A cognate of *monialis* exists in French and did at one time in English also.[48]

The most common term in English for monastic women, "nun," appears to be of Egyptian origin, although its etymology remains obscure.[49] This word appears in both masculine and feminine forms in Greek (*nonnos-nonna*) from the second century A.D. on, and in Latin (*nonnus-nonna*) from the late fourth century. It was not originally an ecclesiastical or even specifically Christian term but was understood, at least as it came into Latin, as an epithet of respect, especially for older persons. Jerome uses it as such in his famous letter to Eustochium (Hier. *epist.* 22,16).[50] It retains this connotation in RB 63.12, where, interestingly, St. Benedict finds it necessary to explain its meaning as *paterna reverentia*.

Thereafter the denotations of the word develop in two quite distinct directions. As an epithet of respect, both masculine and feminine Latin forms survive into the Carolingian period, but, due in part to the influence of Boniface, the feminine form begins to acquire its specific reference to religious women in Frankish and Germanic lands. Probably because of the dominance of the term *monachus*, the masculine Latin form does not develop this kind of reference and drops out of use. In Italian, *nonno-nonna* come to mean grandfather and grandmother. In German, French and English, the feminine form alone survives and refers properly only to monastic women. Given the fact that in the fourth to sixth centuries the term was still a comparatively generalized term of respect for older persons, it is easy to see how it could have developed these quite distinct meanings.

[47] See H. Leclercq "Sanctimonialis" *DACL* 15.747.

[48] See note 2 above.

[49] See J. Hannsens "Nónnos, nónna et Nonnus, nonna" *Orientalia Christiana Periodica* 26 (1960) 26–41; H. Leclercq "Nonne" *DACL* 12.1557, and Adam "Grundbegriffe" pp. 232–233. The evidence assembled by Hannsens shows that Adam is unjustified in denying the Egyptian origin of the word.

[50] The translation "are called chaste nuns" (ACW 33.148), for *castae vocantur et nonnae* is incorrect. The word does not have the specific English meaning of 'nun' at this point, nor does it have any connection with chastity, as its later history demonstrates.

Appendix 2

The Abbot

Two entire chapters of the Rule, 2 and 64, are devoted to the abbot, and he occupies an important place in all its legislation. It is impossible to understand either the spiritual theory of the Rule or its practical regulations without a clear vision of his all-pervasive role. Since this role has been diversely conceived in the course of Benedictine history, it is essential to study St. Benedict's teaching about the abbot, in the light of the tradition upon which he drew.[1]

The title abbas

Although Benedict sometimes uses other terms, such as *prior* and *maior* to refer to the superior of the monastery, he usually, in accord with a number of other Latin monastic sources, gives him the title *abbas*.[2] Like so many other usages in the Rule, this term is derived from Egyptian monasticism, where we find it used already in fourth-century documents. It is almost certainly derived originally from the Aramaic term *abba*, which means 'father.'[3] In Coptic it appears as *apa*, and in Greek and Latin it was simply transliterated and made into a declinable noun, *abbas*. In a similar way the term has been absorbed into modern languages: hence the English word "abbot."

The earliest certain usage of the term in a monastic sense is in

---

[1] In addition to the commentaries on the Rule, see H. Emonds "Abt" *Reallexikon für Antike und Christentum* 1.45–55; J. Gribomont "Abbas" *Dizionario degli Istituti de Perfezione* 1.23–26; Pierre Salmon, *The Abbot in Monastic Tradition*, tr. C. Lavoie, (Washington, D.C.: Consortium Press 1972).

[2] *Abbas* appears 126 times; *prior* 12 times; *maior, pater monasterii*, and *pater spiritalis* once each.

[3] An attempt has been made to derive it from the Greek *papas*, a title applied to bishops in the early Church and eventually restricted to the bishop of Rome. No adequate explanation has been offered, however, for the dropping of the initial *p*. See E. von Dobschütz, *Das Decretum Gelasianum*, TU 3rd series 8,4 (Leipzig: J. C. Hinrichs 1912) p. 227.

Greek papyri found in Egypt, which date from about 330 to 340. Its regular appearance in the *Apophthegmata* (which were collected later but reflect an ancient oral tradition) may indicate a still earlier usage, going back to the origins of Egyptian monasticism. Later in the fourth century, it is used by Palladius and the author of the *Historia monachorum*, as well as by other Greek writers.[4] But it does not appear in the *Life of Antony*, nor in the letters attributed to him, which are very probably authentic. Athanasius, however, uses it elsewhere as a title for a monk (Ath. *narr.Ammon.*). It was not used in Cappadocia; St. Basil, who also does not use the term "monk," called the head of his fraternity *ho proestōs*, 'the one in charge,' which Rufinus translates as *is qui praeest*.

In Egyptian usage the term does not designate the superior of a community, as we understand it today, but an "elder" or "senior," advanced in the wisdom of the desert and gifted with the charism of enlightening others by conferring upon them a *logion*, or 'word.' In the Pachomian sources, both Coptic and Greek, it likewise refers to various elders, but is sometimes used without a proper name ("the Abbot") to designate Pachomius himself. Hence the process of reserving it to the superior of a *coenobium* may have begun in Egyptian cenobitism, though the original use of the term to mean 'elder' takes us back to the semi-eremitical phase of Egyptian monasticism. The older usage still prevails in the Byzantine world, whereas in the West the term "abbot" is applied only to cenobitic superiors.

The term was quickly adopted by Latin writers. Jerome uses it only rarely (never in his translation of the Pachomian materials) and seems originally to have objected to it on the grounds that Matt 23:9 forbids designating human beings as father.[5] While Augustine never uses it (the superior of his monastery is called *praepositus*, 'the one placed over'), it appears frequently in Sulpicius Severus and especially in Cassian. While the former uses it only to designate a cenobitic superior, in Cassian it can still refer to a charismatic elder in the desert, but also serves as the title of the superior of a *coenobium* (Sulpic.Sever. *dial.* 1,10,11,17,18,19,22). By the sixth century, in the *Lives of the Jura Fathers*, the *Regula Magistri* and St. Benedict, it is used exclusively in the latter sense.

The origins of the monastic use of the term are difficult to explain. An Aramaic word, it would be at home in Syria: did it originally come

---

[4] E.g., Evagr. *de orat.* 108, in regard to Theodore of Tabennesi.

[5] He argues thus in Hier. *in Gal.* 4-6, but offers a justification for it in the later Hier. *in Matt.* 23:9. He uses the term himself in Hier. *vita Mal.* 3 and 10, and in Hier. *epist.* 51,2.

to Egypt from Syria at some remote period earlier than our documentation? This would support the hypothesis of those who believe that monasticism originated in Syria rather than in Egypt.[6] Although *abba* in the sense of 'lord' or 'sir' was used as a title of respect in Syria, however, its technical monastic use there and in Palestine is so late that it seems more likely that it results from Egyptian influence rather than vice versa.[7]

On the other hand, its usage may have originated independently in Egypt out of reflection upon the biblical use of *abba*. In the New Testament, Jesus uses this term of endearment when calling upon God, thereby revealing the intimate relationship he enjoyed with him; and the early Christians used it in imitation of him, aware that they had been adopted as sons of God (Mark 14:36; Gal 4:6; Rom 8:15). But it is applied only to God. Its application to the spiritual father who mediates God's word supposes a theology of spiritual fatherhood that would assimilate the role of the *abba* to that of God himself. In the earliest Egyptian texts there is no evidence of such a development, though it does appear in the Pachomian literature. The sources do not tell us clearly where and why the title was first applied to monks. However, the doctrine of spiritual fatherhood that grew up in the monastic tradition developed out of a rich background in the Scriptures and early Christian tradition, to which we must now turn.

Spiritual fatherhood in the Scriptures and early Christian tradition

In both the prophetic and sapiential traditions of Israel, the relationship between master and disciple is presented under the metaphor of father and son. Since both prophecy and wisdom had roots in the culture of the ancient Near East, this metaphor extends far back into history.[8]

---

[6] E.g., A. Vööbus, *History of Asceticism in the Syrian Orient*, CSCO 184 (Louvain: Secrétariat du CSCO 1958); see introduction p. liv. It is noteworthy that the *Apophthegmata* uses the corresponding Aramaic term *amma*, 'mother,' for female ascetics. Some also believe that the term *monachos* is derived from Syriac usage. See Appendix 1, pp. 306–307.

[7] Neither Chrysostom nor Theodoret uses the term *abba* of a renowned monk or of a cenobitic superior. It becomes common only in the sixth and seventh centuries, in writers such as Dorotheos of Gaza, Cyril of Scythopolis and John of Damascus. In the East the accent has always been upon the personal holiness of the monk rather than upon his office, even when it is applied to a cenobitic superior. See I. Hausherr, *Direction spirituelle en Orient autrefois*, Orientalia Christiana Analecta 144 (Rome: Pont. Inst. Orientalium Studiorum 1955) pp. 35–39.

[8] On spiritual fatherhood, see especially L. Dürr "Heilige Vaterschaft im Antiken

It is the role of a father not only to beget children but also to educate them. Consequently, the activity of teaching was seen as the work of the father, and one who performed it could be called "father." The ancient wisdom literature of both Egypt and Mesopotamia is often presented in the form of a father's instructions to his son: not only is the content the traditional paternal advice that was handed down to successive generations, but the form is a paternal monologue that frequently contains the direct address "my son" or "my sons."[9] The frequent use of this literary form in Proverbs and other Old Testament wisdom literature shows Israel's dependence upon the prevailing cultural patterns.[10]

In the ancient world the parents were the principal teachers of their children; scribal schools educated only a small minority chiefly destined for government service.[11] Normally the son learned his father's trade by a kind of apprenticeship, and the daughter learned the domestic arts from her mother.[12] More important than this, however, was the communication of the parents' sense of values, their convictions about the meaning of life and how it was to be lived in practice. For Israel this involved a sense of identification with the people of God and the acceptance of faith in Yahweh, which informed the whole of life. The Old Testament is filled with the idea of the transmission from father to son of the religious heritage of Israel; this is particularly stressed not only by the wisdom tradition but also by the Deuteronomic literature (Deut 6:7,20-23; 32:7,45-47; Josh 4:21-22; Exod 13:8).

Teaching how to live, communicating the fruits of one's own experience, is a continuation of the transmission of life proper to fatherhood. The wisdom handed on by the sage was a gift of life: "The teaching of the wise is a fountain of life, that one may avoid the snares of death" (Prov 13:14). In Israel, wisdom was progressively seen as a gift of God, and finally identified with the Mosaic law, itself consid-

---

Orient" in *Heilige Überlieferung: Festgabe I. Herwegen* (Münster: Aschendorff 1938) pp. 1–20; P. Gutierrez, *La paternité spirituelle selon S. Paul*, Études bibliques (Paris: Gabalda 1968); *La paternité spirituelle: Séminaire pour maîtresses de novices cisterciennes* (Laval: Abbaye Cistercienne 1974; hors commerce).

[9] See the texts translated in J. Pritchard, *Ancient Near Eastern Texts Relating to the Old Testament* (Princeton, N.J.: Princeton Univ. Press 1955), especially the instructions of Ptah-hotep and Merikare.

[10] E.g., Prov 23:19-26; 24:13,21; Prov 1–9 passim; Sir 2:1; 3:12,17; 4:1; 6:18,24,32 and passim. The plural is used in Prov 4:1; 5:7; 7:24; Ps 33(34):11; Sir 3:1; 23:7.

[11] In Israel there is no mention of schools until a late period (see Sir 51:23), but prophets and sages had disciples whom they instructed.

[12] This is the background behind the saying of John 5:19-20.

ered by the Deuteronomist as "your very life" (Deut 32:47; see Sir 24:23).

The metaphor of the father-son relationship appears also among the prophets and their disciples. While the term "sons of the prophets" probably does not have the connotation of spiritual sonship, but simply means "guild" or "brotherhood" of prophets, we find Elisha addressing his master Elijah as "my father" at the moment of the latter's disappearance (2 Kgs 2:12). Elisha had asked for a double share of the master's inheritance, which by right belonged to the eldest son. His sonship is based upon the transmission of the "spirit" that made him a new Elijah. In similar fashion the king of Israel, who sought advice from Elisha, calls him "my father" (2 Kgs 6:21; 13:14). Here, as in the circles of the sages, it is the transmission of teaching that constitutes the father-son relationship.

For the Old Testament, then, instruction is an exercise of fatherhood, especially when it concerns the total formation of a person. To develop his personality and the very life he has received from his parents, every man needs the help of others. To benefit another in this way is to exercise the function of fatherhood on his behalf, to show him "the way of life." That these ideas were current at the time of the New Testament is clear from their appearance in the Qumran literature and in Philo. The metaphor of sonship applied to disciples is also found in Hellenistic literature. But it is principally the religious tradition of the Old Testament that prepared the way for St. Paul, who, however, developed it in a unique fashion.

In his very first epistle Paul compared his behavior at Thessalonica to the way in which a father deals with his children: "You know how, like a father with his children, we exhorted each one of you and encouraged you and charged you to lead a life worthy of God" (1 Thess 2:11-12). From metaphor, however, he advanced to an affirmation of real fatherhood when addressing the Corinthians: "Even if you have ten thousand guardians in Christ, yet you do not have many fathers, for I begot you in Christ Jesus by means of the Gospel. Therefore I urge you, be imitators of me" (1 Cor 4:15-16). Here we have more than a simple comparison. Paul is affirming that the relationship which unites him to the Christians of Corinth is a genuine fatherhood, to be understood by analogy with physical fatherhood.

The father is concerned solely with the welfare of his children, for it is he who has given them life. In this sense he is to be contrasted with the "guardian" or "pedagogue," a slave who conducted the child to and from school and often meted out harsh discipline to him. No one else—not even ten thousand such slaves—can replace the role of the father. For it is he who has *begotten* the child. In the natural order, to beget is to transmit life, to share in the creative process itself. The New Testament often uses the language of physical generation and birth to express the reality of the new divine life conferred upon us in the Christian economy. For St. John, to be a Christian means to enter into this new life, to be born again, from above, of water and the Spirit; this is a gift of God that makes a person the child of God and assimilates him to his only-begotten Son, placing him permanently in the state of adoptive divine sonship (see John 1:12-13; 3:3-8; 1 John 2:29; 3:1-2,9; 5:1,11-12).

Paul speaks of this same reality in a different way. That he is not speaking of sacramental regeneration in baptism, as is St. John, is clear from his explicit exclusion of baptizing from his apostolic role at Corinth (1 Cor 1:13-17). He is father not through baptism but "by means of the Gospel." For Paul, however, word and sacrament are inseparably united. The same transcendent reality is approached from a different aspect than in the Johannine literature.

In this concept of "begetting by means of the Gospel," the Word of God that is proclaimed is the seed that transmits life.[13] The idea is not original in Paul: it appears elsewhere in the New Testament[14] and is related to the metaphorical usage of the image of seed in pagan and Jewish writers (see Plato *phaed.* 248d; 249a; 276e; Phil. *cher.* 43-44), as well as to the Old Testament idea of the efficacy of the Word of God.[15]

The Old Testament does not use the image of the Word as a seed, but it appears to have become quite common in the early Church. James writes: "He brought us forth by the word of truth, that we should be, as it were, the first-fruits of his creation" (Jas 1:18). Peter is

[13] See Gal 3:26-27; Col 2:12; Eph 5:26. St. John also associates the acceptance of the word through faith with baptismal regeneration: John 1:12-13; 3:12; 1 John 2:24-25; 5:1,10-12.

[14] Jas 1:17-18; 1 Pet 1:23; 1 John 3:9, and the explanation of the sower parable: Mark 4:14-20 and parallels.

[15] Deutero-Isaiah especially stresses the power of God's Word (see Isa 55:11). For him and his followers, all creation came about simply by the Word of God (thus Pss 32[33]:9; 147:15,18). Deuteronomy speaks of the Word within man's heart (Deut 30:14). The personification of the Word, which begins already in Deutero-Isaiah, becomes clear in late Old Testament passages such as Wis 18:15 and, outside the Bible, in the concept of the *memra*, which occurs in the Aramaic targums as a means of avoiding anthropomorphisms.

even more explicit: "You have been born anew, not of perishable but
of imperishable seed, through the living and abiding word of God."
He then quotes Deutero-Isaiah: "the word of the Lord abides
forever," and adds, "That word is the Good News which was preached
to you" (1 Pet 1:23-25, citing Isa 40:6-8). Very likely St. John also has
the image of the word in mind when he says, "No one born of God
commits sin, for God's seed abides in him, and he cannot sin because
he is born of God" (1 John 3:9).

The Good News, then, is the seed that brings forth new life in the
Christian, the very life of God because the seed is God's word. Just as
in the natural order a man becomes a father by contributing the seed
that transmits life, so in the supernatural order the apostle who imparts the life-giving word is rightly said to have brought forth the life
of grace in the hearer, and the latter is rightly called his son. Such is
the reasoning of Paul. All life is a gift of God, but the man who confers
life by means of his seed is really a father, and the same is true of the
spiritual father who transmits the seed of his word. The Word of God
is powerful and active, a fertile principle of salvation implanted in a
man's heart, where it engenders life like the virile seed in the womb;
it is the power of God unto salvation for everyone who has faith, the
word of life that makes its recipients children of God (1 Thess 1:5;
Rom 1:16; Phil 2:15-16).

In this transmission of life, the apostle is the indispensable instrument of God. The divine initiative has selected men, as it did in the
Old Testament, to proclaim the living word: they are God's representatives or ambassadors, who speak not their own message but that
of God (2 Cor 2:17; 5:20; 1 Thess 2:13). Therefore, Paul can rightly
claim the Gospel as his own (Gal 1:11-12) while still claiming that it is
God's word. And he can attribute to his own ministry the fertility and
efficacy of the word he preaches (1 Cor 2:4-5; 2 Cor 4:7). It is a case of
the mysterious cooperation between grace and nature: the apostle is a
co-worker with God (1 Cor 3:9; 2 Cor 6:1). Accordingly, the preacher
of the word is God's instrument in communicating the new life, just as
is the minister who confers baptism, the rebirth, and can equally be
designated as spiritual father.

Paul understands this in a very realistic fashion. As in natural
fatherhood, the act of begetting sets up an enduring relationship with
the children. The apostle himself becomes the instrument of salvation
for them: he is a "sacrament" and his whole person becomes a source
of life. He represents the heavenly Father to his children: his whole

life is a means of preaching the life-giving word to them. Therefore Paul can urge them to be "imitators of me" (1 Cor 4:16; 11:1), just as he speaks of their imitating Christ or God (1 Thess 1:6; Eph 5:1). As a natural father remains with his children to teach them by both word and example and thus continues the work of giving life that was begun when he begot them, so the spiritual father continues to confer life by the ongoing proclamation of both his teaching and his life, until his children are fully formed. To this must be added the duty of correcting their errors and failures, and offering comfort, support and encouragement, in the manner of a father who unselfishly has their welfare at heart (see 1 Cor 4:14; 2 Cor 1:3-7).

The early Church took up Paul's teaching about spiritual fatherhood and developed it in the two directions already indicated by the New Testament: the sacramental and the prophetic. We find the fatherhood of the bishop affirmed already, at least in an equivalent way, in the apostolic fathers. Ignatius says "all should respect the deacons as Jesus Christ, even as the bishop is a type of the Father, and the presbyters as the council of God and the college of apostles" (Ign. *Trall.* 3,1). Elsewhere he commands, "All of you follow the bishop, as Jesus Christ [follows] the Father" (Ign. *Smyr.* 8,1). For Ignatius, the bishop is clearly the visible representative of God the Father: when the presbyters defer to him, it is really "not to him, but to the Father of Jesus Christ, the bishop of all. . . . It is right that we offer obedience without hypocrisy, for one does not merely deceive this bishop who is seen, but wrongs the Unseen One" (Ign. *Magn.* 3,1-2).

The fatherhood of the bishop is more explicitly developed in the Church orders. Thus the *Didascalia Apostolorum*, probably an early third-century document, refers to the bishop not only as shepherd and physician but also as father: "Let the bishop love the laity as his children. . . . He is the teacher of piety and, next after God, he is your father, who has begotten you again to the adoption of sons by water and the Spirit" (*Didasc.apost.* 2,20-26). The bishop's role as father, however, is related not only to his administration of the sacraments, as in the preceding text, but also to his proclaiming the word and teaching doctrine. Commenting on the Old Testament command to honor father and mother, the author says: "How much more should the word exhort you to honor your spiritual parents, and to love them as your benefactors and ambassadors with God, who have regenerated you with water, and endued you with the fullness of the Holy Spirit, who have fed you with the word as with milk, who have nourished you

with doctrine, who have confirmed you by their admonitions. . . ."
(*Didasc.apost.* 2,33).[16]

The Fathers also pursued the biblical idea of the generation of children through handing on the word. Irenaeus states clearly the principle that one becomes a son by receiving the teaching of another: " 'Son' has a twofold meaning: . . . one is a son in the natural order because he was born a son; . . . the second is made so . . . by the teaching of doctrine. For when any person has been taught from the mouth of another, he is called the son of the one who instructs him, and the latter is called his father" (Iren. *adv.haer.* 4,41,2).

It is especially in the Alexandrian school, however, that the fatherhood of the teacher and preacher of the word is developed. Given the emphasis of the Alexandrian Fathers upon the Logos, the word of Scripture and the teacher in the Christian community, the development is not surprising. Typically, Clement derives the idea both from Plato and from St. Paul: "As he [Socrates] says in the *Theaetetus*, 'He [the virtuous man] will beget and train men; for some procreate by the body, others by the soul.' For among the barbarian philosophers to teach and to enlighten is also called begetting, just as the Apostle says, 'I have begotten you in Jesus Christ'" (Clem. *strom.* 5,2).

Elsewhere Clement elaborates further, explaining that the word is the seed through which the begetting takes place: "It is a good thing to leave good children to posterity: such is the case with children of our bodies. But words are the progeny of the soul; thus we call those who have taught us 'fathers.' . . . The word that is sown is hidden in the soul of the learner, as in the earth, and this is spiritual planting. . . . I believe that soul united to soul and spirit to spirit in the sowing of the word will make what is sown germinate and grow. And everyone who is instructed is, from the viewpoint of dependence, the son of his teacher. 'Son,' says he [Solomon], 'do not forget my precepts'" (Clem. *strom.* 1,1, citing Prov 3:1; see also Clem. *strom.* 3,15).[17]

There can be little doubt that these concepts developed out of the important place occupied by prophecy and teaching in the early Church. Prophets and teachers are mentioned frequently in the New Testament; while their precise functions in the early Christian community are subject to dispute, they were certainly both concerned

[16] In later Patristic literature the fatherhood of the bishop is a common theme. See, for example, Aug. *in psalm.* 44,32.

[17] Origen frequently makes use of the analogies of the preacher as father and the word as seed. See Orig. *hom. in Ex.* 1-3; *in Ioan.* 32,10.

with the ministry of the word.[18] The teacher's role was probably to expound the Christian faith to those who had received baptism but needed further instruction (*didachē*), and the instruction, especially in Jewish-Christian communities, must have consisted largely in the Christian interpretation of the Old Testament.

The prophet was no doubt so called because he was seen to be in continuity with Old Testament prophecy; therefore he was a charismatic who was moved by the Spirit to utter the word of God, and prophecy was a sign of the Spirit's presence in the Church. Paul ranks prophecy, followed immediately by teaching, directly after apostleship in the hierarchy of ministries (1 Cor 12:28) and says that its purpose is to build up, encourage and console the Church (1 Cor 13:3). It seems that there was a certain institutionalizing of the charism: the prophet was seen as holding an office in the community, though his precise function in the liturgical assembly is not known.

Prophecy was obviously subject to abuse and self-deception, as in the Old Testament, and there were false prophets who posed a threat to the communities. We find a number of references to them in the New Testament (Matt 7:15; 24:11,24; Mark 13:22; 2 Pet 2:1; 1 John 4:1). It thus seems likely that prophets were numerous in the early Church: we find them mentioned frequently in the *Didache*, together with teachers, and by Justin Martyr (*Didache* 11 and 13; prophets in *Didache* 10 and Iust. *dial.* 82). The excesses of Montanism in the second and third centuries may have brought charismatic gifts into some disrepute, but the functions of the New Testament prophets and teachers nevertheless continued in the ministry of the word exercised in the community: the *didascalia*.

It is probably out of this background that the emergence of the *abba* or charismatic elder, the bearer of the inspired word, in the Egyptian monastic circles of the fourth century should be understood.[19] On the one hand, the desert elder exercised the charismatic functions of word-bearer much as the prophets and *didaskaloi* did in the early Church. On the other hand, he is called *abba*, whereas throughout the early Church there is a constant tradition of spiritual fatherhood attributed not only to sacramental and hierarchical ministers but also to those who generate life in the spiritual order by transmission of the

---

[18] See C. H. Peisker and C. Brown "Prophet" *The New International Dictionary of New Testament Theology* (Grand Rapids: Zondervan 1978) 3.74–92.

[19] Thus K. Heussi, *Der Ursprung des Mönchtums* (Tübingen: J.C.B. Mohr 1936) pp. 165–167.

word. There is no evidence in the texts that the name was given because of such a theology of spiritual fatherhood or that the Egyptian elder is a lineal descendant of the early Christian prophet. But both may be deemed highly probable.

The abba *in the Egyptian desert*

The life of the semi-anchorites in the deserts of Nitria and Scete is known chiefly through the *Apophthegmata Patrum*, together with information provided by Palladius, Cassian and the *Historia monachorum*. Nitria was founded around 330 by Amoun, and Scete about the same time by Macarius the Egyptian, and they flourished throughout the fourth century. The life was rather unstructured and could range from total solitude to a fair degree of common interaction. Similar forms of monastic life existed in the Fayyum, the Thebaid, the eastern desert, and the Delta area. What was characteristic of it and essential to its functioning was the role of the *gerōn* or 'elder.'[20]

While the elder, who was called *abba*, was often a man well advanced in years, the determining factor was not chronological age but wisdom born of experience. The chief requisite for the exercise of spiritual fatherhood was that the man be himself spiritual. Spirituality was never considered an intellectual achievement; it could be acquired only by practice. A spiritual man was one who had himself lived the monastic life, come to know himself, struggled against his passions and the onslaughts of the demons, and allowed the power of grace to triumph in him. He had a doctrine, but it was not learned by study; it was the type of wisdom possessed by those who live rightly and learn from life itself. Such persons are able to advise others on the basis of their own experience.

The *abba*, then, was an experienced monk who knew the life from living it himself. He was a holy man, for he had achieved a measure of success in his personal struggle. He was able to be a spiritual father, *patēr pneumatikos*, to beget sons in his own image. He was considered to be a bearer of the Spirit, *pneumatophoros*, because holiness was no personal achievement, but the gift of the Spirit of God who dwells in us.[21] The holy monk was filled with the Spirit because the

---

[20] See *ibid.*, pp. 164–186; G. Colombás, *El monacato primitivo*, BAC 351,376 (Madrid: La Editorial Católica 1974–75) 2.97–104; Hausherr, *Direction spirituelle en Orient autrefois*.

[21] F. von Lilienfeld "Anthropos Pneumatikos-Pater Pneumatophoros: Neues Testament und Apophthegmata Patrum" *Studia Patristica* 5, TU 80 (Berlin: Akademie-Verlag 1962) 382–392.

Spirit's dwelling place in him had been swept clean by the monk's asceticism. He was, then, a true charismatic, a man in whom the Spirit dwelt and who was entirely subject to, and directed by, the Holy Spirit. To father sons, then, meant to communicate the Spirit to others so that they might also open their hearts to his indwelling.

The *abba* begot spiritual sons chiefly through the seed that is the word. Young men thirsting for salvation and the experience of God came to him as to a tested veteran. What they asked for was "a word" (*rhēma*): "Father, give me a word." The request sometimes envisaged a particular problem and asked for specific advice; sometimes it was put in the most general terms: "How can I be saved?" The genuine fathers were the ones who did not seek to be fathers and whose humility made them hesitant to accept the role. Sometimes the disciple had to wait several days for an answer; sometimes the elder spotted him as a fraud and would not answer at all. The "words" were usually brief, pithy pronouncements containing insights of profound wisdom under an appearance of great simplicity. They are preserved in the collections of *apophthegmata*, which have been compared to the "pronouncement stories" of Jesus in the Synoptic Gospels. Their teaching is the fruit of experience.

The desert monks had a strong sense of tradition, which was identified with "the teaching of the elders." This was no systematized body of doctrine, but a kind of unsophisticated unwritten law that prescribed the best way to do things. Its inspiration was strongly evangelical, and it was most probably rooted in the ascetical and charismatic groupings of the pre-monastic period, but it developed out of actual practice in the first monastic generation. Each *abba*, in his own teaching, felt that he was handing on the tradition, and the tradition thus became incorporated in wise sayings that were remembered and propagated. The disciple, formed by the master's teaching, received the tradition from him; when he became an *abba* himself, he passed it on to his disciples. The sayings of the fathers were eventually collected and set down in writing. They have been among the favored reading of monks ever since and have often served to recall monasticism to the purity and simplicity of its origins. When the traditional teaching of the fathers was absorbed by learned intellectuals such as Evagrius of Pontus and John Cassian, they systematized it on the foundations of Greek philosophy and Origen's theories about the development of the spiritual life. But they were very conscious of the obligation to be faithful to tradition.

The elder became a spiritual father through a very personal relationship to an individual disciple. He could have more than one disciple at the same time, and they might all live under the same basic regime, but each was treated as a unique individual. They made their problems known to him through manifestation of thoughts (*logismoi*); this included not merely the bad thoughts by which they were tempted but whatever occupied their interior faculties. It was therefore more inclusive than simply confession of sins or evil thoughts, or even manifestation of conscience in the modern sense. The disciple, who was not yet liberated from slavery to his passions and from the darkness of sin, was often unable to distinguish in himself between what was healthy and positive and what was dangerous and deceptive. He therefore humbly opened his inner self to examination by the spiritual father. The latter's ability to make sound judgments about what the disciple revealed to him was called "discernment of spirits" and was regarded as a charismatic gift.[22] The conflicting forces that compete for control of a man's heart were personified as "spirits": the demons on the one hand (which Evagrius classified into eight principal types) and the Spirit of God on the other. Since the demons disguise themselves as angels of light (see 2 Cor 11:14), they can deceive the uninitiated, but not the *abba* who has the gift of discernment.[23]

The theme of discernment or discretion appears often in the desert literature.[24] The omnipresence of demons, which appears so alien and disconcerting to the modern mind, is a fundamentally mythological way of stating profound spiritual and psychological insights into the human heart. The unmasking of illusions conducted by the fathers is in some respects an anticipation of the procedures of modern psychotherapy, but its purpose was entirely pastoral and spiritual.[25] The elder aimed at helping the disciple to come to a knowledge of himself: by patiently and objectively examining the forces that clamored for control, he showed the youth what he must do if he really wished to extirpate the roots that sin and selfishness had sunk in him,

---

[22] See G. Bardy "Discernement des esprits chez les Pères" *DS* 3.1247–54.

[23] See A. and C. Guillaumont "Démon dans la plus ancienne littérature monastique" *DS* 3.180–212.

[24] The classic treatise on discretion is Cassian. *conl.* 2.

[25] P. Sorokin "The Monastic System of Techniques. Monastic 'Psychoanalysis,' Counseling and Therapy," excerpted from *The Ways and Power of Love* (St. Meinrad, Ind.: Abbey Press 1973); T. Merton "The Spiritual Father in the Desert Tradition" *Contemplation in a World of Action* (Garden City, N.Y.: Doubleday 1971) pp. 269–293; "Final Integration: Toward a Monastic Therapy" *ibid.*, pp. 205–217.

perhaps even masquerading under virtuous pretenses, and to surrender himself in total abandonment to the Spirit of Christ. Thus would he be enabled to know his true self and at the same time to know God. Only in this way could he find an answer to the classic question presented to the fathers: How can I be saved?

The portrait of the desert fathers that the literature reveals to us is an admirable example of the exercise of spiritual fatherhood. They knew, as good natural parents do, that they were dealing with an ineffable mystery that demanded the most profound respect. They gave no advice unasked and were reluctant even to accede to entreaty, for they knew that it is no trivial matter to direct another's life and share in God's own fatherhood on his behalf. They showed no surprise or shock at whatever thoughts a monk might have, for one who has come to a knowledge of himself is realistic about the possibilities of fallen nature.[26] They had a profound respect for every man, for they knew that he carried the image of God in him, no matter how obscured it might be by sin. Each monk was a unique creation of God who was to be dealt with as a distinctive individual. Spiritual direction was not a set of stock solutions to be applied mechanically to every problem; still less was it a subtle way of gaining control over others by manipulating them. It was an honest searching to know the other and help him to know himself, so that he might learn to wrestle on his own with the forces of darkness and surrender his life to the creative power of God. The goal of spiritual fatherhood was the growth of the son to adulthood. Once he had, through harsh experience, absorbed the traditional wisdom that was identical with holiness, he could himself become the father of sons.

Above all, what we discern in the attitude of the desert *abba* is charity: a sincere, personal love for each monk who came to him seeking. The elder was vitally concerned with the ultimate welfare of each disciple. He cared about him; he treated him as a father treats his son. This often comes out in the form of an exquisite tenderness, of compassion in its deepest sense of willingness to suffer with another and to make his suffering one's own, of understanding the other without subtly conveying judgment or rebuke or superiority. It can also take the form of necessary severity, however, or of the unexpected answer that shocks the questioner back into reality.[27] One who truly loves tries to provide what the other needs, not what he wants. The *abba*

[26] The classic story about a pseudo-elder who was shocked and judgmental at the temptations of a young monk is recounted by Cassian. *conl.* 2,13.

[27] M. Matthei "Afflicción y consuelo en los Padres del Desierto" *SM* 5 (1963) 7-25.

respected his disciple as a man and a child of God, and stood in awe
before the mystery that every human person encompasses; hence he
could love him genuinely with a divine charity that was at the same
time intensely human.

If all of this is the fruit of divine grace, it is nonetheless not extraordinary, in the modern sense of "miraculous." However, there are also
in the desert literature a number of accounts of such extraordinary
accomplishments of the fathers.[28] Sometimes they have the gift of
seeing into the heart of another (*kardiognōsis*) and reading his mind.
They are so powerful with God that they can bring about wonders
simply by intense application to prayer. Occasionally they experience
ecstasy and visions and other extraordinary states. They have the gift
of working wonders, such as healings, nature miracles and raising the
dead to life. While these are by no means the most prominent feature
of the *Apophthegmata*, they are intended to emphasize the charismatic nature of the *abba's* gifts and are in continuity with the pre-
monastic Christian charismatics and the New Testament. Indeed, the
wonders of the fathers often reproduce biblical models and are intended to show that the elders fulfill the requirements of a Man of
God, precisely as St. Gregory was later to do in his stories about St.
Benedict in the *Dialogues*.[29]

Similarly, the desert fathers often taught by performing symbolic
actions not unlike those of the Old and New Testament prophets
(*Apoph.*: see Zacharias 3; Moses 2; Pior 3; Ammonas 8 and 9). This
was a deliberate imitation of biblical models in a predominantly oral
culture that still had much in common with that of biblical times. But
it also emphasizes the point, which was so cherished by the fathers,
that teaching is more a matter of deeds than of words. What they had to
teach was no academic discipline but a way of life. An art can be
taught only by showing how to do it. Therefore, the example of the
abba was his principal means of instruction, and imitation was for the
disciple the chief means of learning. The fathers' concern to give
example also protected them against the danger of not practicing what
they preached. The Abba Poemen once summed up the matter clearly
in a memorable pronouncement. When a monk asked him if he should

[28] While Cassian is rather restrained in his attitude toward miracles (see his remarks
in the Preface to the *inst.* and in *conl.* 18,1), Palladius and Sulpicius Severus delight in
recounting them. The *Apophthegmata*, on the whole, is quite reserved.

[29] See B. Steidle "'Homo Dei Antonius': Zum Bild des 'Mannes Gottes' im alten
Mönchtum" *Antonius Magnus Eremita 356–1956*, StA 38 (Rome: Herder 1956) pp.
148–200.

consent to be in charge of some brothers who had so entreated him, the Abba replied, "No. Be their model (*typos*), not their lawgiver (*nomothetēs*)" (*Apoph.*: Poemen 174). We shall see in the Rule how much St. Benedict absorbed this emphasis upon teaching by example.

The abba in Egyptian cenobitism

Community forms of monastic life arose quite early in Egypt. We are best informed about the *coenobia* that developed in the Thebaid around Pachomius, because a substantial body of Pachomian literature has been preserved. There were, however, a number of other cenobitic developments. The Pachomian literature itself testifies to the existence of other monasteries in southern Egypt. We are informed about *coenobia* in northern Egypt by Cassian, Palladius and the author of the *Historia monachorum*. Generally it seems that they developed around a renowned *abba* who attracted numerous disciples. Such was the case of the *coenobium* of Abba Apollos, of which we are informed by the *Historia monachorum* (*Hist.mon.* 8). As the number of disciples grew, the life became more organized, with common ownership of property, common table and sometimes other common exercises. But the spiritual fatherhood of the abbot for each monk remained the constitutive basis of the *coenobium* as it was for the monks of Scete.

It is far from agreed, however, that every manifestation of cenobitic life was the result of this type of development. Armand Veilleux has argued that genuine cenobitism, which he believes was achieved in Egypt only by Pachomius, is in no sense an outgrowth of the solitary life, but an entirely independent development. The monasteries of northern Egypt, which, he agrees, did emerge from semi-anchoritic groups, were not truly cenobitic, but merely larger assemblies of semi-anchorites: they did not share the ideal of the common life that is the hallmark of the Pachomian institute. According to Veilleux's thesis, the role of the *apa* in Pachomius' monasteries was not that of spiritual father to each monk, but of organizer of a common regime, a subculture, that encouraged the personal development of the majority and of the community as such. It was only in Western cenobitism that the head of the community took on the functions of the spiritual father, thus fusing the cenobitic ideal with that of the desert. Veilleux regards this as a deviation due to Cassian's misrepresentation of the northern Egyptian monasteries as genuine *coenobia*.[30]

---

[30] A. Veilleux, *La liturgie dans le cénobitisme pachômien au quatrième siècle*, StA 57

This thesis supposes that the Pachomian literature is not homogeneous and that much of it testifies to a later development that went beyond the intentions of Pachomius himself. It further supposes that Cassian and other writers have attributed to the *coenobia* of northern Egypt features of the common life that in fact they did not possess. The evidence for these assumptions, however, is less than thoroughly convincing.[31] It is clear, indeed, that the Pachomian texts testify to a degree of evolution in the institute, the precise determination of which is still an open question; but that there was a sharp discontinuity between Pachomius and his immediate successors scarcely seems to be supported by the evidence adduced. And while it is true that Cassian probably never visited any Pachomian monastery, he did have personal knowledge of the *coenobia* in the Delta area, and there is no convincing reason to suggest that he distorted their real character. It is true, moreover, that Pachomius himself only rarely speaks of his own function in terms of fatherhood, but his immediate successors attribute such a role to him, and the authors of the *Lives* depict him as constantly exercising it.

In fact, the most abundant testimony regarding the exercise of spiritual fatherhood by the Egyptian cenobitic *apa* is in the Pachomian literature. Pachomius began his own monastic career in the traditional way, by becoming a disciple of the elder Palamon. Once his training had been completed, however, and he himself began to attract disciples, he took a new direction and formed them into a community. His ideal was the primitive Christian community of Jerusalem as described in Acts. He greatly emphasized the value of brotherhood, fraternal charity and mutual assistance, and always referred to his institute as the *koinōnia*. The importance of the community in his monastic vision is stressed much more by him than by other cenobitic founders in Egypt, about whom, however, we know much less. It is derived from his conception of Christian values and from his reflec-

---

(Rome: Herder 1968); "The Abbatial Office in Cenobitic Life" *MS* 6 (1968) 3–45; "Le rôle de la sous-culture monastique dans la formation du moine" *Nouvelle Revue Théologique* 100 (1978) 734–749. His views are shared in part by F. Ruppert, *Das pachomianische Mönchtum und die Anfänge klösterlichen Gehorsams* (Münsterschwarzach: Vier-Türme Verlag 1971).

[31] See A. de Vogüé "À propos de la théologie de l'abbatiat et de ses implications liturgiques" *Vie Spirituelle Supplément* 87 (1968) 612–614; "Les pièces latines du dossier pachomien: Remarques sur quelques publications récents" *RHE* 67 (1972) 26–67; "Saint Pachôme et son oeuvre d'après plusieurs études récents" *ibid.* 69 (1974) 425–453. The issues involved in this question are lucidly explained and discussed by P. Deseille "Eastern Christian Sources of the Rule of St. Benedict" *MS* 11 (1975) 73–122.

tion upon Scripture, which is the source of his inspiration and the real rule of life for his monks.[32] This stress upon the value of the community, however, is not incompatible with the traditional role of the *apa* as spiritual father, and the evidence suggests that the two were already combined by Pachomius himself and not only by later Western founders.

The Pachomian literature speaks of Pachomius himself in much the same way as the *Apophthegmata* speaks of the elders of the desert. He is given the titles "apa" and "man of God" and spoken of as "blessed" and "holy." It is recognized that he possessed the charismatic gifts characteristic of a *pneumatophoros*: absorption in prayer, discernment of spirits, humility, extraordinary asceticism, visions, *kardiognōsis*, power over demons, understanding of the Scriptures. There is also a new element, for he is venerated further as founder and propagator of a way of life by his followers and as intercessor for them.[33] The basis of his recognition as father, however, is certainly his exercise of spiritual fatherhood on behalf of his monks.[34]

To fulfill this function on behalf of others was the vocation of which Pachomius became conscious early in his career. The *Lives* relate that, in response to his desire to know the will of God, he was told in a visionary experience that God's will for him was "that you serve the human race to reconcile it with him." Pachomius, who had been living a semi-anchoritical form of life, was astonished, but then remembered the resolve he had made when he was a conscript and first experienced the charity of Christians. Consequently, he recognized the inspiration as a genuine message from the Lord. From this time onward he sought to become the servant of all, desiring to imitate Christ through *diakonia* and thus bring others to him.[35] The Greek *Life* tells how he not only instructed his first candidates "according to the Scriptures," but personally served them by preparing the meals, attending

[32] On the Pachomian *koinōnia*, see Veilleux, *La liturgie*, pp. 167–197; H. Bacht "Antonius und Pachomius: Von der Anachorese zum Cönobitentum" *Antonius Magnus Eremita*, pp. 66–107 (see note 29 above).

[33] That the veneration of a founder of a religious order by his followers began already with Pachomius has been demonstrated by J.-F. Gilmont "Paternité et médiation du fondateur d'Ordre" *RAM* 40 (1964) 393–426.

[34] On the spiritual fatherhood of Pachomius, see H. Bacht, *Das Vermächtnis des Ursprungs* (Würzburg: Echter Verlag 1972) pp. 213–224; Ruppert, *Das pachomianische Mönchtum*, pp. 159–166; P. Deseille, *L'esprit du monachisme pachômien*, Spiritualité Orientale 2 (Nantes: Abbaye de Bèllefontaine 1968) pp. vii–xix.

[35] The fullest account is in *Vita sa*[3]: Lefort 60–61. See Ruppert, *Das pachomianische Mönchtum*, pp. 30–31, "Die Berufung zum Klostergründer."

to visitors and caring for the sick. He wanted them to be free for studying the psalms and other parts of Scripture, especially the Gospel, and himself found contemplative peace (*anapausis*) "in serving God and you, according to God's command" (*Vita prima* 24). Here we find the familiar concern to teach by example rather than by word.

The accent on service of others, however, on brotherhood and on a humility that would not permit any kind of preference in his own favor is distinctive of Pachomius' understanding of his role. His inspiration is purely evangelical. He had no higher education and in fact shared the Coptic peasant's suspicion of Greek learning, condemning Origen as an arch-heretic (*Vita prima* 3,56). But he understood the simplicity of the Gospel as a way of life and knew that to communicate it to others, he had to act as Jesus did. His overriding concern was to win souls, to deepen the religious life of each of his monks, to promote the growth of persons. The creation of a disciplinary regime was entirely secondary to this end; still lower in the hierarchy of values was the material and economic framework that sustained the temporal life of the monks, necessary as both of these considerations were for the smooth functioning of what became large communities. Pachomius insisted upon a firm, even harsh discipline and could be severe in dealing with delinquency when the case warranted such treatment. His rule at first reading seems harsh and impersonal, but it gives only the external norms of behavior that were required, without conveying the warmth of inspiration that motivated them. The *Lives* and the *Catecheses* are needed to complete the image of Pachomius as teacher and model.

The terminology of fatherhood and sonship is used frequently in the *Lives* to express the relationship of the *apa* to his monks. One of the Coptic *Lives* begins by exalting Pachomius as father: the author quotes Isaiah's "Look to Abraham your father" (Isa 51:2), argues that Jesus' prohibition against giving the title "father" to a man (Matt 23:9) does not apply, and apparently understands the "father of spirits" of Heb 12:9 of Pachomius. All this has been said, he continues, "so that you may know for certain that a man who begets another in the work of God is his father after God, both in this age and in the other." He then speaks of Paul's begetting sons "not only by the gospel, but also by good and admirable deeds," and concludes: "Such indeed is the case of our father Pachomius, because our Father who is in heaven dwells in him. . . . All those who resemble the Apostle in their actions deserve to be called fathers because of the Holy Spirit who dwells in them" (*Vita sa* [3]).

Pachomius himself, while he emphasized the brotherhood of all and firmly resisted any special consideration that would set him apart, seems nevertheless to have thought of himself as a father as well. The terminology appears only rarely on his own lips, as when he says to a man who has come to enter the monastery, "When we shall have seen that you have walked in the way that I shall direct you, then I am prepared to take care of you, like a father, in everything that your salvation requires" (*Vita bo* 115). He also spoke of other monks as fathers: when entrusting a young monk to the care of an elder, he said, "Here is your father after God: everything that you see him do, you shall do. If he fasts, you will fast with him, and you will act just as he does; if he sits at table to eat, you will sit beside him and eat; when he gets up, you will get up with him; you will do nothing without him, and go nowhere without his permission" (*Vita sa*[5] 93). This text is reminiscent of the elder-disciple relationship of the semi-anchorites of Scete and shows the similarity of Pachomius' concept of spiritual fatherhood to that of the desert.[36]

This text also shows how Pachomius shared the burden of spiritual fatherhood with other experienced monks in the community. His institute grew so rapidly that he had to divide the community into "houses," which consisted of smaller groupings of monks under a subordinate superior—the ancestor of the deaneries of St. Benedict. Later he established other monasteries both up and down the Nile, which were not independent but formed a single *koinōnia*; nevertheless, these monasteries at a distance naturally had to be governed by other monks dependent on Pachomius. In choosing these superiors, he was guided solely by the consideration that they be spiritual men, capable of leading others to growth: "He appointed certain ones, among qualified brothers, to help him in what pertained to the salvation of their souls" (*Vita bo* 26). Horsiesius later told the monks: "Brothers, hearing what is written, 'He who exalts himself shall be humbled,' let us watch over ourselves. It is not for everyone to govern souls, but only for perfect men. There is a parable that an unbaked brick laid in a foundation near a river will not last for a single day, but a baked one lasts like a rock" (*Vita prima* 126).

The role of these superiors was, then, not merely disciplinary and

---

[36] If Pachomius only infrequently referred to himself as father, it was because he recognized that he was only a mediator; the real father is God. Thus he said to Theodore upon the latter's arrival at the monastery, "Don't cry, my son, for I am a servant of your Father" (*Vita bo* 30). On another occasion he said, "I have never considered myself to be the father of the brothers, for only God is their father" (*Vita prima* 108).

administrative; they were regarded as true spiritual fathers, though in subordination to Pachomius and his successor. They and the men who took his place as father of the entire *koinōnia* after his death were, in a certain sense, identified with Pachomius, so that it was his fatherhood they exercised. They made his pastoral concern present and operative when and where he could not exercise it directly. Thus Horsiesius, upon the death of Theodore, cried out that Pachomius had been taken from them (*Vita bo* 207); and when he was himself installed in Theodore's place, the brothers rejoiced "as if they saw our father Pachomius and Theodore in their midst" (*Vita bo* 208). The basis for this quasi-identification was the conviction that his collaborators shared in the charism of Pachomius himself.

The appointment of monks to be superiors seems to have been regarded as the choice of God himself: the designation by Pachomius or another, or even the consensus of the brotherhood, was only the recognition of the will of God. Thus when Horsiesius succeeded Theodore, the Coptic author wrote: "The God of our father Pachomius, of Apa Petronius and of Apa Theodore, he who is merciful, compassionate, and of abundant pity, placed his blessing on Apa Horsiesius, and the angels put their hands upon him; and all the brothers as well as the elders of the monasteries received him and confirmed him as their father. . . . After this, the holy archbishop Apa Athanasius heard it reported that the holy father Apa Theodore had died and that God had put Apa Horsiesius in his place to nourish the souls of the brothers" (*Vita sa* [3b]). The source of the father's authority, then, is purely charismatic. We are told, indeed, that the bishop of Tentyra, in whose diocese the first Pachomian monasteries were located, asked St. Athanasius to ordain Pachomius, "a father and man of God," to be "father and priest of all the monks of the region" (*Vita prima* 30). No doubt the bishop was worried about the sudden growth of the monastic movement and saw the need for hierarchical control. Pachomius escaped ordination by hiding, however, and always remained a layman, as was the case with the majority of the desert elders.

The fatherhood of Pachomius and his successors and subordinates was exercised in the way that was traditional in the desert: teaching by both word and example. Pachomius frequently instructed his monks by means of the *catechesis* or conference. In each monastery there were three such instructions weekly, given by the father, and two others given in the "houses" by the subordinate superiors. A number of examples of these catecheses have survived in both Greek and Coptic.[37] Their chief characteristic is their intensely biblical interest; sometimes they are little more than chains of scriptural texts or are entirely devoted to interpreting passages of Scripture. One of the charisms of a Man of God was the understanding of the Scriptures. The Bible was seen, however, as a practical rule of life, and therefore the understanding of it was revealed in the exemplary conduct of the Man of God. Pachomius, although he was "abbot general" of the whole *koinōnia*, lived as a simple monk in one of the houses and was subject to its "dean." He showed his monks how to live by serving as a visible model of the monastic life, and especially of the patience and compassion of Christ. He is accordingly firmly in the tradition of a father's formation of his sons by word and example.

The superior in other cenobitic traditions

Some notable differences distinguish the monastic movement of Cappadocia from that of Egypt. It seems to have originated with groups of Christians who banded together to live the ascetic life. Basil himself began in this way with members of his own family, after the completion of his studies and of a journey to visit the monastic establishments of the East (see Introduction, pp. 31–32). It was an independent movement, no doubt connected with the ascetical currents of Syria, but without dependence upon the monastic developments in Egypt. Basil never uses the Egyptian terminology (e.g., monk, abbot) and declares himself opposed to the solitary life. It was an entirely different situation from that of the desert, where individuals went to an elder to seek guidance. Basil came to occupy a position of leadership among the groups of ascetics after he became a priest and a bishop. He wished to encourage and strengthen the movement, to provide it with a solid theological foundation, and to purge it of error and deviation. His so-called Rules are simply a collection of his answers to the questions and problems submitted by ascetics.[38]

In these circumstances, it is obvious that Basil's relationship to his followers was different from that of the elders of Nitria or the Pachomian *apas* to their respective disciples. The communities did not grow up around a renowned *abba*, as in Egypt; the communities existed

[37] See *Vita prima* 56-57,96-97,102 (Pachomius); 118,126 (Horsiesius); 131,135,140-142 (Theodore).

[38] See J. Gribomont "Saint Basile" *Théologie de la vie monastique*, Théologie 49 (Paris: Aubier 1961) pp. 99–113 and the literature therein cited.

first and then sought an appropriate organization and government. Consequently, the process is inverted: the superior is a product of the community rather than vice versa. As a result, the concept of spiritual fatherhood does not have the same fundamental importance that it assumed in Egypt; and the community itself, based upon the New Testament idea of Christian fellowship, assumes greater prominence. The community, moreover, was the ordinary Christian community, at least at first, for the movement was originally more of an attempt to reform the whole Church than to create a special way of life within it for a minority. Gradually, however, it developed more and more into what we today would call a religious community.

In the first edition of his *Asceticon*, which was known to St. Benedict in the translation of Rufinus, Basil speaks twice of the "one in charge." He emphasizes, on the one hand, his duty to God, namely, to be faithful to the divine will and to the Scriptures in everything he commands; and, on the other, his duty to the members of his community, to be "like a nurse caring for her children," prepared to give not only the Gospel but even his life for their sake (Basil. *reg.* 15). When it is necessary to correct them, he must have the concern of a father and a doctor for a son who is sick (Basil. *reg.* 24). His brother, Gregory of Nyssa, who continued Basil's work in furthering the ascetic movement in Asia Minor, uses similar language in his ascetical works. In the treatise *On Virginity*, he emphasizes the need for the young and immature to find a "good guide and teacher" to advise them in regard to undertaking the ascetic life (Greg.Nys. *virg.* 23). In his later treatise *On the Christian Mode of Life*, he specifies the obligations of the "one in charge": above all he must have humility, serve the brothers in a self-effacing manner, and make his own life an example for them. He is to "provide instruction according to the need of each," but in this he is compared, not to a father, but to a *paedagogōs*, the slave to whom the father entrusts his children to see that they are taught. He is to adapt himself carefully to the individual needs of each (Greg.Nys. *inst.christ*: Jaeger, p. 69; FC, p. 146).

These profoundly evangelical ideas coincide in many respects with the views of the Egyptians. Indeed, the Cappadocians have a different point of departure: the charismatic elder and his role in the formation of spiritual sons does not stand at the center of their preoccupations. Nevertheless, they are concerned that the superior teach both by word and by example and, like Pachomius, insist that he be the first to give an example of humility and *diakonia*. Despite the diversity of situation and approach, in practice the difference between the functioning of a Basilian *proestōs* and that of a Pachomian *apa* was perhaps not very marked, simply because both had independently drunk from the pure source of the Gospel.

Augustine too, despite his respect for the monastic heroes of Egypt, acted quite independently of them in formulating his own concept of monastic life. For him it was a matter of fashioning his own version of the ascetical ideal that he had come to know at Milan and Rome, and that was sweeping all through the West at the end of the fourth century (see Introduction, "Monasticism in Roman Africa," pp. 59f.). His inspiration was the ideal of fraternal unity that he found so impressive in the Acts of the Apostles; hence for him the point of departure was the *community*. After the rather leisurely ventures of Cassiciacum and Tagaste, he fully implemented his ideal of the common life, common ownership and *unanimitas* at the garden monastery of Hippo in 391. The superior of the group was not called *abbas*, but simply *praepositus*, the 'one placed over.'

Only at the end of the *Regula ad servos Dei* does Augustine speak *ex professo* of the *praepositus*. He says that obedience is to be shown to him "as to a father." He is looked upon as representing God to the brothers, for Augustine says that dishonor shown to him would be an offense against God. He is to be outstanding in humility, motivated by charity and not by the wish to dominate others. He is to console, correct or come to the aid of the brothers, as the needs of each determine. He must maintain discipline, but seek to be loved more than feared. His own good example should be the principal means of exercising an influence upon others. He should always remember that he will have to give an accounting to God for the way in which he has fulfilled the duty entrusted to him (Aug. *reg.serv.* 7,1-4).

We do not know how the superior was chosen, but his authority was not supreme, for he was to refer serious matters to the *presbyter*, apparently a priest appointed by the bishop as overseer of the community (Aug. *reg.serv.* 7,2). As in Cappadocia, this Augustinian form of the common life was more integrated into the local church and under hierarchical authority than was generally the case in Egypt. Nothing is said of the charismatic gifts of the *praepositus*, even if he is thought to represent God and to act as a father. Nevertheless, the qualities and the service required of him, precisely because of their intensely biblical inspiration, are scarcely different from what we find in the Pachomian literature. St. Benedict was profoundly influenced by Augustine's assimilation of evangelical values, and we find some of the great Doctor's memorable phrases echoed in the Rule.

Benedict's understanding of the abbot

St. Benedict devotes two entire chapters to the abbot: chapter 2 deals with the nature of his task and the manner of its exercise, and chapter 64 treats of the selection and installation of the abbot, adding further observations on the personal qualities of the man chosen for the role, which complete but do not alter what is said in chapter 2.

The text of St. Benedict's chapter 2 is almost certainly derived from the corresponding chapter (also chapter 2) of the *Regula Magistri*. While some details might be interpreted in such a way as to make a case for the priority of the RB, it has been shown that the order of material in the chapter constitutes an overwhelming argument for its dependence upon the RM.[39] The latter displays a structure that has been very carefully worked out, employing the techniques of repetition, *inclusio* and chiasm. It is divided into four sections of approximately equal length,[40] of which the first and fourth correspond to each other, treating the same subjects in nearly the same order. These introductory and concluding sections deal with the nature of the abbot's role and answer the question "What is an abbot?" The second and third sections also correspond to each other, for each treats, in identical order, of the same two themes: the twofold character of the abbot's teaching and the equality of treatment he should extend to all without prejudice. The first of these themes is embellished, in both sections, though in different locations, with a sub-theme developing the idea that each of the two kinds of teaching suits a particular kind of disciple.

The entire structure, therefore, forms a great chiasm, within which a series of elements forms inclusions or marks off development of thought by carefully placed repetitions. Thus the solemn intonation of the word *abbas* introduces each of the four sections:

"An *abbot* who is worthy to be in charge. . . . (1)
Therefore when anyone takes on the name of *abbot*. . . . (11)
In his teaching, the *abbot* should always observe. . . . (23)
The *abbot* should remember always what he is. . . ." (30)

---

[39] De Vogüé, *La communauté*, pp. 78–186, has analyzed chapter 2 exhaustively. Earlier studies are those of F. Masai "La Règle de S. Benoît et la 'Regula Magistri'" *Latomus* 6 (1947) 207–229; J. McCann "The Rule of the Master" *DR* 57 (1939) 3–22. See also B. Steidle "Abbas/Tyrannus: Zur Abtsidee der Regel St. Benedikts" *BM* 24 (1948) 335–348, and, more recently, "Memor periculi Heli sacerdotis de Silo. Zum Abtsbild der Regel St. Benedikts (Kap. 2,26)" *EA* 52 (1976) 5–18.

[40] More precisely, five sections: the last concerns the question of consulting the community, which forms chapter 3 in the RB. In this section, however, there is little correspondence between the text of the RB and that of the RM.

It is obvious that such a carefully structured literary development must be the work of a single mind, and indeed of a mind that operates with exceptional logic and clarity.

On the other hand, the corresponding chapter of the RB displays a portion of the same clear structure, but in a mutilated form. While the first section is almost identical to that of the RM and the second differs only slightly, the third has disappeared except for the sub-theme and is partially replaced by an exhortation to eliminate evils promptly. The concluding section lacks one of the elements that in the RM forms an inclusion with the introduction, and contains a passage that has no correspondence elsewhere. It is easy enough to see how the text of the RM could have been altered into the present chapter 2 of the RB by someone who either did not perceive the clear structure or else was not concerned to preserve it. On the other hand, it is almost impossible to imagine how a redactor, confronting the text of the RB, could have transformed it into the precise architecture of the RM. Indeed, commentators have never been able to discern a clear outline of the material in RB 2;[41] it is only when it is compared with the RM that the structure emerges and the redactional process can be reconstructed. By omitting three passages of the RM and adding three new ones in adjacent places, St. Benedict has profoundly disturbed the original order, though he has improved the content. This can best be seen in the following outline:[42]

RM	RB
INTRODUCTION (1-10)	INTRODUCTION (1-10)
1. Name ABBOT = one who takes Christ's place (1-3)	1. Name ABBOT = one who takes Christ's place (1-3)
2. Teaching must conform to divine precepts (4-5)	2. Teaching must conform to divine precepts (4-5)
3. Responsible for his teaching and for monks' obedience (6)	3. Responsible for his teaching and for monks' obedience (6)
4. Must account at Judgment for disciples' souls (7-10)	4. Must account at Judgment for disciples' souls (7-10)
FIRST SECTION (11-22)	FIRST SECTION (11-22)
1st theme: Twofold teaching: word and deed (11-15)	*1st theme:* Twofold teaching: word and deed (11-15)
Sub-theme: Different types of teaching for dif-	*Sub-theme:* Different types of teaching for dif-

[41] See the commentaries of A. Lentini, O. Cunill and I. Herwegen.

[42] De Vogüé, *La communauté*, pp. 78–100. See also Appendix 7, pp. 488–493, for comparative texts.

ferent types of person (12b)	ferent types of person (12b)
2nd theme: Equal charity to all (16-22)	*2nd theme:* Equal charity to all (16-22)
	[*1st addition:* Rank of monks (RB 18b-19)]
	[*1st omission:* RM 21]
SECOND SECTION (23-31)	SECOND SECTION (23-29)
1st theme: Twofold teaching: word and deed (23-29)	_____
Sub-theme: Different types of teaching for different types of person (23-25)	*Sub-theme:* Different types of teaching for different types of person (23-25)
2nd theme: Equal charity to all (30-31)	_____
	[*2nd omission:* RM 26-31]
	[*2nd addition:* Eliminate evils promptly (RB 26-29)]
CONCLUSION (32-40)	CONCLUSION (30-40)
1. Name ABBOT = more is required of him (32)	1. Name ABBOT = more is required of him (30)
	[*3rd addition:* Temporal concerns secondary (31-36)]
2. Must account at Judgment for disciples' souls (33-36)	2. Must account at Judgment for disciples' souls (37-38)
	[*3rd omission:* RM 35-38]
3. Teaching must conform to divine precepts (37-38)	
4. Will also have to account for his own soul (39-40)	4. Will also have to account for his own soul (39-40)

As a matter of methodology, therefore, the teaching of the RM on the abbot must first be examined; its author sets forth his doctrine with completeness and clarity. St. Benedict is much more brief and trenchant. For him, mere allusion often replaces detailed exposition. His disagreement with the Master can sometimes be discerned in what he omits or alters, his own concerns in what he adds. Fundamentally, however, except where differences are stated or can reasonably be inferred, it can be assumed that he accepts the Master's teaching. The agreements are more extensive and more important than the differences. Thus it appears that Benedict accepts the Master's theology of the abbatial office, even though he omits a significant passage in which this theology is expounded (RM 1.82-92). This occurs at the end of chapter 1 and forms a link with the chapter on the abbot that follows. Such logical connections between chapters are frequent in the RM and often omitted by the RB in its concern to abbreviate.

In these two paragraphs omitted by St. Benedict, the Master explains that the Lord gave the Church three degrees of *doctrina*: first the prophets, then the apostles, finally the *doctores*. Here he is citing the list of charisms in 1 Cor 12:28 (apostles, prophets, teachers), but has placed the prophets first, understanding this term to refer to the Old Testament prophets.[43] Accordingly, the three categories are taken not simultaneously but successively: the prophets in Old Testament times, the apostles in the days of the early Church, the teachers today. The latter continue the mission of the apostles to be shepherds of the Lord's flock; to them are addressed the words, "Feed my sheep" (John 21:17). The Lord's sheepfolds are of two kinds: "churches" and "schools of Christ." The former term refers to local churches; the latter, to monasteries. It is explained elsewhere in the RM that each of these has its own hierarchy: the former has bishops, priests, deacons and clerics; the latter, abbots and provosts (RM 11.6-12).

The monastery, therefore, is analogous to a local church, and the abbot to a bishop. Both receive from the Lord the authority to rule over their respective sheepfolds, as well as the *doctrina* they hand on to their sheep. To both are addressed the words of Christ: "He who hears you, hears me" (Luke 10:16). The abbot, then, like the bishop, has a divine commission to preside over the school of Christ entrusted to him. He is in the line of apostolic succession, heir to that teaching that comes down from the apostles and that they in turn received from Christ. Accordingly it is called "the commands of the Lord" and "the divine precepts" (RM/RB 2.12). Since the abbot is a layman, it is not by virtue of sacramental ordination that he inherits the promise of

---

[43] This was in fact a variant reading, attested to by Hier. *in Zach.* 1. A similar inversion is found in variant texts of Eph 2:20: the variant indicates a tendency of scribes to understand these "prophets" as Old Testament personages rather than New Testament figures. See A. de Vogüé, *La Règle du Maître*, SC 105,106,107 (Paris: Éditions du Cerf 1964–65) 1.348, n.82; 2.50, n.14.

Christ: he belongs not to the sacramental but to the charismatic hierarchy.

If Benedict does not develop this teaching in detail, there are nevertheless indications that he tranquilly accepted it, though with some nuances. For him, too, the monastery is a "school" (Prol.45) and the abbot a *doctor* (5.6), even though these terms are used only once each and never explained. Further, the apostolic succession is presupposed, as is clear from the application of "He who hears you, hears me" (Luke 10:16) to monastic superiors (5.6), as in the RM (11.11). The abbot of the RB is likewise a shepherd to whom the *paterfamilias* has entrusted a flock, which he is to feed with his *doctrina* (2.6-10; see 27.8). St. Benedict has adopted almost unchanged the first ten verses of the RM's chapter 2, in which the latter builds upon the theory of apostolic mission just enunciated at the end of the preceding chapter.

In this passage St. Benedict makes it clear from the outset that the abbot's function is to make Christ present to his monks. He "holds the place of" or "fulfills the role of" Christ in the monastery. That this is so is strictly a matter of faith: "it is believed that . . . ." Reason cannot establish the abbot's role in the cenobitic life; the whole question is a supernatural one. The monk must believe that the abbot is for him the mouthpiece of Christ, as the bishop is for the faithful of his local church, as the apostles were for the primitive Christian community and the prophets for the people of Israel. He is a mediator who bridges the gap between Christ and the monk, interpreting for him the Gospel teaching as it applies specifically to him, making the word of Christ alive and actual in the present moment. He is a channel through whom the word and will of Christ come to the monk.

The Rule relates this essential function of the abbot to his title *abbas*: this name means 'father,' and the essential role of the abbot is to be a father to his monks. The teaching is supported by reference to a biblical text in which the term *abba* is associated with the sonship of the Christian: "You have received the spirit of the adoption of sons, in which we cry out, 'Abba, Father!'" (Rom 8:15). That the abbot should be spoken of as father to his monks is not surprising in view of what has already been said of the monastic tradition of spiritual fatherhood exercised by the elder. What is surprising, however, at least at first sight, is that this name "Father" is said to be *Christ's* name: "He takes Christ's place in the monastery . . . when he is called by his name" (2.2). Hence the cry of the Christian to his heavenly Father is directed to Christ rather than to God the Father! This question of the fatherhood of Christ will be discussed in the next section.

The definition of the abbot as father must, of course, be understood in the light of the tradition of spiritual paternity that we have previously sketched. Just as the Egyptian cenobitic founders absorbed this tradition from the elders of the desert and adapted it to their own situation, the Western legislators likewise derived it from their Eastern models. As in the East, the analogy is based upon the transmission of teaching, and precisely the kind of teaching ("formation" is perhaps a better term) that a parent gives to his children. Consequently, the abbot is primarily a *doctor*, as the RM makes clear. St. Benedict does not use this term in chapter 2, but the entire treatment is filled with other terms that belong to the vocabulary of teaching and learning: the abbot hands on *doctrina, veritas, iussio, admonitio, praecepta* and *mandata*; his activity is called *docere, monstrare, proponere* and *animas regere*; the monks are called *discipuli* and *filii*. The abbot is called *pater* and *magister* (2.24; see Prol.1). The response of the monks to him should be that of *oboedientia*.

Another analogy occurs throughout the chapter: the abbot is related to his monks as a shepherd is to the sheep under his care. This is, of course, one of the most familiar biblical metaphors. David, who tended the sheep of his father Jesse, was taken from the domestic sheepfold to be put in charge of the flock of Israel by Yahweh their owner (2 Sam 7:8; Ps 77 [78]:70-71). For this reason, his descendants, the kings of Judah, were referred to as shepherds to whom God had entrusted his sheep (Jer 2:8). When the shepherds proved unfaithful and untrustworthy, Yahweh took back his flock and shepherded it himself until a new shepherd might be sent who could be relied upon to safeguard the sheep (Ezek 34:1-24; Jer 23:1-4). This was his own Son, who identifies himself as the Good Shepherd (John 10:1-16) who enters into a personal relationship with each of his sheep. To continue his work of shepherding, Christ commissioned his disciples to feed his sheep (John 21:15-17). The successors of the apostles continue the task of shepherding the flock Christ has assembled (Acts 20:28-29; 1 Pet 5:1-4), trying to ensure that none goes astray (Matt 18:12-14; Luke 15:3-7).

The shepherd's role is carried out in the various churches by the bishops, who are the mediators of grace for their flock. In the "school for the service of the Lord" (i.e., Christ), it is the abbot who fulfills the task of the shepherd, taking the place of the Supreme Shepherd. Here, however, Christ is the *paterfamilias*, the head of the family and of the entire estate, to whom the flock belongs. The abbot is a subordinate, an employee, so to speak, of the *paterfamilias*; to him is entrusted the care of the flock. If they do not turn out well, their defects are laid to the blame of the shepherd, who shall have to give an accounting to the owner, unless, indeed, the shepherd did the best he could but the sheep refused to obey (RB 2.7-10). The sarabaites are regarded as false cenobites because they lack the one element most necessary to a real *coenobium*: a shepherd (1.8). Hence the monasteries in which they live are not "the Lord's" sheepfolds but only their own; he is not the *paterfamilias* of these sheep, for his representative, the abbot, is not there to act for him on their behalf. The Rule sketches the image of Christ the loving Shepherd as a model for the abbot to follow (27.8-9).[44]

Still another metaphor introduced to explain the abbot's task is that of physician, which occurs in chapter 28, though in the very last verse the sheep metaphor returns. Here he is advised to act as a doctor would in dealing with "sick" brothers, i.e., those who refuse to amend their evil ways even after being corrected and disciplined. The wise doctor uses various remedies, which increase progressively in severity and in the violence they do to the patient, inflicting pain on him, however, only in order to benefit him by effecting a cure. The last step is amputation; it is invoked only if all else fails. Likewise the abbot must vary his remedies according to the nature of the disease and the constitution of the patient, applying progressively more severe disciplinary penalties. His motive is solely medicinal: if his remedies are painful, it is only because he wants to cure the sickness. Only as a last resort does he amputate "so that one diseased sheep may not infect the whole flock." In fact, the chapter concludes with a mixing of metaphors.

Finally, the abbot is compared to a trusted servant or steward of the household. In 64.7, St. Benedict says that the abbot will have to give an accounting of his stewardship, *vilicatio*: the word used in the Latin versions to translate the Greek term *oikonomia*, 'the management of the household.' In the New Testament it is used only in Luke 16:1, to refer to the "unjust steward." This official was manager of the entire

---

[44] The portrait of the shepherd in 27.8-9 is clearly meant to be Christological: he is called "the Good Shepherd" and his shoulders are "sacred." It borrows elements from Matt 18:12-13 (the mountains, the strayed sheep, the searching), from Luke 15:4-7 (the carrying on the shoulders), and from John 10:1-16 (the Good Shepherd). The Fathers frequently gave a Christological interpretation of the sheep parable: Orig. *hom. in Iesu Nave* 7,6; Meth. *conviv.* 3,6; Greg.Nys. *adv.Apoll.* 16, *cont.Eun.* 4,12, *in Eccl.* 2; Hier. *in Matt.* 18,12; Ambr. *in Luc.* 15,4; Iren. *demonstr.apost.praedic.* 33, *adv.haer.* 3,19,3; 3,23,8; Tert. *pud.* 7,1.

property of a wealthy owner, who trusted him to administer his household. The same idea is further developed in 64.21-22: ". . . when he has ministered well he will hear from the Lord what that good servant heard who gave his fellow servants grain at the proper time: 'I tell you solemnly,' he said, 'he has set him over all his possessions.'" The reference here is principally to Matt 24:45-47, with allusion to Matt 25:21 and 1 Tim 3:13. The servant in question has been singled out by the owner of the household for a task involving responsibility: to dispense rations to all the members of the household during the owner's absence. He acquits himself well, and upon his return the owner makes him chief steward, putting him over all his property. This metaphor, then, points to the abbot's task as administrator of the community and all its property and affairs, both spiritual and temporal. Again, the abbot is not the owner but a subordinate who must give an accounting to Christ, his Master, of his stewardship.

Father, teacher, shepherd, doctor, steward — these are the titles and functions attributed to the abbot analogically in order to elucidate his role. The RM contains one other that St. Benedict omitted: that of mother. The Master says that the abbot should show the brothers the tenderness of a father and the love of a mother (RM 2.31). The image is not unusual in Patristic literature and is rich in significance. It occurs in the six verses of the second section of the RM (2.26-31) that the RB omits entirely to make room for 2.26-29. Given Benedict's penchant for abbreviating, especially to compensate for an addition to the text of the RM, the omission does not necessarily imply the author's rejection of the analogy.

It should be noted that all the imagery of the two Rules is eminently biblical; the entire description of the abbot is drawn from biblical themes and in no sense from profane sources. Further, most of these are images that have traditionally been applied to Christ, either in Scripture itself (teacher, shepherd, doctor) or by the Fathers (father, mother). The abbot is identified as another Christ—as the one who represents him in the monastery—by application to him of the very titles that define the role of Christ himself.

This observation about the biblical source of the themes employed has in fact considerable methodological significance. Scholars seeking to elucidate the RB have often turned to profane documents and to the secular culture of the time to which they witness.[45] They have accord-

---

[45] See C. Butler, *Benedictine Monachism: Studies in Benedictine Life and Rule* (London: Longmans, Green and Co. 1919); J. Chapman, *St. Benedict and the Sixth*

ingly taken the society of the late empire and its surviving social institutions as the background out of which the Rule is to be understood. The order and severity reflected in Benedict's legislation are seen as a product of the Roman legal mind and the *Nursina durities* of its author. Therefore, monastic profession can be compared to the oath of the Roman soldier, the monastic chapter to the corporation in Roman law, the cenobitic community to the *familia* of late Roman society, and the abbot to the *paterfamilias* of the household. The plenary authority of the abbot is thus comparable to the provisions of Roman law, the *domesticus magistratus*, by which the *paterfamilias* had complete control over his children and slaves, even the power of life and death, and responsibility for their actions likewise fell upon him.

At first sight this comparison seems illuminating. In fact, however, there is not the slightest evidence for it in the texts. The only time the term *paterfamilias* occurs in the RM and RB it does not refer to the abbot but to Christ: the abbot is only the shepherd to whom the *paterfamilias* entrusts his sheep. This passage, in fact, shows that the image of the *paterfamilias* is not really appropriate for the abbot, for the latter is never envisaged as the owner whose authority is absolute and all-embracing. His role is more humble: he is only a *vices gerens*, one who takes the place of, and tries to discern and execute the will of, the real owner, Christ. Envisaged in political terms, it is true that the abbatial office looks like an unlimited monarchy in which one man holds sway; from this point of view, he may seem to resemble the Roman *paterfamilias*. But the whole issue is precisely that this point of view is incapable of penetrating to the reality: the abbot cannot be understood in purely political terms, for his function transcends the political sphere.

To say this is not to deny that the abbatial office is, like all human institutions, culture-conditioned and therefore subject to variations of understanding and execution with the passage of time. On this score, history is richly instructive. To this extent the analogy with profane institutions is not totally beside the point, for it is scarcely possible for people of any period to be uninfluenced in their perception of religious institutions by the pre-understanding they have gained from their environment. But a close examination of the RB reveals that its author derived his understanding of what an abbot should be, not from

---

Century (1929; rpt. Westwood, Conn.: Greenwood Press, Inc. 1972); I. Herwegen, *Sinn und Geist der Benediktinerregel* (Einsiedeln: Benziger 1944).

profane analogies, but from a religious tradition deeply rooted in the Bible. Every theme and image that he invokes is biblical. The monastic legislators were heirs of a tradition; they read, cited and built upon their predecessors, and thereby gradually accumulated a fund of highly traditional doctrines and institutions, rooted in the Scriptures and always seeking their justification in the Word of God. They developed and lived in what can rightly be called a religious subculture, and it was this rather than the dominant culture of the world outside that formed the principal influence upon their thought and institutions. In order to understand these, therefore, we must explore their monastic background and environment in preference to the secular structures of the period, without denying that the latter also exercised some influence.

What an abbot ought to be, however, what he should do and how he should do it were clearly mapped out long before the sixth century dawned. The Western rules are in this respect, as in most others, derived from the Eastern doctrine and practice. We have seen, however, that Eastern monasticism was by no means univocal. What precisely, then, is the source of Benedict's concept of the abbot, which he has taken over with only minor nuances?

Clearly, the RB and the RM are in the tradition of spiritual fatherhood. We have seen that this, and the use of the title *abba* to designate the bearer of it, originated in Egypt, so far as our documentation permits us to judge, and first flourished among the semi-anchoritic elders. It is probably the full-blown development of the charisms of prophecy and teaching that had been exercised by holy men in Christian communities from the beginning. When cenobitism developed, the spiritual fatherhood of the *abba* was extended to a greater number of disciples. In the Pachomian institute, new elements were added, notably the emphasis upon the importance of the *koinōnia*, and adjustments such as the introduction of subordinates had to be made when the number of disciples increased. But, while these differences may have altered the manner in which the *abba's* fatherhood was actually exercised, they did not change the essential relationship between abbot and monk-disciple. The *coenobium* was an extension of the elder-disciple relationship on a scale that inevitably produced alterations, but this relationship remained the very essence of the cenobitic life.

The first thing that defines an abbot, then, is not his position at the head of a community or an institution but his relationship to persons.

He is a mediator between Christ and each of his monk-disciples. It is through him that Christ reaches into the life of the monk: his word and command come to the monk through the abbot's voice. In him the monk must—by faith—see Christ personified and, as it were, newly made incarnate in quasi-sacramental fashion. The entire purpose of this relationship is educative, in the sense of total spiritual formation. The monastic tradition knew by experience how difficult it is for a Christian, despite good will, to follow God's law and come to salvation unaided. The normal way of working out one's salvation is to learn from another human being who has himself made the journey and is able to guide another along the right path. The abbot is primarily the spiritual father who provides such direction—this is his chief reason for being. He is seen in terms of the biblical tradition of wisdom teacher, prophet and apostle, and of the concept of spiritual father-hood that grew out of it in the early Church.

Since the father-analogy rests upon the transmission of teaching as primary analogue. the abbot's relationship to Christ, on the one hand, and to each monk, on the other, can also be described as *doctor*, 'teacher,' but one who teaches a doctrine that he has himself received from Christ, the real Teacher. The abbot is only a mediator. The same may be said of the images of shepherd and steward: these biblical metaphors also underscore the abbot's position as mediator. His authority is delegated; he is functioning on another's behalf. The *coenobium* exists in order to lead men to salvation by showing them Christ, his teaching and his will. Any other goal it sets for itself is secondary and must remain subordinate to this supreme end. It is a *school*, a place where people come together for their own formation at the hands of a master, a teacher qualified to guide them. Its purpose is achieved to the extent that the ideal is realized in practice. On the one hand, the abbot must be another Christ, a man of authentic and profound Christian conviction and experience, so thoroughly molded by the Word of God that his very being as well as his speech proclaims it unceasingly; a man with a clear understanding that his essential task is the formation of his disciples. The monk, on the other hand, must not only come with this purpose in view but maintain it throughout his life, and, through all the *dura et aspera*, keep firm his faith that the abbot represents and functions as Christ for him.

The fatherhood of Christ

The abbot's role as father is derivative: he is father because he takes the place of Christ, the real Father of the monks. The practice of designating the Second Person of the Trinity as Father may seem theologically eccentric and at variance with the Scriptures. In fact, however, it was a common theme among the Fathers, and the Rule is drawing upon an already rich tradition. Far from moving in a direction other than the Scriptures, the Fathers were developing an idea that seems at least implicitly contained in the New Testament.[46]

The New Testament never applies the title "Father" directly to Christ. This title is reserved to the First Person of the Trinity, who is Creator of all that is and Father of the Son. From the viewpoint of inner Trinitarian relationships, he alone can be Father, and the Second Person, eternally begotten by him, can alone be called Son. From the viewpoint of God's activity outside the Trinity, however, we may consider the Second Person not only in his relation to the Father but also in his relation to us. He is the Mediator through whom God's word and grace descend to us and our response and prayer ascend to the Father. Jesus Christ is truly human like ourselves and at the same time is the Eternal Son.

Insofar as he comes to us as representative of his Father, Jesus exercises the role of fatherhood on our behalf. It is from him that we receive the commandments of God in the Good News of God's complete revelation. He is the complete manifestation of the Father. Therefore, he is the supreme Teacher and as such exercises a role that can be compared to fatherhood. If the New Testament does not call him Father, it does refer to his disciples as his sons. Mark records Jesus as saying, "Children (*tekna*), how hard it is to enter the Kingdom of God!" (Mark 10:24). The usage is more frequent, however, in the Johannine literature. Jesus says to his disciples, "Little children (*teknia*), yet a little while I am with you" (John 13:33); "I will not leave you orphans" (John 14:18); and "Children (*paidia*), have you any fish?" (John 21:5). Strictly speaking, this need be nothing more than a term of endearment for those to whom one feels closely bound; the author of 1 John uses the same diminutive in addressing the Christians to whom he writes.

Divine sonship, however, is a prominent theme both in Paul, who speaks of adoptive sonship, and in John, for whom Christians are children of God because they are begotten of him. Both writers, how-

[46] This question was first explored by H. S. Mayer, *Benediktinisches Ordensrecht in der Beuroner Congregation* (Beuron: Archabbey 1932) 2/1.88–97; it was then taken up by B. Steidle "Heilige Vaterschaft" *BM* 14 (1932) 215–226; "Abba Vater" *ibid.* 16 (1934) 89–101; *The Rule of St. Benedict* (Canon City: Holy Cross Abbey 1967) pp. 82–89. See also O. Casel "Bemerkungen zu einem Text der Regula sancti Benedicti" *SMGBO* 61 (1947) 5–11

ever, speak of children of God, not of Christ; Jesus is Son par excellence, and therefore our elder brother. There is one text, nonetheless, that has perhaps not been sufficiently considered: "Little children, abide in him, so that when he appears we may have confidence . . . . you may be sure that everyone who does right is born of him" (1 John 2:28-29). Though the context suggests that the Christian is born of Christ, the commentators generally recoil from this conclusion on the grounds that Johannine thought, which insists so much upon birth from God, could not tolerate such an idea.[47] There is, however, a respectable history of Patristic interpretation in this sense.[48] Whatever may have been the original author's intent, the Fathers found justification in such New Testament passages for speaking of the fatherhood of Christ.

This idea was also deduced from the text of Isa 9:6, in which the messianic King announced by the prophet is called "Father of the world to come." Since this passage was seen to be fulfilled in Christ by the New Testament (Matt 4:15-16), the Fathers understood this as a title of Christ.[49] Another text of Isaiah (8:18) is quoted by the author of Hebrews: "Here am I, and the children God has given me" (Heb 2:13), who puts it in the mouth of Christ. Although the point of Hebrews is that Christians are children of God and Christ is our brother by reason of assuming our humanity, the quotation from Isaiah can be interpreted in the sense of Christ's fatherhood. In a similar way, the Pauline theme of Christ as second Adam lent support to this view. Since Adam was father of the human race, and Christ has now assumed the role of the new Adam, he can likewise be considered our father.[50]

Patristic developments on the fatherhood of Christ began already in the second century and became increasingly abundant thereafter. In

[47] Among modern commentators, only A. Brooke, *The Johannine Epistles*, ICC (Edinburgh: T. and T. Clark 1912) p. 68 seems to consider seriously that birth from Christ was intended. See the excellent treatment of R. Schnackenburg, *Die Johannesbriefe*, Herders Theologisch. Komm. zum NT 13,3 (Herder: Freiburg 1953) pp. 146–147 and the excursus "Gotteskindschaft und Zeugung aus Gott," pp. 155–162.

[48] Thus, Ambr. *fid. ad Grat.* 4,154; Aug. *tract. in Ioan.* 4,3; Baedae *in 1 Ioan.* 2,29. The latter follows Augustine almost verbatim.

[49] See Orig. *hom. in Num.* 27,2: GCS 30, "The Father of the world to come, who says of himself, 'I am the door. No one comes to the Father except through me.'"

[50] Thus the early apologist Aristides affirms that the Christians trace the origin of their race to the Lord Jesus Christ as the Jews trace theirs to Abraham: Arist. *apol.* 15,1; 14,1. Likewise, Justin Martyr says that Christ has begotten us as Jacob begot Israel: Iust. *dial.* 123,9; 138,2.

the *Acts* of Justin Martyr and his companions, which date from shortly after the middle of the second century, Hierax, when asked about his parents, replies: "Christ is our true father, and our faith in him is our mother" (*Passio Iust.*, recension B,4). Another witness, possibly from even earlier in the second century, is the *Epistula Apostolorum*, in which the apostles say to the risen Lord, "You are our father," and Christ responds by showing how they also are to become fathers and teachers through him by dispensing the word of God, baptism and the forgiveness of sins (*Epist.apost.* 41-42). The apocryphal *Second Letter of Clement* says, "He gave us the light; as a father he called us sons; he saved us when we were perishing" (Ps-Clem. *ad Cor.* 2,1,4). Irenaeus compares Christ to Jacob: as the latter brought forth the twelve tribes, so Christ begot the twelve-pillared foundation of the Church and raised up sons of God (Iren. *adv.haer.* 4,21,3); "the Word of God is the Father of the human race" (*ibid.* 4,31,2). Melito of Sardis, in a list of titles given to Christ, includes that of "father insofar as he begets."[51]

The fatherhood of Christ is especially developed by the Alexandrian Fathers. While for Clement Christ is primarily the *Paedagogos*, the Teacher to whom the Father entrusts his children's instruction, he describes the activity of the Teacher as characterized by tender care and concern like that of a father or mother (Clem. *paed.* 1,6). In the lyrical concluding hymns of the *Paedagogos*, he exalts Christ as Creator, King, Lord and Father, and refers to Christians as "the Christ-begotten" (*ibid.* 3,12). In the *Stromata*, citing Matt 23:9, he says, "'you have only one Father who is in heaven,' but he [Christ] is also the Father of all through creation." The prohibition against calling anyone father on earth means that our human father is not the true cause of our being; "thus he wants us to turn and become children again, recognizing him who is truly our father, when we are reborn through water" (Clem. *strom.* 3,12).

Reference to Christ as Father in the works of Origen, fragmentary as they are, is so frequent as to be almost commonplace. In the *Homilies on Exodus* he explains the phrase "He is my God and the God of my father" of Exod 15:2 as follows: "Our Father who created us and has begotten us is Christ, for he himself tells us, 'I am going to my Father and your Father, to my God and your God.' Hence if I acknowledge

---

[51] G. Racle "À propos du Christ-Père dans l'Homélie Paschale de Méliton de Sardes" *RechSR* 50 (1962) 400–408 shows that this is not an expression of modalistic theology, as some have thought, but concerns the saving activity of Christ.

that God is my God, I will glorify him; but if I further acknowledge that he is the God of my Father, Christ, I will exalt him" (Orig. *hom. in Ex.* 6,2). Commenting elsewhere on the Lucan genealogy, he says, "The origin of all families descended from the God of the universe began with Christ, who came next after the God and Father of the whole universe, and is thus the Father of every soul, as Adam is the father of all human beings" (Orig. *prin.* 4,3,7). In his exegesis of the Gospel parables in which the *paterfamilias* appears, he understands him to be Christ. Thus he interprets the householder of Matt 13:52, who brings forth both new and old from his treasure-house (Orig. *in Matt.* 10,15), and the owner of the vineyard in Matt 20:1-16, who hires laborers to work for him (*ibid.* 15,28). This Christological interpretation became widespread in the West owing to the great influence exercised by Origen upon subsequent exegesis (see Hil. *in Matt.* 20,5; Aug. *serm.* 87,9; Hier. *in Matt.* 4,25).

The theme of Christ's fatherhood appears quite frequently in the Latin Fathers and seems to have been tranquilly accepted as traditional (Ps-Cyp. *adv.Iud.* 2,19; Ambr. *epist.* 76,4; Aug. *epist.* 187). Augustine is typical: "Although God's Son adopted us as sons for his Father, and wished us to have this same Father through grace who was his Father through nature, yet he also shows, as it were, a fatherly attitude toward us when he says, 'I shall not leave you orphans'" (Aug. *in Ioan.* 75). St. Leo the Great, without directly giving the title "Father" to Christ, speaks in a similar way, combining this theme with that of the Shepherd (Leo.M. *tract.* 63,6).

The fatherhood of Christ is but one aspect of a broader phenomenon of devotion to Christ in the early Church, as reflected especially in popular piety. The early Christians did not think of him as a remote and transcendent figure, but as a loving Savior with whom they enjoyed a close personal relationship. As a consequence, they spoke to him intimately in prayer and thought of him with love and affection. This disposition is evident in the earliest acts of the martyrs, which are representative of popular piety.[52] It can also be found, however, in highly sophisticated thinkers among the Fathers, particularly in oblique remarks through which we catch a glimpse of their personal devotion.[53] It is frequent in Origen. A typical example is his well-known statement about the Fourth Gospel: "No one can understand

[52] K. Baus "Das Gebet der Martyrer" *Trierer Theologische Zeitschrift* 62 (1953) 19–32.

[53] K. Baus "Das Gebet beim hl. Hieronymus" *ibid.* 60 (1951) 178–188.

this Gospel unless he has leaned against the breast of Jesus and taken Mary as his Mother" (Orig. *in Ioan.* 1,4).

It is above all in monastic literature that we find evidence of this Christocentric piety. Monasticism grew out of the most devout circles of the second- and third-century Church, the virgins and ascetics, and was strongly marked with the imprint of the spirituality of martyrdom. At a fairly early stage of its development, monastic theorists made extensive use of Origen to explain the ascetical and mystical life. It is not surprising that the tender devotion to Christ that we find in these sources was inherited by the monks.

The concept of Christ as Father seems to have been held in particular honor in monastic circles. An important text of Evagrius of Pontus reveals not only the use of the title "Father" to designate Christ but also its extension in monastic circles to the human spiritual father. His letter seems to be an answer to some monks who had written asking for spiritual counsel, "the fruits of charity." He replies: "It is more fitting for you to seek the fruits of charity among yourselves, since divine charity possesses you as a result of *apatheia*, and indeed the sons do not provide riches for their fathers, but fathers for their sons. Therefore, since you are fathers, imitate Christ your Father, and nourish us at the appointed time with barley loaves through instruction for the betterment of our lives" (Evagr. *epist.* 61).[54] That a similar concept was current in Syria seems clear from its frequent appearance in St. Ephraim, who stresses especially the parallelism with Adam and the function of baptism as the rebirth in which Christ begets sons and daughters to be brought to birth by the Church.[55]

The position of the Rule, then, is to be evaluated in the light of its extensive background of Christocentric piety in the early Church and in the previous monastic tradition.[56] For St. Benedict, Christ is primarily God: he is Father, King, Shepherd, and *Paterfamilias*. The name *Iesus* never appears in the RB; he is called *Christus, Dominus* or *Deus*. The term *Dominus* usually refers to Christ, and *Deus* sometimes

[54] The importance of this text was first pointed out by M. Rothenhäusler "Der Vatername Christi" *SMGBO* 52 (1934) 178–179. See also Hil. *vita Hon.* 4; Porcar. *mon.*; Arnob. *ad Greg.* 19.

[55] Texts of Ephraim are cited by B. Steidle "Abba Vater" *BM* 16 (1934) 89–101, especially 100. See also Philox. *ad Pat.* 99; *Lib.grad.* 29,19.

[56] On Benedict's concept of Christ, see A. Kemmer "Christ in the Rule of St. Benedict" *MS* 3 (1965) 87–98; A. de Vogüé "The Fatherhood of Christ" *ibid.* 5 (1968) 45–57; A. Borias "'Dominus' et 'Deus' dans la Règle de saint Benoît" *RBén* 79 (1969) 414–423; "Christ and the Monk" *MS* 10 (1974) 97–129.

does. There is a warm devotion to Christ, which is summed up in the axiom: "the love of Christ must come before all else" or "Let them prefer nothing whatever to Christ" (RB 4.21; 72.11; see also 5.2). The monk meets him in the person of guests and of the sick, and above all in the abbot. There is no hesitation about praying to him; often, though not always, the psalms are prayed to Christ as God.[57] The Scriptures, including the Old Testament, are often taken to be the word of Christ.

This Christocentric vision derives from two sources. One is the piety of the early Church and its devotion to Christ, which, as we have seen, was especially cultivated in monastic circles. The other is the influence of the reaction against Arianism, an important factor in the West in the fifth and sixth centuries, which led to increasing emphasis upon the divinity of Christ. This brought about the frequent use of formulas that equated Christ with God, and abandonment of familiar reference to his humanity. As a result, we find in the RB none of the intimate personal address to Jesus that is frequent in Origen. The RB, however, is more moderate in this respect than the RM. The latter is marked not only by Christocentrism, but by what has been called pan-Christism.[58] Christ is Creator, Author of the Scriptures, Provider and eschatological Judge. The commentary on the Lord's Prayer that the Master includes in his introductory material shows quite clearly that "Our Father" means Christ and that the prayer is addressed to him.[59] St. Benedict, who sometimes changes the RM's "Lord" to "God," is more reserved.[60] While Benedict shows greater discretion

---

[57] B. Fischer "Die Psalmenfrömmigkeit der Regula s. Benedicti" *Liturgie und Mönchtum* 4 (1949) 22–35; 5 (1950) 64–79. Fischer somewhat overstates his case, as has become clear from later studies (see the articles cited in the preceding note): St. Benedict does not conceive the entire liturgical prayer of the monastery as directed to Christ, and it is unlikely that "opus Dei" means 'the work of Christ.' His approach is more nuanced. On the question of praying the psalms to Christ, see B. Fischer "Le Christ dans les psaumes: La dévotion aux psaumes dans l'Église des Martyrs" *La Maison-Dieu* 27 (1951) 86–113. The oldest understanding of the psalms as prayer to Christ is in Clem. *ad Cor.* 22,1-8, in which the "Come, children, listen to me" of Ps 33(34) is placed in the mouth of Christ. It is used similarly in RB Prol.12-17, following RM Ths. 8-13. See also F. Vandenbroucke, *Les Psaumes, le Christ et Nous* (Louvain: Mont-César 1965²).

[58] Thus de Vogüé "The Fatherhood of Christ," p. 48.

[59] The earliest instance of directing the Lord's Prayer to Christ appears to be *Acta Thomae* 144. For the appearance of this phenomenon in liturgical texts, see J. Jungmann, *The Place of Christ in Liturgical Prayer* (Staten Island: Alba House 1965) pp. 49, n. 1; 98, n. 5; 168, n. 7; 220, n. 3.

[60] The RB does not have the commentary on the Lord's Prayer, but refers to the prayer in 7.20 and 13.13-14. In the former place it alters the RM's "Lord" to "God." This may indicate an intention to direct the prayer to the Father rather than to Christ. Elsewhere,

and more variety of usage, however, the difference is mainly one of degree.

The Prologue of the RB offers a good example of the place that Christ holds in its author's teaching. It addresses those who want to serve "the true King, Christ the Lord" (3). It is he to whom we pray to bring to perfection the good we initiate, so that we, who are his sons, may not be disinherited by an angry Father (4-7). It is this same Christ who calls out to us in the Scriptures (both Old and New Testaments!), inviting us; he is the *paterfamilias* of the parable of the vineyard, looking for workmen. In this invitation Christ shows us the way to life (8-20). Taking his Gospel as our guide, we hope one day to see him (Christ) who has invited us (21). In the words of Psalm 13(14), we ask what we must do, and Christ answers us through the same psalm (22-27). Our evil thoughts must be dashed against Christ (28), and we must attribute to his work whatever good is found in us (29-34).

When Christ has finished saying all this, he waits for our answer (35), but patiently gives us time to repent (36-38). We must do what he has told us, asking him for his grace to help us (39-44). We enter a "school for the Lord's [Christ's] service," which will involve some difficulties; but as our love increases, it will be a delight to follow his commands (45-49). Persevering in Christ's teaching and sharing in his sufferings, we will one day reign with him (50). Throughout this entire development the author is thinking of Christ, and both *Dominus* and *Deus* refer to him exclusively. He is Father, Teacher, *Paterfamilias*, Author of Scripture.

It is no surprise, then, when we come to chapter 2, to find Christ designated as Father of the monks, and the abbot's role understood to be that of derivative or surrogate father, the one who "holds the place of Christ" (2.2).

How the abbot exercises his office

While the first and fourth sections of chapter 2 of the RM/RB explain what an abbot is, the second and third sections deal with the question, "How does he go about the fulfillment of his responsibility?" How, in practice, does he exercise the role of father, teacher, shepherd, physician and steward in order to make Christ present to his monks? We have seen that these two sections, which closely parallel one another in the RM, deal with two related questions: the abbot's twofold teach-

---

however, the same change is made without a clearly discernible reason, as in RB 7.29; 7.67; see also 2.6.

ing and the equal charity he must display toward all. We shall now examine the Rule's doctrine on these points.

The abbot's essential role is that of teacher: he is called *doctor* and *magister*.[61] In this he reflects Christ, whose place he holds, for he too is a Teacher: as he handed down the word of God to his disciples, the *doctores* must do likewise for their contemporaries. The RB never calls Christ "Teacher," but it speaks of his *magisterium* (Prol.50), and throughout the Prologue it is he who does the teaching, offering the "way of life." Christ teaches through the Scriptures, the Rule and the abbot. Therefore the abbot is a teacher in a derivative sense, a channel for transmitting the teaching that Christ gave in the Gospel: "He must never teach or decree or command anything that would deviate from the Lord's instructions" (2.4).[62]

Now Christ is Father as well as Teacher, and the abbot likewise is teacher of the monks insofar as he is their father. This means that the teaching role assigned him is a particular kind of teaching, which must be specified. It is not simply what we ordinarily mean by teaching. When the abbot is called "father" and "teacher" and the monastery a "school," we are in the realm of analogy, and the precise content of the analogy needs to be specified if we are not to fall into error. The teaching to which an abbot is obliged is the kind of teaching a father gives his children rather than the kind a professional teacher gives the student. It is not academic but existential. Its content is not speculative knowledge (though it may well be based upon this and may sometimes include it) but the practical knowledge of how to live. It is not clearly structured and formally presented as a professor's lectures are, but is communicated in numerous informal and often subtle ways, through personal contact.

Reference to the monastery as a school can easily mislead us. For us today, a school is a rather clearly defined type of institution, having to do with what we call "formal education"; in practice we often tend to equate "education" with "school" and to make the mistake of assuming that people who have been through school are educated and, conversely, that people cannot be educated unless they have been through school. In fact, much of our education, particularly the type

---

[61] *Doctor* only in 5.6; *magister* in 2.24; 3.6; 5.9; 6.6. Some hold that the *magister* of Prol.1 also refers to the abbot.

[62] In regard to the abbot's role as teacher, the RB is much more reserved than the RM, which makes every chapter of the rule a kind of oracular pronouncement coming from Christ through the abbot: "Respondit Dominus per magistrum." See A. Borias "Le Christ" pp. 114–116 (note 56 above).

that is not "formal," is accomplished apart from school. Education begins at birth, and we all learn some of the most important things (how to speak, walk, eat and behave) before we are sent to school. As a result, we have many teachers, of whom the most important are our parents.

The word *schola*, which occurs but once in the RB (Prol.45), does not mean quite the same thing as our word "school."[63] The term originally designated a place, a room or hall in which a group of people assembled, a meeting place. The group gathered for a common purpose, which could be of diverse nature: it could, indeed, be a teacher meeting with students to instruct them, but it could also be a group of workers or athletes or soldiers or any group with a common concern (See note to Prol.45). *Schola* could also designate the group itself, and thus came to mean an assembly of people gathered for a common purpose. In our ordinary usage today, it has been restricted to a single purpose, that of education.[64] But in the Rule it does not have this precision, and there is no nuance of "formal education." It means a group of people who have come together for the common purpose specified by the Rule: to seek God, to imitate Christ, to obey his commands, to persevere in his teaching. In the *schola*, which is both a place, i.e., an institution, and a human grouping, we learn how to do these things, to follow the "way of life."[65] The process can perhaps be more fittingly compared to an apprenticeship by which a person learns a skill from another through long association with him than to a school in the modern sense.[66]

[63] See B. Steidle "Dominici schola servitii. Zum Verständnis des Prologes der Regula St. Benedikts" *BM* 28 (1952) 397–406. A different view is presented by C. Mohrmann "La langue de saint Benoît" in P. Schmitz, *Sancti Benedicti Regula Monachorum* (Maredsous: Editions de l'Abbaye 1955²) pp. 31–33. E. Manning denies that St. Benedict thought of the monastery as a *schola*, since he considers Prol.40-50, where the term occurs, as inauthentic. See "L'étude de la Regula Sancti Benedicti dans la perspective du centenaire de 1980" *CollCist* 41 (1979) 141–154. This opinion is refuted, however, by A. de Vogüé "La Règle d'Eugippe et la fin du Prologue de S. Benoît" *CollCist* 41 (1979) 263–273. See also G. Penco "Sul concetto del monastèro come 'schola'" *ibid.* 32 (1970) 329–333. See the note to Prol.45.

[64] The term can still designate both the place and the group of people, and can also refer to a wider reality than an instructional institution, but this broader connotation is less usual in common parlance.

[65] Monastic use of the term *schola* had been long established. Cassian uses it in *conl.* 3,1; 18,16; 19,2. Other examples are given by Steidle (see note 63).

[66] In the ancient world and especially in Semitic culture, skills were usually handed down from father to son; hence apprenticeship to a master was conceived of as a father-son relationship. The monastic tradition reflects this not only in its use of the father-analogy but also in its stress on imitation as the primary means of learning. See C. H.

The primary analogy, however, is that of a father "teaching" his sons. In modern terminology "formation" is perhaps a better word than "teaching" to convey what is intended, because it is more comprehensive. What a parent conveys to his children is not confined to the level of the intellect, as "teaching" suggests. Indeed, it includes this area, for every child acquires a great deal of information from his parents, whether correct or not, depending upon their intellectual culture. But even more significant is the less tangible sphere of attitudes, outlook, moral standards, sense of values, vision of reality. Everyone who deals with youth is aware of the decisive importance of early parental formation. Such qualities as neatness, politeness, respect for authority, sensitivity to others, honesty and reliability are instilled by good parents from earliest infancy, not by any formal instruction, but by the continuous influence they exercise simply by what they are and through the countless intimate personal encounters of everyday life. Such formation affects every aspect of human development: intellectual, volitional, emotional, physical, moral and religious. It conveys a whole vision of the meaning of life and a sense of what is valuable and to be pursued. In highly unsophisticated form, it is a kind of existential philosophy of man.

All this is the work of formation: this is what the Rule means by "teaching." The abbot, then, is not a scholar or professor, not even of the sacred sciences. What he wants to communicate is not primarily knowledge but wisdom. What he wants to bring about in his disciples is their total personal conversion. His primary qualifications, then, are not intellectual brilliance or academic achievement but "sapientiae doctrina et vitae meritum" (64.2). These two qualities, wisdom and virtue, are closely related, for the "wise doctrine" is that of the Gospel, that "folly" which is wiser than human wisdom (1 Cor 1:18-24), and the "goodness of his life" is the actualizing of the Gospel, the existential wisdom. The Gospel is the kind of "doctrine" one acquires more by living it and reflecting on one's experience than by studying. The abbot, like the spiritual father of the desert, is a man of proven holiness who can help others to discover God's will and to discern the spirits at work in them because he has himself assimilated the Gospel through his own reflection and experience.

The communication of such *doctrina* is a very subtle process. The Rule appropriately compares it to the hidden and mysterious action of

Dodd "A Hidden Parable in the Fourth Gospel" *More New Testament Studies* (Grand Rapids, Mich.: Eerdmans 1968) pp. 30–40.

leaven in a mass of dough (2.5). The manner of its communication is twofold: by word and by example. Benedict makes much of the importance of the abbot's teaching by means of his own life, by the way he conducts himself. The sub-theme (RB 2.12b,23-25) develops the need for the abbot's adapting himself to the individual differences of his monks: some will be successfully influenced through verbal instruction, appeal and admonition; others will be affected but little by words and can be reached only by example. But the teaching through action is not meant only for the latter; it is specified that "he must point out to them all that is good and holy more by example than by words" (2.12). The message of his own life is more effective than what he says, even for those who understand his words. The very nature of the wisdom he presents is such that it is not genuine, is not fully itself, unless it is translated into practice. The doing of it is essential to what it is. The Gospel is not a philosophy—we do not really know it until we know it by experience.[67]

The other concern of the central sections of chapter 2 is that favoritism be banished. While St. Benedict retains this point, he has eliminated much of the RM's development of it; he is much more insistent upon the need for diversity of treatment of different individuals than upon equality of treatment. However, he too affirms that the abbot must show equal *charity* to all (2.22). Benedict is especially insistent that social status should not influence the abbot's attitude toward anyone, and the New Testament is invoked to show that all purely human distinctions are obliterated by our oneness in Christ (2.20). The only valid standard of judgment is the monk's fulfillment of the religious commitment he has made. Accordingly, preference may be shown (and by "preference" Benedict understands primarily promotion in rank) only to those who show greater virtue. Equality of charity does not imply equality of treatment: the abbot must take account of individual differences and treat each monk according to his needs. But he must love each one and deal with him in a way best calculated to develop his own unique potentialities.

From all this it is clear in what sense the abbot's teaching can rightly be compared to that of a father. The comparison is forceful and il-

---

[67] In biblical thought there is a close relationship between word and action: Hebrew uses the term "word" (*dabar*) to mean 'thing' or 'deed.' The *mirabilia Dei* are revelatory insofar as they are "words" that convey meaning. The deed and the word together (such as prophetic actions accompanied by explanation) constitute a whole, a single revelatory phenomenon.

luminating. But it is only an analogy, and it needs to be added that, as in all analogies, the two situations are comparable but not identical. There are also differences that should be recognized; if they are not, distortion inevitably results. The first difference is that a father is dealing with children and the abbot with adults. The analogy does not provide any excuse for the abbot to treat his monks like children. Indeed, they still have something to learn—as the abbot himself does—but they must learn it as adults and not as children. The Rule offers no justification for the abbot's assuming an attitude of paternalism, in the pejorative sense of the term. Still less does it assume his infallibility; on the contrary, it stresses that he is a weak and sinful human being who must be on his guard and concerned for his own salvation. The humility that allows him to admit his own error is itself an important aspect of his teaching.

Secondly, the masculine feature of the analogy is not essential. Spiritual "fatherhood" is not a male prerogative. It involves the relationship between one human being and another, and neither sex is privileged in its exercise either by nature or by status in the Church. The Rule was written for a male community, but its provisions are equally applicable to either sex. Both the Bible and the Fathers sometimes compare God to a mother as well as to a father.[68] The RM compares the abbot to both in a phrase which is meaningful in itself but which the RB has omitted.[69] The Scriptures use both the metaphor of begetting and that of giving birth.[70] Historically, spiritual parenthood has been exercised by both sexes, both in the Egyptian desert and in later Western abbeys.[71]

The abbot as administrator

The abbot's task is defined by his essential role as father and teacher: his overriding concern is the spiritual formation and growth of his disciples. The abbot of the RB is the transposition into cenobitic

---

[68] See Hos 11:3-5; Isa 66:13; Matt 23:37; 1 Cor 3:1-2; Origen wrote, "Christ can be called father and mother" (Orig. *in Prov.* 20).

[69] "He will show all his disciples and sons the realization of both parents in his own person: showing his love equally to them as a mother, he shows himself a father to them by uniform tenderness" (RM 2.30-31).

[70] The variation of metaphor is facilitated by the fact that the Greek verb *gennaō* can mean both 'beget' and 'give birth.'

[71] The *Apophthegmata* lists the sayings of a number of female elders. Women not only functioned as mothers of female communities, but in the Middle Ages sometimes ruled double monasteries, exercising jurisdiction also over male subjects. Especially significant was Robert of Arbrissel's institute of Fontevrault (1099), in which the abbess held supreme authority over the monks as well as the nuns.

terms of the spiritual father of the desert monks. The transposition, however, has brought with it factors that do not really alter the essential purpose of the office, but nevertheless modify the concrete circumstances of its exercise. When the disciples become a community, the monastery becomes an institution. While there may be almost infinite variety in the size and complexity of Benedictine monasteries, even the simplest requires some degree of government and administration. The role of the abbot is not purely in the spiritual order; he is also the administrator of all the monastery's affairs. Throughout the RB the abbot is given ultimate responsibility for everything that concerns the life of the community, whether in the spiritual or in the temporal order.

The chapters of the Rule that concern the ordering of the daily life—common prayer, discipline, food, sleep, work, travel, reception of guests—uniformly place the making of policy and decisions in the hands of the abbot. On the other hand, the two chapters that deal *ex professo* with the abbot speak primarily of his personal relationships with his monks and say almost nothing of his administrative tasks. At first sight this omission is puzzling, for in practice the burdens of administration occupy much of an abbot's time and concern. Upon closer examination, however, we find that the silence of chapters 2 and 64 on this matter actually reveals an important aspect of Benedict's mentality. For him, administration of the monastery's affairs, even temporal affairs, is not a separate task—it is an integral aspect of his responsibility for the formation of his sons.

In this respect the father-analogy once again becomes illuminating. The father of a family also has to provide for every aspect of his children's lives: he must feed, clothe and house them, provide medical care and recreation, see to their education and social needs, determine his family's relationships to the larger society. This is not a separate compartment of life; it is an aspect of his responsibility for their formation. For much of the "teaching" that he imparts, the sense of values and relative priorities that he inculcates, is communicated precisely by means of the way in which he deals with these administrative problems. In this area, indeed, the parallel between the abbot and the *paterfamilias* of the Roman family may be conceded a certain validity. There is no relationship of dependence, but there is a similarity of function: the abbot is in charge of all the spiritual and temporal affairs of the monastery in much the same way as the *paterfamilias* presided over the extended family of late Roman society.

What is reflected in this concept of the abbot's function is the holistic worldview of the Bible and early Christianity. Human life is a whole, and everything in creation is good. There is no aspect of life in this world that cannot, if rightly understood and used, contribute to leading us to our final end. Temporal reality and human endeavor are reflections of the perfections of God. Material things are *sacramenta*, symbols that reveal the goodness and beauty of the Creator. Consequently, Benedict can say that ordinary tools for work should be treated like the sacred vessels intended for liturgical use (31.10). It is only sin that has disfigured the beauty of creation and diverted things from their purpose. The monastic life is an effort to restore the lost paradise, to regain the image of God in man that has been distorted. Therefore, the temporal order cannot be despised or neglected. In the monk's life there is no area that can be exempted from subjection to the divine precepts and the regime of grace. This is no disincarnate spirituality; conversion embraces the whole of life.

Administration, then, is not a purely profane art that can be left to anyone who is knowledgeable about business. In the New Testament, "administration" is one of the charisms mentioned together with prophecy and teaching (1 Cor 12:28; Rom 12:6), a gift the Holy Spirit confers for the good of the community. Benedict likewise supposes that what is most important for temporal administration in the monastery is not simply human skill but spiritual qualities arising from faith and a resolute commitment to a Christian vision. It is significant that the requirements for the cellarer are practically the same as for the abbot and the deans: wisdom, fear of God, humility, conducting himself "like a father" (RB 31). Indeed, the management of business affairs is an art that can be learned, and today professional training in some degree is needed to master the complexities of temporal administration. But the supernatural outlook that perceives the purpose of the process is of supreme importance. It is the abbot who sets the tone and oversees everything, for he is the father who bears ultimate responsibility, even if he may delegate much of the detail.

The choice and installation of the abbot

Since the abbot is representative of Christ in the *coenobium*, the selection of a person to fill the office must reflect the will of God. As God by a special call chose the prophets and kings who acted as mediators of his word and will in the Old Testament, and Christ personally selected the apostles who handed on the Gospel to the early Church, so the divine will must be operative in the choice of the *doctores*—bishops and abbots—who now mediate the divine precepts. The will of God, however, has to be made known through human channels in this case as in others. The early Church, therefore, recognized a number of ways in which bishops and abbots might be chosen, and believed that the will of God was manifested in their election or appointment by human agents. In modern times we are accustomed to majority vote of the community in the case of abbots and direct appointment by the Holy See in the case of bishops;[72] in ancient times the situation was more complex.[73]

In the monastic tradition a number of different procedures were in use. Pachomius appointed his own successor, although he first consulted the elders, and Petronius did the same (*Vita prima* 114; 117; *Vita sa*[5] and *sa*[7]). Honoratus likewise designated his successor at Lerins, and there are many later examples. This is also the system followed by the RM. The abbot is to choose the most virtuous monk in the community and designate him as abbot-elect. He is to encourage the monks to compete with one another for this honor by striving to be the most obedient. When the appointment has been made, the bishop and his clergy are summoned to install the new abbot by means of a liturgical rite. If the old abbot then recovers, the new one is to act as "second" until his predecessor's death. But he may still be deposed by the old abbot if he misbehaves, and another appointed in his place. If the abbot dies suddenly, without having designated a successor, the bishop brings in an abbot, presumably from another monastery, who governs the community for thirty days. At the end of that time he chooses the most observant monk and presents him to the bishop to be installed as abbot.

St. Benedict does not mention designation by the previous abbot. He prefers to involve the community in the choice of their abbot. What he says about this, however, is subject to diverse interpretation,

---

[72] In an abbatial election, if a majority is not achieved after a certain number of ballots, usually six, the office is filled by appointment. Appointment by the Holy See after consultation as a regular method of choosing bishops is found only in the Latin Church; in the Eastern Churches electoral procedures are still in use. The Bishop of Rome is also elected, and the papal law still provides for the possibility of his being chosen by acclamation.

[73] The case of St. Ambrose is well known. As civil governor, he went to the church to maintain order. When a child cried out, "Ambrose bishop," the whole assembly took up the cry, even though he was only a catechumen. The divine will became known through this spontaneous outburst, so that the agreement upon Ambrose transcended the Arian-Catholic division of the Milanese Christian community. The story is told by Paulin. *vita Ambr.* 3.

and there is no agreement at present about the precise meaning of the passage in RB 64.1-6. Even the definition of the terms *eligere, ordinare* and *constituere* is disputed. Benedict says that the person placed in office should be either (1) selected by the whole community acting unanimously in the fear of God; or (2) selected by some part of the community, no matter how small, that possesses "sounder judgment" (*sanius consilium*). Rank is to count for nothing; the sole qualifications are "goodness of life and wisdom in teaching." If it should happen that the whole community selects an unworthy abbot, then the bishop of the diocese or neighboring abbots or lay people should intervene to depose him and put a good abbot in his place.

The differing interpretations of this passage depend upon diverse views of the author's intention. Did he intend to give precise regulations for the procedure to be followed, so that the text is juridically accurate and its meaning can be determined by comparison with other passages of the RB and with other contemporary texts? Or is the Rule deliberately vague and without strict juridic intent, because the actual practice was well known to those for whom it was written and did not have to be defined? Or does it perhaps simply ignore the question of procedure entirely and address itself solely to the spiritual problem involved in the choice of an abbot? In comparison with other rules and contemporary texts, the RB is notoriously obscure, whatever be the explanation of this.[74]

One view holds that the community did not have the right of election, but only of postulation. The bishop was the final authority. To him the community presented the candidate whom they had unanimously chosen, or a candidate chosen by a minority, the *sanior pars*. The bishop would also be the arbiter who determined which monks constituted the *sanior pars* or electoral body. He would have the right to examine the candidate proposed to him by the electors and confirm the choice. If he felt that the candidate postulated was not worthy, he would reject him, and himself appoint an abbot; in this he might be assisted by the advice of other abbots and interested lay Christians from the vicinity. The new abbot would then be installed by the bishop, assisted by other abbots (65.3). This view supposes that the Rule legislates accurately: the term *eligere* means to postulate; *ordi-*

---

[74] A survey of opinions on this question is provided by J. Lienhard "*Sanius Consilium*: Recent Work on the Election of the Abbot in the *Rule* of St. Benedict" *ABR* 26 (1975) 1-15.

nare means to appoint or to place in office; *constituere* means to install.[75]

Another opinion holds that the bishop's function was merely to confirm and install the abbot; he had nothing to say of the choice of the candidate except in special circumstances, when an unworthy abbot had to be deposed or when the election was indecisive. The choice of the candidate was up to the monastic body: the Master, who is more authoritarian, entrusts it solely to the previous abbot (or an abbot from another monastery); St. Benedict, who is more conscious of the abbot's fallibility, places confidence in the community to make the choice. In either case, the choice is really that of God; the human agents are merely intermediaries who try to discern his will. The abbatial office is still charismatic, as it was in its origins and in the case of the great spiritual fathers raised up by God, like Pachomius. It is not an "ecclesiastical" office, and the bishops have no determination of it aside from exceptional cases which require their intervention. For St. Benedict, it is the community that discerns the divine choice, and the bishop must confirm and install their candidate. The bishop's right to intervene in the affairs of monasteries was not yet clearly defined in canon law.[76]

This approach, however, does not clarify the meaning of the *sanius consilium* nor determine what procedure was to be followed when the community could not agree with quasi-unanimity. Some argue that the Rule is obscure on this point because the practice was so well known that it was not necessary to describe it. Kassius Hallinger maintains that all the methods of choosing an abbot known from contemporary documents were "undemocratic" ones: designation by a single individual (abbot or bishop or lay founder) or election by a minority.[77] He suggests that even the unanimous "election" mentioned by RB 64.1 is really only the community's ratification of a candidate already chosen by appointment or elected by a minority. Minority elections were provided for in the Code of Justinian in 546[78] and must have been known from actual usage. If the Rule does not specify how the electors

[75] The clearest exposition of this view is that of H. Brechter "Die Bestellung des Abtes nach der Regel des heiligen Benedikt" *SMGBO* 58 (1940) 44–58.

[76] B. Steidle "'Wer euch hört, hört mich' (Lk 10,16): Die Einsetzung des Abts im alten Mönchtum" *EA* 40 (1964) 179–196.

[77] K. Hallinger "Das Wahlrecht der Benediktusregula" *ZKG* 76 (1965) 233–245.

[78] *Novellae* 123,34: R. Schoell and W. Kroll, *Corpus Iuris Civilis* (Berlin: Weidmann 1959[6]) 3.618. The Latin text reads: "Abbatem ... omnes monachi [aut?] melioris opinionis existentes eligant."

are to be chosen, it is only because this was understood by everyone: the *seniores* or *decani*, of whom the RB often speaks, constituted the electoral body, as being the monks who best possessed the spiritual qualities that enabled them to discern the divine will.[79]

It has recently been proposed that all of these views mistake the real intention of St. Benedict by supposing that he wished to lay down a procedure for choosing an abbot or that he assumed that such a regular procedure was followed. Herbert Grundmann has suggested that the author had no such intention and was concerned solely with the spiritual problem involved, not at all with canonical procedure. St. Benedict was convinced that the supremely important factor in an abbatial election is the will of God, and he wants the community to be open to discerning the divine intention. Consequently, they are to act "in the fear of God," consider solely the virtue and wisdom of the candidate, and be prepared to accept even the youngest if God's choice should fall upon him (RB 64.1-2). God's will may be manifested in different ways: through the whole community, through a *sanior pars*, or even through an individual. One cannot determine in advance how God will manifest his will; therefore, rather than intending to specify an election procedure, St. Benedict feels that this ought not be too clearly defined, for fear that the freedom of the Spirit may be constrained by human regulations. According to Grundmann, the RB represents a purely charismatic point of view and is not at all concerned with juridical procedure.[80] He notes that in a parallel case, the

[79] Evidence that the deans constituted the electoral body is cited by Hallinger in the cases of Murbach and Fulda, but only from the eighth and ninth centuries. His thesis is rejected by H. Grundmann "Zur Abt-Wahl nach Benedikts Regel: Die 'Zweitobern' als 'sanior pars'?" ZKG 77 (1966) 217–223. In the Middle Ages the community often entrusted the choice of the abbot to a group of electors; an interesting twelfth-century example from Bury St. Edmund can be found in *The Chronicle of Jocelin of Brakelond*, ed. H. E. Butler (London: Nelson 1949) pp. 16–24. See also A. Gasquet, *English Monastic Life* (London: Methuen 1904) pp. 44–48; H. Leclercq "Élections abbatiales" DACL 4.2611–18. The use of a small electoral body (*electio per compromissum*) has survived in the provisions of the U.S. Constitution for the election of the President; in fact, modern political electoral methods developed out of ecclesiastical practice. See L. Moulin "Les origines religieuses des techniques électorales et délibératives modernes" *Revue internationale d'histoire politique et constitutionelle* n.s. 3 (1953) 106–148; "Sanior et maior pars. Note sur l'évolution des techniques électorales dans les Ordres religieux du VIe au XIIe siècle" *Revue historique de droit français et étranger*, 4e série 36 (1958) 368–397, 491–529. On past and present methods of electing abbots, see B. Hegglin, *Der benediktinische Abt in rechtsgeschichtlicher Entwicklung und geltendem Kirchenrecht* (St. Ottilien: Eos Verlag 1961) pp. 45–51, 130–135.

[80] H. Grundmann "Pars Quamvis Parva: Zur Abtwahl nach Benedikts Regel" *Festschrift Percy Ernst Schramm* (Wiesbaden: F. Steiner Verlag 1964) 1.237–251.

choice of the Holy Roman emperor, no clear law of succession was ever formulated, precisely in order to give free play to the divine will.

It is also uncertain whether St. Benedict intended a liturgical rite of abbatial blessing and installation by the bishop. He does not mention such a rite. Is it legitimate to interpret this silence to mean that he takes such a ceremony for granted because it was already customary?[81] There is no mention of the abbatial blessing in liturgical books until the *Gregorian Sacramentary*, which contains chiefly seventh- and eighth-century material, but this does not prove that the rite could not have been in use earlier. In fact, a rite of this kind is described in RM 93 and 94: the bishop is the officiant, and it includes the celebration of Mass as well as an installation ceremony. One cannot conclude, however, that the rites known to the RM must have also been practiced in St. Benedict's monastery except in cases where there is evidence to the contrary.[82] Liturgical practice may have differed considerably from one monastery to another at this period. Later the rite of abbatial blessing underwent a vast development owing to the important social position occupied by abbots in the Middle Ages. This development injected confusion into the understanding of the abbot's role by patterning the blessing upon the consecration of a bishop and thus making it appear that the abbot was part of the sacramental hierarchy. The recent revision of the rite according to the principles of Vatican II has restored its simplicity and original meaning.[83]

Given the diversity of practice at the time and the laconic character of Benedict's statements on the subject, it may well be impossible for us ever to determine with certitude what he intended in regard to the manner of determining abbatial succession. The debate about it, however, is not just an idle dispute among scholars, but is important for understanding the role of the abbot: the manner in which he is selected and installed tells us something about the nature of his office.

[81] This view is defended by Chapman, *St. Benedict and the Sixth Century* and by R. Somerville "'Ordinatio Abbatis' in the Rule of St. Benedict" *RBén* 77 (1967) 246–263. Gregory the Great speaks of the *ordinatio* of an abbot by a bishop that involves the celebration of Mass (*Registrum epistolarum* 11,48: *PL* 77.1168). Directives for a similar rite are found in the seventh century in the *Penitential* of Theodore of Canterbury: *PL* 99.928–929.

[82] A. Mundó "À propos des rituels du Maître et de saint Benoît: La 'Provolutio'" *SM* 4 (1962) 177–191.

[83] On the abbatial blessing, see S. Hilpisch "Entwicklung des Ritus der Abtsweihe in der lateinischen Kirche" *SMGBO* 61 (1947) 53–60; J. Baudot "Bénédiction d'un abbé et d'une abbesse" *DACL* 2.723–727; D.C. "Ordo Benedictionis Abbatis et Abbatissae: Decretum, Praenotanda, Commentarium" *Notitiae* 7 (1971) 32–36; A. Nocent "Benedizione dell' abate" *Dizionario degli Istituti di Perfezione* 1.8–14.

There can be no question that for Benedict the abbot is the successor of the spiritual father of the desert. He is the "holy man," the "Man of God," the charismatic elder, the teacher who from his experience is able to provide a "word" for the upbuilding of others. It is true that Benedict has been influenced also, in a fruitful and enriching way, by the Basilian and Augustinian traditions, for which the community rather than the abbot is the starting point. They have had but little effect, however, on his vision of the abbot, which remains predominantly in the tradition of Egypt that came to the West through Cassian. Everyone admits that for St. Benedict the abbot is primarily the spiritual father.[84]

Is the abbot, then, a purely charismatic figure? Indeed, if his principal function remains the spiritual formation of each of his monks, nevertheless the situation has undergone modification from the status of the charismatic in the desert. The spontaneous appearance of a "Man of God" cannot be duplicated by putting someone into office, no matter how carefully he is chosen. The Spirit, while its operation is compatible with the institution, cannot be institutionalized. An abbot chosen to govern a community is in a different position from that of the original founder: the latter had attracted disciples by his personal qualities; the former assumes the direction of an already existing community. He may find it impossible to develop the same kind of personal relationship with each individual that the founder had. Further, he assumes an obligation to teach and direct his community, whereas the desert father taught only when asked for advice, and even then it was often with great reluctance. The institutionalized task also assumes dimensions such as sheer size and administrative burden that

[84] A. Veilleux "The Abbatial Office in Cenobitical Life" *MS* 6 (1968) 3–45 concedes that this is true of the RB, even though he considers it a deviation. In the East (Syria, Basil, Pachomius), he maintains, the cenobitic superior was originally a *primus inter pares*, the center or "eye" of the community, whose relationship to the monks was horizontal rather than vertical. It was Cassian who, having no acquaintance with real cenobitism, transplanted the desert *abba* into the *coenobium* for purposes of his own, viz., to reform the monasteries of Provence along the lines of his Egyptian eremitical ideals. The Master, with his usual excess of logic, carried the idea to extremes by putting the abbot on the same plane as the bishop—a most unfortunate step whose disastrous effects last right down to the present. St. Benedict innocently inherited the idea of the abbot as spiritual father from Cassian and the RM, but he had the good sense to steer clear of the latter's excessive conclusions. Moreover, his knowledge of Basil enabled him to introduce a corrective that went far toward neutralizing the nefarious influence of Cassian. It follows that the RB presents a moderate view of spiritual fatherhood and should be understood as repudiating material in the RM that it does not explicitly reproduce, specifically the abbot-bishop comparison.

alter the functioning of the abbot in practice. While he must be concerned about each individual, his teaching is often directed more at the community as a whole.[85] The abbot of the RB is the lineal descendant of the charismatic *abba* and still reproduces the essentials of his role, but he is not exactly the same thing.

Did the Rule regard the abbot as belonging to the purely charismatic element in the Church? In fact, while monasticism had begun as a charismatic phenomenon outside the hierarchical structure of Church authority, it had been brought into it in varying degrees at different times and places.[86] It was not until the Middle Ages that it became thoroughly institutionalized, though then and often since it has periodically been revivified by new stirrings of the Spirit. In the sixth century the situation was still fluid: the bishops exercised some control over monasteries, as the letters of Gregory the Great testify, but there was no clear-cut and universal canonical pattern. Abbots were most often still laymen, and the monastic hierarchy was clearly distinct from the ecclesiastical, though the two interacted in varying degrees.

The fact that there was no fixed pattern is precisely the nub of the difficulty in determining what Benedict intended the bishop's role to be. The RM allows him no voice in selecting the abbot; this decision is made by an abbot. Did Benedict believe likewise that the will of God was to be mediated solely through monastic channels and exclude the bishop from the normal selection process (Steidle), or did he leave the ultimate decision up to episcopal authority and allow the monks only to propose a candidate (Brechter)? It is difficult to decide.

If the bishop not only installed the abbot but actually appointed him, then it would seem that the abbot's authority was conferred upon him by the Church through the hierarchy. Such was not the idea of early monasticism, which believed that the foundation of an abbot's authority was a charism given to him directly by the Holy Spirit and quite distinct from the jurisdiction of the hierarchical Church.[87] It is

[85] R. Weakland "The Abbot in a Democratic Society" CS 4 (1969) 95–100; "Obedience to the Abbot and the Community in the Monastery" *ibid.* 5 (1970) 309–316; "The Abbot as Spiritual Father" *ibid.* 9 (1974) 231–238; "Amtsautorität und Seelenführung" EA 51 (1976) 85–91; G. Dubois "Authority and Obedience in Contemporary Monasticism" CS 8 (1973) 101–108.

[86] The seventh canon of the Council of Chalcedon had already declared, "Placuit . . . monachos vero per unamquamque civitatem aut regionem subiectos esse episcopo" (Mansi 7.374).

[87] J. Bonduelle "Le pouvoir dominatif des abbés" *La Vie Spirituelle Supplément* 69 (1964) 201–223.

not easy to determine what the Western monastic legislators thought about this point. The question arises even if the bishop had no role in the selection of the abbot, as in the RM, for he still presided at the installation (RM 93-94; RB 65.3). The Master does not pronounce clearly on this point; what he says can be understood to attribute the abbatial authority to the liturgical rite conducted by the bishop, but it may also mean that he derived it from a charismatic gift received directly from God.[88] Since Benedict says nothing of the installation rite beyond the allusion in 65.3, we have no clear way of determining his view of the matter.

In either hypothesis, however, the authority of the abbot is deemed to come, in the final analysis, from God, either directly by virtue of a charism or indirectly through the jurisdictional power of the hierarchy. It does not originate from the community. The abbot is father of his monks because God has chosen him and placed him in office (through whatever intermediaries), and the monks owe him obedience because they *believe* this: "Since he is believed to hold the place of Christ in the monastery, he is addressed by a title of Christ, as the Apostle indicates: 'You have received the spirit of adoption of sons by which we exclaim, abba, father'" (RB 2.2-3). In ancient times, when different methods of selection were in use, there was less danger of confusing the election of an abbot with the modern political practice of electing officials by majority vote. The latter derive their authority from the will of the electorate; the abbot does not. Whatever political process may be employed in his selection is of only secondary importance; St. Benedict may even have been relatively indifferent to it. He is more concerned that the right person be chosen, and that God's will be done. "They must ... set a worthy steward in charge of God's house" (RB 64.5).

---

[88] P. Tamburrino "La Regula Magistri e l'origine del potere abbaziale" *CollCist* 28 (1966) 160–173; B. Jaspert "'Stellvertreter Christi' bei Aponius, einem unbekanntem 'Magister' und Benedikt von Nursia: Ein Beitrag zum altkirchlichen Amtsverständnis" *ZThK* 71 (1974) 291–324. De Vogüé has changed his mind on this question and now holds that according to the RM the abbot derives his power from the liturgical installation by the bishop: "L'origine du pouvoir des abbés selon la Règle du Maître" *La Vie Spirituelle Supplément* 70 (1964) 321–324.

Appendix 3

The Liturgical Code in the Rule of Benedict

From earliest times Christians have been conscious of the privilege and the responsibility of prayer. Paul exhorted the community at Thessalonica to "pray constantly" and to "give thanks in all circumstances" (1 Thess 5:17-18). In the theology of Luke's Gospel, Jesus himself is portrayed as a man of prayer and as a teacher of prayer: "In these days he went out to the mountain to pray; and all night he continued in prayer to God" (Luke 6:12). It is not surprising, then, that in early Christian sources outside the New Testament we find an emphatic interest in prayer, personal and public. A survey of these sources will reveal four principal lines in the development of what we today call the Liturgy of the Hours or the Divine Office—an officially established pattern of common prayer (psalms, hymns, Bible readings, petitions) that punctuates the various hours of the day and night. With Juan Mateos, we may identify these four lines of development in the Liturgy of the Hours as follows: [1]

1. times for prayer in the primitive Church;
2. the development of a "monastic tradition" of prayer-times in fourth-century Egypt;
3. the "cathedral tradition," i.e., public prayer as celebrated in parochial or cathedral churches;
4. the rise of an "urban monastic tradition" of prayer-times.

Each of these four stages merits some attention.

Times for prayer in the primitive Church

From the beginnings of Christianity until the early fourth century, there is scant testimony for large-scale, formal celebrations of the

[1] J. Mateos "The Origins of the Divine Office" *Worship* 41 (1967) 477–485.

379

Liturgy of the Hours. This does not mean, however, that the hours of prayer did not exist in the earliest era of Christian life. Indeed, there is a great deal of evidence for the Christian custom of praying, privately and/or in common, at definite times of the day and night. For example, the *Didache*, a small manual of Christian catechesis and liturgical customs dating from the late first or early second century, instructs Christians to pray the Lord's Prayer three times a day (*Didache* 8,3). About a century later, Clement of Alexandria, a prominent Christian theologian and apologist († c. 215), mentions the custom of praying at the third, sixth and ninth hours of the day, as well as at morning, evening and night (Clem. *strom.* 7,7).

Some of the early Church Fathers attempted symbolic explanations of why Christians pray at certain hours. One such explanation can be found in the treatise on prayer by Tertullian († c. 225), a passionate representative of Latin Christianity in North Africa. For Tertullian, as for most of the early Fathers, the supreme law of Christian prayer is the continual prayer of the heart. The Christian is one who should pray "at all times and everywhere" (Tert. *de orat.* 24). Still, there are moments during the day that have been hallowed by tradition as times particularly appropriate for prayer. Concerning these times, Tertullian comments:

> It was at the *third hour* that the Holy Spirit was poured upon the assembled disciples. Peter, on the day he had the vision of all [the creatures] in the sheet, climbed up to higher places through the grace of prayer at the *sixth hour.* Likewise John: at the *ninth hour* he went to the temple, where he restored a paralytic to health (Tert. *de orat.* 24-25).[2]

Although these customary prayers at the third, sixth and ninth hours are best said in common, Tertullian does not regard them as juridical obligations that bind Christians. More important, in his view, are the morning and evening prayers. These he calls the *legitimae orationes*, prayers of such fundamental importance for the daily life of Christians that they possess what amounts to the prescriptive force of law.

Among Western Christian writers, Tertullian was not alone in his emphasis on the importance of prayer in the morning and evening, and at the third, sixth and ninth hours of the day. The *Apostolic Tradition* (c. 215), another manual of liturgical customs that seems to reflect the traditions of the Roman Church, also offers a symbolic interpretation of the customary times for prayer. Hippolytus, the reputed author

---

[2] Tertullian, *De oratione*:CCL 1.272.

of the *Apostolic Tradition*, relates the prayer-hours to events surrounding the passion of Jesus:

> If you are at home at the *third hour*, you should pray to God and offer him praise . . . for it is the time when Christ was nailed to the cross. . . . In the same way, you should pray at the *sixth hour*, thinking of Christ hanging on the cross while the sun was checked in its course and darkness reigned supreme. . . . At the *ninth hour*, your prayer and praise should be protracted. . . . It was at this time that Christ, pierced with the spear, poured forth water and blood, and lighted the rest of the day's span and brought it to evening. By making the light return as he went to sleep, he gave us an image of his resurrection. Pray, too, *before you lie down to rest*. About *midnight*, get up again, wash your hands with water and once more set about your prayer. . . . About *cock-crow*, get up once more and pray again, for it was at this time . . . that the children of Israel denied Christ. . . ." (Hippol. *trad.apost.* 35).[3]

In the middle of the third century, St. Cyprian, bishop of Carthage († 258), adds further testimony to the practice of Christian prayer at prescribed hours of the day and night. In his treatise *On the Lord's Prayer*, Cyprian gives two different symbolic interpretations of prayer at the third, sixth and ninth hours: one based on the mystery of the Trinity, and another that seems to combine the interpretations of both Tertullian and Hippolytus. Cyprian notes that these customary hours of prayer were already known to the people of Israel, but that for Christians "both the times and the sacraments have increased." Thus Cyprian also prescribes prayer for morning, evening and night:

> . . . we must also pray in the *morning*, that the resurrection of the Lord may be celebrated by morning prayer. . . . Likewise *at the setting of the sun* and *at the end of the day* necessarily there must again be prayer. For since Christ is the true Sun and the true Day . . . we pray for the coming of Christ to provide us with the grace of eternal light. . . . Moreover, let us who are always in Christ, that is, in the light, not cease praying even *in the night*. Thus the widow Anna without intermission always petitioning and watching, persevered in deserving well of God. . . . (Cypr. *domin.orat.* 35).

Other historical testimonies could be cited, but these few examples reveal that at an early stage in the life of the Church, the scriptural principle of "incessant prayer" was reinforced by the Christian custom of prayer (public and/or private) at definite times of day and night.

---

[3] Translation from A. Hamman, *Early Christian Prayers* (Chicago: Henry Regnery Co. 1961) pp. 254–255.

Some scholars have contended that these prayer-times originated in the liturgy of the synagogue or that they were rooted in apostolic custom.[4] Whatever their origin, it is clear that the early Church Fathers acknowledged these times of prayer as a serious, if not juridically obligatory, responsibility for all Christians. Nor were such hours of prayer considered the special duty of ascetics and clergy; they were part of every Christian's effort "always to pray and not lose heart" (Luke 18:1).

Egyptian monastic tradition (fourth century)

The fourth century was an especially critical period for the development of Christian life and doctrine. It was a century that saw the emergence of Christianity as a "licit religion" in the Roman Empire (through the so-called Edict of Milan in 313). It was also a time of intense theological turbulence, witnessed by the debates about the person and nature of Christ at the Council of Nicaea (325). Outstanding teachers, theologians and pastors like Ambrose, Basil, Gregory of Nyssa, Augustine and Jerome were at work. Moreover, the fourth century was an epoch of vigorous liturgical development. The classical descriptions of Christian initiation, preserved in the mystagogic catecheses of bishops like Ambrose and Cyril of Jerusalem, date from this period. At the same time, the fourth century was an era of bold experimentation in Christian lifestyles. Antony († 356), the great eremitical hero, was still very much alive; Pachomius (c. 290–346), commonly, if incorrectly, called the father of cenobitic monasticism, was organizing his communities in the Thebaid region of Egypt.

Such is the background for some of our earliest accounts of what Mateos has called the "monastic tradition" in the Liturgy of the Hours.[5] In the last twenty years these accounts, especially those that deal with prayer-times among the Egyptian monks, have been subjected to a considerable amount of scrutiny by scholars. Some comments about the results of this recent research are in order.

How did the Egyptian monks, especially those who followed the Pachomian tradition, pray? The answer to this question depends, to a great extent, on how we evaluate the evidence contained in docu-

[4] See C. W. Dugmore, *The Influence of the Synagogue upon the Divine Office*, Alcuin Club Collection 45 (London: Faith Press 1964) and D. Hadidian "The Background and Origin of the Christian Hours of Prayer" *Theological Studies* 25 (1964) 59–69.

[5] Mateos "The Origins of the Divine Office" pp. 481–482 and W. Storey "The Liturgy of the Hours: Cathedral versus Monastery" *Christians at Prayer*, ed. J. Gallen (Notre Dame, Ind.: Univ. of Notre Dame Press 1977) pp. 61–82.

ments like the various "Lives" of Pachomius, the so-called *Rule of Pachomius*, the *Rule of the Angel* (preserved in Palladius' *Lausiac History*) and the descriptions of Egyptian monastic life provided by John Cassian (c. 360–435) in his *Conferences* and *Institutes*. The liturgy of the fourth-century Pachomian communities has been thoroughly studied by Dom Armand Veilleux.[6] His conclusions are significant for two reasons. First, they reveal a picture of Egyptian monastic liturgy that is rather different from that often assumed by historians who study the Liturgy of the Hours. Secondly, Veilleux's studies have called into serious question Cassian's reliability as a witness to Egyptian monastic practice. While it will not be possible to outline all of Veilleux's conclusions, some of them must be discussed because of their impact on our interpretation of the liturgical code in RB.

In 1957, A. van der Mensbrugghe published an article in which he argued that the Egyptian monks categorically repudiated the notion of "discontinuous" periods of prayer scattered throughout the day.[7] It was his contention that the Egyptian ascetics adhered staunchly to the ancient Christian principle of incessant prayer and that they therefore opposed the introduction of "official" hours of prayer, even though these hours were being widely adopted by monks in other regions of the world (e.g., West Syria, Cappadocia and Palestine). On the basis of this argument, van der Mensbrugghe attempted to show that the Egyptian prayer-hours developed in three stages:[8]

a) the "pre-Pachomian" stage, which steadfastly adhered to the ideal of incessant prayer for the individual monk through the discipline of vigils and the recitation of the psalter;

b) the "first-generation Pachomian monks," who celebrated three periods of common prayer daily: after work in the late afternoon, after supper (a "household" assembly for prayer) and at dawn;

c) the "second-generation Pachomian monks," i.e., those who were influenced by the *Rule of the Angel* (c. 380) and who therefore celebrated two periods of common prayer daily, morning and evening, at each of which twelve psalms were said. To these two "hours" were added psalms said during the day, while the monks were working, as

---

[6] A. Veilleux, *La liturgie dans le cénobitisme pachômien au quatrième siècle*, StA 57 (Rome: Herder 1968) pp. 276–323.

[7] A. van der Mensbrugghe "Prayer-Time in Egyptian Monasticism" *Studia Patristica* 2, TU 64 (Berlin: Akademie-Verlag 1957) 435–454.

[8] *Ibid.*, pp. 450–451.

well as three psalms said at the ninth hour, before the community
meal.

Van der Mensbrugghe's theory about the development of prayer-
times in Egyptian monasticism has been severely criticized by Veilleux. First, Veilleux contends that van der Mensbrugghe is inaccurate
about the complicated matters of chronology and authenticity among
the numerous documents that make up the Pachomian dossier of
sources. Secondly, Veilleux argues that the presumed Egyptian opposition to definite hours of prayer is largely without foundation in the
sources. Thirdly, Veilleux maintains that Cassian, whose description
of monastic life in fourth-century Egypt has often been accepted un-
critically, is an unreliable guide.[9] It must be remembered that Cassian was engaged in a polemic against monks in Gaul, some of whose
observances he found objectionable. This polemic sometimes led
Cassian to paint a uniform, idealized portrait of monastic life in
Egypt—a portrait at variance with the actual facts.

On the basis of his own research into the Pachomian sources,
Veilleux suggests a somewhat different interpretation of the early
Egyptian monastic tradition of prayer. We may summarize some of
his conclusions as follows:[10]

1. The collection of precepts known as the *Rule of Pachomius* reveals only two gatherings for prayer each day—morning and evening.
The morning synaxis brought all the brothers of the monastery together. In addition to prayer, this morning office included additional
elements such as work, manifestation of faults, and, perhaps,
catechesis. Evening prayer was celebrated in the individual households and was apparently done just before retiring for the night.

2. Some historians of the Divine Office have thought that there
were two evening gatherings in the Pachomian system: a "major" one
that involved all the brothers of the monastery, and a "minor" one that
concerned each household separately. Veilleux rejects this opinion
and suggests that it has been based on a gloss that Jerome made in his
Latin version of the Coptic text of the *Rule of Pachomius*.

3. Unlike other monastic groups, the Pachomian houses had *two*
meals daily, one at the middle of the day and another toward evening.
Sometimes the Pachomian sources used the technical term *synaxis*
(usually reserved for a "liturgical assembly" or a "place of prayer") in
reference to the common meals rather than times of prayer.

[9] Veilleux, *La liturgie*, pp. 282–283.
[10] *Ibid.*, pp. 292–315.

4. The morning synaxis in the Pachomian monasteries involved the following elements:

—After the signal for prayer had been given, the monks gathered informally and took their seats in order of seniority.

—Starting with the seniors, the monks took turns reading sections from the Scriptures. These biblical texts were not necessarily psalms; indeed, Veilleux feels that the Pachomian "office" was not composed principally of psalms.

—After each section of Scripture was finished, the reader gave a signal and all the monks rose. Standing, they prayed the Lord's Prayer with arms outstretched. Then they prostrated for silent interior prayer. After a brief time the monks rose again and continued to pray interiorly.

—Then another signal was given and the monks sat once more to listen to the Scriptures.

Veilleux points out that the earliest descriptions of the Pachomian morning office refer to the use of the Lord's Prayer, but not to the use of "psalter collects" (i.e., prayers based on the text of the psalm and said aloud following the period of silent interior prayer).

5. The Pachomian evening synaxis is more difficult to describe. The sources refer to "six prayers" said in the evening, and this has led many writers, including St. Jerome, to assume that "six *psalms*" were chanted. After a close examination of the Coptic sources, however, Veilleux maintains that the evening prayer in the Pachomian households refers to an office wherein several readers each recited six sections from Scripture. These biblical sections were not necessarily psalms.

6. What, then, of the famous *Rule of the Angel* and its tradition of "twelve psalms (prayers)" at both the morning and evening offices? Veilleux argues that this *Rule* does not represent the liturgical usages of Pachomian cenobites, but rather the practices of semi-anchorite monks in Lower Egypt—monks who were familiar with only one weekly gathering for common prayer, the Saturday-Sunday vigil that accompanied the weekly celebration of the Eucharist. Originally, then, the "twelve prayers" may simply have meant: "Pray at each of the twelve hours of the day and at each of the twelve hours of the night; in other words, pray incessantly at all hours of day and night." According to this interpretation, the *Rule of the Angel* originally referred to the ancient principle of incessant (private) prayer, not to the morning and evening hours of common prayer. Later on, these

"twelve *prayers*" were identified as "twelve psalms" said at the morning and evening synaxes. This later development would have been the practice commented upon as "Egyptian" by Cassian in Book II of his *Institutes*.

According to Veilleux, then, the Egyptian monastic tradition of common prayer was not nearly so ancient or so uniform as Cassian would have us believe. There was still a great deal of variability in the manner of gathering for public prayer among the monastic communities in fourth-century Egypt. Furthermore, there is little hard evidence to support van der Mensbrugghe's thesis that the Egyptian monks resisted the introduction of definite hours for prayer.

The cathedral tradition of the Divine Office (fourth century)

We have already mentioned that from the beginning the Christian hours of prayer were not considered the special prerogative of monks and clerics. *All* Christians were called upon to sanctify the hours of the day with prayer. Still, as time went on, important differences arose between the pattern common among monks and the pattern of prayer practiced by other Christians. The "cathedral tradition" is a term widely used today to identify that specific pattern of public prayer-hours celebrated by Christians in parish or cathedral churches. It may be useful, first of all, to indicate how this cathedral tradition differed from celebrations by ascetics.[11]

a) *Use of the psalter.* Cathedral offices tended to adopt a more selective approach to the psalter. The psalms were not read in order (*lectio continua*), but rather were selected for their appropriateness to the time of day and the season of the year. Efforts were made to underscore the Christological meaning of the psalms, i.e., to make the psalms Christian prayer by relating them to the mystery of Jesus risen and alive in his people. Further, it was not considered essential to recite the whole psalter in a specified period of time, e.g., a week.

b) *Ritual development.* The cathedral tradition gave scope to a more elaborate ceremonial development in the hours of common prayer. Though such ritual developments were not absent in monastic circles, they seem to have been encouraged more strongly in parochial celebrations. Use of lights, incense and vestments enhanced the hours of prayer.

c) *Variety.* The cathedral tradition stressed the use of texts and songs that could easily be recognized and remembered by the congre-

---

[11] See Storey "The Liturgy of the Hours" pp. 65–66.

gation. The repetitive patterns of song and rite in cathedral celebrations were designed to encourage easy and immediate participation by all, and this often resulted in a reduction in the number of variable elements in the office.

d) *Length.* The principal daily hours of prayer in the cathedral tradition were morning (Lauds) and evening (Vespers). As we shall see, there also developed a weekly "vigil of the resurrection" early Sunday morning, but this vigil was different from the lengthier monastic vigils. Moreover, as time went on, it became customary for monks in the West to celebrate prayer at the third (Terce), sixth (Sext) and ninth (None) hours in common. By contrast, the cathedral tradition tended to limit itself to common prayer in the morning and in the evening.

e) *Readings and prayer.* While the monastic offices customarily included readings from the Bible, the prayer-hours in the cathedral tradition often omitted such readings altogether. The cathedral office was not designed to instruct but to give public expression to the community's praise and petition. Litanies of petition, with the popular response "Lord, have mercy," became a familiar element in the cathedral tradition.

What documentary evidence do we possess that exemplifies this cathedral tradition of prayer-hours? One of the earliest witnesses is Eusebius († 339), best known for his *History of the Church.* In his commentary on Psalm 90(91), Eusebius explains that Christians celebrate morning prayer in order to give thanks and praise for the Lord's mercy; at evening prayer they confess their faults and seek forgiveness:

> In the *morning,* at the rising of the light, we proclaim the mercy granted us by God; at *night,* we manifest his truth through a sober and chaste way of life.[12]

Later in the fourth century St. John Chrysostom reaffirms Eusebius' interpretation of the two chief hours of daily public prayer in a sermon delivered to newly baptized Christians at Antioch:

> I urge you to show great zeal by gathering here in the church *at dawn* to make your prayers and confessions to the God of all things, and to thank Him for the gifts He has already given . . . strengthened with this aid, let each one leave the church to take up his daily tasks. . . . let each one approach his daily task with fear and anguish, and spend his working hours in the knowledge that *at evening* he should return here to the church, render an account to the Master of his whole day, and beg

---

[12] Translation from the Greek text: *PG* 23.1172.

forgiveness for his falls. . . . each evening we must beg pardon from the Master for all these faults. . . .[13]

In addition to the morning and evening hours of prayer in the cathedral tradition, there also arose, in the fourth century, the custom of the "resurrection vigil," celebrated in the early hours of Sunday morning. The first document that alludes to this celebration is the *Apostolic Constitutions*, a Syrian manual of Church discipline and liturgical customs that dates from the second half of the fourth century. There we read:

> . . . *assemble together every day, morning and evening*, singing psalms and praying in the Lord's house: *in the morning say Psalm 62 and in the evening say Psalm 140*. . . . *On the day of our Lord's resurrection*, give praise to God, who made the universe through Jesus, sent him to us, permitted him to suffer and raised him from the dead. For what excuse will a person make to God if he fails to assemble on that day to hear the saving word concerning the resurrection? *On that day we pray three times* in memory of him who rose after three days. . . . (*Didasc.apost.* 2,59).[14]

According to Mateos, this reference to three times of prayer on Sunday is actually an allusion to the resurrection vigil that preceded the Eucharistic celebration. This vigil is described much more fully in another fourth-century source known as Egeria's *Travels*, written sometime between 381 and 384. A lady with a keen eye for liturgical detail, Egeria was a pilgrim to the Holy Land. While in Jerusalem she attended numerous services and included descriptions of them in the diary she kept while travelling. Here is Egeria's description of the vigil that took place at cock-crow on Sunday morning in Jerusalem:

> On the seventh day, the Lord's Day, there gather in the courtyard before cock-crow all the people, as many as can get in, as if it was Easter. . . . Soon the first cock crows, and at that the bishop enters, and goes into the Anastasis. The doors are all opened, and all the people come into the Anastasis, which is already ablaze with lamps. When they are inside, a psalm is said by one of the Presbyters, with everyone responding, and it is followed by a prayer; then a psalm is said by one of the deacons, and another prayer; then a third psalm is said by one of the clergy, a third prayer. . . . After these three psalms and prayers they take censers into the cave of the Anastasis, so that the whole Anastasis

---

[13] John Chrysostom, *Baptismal Instructions*, ACW 31.126–127.
[14] Translation from the Greek text: *Didascalia et Constitutiones Apostolorum*, ed. F. Funk (1905; rpt. Turin: Bottega D'Erasmo 1964) pp. 171–173.

basilica is filled with the smell. Then the bishop, standing inside the screen, takes the Gospel book and goes to the door, where he himself reads the account of the Lord's resurrection. . . . When the Gospel is finished, the bishop comes out, and is taken with singing to the Cross, and they all go with him. They have one psalm there and a prayer, then he blesses the people, and that is the dismissal (Eger. *peregr.* 24,9-10).[15]

One can see in this description several of the elements characteristic of the cathedral tradition in the Liturgy of the Hours, e.g., the use of incense and lights, the rather elaborate ceremonies. As we shall see, this resurrection vigil seems to have had some influence on the Rule of Benedict, particularly on its directions for the last segment of vigils on Sunday.

Urban monastic tradition

The final line of development in the Liturgy of the Hours has been characterized by Mateos as the "urban monastic tradition."[16] Monks who lived in cities could hardly help being influenced by the liturgical customs of parochial churches. The urban monks tended to adopt cathedral customs associated with morning and evening prayer. To these they added the public celebration of the daytime prayers (at the third, sixth and ninth hours) already referred to by writers like Tertullian, Hippolytus and Cyprian. The monks also celebrated vigils ("nocturns," the "night office," the "midnight office") and, perhaps, Compline. The urban monastic tradition thus combines elements traditional among ascetics (e.g., vigils) with popular customs derived from the cathedral tradition. This mixture of elements had its influence, as we shall note below, on the structure and content of the Divine Office in the Rule of Benedict.

The historical outline given above shows that by the time the RB appeared, there were already well-established patterns of common prayer in both the monastic and cathedral traditions. Quite obviously, these patterns of prayer had an impact on the liturgical code of the RB. In the notes that follow, based largely on the extensive commentaries of Dom Adalbert de Vogüé, we shall attempt to identify both the distinctive contributions made by the RB to the structure and content of the Liturgy of the Hours, as well as those elements borrowed by the RB from other sources, e.g., the *Rule of the Master* and the customs of Roman basilical monasteries.

[15] *Egeria's Travels*, tr. J. Wilkinson (London: SPCK 1971) pp. 124–125.
[16] Mateos "The Origins of the Divine Office" pp. 484–485.

The hours of prayer in the RB

Before discussing the sources used by Benedict in the liturgical code, it may be useful to outline the structure of the Liturgy of the Hours found in RB 8–20. There are eight "hours" in Benedict's arrangement: Vigils, Lauds, Prime, Terce, Sext, None, Vespers and Compline. In the outline that follows, references are given in the right-hand column to the appropriate chapter and verse in RB where one may find further detail about the hours of prayer and their content. In the left-hand column references are given to the RM, one of RB's sources.[17]

RM		RB
	I. VIGILS (RB 9,10,11)	
32–33;44	A. *Vigils: Weekday in winter*	9
	1. Introduction	
32.13	Opening verse ("Lord, open my lips"), three times	9.1
	Psalm 3	9.2
32.14	Psalm 94(95)	9.3
	Ambrosian hymn	9.4
	2. "First Nocturn"	
33.29;44.2	Six psalms with refrain	9.4
(9 psalms)	Versicle	9.5
	Blessing by abbot	9.5
	Three readings	9.5
	Three responsories (one after each reading)	9.5
	3. "Second Nocturn"	
44.2	Six psalms with "alleluia" refrain	9.9
(4 psalms)		
44.4	Reading from the Apostle	9.10
44.4	Versicle	9.10
44.4	Litany ("Lord, have mercy")	9.10
("rogus Dei")		
33;44	B. *Vigils: Weekday in summer*	10
	All as for a weekday in winter (see above), except: the three readings and responsories are replaced by:	
	One reading from the Old Testament, recited by memory	10.2
	A short responsory	10.2

[17] This table is an expansion of the comparative diagram of the Roman, RM and RB versions of the vigils as given in de Vogüé, 5.435–436.

RM		RB
49	C. *Vigils: Sundays, summer and*	11
(all-night	*winter* [18]	
vigil on	1. Introduction (inferred from the	
Saturday-	structure of weekday vigils;	
Sunday)	not explicitly mentioned in	
	RB 11)	
	2. "First Nocturn"	
	Six psalms (with refrain: cf.	11.2
	RB 11.4)	
	The first psalm of Sunday	
	vigils is always Psalm 20	
	(21): (see RB 18.6,23).	
	Versicle	11.2
	(Blessing by abbot? See	
	weekday vigils, above)	
	Four readings	11.2
	Four responsories (one after	11.2
	each reading)	
	3. "Second Nocturn"	
	Six psalms with refrain	11.4
	Versicle	11.4
	(Blessing by abbot? See	
	weekday vigils, above)	
	Four readings	11.5
	Four responsories (one after	11.5
	each reading)	
	4. "Third Nocturn" (cf. the "resur-	
	rection vigil" of the cathe-	
	dral tradition described in the	
	Apostolic Constitutions and	
	in Egeria's *Travels*)	
	Three canticles with "alle-	11.6
	luia" refrain	
	Versicle	11.7
	Blessing by abbot	11.7
	Four readings from the New	11.7
	Testament	
	Four responsories (one after	11.7
	each reading)	
	The hymn "We praise you,	11.8
	God"	
	Reading from the Gospel	11.9
	The hymn "To you be praise"	11.10
	Final blessing	11.10

[18] *Ibid.*, p. 471.

RM		RB
33;35;39	II. LAUDS (RB 12–13)	
	A. *Lauds: Sunday*	12
	1. Introduction	
	Psalm 66(67) without refrain	12.1
	Psalm 50(51) with "alleluia" refrain	12.2
	2. Psalmody	
	Psalm 117(118)	12.3
	Psalm 62(63) (cf. the morning psalm of the cathedral tradition described in the *Apostolic Constitutions*)	12.3
	3. Canticle and "praises" (*Benedictiones et laudes*)	12.4
35.5	Canticle of the Three Young Men (Dan 3:52-56,57-90; RB uses the term *Benedictiones* for this canticle)	12.4
39.4	Psalms 148, 149, 150 (RB uses the term *laudes* to refer to these three psalms, which were a familiar part of Lauds in the old Roman Office)	12.4
	4. Reading and concluding prayers	12.4
39.2 (different reading)	A reading from the Book of Revelation	12.4
39.1	A responsory	12.4
	Ambrosian hymn	12.4
	Versicle	12.4
39.2	Gospel Canticle (almost certainly the *Benedictus* or "Song of Zechariah"— Luke 1:68-79)	12.4
35.1 ("rogus Dei")	Litany (perhaps a full litany rather than simply the "Lord, have mercy")	12.4
	Conclusion (Lord's Prayer? See RB 13.12)	
	B. *Lauds: Weekdays*	13
	1. Introduction	
	Psalm 66(67) without refrain	13.2
	Psalm 50(51) with refrain	13.2
	2. Psalmody (variable)	13.3-9
	Monday: Psalms 5 and 35(36)	13.4

RM   RB

	Tuesday:	Psalms 42(43) and 56(57)	13.5
	Wednesday:	Psalms 63(64) and 64(65)	13.6
	Thursday:	Psalms 87(88) and 89(90)	13.7
	Friday:	Psalms 75(76) and 91(92)	13.8
	Saturday:	Psalm 142 (143) and the Canticle from Deuteronomy divided into two sections	13.9

3. Canticle and "praises"   13.10
   The canticle follows the variable psalms and follows the "practice of the Roman Church" (13.10). On Saturday, the canticle is actually the second section of the Canticle from Deuteronomy (RB 13.9).
   Psalms 148, 149, 150   13.11
4. Reading and concluding prayers   13.11
   A reading from the Apostle   13.11
   A responsory   13.11
   Ambrosian hymn   13.11
   Versicle   13.11
   Gospel Canticle (probably the "Song of Zechariah")   13.11
   Litany   13.11
   Conclusion   13.11
   Lord's Prayer (recited aloud by the superior)[19]   13.12

34;35;40   III. PRIME (RB 17.2-4; 18.2-5)
                    (Sunday and weekdays)[20]
                    1. Opening verse: "God, come to   17.3
                       my assistance"
                    2. Hymn   17.3
35.2; 40.1-2   3. Psalmody (variable) (with or   17.2; 18.2-5
                       without refrain: 17.6; "alleluia" on Sunday: 15.3)

---

[19] On Benedict's use of the Lord's Prayer at this point in the office, see *ibid.*, 2.251.

[20] On the question of the origins of the office of Prime and its place in Benedict's system of prayer-hours, see *ibid.*, 5.516–518.

RM			RB
(2 psalms with refrain; 1 psalm with alleluia)	Sunday:	Psalm 118 (119) (four sections)	18.2
	Monday:	Psalms 1, 2, 6	18.4
	Tuesday:	Psalms 7, 8, 9A(9)	
	Wednesday:	Psalms 9B (10), 10(11), 11(12)	Psalms for Tuesday
	Thursday:	Psalms 12 (13), 13(14), 14(15)	through Saturday
	Friday:	Psalms 15 (16), 16(17), 17A (18A)	inferred from RB 18.5
	Saturday:	Psalms 17B (18B), 18(19), 19(20)	
35.3;40.3 (2 readings; 1 responsory)	4. Reading (only *one*; note the difference from RM)		17.4
	5. Concluding prayers		
40.3		Versicle	17.4
35.3;40.3 ("rogus Dei")		Litany ("Lord, have mercy")	17.4
		Dismissal	17.4

RM			RB
35;40	IV. TERCE (RB 17.5; 18.1,3,7,9)		
	1. Opening verse: "God, come to my assistance"		17.5; 18.1
	2. Hymn		17.5
35.2;40.1-2 (2 psalms with refrain; 1 psalm with alleluia)	3. Psalmody (partial variability) (with or without refrain: 17.6; "alleluia" on Sunday: 15.3)		
	Sunday:	Psalm 118 (119) (three sections)	18.3
	Monday:	Psalm 118 (119) (three sections)	18.7
	Tuesday | Saturday:	Psalms 119(120), 120 (121), 121 (122) (inferred from 18.9-10)	
35.3;40.3 (2 readings; 1 responsory)	4. Reading (only *one*; note the difference from RM)		17.5

RM		RB
	5. Concluding prayers	
40.3	Versicle	17.5
35.3;40.3	Litany ("Lord, have mercy")	17.5
("rogus Dei")		
	Dismissal	17.5

RM			RB
(cf.	V. SEXT (RB 17.5; 18.1,7, 9, 10)		
RM's	(Sunday and weekdays)		
outline	Same structure as for Terce, except:		
for Terce)	Psalmody: (with or without refrain:		
	17.6; "alleluia" on Sunday: 15.3)		
	Sunday:	Psalm 118(119)	18.3
		(three sections)	
	Monday:	Psalm 118 (119)	18.7
		(three sections)	
	Tuesday		
	⎮		
	Saturday:	Psalms 122(123),	18.9-10
		123 (124),	
		124 (125)	

RM			RB
(cf.	VI. NONE (RB 17.5; 18.1,7,9,10)		
RM's	(Sunday and weekdays)		
outline	Same structure as for Terce and		
for Terce)	Sext, except:		
	Psalmody: (with or without refrain:		
	17.6; "alleluia" on Sunday: 15.3)		
	Sunday:	Psalm 118 (119)	18.3
		(three sec-	
		tions)	
	Monday:	Psalm 118 (119)	18.7
		(three sec-	
		tions)	
	Tuesday		
	⎮		
	Saturday:	Psalms 125 (126),	18.9-10
		126 (127),	
		127 (128)	

RM		RB
36;41	VII. VESPERS (RB 13.12; 17.7,8; 18.12-18)	
("lucernaria")	(Sunday and weekdays)[21]	
	1. Introduction: (RB makes no	

[21] One will notice a lack of symmetry between Lauds and Vespers in RB. See *ibid.*, 5.495–498.

RM   RB

RM		RB
	explicit references to either an opening verse or introductory psalms)	
36.1;41.1-2 (4 psalms with refrain; 2 psalms with alleluia)	2. Psalmody (variable) (with refrain: 17.7; "alleluia" is *not* used on Sunday: 15.3)	18.12-18
	Sunday: 109 (110), 110 (111), 111 (112), 112 (113)	18.13
	Monday: 113 (114-115), 114 (116A), 115 (116B), 116 (117), 128 (129)	18.17
	Tuesday: 129 (130), 130 (131), 131 (132), 132 (133) (inferred from 18.13-14)	
	Wednesday: 134 (135), 135 (136), 136 (137), 137 (138) (omit 133[134]: 18.14)	
	Thursday: 138A (139A), 138B (139B) 139 (140), 140 (141)	18.16
	Friday: 141 (142), 143A (144A), 143B (144B), 144A (145A) (omit 142[143]: 18.14)	
	Saturday: 144B (145B), 145 (146), 146 (147A), 147 (147B), (inferred from 18.13-14)	
	3. Reading and concluding prayers	18.18
36.1;41.3	Reading	18.18
36.1;41.3	Responsory	18.18

RM		RB
	Ambrosian hymn	17.8; 18.18
36.1;41.3	Versicle	18.18
36.1;41.3	Gospel Canticle (almost certainly the *Magnificat* or "Song of Mary": Luke 1:47-55)	17.8; 18.18
36.1	Litany	17.8
("rogus Dei")		
	Lord's Prayer	13.12; 17.8
	Dismissal	

37;42	VIII. COMPLINE (RB 17.9-10; 18.19) (Sunday and weekdays)	
	1. Introduction: (RB gives no explicit directions)	
37.1;42.1-2 (2 psalms with refrain; 1 psalm with alleluia; 1 responsory)	2. Psalmody (invariable) (without refrain: 17.9) Psalms 4, 90 (91), 133 (134)	17.9; 18.14; 18.19
	3. Hymn, reading and concluding prayers	
	Hymn	17.10
37.2	Reading	17.10
	Versicle	17.10
37.2	Litany ("Lord, have mercy")	17.10
("rogus Dei")	Blessing	17.10
	Dismissal	17.10

The relation between RM and RB

In the liturgical code, as in other matters of monastic life and discipline, the chronological priority of RM over RB seems well established. In other words, the liturgical code of the Master (RM 33–49) seems more primitive than the code outlined in Benedict (RB 8–20).[22] A couple of examples will help illustrate this point.

a) *Sunday vigils.* The more ancient monastic tradition of keeping vigils for Sunday involved praying through the whole night from

[22] References to the Rule of the Master and its liturgical materials will be given according to the edition of A. de Vogüé, *La Règle du Maître*, SC 105–107 (Paris: Les Éditions du Cerf 1964–65), cited as de Vogüé, RM with volume and pages.

For the comparison between the general shape of the office in RB and RM, see de Vogüé 1.101–103 and "Scholies sur la Regle du Maître" *RAM* 44 (1968) 121–159.

Saturday evening until Sunday dawn. The RM has maintained this tradition: "Every Saturday, vigils should be celebrated in the monastery from evening until the second sound of the cock-crow; then Lauds are said" (RM 49.1). In contrast, however, RB replaces the all-night vigil on Saturday-Sunday with an office at the end of the night that is very much like vigils on ordinary weekdays, only a bit longer (RB 11).

b) *Use of "alleluia."* RM's instructions for the use of the "alleluia" at the Liturgy of the Hours are extremely detailed (see RM 39–45). According to the Master, "alleluia" is to be used every day with at least some part of the office, except during the period from Epiphany to Easter. RB, however, devotes but a brief chapter to the subject of "alleluia" (RB 15). Moreover, Benedict restricts the use of "alleluia" to the following instances: Eastertide (RB 15.1); the second six psalms of vigils on Sundays and weekdays (RB 15.2); the hours of office on Sundays outside Lent, except for Vespers and Compline (RB 15.3). The more prominent use of "alleluia" in RM appears to reflect an old monastic tradition that viewed the time after Pentecost as a kind of extension of the paschal season.[23]

These two examples, as well as other details analyzed extensively by de Vogüé,[24] make it likely that RB used RM as a source for its liturgical code, and not vice versa. This does not mean, however, that Benedict relied exclusively on the Master for his liturgical material. For there is another source of vast importance in understanding RB 8–20: the Roman Office.

Benedict and the Roman Office

In saying that the Roman Office was a source for RB's liturgical code, we need to be rather precise about what we mean by "Roman." Two traditions existed simultaneously at Rome: one, the office as recited by urban monks in various churches in the City; another, the cathedral tradition of the Roman Church followed by clergy and laity. Characteristically, the Roman monastic offices included the common celebration of Vigils and the "Little Hours" (Terce, Sext, None). The Roman cathedral tradition was organized around the principal hours of Lauds and Vespers.[25] Benedict uses the Roman monastic tradition

[23] De Vogüé, RM, 1.55, n.4.
[24] De Vogüé, 5.383–418.
[25] A. de Vogüé "Origine et structure de l'office benedictin" *CollCist* 29 (1967) 195, n.1.

as a basic source, though he occasionally manifests some influence from the cathedral tradition.[26]

It is important to notice, however, that while Benedict uses the Roman Office as a source, he changes it in some important respects. The following are a few examples of the way the liturgical code in RB has modified its Roman model.

a) *Vigils and Vespers.* At Rome, as in the RB, the custom was to recite the entire psalter within a week's time.[27] But the Roman practice was to divide the weekly psalter between only two of the prayer-hours: Vigils and Vespers.[28] Thus, Psalms 1–108(109) were recited at Vigils each week, and Psalms 109(110)–150 were said at Vespers.[29] This meant that the other hours of the Roman monastic office were composed primarily of invariable psalms repeated at the same hours each day.

Shortly before the appearance of the RB, this Roman tradition of the weekly psalter had undergone a reform.[30] What RB 8–20 proposes is, then, a "reform of a reform." Benedict maintains the principle of the weekly psalter, but introduces two significant modifications: (1) he limits the number of psalms at Vigils to twelve on all days, including Sunday, and reduces the number of psalms at Vespers from five (the Roman custom) to four; (2) since this reduction in the number of psalms at Vigils and Vespers left several unused, Benedict introduced variable psalmody at the hours of Lauds, Prime, Terce, Sext and None.[31] These two changes—firm regulation of the number of psalms at Vigils and Vespers, and the introduction of variable psalms at the other hours—allowed Benedict to eliminate some of the repetitions in the Roman monastic office, while at the same time maintaining the principle of the weekly recitation of the psalter.

b) *The "third nocturn" of Sunday Vigils.* We have already seen that in the fourth century there developed a popular Sunday morning office known as the resurrection vigil. This practice from the cathedral tradition seems to have influenced Benedict's arrangements for the

---

[26] See RB 13.10, where the reference to the canticles used at Lauds on weekdays seems to be an influence of Roman cathedral practice.

[27] See RB 18.23-25, where the principle of weekly recitation of the whole psalter is staunchly defended.

[28] See de Vogüé "Origine et structure" p. 195 for a discussion of the Byzantine custom. See de Vogüé 1.102–104 for a table comparing the Roman Office, RB and the Byzantine Office.

[29] De Vogüé "Origine et structure" p. 195.

[30] *Ibid.*, pp. 195–196.

[31] *Ibid.*, p. 196, n.2.

"third nocturn" (third section) of Sunday Vigils. While the old Roman Office may have had something similar,[32] it seems more likely that Benedict was influenced at this point by popular customs from Jerusalem, Constantinople and Milan. The presence of the hymn "To you be praise" (*Te decet laus*: RB 11.10) also points to the impact of Eastern liturgical forms on RB.[33]

c) *The Lord's Prayer at Lauds and Vespers.* Benedict's insistence that the Lord's Prayer be recited aloud by the superior at the conclusion of Lauds and Vespers (RB 13.12) may also represent a departure from Roman custom, which directed that the Lord's Prayer be recited silently at the end of Vespers.[34] On this point it is possible to see the influence of Spanish liturgical customs of the sixth century.[35]

d) *The presence of hymnody in RB.* At all the liturgical hours of both night and day, RB directs that a hymn (sometimes "an Ambrosian hymn") be sung. This is interesting, because no Roman source earlier than the twelfth century mentions hymnody as a regular feature of the Liturgy of the Hours.[36] It is possible that Benedict picked up this tradition of hymnsinging from other sources, notably Lerins or Milan.[37]

These few examples show that while the Roman monastic tradition was a major source of influence on the liturgical code in RB, it was not the only one. Furthermore, Benedict did not hesitate to modify that tradition in significant respects.

Liturgical vocabulary in RB

The liturgical vocabulary found in RB 8–20 involves some rather technical terms. The list that follows is not meant to be exhaustive, but it does include some of the terms that are either difficult to translate into English or problematic because of a lack of certainty about their meaning in the sixth-century Latin used by Benedict. The list will indicate the Latin word, followed by a reference to its first appearance in the liturgical code of RB; then the English rendering used in this edition will be cited and, finally, comments on its meaning will be given.

[32] De Vogüé, 5.476–477.
[33] For the text of this hymn, see *Didasc.apost.* 7,48.
[34] De Vogüé, 5.493.
[35] *Ibid.*, p. 493, n.25.
[36] *Ibid.*, p. 535.
[37] *Ibid.* For some further examples of the way the monastic tradition of Arles and Lerins influenced RB, see *ibid.*, pp. 449–450, 478, 491.

a) *Ambrosianum* (9.4). Translated here as "Ambrosian hymn." This term, which occurs four times in the liturgical code (9.4; 12.4; 13.11; 17.8), is used to designate only the hymns assigned for Vigils (9.4), Lauds (12.4) and Vespers (17.8). When the hymn for other hours of the Divine Office is designated, Benedict uses the term *hymnus* (see, e.g., 17.3). We know that even in his lifetime Ambrose had a reputation for hymnwriting, partly because Augustine, his contemporary, makes admiring references to his work (Aug. *conf.* 9,7). Many hymns attributed to Ambrose, however, cannot definitely be proved authentic, since the bishop of Milan had many imitators, especially in the medieval period.[38] For this reason it is difficult to know exactly which "Ambrosian hymn" Benedict had in mind.

b) *Antiphona* (9.3). Translated throughout the liturgical code as "refrain(s)." The exact meaning of *antiphona* (usually translated "antiphon") has been widely disputed. An accurate interpretation of the term demands that we examine the manner of performing the psalmody in RB.

In the early centuries of Christian worship, at least five different methods of performing psalmody were known. These included:[39]

1. psalms sung by the whole congregation;

2. psalms sung by a single person, while all others listened;

3. psalms sung alternately by the halves of the congregation or by two choirs ("antiphonal style");

4. psalms sung by one person for one verse (or half-verse), with the congregation singing the next verse (properly speaking, a "responsorial style");

5. psalms sung with a soloist chanting the verses, while those assembled respond with a refrain ("Alleluia," "Amen" or some other text; this too is a form of responsorial style).

It must be noted that a transformation of the antiphonal style (3, above) occurred. The ancient sense of "antiphon" referred to an alternation between two choirs (or two halves of the congregation). Later the term "antiphon" was used for a short text sung before and after a psalm or canticle. It is this latter sense of antiphon that has become familiar to most modern Christians.

Our question, of course, is, what did *antiphona* mean, particularly in monastic circles, in the epoch that produced the RB? Various

[38] Erik Routley, *Hymns and Human Life* (London: John Murray 1952) pp. 21–23.

[39] For these five methods of performing psalmody, see J. A. Lamb, *The Psalms in Christian Worship* (London: Faith Press 1962) pp. 38–45.

hypotheses have been advanced by scholars. In an article published in 1957, Corbinian Gindele argued that "antiphon" refers to a set of three psalms (thus, e.g., "three antiphons" would equal "nine psalms").[40] Although the proposal may seem preposterous, it is not to be dismissed out of hand. In the ancient Byzantine and Syrian liturgical traditions, for example, there is a tendency to group psalms together in sets of three or more.[41] De Vogüé, however, has argued against Gindele's interpretation, at least as it affects monastic sources like RM and RB.[42] According to de Vogüé, the meaning of "antiphon" in RM is simply this: "one antiphon" equals "one psalm"; the terms *antiphonae*, without further reference, and *psalmi cum antiphonas* are equivalent terms in RM.[43]

But this still leaves us with the question: what sort of performance is implied by the expression "psalm(s) with antiphon(s)," which appears several times in RB (e.g., 9.4; 11.4; 13.2)? De Vogüé has argued that the manner of performing the psalmody used almost exclusively today (the psalm chanted between two sides of the choir) was not common in Benedict's time. Rather, he maintains, the psalms were customarily recited by one or two soloists, with active participation by the assembly in the form of a "response" or "antiphon." "Antiphonal psalmody" thus implied the use of a responsorial refrain with which the whole community responded as the soloist(s) chanted the verses of the psalm.[44] Occasionally, indeed, the term "antiphon" refers only to the congregation's refrain, as distinguished from the verses of the psalm.[45] If this interpretation is correct, it means that the use of "psalms with antiphons" would have required a fairly large group of people who could reply with a refrain to the verses of a psalm chanted by one or two soloists.[46] This may be the reason why RB directs that "antiphons" are not to be used if the community is small (cf. RB 17.6).

Thus RB seems to know two basic types of psalm-performance: (1) psalms "with refrain (antiphon)" or with "alleluia"; and (2) psalms

[40] C. Gindele "Die Römische und monastische Überlieferung im Ordo Officii der Regel St. Benedikts" StA 42 (1957) 171–222.

[41] For examples, see J. Mateos "La psalmodie dans le rite byzantin" *Proche-Orient chrétien* 15 (1965) 107–126; "Les matines chaldéennes, maronites et syriennes" *Orientalia Christiana Periodica* 26 (1960) 51–73.

[42] A. de Vogüé "Le sens d'antifana' et la longueur de l'office dans la 'Regula Magistri'" *RBén* 71 (1961) 119–124.

[43] De Vogüé, RM, 1.60–61.

[44] De Vogüé, "Origine et structure" p. 198.

[45] De Vogüé, 2.522, note on RB 14.2.

[46] De Vogüé, 5.532.

"without refrain (antiphon)" (psalms chanted *in directum*: cf. RB 12.1; 17.6). The present translation renders the expression *psalmi cum antiphonas* by "psalms with *refrain*" (e.g., 9.4), in the hope of overcoming the mistaken impression that the later sense of "antiphon" often creates in the minds of modern readers. Benedict's *antiphona* was not a short text recited only at the beginning and end of a sung psalm, but a refrain sung by the assembly in response to the verses of a psalm chanted by soloists. Sometimes this refrain was an "alleluia" (cf., e.g., RB 9.9; 11.6; 12.2).

Similarly, the present translation uses the phrase "(psalm) without refrain" to render the Latin *psalmus sine antiphona*, as well as the Latin *psalmi directanei* (17.9) and *in directum psalluntur* (17.6). This "direct" method of psalm-performance involved the recitation of a psalm, either by a soloist or by the entire assembly, without the use of any refrain or response.[47] Thus the terms *in directum, sine antiphona,* and even the problematic *decantandum* (9.3) all seem to refer to the "direct" method of singing psalms without refrain.[48]

One final item should be noted before leaving the question of psalm-performance in RB. Benedict uses a variety of words to express how the psalms are to be performed. Sometimes, for instance, he will say "four psalms are *sung*" (e.g.: "Vespera . . . quattuor psalmorum modulatione *canatur*" in 18.12), sometimes "(psalms) are *said*" (e.g.: "reliqui omnes in vespera *dicendi sunt*" in 18.15). It was the opinion of Cuthbert Butler that RB made no hard and fast distinctions in the use of words like *dicere* ('say'), *canere* ('sing'), *cantare* ('sing'), *modulare* ('make music'), and *psallere* ('chant [psalms]').[49] Butler's opinion seems to be a valid one, and it should be kept in mind while reading the present translation. When one reads that canticles at Sunday Vigils "are *said*" (11.6; Latin: "*dicantur* . . . cantica"), one should not interpret this as a prohibition against singing the canticles! Similarly, when one reads in the Latin text of RB 11.3, "*dicatur a cantante* gloria" (literally: "*said* by the one *singing*"), one should not assume that the cantor is being instructed to speak rather than sing. Benedict seems to have used these words freely, without following any rigid rules of classification between things spoken and things sung.

c) *Benedictiones* (12.4). Translated here as "the Canticle of the

---

[47] Mateos "La psalmodie dans le rite byzantin" p. 107.

[48] De Vogüé, 2.511, note on RB 9.3.

[49] *Sancti Benedicti Regula Monachorum*, ed. C. Butler (Freiburg im Breisgau: Herder 1912) p. 205, n.1.

Three Young Men" (Dan 3:52-56,57-90). The use of this same liturgical text as a part of the celebration of Lauds is found in RM.[50] It might
also be noted that in the old Spanish liturgy, the Canticle of the Three
Young Men was used at the Eucharist on Sundays and the feasts of
martyrs.[51] In the seventh century, for example, the Fourth Council of
Toledo (A.D. 633) insisted on the singing of this canticle (against those
priests who were neglecting it at Mass).[52] It is possible that the liturgical use of the *Benedictiones* became popular as a result of influence
from the Jerusalem church, where the canticle was sung at the Paschal
Vigil.[53] Finally, it should be observed that the sixth-century monastic
tradition at Arles, represented by Bishops Caesarius and Aurelian,
used this canticle at Lauds during the Easter season.[54]

d) *Canticum* (11.6). Here translated as "canticle(s)" in every instance except at RB 15.3, where, by way of metonymy, it has been
rendered "Vigils." Benedict's provision for the use of three canticles
at Sunday Vigils (11.6) recalls the resurrection vigil at Jerusalem as
described in Egeria's *Travels* (Eger. *peregr.* 24,9-10).

e) *Laudes* (12.4). In the plural this term has a technical meaning:
Psalms 148, 149, 150 (cf. RB 12.4; 13.11).[55] (At RB 16.5, however, this
technical meaning of *laudes* is *not* found; thus the word has been
rendered "praise"). The use of the term *laudes* to refer to the last three
psalms of the psalter probably stems from the fact that in the Vulgate
the first (Ps 148) and the last (Ps 150) begin with the Latin word *Lau-
date* ("Praise!").

f) *Lectio, lectiones* (8.3). Throughout the liturgical code these
words have been translated "reading(s)" (cf. 8.3; 9.5; etc.). It seemed
preferable to use "reading" rather than "lesson" in keeping with current English liturgical terminology. De Vogüé has noted that Benedict's system of readings at the Divine Office differs from that of both
RM and the Roman Office.[56] For example, these latter two traditions
place the readings at the end of the psalmody at weekday vigils, while

[50] De Vogüé, RM, 1.59.
[51] See L. Brou "Les Benedictiones ou cantique des trois enfants dans l'ancienne
messe española" *Hispania Sacra* 1 (1948) 26–33.
[52] For the text of the canons of the Fourth Council of Toledo on this matter, see J.
Mansi, *Sacrorum Conciliorum nova et amplissima collectio* (Graz: Akademische Druck
1960) 10.623.
[53] Brou "Les Benedictiones" p. 22.
[54] De Vogüé, RM, 1.59.
[55] *Ibid.*
[56] See, for example, de Vogüé, 5.443–450 on the readings at weekday Vigils.

RB places the readings between the two sets of six psalms at this office. Since RB provides us with no lectionary, we cannot be sure how Benedict distributed the Bible readings during the course of the Church year.

g) *Matutini* (8.4). Translated throughout the liturgical code as "Lauds," the "dawn" hour of the Divine Office that follows Vigils in Benedict's system. Similarly, the expressions *matutinorum sollemnitas* [57] (13.1) and *agenda matutina* (13.12) have been rendered "Lauds." In the past, *matutini* has sometimes been translated "Matins," but this creates confusion, since, in later monastic parlance, "Matins" was used for what Benedict calls "Vigils" or "Nocturns." Lauds and Vespers together form the two principal hinges of the Liturgy of the Hours, especially—though not exclusively—in the cathedral tradition. Benedict's arrangement for Lauds (cf. RB 12,13) is heavily indebted to the classical Roman Office, as the following comparison will indicate: [58]

Roman	RB
	Psalm 66(67)
Psalm 50(51)	Psalm 50(51)
Variable psalms	Variable psalms
Psalms 62(63), 66(67)	Variable psalms
Canticle	Canticle
Psalms 148–150	Psalms 148–150

As one can see, Benedict's arrangement permits a bit more variability (two variable psalms each day), while keeping most of the elements familiar in the Roman Office: Psalm 50(51); Psalm 62(63) on Sundays (RB 12.3); the canticle; the *laudes*. The practice of beginning Lauds with a psalm recited without refrain (cf. RB 12.1; 13.2—Psalm 66[67]) may have been derived from the monastic tradition of Arles. [59]

h) *Opus Dei*. This term, hallowed in Benedictine tradition, does not actually appear in the liturgical code (RB 8–20). It does surface in a number of places outside the code (e.g., RB 7.63; 22.6; 43.t,3; etc.). In the liturgical code itself, other phrases are employed to refer to the Liturgy of the Hours or the Divine Office. For example, the title of RB 8 uses *officium divinum* (in the plural), here translated as "Divine Office." The title of RB 16 has *divina opera* (in the plural), here translated as "Divine Office" (cf. 19.2). In RB 16.2 the term *servitutis*

---

[57] This expression was used by Cassian, *inst.* 3,3; see the reference in Butler, *Sancti Benedicti*, p. 44.

[58] The comparative table is taken from de Vogüé, 5.487.

[59] *Ibid.*, 5.491.

officia appears, here translated as "obligations of service."[60] Finally, in RB 17.7, the Greek liturgical term for an "assembly" (*synaxis*) appears in reference to Vespers only. Thus the present translation renders the Latin of 17.7 ("Vespertina . . . *synaxis*") simply by "Vespers." For a fuller account of the history of the term *opus Dei*, readers are referred to the almost classic article on the subject by Irenaeus Hausherr.[61]

i) *Vespera* (13.12: "agenda . . . vespertina"; 15.3). Translated throughout as "Vespers." As is usually the case in the liturgical code, Benedict shows his indebtedness to the Roman Office in his format for Vespers. However, while the classical Roman Office had five psalms at this service, RB reduces the number to four.[62] Vespers in RB also differs from the evening prayer described in RM 36 and 41, where six psalms are assigned for each day.[63] It may also be noted that RM and RB differ in their terminology for this evening hour of the Divine Office. RM ordinarily uses *lucernaria* (literally, 'lamp-lighting') to refer to the hour of office and reserves *vespera* ('evening') as a designation for the time of day.[64] On the other hand, Benedict never uses the term *lucernaria*. De Vogüé has written that the term *lucernaria* (or: *lucernarium*) seems not to have been known in Rome.[65] There, *Vespera* was used to designate both time of day and the evening hour of the office (the counterpart of Lauds). Some scholars have argued that the presence of a term like *lucernaria*, in RM and other sources, is a sign of "high antiquity." De Vogüé disputes this claim and insists that use of the term *lucernaria* simply indicates "non-Roman provenance" and nothing more.[66] Thus, while the ancient Church certainly knew a "lamp-lighting" service of prayer and praise, the *lucernaria* of a sixth-century document like RM means simply "the evening psalmody." RB's use of the alternative term, *vespera*, simply situates the document in the "pure Roman" tradition.[67]

[60] The phrase *servitutis officia* may be found in a postcommunion prayer for Palm Sunday in the ancient Gelasian Sacramentary. For Latin text see *Liber Sacramentorum Romanae Aeclesiae ordinis anni circuli*, ed. C. Mohlberg, Rerum Ecclesiarum Documenta, Series Major: Fontes 4 (Rome: Herder 1960) p. 54, n.332.

[61] I. Hausherr "Opus Dei" *Orientalia Christiana Periodica* 13 (1947) 195–218.

[62] De Vogüé, 5.497.

[63] *Ibid.*, for the proposal that RM's six-psalm arrangement for Vespers is in accord with the more ancient, pre-classical Roman tradition.

[64] *Ibid.*, 5.519–525.

[65] *Ibid.*, 5.522.

[66] *Ibid.*, 5.524–525.

[67] *Ibid.*

j) *Vigiliae* (8.3). Translated here as "Vigils." Besides *vigiliae*, a number of different terms are used in RB to indicate the night office: *vigiliae nocturnae* (9.11); *nocturna laus* (10.t); *nocturnos* (15.2); *nocturnis vigiliis* (16.4). All these terms have been rendered by the English "Vigils" in the present translation, with the exception of *nocturna laus* ("Night Office": 10.t). The variance in terminology for this office in RB is reflected as well in other monastic sources of the same period. For example, Caesarius and Aurelian of Arles call the ordinary weekday night office *nocturni*, while reserving the term *vigiliae* for Saturdays, Sundays and feasts.[68] RM keeps the term *vigiliae* for full-length vigils, i.e., for the vigils that begin on Saturday evening and end in the early hours of Sunday morning (RM 49).

Some remarks have already been made about the difference between RM and RB in the matter of vigils. RB's abandonment of the "all-night" vigil distinguishes it from an almost universal custom among monks in the East, in Gaul and in Italy. Indeed, throughout the fifth and sixth centuries, one can say that monks kept the practice of all-night vigils not only on great festivals but weekly.[69] How, then, can one explain Benedict's departure from this sacrosanct custom?

De Vogüé has noted that, like the Roman Office, Benedict has replaced the all-night vigil (one spread throughout the entire night) with an office of fixed structure and predictable duration—an office that comes at the end of the night after the monks have had an opportunity for a full night's sleep.[70] Thus, while RM tries to maintain vigils at least on some occasions, RB rallies to the practice of Rome, where we seem to find the earliest evidence for abandoning vigils.[71] It would be idle to speculate on the reasons why all-night vigils were abandoned in RB. Suffice it to say that in calling his night office "Vigils," Benedict is following a tradition which, in the opinion of de Vogüé, is just as ancient and legitimate as restriction of the term to the all-night office described in RM.[72]

One final remark may be made on the subject of Vigils in RB. While Benedict's sources for the structure of weekday Vigils include RM, the Roman Office and the tradition of Arles and Lerins, his source for Sunday Vigils is exclusively the Roman Office. Even so, Benedict has modified his Roman source. Whereas the Roman Office sometimes

[68] *Ibid.*, 5.465.
[69] *Ibid.*, 5.455.
[70] *Ibid.*, 5.457.
[71] *Ibid.*, 5.462.
[72] *Ibid.*, 5.467–468.

lengthened the first part of the psalmody for Sunday Vigils (12, 14 or 19 psalms), Benedict adhered strictly to twelve psalms for the entire office.[73]

Times and seasons in the Rule of Benedict

a) *The Church year in the Rule of the Master.* According to the provisions found in RM, the year had two basic divisions: (1) winter: from the autumnal equinox until Easter; and (2) summer: from Easter until the autumnal equinox. This basic rhythm of two seasons is modified somewhat by a specifically religious and liturgical concern, the celebration of Easter. Easter is always the point at which the changeover from the winter season to the summer season occurs. It thus marks both the change of natural season (winter to summer) and the change of liturgical time (Lent to Paschaltide).[74] Related to the Easter festival in RM is the Christmas-Epiphany cycle. Both Easter and Christmas are preceded by a period of penitential preparation. Eight days of fast and abstinence are observed before Christmas (RM 45.4-7). As one might expect, the period of preparation for Easter is much longer. On the day after Epiphany, RM directs that the singing of "alleluia" be discontinued (RM 45.9); at the same time, there begin the "one hundred days" of fasting before Easter (*centesima Paschae*: RM 45.11).[75] Lent proper begins six weeks before Easter. RM also makes explicit reference to observances on the days of the "paschal triduum": Holy Thursday (e.g., RM 53.26), Good Friday (e.g., RM 53.47) and Holy Saturday (e.g., RM 53.47). Moreover, RM refers to other prominent liturgical days like the Octave of Easter (RM 53.55) and the Vigil of Pentecost (RM 28.45).

The central focus of the week in RM is, of course, Sunday with its all-night vigil beginning Saturday evening, its celebration of the Eucharist, its provision for *two* meals, and its use of the "alleluia."[76]

b) *The Church year in RB.* RB's organization of the year is similar to that of RM. There are two basic seasons, summer and winter (see, e.g., RB 8–10). Unlike RM, however, RB is not uniform in its directions for the beginning of the winter season. Liturgically, winter begins on the "first of November" (8.1), while the winter season of fasting begins in September and the winter schedule for work begins on the first of

[73] *Ibid.*, 5.470–472.
[74] De Vogüé, RM, 1.38–39.
[75] See discussion, *ibid.*, 1.41–42.
[76] *Ibid.*, 1.39.

October. It should be observed that the variable dates for the beginning of the winter season have their parallels in other monastic and ecclesiastical sources. For example, the Augustinian *Ordo monasterii* parallels RB's dating of Vigils during the winter season (Aug. *ord.mon.* 2).[77]

The Easter-Pentecost season is mentioned in the liturgical code (see, e.g., 15.1), as is Lent (15.2-3). But unlike RM, RB is silent about the Christmas-Epiphany cycle.[78] Nor are the days of the paschal triduum described. Further, as we have already noticed, RB has abandoned the weekly all-night vigil on Saturday-Sunday.

Of some interest is Benedict's use of the term *caput quadragesimae* (translated here as "the beginning of Lent": 15.2). This phrase appears four times in RB (15.2; 41.6; 48.10,16). *Caput quadragesimae* was, of course, an expression frequently found in ancient liturgical books, where it ordinarily designated the sixth Sunday before Easter.[79] But Benedict fails to supply any exact date for this beginning of Lent, nor does he repeat the mathematical calculations of RM, which sought to make up the full complement of forty days in Lent by adding some supplementary fast days in advance of the sixth Sunday before Easter.[80]

Finally, it may be noted that while RB makes a general reference to saints' days and festivals (RB 14), there is no mention of specific saints or feasts (other than Easter and Pentecost) in the liturgical code.

c) *The computation of time in RB.* A word should be said about the way RB computes the various hours of day and night (see, e.g., RB 8.1: "the eighth hour of the night"). In the ancient world there were two basic divisions to each day: the period from sunup to sundown ("day"), and the period from sundown to sunup ("night"). Each of these periods was divided into twelve segments called *horae* ('hours'). There were, therefore, "twelve hours of day" and "twelve hours of night." But since sunup and sundown varied constantly throughout the year, these hours would not always have been equal in length. For example, in the summer an hour during the day would have been longer than an hour during the night, for the simple reason that the nights are shorter at that time of year. Similarly, an hour during the

---

[77] De Vogüé, 1.86.

[78] The absence of references to Christmas and Epiphany does not mean that these feasts were not celebrated at this period. See A. A. McArthur, *The Evolution of the Christian Year* (London: SCM Press 1953) pp. 31–76.

[79] De Vogüé, 1.96.

[80] *Ibid.*, 1.96–97.

day in summer would have been longer (roughly eighty minutes) than an hour during the day in winter (roughly forty minutes). Only at the two equinoxes would the hours of day and night have been nearly equivalent. Thus, the "eighth hour of the night" (8.1) would have varied, according to modern measurements of "clock time," as much as forty minutes, depending upon whether the season was summer or winter.[81] Because of these variables in the computation of time, the present translation has rendered the time references in the liturgical code literally (e.g., "the *eighth hour* of the night": 8.1; "the *middle of the night*": 8.2).

The Eucharist in RB

To the modern reader, the scarcity of references to the Eucharist in the RB may seem scandalous. The term *eucharistia* never appears in RB, although it does occur in RM (72.8). But there are other differences between RB and RM in this matter as well. Some of these are discussed in the paragraphs that follow.

a) *The Eucharist in RM.* The Master provides for the monks to receive Communion under both species each day. The abbot of the monastery, even if he is not an ordained cleric, is responsible for distributing the Eucharist. According to de Vogüé, this distribution took place "at a Communion service held between part of the office—Sext, None or Vespers—and the common meal."[82] Concerning this practice in RM, de Vogüé goes on to comment:

> This communion *extra missam* seems to have been performed according to a short rite of which the only part familiar to us is the kiss of peace. As for the eucharistic sacrifice, the monks appear to have attended it only on Sundays, and doubtless went to the parish church to do so. Mass was celebrated in the oratory of the monastery only on rare and special occasions, when the secular clergy were invited.[83]

That the ancient monks did not celebrate the Eucharist every day can be shown from literature both monastic and non-monastic.[84] Even after the custom of ordaining large numbers of monks developed, priest-monks did not necessarily celebrate (or concelebrate) the Eucharist every day. A study of medieval monastic customaries, for example, has revealed that ordained monks frequently communicated

[81] See B. Steidle, *The Rule of St. Benedict*, tr. U. Schnitzhofer (Canon City, Colo.: Holy Cross Abbey 1967) pp. 132–134.
[82] A. de Vogüé "Problems of the Monastic Conventual Mass" DR 87 (1969) 328.
[83] *Ibid.*
[84] *Ibid.*, pp. 327–330 for some of this evidence.

with the rest of the community at the conventual Eucharist. It was certainly not considered obligatory for a priest-monk to "say his Mass" every day.[85]

b) *The Eucharist in RB*. What, then, can be said about the celebration of the Eucharist in RB? As we have seen, the liturgical code of RB makes no references at all to Mass. The term *missa* does appear in the code (17.4,5,8,10), as well as in three places outside the code (35.14; 38.2; 60.4). But in none of these instances is it clear beyond all doubt that *missa* means "Mass."[86] At this period in the development of liturgical terminology, *missa* can simply mean 'dismissal' or the concluding blessings and prayers that are said before the conclusion of a liturgical service (whether Mass or office). The same thing can be said about the term *oblatio*, which does appear in RB but not in the liturgical code (59.1,8). Although *oblatio* was used of the Eucharistic celebration in literature of the period, it does not necessarily have this meaning in chapter 59, where the subject is noble parents who want to present their sons to the monastery.[87]

One does find in RB, however, the term *communio*. This word occurs three times, but never in the liturgical code. In RB 63.4, the monks are directed to approach the "kiss of peace" and the "Communion" according to their rank in the community. Almost certainly this is a reference to the reception of the Eucharist. But it does not necessarily refer to the celebration of Mass, since, as we have seen, RM gives similar instructions for the reception of Communion daily after office and before the meal. In other words, RB may simply be following RM at this point—a ritual of Communion (outside Mass) that includes the exchange of the kiss of peace.

Again, in RB 38.10, the term *communio* appears, this time in reference to the weekly reader at table. The reader is to be given a *mixtum* (a drink of wine, most probably) "because of the holy Communion" (*propter communionem sanctam*). Once more RB follows RM, where a similar practice is mentioned (RM 24.14). The reference in RB 38.10 may, then, signify a daily reception of the Eucharist along the lines indicated in RM.[88]

Finally, *communio* occurs in RB 38.2 in the phrase *post missas et*

---

[85] R. Grégoire "La Communion des moines-prêtres à la messe d'après les coutumiers monastiques médiévaux" *Sacris Erudiri* 18 (1967–1968) 524–549.

[86] De Vogüé "Problems of the Monastic Conventual Mass" p. 327.

[87] *Ibid.*, pp. 327–328, where de Vogüé seems to accept *oblatio* as a reference to Eucharist. For a contrasting opinion see Steidle, *The Rule of St. Benedict*, pp. 260–262.

[88] See E. de Bhaldraithe "Problems of the Monastic Conventual Mass" *DR* 90 (1972) 170.

communionem. De Vogüé seems to feel that this phrase means "after Mass and Communion," especially since the verse (38.2) deals with Sunday.[89] But as Eoin de Bhaldraithe has pointed out, *missas* here "may very well mean the end of Sext, for this is exactly how it is described in 17, 13" (17.5 according to the versification used in this edition).[90] Even RB 38.2, then, may not actually be a reference to the full Eucharistic celebration, though de Vogüé's opinion cannot be dismissed lightly.

Should we conclude that RB knows nothing at all about a Eucharist in the monastery, even on Sundays? Probably not. De Vogüé's conclusion on the matter seems both sound and cautious. He writes: "At most it is possible that a conventual Mass in St. Benedict's monastery was celebrated on Sundays and feast days. But perhaps Mass was celebrated less often, even without fixed regularity."[91]

Psalmody and prayer in RB

Before concluding these notes on the liturgical code, some comments should be offered on the relationship between psalmody and "prayer" in RB. RB 20.4-5 reads:

> Prayer should therefore be short and pure, unless perhaps it is prolonged under the inspiration of divine grace. In community, however, prayer should always be brief; and when the superior gives the signal, all should rise together.

What is this "short," "brief" prayer that Benedict describes in chapter 20? Earlier in the liturgical code, at RB 17.5, *oratio* ("prayer") seems to be a global reference to the entire Divine Office.[92] Do the references to prayer found in chapter 20 mean that the whole Divine Office should be characterized by brevity? Or is there another meaning for "prayer" in RB 20?

Some assistance in answering these questions may be sought in the ancient use of psalmody in both the monastic and the cathedral traditions. St. Athanasius, John Cassian and Egeria's *Travels* all refer to the "prayer" that followed the singing of a psalm.[93] The practice of offering prayer after the psalm was one way to "Christianize" the psalter. Prayer permitted the community to appropriate the meaning of the psalm in the light of Jesus' life, ministry, mission and destiny. In the

---

[89] De Vogüé, 2.574, note on RB 38.2.
[90] De Bhaldraithe "Problems" p. 170.
[91] De Vogüé "Problems of the Monastic Conventual Mass" p. 328.
[92] De Vogüé, 2.527, note on RB 17.5.
[93] *Ibid.*, 5.581.

cathedral tradition especially, this "psalm-prayer" involved both a brief period of silent personal prayer following the psalm and a collect or oration said by the presiding minister. The so-called psalter collects developed significantly in the fifth to the seventh centuries. They were written down and circulated in a number of different churches.[94]

Whether or not such formal psalter collects were known in monastic circles is a debated point. While Cassian seems to be familiar with them, RB makes no clear references to these collects. Nor are Benedict's allusions to the silent prayer after the psalms as clear as those found in the Master (see RM 14.1,20; 33.44; 55.6,18; 56.3-7). De Vogüé comments that, unlike the cathedral tradition, psalter collects may not have been customary in monastic circles.[95] But at the same time he argues that silent personal prayer following the psalm was very much a part of the monastic tradition.

The references to prayer in RB 20.4-5 may, therefore, be an allusion to the monastic custom of prostrating for silent prayer after the psalm, even if no psalter collect was to follow. According to de Vogüé, these periods of silent prayer were an intrinsic part of the psalmody in monastic tradition.[96] The psalms acted as invitations to prayer (the silent prayer of the heart). For in the older monastic practice, the psalm was not regarded as human homage rendered to God but rather as God's message to humanity, awakening the response of prayer. Like other parts of Scripture, the psalms were readings that invited and encouraged the prayer of the heart. Thus the psalm (reading) awakened a response (interior prayer) that was sometimes gathered up into the words of a public prayer (psalter collect). This three-stage movement—reading, personal prayer, collect—was an important way for Christians to appropriate the deeper meaning of the psalms. Sometimes the "Glory be to the Father" was also used as a way to "Christianize" the psalter. The liturgical code of RB directs the use of the "Glory be" with the psalms (see, e.g., 9.2,6; 11.3; 13.9; 17.2; 18.1).[97]

Summary

Overall, it can be said that the liturgical code in RB reflects both originality and faithfulness to the earlier monastic tradition. Benedict was not afraid to draw upon a variety of sources for his liturgical

[94] Several different series of such psalter collects were compiled during this period: an African series, an Italian series and several Spanish series. See de Vogüé, 5.584–585.

[95] De Vogüé, 5.582–583. See also A. de Vogüé "Le sens de l'office divin d'après la Règle de s. Benoît" RAM 42 (1966) 391–404; 43 (1967) 21–33.

[96] De Vogüé "Le sens de l'office divin" pp. 21–28.

[97] Ibid., pp. 27–28.

material: RM, the Roman Office, the monastic tradition of Arles and Lerins, cathedral usages from Jerusalem, Milan, Spain. Nor was he hesitant about introducing new elements into the liturgy for monks (e.g., hymnody). While maintaining traditional elements (e.g., the weekly psalter from the Roman Office) he adapted and modified those elements, shaping them to his own purposes. RB is, therefore, a good example of the way Christians have remained faithful to a liturgical tradition precisely by adapting it to meet changing circumstances.

Appendix 4

The Disciplinary Measures in the Rule of Benedict

The end of the "Age of Martyrs" marked the beginning of a surge of penitential practices and developments in the early Church.[1] Linked to this was the accelerated growth of monasticism and monastic forms of life, typified by the desert hermit and culminating in the *coenobium*. Here ascetics gathered to live a common life under the guidance of a spiritual master and a rule of life.[2] From the abundant literature by and about these ascetic sages, it is clear that they saw in their austere lives a perpetuation of the spirit of the martyrs,[3] who achieved the fullness of Christian life and hope by crowning their baptism in water with their baptism in blood. This was to make a virtue of a necessity. But the virtue proved too precious to be permitted to pass away with the end of the persecutions. The monk thus came forward as the "white martyr,"[4] who sought the perfection of the baptismal life through cultivating the "way of penance" (*paeni-*

---

[1] Of the many writings that treat the early Church's penitential developments, the classical work remains B. Poschmann, *Paenitentia Secunda: Die kirchliche Busse im ältesten Christentum bis Cyprian und Origenes* (Bonn: Hanstein 1940).

[2] It remains uncertain whether persecution of Christians or the end of the persecutions was the actual stimulus to monastic growth at this period of history. Anchoritic and cenobitic monasticism developed from various lines of early Christian asceticism and do not represent the origin of monasticism, "but rather successful forms on which others patterned themselves" (J. Gribomont "Monasticism" *New Catholic Encyclopedia* 9 [1967] 1036). See also Introduction, pp. 11f.

[3] Cf. E. Malone, *The Monk and the Martyr: The Monk as the Successor of the Martyr* (Washington, D.C.: Catholic Univ. Press 1950).

[4] The expression "white martyrdom" arose among the early monks of Ireland, who, in addition to distinguishing "white" and "red" martyrdom, also spoke of "green" martyrdom—that is, one who "separates from his desires or suffers toil in penance and repentance." See *ibid.*, p. 71.

tentia secunda)[5] as the primary means to regenerate one's *paenitentia prima*, i.e., baptism.

The association between monastic life and penance was therefore not contrived. But it needs proper understanding through careful study of the sources and forces that constitute the essence of a life of participation in the sufferings of Christ (RB Prol.50). In this perspective, it is readily seen that the RB should be no exception to its times when it treats at length the penalties one may incur in the monastery. Yet, compared to his most immediate sources, Cassian and the *Rule of the Master*,[6] St. Benedict is quite brief and concise in his disciplinary legislation, but also more thorough, circumspect and humane.

The historical context

During the third century, the West developed a rather uniform penitential practice as a public act within the Church's liturgy under the watchful direction of the hierarchy.[7] At the same time, in the East, an alternate approach to penance was evolving. Here the "spiritual person" (*pneumatikos*) emerged as the foremost minister of the Church's role in the forgiveness of sins. The East did not generally succumb to the rigorism that predominated in the West; rather, it allowed for more than a single reception of sacramental penance within a lifetime, and distinguished several degrees of penitents: (1) the "weeping" (*flentes*), who remained outside the liturgical assembly and wept for forgiveness; (2) the "listeners" (*audientes*), who had to leave with the catechumens after hearing the "liturgy of the word"; (3) the "prostrate" (*substrati*), who had to kneel or lie prone, begging forgiveness of the assembly; (4) the "standing" (*stantes*), who could remain standing for the entire liturgy with those in full communion, without, however, being permitted to receive the Eucharist. These steps can be seen developing already in Origen and Dionysius of Alexandria, and

[5] Tertullian, writing around the year 200, gives witness to the use of this expression among Christians. In his *De paenitentia* (6,14) he says that he is hesitant about informing catechumens of the *paenitentia secunda* lest they view it simply as an opportunity to continue sinning, just as some of them used the time before baptism as an outstanding period to sin, believing that all would be forgiven them in baptism.

[6] Cassian. *inst.* 2,15-16; 3,7; 4,16; and *conl.* 18,15; and RM 12–14, which contains 169 verses as compared to the 53 verses of RB 23–30 and 44. See de Vogüé, 7.275.

[7] Cyprian of Carthage († 258) and his contemporary churchmen provide ample witness to this contention. For a more complete treatment, see K. Hein, *Eucharist and Excommunication: A Study in Early Christian Doctrine and Discipline* (Frankfurt am Main: Peter Lang 1975²) pp. 365–410.

are fully present in Basil of Caesarea.[8] Origen, a persuasive proponent of the *pneumatikos* in the Church,[9] still concedes to the bishop the most prominent role in the exercise of sacramental penance. But in the bishop Dionysius of Alexandria, the penitential system is found to be rather flexible. By securing a "letter of recommendation" from a martyr,[10] a repentant apostate could obtain readmission to the Church without the mediation of the hierarchy. Eventually, under the influence of such practices, the public character of penance gave way to "private" forms, especially under the direction of the "successors to the martyrs," the monks.[11]

In the West, by the end of the fourth century, penitential practices began to declir.· –not through laxity, but because they became too demanding. First, there were those who denied altogether the Church's power to forgive certain sins.[12] In turn, Popes Siricius (384–399), Innocent I (401–417), and in particular Leo I (440–461) issued decrees allowing for the reduction of public penance, while maintaining it for especially serious sins; these, however, were still considered forgivable only once after baptism. At the same time, extremely hard sanctions were imposed upon these sinners. They were not permitted to marry or hold public office or to use the baths,[13] and so on. Soon

---

[8] See Origen († 253), *in Ioan.* 28,4–7; Dionysius of Alexandria († 264), see note 10 below; Basil of Caesarea († 379) *epist.* 217, canons 56–83.

[9] See G. Teichtweier, *Die Sündenlehre des Origenes* (Regensburg: Pustet 1958) p. 253.

[10] In a letter to Fabius of Antioch, preserved by Eusebius, *hist.eccles.* 6,42,5-6, Dionysius attests how the martyrs, through a "letter of recommendation," influenced the penitential system so strongly that one's readmission to communion with the Church could by-pass the bishop.

[11] See P. Meinhold "Busswesen" *Die Religion in Geschichte und Gegenwart*, 1.1548. As early as Ignatius of Antioch, the reverence accorded the ascetic, sometimes to the discontent of the bishop, is clearly noted. Likewise, the *Pastor Hermae* and Justin Martyr witness to the ascetics' esteemed and influential presence in the Church. See H. Leclercq "Monachisme" *DACL* 11.1783-84. In his *vita Anton.* 46, Athanasius notes how Antony ministered to the confessors in prison while hoping himself to gain martyrdom. Failing this, it is explained how the monastic life is nevertheless the life of martyrdom (47). Antony, whom Athanasius himself sought out for spiritual edification and guidance, is filled with the Holy Spirit (14 and 22) and has the ability to discern spirits (88). The development of "private confession" under the influence of monks and monk-confessors was much slower in the West, but is obvious in the case of the Celtic monks on the continent, who introduced many penitential books in the early Middle Ages. See L. Bieler "Penitentials" *New Catholic Encyclopedia* 11.86-87.

[12] Novatianism was a heretical, rigorist system in Benedict's day.

[13] The infrequent use of the bath or total abstention from it (see *vita Anton.* 93) was viewed as an ascetical practice as well as a protest against the luxury and abuses connected with the public Roman baths.

sacramental penance was generally viewed primarily as immediate preparation for death or to be used only in case of serious illness.[14] Penitents, because they were refused marriage and public positions, were looked upon more and more as a type of monk. This association between the penitent and monastic life often encouraged pious laypersons, particularly in France and Spain, to take up the life of penance voluntarily and to associate themselves as *conversi* with a monastery, while continuing their life in the world.[15]

Finally, the barbarization of society at St. Benedict's time further stimulated ecclesial and religious institutions to produce detailed and stringent penal legislation, for the Church, more than the civil institutions, had the stability and capacity to bring about some state of "law and order."

Under these conditions and, to a large extent, in response to them, the Patriarch of Western Monasticism drafted a Rule that brought together many of the best and most balanced disciplinary measures of the Church's tradition and practice in both the East and the West. These he supplemented and modified with his own experiences and scriptural insights. The outcome was such a well-formed alliance of asceticism and moderation that the RB has survived the test of the centuries beyond numerous other monastic rules.[16]

But it was not interest in civil law and order or in longevity of his Rule that motivated Benedict's disciplinary legislation; rather, it was simply the Christian life itself as lived in a monastery and as founded in its most outstanding source—revelation. Even when other monastic and spiritual traditions of the Church occur point for point in the RB's disciplinary provisions, it is clear that St. Benedict made use of them only because they were, in his mind, adequate expressions of the motives he found in Scripture: "What page, what passage of the inspired books of the Old and New Testaments is not the truest of

[14] See Meinhold, p. 1548, and C. Vogel, *La discipline pénitentielle en Gaule des origines à la fin du VII*[e] *siècle* (Paris: Letouzey et Ané 1952) p. 51.

[15] See É. Amann "Pénitence" *Dictionnaire de théologie catholique* 11.834. In this we readily see the seed of the later *fratres conversi* and today's "oblates." Many examples and descriptions of *conversi* are furnished by Vogel, *La discipline*, pp. 128–138.

[16] Since monastic life is interested not only in the avoidance and forgiveness of sin but also in eradicating attachment to sin and its occasions, it is not surprising that the fathers of monasticism applied the severe ecclesial discipline taken against major sins to the faults and imperfections one may encounter in the monastic life. St. Benedict expresses this in concise disciplinary measures, generally made abruptly and without explanation, which give the Rule a harsh tone. See de Vogüé, 5.785–786. Nevertheless, the moderation and balance in the RB made the monastic life accessible to many who could not have borne the rigors of other rules.

guides for human life? What book of the holy catholic Fathers does not resoundingly summon us along the true way to reach the Creator?" (RB 73.3-4).

Therefore, our interest here is directed principally toward gaining a deeper insight into St. Benedict's spiritual motivation. The reconstruction of the traditions and history that finally resulted in the Rule is not the object of our pursuit[17] except to the extent that it serves to illuminate or illustrate the point at hand.

Main characteristics of corrective legislation in RB

The major portion of St. Benedict's corrective legislation is found in RB 23-30 and 44, often referred to somewhat inaccurately as the "penal code." In addition, there are many other statements of a disciplinary nature found dispersed throughout the Rule. These all provide for the correction of various faults, large and small, through several forms of sanction, including corporal punishment and expulsion from the monastery. However, it would be incorrect to view this disciplinary legislation as if it had from its inception "canonical status" that gave it recognition and force throughout the Church.[18] Instead, the RB applies the elements of ecclesial discipline to monastic life without claiming that it thereby also imposes these penalties with the same canonical force that they otherwise held in the Church. Often the disciplinary legislation of the RB reflects more the spirit of an earlier age than of its own times. This is largely due to Benedict's choice of

[17] This is a special task that others have undertaken, especially in the monumental work of de Vogüé, 1-7.

[18] Many commentators on the RB have depicted Benedict with a juridical and canonical status in the Church of his day that he as a matter of fact cannot be said to have had. Their conclusions depend on unfounded or erroneous premises, such as the claim that St. Benedict was a priest, and that priests had the power to excommunicate one from the Church. This argument was bolstered with a reference to the *Decretum Gratiani* (c. 32 2. XI qu. 3), which purported to be quoting St. Augustine: "Omnis christianus, qui a sacerdotibus excommunicatur, satanae traditur: quomodo? scilicet, quia extra ecclesiam diabolus est sicut in ecclesia Christus: ac per hoc quasi diabolo traditur, qui ab ecclesiastica communione removetur." However, this text is now acknowledged as pseudo-Augustinian. See R. Spilker "Die Busspraxis in der Regel des hl. Benedikt, II. Die Exkommunikation" *SMGBO* 57 (1939) 14. Others have held that Gregory's account (*dial.* 23) indicates that Benedict's excommunication of two nuns had canonical recognition in the Church. Aside from the naïve historicism implicit in this argument, it must be noted that St. Benedict only threatened to pronounce excommunication (without ever actually doing so). The purpose of the account is to depict Benedict as the man of God filled with the Spirit of God and whose charismatic word claimed the respect and attention of ecclesial authority. For fuller discussion, see G. Oesterle "De codice poenali in Regula S. Benedicti" *StA* 18/19 (1947) 173-193, esp. 185f.

sources and traditions and especially his very conscious effort to shape monastic life and discipline according to the Gospel (RB Prol.21; 11.9; 23.2).

St. Benedict notes (RB 23.2) that monastic discipline is to be "in accord with our Lord's injunction" (Matt 18:15-17). Therefore, two secret admonishments are to be given to a brother "found to be stubborn or disobedient or proud, if he grumbles or in any way despises the holy rule and defies the orders of his seniors" (RB 23.1). If that proves ineffective, the wrongdoer is to be rebuked "in the presence of everyone."[19]

The *Rule of the Master* (12.2-3) speaks of "two or three warnings" (with no mention of their being given in secret) before the recalcitrant is brought to the abbot for excommunication, pronounced in the presence of the superiors and the community.[20] St. Benedict reshapes the RM to bring the ruling more exactly in line with the New Testament, without, however, succumbing to a fundamentalist use of Scripture. This is seen in the case of a remiss prior, who is to be verbally corrected up to four times (RB 65.18). After that, if he still has not responded properly, he is to undergo the *correptio disciplinae regularis* (RB 65.19), that is, the "public" process of correction,[21] which could even conclude with the prior's removal from office and expulsion from the monastery.

The RM, in an analogous situation of the abbot's hand-picked successor, prescribes that if he does not amend after being warned by the abbot (RM 93.77), he is to have his name stricken from the diptych, be deposed and undergo punishment, namely, excommunication, as any other negligent member of the community would (RM 93.78-79).

The Master seems to have an indefinite number of warnings in mind for a neglectful abbot-designate. But St. Benedict, who characteristically refrains from stipulating specifics (leaving them to the discretion of the abbot), wishes to set definite limits and guidelines for dealing with a superior in need of correction. Clearly, he has had unfavorable experiences with priors (RB 65). Yet, greater than usual patience is required in correcting them, lest the abbot make a hasty or imprudent decision because of some envy or jealousy in himself (RB 65.22).

[19] See RB 23.3: *coram omnibus*, which also calls to mind 1 Tim 5:20, and is not used in Benedict's monastic sources.

[20] RM 13.5: "praesentibus suis praepositis vel cetera congregatione circumstante."

[21] See de Vogüé, 2.658. Fuller treatment of this and related expressions follows in this study.

Excommunication in practice and in theory

In both the RM and the RB, varying degrees of excommunication may follow upon the verbal warnings, corresponding to Matt 18:17: "Let him be to you as a gentile and a tax collector." However, this amounts to an accommodation of the text, for the excommunication that follows is not yet a matter of expulsion from the community, even though that is the literal force of Matt 18:17. Instead, it is at first only a matter of exclusion from the common table for lighter faults, and, in RB 24, of refraining from active participation in the Divine Office. Full exclusion from the oratory follows upon serious faults (RB 25.1), according to the abbot's judgment as to the gravity of the fault (RB 24.2). Such an offender is also deprived of general association with the community (RB 25.2-6).

If the process of graduated excommunication remains ineffective, then expulsion from the community is in order. But even this is a matter of "degree" inasmuch as Benedict allows for a threefold expulsion from the monastery before the action is definitive (RB 29). After the third departure of the unrelenting monk from the monastery, the Master declares: "Let him be as a gentile and publican" (RM 64.4). It is clear that this process also is a further adaptation of Matt 18:17.

The practice of distinguishing between "minor" and "major" excommunication [22] had ample precedent in monastic tradition by St. Benedict's time. The New Testament passage "If your eye scandalize you ..." (Matt 5:29-30) furnished Basil the Great with a scriptural basis for the final expulsion of impenitent monks if other measures failed.[23] St. Benedict may well have this text and application in mind when he says in RB 28.6: "The abbot must use the knife and amputate. For the Apostle says: 'Banish the evil one from your midst' (1 Cor 5:13); and again, 'If the unbeliever departs, let him depart' (1 Cor 7:15), lest one diseased sheep infect the whole flock."[24]

---

[22] This is not to be confused with the classification of excommunicants as *tolerati* or *vitandi*—a distinction first made by Martin V in 1418. Cf. Gasparri, *Fontes* I,58 ("Ad Evitanda").

[23] *Reg.fus.* 28.1; *reg.* 57.

[24] At this point, St. Benedict seems to be dependent on Origen's *hom. in Iesu Nave* 7,6. After citing Matt 5:30, the Alexandrian theologian remarks that when all other efforts at correcting someone fail, then there "remains only the remedy of surgical operation" (*solum superest remedium desecandi*). This is for the good of all, to prevent their being infected "by the one diseased sheep" (*sicut ex una ove morbida grex universus inficitur*). See F. Hockey "Origen—Used by St. Benedict in His Rule?" *RBén* 72 (1962) 349–350. RM 13.4 likewise speaks of the excommunicated monk "velut quaedam

The complete and one-time expulsion that Paul uncompromisingly demands for the incestuous Corinthian (1 Cor 5:1-13) is here, as already in Basil, reinterpreted to allow for more than one expulsion or degree of excommunication.[25] Accordingly, one whose offense is so serious as to deserve excommunication "from the table and the oratory" is to be left alone at his work (RB 25.4) in order better to impress upon him the words of Paul: "As for such a fellow, he has been given over to the destruction of his flesh, so that his spirit may be saved in the Day of the Lord" (1 Cor 5:5).

It is significant that St. Benedict omits from the quoted passage any mention of one's being handed over "to Satan."[26] The RM makes no allusion at all to 1 Cor 5:5 in this context. Instead, it speaks of the excommunicated monk as one who is not to be addressed as "brother" but as a "heretic," and not as a "son of God" but as a "demon's workman."[27] He is compared to Judas, and is one who follows the devil (RM 13.14). In all this the Master is developing a theology of excommunication that is rejected by the RB.

Not only does the RB refrain from calling excommunicated monks "heretics"—a term that would have been quite out of proportion to the crime at this period of history when heretics could even be faced with

---

scabies est procreata in grege." While this expresses much the same idea as RB 28.8, Benedict's choice and arrangement of words (*ne una ovis morbida omnem gregem contagiet*) are strikingly similar to Origen's.

[25] See de Vogüé, 7.273.

[26] De Vogüé, 5.748, believes the omission is due to St. Benedict's abhorrence of the idea of abandoning one to the devil. Later in the text (p. 846), he adds that the omission is more readily explained by a textual variation of 1 Cor 5:5 found among some Latin authors. However, these explanations fail to convince, since it seems certain that Benedict takes his cue from Cassian (*inst.* 2,16) for the use of 1 Cor 5:5 in RB 25.4. Cassian speaks exclusively of one's being "handed over to Satan." This expression, as pointed out in the text above, can evoke several New Testament passages—among them, 1 Cor 5:5. Thus, St. Benedict is stimulated by Cassian's language to think of 1 Cor 5:5, while, at the same time, omitting precisely Cassian's words in quoting this passage. We must conclude that he does so intentionally, because the connotations the expression would suggest would not serve his purposes or theology. As with Paul, "to be handed over to Satan" could only mean to Benedict expulsion not only from the monastery but also from the Church—analogous to expulsion from Paradise and to being given over to the realm and power of Satan. But as long as the monk is in the monastery, though being subjected to some form of excommunication, he is certainly in the Church and not "handed over to Satan." Moreover, even a monk who has been expelled from the monastery could hardly be considered excommunicated from the Church, since faults that may lead one out of the monastic life do not necessarily lead one out of the Church itself. Ultimately, Benedict accommodates 1 Cor 5:5 to the monastic context, without doing violence to Paul or to the monk being subjected to correction.

[27] "Iam non dicendi fratres sed heretici...iam non dicendi filii Dei sed operarii daemonis" (RM 13.2-3).

the death penalty according to the laws of Justinian[28]—but it designates them as "brothers," albeit as *fratres delinquentes* (RB 27.1). As a result, the excommunicated monk is to be viewed in moral rather than dogmatic categories: he is a sinner, but not necessarily a heretic. Loving concern for the sinner is a foremost duty of Christians according to tradition and the RB (Prol.36-38).

Although Paul demands the full and permanent expulsion[29] of the evildoer for the protection of the Christian community, since "a little leaven leavens the whole lump" (1 Cor 5:6), his primary concern is "that his spirit[30] may be saved in the day of the Lord Jesus" (1 Cor 5:5). It is this soteriological aspect that St. Benedict wishes to realize (RB Prol; 72.11-12). At the same time, Paul's statement contains an urgent eschatological note, since he expects the "Day of the Lord" (the return of Christ) to be quite near (1 Cor 7:27,31; 11.26). From RB Prol.35-38, it is evident that Benedict does not have the same attitude about the nearness of the end, but adapts it (in keeping with 2 Pet 3:9 and Rom 2:4) to the soteriological thrust of 1 Cor 5:5. As a result, the recalcitrant's isolation from the community is not only to move him to repentance (RB 25.2-3), but to serve as a reminder that continued and further hardening in his fault could eventually exclude him from salvation—the *terribilis sententia* of Paul (RB 25.3).

This isolation, especially from the table (cf. also RM 13.62), has its scriptural precedent in 2 Thess 3:10,14. But St. Benedict probably has 1 Cor 5:11 ("not even to eat with such a one")[31] equally in view. This action would include the withholding of a blessing or greeting (RB

---

[28] In his *Code of Law* from 527, Justinian revived all earlier laws against heretics (including pagans, Jews and Samaritans) and subjected Manichaeans to capital punishment (cf. *Codex Justinianus*, C.S. 80 v.9, edited by Krüger). None of these could accept a political or military honor or office; nor could they act as rhetoricians or lawyers. The task of enforcement of the laws was left in the hands of bishops. See H. S. Alivisatos, *Die kirchliche Gesetzgebung des Kaisers Justinian I* (1913; rpt. Aalen: Scientia Verlag 1973) pp. 32–33.

[29] The intent of 1 Cor 5:5 could only be full and permanent excommunication as Paul wrote it and as implied in v.2 ("Let him who has done this be removed from among you") and reaffirmed in v.13: "God judges those outside. 'Drive out the wicked person from among you'" (cf. Deut 13:5).

[30] "Spirit" is never used in Paul to mean the "soul" in contrast to the material body. Rather, it means here "the person as converted to Christ." See Hein, *Eucharist and Excommunication*, p. 95. Likewise, Benedict never uses "spirit" to mean "soul" (RB Prol.11; 2.3; 7.70; 25.4; 38.2; 49.6; 58.2; 65.2).

[31] As in RB 24.4, it may well be that Paul intends non-association at table as the first and foremost step (rather than the last step) in dealing with a wrongdoer. See Hein, *Eucharist and Excommunication*, pp. 96–97. It is also noteworthy that Paul's lists of sins that exclude one from the Kingdom of God correspond to the lists that sever one from association with the community. Cf. Gal 5:19-21; Eph 5:5; 1 Cor 6:9-10; Col 3:5-8.

25.6; 2 John 10-11). The order that the food given to the excommunicated person is not to be blessed is consonant with the early Church's concept of the "communion of saints," which was not a matter of communication between Christians on earth and the consortium of saints in heaven, but of the sacramental sharing among Christians at any time: "holy things to holy people."[32]

Excommunication and the New Covenant[33]

The preceding treatment of excommunication in the RB has brought to light the strong moral rather than dogmatic character of this action as implemented by St. Benedict. But this is not to say that the wrongdoer is merely an errant brother. Ultimately, his misbehavior can lead to severance not only from the monastic community but also from the community of all the faithful and from the covenant with Christ. The import of this "covenant theology," implicit throughout the RB,[34] is evident in chapter 29, which provides for three departures (expulsions) from the community before the process is considered irreversible. In RB 28.7, the sundering of the malcontent from the community is reinforced with Paul's statement in 1 Cor 7:15: "If the unbeliever (infidelis) departs, let him depart."

In context this passage deals with the problem of a non-Christian partner in marriage who refuses to continue peacefully in marriage. The word that seems to capture St. Benedict's attention and is accommodated to the monastic situation is infidelis—an apt description of the monk who refuses to live the monastic state in peace.[35] However, Benedict interprets the term as "unfaithful" rather than as "infidel." Such an understanding of the term is consistent with his reluctance to place the excommunicated party in a doctrinal rather than moral con-

---

[32] Ta hagia tois hagiois. See W. Elert, Abendmahl und Kirchengemeinschaft in der alten Kirche hauptsächlich des Ostens (Berlin: Lutherisches Verlagshaus 1954) pp. 65–66.

[33] The concepts developed in this section were stimulated by Abbot Martin J. Burne's paper "Sacred Scripture in the Rule of Benedict," First Lecture (p. 15), delivered at the Formation Directors' Workshop, Saint Paul's Abbey, Newton, N.J., 1975. Any misrepresentation of that material here is to be attributed only to the fault of the present writer.

[34] Explicit mention of "covenant" is made only in RB 2.14 in a quotation from Ps 49(50):16-17. However, the very concept of excommunication derives from the idea of covenant and the possibility that one can be severed from it. Cf. Num 15:30; Heb 6:4-6; also Hein, Eucharist and Excommunication, pp. 136–147.

[35] We cannot but think here of the Benedictine motto, Pax. Peace is not only the requirement for life in community, but the pax is also the sign and seal of a life of penance and conversion.

text. Likewise, the concept of unfaithfulness or infidelity has a particular significance in a marital or covenant-oriented setting. The monk's life, like marriage, requires great faith (trust) and fidelity (loyalty) for its success. Both chapters 5 and 7 of 1 Corinthians treat of marital matters, and marriage is the sign of God's covenant of love with the "faithful"—the Church (Eph 5:25-32).

Repeatedly St. Benedict applies St. Paul's covenant theology.[36] It is in this framework that RB 33.4 ("monks may not have the free disposal even of their own bodies and wills")[37] and RB 58.25 ("from that day he will not have even his own body at his disposal")[38] can be best understood. These statements, often so alien to the ideas of an individualistic age, recall several passages from Paul's writings concerning the relationship of husband and wife, and of Christ and the Church.[39] In the final analysis, St. Benedict states far more thoroughly than his immediate monastic sources the notion of the offender's severance from salvation, without, however, labeling the wrongdoer as a heretic or one who is to be immediately abandoned to his unfortunate lapse.

As in his "theology of excommunication," so also in his "theology of concern" (see Thematic Index; CARE and CONCERN) for the excommunicated, St. Benedict proves himself independent of the Master and Cassian. In RB 27.3-4, a quotation is taken from 2 Cor 2:7-8 ("Let them console him lest he be overwhelmed by excessive sorrow . . . let love for him be reaffirmed"), to which is immediately added by way of explanation of this "love": "and let all pray for him."[40] An important part of St. Benedict's concern for the excommunicated brother is the abbot's sending of the *senpectae*[41] to console the fellow monk and to encourage him to a change of heart. This practice recalls Paul's advice to the Galatians: "Brothers, if a man is overtaken in any trespass, you

---

[36] In this same context, the RM quotes rather exclusively from Matthew. Benedict's independence from the Master and his preference for Paul indicates his deliberate intention to view excommunication in a more theological light than many of his monastic sources did.

[37] "Nec corpora sua nec voluntates licet habere in propria voluntate."

[38] "Ex illo die nec proprii corporis potestatem se habiturum scit."

[39] Eg., 1 Cor 6:12,19; 7:4; Eph 5:21,28–33. See de Vogüé, 7.394–395 for further consideration of monastic fidelity to the covenant with Christ, sealed in baptism and lived out through the monastic way of life.

[40] *Consolentur* eum *ne abundantiori tristitia absorbeatur . . . confirmetur in eo caritas* et oretur pro eo ab omnibus. RM 15.26 also mentions the prayers of all for the excommunicated.

[41] See note to RB 27.2.

who are spiritual (*hymeis hoi pneumatikoi*) should restore him in a spirit of gentleness" (Gal 6:1).

Although it is not likely that Paul is referring to the incestuous man of 1 Cor 5 when he advises the Corinthians in 2 Cor 2:7-8 to accept a repentant offender again into their midst, it is likely that St. Benedict, as many Church Fathers before him, identifies them as one and the same.[42] In doing so, it is clear that his foremost concern is the repentance of the offender and the ensuing forgiveness of the community, rather than a vindictive proceeding against such weak persons, for that would endanger rather than promote their salvation (RB 27.5-9; 64.11-14,17-18). This also fits well into Paul's interpretation of the community's role in forgiveness in 2 Cor 2:11: "to keep Satan from gaining the advantage over us; for we are not ignorant of his designs."

From the preceding presentation, it is amply clear that St. Benedict is thoroughly acquainted with Pauline thought and most capable of applying it to monastic life. His appreciation for the Apostle's insights and theology moves him to produce a rule for monasteries that is sane, balanced and firmly founded on Paul's thinking; and he does this independently of his monastic sources and predecessors.

Exclusion from prayer

Closely related to the practice of exclusion from the table is the exclusion from prayer with the community. Although the practice is introduced without any explicit scriptural references, it is easily understood as included in many biblical restrictions regarding wrongdoers or people under some cultic censure,[43] and has a well-documented history by St. Benedict's time.

The Gospel according to John (9:22; 12:4; 16:2) shows the synagogue procedure for preventing certain persons from participation in the prayer and worship of the community.[44] St. Paul, apparently trained in rabbinical thought and practice (Acts 22:3), advises the Corinthians "not to associate with immoral men" or "with anyone who bears the name of brother if he is guilty of immorality or greed ... not even to eat with such a one" (1 Cor 5:9,11). These measures would clearly preclude community in prayer with such persons.

[42] See de Vogüé, 5.749.

[43] Especially during the third century, Western Christianity often developed concepts and practices of cultic purity taken from the Old Testament, perhaps as a reaction to Gnostic and heretical depreciation of Yahweh and the experiences of Israel.

[44] Cf. H. Strack and P. Billerbeck, *Kommentar zum Neuen Testament aus Talmud und Midrasch*, 6 vols. (Munich: Beck 1922–61) 4.293–333.

Various early Christian writings and Church Fathers clearly spell out their reasons for non-association in prayer with the excommunicated. Often they assert that the purity and effectiveness of prayer and cultic action require the presence of only those properly disposed. The *Didache* gives the following instruction: "Having gathered together on the Lord's Day, break bread and give thanks after having confessed your faults, so that your sacrifice may be pure. But anyone having a quarrel with an associate of his is not to join you until they are reconciled, so that your sacrifice may not be profaned" (14,1-2).

Though it remains unclear in what way the sacrifice (the Eucharist) would be profaned and made impure by the presence of certain persons,[45] the emphasis of the passage is on ethics and morals, and not on some magical devaluation of the sacrifice itself. The demand for "purity of cult" at least makes it clear that the moral state of a Christian can never be a merely "private matter" that concerns only the individual and God to the exclusion of the common good of the community. This principle is basic to cenobitic monasticism, where *community* prayer and *mutual* concern for the moral status of all form the *raison d'être* of the religious community.

Tertullian, writing at the beginning of the third century, specifies that the Christian gathering is not only for prayers but also for enacting disciplinary measures when someone has sinned so seriously as to be deprived of all association in prayer or the Christian assembly. "This is the foremost sentence before the future judgment."[46] In other words, excommunication is indeed meant to be a foretaste of eternal exclusion from the community of the saved.

According to Hippolytus,[47] catechumens must remain apart from the faithful during prayer and are not to receive the kiss of peace. The significance of this lies in the fact that the early Church, especially in the West, likened the status of the penitents to that of the catechumens

---

[45] The idea of profaning the Eucharistic sacrifice is found explicitly in 1 Cor 11:27. In the ancient world, the presence of a person incapable of proper association with the divine (that is, "impure") invited the wrath of God not only upon himself but also upon all those near him. See Jon 1:4-15; G. B. Miles and G. Trompf "Luke and Antiphon: The Theology of Acts 27-28 in the Light of Pagan Beliefs about Divine Retribution, Pollution and Shipwreck" *Harvard Theological Review* 69 (1976) 259-267; also M. Douglas, *Purity and Danger: An Analysis of Concepts of Pollution and Taboo* (1966; rpt. New York: Praeger 1970).

[46] "Summumque futuri iudicii praeiudicium est." *Apologeticum* 39,4:CC 1.150. On avoiding all contact with heretics, see Ign. *Smyr.* 7,2; *Trall.* 7,2; and Iren. *adv.haer.* 1,16,3.

[47] Hippol. *trad.apost.* 2,22,5 and 2,18,1-3. On the exclusion of sinners from prayers, see Orig. *c.Cels.* 4,27; *in Matt.* 89; Cypr. *de laps.* 15-25.

up to the sixth century, owing to the analogy drawn between baptism (*paenitentia prima*) and the sacramental forgiveness of sins (*paenitentia secunda*). In the same vein, *paenitentia secunda* was generally considered to be as incapable of repetition as baptism. It is "natural" then that monastic life, as recommitment to the baptismal covenant, should also be a life of *paenitentia*—a "continuous Lent" (RB 49.1). The life of penance is consequently not a matter of morbid sorrowing over one's sins (though sorrow for sin is certainly not excluded), but rather an aversion from self-centered isolation and conversion to Christ who is found in the community of the covenant (John 20:19-29). It is joyful longing and preparation for Easter (RB 49.7)—the day when catechumens received baptism and full reception into the community of believers.

These witnesses of the early Church amply demonstrate the practice of excluding certain persons (sinners and heretics in particular) from full participation in the life of the Christian community, especially in the matter of prayer and worship. However, not every writing of this period arrives at the same conclusion by the same means—that is, by expounding on "cultic purity." The *Didascalia Apostolorum*,[48] a third-century document, takes a very negative stance against those who subscribe to the Old Testament's understanding of cultic purity.[49] But its procedures for treating wayward Christians are most interesting, since there are parallels or analogies to both the RM and the RB. Thus, one who is found to be remiss should be dealt with according to the prescriptions of the Gospel (Matt 18:15-17). If, after two private rebukes and the rebuke before the whole assembly, the one in question still does not obey, he is to be treated as a "heathen and a publican": "For the Lord has commanded you, O bishops, that you should not henceforth receive such a one into the Church as a Christian nor communicate with him. For neither dost thou receive the evil heathen or publicans into the Church and communicate with them except they first repent."[50]

[48] This document was probably written by a Jewish Christian bishop for a community in North Syria sometime during the third century. Quotations in the text are from the translation provided by R. H. Connolly, *Didascalia Apostolorum: The Syriac Version Translated and Accompanied by the Verona Latin Fragments* (Oxford: The Clarendon Press 1929). It seems to be a serious oversight on the part of most commentators and historians of monastic rules when they fail to consider this work. Connolly, p. xix, believes it was translated into Latin during the age of Ambrose. If that is so, it is very probable that St. Benedict was acquainted with the work.

[49] See *Didasc.apost.* 26.

[50] *Ibid.*, 10; Connolly 102–103.

An unrepentant evildoer is to be considered a liar rather than a Christian and is to be avoided.[51] Even his gifts for the support of the Church are to be rejected, lest others be deceived into offering prayers for one who refuses to repent.[52] But if a sinner does repent, he should be received back into the fold in accord with the prescribed penitential system:

"As a heathen," then, "and as a publican let him be accounted by you" who has been convicted of evil deeds and falsehood; and afterwards, if he promise to repent—even as when the heathen desire and promise to repent, and say "We believe," we receive them into the congregation that they may hear the word, but do not communicate with them until they receive the seal and are fully initiated: so neither do we communicate with these until they show the fruits of repentance. But let them by all means come in, if they desire to hear the word, that they may not wholly perish; but let them not communicate in prayer, but go forth without. For they also, when they have seen that they do not communicate with the Church, will submit themselves, and repent of their former works, and strive to be received into the Church for prayer; and they likewise who see and hear them go forth like the heathen and publicans, will fear and take warning to themselves not to sin, lest it so happen to them also, and being convicted of sin or falsehood they be put forth from the Church.

But thou shalt by no means forbid them to enter the Church and hear the word, O bishop; for neither did our Lord and Saviour utterly thrust away and reject publicans and sinners, but even did eat with them. And for this cause, the Pharisees murmured against Him, and said: "He eateth with publicans and sinners." Then did our Saviour make answer against their thoughts and their murmuring, and say: "They that are whole have no need of a physician, but they that are sick" (Mk 2.16-17). Do you therefore consort with those who have been convicted of sins and are sick, and attach them to you, and be careful of them, and speak to them and comfort them, and keep hold of them and convert them. And afterwards, as each one of them repents and shows the fruits of repentance, receive him to prayer after the manner of a heathen. And as thou baptizest a heathen and then receivest him, so also lay hands upon this man, whilst all pray for him, and then bring him in and let him communicate with the Church. For the imposition of hands shall be to him in the place of baptism: for whether by the imposition of hands, or by baptism, they receive the communication of the Holy Spirit.[53]

[51] *Ibid.*, 5; Connolly 38.
[52] *Ibid.*, 18; Connolly 158–159.
[53] *Ibid.*, 10; Connolly 103–104.

While the similarities between the *Didascalia* and the RB do not necessarily indicate a line of direct dependence, it is abundantly clear that the RB has much of the same spirit, providing for freedom from the prevailing rigorism and cultic formalism. It must also be remembered that monastic life in the West had many roots in the East[54] that were otherwise not so well known or appreciated in the Western Church. The *Didascalia* appears to be one such root.

Corporal punishment

Both the RM and the RB appear equally dependent on Cassian for the employment of corporal punishment, but each in its own way. Cassian provides a long list of offenses for which one is to be either beaten or expelled.[55] The Master orders blows *usque ad necem*[56] for a monk who remains impenitent for three days after excommunication (RM 13.68-71). The abbot may then also expel him from the monastery. Boys up to fifteen years of age, however, are to receive blows in lieu of excommunication (RM 14.79-80).

St. Benedict makes several distinctions and adaptations in his use of corporal punishment in order to remove the vindictiveness and formalism found in his sources. Similar to the Master, he prescribes blows for those who remain unrepentant even after excommunication (RB 28.1). But there is no specified duration of time after which the abbot is to proceed with corporal punishment. And if the monk remains hardened even after this, it is not yet a question of expulsion from the monastery. Instead, the abbot is to act as a "wise physician"[57] and apply his own prayers and ask the prayers of the brotherhood for the "sick brother" (RB 28.4-5). If there are still no positive results, then expulsion from the monastery may ensue (RB 28.2-7). But again,

[54] See Introduction, pp. 1–41.

[55] "vel plagis emendantur, vel expulsione purgantur" (Cassian. *inst.* 4,16,3).

[56] Certainly this is not to be construed to mean "to the point of death" except as an expression that approximates the Americanism "to beat the living daylights out of someone." Perhaps a definite number of blows is foreseen in this expression. The Synod of Mâcon in 583 (canon 3) prescribed "uno minus de quadraginta ictus accipere" (Deut 25:3; 2 Cor 11:24) for a young cleric who appeals a case to a civil judge. See Vogel, *La discipline*, p. 173.

[57] *Sapiens medicus*: RB 27.2 and 28.2. Though Jesus is associated with the concept of physician in the Gospels (Matt 9:12; Mark 2:17), the expression being investigated here probably stems from Origen's polemic in *Contra Celsum* against the pagan cult to Asclepius, "Savior and Healer." To this is contrasted *Christus medicus*. By Augustine's time, the expression has lost its polemic character. See R. Arbesmann "The Concept of 'Christus medicus' in St. Augustine" *Traditio* 10 (1954) 3–6.

no time limit is set on the period of prayers that precede the act of expulsion.

Since understanding does not necessarily come when a boy turns fifteen, St. Benedict simply prescribes that boys too young to realize the meaning of excommunication, along with any older persons who lack the understanding, be given blows instead, or, if more appropriate and effective, made to fast[58] for a time, "that they may be healed" (RB 30.3).

No immediate scriptural basis is given for the use of corporal punishment. Yet, it is implied in RB 2.28-29 through quotations from Prov 29:19 and 23:14. Also, the practice of the Church in St. Benedict's time in regard to the handling of recalcitrant clerics[59] and the example of earlier monastic sources[60] could well supply a precedent for corporal punishment in the RB. The bishops in council at Epaone (517) decreed that young clerics who assist at meals of heretics or Jews should be beaten (canon 15). Likewise, the council of bishops at Agade (506) provided for corporal castigation of intoxicated clerics or of clerics and monks who presumed to travel without the proper letters of recommendation from their ecclesial superiors (canon 41). Even bishops engaged in unseemly discord with each other could be subjected to such punishment according to the Council of Tours held in 567 (canon 2). It is difficult to determine to what extent these examples from France were known and practiced in Italy at St. Benedict's time.[61] But it would seem to be more likely than not that such practices were known and employed throughout the Roman Church, and that they were in the "spirit of the times."

Application of penalties in specific instances

The miscellaneous faults and penalties outside of RB 23–30 and 44 may be summarized as follows:[62]

---

[58] The penitential practice of fasting replaces beatings in some monastic rules. The *Regula Ferioli*, ascribed to Bishop Ferreolus of Uzès in southern France († 581), prescribes fasts in all cases except thievery, which it calls "quasi adulterium secundum." See G. Holzherr, *Regula Ferioli: Ein Beitrag zur Entstehungsgeschichte und zur Sinndeutung der Benediktinerregel* (Einsiedeln: Benziger Verlag 1961) pp. 129–130.

[59] See Vogel, *La discipline*, pp. 55–57.

[60] B. Steidle, *Die Regel St. Benedikts* (Beuron: Herder 1952; English tr. Holy Cross Abbey 1967) pp. 203f., gives a number of examples of corporal punishment from various monastic traditions.

[61] Apparently because of the vicissitudes of the Church in Rome and Italy during the barbarian invasions, much documented material was irretrievably lost, leaving a hiatus that has frustrated historians ever since.

[62] This list is basically the one given by de Vogüé, 5.773–774.

2.26-29	All faults (one or two verbal admonitions, the obstinate are to receive corporal punishment).
3.10	Disputing with the abbot (*disciplina regularis*).
11.13	Tardiness in giving the signal to rise (satisfaction in the oratory).
21.5	Proud dean (three reprimands, deposition for failure to amend).
32.4-5	Mishandling of monastic goods (reprimand, *disciplina regularis* for failure to amend).
33.7-8	Appropriation of anything (two warnings followed by *correptio*).
34.7	Grumbling (*disciplina districtior*, 5.19 *poenam murmurantium*).
42.9	Speaking after Compline (severe punishment).
43.4-9	Arriving late for Vigils (satisfaction in the last place or in the place set apart).
43.10-12	Tardiness for the day hours (take last place and intone no psalm until satisfaction has been made).
43.13-17	Absence from prayer before or after meal (reprimand, meals apart and no wine for failure to amend until satisfaction and amendment have been made).
43.19	Asking for some food offered earlier by a superior but refused (deprivation of it and other extra food until amendment has been made).
45.1-3	Mistake in the oratory (satisfaction in the presence of all, severe punishment for adults and beating for children for failure to make satisfaction).
46.1-4	Failure to make voluntary satisfaction for damaging anything or for some other transgression (harsher than usual correction).
48.19-20	Idleness or gossiping (reprimand, *correptio regularis* for failure to amend).
51.3	Eating outside the monastery without permission (excommunication).
54.5	Accepting an object without permission (*disciplina regularis*).
55.17	Object hidden in the bed (*disciplina gravissima*).
57.2-3	Proud artisan (removal from work until humbled and permitted to return).
62.8-11	Violation of the Rule by a priest (frequent warnings, appeal to the bishop for refusal to correct self, expulsion for failure to amend).
65.18-21	Rebellious prior (four verbal warnings, *correptio disciplinae regularis* for failure to amend, deposition from office for refusal to correct himself, expulsion for disobedience).
67.6	Talking about one's visit outside the monastery (*vindicta regularis*).
67.7	Going somewhere or doing something without permission (*vindicta regularis*).
69.4	Defending another at fault (severe punishment).
70.1-3	Striking or excommunicating another without permission (public reprimand).

70.6   Striking an elder or a child in anger (*disciplina regularis*).

71.5   Refusal to obey an elder (reprimand).

71.9   Refusal to make satisfaction to an elder (corporal punishment, expulsion for resistance).

a) *Eating.* In general, these disciplinary measures are clear and in accord with the stipulations of the disciplinary code in the RB. However, in addition to the *disciplina regularis* and similar statements left untranslated in the above list (and discussed below), several other offenses and penalties are not immediately transparent.

It is difficult to see what is behind the punishment for asking for food from a superior that had been at first refused (RB 43.19). Perhaps St. Benedict has in mind particular experiences unknown to modern readers, but which would furnish a key to better understanding. Possibly it is a question of eating at the proper times. Cassian lists "the inordinate and secret consumption of food"[63] among the faults to be punished with blows or expulsion. He further advises the monk to be very careful not to eat outside regular meals, as one might be inclined to do while walking through an orchard, for that would be to give in to concupiscence.[64] At this point, however, St. Benedict does not appear so much concerned with *unseemly* eating that may lead to overindulgence of appetites—he warns of that in connection with the meal itself (RB 39.7-9)—as with *untimely* eating that would upset the good order of the house (RB 31.18-19) unless properly controlled (RB 41). Eating outside regular mealtimes could possibly encourage disregard for the common meals with the brotherhood (RB 43.13-17), and also render the whole system of excommunication from the table less effective.

Further insight in regard to eating at inappropriate times and places is found in RB 51. A monk may be excommunicated (though the degree is not specified) for eating outside without the abbot's permission (RB 51.3). While this may appear too stringent to present-day monks, it is probable that St. Benedict wishes only to simplify the whole matter of eating at irregular times or outside the monastery and to correct abuses that can easily arise from such practices. The Master supplies lengthy and complex prescriptions about such eating, noting when it is permissible and when not in view of the days of fast and the regular hours for eating, and with whom one may or may not eat, and so on (RM 59–62). The RB eliminates this complex formalism and replaces it

---

[63] "extraordinaria, ac furtiva cibi refectio." Cassian. *inst.* 4,16.

[64] *Ibid.*, 4,18; 5,20.

with the abbot's personal judgment of the needs of the monk, who, at any rate, can seek permission to eat outside or at a time other than the ordinary times for meals (RB 37).

b) *Priest-monk.* The admission of a priest into the monastery added a note of complication to matters of discipline (RB 62.8-11), since a priest has "canonical status" (in the hierarchy), while monasticism was originally a "lay movement" without canonical status,[65] as seen earlier in this study. Thus, the bishop of the area is to be called in for the public reprimand of a misbehaving priest-monk, for his presence would add a note of persuasiveness and ecclesial recognition to the public rebuke, and assure that he would be adequately informed of the situation and any additional possible consequences. If the priest is eventually expelled from the monastery, the bishop must be prepared to take charge of him and provide him, if the bishop is so inclined, with a "letter of recommendation."[66]

c) *Disciplina regularis.* The Master does not use the expression *disciplina regularis*, but *disciplina regulae*, in speaking of the disciplinary measures of his Rule. St. Benedict uses this latter expression in the sense of discipline as 'good order' or 'good conduct,' or 'the norms of the Rule' (RB 60.2; 62.4). In RB 60.5 and 62.3 (on priests in the monastery), *disciplina regularis* is used in a general sense to designate the monk's life under the Rule. Otherwise, in a disciplinary context, the term seems to refer especially to the penalties that are of a public character within the monastery—that is, the rebuke "in the presence of all" (*coram omnibus*) and other measures that may follow.[67]

In speaking of *districtior disciplina* and *gravissima disciplina*, St. Benedict apparently wishes to emphasize a greater degree of severity in the chastisement. Accordingly, *disciplina* would not have the sense of law but of chastisement.[68]

The other terms or expressions left untranslated in the list of penalties above seem generally equivalent to *disciplina regularis*. The

[65] This is not to ignore the promotion of monasticism by such prominent ecclesiastical figures as Athanasius, Basil the Great and Gregory I. But the fundamental origins of monasticism, including Benedictine monasticism, lie beyond the immediate direction of and incorporation into the Church's hierarchy.

[66] See de Vogüé, 6.1381. Such letters have their origins in 2 Cor 3:1 and Rom 16:1. But as a standard form and practice, they begin with Cyprian's time and become common for Christian travelers of the fourth century and for some time thereafter. See Elert, *Abendmahl*, pp. 108–112; L. Hertling "Communio und Primat" *Una Sancta* 17 (1962; orig. *Miscellanea historiae pontificae* 7, Rome 1943) 102–106.

[67] This is the judgment of de Vogüé, 5.777–785, which we accept here.

[68] *Ibid.*

employment of the public disciplinary measures is to be carefully controlled. Anyone who presumes to mete out corporal punishment or to proclaim another excommunicated without the abbot's permission is himself liable to the public correction of the Rule (RB 70.1-3,6). This prescription is probably directed especially toward superiors under the abbot, since they would be the most likely ones to use their authority rashly.

d) *Satisfaction and amendment.* These two closely related concepts, expressed particularly in the words *satisfactio, satisfacere,* and *emendatio, emendare,* generally designate respectively the objective procedure of discipline and self-correction and the ensuing expected change of behavior and attitude, as in RB 5.19, where the grumbler is to "change for the better and make amends" (*cum satisfactione emendaverit*). "Amends," or satisfaction, is the procedure whereby one acknowledges a fault (RB 7.44) and carries out the imposed penalties (RB 43.12; 44; 46.3; 71.8). This action is concerned with the interior and exterior attitude of humility (RB 27.3; 45.1; 71.8), making it an appropriate penitential act (RB 24.7) intended to repair the damage caused by the fault in the one who committed it (RB 43.12). This includes regaining one's right relationship with God (RB 11.13; RM 14.26) and obtaining forgiveness of the injured (RB 44). Satisfaction is clearly more than a mere formality. It is a concrete and, as it were, "sacramental" procedure that should normally repair damaged relationships and eradicate pride in the offender. While being predominantly procedural and external, its direction is nevertheless inward to uproot the source of the evil.

"Amendment" can also signify the objective corrective measures to be undertaken (RB 2.40; 46.4).[69] But its predominant meaning is reformation or correction of one's behavior as a result of an internal change of attitude.[70] It thus rids one of faults (RB 4.58), and may designate the *completed* correctional measures (RB 43.19), much in the sense of "satisfaction" (RB 24.4; 43.11,16).

Conclusion

"Of all the parts of the Rule, this one that we are about to consider is without doubt the most outmoded." With this statement, Adalbert de

---

[69] "Amend" in the sense of imposed correction or penalty is the result of the probable influence of St. Augustine on the RB; for, in *reg.serv.* 11,119, he speaks of *gravius emendatur* in regard to one who has committed a fault without admitting it but is still found out. See de Vogüé, 5.826.

[70] Cf. RB 21.5; 23.3; 28; 32.5; 33.8; 43.7,9,15-16; 48.20; 62.9-10; 65.19.

Vogüé introduces his commentary on the RB's disciplinary code,[71] pointing to the fact that excommunication and blows find little acceptance or appreciation in modern monasticism. Yet, the study and understanding of these elements, so central to the RB, are essential to the renewal of modern Benedictine life as encouraged by Vatican II.[72]

The system of discipline in the RB seeks to preserve the proper order and functioning of monastic life and above all the correction of vices and negligences. These are goals and values that any modern adaptation of the disciplinary measures must maintain and promote, for the whole of monastic life is meant to lead one to a change of behavior and attitude—a deep conversion. It is the way of penance, of conversion. If that is properly understood, accepted and practiced, then the liberty, the spontaneity and the joy of life that some may otherwise feel to be suppressed in the Rule will proceed more genuinely and forcefully from a deeper and fuller level of one's existence, just as surely as Christ came forth from the confines of death to the fullness of life that all are invited to share with him (Prol.49-50).

[71] See de Vogüé, 7.263.

[72] See *Perfectae Caritatis*, n.2; A. Flannery, *Vatican Council II: The Conciliar and Post Conciliar Documents* (Collegeville, Minn.: The Liturgical Press 1975) p. 612.

Appendix 5

Monastic Formation and Profession

Four chapters of the Rule, 58–61, treat of the process of receiving new members into the community. The first of these chapters is the most important: it deals with what may be considered the normal case, that of an adult lay postulant. The other chapters provide for three exceptional cases: those of children (59), priests (60), and men who are already monks (61). The recruitment and formation of new members were regulated by most monastic legislators. The provisions of the Rule grew out of previous monastic teaching and experience.

Formation and profession before St. Benedict

A man's intention to live as a monk was the result of a personal decision. In earliest times one could simply go to the desert and assume a monastic mode of life. Each monk sought out an elder who clothed him in the monastic habit and taught him how to conduct his life. There was no established pattern of formation, and the profession of the monastic way of life was sufficiently indicated by assuming the habit.

It was natural that cenobitic monasteries should develop more formal procedures for admission: experience gradually revealed the importance of careful testing of candidates as well as of instruction. These two necessities gradually brought about a longer period of time allowed for admission and formation. The candidate's motivation was tested first, and he was admitted only when there was reasonable certainty about his sincerity. Then he had to be taught all the things he would need to know in order to share the community's life, and be trained in virtuous conduct. At first this instruction was given *after* admission to the community.

The Pachomian rule specifies that before admission "he shall not be free to come in, but first it shall be reported to the father of the monastery, and for a few days he shall stay outside, in front of the door" (Pachom. *reg.* praecepta 49). During these days careful inquiry was made to learn whether the person might be a criminal or a slave fleeing out of fear. He was also tested to determine "whether he is able to renounce his parents and despise his property" (*ibid*).

In the Pachomian houses, most of the instruction was given after admission. The Pachomians accepted pagan candidates who remained catechumens until they were baptized at the following Easter celebration.[1] They were in need of instruction in the most elementary truths of the Christian faith and norms of behavior (*Vita sa*[10]). Whether pagan or Christian, moreover, they had to be taught the discipline and customs of the house (Pachom. *reg.* praecepta 49) and the psalms and biblical readings needed for the liturgy (*ibid.* 139). If illiterate, they had to learn how to read; the minimum that each monk had to memorize was the psalter and the New Testament (*ibid.* 139-140).

Other monastic sources confirm these practices of Egyptian cenobitism. Cassian says that in Egypt one who sought entrance was not admitted until he had spent "ten days or more" outside to prove his sincerity and perseverance, as well as his humility and patience. Meanwhile insults and reproaches were directed at him to try his constancy (Cassian. *inst.* 4,3). In his two accounts of Pinufius' attempt to enter a Pachomian monastery, he says that the elder was kept waiting outside the gate "for a rather long time" (*diutius*, Cassian. *inst.* 4,30) or, in the second account, "for many days" (*multis diebus*, Cassian. *conl.* 20,1). Palladius' story of Macarius the Alexandrian's attempt to enter Tabennesi is similar: he is rebuffed and made to wait, finally being admitted on the seventh day (Pallad. *hist.laus.* 18,12-13). Sulpicius Severus, without mentioning a specific length of time, likewise says that postulants were admitted by the abbot only after being tried and proved (Sulpic.Sever. *dial.* 1,17).

St. Basil is also basically in agreement with this procedure, though he says nothing of the lapse of time involved in acceptance and formation. He believes that the motives of a postulant must be carefully tested. If he willingly does the manual work assigned him, displays a disciplined behavior and readily admits his faults, these are favorable signs and he may be received. But before he is introduced into the community, he should be given some menial and humiliating tasks as a test of his resolve (Basil. *reg.* 6). Augustine's *Regula ad servos Dei*,

---

[1] This is demonstrated from the texts by A. Veilleux, *La liturgie dans le cénobitisme pachômien au quatrième siècle*, StA 57 (Rome: Herder 1968) pp. 198–206.

on the other hand, says nothing at all about the acceptance and formation of candidates.

After this preliminary period of testing, it was the Egyptian practice
to clothe the candidate in the monastic habit as soon as he was accepted. This was the practice of the anchorites, and thus Pachomius
began his monastic career: after Palamon had told him all the reasons
why he would be unable to endure his way of life, he finally gave in to
his entreaties, opened the door to admit him, and clothed him in the
schema, or monk's habit (*Vita prima* 6). Later, when postulants came
to Pachomius, he tested their worthiness, then clothed them in the
habit and admitted them to the community (*ibid.* 24; *Vita bo* 23). This
became the practice in Pachomian monasteries (Pachom. *reg.*
praecepta 49). The change of clothing symbolized, as for the anchorites, the monk's resolve to change his whole way of life and sense of
values—in short, to undergo *conversion*.[2]

The only requirement, then, for receiving the habit was the brief
test of motivation, to be sure that the candidate was sincere in seeking
conversion, and the instruction, which was apparently also brief. Cassian also speaks of conferring the habit immediately after the short
period of testing: "Brought into the assembly of the brothers, there in
the midst he is stripped of his own clothes and by the hand of the
abbot is garbed in those of the monastery" (Cassian. *inst.* 4,5). For
Cassian, this rite symbolizes the renunciation of all worldly possessions, even the monk's clothing, and the complete detachment from
ownership. The uniform habit is also a sign of poverty for St. Basil, but
he does not say at what point it was conferred (Basil. *reg.* 11).

Therefore, investiture with the habit had a quasi-sacramental meaning: it was the outward sign signifying that a man had become a
monk.[3] Both Pachomius and Cassian prescribe that the candidate's
secular clothes should be set aside and kept (Pachom. *reg.* 49; Cassian.
inst. 4,6); the latter specifies that if he should later fail to live up to his

---

[2] P. Oppenheim "Die religiöse Bedeutung des Mönchskleides im christlichen Altertum" *BM* 14 (1932) 268–272; *Symbolik und religiöse Wertung des Mönchskleides im
christlichen Altertum* (Münster: Aschendorff 1932).

[3] This sacramental meaning of the habit has been restored by the new rite of religious
profession approved by Pope Paul VI in 1970: "The rite of first profession provides for
the presentation of the habit and other signs of religious life, following the very ancient
custom of giving the habit at the end of the period of probation; for the habit is a sign of
consecration." *The Rite of Religious Profession* (Washington, D.C.: USCC 1971) intro.
n.5; see *Perfectae caritatis* n.17. This meaning had been long obscured by the practice,
sanctioned by canon 553, of giving the habit to novices, although the RB prescribes that
investiture should occur at profession.

profession, he should be stripped of the monastic garb, clothed in his former secular garments and expelled.

The Egyptian practice, then, seems to have permitted admission within some days after a candidate's arrival. Cassian states this quite formally (Cassian. *inst.* 4,32); the Pachomian rule is not quite so clear, as it supposes that some instruction has been given before investiture (Pachom. *reg.* praecepta 49), but it probably also refers to a short period of time. When invested, the new monk entered into the community as a full-fledged member. If he received further instruction, the texts do not refer to this explicitly. Probably there was a gradual development; as the need for instruction became apparent, the period of formation was lengthened. One Pachomian text speaks of a period of a month (Theod. *catech.* 3,28-29). Cassian affirms that after investiture the monk did not yet enter the community, but for a whole year was under the supervision of the guestmaster, a senior who lived near the gate and cared for the pilgrims and guests. The new monk was to learn humility and patience by caring for the guests. After a full year thus engaged, he was finally admitted to the community and placed under another senior who was in charge of the younger monks (Cassian. *inst.* 4,7).[4] Here we find for the first time the one-year formation period, but it comes after admission rather than before. Once placed before admission, as in the RB, the one-year novitiate became the norm in the Western Church.

There was also another tradition in Egypt that is attested before the end of the fourth century, that of a three-year formation period. It is found only in the so-called *Rule of the Angel*, a collection of monastic practices said to have been dictated to Pachomius by an angel.[5] Here it is prescribed that a candidate should not be received into the community until he has spent three years doing hard work. It is not specified whether this three-year period is before or after investiture. We find the three-year norm again in the legislation of Justinian of 535 (*Novellae* 5,2), in which it is clear that the three-year period *precedes*

---

[4] In his accounts of Pinufius' entry into a Pachomian monastery, however, nothing is said of this year under the guestmaster; immediately after his acceptance he is assigned to the garden under the supervision of a younger brother (Cassian. *inst.* 4,30; *conl.* 20,1). Is the one year a later development, or does it reflect a different practice among the cenobites of northern Egypt?

[5] This rule appears in Pallad. *hist.laus.* 32; Cassian. *inst.* 2,4-6; Soz. *hist.eccles.* 3,14; *Vita tertia* 30-32; *Vita Pach.* 21-22. It does not seem to have originated in a Pachomian environment, since some of its provisions contradict practices known from Pachomian literature.

investiture.[6] Gregory the Great was familiar with this law and prescribed in one of his letters that ex-soldiers should be given the habit only after three years' probation (Greg. *epist.* 8,5).[7]

The development that took place in regard to monastic profession is analogous to that of baptismal practice. In the New Testament it is clear that as soon as a person had been moved to conversion by the preaching (*kerygma*), he was baptized (Acts 8:35-38; 10:44-48). He still needed instruction (*didachē*), but this was given *after* baptism (Acts 2:37-42). In the course of the second century, however, instruction was required before baptism, and the sacrament accordingly postponed. This was probably due, at least in part, to the danger of Gnosticism; experience showed that it was advisable to test the motives of candidates more rigorously and instruct them more thoroughly. By the beginning of the third century there was a developed catechumenate in preparation for baptism (Hippol. *trad.apost.* 15-20). In a similar way, the monks seem to have realized gradually the need for further testing and instruction of candidates, and to have required this teaching before the conferral of the habit, thus postponing profession. Cassian already knows of the full year under an elder's direction, but he still places it after profession. By the beginning of the sixth century, the Western practice required a full year's training *before* investiture with the habit (Caes.Arel. *reg.virg.* 4; RM 90.79-80).

In the *Regula Magistri* we find the basic features of the Egyptian system, as reported by Cassian, but in a quite developed form. The program has now become complex, and the Master's penchant for detail does not facilitate the understanding of the five chapters he devotes to the question of recruitment (RM 87-91).[8] The lay postulant

---

[6] A later law (*Novellae* 123,35) of 546 restricted the three-year trial to slaves and civil servants. An echo of this legislation occurs in canon 19 of the fifth council of Orléans (549), which speaks of investiture after three years as well as of investiture after one year.

[7] Was Gregory perhaps thinking of this already four years earlier, at the time of the composition of the *Dialogues*, when he described St. Benedict as spending three years in the cave at Subiaco in a kind of monastic probation (Greg. *dial.* 2,1)?

[8] Chapters 87-89 seem to contradict ch. 90 and prescribe a different procedure. It is possible that they represent two separate systems, one of which succeeded the other chronologically. But it seems more probable that they should be understood as complementing one another and forming a single coherent system. This interpretation, which we follow here, is favored by the titles: ch. 90 concerns the lay candidate and ch. 87 the *conversus*, i.e., one who had already been living a quasi-religious life in the world, and who may have been exempted from the provisions of ch. 90. The provisions of chs. 87-89, however, applied to all candidates. See de Vogüé, 6.1289-1307.

who came to the monastery was met by the abbot, who feigned rejection of his request as a matter of policy (RM 90.2). He then explained the difficulties of the life in detail, read the entire rule to him, and exacted a promise to obey it (90.64) as well as the abbot (90.67). We learn from chapters 87–88 that this entire procedure lasted for two months (88.3) and included precise arrangements for the candidate to dispossess himself of everything he owned (87.4-74). During this time he lived in the guesthouse, under the supervision of the two guestmasters (88.7-9), but shared the life of the community (88.4-5). At the end of these two months, he made the promise that constituted his profession (90.64-67; 89.8); this was celebrated in a public rite conducted in the presence of the community (89.3-28). Thereupon he was assigned to a deanery and officially received into the community (89.28).

The profession rite, however, did not include investiture; the candidate had to be further tested for a whole year (90.79) and only then received the habit and the tonsure (90.80-81). During this time he remained in his deanery, but his daily instruction and testing were carried out by the abbot (90.74). There was no novice master (*senior*). The full year came between profession and investiture, which the Master separates. The new monk's secular clothes were kept in case he should leave. Clearly the basic features of this system were derived from Cassian, but they have been reworked, in a rather original way, into a new synthesis.

Reception and formation in the RB

The provisions of the RB for the reception and training of postulants retain most of the elements found in the RM and earlier sources, but St. Benedict rearranges them into a new program. The RB is more developed in some respects, suggesting a further stage of evolution, but is also simpler and more coherent. The principal difference is that profession and investiture are combined into a single rite, with the full year of formation preceding.

The RB continues the tradition of making admission difficult, which goes back to the earliest days of Egyptian monasticism. Rather than the merely *pro forma* refusal of the RM, it prescribes a genuine test of perseverance: the person is not admitted for four or five days, and during this time he is subjected to harsh treatment (*iniurias*) and "difficulty of entry" (*difficultatem ingressus*). St. Benedict is not specific about the nature of the "harsh treatment" and "difficulty of entry," but clearly wants a searching examination of the man and his motives for coming, and a preliminary test of his patience and persistence. As a biblical justification for this procedure, he adopts the same passage of 1 John as is used by the RM: "Test the spirits to see if they are from God" (1 John 4:1; RM 90.71; RB 58.2).

During these four or five days (a reduction by half of the period prescribed by Cassian), the candidate is apparently left outside. Then, if he has shown patience and humility during this time of probation, he is admitted to the guesthouse "for a few days" (*paucis diebus*). Nothing is specified about this period. It is followed by a full year, divided into periods of two, six and four months. At the end of each of these intervals, the Rule is read to the candidate. He is now called a "novice" and lives in a special area of the monastery called the "novitiate" (*cella noviciorum*), where his formation is entrusted to a monk described as "a senior chosen for his skill in winning souls" (RB 58:5-6).

At this point the text of the Rule presents a problem of interpretation, especially if the provisions of the RM are kept in mind. Verse 4 speaks of the "few days" in the guesthouse and verse 9 of the "two months" after which the Rule is read, following which the candidate is taken to the novitiate (v.11). In between these passages, however, verses 5-7 introduce the subject of the novitiate, the *senior*, and what is to take place there under his direction. This passage seems intrusive insofar as it suddenly speaks of "novices" in the plural (vv.5-6), only to revert to the singular again in verse 7.[9]

There are two ways in which this section can be understood. The usual interpretation (which is presupposed by our translation) understands it to describe a consecutive order of events: after a few days in the guesthouse (v.4), the candidate goes to the novitiate area (v.5), and there spends the two months that culminate in the first reading of the Rule (v.9). The two months are therefore spent in the novitiate. This seems the most natural way to read the text: since verse 5 introduces the novitiate immediately after the few days in the guesthouse, the reader is led to understand the *postea* to mean "directly after this." Such is in fact the understanding of the vast majority of commentators and the practice of nearly all Benedictine monasteries.[10]

---

[9] Seeing this difficulty, the copyists frequently changed all the verbs and pronouns of vv.5-6 to the singular in order to correct the passage. See the apparatus of Hanslik's edition and de Vogüé, 3.349.

[10] Thus Smaragdus, the oldest commentary: "The fact that he says 'Then let him be taken to the novitiate' when he has previously said 'let him be in the novitiate' should

The other interpretation—that the two months were spent in the guesthouse—goes back to ancient times. It is adopted by the ninth-century commentary on the Rule that appears in various recensions under the names of Basil, Hildemar and Paul the Deacon.[11] While it offers a better explanation of verses 10-11 and provides a closer parallel to the RM, it requires verses 5-7 to be understood as parenthetical, anticipating information about the novitiate that chronologically belongs later, after verse 11. The reader would quite naturally understand the candidate to be in the novitiate from verse 5 onward, and in fact this is what St. Benedict has generally been taken to mean.

The twelve months of formation are divided into three periods, of two, six and four months, respectively. At the conclusion of each of these periods, the Rule is solemnly read to the novice. St. Benedict here amplifies the program of the RM, which has only two months and a single reading of the Rule before profession. The repeated stress upon the Rule is intended to let the candidate know precisely what obligations he is undertaking, and the increase in the length of time and emphasis upon his deliberation show a concern that he make the decision to commit his life with full knowledge, reflection and freedom.

Whereas the RM has but a single promise, which comes at the end of the two months and constitutes profession, the RB mentions two promises during the formation period (58.9,14), in addition to the formal promise at the profession rite (58.17). The first of these is a promise *de stabilitate sua perseverantia* made at the beginning (or perhaps the end) of the initial two-month period. The second comes at the end of the year, following the third reading of the Rule, and is a promise "to observe everything and to obey every command given him." What is the meaning of these promises, which seem redundant? They are not binding commitments: at least in the case of the first, the novice is still free to leave after promising (58.10). The second is scarcely independent of profession, which follows immediately. The first promise explicitly mentions perseverance, the second obedience.

These promises express scarcely more than the intention to remain

be understood to mean that he has left the novitiate and come to the parlor or whatever place the abbot chooses, to listen to the precepts of the Rule; and then he is taken back again to the novitiate" (Smarag. *expos. in reg.* 294).

[11] Hildemar declares categorically, "In this chapter St. Benedict distinguishes three stages: at the monastery gate for four or five days before he is told he may come in; then two months in the guesthouse; and finally ten months in the novitiate" (Hild. *exp.reg.* p. 537).

for the present and subject oneself to everything the monastic life entails during the time of formation. The difficult expression "to promise perseverance in his stability" simply means that the candidate, after the few days he has spent in the guesthouse (or after the two months?), has decided to stay and wants to persevere through the novitiate to profession. The second promise, at the end of the year, means that he wants to make profession and bind himself permanently to all the obligations of the monastic life.

St. Benedict, as we have seen, placed the full year of formation before profession and investiture. His legislation in this regard has been decisive for all religious life in the Western Church (*CIC* 555). In addition to this, however, he made two other influential contributions: a special area for the novices (*cella noviciorum*) and a special official to supervise them (*senior*). The RB accepts neither the solution of Cassian, who has the candidate spend his year in the guesthouse learning humility by performing humble tasks under the direction of the guestmaster, nor that of the Master, who places him, like the other monks, in a deanery under a *praepositus*. St. Benedict prescribes instead a special regime suited to his needs and directed by a monk whose primary qualification is "skill in winning souls."

For the RB there is no question but that the novice is to be separate from the community in some important respects. He is not separated in *every* respect: he takes part in the Divine Office with the other monks (58.7) and presumably in such other common exercises as instruction by the abbot and the pre-Compline reading (42.3-6). He may have been with them during manual labor—the Rule does not specify this point. But his living quarters are separate: he is to sleep and eat in the novitiate (58.5). The latter point may seem surprising to those accustomed to modern practice, but the Rule is quite clear about it, and medieval monasteries often had a separate refectory in the novitiate.[12] No doubt the intention of St. Benedict in prescribing such extensive separation of the novice from the community was to provide him with a genuine experience of solitude and silence. The separation was considered necessary to create an atmosphere suitable for what the novice was to accomplish in the novitiate. This is defined by the RB as *meditatio* (58.5).

[12] This can be seen on the plan of St. Gall: see W. Horn and E. Born, *The Plan of St. Gall*, 3 vols. (Berkeley: Univ. of California Press 1979). It is also mentioned in the medieval customaries; see E. Martène, *Commentarius in Regulam S. Benedicti: PL* 66.812-813.

For the ancients, the term *meditatio* meant something different from what it does for us today.[13] It was not a purely interior activity ("thinking about" or "reflecting on"), but involved the repetition of a text aloud. Associated with reading (which was also done aloud), it meant that the reader repeated passages over and over again in order to learn them by heart. Once learned, these texts could then be repeated from memory without a book. This latter activity, which could be carried on during work or other activities, was also called *meditatio*. The "meditation" or "rumination" of scriptural passages while performing other tasks, which required extensive memorization of Scripture, was an important activity among the Pachomians. While it is still mentioned, albeit rarely, in the RM (50.26,43), the RB no longer speaks of it; St. Benedict never mentions *meditatio* in connection with work, but always with *lectio* (8.3; 48.23).[14] These two activities go together: while reading from a book, the monk is to repeat passages again and again until he has them memorized.

The novice had a good deal to learn during his year's training. He may have had to begin with learning to read; some candidates, at the end of their year's formation, were still unable to write their own profession formula (58.20). He then had to memorize those portions of Scripture that monks had to know by heart for use in the office. These included the psalms (8.3) and the short readings that were recited without a book (9.10; 10.2; 12.4; 13.11). He may also have memorized passages that were to be "chewed over" or "ruminated upon" later as a stimulus to private prayer; the RB does not speak of this, but it was a common monastic practice both before and after St. Benedict.[15] The novice's *meditatio*, then, was a kind of study, but not in the modern sense; it was confined to sacred texts, principally Scripture, and its goal was not purely intellectual, but an existential appropriation of the

[13] See E. von Severus "Das Wort 'Meditari' im Sprachgebrauch der Heiligen Schrift" *Geist und Leben* 26 (1953) 365–375; "Das Wesen der Meditation und der Mensch der Gegenwart" *ibid.* 29 (1956) 108–116; H. Bacht "'Meditatio' in den ältesten Mönchsquellen" *ibid.* 28 (1955) 360–373; *Das Vermächtnis des Ursprungs* (Würzburg: Echter Verlag 1972) pp. 244–264.
[14] See A. de Vogüé "Les deux fonctions de la méditation dans les règles monastiques anciennes" *Revue d'histoire de la spiritualité* 51 (1975) 3–16.
[15] See J. Leclercq "Meditation as a Biblical Reading" *Worship* 33 (1958–59) 562–569; *The Love of Learning and the Desire for God* (New York: Fordham Univ. Press 1961) pp. 13–30; A. Louf "The Word beyond the Liturgy" *CS* 6 (1971) 353–368; 7 (1962) 63–76; *Teach Us to Pray* (Chicago: Franciscan Herald Press 1976) ch. 4; F. Ruppert "Meditatio-Ruminatio: Une méthode traditionelle de méditation" *CollCist* 39 (1977) 81–93.

Word in view of forming his life. It was an activity as closely related to prayer as to study: medieval monastic writers considered *lectio*, *meditatio*, *oratio* and *contemplatio* to be four successive phases of a single movement involving the mind, the heart, the will and the body.[16]

The Rule does not specify other studies for novices. No doubt they became acquainted with the Fathers and the monastic literature through their *lectio*. We may suppose that beginners received appropriate guidance in their reading. The *senior* in charge of them is directed to "look after them with careful attention." The principal responsibility for their formation fell upon him, though probably the abbot retained a certain role for himself. Hence it is probably the novice master who is to "preach" (*praedicentur*) the "hardships and difficulties that will lead him to God." While this may have involved a certain amount of teaching in the modern sense, ancient monastic formation was more oriented toward the development of virtue: to learn humility, patience, obedience and self-denial (see Cassian. *inst.* 4,8; Basil. *reg.* 6). This was the work of experience, not of any academic instruction. As at the origins of monasticism in Egypt, formation is accomplished by a kind of apprenticeship to an experienced elder.

The elder, certainly, is not supposed to drive candidates away; "winning souls" is his task. But he is not to leave them under any illusions; they must be tried seriously and exposed to the *dura et aspera*. The RB specifies certain criteria by which the development of a novice may be judged: "Whether the novice truly seeks God and whether he shows eagerness for the Work of God, for obedience, and for trials."[17] The primary criterion is the seeking of God: the novice's motives must be probed to be sure that he has come to the monastery for the right reason. The ancients were aware of the subtle intrusion of self-deception, and in an unscientific but intuitive fashion recognized the varieties of subconscious motivation that are studied by modern psychology. Often the novice is unaware of his own motivation, and his intentions have to be brought to light and purified.

Eagerness for sincerely seeking God is ordinarily manifested by

[16] The clearest statement of this position is in the *Scala claustralium* of Guy II the Carthusian: see E. Colledge and J. Walsh, *The Ladder of Monks and Twelve Meditations by Guigo II* (Garden City, N.Y.: Doubleday Image Books 1978).

[17] See A. de Vogüé "Les trois critères pour l'admission des novices (RB 58)" *CollCist* 40 (1978) 128–138.

one's concrete behavior in regard to the essential features of the monastic life. The Rule singles out three that are especially important, though not exclusive. The "Work of God" in the RB always means the divine office, although in earlier monastic literature it had a wider connotation.[18] The novice must come to love the common prayer of the community, prepare himself for it industriously through *meditatio*, take part in it with attention and devotion, and extend the prayer of the office throughout his life in constant attention to God (7.10-30; 43.3). Obedience, in all the monastic rules, is the primary qualification of the cenobite; both Cassian and the RM insist upon it in the formation of novices (Cassian. *inst.* 4,8,10,23-31; RM 90.55-67). The RB regards it as the means "by which we return to God" (Prol.2) and makes it one of the three great virtues treated in chapters 5–7.

The third criterion is eagerness for trials (*opprobia*). The term is never used elsewhere in the RB or the RM, except twice in biblical citations (RB Prol.27; 7.52; RM Ths. 23; 10.69). What does it mean here? De Vogüé has suggested that the RB is here dependent upon St. Basil (Basil. *reg.* 6-7), where the terms *opus Dei* and *opprobrium* occur and there is also insistence upon obedience.[19] The *opprobria* in the Basilian context are not insults or injuries, but humble tasks, "laborious jobs that people in the world consider humiliating" (*ibid.* 6). It may be recalled that Cassian also assigned the novice to the guest-house, to perform humble services by which he might learn humility and patience (Cassian. *inst.* 4,7). Therefore, this criterion seems to be one of humility. The novice must be willing to show that he is not above doing things that are unattractive and unpleasant, the kinds of things that were left for slaves in the ancient world.

The RB does not envision "fictitious humiliations," devised to test the novice's endurance; but the *opprobria* certainly do not exclude bearing insult and injury when these arise spontaneously, nor the acceptance of correction when it is needed.[20] The Work of God, obedience and the acceptance of humiliation correspond strikingly to the degrees of humility in chapter 7: the Work of God to the first

[18] See I. Hausherr "Opus Dei" *MS* 11 (1975) 181–204.

[19] *Art. cit.* in note 17.

[20] It must be noted that Cassian, *inst.* 4,3, also speaks of *obprobriorum tolerantia* as evidence of the candidate's constancy, showing how he will bear up in temptations. In the context these *obprobria* are injuries and rebukes. Since obedience is emphasized in the same context, it cannot be excluded that St. Benedict was influenced by Cassian also, as well as by Basil, in his choice of the three criteria. *Opera Domini* (the *Opus Dei* of RB), understood in the wide sense, as in Basil, also occurs in Cassian. *inst.* 4,33.

degree, obedience to degrees 2-4, and humiliation to degrees 5-7.[21] In that way the novice is expected to grow in that spiritual program which marks the monk's ascent to charity.

Monastic profession according to the RB

For St. Benedict, the act of profession is of decisive importance. It comes at the end of the complete process of testing and formation that has been described, and it binds the monk for life. The decision so to bind himself is an exercise of the monk's free choice; he has had leisure to reflect and has been free either to stay or to leave (58.16). But from the moment he makes profession he will have voluntarily limited his freedom by agreeing no more "to leave the monastery, nor to shake from his neck the yoke of the rule" (58.15-16). The importance of profession is underlined by the fact that the Rule provides an unusual wealth of detail about the rite.[22]

From earliest times the symbol of "conversion," of becoming a monk, was the reception of the habit, which publicly indicated an intention of living the life of a monk. While some simply assumed the habit themselves, it was usually given by a person who was already a monk, as St. Gregory relates of St. Benedict (Greg. dial. 2,1). The assumption of the habit did not necessarily involve a lifelong obligation to remain in the monastic life. The Pachomian rule prescribes the clothing, after the testing and instruction of the candidate, in this way: "Then they shall strip him of his secular clothes and clothe him in the habit of monks; and he shall be entrusted to the porter, who, at the time of prayer, is to bring him before all the brothers, and he shall sit in the place assigned to him" (Pachom. reg. praecepta 49).

It is not entirely clear whether this clothing constituted a profession rite. The use of the plural ("they shall . . . clothe him") indicates that it was not simply a private conferral of the habit. On the other hand, the postulant is brought into the community only later, at the time of public prayer; this suggests that the investiture does not have the

---

[21] Thus de Vogüé, art. cit., pp. 135–136 in note 17.

[22] On the profession rite, see M. Rothenhäusler, Zur Aufnahmeordnung der Regula S. Benedicti, Part I of Studien zur benediktinischen Profess, Beiträge zur Geschichte des alten Mönchtums und des Benediktinerordens 3 (Münster: Aschendorff 1912); "Die Anfänge der klösterlichen Profess" BM 4 (1922) 21–28; "Der heilige Basilius und die klösterliche Profess" ibid. 280–289; H. Frank "Untersuchungen zur Geschichte der benediktinischen Professliturgie im frühen Mittelalter" SMGBO 63 (1951) 93–139; P. Ernetti "La professione monastica" Vita Monastica 11 (1957) 152–162; 12 (1958) 3–12; B. Sause "The Rite of Monastic Profession" Benedictine Review 18 (1963) 20–29; 40–52; P. Hofmeister "Benediktinische Professriten" SMGBO 74 (1963) 241–285.

significance of making him a member of the community. The precise
content and binding force of the commitment are also unclear in the
Pachomian literature. Certainly the monk bound himself to follow the
life of the community, and this involved the renunciation of marriage
and private possessions, and the acceptance of the regime of prayer,
work and silence. It is not clear, however, that these were lifelong
obligations or that they were guaranteed by a vow or an oath, at least at
the beginning. Such an understanding developed gradually, however,
and there are some texts in the literature which suppose that a binding
promise has been made to God to remain in the monastic life.[23]

The first known example of requiring a commitment in writing is
found in Shenoute of Atripe, who governed the "White Monastery,"
some distance down the Nile from the Pachomian houses, at the end
of the fourth century. In many respects the mentality of Shenoute is
more primitive and less evangelical than that of Pachomius. The written document, which is in the form of an oath rather than a vow, is
intended to put additional pressure upon the monks to fulfill what
they have promised. This is characteristic of Shenoute, who habitually
made abundant use of threats and violence to control his restless flock.
An element of juridical constraint is introduced by means of the written formula. The monk's agreement is called a "covenant."[24]

Cassian says nothing about a formal promise upon the monk's entry
into the community; he can later be expelled at any time, though to
leave of his own accord seems to be regarded as an infidelity (Cassian.
inst. 4,6). Cassian does know of a rite of investiture, however; the
habit is presented by the abbot in the presence of the whole community (ibid. 4,5). The abandonment of his secular clothing is symbolic of
his renunciation of all worldly property. Basil, on the other hand,
provides no directives for a rite of investiture, but quite clearly prescribes a promise of virginity, which he calls professio virginitatis,
propositum, and pactum, in his Small Asceticon (Basil. reg. 11). He
regards this as a binding commitment and its violation as an infidelity
to God. It is to be made with full freedom, and only when a person is
of adult age. The Large Asceticon has further developed the prescrip-

---

[23] These questions are discussed, with reference to the relevant texts, by Veilleux, La
liturgie, pp. 206–220.

[24] On Shenoute, see J. Leipoldt, Schenute von Atripe und die Entstehung des
national-ägyptischen Mönchtums, TU 25,1 (Leipzig 1903). The Coptic text of his works
has been published by J. Leipoldt and W. E. Crum, Sinuthii archimandritae vita et
opera omnia, CSCO 41,42, and 73 (1906, 1908, 1913); Latin trans. by H. Wiesmann,
CSCO 96,108,129 (1931, 1936, 1957).

tions for this "profession," adding that the "officials of the Church" (undoubtedly the bishops) are to be brought in as witnesses of the "consecration of the body" (Basil. *reg.fus.* 14-15; see *epist.* 199, canon 18; 217, canon 60; 46). There is no mention of a written promise; presumably this "profession" was made orally. It certainly involved a lifelong commitment to celibacy. This *propositum* contains all the essential elements of a vow.

The RM offers a rather complete description of the profession rite, and is also quite clear about the nature of the obligation assumed (RM 89). At the end of the two-month trial period, after the postulant has told the abbot of his decision to remain, the profession is held on the following day after Prime. The postulant first asks for the prayers of the abbot and community, then formally petitions for admission. The abbot's reply clearly indicates the nature of the obligation involved: "See, brother, you are not promising anything to me, but to God and to this oratory and holy altar" (RM 89.11). A document in which the postulant has listed the possessions he is conferring upon the monastery is placed upon the altar. He then says a "responsory" taken from Ps 118(119):116 (the *Suscipe*), and the abbot replies with a text from Ps 67(68):29 (*Confirma hoc*). After everyone has given the postulant the kiss of peace, the abbot says the concluding prayers, takes the inventory from the altar and entrusts the new brother to the dean who will be his immediate superior. A year later, if he has been perfectly observant, he is tonsured and given the monastic habit (RM 90.79-81).

As with most of the admission and formation procedures, so also in regard to profession St. Benedict received the elements from his predecessors. But through some rearrangement and reinterpretation he succeeded in giving a greater coherence and simplicity to the process.

We are told nothing of the liturgical setting of profession, except that it takes place in the oratory, where there is an altar and relics of the saints (58.17-20). In a later chapter, however, in dealing with the oblation of a boy, the Rule prescribes: "At the presentation of the gifts, they wrap the document itself and the boy's hand in the altar cloth. That is how they offer him" (59.2). If the oblation of a child took place at the offertory of a Eucharistic celebration, it is reasonable to suppose that the profession of an adult monk would also occur during Mass. Benedictine tradition has drawn this conclusion and generally prescribed that profession should take place at the offertory.[25] The

---

[25] The earliest evidence is in the *Canons* of Theodore, archbishop of Canterbury from

celebration of the Eucharist, like much else in liturgical practice, is rarely alluded to by the RB, which apparently takes contemporary practice for granted as known to its readers.

St. Benedict's rite consists of four elements. The first is the *promissio*, the monk's formal promise. Whereas in the RM it is clear that this promise is made to God, in the RB it seems to be made rather to the abbot. This is not stated formally, but is the most natural inference from the fact that he "makes a promise . . . *in the presence of* God and his saints" (58.17-18). Strictly speaking, then, the Rule does not prescribe a *vow*, but rather an *oath*: a vow is a promise made to God, whereas an oath is made to another human being in the presence of God, who is invoked as witness. Later tradition has generally interpreted the promise as a vow.[26] In practice, the distinction is not of great significance. In the early Church, the concept of vow was not yet clearly delineated and the terminology was still indeterminate. The consequences of the *promissio* scarcely differ from those of a vow: the monk solemnly binds himself for life (58.15-16), and infidelity to what he promises is regarded as sacrilegious: "If he ever acts otherwise, he will surely be condemned by the one he mocks" (58.18). Moreover, for the RB the abbot holds the place of Christ so realistically that to make a promise to the abbot is in effect to make it to Christ (see RB 2.2; 5.2-3; 5.15).

The content of the *promissio* will be discussed in the next section. We do not know exactly what form it took. It seems likely that it was cast in the form of questions and answers, both because this procedure was common in the early Church (as in the baptismal rite), and because it appears in this form in the earliest commentaries on the RB and earliest profession rituals that have survived.[27] The RM, too, has

---

668 to 690. Hildemar mentions the Mass in connection with the oblation of a child, but not in speaking of the profession of an adult monk. In the Middle Ages, profession sometimes occurred after the Collect, in imitation of minor orders: see I. Herwegen, *Sinn und Geist der Benediktinerregel* (Einsiedeln: Benziger 1944) p. 344. The reform of Vatican II has restored the rite of religious profession to its earlier form, and also situated it immediately following the Gospel; a recent practice of making profession to the sacred host just before communion is strongly discouraged. See *The Rite of Religious Profession*, intro. nn.14-15. Since both the Creed and the Prayer of the Faithful are omitted, the profession immediately precedes the offertory procession.

[26] Contemporary practice in most Benedictine monasteries retains the wording of the RB, but inserts a mention of vows: "I, N., pronounce with vows valid for three years (or with solemn vows), before God and his saints, in the presence of our Father in Christ, N., and the monks of this monastery. . . ."

[27] See I. Herwegen, *Geschichte der benediktinischen Professformel*, Part II of *Studien zur benediktinischen Profess*, Beiträge zur Geschichte des alten Mönchtums und

a dialogue between abbot and monk. Derived perhaps from the classical Roman usage of the *stipulatio* to bind a person to an obligation in the presence of witnesses and create a unilateral contract, it was widely used in liturgical practice, as it still is today. Most monasteries today use the interrogation form for the *promissio*, and it has been adopted in the 1970 *Rite of Religious Profession.*

The second stage in the rite was that of the *petitio*, a written document in which the novice formally stated the terms of his promise. St. Benedict's insistence on this is an important step in the development of a consciousness of the juridical character of profession. We have seen that a document was required by Shenoute of Atripe, but there is no evidence that his example had any following. In the RM there is a document called a *brevis vel donatio*, but it is merely an inventory of the candidate's possessions and a deed transferring them to the monastery.[28] Its purpose is to make the transfer a legal act, so that the monk cannot later lay claim to the property he has renounced; a similar concern appears in RB 58.24-25; 59.3-6. In view of this, it appears that the use of a document arose from the need of conferring legal validity and sanction upon the monk's renunciation of property. St. Benedict has taken a notable step forward in expanding the purpose of the document; it is not merely a formal donation of property but of the monk himself. It states his promise in written juridical form, formalizing his free gift of himself to the service of God.

The Rule is not explicit about the rite of the *petitio*. It may be that the novice wrote it out then and there, but it seems more likely that it had been prepared in advance, as is done today, with only the signature left for the ceremony itself. The Rule does specify that he shall himself place it on the altar. This symbolizes his voluntary act of offering himself to God, whose presence is represented by the altar. Again, this shows that for St. Benedict the monk's promise is effectively directed to God. The document remains on the altar until the end of the profession rite. Today it is commonly said that this sym-

---

des Benediktinerordens 3 (Münster: Aschendorff 1912); J. Leclercq "Profession According to the Rule of St. Benedict" *CS* 5 (1970) 252–277; also in *Rule and Life: An Interdisciplinary Symposium* (Spencer, Mass.: Cistercian Publications 1971) pp. 117–150; C. Capelle, *Le voeu d'obéissance des origines au xii siècle* (Paris: Pichon et Durand-Auzias 1959) pp. 103–116.

[28] The RM, moreover, includes the "monk's soul" in the offering formula that he recites while placing his document on the altar (RM 89.18). The use of the document is nevertheless restricted to cases in which the novice bestows property upon the monastery (RM 89.17).

bolizes the union of the monk's self-offering with the sacrifice of Christ, but there is nothing of this in the RB. It is significant that at the end it is the abbot who takes the *petitio* from the altar. The monk, who has given himself totally, has no more control over it, and it is effectively the abbot into whose hands he has committed himself, for God's will is manifested through him. The *petitio* is to be kept in the archives as legal proof of the monk's profession; if he ever leaves, it is not returned to him, but serves as a witness against his apostasy (RB 58.29).

The third part of the rite is the specifically religious and liturgical element of the profession: the *oratio*. The novice addresses himself to God in the words of Ps 118(119):116, the same text used by the RM: "Receive me, Lord, as you have promised, and I shall live; do not disappoint me in my hope."[29] It is an eloquent prayer, asking that his gift of himself may be acceptable and that God may respond to it by fulfilling the hopes of the monk. St. Benedict adds to the RM's directive a threefold repetition of this verse, concluding with the doxology. The words *tertio respondeat* suggest that he means that the choir should reply three times to a threefold recitation by the novice, as is done today, i.e., six times altogether, followed by the *Gloria*. After the monk has prayed that his offering may be acceptable, he asks for the prayers of the monks, prostrating before each of them. There is no mention of the *Confirma hoc*, the sign of peace, nor the concluding prayers by the abbot, all of which are prescribed by the RM (89.25-26).

Subsequent Benedictine tradition found this simple *oratio* too jejune and hastened to fill the vacuum already at an early date. Smaragdus, who cites the text of the RM, prescribes the Lord's Prayer followed by an oration (of which he provides the text) and then the kiss of peace by all (Smarag. *expos. in reg.*, on 58.23, p. 297). The latter signifies the new monk's acceptance into the community (RB 58.23).

The major modification of St. Benedict's ritual, however, was the addition of the *consecratio monachi* at this point. Monastic profession in the West, as in Egypt of the fourth century, was an act of the monk, not a sacramental rite or act of the Church. It began to be conceived as such, however, in the East; such a rite is mentioned by St. Nilus in the

---

[29] Both the Master and St. Benedict insert "Lord" into this text, though it is not found in Scripture. It may, however, have appeared in the Latin text known to them, for it is found in one manuscript of the Old Roman Psalter, the tenth-century Bosworth Psalter, now in the British Museum, which is thought to have belonged to St. Dunstan. It is possible that the RM and RB conceive of this prayer as being directed to Christ, for *Domine* often signifies Christ in both rules.

fifth century and first described by Pseudo-Dionysius in the sixth
(Ps-Dion. *eccl.hier.* 6,3).[30] Some scholars have suggested that it must
have been known to St. Benedict, and that he does not mention it
because he took it for granted.[31] There is, however, no evidence for
such a view. It is first mentioned in the West by Theodore of Canterbury in the late seventh century (Theod.Cant. *can.* 2); it is significant
that he was an Oriental. The Eastern ceremony consisted of an epi-
clesis, the monk's profession, tonsure, conferring of the habit, and
kiss of peace; sometimes there was also an imposition of hands.

Theodore prescribes that the abbot shall celebrate Mass (it is supposed that he is a priest) and pronounce "the three orations" over the
monk's head. For seven days the monk shall keep his head covered
with the cuculla, in imitation of the neophytes after baptism. We are
not certain that this consecration was combined with the profession
rite of the RB. But that step had been taken by the time of Hildemar.
After the *Suscipe*, the novice prostrates and the others kneel. Then
three *Kyries* and five psalms are sung, followed by a number of versicles and an oration. After the investiture the novice receives the kiss of
peace from all the monks (Hild. *exp.reg.* p. 547); then he wears his
cuculla for three days. Besides the Gallican predilection for multiplication of psalms and versicles, this rite shows the influence of baptismal symbolism: the prostration accompanied by the *Miserere* and *De
profundis* symbolizes death to sin. A later medieval development that
lasted until modern times had the prostrate monk covered with a funeral pall and surrounded by lighted candles.[32]

Both the *consecratio monachi* and the baptismal analogy are in
themselves legitimate developments if they are kept within bounds.
The modern rite of monastic profession includes the consecratory
prayer, considerably simplified. Neither of the two official formulas in

[30] On the *consecratio monachi*, see R. Molitor "Von der Mönchsweihe in der lateinischen Kirche" *Theologie und Glaube* 16 (1924) 584–612; P. Oppenheim "Mönchsweihe
und Taufritus. Ein Kommentar zur Auslegung bei Dionysius dem Areopagiten" *Miscellanea Mohlberg* (Rome: Ediz. Liturgiche 1948) 1.259–282.

[31] O. Casel "Die Mönchsweihe" *Jahrbuch für Liturgiewissenschaft* 5 (1925) 1–47;
Herwegen, *Sinn und Geist*, pp. 341–344.

[32] R. Molitor "Symbolische Grablegung bei der Ordensprofess" *BM* 6 (1924) 54–57;
B. Neunheuser "Mönchsgelübde als Zweite Taufe und unser theologisches Gewissen"
Liturgie und Mönchtum 33–34 (1963–64) 63–69; S. Feldhohn "Gestorben der Sünde—
Lebend für Gott. Gedanken zum Taufbewusstsein in den ältesten Mönchsviten und
Regeln" *ibid.* 52–62; J. Leclercq "Professione religiosa secondo battesimo" *Vita Re-
ligiosa* 3 (1967) 3–8; "Baptême et profession. Genèse et évolution de la vie consacrée"
Aspects du monachisme hier et aujourd'hui (Paris: La Source 1968) pp. 69–97; "Monas-
tic Profession and the Sacraments" *MS* 5 (1968) 59–85.

the 1970 *Rite of Religious Profession* contains an explicit mention of baptism, but it is referred to elsewhere in the rite, echoing the teaching of Vatican II (*Lumen gentium* n.44; *Perfectae caritatis* n.5). These theological and liturgical developments, however, are quite beyond the horizons of the RB.

One more step remains in the profession rite: that most ancient gesture of all, the conferring of the habit. For the RM it is a "holy" garment; the newly professed must give evidence of virtue for a whole year before he may wear it (RM 90.68-80), and the monk who leaves must give it back, lest "the garb of Christ . . . be carried off and be contaminated in the world" (90.84-86). St. Benedict has nothing of this perspective nor of the tonsure that accompanies the clothing. He returns to the view of Cassian, for whom the clothing is a symbol of dispossession: the monk renounces even his own clothes and wears those of the monastery (Cassian. *inst.* 4,5). This is clear from the context in RB and explains the apparent interruption of verses 24-25.

These verses deal with the question of disposing of property, which has already been taken care of and really pertains to the question of the *petitio*. Like the RM, St. Benedict allows the monk either to confer it upon the poor or to transfer it to the monastery; Cassian would not allow the monastery to accept any of it (Cassian. *inst.* 4,4). This was no doubt provided for by a clause in the *petitio*. The RB speaks of this matter in verses 24-25 because it is related to the matter of the habit: the stripping off of the monk's secular clothes symbolizes his renunciation of all possessions. As with Cassian and the RM, the clothes he has given up are to be kept so that if he ever leaves (Cassian speaks only of expulsion in *inst.* 4,6; the RM 90.84 and RB 58.28 of voluntary departure), they may be returned to him and the habit kept in the monastery. St. Benedict is not concerned about the profanation of the "holy" habit, but wants to show that the monk has gone back on his renunciation.

This difference of outlook also explains why Benedict prescribes that investiture should accompany profession and admission to the community. Cassian did not admit the monk to a deanery until a year after investiture, whereas the Master postponed investiture until a year after profession and admission to a deanery. The RB differs from Cassian in placing the year of formation before investiture, and from the RM in not requiring the monk to prove his "holiness" before receiving the habit. Since the habit represents dispossession rather than holiness, it can be conferred as soon as the novice has renounced his property. Thus the entire ritual of profession and admission becomes more coherent. It is interesting to note, however, that a vestige remains of the earlier separation between admission and investiture. Whereas we should expect that admission to the community would come at the end of the entire rite, it is, curiously, mentioned *before* the habit is given: "From that very day he is to be counted as one of the community" (58.23).

The content of profession in the RB

The question remains: what precisely does the monk promise at his profession, according to the RB? What does he say in his *promissio* and put into writing in his *petitio*, and to what does it bind him?

The Rule addresses this question in 58.17, where it gives the directive: "he promises stability, *conversatio morum suorum*, and obedience" (*promittat de stabilitate sua et conversatione morum suorum et oboedientia*). This is one of a number of three-member formulas in chapter 58.[33] It has frequently been understood, at least in modern times, as a list of the "three Benedictine vows." It is thus taken to mean that the monk formally undertakes three distinct obligations, each of which is the object of a solemn promise to God. Since the Middle Ages, religious have generally promised to observe poverty, celibacy and obedience, the three "evangelical counsels," and these have been seen as distinct promises, binding them under the virtue of religion and each having clear juridical consequences (Thom.Aq. *summa theol.* II-II, 186, a.6-7). Some institutes add an additional vow, expressing a particular aspect of their life (e.g., to serve the poor, to work in foreign missions). In this perspective, the "Benedictine vows" were seen as distinct obligations peculiar to the monastic life while implicitly including the three evangelical counsels.[34]

It is impossible, however, that the author of the RB could have understood the matter in this way. If the very nature of a vow was still unclear at his time, as we have seen, the concept of distinct "vows of religion" was still more remote. It did not develop until the speculative theological ferment of the thirteenth century prompted analysis and definition of such questions. The ancient monks promised simply

[33] The novices "study, eat and sleep" (58.5); they are to show zeal for "the Work of God, for obedience and for trials" (58.7). There are also three readings of the Rule and a threefold repetition of the *Suscipe*.

[34] See J. Leclercq "Evangelio y cultura en la historia del compromiso en la vida religiosa" *Los consejos evangelicos en la tradición monastica*, Studia Silensia I (Silos: Abadia de Silos 1975) pp. 327–342.

to live the full monastic life as it was practiced in a particular monastery and defined by a particular rule. Sometimes there was special emphasis upon a particular feature of the life, such as virginity. The RB conceives of the monk's obligation as embracing all that is required by the Rule.

The three-member phrase of RB 58.17, then, is not a profession formula. We do not know precisely what St. Benedict's monks stated in their *promissio* and wrote in their *petitio*. Later the three-member phrase was often incorporated into the profession formula, though we sometimes find versions containing only two members, stability and obedience.[35] The three-member formula is still used today. In the Rule, however, it is not a profession formula, but rather a rubric that is intended to describe the content of the *promissio* in terms of the monastic realities it encompasses. It is not a list of distinct obligations and is not exhaustive, but is simply a statement singling out some of the principal features of the monk's promise.[36] The profession consisted of a promise to live the entire life prescribed by the Rule. That life is specified, but not exclusively, by the three elements mentioned. Their content is not necessarily mutually exclusive, since they are not perceived as distinct obligations.

Much discussion has been devoted by recent Benedictine writers to the precise meaning of *stabilitas, conversatio morum suorum*, and *oboedientia*. Often the discussion has been colored by the assumption that the three elements represent three distinct "Benedictine vows." Once this supposition is dismissed, the question becomes at once clearer and less urgent, for there is no real doubt about what the monk promised: the full observance of monastic life as defined by the Rule. Nevertheless, the meaning of the threefold rubric still needs to be elucidated.[37]

Of the three aspects of the monk's commitment, the one whose meaning is clearest is obedience. It had long been an important ele-

[35] The *conversatio morum* was apparently dropped from the formula when its meaning was no longer understood. The history of the profession formula has been traced by Herwegen: see note 27 above.

[36] See B. Steidle "Das Versprechen der 'Beständigkeit,' des 'Tugend-Wandels' und des 'Gehorsams' in der Regel St. Benedikts (Kap. 58,17)" EA 36 (1960) 105–122.

[37] In addition to the standard commentaries on the Rule, see C. Peifer, *Monastic Spirituality* (New York: Sheed and Ward 1966) pp. 272–306; "Commitment, Stability, Conversion, Obedience: Proceedings of Regional Symposium, Nunraw" CS 12 (1977) 3–167; *Consider Your Call: A Theology of Monastic Life Today*, ed. D. Rees (London: SPCK 1978) pp. 128–220; A. Roberts, *Centered on Christ: An Introduction to Monastic Profession* (Still River, Mass.: St. Bede's Publ. 1979).

ment in the monastic tradition, though the conception of it differed at various times and places.[38] For Cassian, it is the specific virtue of cenobites (Cassian. *inst.* 4,10,23-31; *conl.* 19,6). St. Benedict devotes chapter 5 of the Rule to obedience, as well as degrees 2-4 of the ladder of humility in chapter 7. In these passages he is dependent upon the RM, though he qualifies the teaching of the Master, and also drastically abbreviates it.[39] His own contribution appears in several passages that are proper to the RB (Prol.2-3; 68; 71; 72.6). As we have seen, obedience is also one of his three criteria for the acceptance of a novice (58.7).

The most controverted of the three elements is the concept of *conversatio morum suorum*. This grammatically difficult phrase appears to be an idiomatic expression that was no doubt clear to St. Benedict's contemporaries. In later times, however, it was no longer understood, and copyists changed it to the easier formula *conversio morum suorum*.[40] The correct reading was first restored by Cuthbert Butler in his critical edition of 1912, and the modern discussion of the meaning of the phrase dates from that time. The phrase *conversio morum* presents no difficulty; it means a 'conversion of one's behavior,' the abandonment of secular habits and adherence to monastic practice. The term *conversatio*, 'way of life,' in itself is likewise quite normal; it is often used in Christian literature to translate the Greek *askēsis* and hence can mean 'the ascetic life' or 'the monastic life.' St. Benedict uses it in this sense nine other times in the Rule. Thus he writes: "Do not grant newcomers to the monastic life (*ad conversationem*) an easy

---

[38] See Capelle in note 27 above; J. Tillard "Aux sources de l'obéissance religieuse" *Nouvelle Revue Théologique* 98 (1976) 592–626; 817–838; S. Frank "Gehorsam und Freiheit im frühen Mönchtum" *Römische Quartalschrift* 64 (1969) 234–245; "Gehorsam" *Reallexikon für Antike und Christentum* 9.390–430; A. Louf "L'obéissance dans la tradition monastique" *Vie Consacrée* 48 (1976) 197–210; J. Gribomont "L'obéissance et évangile selon saint Basile" *La Vie Spirituelle Supplément* 21 (1952) 192–215; J. Rippinger "The Concept of Obedience in the Monastic Writings of Basil and Cassian" *SM* 19 (1977) 7–18.

[39] See A. de Vogüé "La doctrine du Maître sur l'obéissance. Sa genèse" *Revue d'histoire de la spiritualité* 50 (1974) 113–134; *La communauté*, pp. 207–288; 7.135–164; E. Heufelder "Vom Gehorsam im Geist der Benediktus-Regel" *EA* 42 (1966) 477–481; J. Lebourlier "Obéissance selon la Règle bénédictine" *Lettre de Ligugé* 120 (1966) 8–17.

[40] Both the Oxford and the St. Gall manuscripts read *conversatio*: the reading *conversio* is characteristic of the *textus receptus*. It is found in the commentary of Hildemar, who says, "*Conversio morum* is the eradication of vices and cultivation of virtues" (Hild. *exp.reg.* p. 541). That commentators were puzzled by the expression *conversatio morum* is clear from the fact that it was simply omitted in some cases. Already in the seventh century the *Rule of Donatus* reduces the promises to two (Donat. *reg. ad virg.* 6). The same solution appears in the two-member profession formula (see note 35).

entry" (58.1). The combination with *morum suorum*, however, is difficult. What can be the meaning of "the way of life of his behavior" or "the monastic life of his behavior"?

A number of solutions to this problem have been proposed. Here we cannot detail the many intricacies of the question or the nuances introduced by the scholars who have studied it. We shall merely describe the general types of solution proposed and refer the reader to the appropriate literature for the details. The solutions can be divided into three general classes.

First, one group holds, though for different reasons, that *conversatio* in this context is equivalent to *conversio*. This has been argued on the basis that it was traditionally understood in this sense.[41] From a philological viewpoint, it has been explained that, in addition to the noun *conversatio* derived from *conversari*, there is another *conversatio* derived from the verb *conversare*, a frequentative of *convertere*; this second *conversatio* means the same thing as *conversio* and is the word used in RB 58.17.[42] It has been forcefully argued by Hoppenbrouwers, however, that this meaning of *conversatio* is very rare and seems to have been confined to translation language; it is unlikely that an ordinary late Latin writer would have chosen it instead of *conversio*.[43] Finally, it has been suggested that the use of *conversatio* in the RB is quite simply a mistake for *conversio*: the scribe who wrote the archetype (St. Benedict's secretary?) was incompetent and careless and often confused similar words.[44] Where the RM has *conversio* in 1.3, the RB has *conversatio*, with no apparent reason for the change. This is the only one of the ten occurrences of *conversatio* in the RB that has an exact parallel in the RM,[45] which in fact never uses the term. How-

[41] Thus P. Schmitz "Conversatio (conversio) morum" *DS* 2.2206–12; A. Lentini, *S. Benedetto: La Regola* (Montecassino 1947) pp. 489–490. M. Rothenhäusler argued that it is equivalent to Cassian's *vita actualis*, but sees this as essentially involving conversion.

[42] Thus B. Linderbauer, *S. Benedicti Regula Monachorum, herausgegeben und philologisch erklärt* (Metten: Verlag des Benediktinerstiftes Metten 1922); C. Mohrmann "La langue de saint Benoît" in P. Schmitz, *S. Benedicti Regula Monachorum* (Maredsous: Éditions de l'Abbaye 1955) pp. 33–39.

[43] H. Hoppenbrouwers, *Conversatio: une étude sémasiologique*, Graecitas et Latinitas Christianorum Primaeva, Supplementa (Nijmegen: Dekker & Van de Vegt 1964) pp. 45–95. Hoppenbrouwers shows that most of the examples cited by the *Thesaurus Linguae Latinae* for this usage are invalid.

[44] J. Winandy "Conversio (conversatio) morum" *Dizionario degli Istituti di Perfezione* 3.106–110, who refers to the observations of J. Neufville, in de Vogüé 1.354–355.

[45] However, the *noviter veniens quis ad conversationem* of RB 58.1 is comparable to the *cum aliquis . . . indicaverit se velle converti* of RM 90.1.

ever, since the RB uses it eight other times in proper passages, in a perfectly correct way, it is surely arbitrary to hold that all of these occurrences are due to error. At the very least, the scribe must have been unusually consistent in his carelessness! An attempt to equate *conversatio* with *conversio* is based upon insufficient evidence.

A second approach was suggested by Odo Lottin of Mont-César.[46] Rather than deriving the meaning of the phrase from grammatical analysis and contemporary usage, he looked to the context of the Rule itself. Lottin compared the profession formula to the three types of monks mentioned alongside the cenobites in RB 1, and suggested it was meant to eliminate them from the cenobitic program. Since stability distinguishes the cenobite from the gyrovague and obedience distinguishes him from the sarabaite, it seems likely that *conversatio morum suorum* was meant to distinguish him from the hermit. It is true that *conversatio* can have a social meaning ('life together with,' 'association with'); hence Lottin concluded that the phrase means 'life in community' in RB 58.17. But the term in itself never means that without some qualifier identifying the associates, and the *morum suorum* not only fails to fulfill this function, but also becomes unintelligible. Moreover, this hypothesis requires the unlikely supposition that the Rule is opposed to a monk's passage to the desert.[47]

A third type of solution holds that *conversatio* is a term quite distinct from *conversio* and means 'way of life,' 'behavior'; in a monastic context it can mean 'the monastic life.' The promise is general, not specific; the novice simply commits himself to follow the way of life observed in the monastery, with all that it entails. Various scholars have arrived at this conclusion in different ways and have suggested various translations. Rothenhäusler, in a second opinion, held that it means 'the conduct of his behavior';[48] Butler thought it was untranslatable but equivalent to something like 'the conduct of one's life';[49]

[46] O. Lottin "Le voeu de 'conversatio morum' dans la Règle de saint Benoît" *Recherches de théologie ancienne et médiévale* 26 (1959) 5–16; reprinted in *Études de morale, histoire et doctrine* (Gembloux: J. Duculot 1960) pp. 309–321, with reply to critics, pp. 321–328; "À propos du voeu de 'conversatio morum' chez saint Benoît" *Recherches de théologie ancienne et médiévale* 28 (1961) 154–160. A similar view, interpreting *conversatio* to mean 'community life,' is upheld by P. Hickey "The Theology of Community in the Rule of St. Benedict" *ABR* 20 (1969) 431–471.

[47] See the refutations by J. Winandy "Conversatio morum" *Coll. Ord. Cist. Ref.* 22 (1960) 378–386; and T. Merton "Conversatio Morum" *CS* 1 (1966) 130–133.

[48] M. Rothenhäusler "Conversatio Morum" *BM* 12 (1930) 145–146.

[49] C. Butler, *Benedictine Monachism* (London: Longmans Green and Co. 1919) pp. 134–139.

Chapman suggested 'monasticity';[50] McCann proposed 'self-discipline';[51] Würmseer, 'disciplining of his behavior';[52] Friedrich, 'exercise of monastic behavior.'[53]

What was lacking to these opinions was any satisfactory philological explanation of the phrase. This was provided by Steidle, who argued convincingly that it is a case of the "genitive of identity" or "epexegetical genitive," which is common in low Latin and in the RB itself.[54] In this usage two nouns that are synonymous are linked together by placing one of them in the genitive instead of joining them with a conjunction. Thus *factorum nostrorum opera* (RB 7.28) does not mean 'the actions of our deeds' but rather 'our actions and deeds' or simply 'our deeds.' Likewise *supplicatio litaniae* (RB 9.10) should not be translated 'the petitionary prayer of the litany,' but 'the petitionary prayer that is the litany' or simply 'the litany.' It is equivalent to *supplicatio seu litania*.[55]

Applied to the phrase *conversatio morum suorum*, this explanation permits us to treat it as equivalent to *de conversatione et moribus suis* and to translate it as 'about his manner of life and moral conduct' or 'about his manner of life, that is to say, his moral conduct.' *Conversatio* and *mores* are here considered synonyms. Neither has a specifically monastic meaning in itself (though *conversatio* can have such a meaning), but in the context, of course, the "behavior" or "manner of life" in question is that required in the monastery. Hence it is a gen-

---

[50] J. Chapman, *St. Benedict and the Sixth Century* (1929; rpt. Westport, Conn.: Greenwood Press 1971) pp. 207–231.

[51] J. McCann, *Saint Benedict* (1937; rpt. Garden City, N.Y.: Doubleday Image Book 1958) pp. 147–167. In a later treatment of the question, *The Rule of Saint Benedict in Latin and English* (London: Burns Oates 1952) pp. 202–208, McCann holds that *conversatio* means 'conversion' in four of its occurrences in the RB, including 58.17.

[52] N. Würmseer "Conversatio Morum Suorum" *SMGBO* 57 (1939) 99–112.

[53] F. Friedrich "Conversatio Morum. Das zweite Gelübde des Benediktinermönches" *SMGBO* 59 (1941–42) 200–326.

[54] B. Steidle "'De conversatione morum suorum.' Zum philologischen Verständnis von Regula S. Benedicti Kap. 58,17" in *Regula Magistri — Regula S. Benedicti*, StA 44 (Rome: Herder 1959) pp. 136–144. See also his *The Rule of St. Benedict* (Canon City, Colo.: Holy Cross Abbey 1966) pp. 254–257.

[55] In the RB there are a dozen or more instances of the genitive of identity. See the list in the *Index Grammaticus* of Hanslik's edition; and B. Steidle "Der Genetivus Epexegeticus in der Regel des heiligen Benedikt" *SM* 2 (1960) 193–203. A similar usage occurs in English in a phrase such as "the age of fifteen," in which "age" is really identical to "fifteen." The equivalent Latin expression occurs in RB 70.4: *usque quindecim annorum aetates*. Likewise, expressions such as "the city of Paris," "the month of June." The genitive of identity also occurs in New Testament Greek: "the sign of Jonah" (Matt 12:39), "the gift of the Holy Spirit" (Acts 2:38). See M. Zerwick, *Biblical Greek* (Rome: Pont. Biblical Inst. 1963) pp. 45–46.

eral promise to live the life that the Rule and the abbot specify in that particular monastery. Hoppenbrouwers has supported this interpretation by a thorough analysis of the range of meanings of *conversatio*, and has produced a number of examples of its use in the same way, with *mores, vita* or *actus* as a synonym joined to it either by a conjunction or by a genitive of identity. Thus Cyprian writes *de conversatione et moribus suis* (Cypr. *epist.* 4,3; 62,3), 'concerning their manner of life and behavior' or 'concerning their moral behavior,' whereas Maximus of Turin says the same thing with the genitive: *morum conversatio, morum nostrorum alacrem conversationem* (Max.Tur. *sermo* 27,42; 70,28).[56] In the light of this background, it is highly probable that the phrase of RB 58.17 directs the novice to make a promise "concerning his moral behavior."[57]

There remains the question of stability.[58] The RB uses this term in four other places (4.78; 58.9; 60.9; 61.5), and it appears seven times in the RM. The latter also uses *firmitas* three times as a synonym. It can be deduced from both rules that the basic meaning of the concept of stability is *perseverance*. One passage of the RB mentions stability and perseverance together as equivalent ideas: "If he promises perseverance in his stability . . ." (58.9), *si promiserit de stabilitate sua perseverantia*.[59] The RM supports the identification of the two terms

[56] See Hoppenbrouwers, p. 82, as in n. 43 above; other examples in Steidle, *art. cit.* in note 54.

[57] This interpretation is also admitted by de Vogüé, 6.1324–26; and A. Wathen "*Conversatio* and Stability in the Rule of Benedict" MS 11 (1975) 1–44.

[58] On stability, see M. Rothenhäusler "Ältestes Mönchtum und klösterliche Beständigkeit" BM 3 (1921) 87–95; 223–237; "Die Beständigkeit des Benediktiners" *ibid.* 345–357; "Die rechtlichen Wirkungen der benediktinischen Beständigkeit" *ibid.* 440–454; Butler, *Benedictine Monachism*, pp. 123–134; J. McMurray "Monastic Stability" CS 1 (1966) 209–224; "On being 'at home.' Reflections on Monastic Stability in the Light of the Philosophy of Gabriel Marcel" MS 4 (1966) 81–88; M. Löhrer "Towards a Meaning of Monastic Stability" *Benedictine Confluence* 3 (1970) 4–8; A. Roberts "The Meaning of the Vow of Stability" CollCist 33 (1971) 257–269; P. Miquel "De la stabilité" CollCist 36 (1974) 313–322; A. Wathen "Monastic Institute of Federation of Americas 1973" ABR 25 (1974) 246–286; *art. cit.* in note 57; J. Leclercq "La stabilité selon la Règle de saint Benoît" CollCist 37 (1975) 197–204. A major work on stability, which has not been published, was defended as a canon law dissertation at the Gregorian University in the early 1970s by G. Veloso, "Usque ad mortem in monasterio perseverantes (*Regula Benedicti* Pr. 50). The Obligation of Monks to Persevere and to Reside in Their Monastery: A Historico-legal Study of the Discipline in the West from the 4th to the 7th Century, Mainly on Monastic Rules, Conciliar Canons, Papal Decretals, and Imperial Constitutions." See Leclercq, *ibid.*, p. 197.

[59] Dom Germain Morin maintained that the original reading of the St. Gall codex was *de stabilitate sive perseverantia*, and printed this in his diplomatic edition. This reading makes the two terms clearly synonymous. An erasure has made the passage difficult

APPENDIX 5

in a passage that reads: "If they choose stability as a pleasing discipline . . . and wish to commit themselves to perseverance . . ." (89.1);
surely the two phrases are saying the same thing.

It has often been said that the introduction of stability was one of St.
Benedict's major contributions to the development of Western monasticism. The idea, however, was hardly new to him. It is equally required by the RM and other sixth-century rules, and is at least implicit
already in Egyptian cenobitism. In fact, the insistence in the
Apophthegmata on "staying in the cell" shows that the spiritual content of the concept is very ancient. It is true that exile and wandering
as ascetical practices were widely accepted. They sometimes led to
abuse, but not all wandering monks were unworthy. Bishops and
councils tried to regulate the practice, and it may be that in the sixth
century, because of the social upheavals of the times, wandering
monks had a deservedly bad reputation. The Rule does not condemn
all *monachi peregrini* (see RB 61), but requires its own monks to
remain in the *coenobium* except for necessary journeys (RB 50–51;
67). It condemns *gyrovagi*, who are by definition bad monks, but it
equally disapproves of sarabaites, who do stay in one place but do not
live as monks should, since they do not obey an abbot or a rule.

To avoid these pitfalls, Benedict requires that the monk "observe
his [Christ's] teaching in the monastery until death" (Prol.50). It is not
simply a question of remaining physically in the *coenobium* throughout life, but of persevering in living the monastic life there, in accepting the *doctrina* and conforming one's behavior to it. The later distinction between *stabilitas loci* and *stabilitas cordis* represents the view
of the RB accurately, even if these terms are not found in it. The idea
is there equivalently, at the conclusion of chapter 4, where the tools of
good works (the RM calls them tools of the *ars sancta*) are said to be
employed in that "workshop" which is "the enclosure of the monastery and stability in the community" (4.78). The *claustrum monasterii*
means actual physical presence in the *coenobium*, whereas *stabilitas
in congregatione* means to persevere in living the cenobitic life as it is
followed in that community, observing poverty, silence and humility,
and joining in the daily round of prayer and work. Above all, it is

to read, but subsequent critics, beginning with Plenkers, agree that the original reading
was *sua* rather than *sive*. A later corrector changed it to *de stabilitatis suae perseverantia*, the reading of the interpolated codices. Here it is a genitive of identity, which
retains the same meaning. Other copyists chose a different way of improving the
difficult grammar, by writing *de stabilitate sua perseverantiam*. In any case, the passage
effectively identifies stability with perseverance.

perseverance in *obedience*, for this is the primary characteristic of the cenobite. The two elements go together: the place and the life that goes on there; and stability includes both.

Whatever legal distinctions may have been introduced later, St. Benedict's notion of stability is not satisfied by a purely juridical bond to a monastery; one cannot live the life of a *coenobium* unless one stays there and submits in obedience to its regime.[60] On the other hand, passage to another monastery or to the eremitical life is not condemned by the RB. The former is not mentioned at all,[61] while the latter is referred to in such a traditional way in chapter 1 that St. Benedict's view of it can scarcely have been different than that of Cassian, for whom the *coenobium* is, in principle, the apprenticeship for the desert.

We can now examine the formula of 58.17 as a whole. We may first note that two of the three elements contained in it have already been mentioned in the two promises that precede profession. At the beginning (or end) of the two-month period, the novice promises "perseverance in his stability" (58.9), whereupon the Rule is read to him. After twelve months, he promises "to observe everything and to obey every command given him" and never "to shake from his neck the yoke of the rule" (58.14-15). The first promise is one of stability, the second one of obedience, and both explicitly refer to the Rule. Obviously, these are not two separate and distinct obligations. Stability adds to obedience the element of perseverance in it, as well as connoting the cenobitic context and specific place in which that obedience is normally to be rendered.

The third and most important promise, that which constitutes profession, is described by the mention of these two elements, together with a third, *conversatio morum*. This last is the most general of the three. The monk makes a promise that concerns his "moral conduct or behavior," that is to say, he promises to live the kind of life followed in the monastery that he proposes to enter and that is specified by the Rule that has been read to him three times. More specifically, this life

---

[60] On the juridical aspects of stability, see J. Lahache "Stabilité monastique" *Dictionnaire de droit canonique* 7.1078-86.

[61] RB 61 deals with the case of a *monachus peregrinus* and says that if his life is edifying, he may be received into the community, but with the proviso that his abbot must first give consent if he is from a "known" monastery (61.13). It does not explicitly treat the opposite case of a monk from Benedict's monastery who wishes to transfer elsewhere. Can St. Benedict's tolerance of the latter be inferred from the fact that he says, "Never do to another what you do not want done to yourself" (Tob 4:16; RB 61.14), or is this merely a kind of cliché to provide biblical justification for his regulation?

is one of obedience, for it is determined by the traditional observances laid down by the Rule and by the teaching and directives of the abbot, which apply the Gospel and the Rule to the details of everyday life. Finally, he is to live out this obedience in the context of his own *coenobium*, persevering in that obedience in this same place and with this same community, following its observances. The promise is binding for life (Prol.50; 58.15-16).

While the RM does not have this three-member description of the promise, it has an equivalent formula, comparison with which bears out this interpretation: "I want to serve God, by the discipline of the rule that has been read to me, in your monastery" (RM 89.7). For the RM, this is the actual text the novice is to say in the profession rite, i.e., his *promissio*. It too consists of three parts: one is general (service of God), the other two are more specific and define the means by which the first is to be brought about. These are the rule and the monastery. The correspondence with the RB is quite striking: the service of God is parallel to *conversatio morum suorum*; obedience to the rule; stability to the monastery.[62] These two authors conceive of the monastic life in such a similar way that their respective statements of the promises by which a monk binds himself to it have substantially the same content. Both have in mind a monastic form of the Christian communal life that consists in obedience to a rule and an abbot, and that is to be followed perseveringly until death in the same monastery.

[62] See de Vogüé, 6.1326–29.

Appendix 6

The Role and Interpretation of Scripture
in the Rule of Benedict

Whatever other factors may have been involved in the rise and development of the monastic movement, there is no doubt that the central factor, without which the monastic movement is simply unthinkable, is the Scriptures of the Old and New Testaments.[1] The monastic way of life was conceived as a response to the precepts of Scripture and was oriented toward the progressive assimilation of the truths of Scripture. Athanasius portrayed Antony as taking up the monastic form of life in simple obedience to hearing the words of Scripture.[2] Pachomius and his successors were famous for their ability to interpret the Scriptures (e.g., *Vita bo* 190; *Vita sa*[5] 129). The fame of many of the monks who appear in the *Apophthegmata* was due to their ability to interpret Scripture and apply it to practical situations. The study of Scripture was likewise the central activity of the more learned representatives of the movement such as Jerome, Rufinus, Basil and Evagrius. Monastic culture was built out of the materials of Scripture and was centered on its study and assimilation.

To perceive the centrality of Scripture to monastic culture, one need only advert to the role Scripture has always played in the activity that is at the heart of monastic life—prayer. Both personal and common prayer were from the beginning constructed from, and nourished by, the texts of Scripture. The poetic texts of the Old Testament, especially the psalms, came to form the heart of the Divine Office at an early date, and the narrative materials of both Testaments provided material for the liturgical readings. The personal reading of monks was also centered on Scripture. *Lectio* was termed *divina* because it was the

[1] See the Introduction, pp. 4, 31–33.
[2] See the Introduction, pp. 18–20.

reading of Scripture. Meditation in antiquity was conceived essentially as an effort to digest and assimilate the biblical text through repeated recollection of it. And contemplation was to attain the steady vision of those realities presented by Scripture.[3]

The early monks thought that Scripture could provide not only material for the life of prayer but also guidelines for organizing the whole of life. It is the ultimate rule, the *rectissima norma vitae humanae*, as St. Benedict terms it (RB 73.3). It provided the principles for dealing with all sorts of practical situations, such as the number of hours of prayer (RB 16), the distribution of goods (RB 33–34), disciplinary matters (RB 25, 27), the amount of food and drink (RB 39–40). The Bible, however, is a vast compilation of disparate, sometimes seemingly contradictory materials. Those who sought to live by the Gospel needed a practical compendium, an abridged version, containing those precepts that applied most directly to the organization of monastic life. This was the function of some of the monastic rules. The scriptural quotations contained in them are cited not just to provide embellishment but because they are considered normative. They are part of the rule. It is hardly surprising, then, that these early rules contain so many quotations from, and allusions to, biblical texts.

The number of citations and allusions found in the Rule of St. Benedict by modern editors has varied greatly. While Butler found 94 citations and allusions from the Old Testament and 104 from the New Testament, more recently Hanslik found 145 from the Old Testament (88 citations and 57 allusions) and 165 from the New Testament (65 citations and 100 allusions).[4] De Vogüé found 124 from the Old Testament (86 citations and 38 allusions) and 168 from the New Testament (104 citations and 64 allusions).[5] The present edition of the Rule lists 132 references to the Old Testament and 189 to the New Testament. Clearly, the determination of the exact number is somewhat subjective and depends upon the criteria used by editors. It is often impossible to determine whether a passage contains an allusion to a biblical text or simply biblically flavored language. A few examples may serve to illustrate this. In Prol.3 the phrase "weapons of obedience" finds a certain resonance in 2 Cor 10:4-6. The phrase "has

---

[3] For a discussion of the technical terms *lectio, meditatio, oratio* and *contemplatio*, see Appendix 5, pp. 445–447.

[4] C. Butler, *Sancti Benedicti Regula Monachorum* (Freiburg im Breisgau: Herder 1912) pp. 173–175; R. Hanslik, *Benedicti Regula*, CSEL 75 (Vienna: Hölder-Pichler-Tempsky 1960, 1977²) pp. 180–186.

[5] De Vogüé, 2.882–886.

counted us as his sons" (Prol.5) resembles Wis 5:5. One is reminded of Deut 6:7 by the style of RB 7.63. But it is not at all clear that the authors of RM and RB had such texts in mind as they wrote.

The modern reader is often hampered in his recognition of scriptural citations and allusions by two factors that distinguish modern reading from that of the sixth century. First, in antiquity there was far less reading material to be consumed than there is now. The Venerable Bede had at his disposal a library of about two hundred volumes, a distinguished collection for his day but very small by modern standards. Second, reading was almost always done aloud, even in private. St. Augustine expressed some astonishment when he discovered St. Ambrose reading silently (conf. 6,2). In the Rule itself (48.5), the brothers are cautioned to read so as not to disturb others, that is, by reading too loudly. This manner of reading inevitably helped to fix phrases in the reader's mind far more easily than does the rapid silent scanning of great quantities of print that is the modern practice.

In recent times there has been a multiplication of new translations of the Bible, especially in the major modern languages, both for private and liturgical use. This also tends to decrease the possibility of recognizing scriptural allusions. In the sixth century this was not the case. There were basically only two Latin versions available (although these may have contained many variant readings): the old Latin (Vetus Latina) and Jerome's great revision of the Latin Bible, known as the Vulgate. Many of the liturgical texts had become fixed in the old Latin version, but the Vulgate version came to supplant the old Latin for both public and private reading. The version quoted in the Rule is most often the Vulgate, but nineteen of the citations from the Old Testament and eighteen of those from the New Testament depart from the Vulgate.[6] It is not always possible to determine whether this is due to a distinct version or to quotation from memory. In any case, the vernacular biblical text was far more standard than it is today.

In the Rule, Scripture is often considered to be speaking directly to the reader or hearer. It is not merely a source of information about the past or even of revelation about the past, but a guide to life here and now. The Patristic writer thought it obvious that many passages of Scripture were directed to his contemporaries as much as to the contemporaries of the human author of the biblical book, and consequently they were not thought to need any elaborate historical in-

---

[6] S. Pawlowsky, Die biblischen Grundlagen der Regula Benedicti (Vienna: Herder 1965) pp. 30–33.

terpretation. In Prol.8 it is said that "the Scriptures rouse us when they say: 'It is high time for us to arise from sleep.'" It is possible that a citation such as this is intended to recall the whole passage of Rom 13:10-13 to mind.[7] In any case, the author of the Rule sees in it not just an exhortation by St. Paul to the church in Rome to whom he was writing but a word addressed to later generations as well. We too must be roused from our "sleep" by the Word of God. The idea that Scripture is speaking directly to the reader or hearer is very common in the Rule. Out of the 94 instances where a citation is introduced by a formula, 28 begin with a reference to Scripture addressing the monk. In 23 cases it is the Lord who addresses the monk (through the Scriptures).[8] In RB 7 alone, Scripture is said to speak to us (7.19,21,25,33,36,38,41,45), to cry to us (7.1), to command us (7.25), to exhort us (7.45), and to warn us (7.57).

Scripture is described in a variety of ways in the Rule, indicating both the regard in which it is held and the uses it is seen to have. In Prol.9 it is described as "the light that comes from God" (*deificum lumen*) and "the voice from heaven" (*vox divina*). The last phrase refers especially to the exhortation of the invitatory psalm (Ps 94 [95]) heard daily: "If you hear his voice today, do not harden your hearts" (Prol.10). In fact, in Prol.8-10 an elaborate analogy is drawn between the daily rising from sleep to hear the words of Scripture and the taking up of the monastic life in general as a rising from sleep. Hence Scripture can be described as the "light" that awakens us as well as the "voice" that rouses us. The whole of monastic life is thus conceived in these verses as an attempt to respond to the word of Scripture addressed to us.

In Prol.21 the Gospel is described as "our guide." The teaching of both the Rule and the abbot is intended to reflect the teaching of the Gospel. A related phrase, "the Lord's instructions," is contained in a warning in RB 2.4; the abbot is warned not to teach anything at variance with these. Thus the Rule is intended simply as an aid for monks to live by the Scriptures. This is made even more explicit in RB 73, where the Rule is described as "this little rule . . . for beginners." But it is Scripture itself, which has divine authority (*sermo divinae auctoritatis*), that is "the truest of guides for human life" (73.3).

Scripture is also regarded in the Rule as a law. The abbot is required to be learned in "the divine law" (RB 64.9). The Lord's instructions

[7] *Ibid.*, p. 36.
[8] *Ibid.*, pp. 68f.

are understood to be binding (2.4). It is the duty of the abbot to teach the monks how to live by the Scriptures (2.6). He is to put before his monks the "commandments of the Lord" both by his words and his example (2.12). The deans of the monastery are to carry out their tasks according to the "commandments of God" (21.2). The "divine law" is to be read to guests for their instruction when they arrive (53.9). Finally, the monastery, conceived as a school for the Lord's service (Prol.45), is the place where the monks learn to "run on the path of God's commandments" (Prol.49).

The Rule also describes Scripture as "medicine" (28.3). It is one of the remedies that the abbot, acting as a wise physician, is to use in trying to cure his disciples of their faults. This notion is deeply embedded in the monastic tradition and indeed in the New Testament, where Jesus is compared to a physician (Matt 9:12; Mark 2:17). Monastic life can be conceived in its entirety as an effort to heal the wounds of sin or to cure the spiritual diseases to which we are subject. These include especially the eight principal thoughts (see note on RB 1.5). The ability to bring forth the right word from Scripture for the occasion or a saying derived from Scripture was the principal attribute that characterized an "abba" among the early monks.[9]

The literal and non-literal interpretation of Scripture

The modern study of Scripture has come to be dominated, especially during the past century, by what is termed the historical-critical method. In this methodology it is accepted that the only valid sense of Scripture is the literal sense, that is, the meaning intended in the text by the original human author. To determine this meaning, it becomes important to reconstruct, to the extent that it is possible, the historical situation in which the author was writing, to discover successive stages or layers of authorship, etc. This increasingly complex methodology has produced considerable gains in our historical knowledge, in our knowledge of the history of Israel and of the development of Israelite religion, and in our ability to understand the individual texts of both the Old and New Testaments. We have become increasingly aware of the distinctive literary genres in the biblical literature and of the subtleties of theological vision in these texts. All these gains in historical knowledge, however, have also raised in

---

[9] See K. Heussi, *Der Ursprung des Mönchtums* (Tübingen: J.C.B. Mohr 1936) pp. 164f.

the minds of many the question of what relevance the knowledge has to actual religious life today.[10] Even when these texts are viewed as a record of God's dealings with his people, does our greater historical awareness make the texts more relevant to our religious situation? Do these texts still have something to say to us today, or are they simply a record of the past? Such questions have led to the further complexities of the so-called hermeneutical problem.

These are not altogether new questions, although they may be formulated in new ways and for new reasons. They were present implicitly or explicitly in the Patristic period and to a certain degree even in the New Testament. The process of reinterpreting many of the theological concepts of the Old Testament, begun in the ministry of Jesus and continued in the writings of the New Testament, inevitably led to the question of the relevance of many of the older texts. Although there is a strong sense of the continuity of God's design in the history of Israel and in his dramatic intervention in history through Jesus Christ, there is also a sense of discontinuity caused precisely by the dramatic quality of this intervention. Is not much of the Old Testament now out of date? At a very early date Paul found it necessary to argue in his letters to the Galatians and Romans both that there was something radically new in what God had done through Jesus Christ that invalidated the old law, and yet that there was a basic unity and continuity in God's design, that in fact the old dispensation had foreshadowed the new.

It was similar questions that led Marcion to draw up a much restricted canon of Scripture in the second century. But the dominant response of the Patristic period to these questions of continuity and relevance was to interpret the biblical texts, especially those of the Old Testament, in multiple senses.[11] The roots of this methodology were to be found within Scripture itself. A piece such as the Song of Songs, originally composed, it seems, as love poetry, had probably come to be included in the Hebrew canon of Scripture because of the allegorical interpretation attached to it. In this interpretation, the Song was thought to represent the love-relationship between God and his

---

[10] See, for example, D. J. McCarthy "Exod 3:14: History, Philology and Theology" *Catholic Biblical Quarterly* 40 (1978) 311–322.

[11] For discussions of Patristic exegesis, see *The Interpreter's Dictionary of the Bible*, ed. G. A. Buttrick (Nashville: Abingdon 1962) 2.718–721; L. Pirot and A. Robert, *Dictionnaire de la Bible, Supplément* (Paris: Letouzey et Ané 1949) 4.569–591; *The Cambridge History of the Bible. From the Beginnings to Jerome*, ed. P. Ackroyd and C. Evans (Cambridge Univ. Press 1970) pp. 412–453, 465–489.

people Israel, personified as a woman. This was an idea present already in many of the prophets, e.g., Hosea, Isaiah, Jeremiah, Ezekiel. Its deeper roots probably lay in Canaanite mythology. Likewise, in the New Testament Paul had given to many of the Old Testament texts a figurative or allegorical meaning. Thus, Hagar prefigures the earthly Jerusalem, and Sarah the heavenly Jerusalem (Gal 4:21-31). Of course, the notion of a "heavenly" Jerusalem is itself already an allegorical interpretation. Similarly, the rock that Moses struck to provide water for the Israelites is seen by Paul to represent Christ (1 Cor 10:4).

The Book of Psalms in particular received a special interpretation that helped to adapt it to the needs of Christian worship. In modern times we have become accustomed to think of the psalms as a collection, or several collections, of rather heterogeneous religious poetry, much of which was composed for specific cultic or ritual circumstances over a period of many centuries. These poems contain frequent references to different types of Israelite sacrifice and ritual, or to occasions for offering sacrifice, such as thanksgiving, lamentation, etc. In the Patristic period, however, the psalter was regarded as the work of a single author, David, who, it was thought, had composed it as a work of prophecy. This idea is present already in the New Testament (e.g., Acts 2:30; Heb 7:17). At first it was a matter of applying specific verses to Christ, such as Ps 110:1. Then the way was open to try to interpret all of the psalter as prefiguring the Christian dispensation. This approach to the psalms helps to explain how these songs, which often contained theological ideas rather at odds with Christian ones, could so easily have been adapted to the needs of Christian worship.

The tradition of Davidic authorship is reflected in the Rule, where quotations from the psalms are frequently introduced by a formula such as "the Prophet indicates" (e.g., Prol.23,30; 2.9; 6.1; 7.3,14,23; 16.1; 19.3). This, in addition to the fact that in monastic circles it was expected that the entire psalter would be committed to memory, also helps to explain the great frequency with which the psalms are cited in monastic literature as providing guidance for correct living.

The indication, already present in the New Testament, of how Christians could read the Old Testament in a Christian sense had been fully developed into an elaborate method in the Patristic period, before the time of St. Benedict. This was the work especially of the Alexandrian school, of which the most outstanding and influential representative was Origen. His innovations in interpretation have been described elsewhere in this volume.[12] Origen was convinced that the "spiritual" meaning of Scripture was as important as the literal or historical one. The man who saw only the latter meaning was like the Israelite; he did not look beneath the surface of Scripture. But the Christian who was spiritually minded could have the veil removed from his eyes by the Holy Spirit, and then beneath the letter of Scripture he could find food for his soul.

This tradition of spiritual interpretation had become quite popular in the last quarter of the fourth century in monastic circles in Egypt and Palestine, where it was promoted especially by Evagrius and Rufinus. It was brought into the Western monastic tradition by Cassian in a form that became standard. The central role that the "spiritual" meaning held in this tradition is clearly indicated in the following passage:

> You should show yourself diligent, indeed constant, in the reading of Scripture until continual meditation fills your heart and forms you as it were after its likeness; while you make out of it in some way an ark of the covenant, having within two tables of stone, which are the two testaments eternal and sure; and a golden pot that signifies a pure and sincere memory preserving with continual carefulness the manna hidden within it, the manna of the everlasting and heavenly sweetness of the spiritual meaning and the bread of angels; the rod of Aaron, too, which represents the saving standard of our supreme and true high priest, Jesus Christ, which forever buds with freshness of immortal memory. . . . All these are guarded by two Cherubim, the fulness of historical and spiritual knowledge (Cassian. *conl.* 14,10,2-3; tr. by Gibson).

In fact, Cassian recognizes four senses of Scripture, three of which are the spiritual senses: (1) the literal or historical sense, (2) the allegorical or Christological sense, (3) the tropological or moral or anthropological sense, and (4) the anagogical or eschatological sense.[13] To illustrate these senses, Cassian uses the example of the city of Jerusalem: ". . . one and the same Jerusalem can be taken in four senses: historically, as the city of the Jews; allegorically as the church of Christ, anagogically as the heavenly city of God 'which is the mother of us all,' tropologically, as the soul of man, which is frequently subject to praise or blame from the Lord under this title" (*conl.* 14,8). The roots of this type of exegetical methodology are to be

---

[12] See the Introduction, pp. 34–37.

[13] In the medieval period this was enshrined in the commonplace jingle:
Littera gesta docet, quid credas allegoria;
Moralis quid agas, quo tendas anagogia.

found, as has been indicated above, in the New Testament. Paul had spoken explicitly of the "Jerusalem above" (Gal 4:26), and Jerusalem as a symbol for the eschatological reality had been fully developed in Rev 19–21, but there had been no suggestion that every text should be interpreted in these multiple senses. This development led to a proliferation of ingenious and highly imaginative interpretations.

Nevertheless, there were certain controls in this methodology. These were provided chiefly by the practice of comparing one text with another that contained a similar figure or idea. In fact, there developed a remarkably consistent or traditional Patristic interpretation of many texts. An example that occurs in the Rule may serve to illustrate these generalizations. Prol.28 reads: "While these temptations were still *young, he caught hold of them and dashed them against* Christ." The italicized words are taken from Ps 136(137):9, where they express the pious Israelite's hope that the Babylonian babies may be dashed on the rocks before they have a chance to grow up and become oppressors like their fathers. The same verse, with the same interpretation, is alluded to in RB 4.50: "As soon as wrongful thoughts come into your heart, dash them against Christ and disclose them to your spiritual father." The clue to this interpretation had been provided originally by 1 Cor 10:4, which interpreted "the rock" (the one that Moses struck in the desert) as Christ. In 1 Pet 2:4-7 Christ was also described as "a living stone." Since the desire that real Babylonian babies be smashed on real rocks was both historically no longer relevant and hardly consistent with the teaching of Jesus, it was obvious to the Patristic interpreter that the verse must have a "spiritual" meaning. There were spiritual rocks readily available in the New Testament; it remained only to spiritualize the babies into wrongful thoughts. It must also be remembered that for Christians the focus of the struggle between good and evil was no longer against the powers and principalities of this world but within the individual soul. It appeared natural, therefore, to seek the meaning of such a verse by applying it in a tropological sense. This interpretation of Ps 136(137):9 probably originated with Origen and had already appeared in the writings of Latin authors such as Hilary (*in psalm.* 136,14), Jerome (*epist.* 22,6), Ambrose (*paenit.* 2,106), Augustine (*in psalm.* 136,21), and Cassian (*inst.* 6,13) before it reached the sixth-century monastic rules.

Another instance of this kind of "spiritual" interpretation in the Rule is the use of the image of Jacob's ladder (Gen 28:12). Jacob had dreamt that he saw a ladder or staircase stretching up to heaven, with angels ascending and descending upon it. In John 1:51 this text is made to refer to Christ. But in RM and RB the ladder is given an elaborate spiritual interpretation in which it is understood to represent our life on earth. Its sides are our body and soul, and the steps are the twelve stages of humility (RB 7.8-9).

Although this kind of explicit spiritual interpretation of biblical texts is comparatively rare in the Rule—about ten percent of approximately three hundred references—it was probably taken for granted by both the author and his readers that many of the other biblical texts quoted or alluded to would be given this kind of interpretation.[14] This was the dominant methodology practiced by most of the principal earlier Latin writers, e.g., Hilary, Ambrose and Augustine, and it had the strong recommendation of Cassian, whose authority in monastic circles was well established.[15]

An example from Cassian will serve to illustrate this point. Readers sometimes express surprise that a command such as the prohibition against adultery would be included in the list of the tools for good works (RB 4.4) recommended to monks. Surely they did not need to be reminded that this was not in keeping with the monastic vocation. Cassian had explained that this command should of course be observed in the literal sense by those still in bondage to passion, but it could also be observed in a spiritual sense by those who were more spiritual. Thus it could be interpreted as a prohibition against the worship of idols and all kinds of heathen superstition, against vain speculation that destroys the simplicity of faith and against the superstitions of the law of which Paul had written (Gal 4:10; Col 2:21). It could also be understood as a prohibition against "adulterous intercourse with heretical teaching" and, finally, even as a prohibition against wandering thoughts (Cassian. *conl.* 14,11). The roots of this interpretation were, of course, already present in the Old Testament, where the prophets had often used the image of adultery for false worship (e.g., Hos 4:12; Isa 47:13; Jer 3:6).

[14] See L. Leloir "La lecture de l'Écriture selon les anciens Pères" *RAM* 47 (1971) 183–200; and especially H. de Lubac, *Exégèse médiévale: Les quatre sens de l'Écriture*, 3 vols., Théologie 41,42,59 (Paris: Aubier 1959, 1961, 1964).

[15] See A. Kristensen "Cassian's Use of Scripture" *ABR* 28 (1977) 285, who suggests that the sections in the *Conferences* and *Institutes* dealing with cenobitic life tend to use the Scriptures in the literal sense (the cenobitic life being conceived as a life according to the precepts of the Lord), while those sections dealing with the eremitical life tend to make more frequent use of the non-literal sense.

The rejection of the spiritual interpretation of scriptural texts is not an altogether modern phenomenon or even one of the Reformation. Already in antiquity there were voices raised to challenge this methodology. This was done chiefly by the so-called Antiochene school, of which the chief representatives were Diodorus of Tarsus, Apollinaris of Laodicea and Theodore of Mopsuestia. These writers insisted upon the primacy of the literal sense (*historia*), but also admitted a typological sense for many Old Testament passages. This was difficult to exclude in view of its use by New Testament writers. The Antiochene point of view is represented among Latin writers by Junilius Africanus and especially by Jerome (*epist.* 84). In his later works Jerome had come under the influence of Apollinaris, whom he had heard lecture at Laodicea, and came to reject the validity of interpretations other than the historical or literal sense.[16] In the later medieval period, although considerable confusion generally reigned over the uses of the various senses of Scripture, Thomas Aquinas set forth what became the classical position. He insisted that, while the other senses of Scripture might be useful for conveying spiritual or moral teaching and for hortatory or homiletic purposes, for purposes of determining doctrine (what pertains to faith) only the literal sense could be invoked (*summa theol.* I, 1, a.10).

It is generally accepted today that the kind of spiritual interpretation described above is not valid as exegesis of a text (unless of course the allegorical or spiritual meaning is the one intended by the author as, for example, in Ezek 16). It is regarded rather as *eisegesis* (reading into a text). Nevertheless, this does not mean that such interpretations should be dismissed as valueless. They may have considerable value as expression of the spiritual experience of many generations and as pedagogical devices. After all, the ten commandments have served throughout the Christian era as pedagogical devices to convey teaching never intended in the Old Testament context. This does not mean the teaching is wrong, but simply that it cannot be regarded as valid exegesis. In any case, if one is to appreciate the wisdom and the beauty of many Patristic texts, one must recognize and appreciate the fact that the scriptural texts are often being used as vehicles for all sorts of spiritual teaching and moral exhortation not originally intended by the text but having a validity in their own right.

---

[16] See J.N.D. Kelly, *Jerome* (New York: Harper & Row 1975) pp. 59–60.

Appendix 7

The Rule of St. Benedict
and the Rule of the Master

The relationship between the Rule of St. Benedict and that of the Master has been discussed at length in the Introduction, pp. 79–83. The additional material provided in this Appendix is for the purpose of illustrating that relationship and for the sake of further study of the relationship between the two rules. The material is in two parts: (1) a table showing the sequence and correspondences of the two rules; (2) the Latin text of chapter 2, on the abbot, from both rules, arranged to facilitate the study of the redactional activity of St. Benedict, i.e., his omissions and additions.

1. A TABLE OF CORRESPONDENCES

The following table of correspondences between the Rule of St. Benedict and the Rule of the Master has been adapted from that compiled by de Vogüé (1.174–185). It is, as he notes, the fruit of a lengthy comparative study of the two rules. The left-hand column under RM shows those passages that correspond to those of RB not only in content but also by at least approximate position. The right-hand column shows those passages whose location interrupts the parallel sequence of the two rules or those cases where the same subject is treated in more than one place. The parentheses in the two RM columns indicate doubtful or distant relationships and cases of open contradiction. The Roman numerals indicate instances of deliberate structural repetition of themes in RM.

RB	A TABLE OF CORRESPONDENCES	RM
Prol.1	Listen and put into practice	Prol.1,5,8,22 Prol.15,19,22
Prol.2	in order to return to God	Prol.3,11; Thp.6
	from whom you had drifted	Prol.3,7; Thp.6
Prol.3	Engage in the service of Christ through the renunciation of your own will	Th.18,21; Thp.24-53
Prol.4	Ask for divine assistance	Thp.69-72,79
Prol.5-44	Commentary on Psalms 33 and 14	Ths.2-44
Prol.45	Foundation of the school	Ths.45
Prol.46	Hope of not being too harsh	
Prol.47	If it seems a little strict	
Prol.48	it is because the way at first is narrow	(Prol.14)
Prol.49	At length love expands	
Prol.50	Persevere until death	Ths.46
1.1-9	**Kinds of monks:** first three	1.1-9
1.10-11	fourth kind (gyrovagues)	1.13-74
1.12	It is better to say nothing of them	1.13
1.13	Return to the cenobites	1.75
2.1-10	**The abbot:** his name. Looking toward the judgment (I)	2.1-10
2.11-15	He is to adapt himself to different characters (I)	2.23-25
2.16-22	He is not to show favoritism	2.16-22
2.23-25	He is to adapt himself to different characters (II)	2.23-25
2.26	He is to correct faults	
2.27-29	He is to adapt himself to different characters (III)	
2.30	His name. Looking toward the judgment (II)	2.32
2.31-32	He is to adapt himself to different characters (IV)	
2.33-36	The primacy of the spiritual	
2.37-38	Looking toward the judgment (III)	2.33-34
2.38-40	The amendment of others and of himself	2.39-40

RB	A TABLE OF CORRESPONDENCES	RM	
3.1-11	Counsel with the whole community	2.41-50	
3.12-13	Counsel with the seniors		
4.1-74	The tools for good works	2.52; 3.1-77; 4.t	
4.75-77	Conclusion: eternal reward	3.78-94	
4.78	The workshop	6.1-2	
5.1-9	Obedience without delay	7.1-9	
5.10-13	The narrow way	7.47-51	
5.14-19	Obedience without murmuring	7.67-74	
6.1-6	Restraint in speaking: even of good words	8.31-37	
6.7	Questions put to the superior	9.1-50	
6.8	Vulgarity forbidden	9.51	
7.1-9	Humility: preamble: the ladder	10.1-9	
7.10-13	First step. Description	10.10-13	
7.14-18	God present to the thoughts	10.14-19	
7.19-25	God present to volition and desire	10.30-36	
7.26-30	Conclusion of the first step	10.37-41	
7.31-66	Steps 2-12	10.42-86	
7.67-70	Conclusion: love	10.87-91	
8.1-2	The night office: hour in winter		33.3-9
8.3	Study after the office		44.12-19
8.4	Hour in summer		33.10-26
9.1-11	Vigils in winter		33.27-34; 44.1-4
10.1-3	Vigils in summer		33.35-41; 44.5-8
11.1-11	Vigils on Sunday		49
11.12-13	Abridgement in case of lateness		(33.42-54)
12.1-4	Sunday Lauds		35.1; 39.1-5; 45.12
13.1-11	Lauds on ordinary days		35.1; 39.1-4
13.12-14	The Lord's Prayer at the end of the hours		
14.1-2	Feasts of the saints		(45.16-18)
15.1	Alleluia: Easter season		45.1
15.2	Pentecost to Lent: second nocturn		44.2-7
15.3	Sunday at all hours except Vespers		45.12
15.4	Responsory only during Easter season		45.1 (44.3,7)

RB	A TABLE OF CORRESPONDENCES		RM
16.1-3	Office during the day: "seven times a day"		34.1-3
16.4	"In the middle of the night"		33.1
16.5	Synthesis: day and night		
17.1-5	Hours of the day: Prime–None		35.2-3 (40.1-3)
17.6	With and without refrains		(55.6)
17.7-8	Vespers		36.1-9 (41.1-4)
17.9-10	Compline		37.1-2 (42.1-4)
18.1-4	Distribution of the psalms. Prime		
18.7-11	Terce, Sext, None		
18.12-18	Vespers		
18.19	Compline		
18.20-21	Vigils		
18.22-25	The full psalter weekly		
19.1-2	Conduct during psalmody. God present		
19.3-7	Citations. Harmony of mind and voice		47.1-24
20.1-4	Reverence at prayer		48.1-14
20.4-5	Private and communal prayer		
21.1	The deans. Qualities required	11.4	
21.2	Supervision of groups of ten	11.27-30	
21.3-4	Criteria for selection	(11.20-21)	
21.5-6	Correction and removal of deans		
22.1	The dormitory: individual beds	11.109	
22.2	Suitable bedding		
22.3	Single dormitory or smaller ones	(11.108)	29.2-4
22.4	With a lamp burning		29.5-6
22.5	Sleep clothed and belted. No knives	11.111-112	
22.6	Reason: to be ready for office	11.114	
22.7	Young and old interspersed	(11.121)	
22.8	Rising: encourage one another		
23.1-3	Excommunication. Triple warning	12.1-2	
23.4-5	Excommunication or corporal punishment		(14.79-86)
24.1-2	Degree of punishment. The abbot judges	12.4-7	

RB	A TABLE OF CORRESPONDENCES	RM
24.3	Less serious faults. Minor punishment	13.60
24.4	No public recitation for those excommunicated	13.66-67
24.5-6	Meals later than others	13.50-52
24.7	Until satisfaction is made	13.61
25.1	**Serious faults.** Major punishment	13.41-42, 62
25.2-3	Complete isolation	13.43-45, 49
25.4	Sentence of the Apostle	
25.5	Meals: time and amount	13.50-53
25.6	No blessing	13.46-47
26.1-2	**Associating with the excommunicated**	13.54-56
27.1	**Care for the excommunicated.** The abbot as physician	(14.12)
27.2-3	Send *senpectae*	
27.4	All pray for him	(15.19-27)
27.5-7	Solicitude required of the abbot	
27.8-9	Example of the Good Shepherd	(14.7-8)
28.1	**Recidivists.** Corporal punishment	(13.69; 14.87)
28.2-5	Let all pray	(15.19-27)
28.6-8	Expulsion	13.70-73
29.1	**Return of an apostate.** Promise required	
29.2	Put in the lowest place	
29.3	As many as three times	64.1-4
30.1-3	**Reproving boys:** corporal punishment	14.79-86
31.1-2	**The cellarer:** qualities required	16.62-66
31.3-5	Submission to the abbot (I)	16.32-37
31.6-7	Relationship with the brothers (I)	
31.8	Keep watch over his own soul	(16.53-56)
31.9	The sick, etc. The day of judgment	16.27-37
31.10-12	Care for material goods	
31.13-14	Relationship with the brothers (II)	
31.15	Submission to the abbot (II)	16.32-37
31.16	He is not to "scandalize"	
31.17	Helpers to be given him	

RB	A TABLE OF CORRESPONDENCES	RM	
31.18-19	Do everything at proper times		
32.1-2	**The tools and movable goods.** Those in charge	17.1-4,10-20	
32.3	Inventory kept by the abbot	17.5	
32.4-5	Punishment for negligence	17.6-9	
33.1-6	**Private ownership**	16.58-61	82
33.7-8	Punishment for violation of ban		(82.16-27)
34.1-5	**Distribution according to need**		
34.6-7	No grumbling. Punishment		
35.1-2	**Weekly servers.** All to take turns	18.1-12	
35.3-4	Helpers to be given them	19.18	
35.5-6	All to take turns. Exceptions	(18.1-12)	
35.7-8	Saturday: cleaning	19.19-27	
35.9	Washing of the feet	(19.20-21)	(30.4-7)
35.10-11	Utensils returned to cellarer	16.39-40	
35.12-14	Early portion for the servers	(21.11-14)	
35.15-17	Sunday morning. Blessing of servers	25.3-7	
35.17-18	Blessing of new servers	19.1-8	
36.1-3	**The sick.** To be served as Christ	(28.13-18)	70.1-3
36.4-6	Those cared for and those caring for them		
36.7	Infirmary and infirmarian		
36.8-9	Baths and meat		
36.10	Responsibility of the abbot		
37.1-3	**The elderly and children.** No fasting	28.19-26	
38.1	**Reading with meals.** The weekly reader	24.1-4	
38.2-4	Prayer and blessing of reader	24.6-12	
38.5-7	Silence in the refectory		
38.8-9	No questions. Words of commentary	24.19	
38.10	Diluted wine for the reader	24.14	
38.11	Meal afterwards for the reader	24.30,40	
38.12	Selection of reader for ability	(24.1-4)	
39.1-3	**Food.** Two dishes and fruit	26.1	
39.4	A pound of bread	26.2	
39.5	A third set aside for supper	26.3	
39.6-9	Increased allowance. No over-indulgence	26.11-13	
39.10	Children: smaller portions	26.14	
39.11	No meat except for the sick		(53.26-33)

RB	A TABLE OF CORRESPONDENCES		RM
40.1-2	**Drink.** Reservations about pre-scribing measure		
40.3	A half bottle of wine	27.39-40	
40.4	Voluntary abstinence	27.47-51	
40.5-7	Increased allowance. Avoid-ance of satiety	27.43-46	
40.8-9	When not available, avoid grumbling	27.52-54	
41.1	**The times for meals.** Easter season	28.37-40	
41.2-3	Summer. Fast on Wednesday and Friday		
41.4-5	Dispensing from the fast		
41.6	Winter. Daily fast (None)	28.1-2	
41.7	Lent. Daily fast (Vespers)	28.8	(53.34)
41.8-9	Evening meal before dark		(34.12-13; 36.10; 50.70-71)
42.1	**Silence after Compline.** Prin-ciple	(30.8-10)	
42.2-7	Reading before Compline		
42.8	Compline and beginning of silence	30.12-13	
42.9	Breaking the silence. Punish-ment	(30.28-30)	
42.10	Exceptions: guests, the abbot's orders	30.24-27 (17-22)	
42.11	Careful restraint	30.19,25-26	
43.1-3	**Those coming late** to office or meals. Nothing put before office		54.1-2
43.4-9	Those late for Vigils	(32.9-15)	73.1-5
43.10-12	Those late for day hours		73.6-7
43.13-16	Those late for meals		73.8-10
43.17	Prayers after meals		73.11
43.18	Nothing between meals		(21.8-10; 30.23)
43.19	Refusing what is offered. Pun-ishment		(22.7-8; 74)
44.1-3	**Major satisfaction.** Prostration (I)		14.20-22
44.4	At the feet of all		14.17
44.5	Readmittance to choir		
44.6	To refrain from intoning or reading		(13.66; 73.17)
44.7-8	Prostration after the office (II)		(14.20-22)

RB	A TABLE OF CORRESPONDENCES		RM
44.9-10	Minor satisfaction		13.61
45.1-2	**In the oratory.** Penalties for not making satisfaction		
45.3	Children: corporal punishment		(14.79)
46.1-4	**Satisfaction for faults at work**		
46.5-6	Hidden sin and its cure		15.1-17
47.1	**The signal for office**	31.1-9	
47.2	Intoning the psalms according to seniority	46.1-2	
47.3	Qualifications for reading and singing	(46.1-7)	
47.4	The manner of reading and chanting	47.1-6	
48.1	**Manual labor.** Necessity	50.1-7	
48.2-6	Summer schedule	50.39-69	
48.7-9	The harvest		(86)
48.10-13	Winter schedule	50.8-38	
48.14	Lenten schedule		
48.15-16	Reading in Lent		
48.17-21	Supervision during the reading		
48.22	Sunday reading		75.1-7
48.23	Those unable to read	50.76-77	
48.24-25	Work for the sick	50.75,78	
49.1-3	**Lent:** Time of purification		
49.4-7	Prayer and abstinence	51–53	
49.8-10	Control by the abbot	(53.11-15)	(74.1-4)
50.1-3	**Office outside of choir.** At work	55	
50.4	On a journey	56	(58)
51.1-2	**Meals forbidden on a day trip**	61	
51.3	Penalty		
52.1	**The oratory.** Not a place for work		
52.2-5	Silence while leaving it	68	
53.1-2	**Guests.** All to be received as Christ		
53.3-4	Welcome	65.1-8	
53.4-5	Prayer before kiss of peace	71.1-10	
53.6-7	Humble greeting	65.1-8	
53.8-9	Prayer. Reading. Kindness		
53.10-11	Breaking the fast	72	
53.12	Washing the hands		
53.13	Washing the feet		(30.5,26; 53.43)
53.14	Recitation of Ps 47:10	(65.9)	

RB	A TABLE OF CORRESPONDENCES		RM
53.15	Reception of the poor		
53.16-17	The kitchen for the abbot and guests		
53.18-20	Distribution of this work		(16.45-46)
53.21-22	Guest quarters and guest-masters	79	
53.23-24	Speaking with guests restricted		
54.1-5	**Reception of letters and gifts**	(76)	
55.1-3	**Clothing.** Adapted to diverse locales		
55.4-6	Items of clothing and shoes	81.1-30	
55.7	Use of available materials		
55.8	The abbot to ensure correct measurements		
55.9-12	Used clothing. Avoidance of superfluity		
55.13-14	Clothing for a journey	(81.7)	
55.15	Bedding	81.31-32	
55.16-17	Inspection of beds. Penalties	82.23-31	
55.18-19	Necessary items to be provided	(82.1-22)	
55.20-22	Distribution according to need		
56.1-3	**The abbot's table**	84	
57.1-3	**Artisans.** Humility required		
57.4-6	Fraud to be avoided	85.8-11	
57.7-9	Price of goods sold	85.1-7	
58.1-4	**Candidates.** Admission made difficult	87.2	90.1-71
58.5-7	The novitiate and novice master		
58.8	Hardships and difficulties to be set forth	87.4	90.3-67
58.9	After two months	88	
58.9-10	Reading of the Rule	87.3-4	
58.12	Second reading of the Rule	(89.1)	
58.13	Third reading		(90.64)
58.14	Promise and admission		90.67
58.15-16	Stability. No longer free to leave		(90.66)
58.17-23	Ceremony of profession	89.3-28	
58.24-25	Liquidation of goods	87.5-75; 89.17-23	
58.26	Clothing		90.80
58.27	Preservation of his old clothing		90.83
58.28	Restitution of clothing in case of apostasy		90.84-87

RB	A TABLE OF CORRESPONDENCES		RM
58.29	The abbot keeps profession document	89.27	(90.88-95)
59.1-6	**The offering of sons of nobles**	91	
59.7-8	The case of poor people		
60.1-7	**The admission of those in holy orders**		83
60.8-9	The case of clerics		
61.1-4	**Visiting monks**		79.29-34
61.5-10	Reception of visiting monks as members of the community		79.23-28
61.11-12	Promotion of such a one to a higher rank in the community		
61.13-14	Reception of visiting monks from a known monastery		
62.1-7	**Monks ordained priests**		
62.8-11	Insubordination. Penalties		
63.1-9	**Rank in the community**	(92)	
63.10-17	Respect and love among juniors and seniors		
63.18-19	Supervision of children		
64.1-6	**The choice of an abbot**	92–93	
64.7-22	Admonitions for a new abbot	(93.15-23)	
65.1-10	**The prior.** Unsuitable arrangements	92–93	
65.11-13	To be avoided if possible	92	
65.14-15	Selection by the abbot	(93.56-68)	
65.16-17	Subordination to the abbot	93.69-70	
65.18-21	Penalties. Removal from office	93.74-79	
65.22	The abbot to avoid jealousy		
66.1-5	**The porters.** Lodging and function	95.1-3	
66.6	Everything necessary within the enclosure	95.17	
66.7	Avoid leaving the enclosure	95.18-21	
66.8	The Rule to be read often in the community	(95.24)	24.15-17, 26-27, 31-33
67.1	**Going on a journey.** Prayer before departure		66.1-4
67.2	Commemoration at the office of those absent		20.1-13
67.3-4	Prayer on return		66.5-7
67.5-6	Relating incidents forbidden. Penalties		

RB	A TABLE OF CORRESPONDENCES	RM
67.7	Leaving without permission. Penalties	
68.1-5	**Obedience in difficult tasks**	
69.1-3	**Not to defend one another**	
69.4	Penalty	
70.1-2	**Reservation of power to correct or punish**	
70.3	Correction in public	(12–13)
70.4-5	Correction of children	
70.6-7	Unauthorized correction. Penalty	
71.1-4	**Mutual obedience**	(3.76)
71.5	Refusal of this. Correction	(3.74)
71.6-8	Reproval and satisfaction	
71.9	Refusal of satisfaction. Penalty	
72.1-12	**Good zeal**	(92.51)
73.1-7	**A rule for beginners only**	
73.8-9	Begin by fulfilling it	95.24

2. RM 2 AND RB 2–3 ARRANGED FOR COMPARATIVE STUDY

The passages in boldface type indicate those sections where RM and RB are identical. The redactional activity (omissions, additions, revisions) on the part of the author of RB is thus made clear at a glance. See Appendix 2, pp. 346–355, for a fuller discussion of the relationship of RB to RM in treating of the abbot.

Interrogatio discipulorum:

II. Qualis debeat esse abbas

Respondit Dominus per magistrum:

[1] Abbas, qui praeesse dignus est monasterio, semper meminere debet quod dicitur, et nomen maioris factis implere. [2] Christi enim agere creditur vices in monasterio, quando ipsius vocatur pronomine, [3] dicente apostolo: *Sed accepistis spiritum adoptionis filiorum, in quo clamamus* Domino: *abba, pater.* [4] Ideoque hic abbas nihil extra praeceptum Domini quod sit, debet aut docere aut constituere aut iubere, [5] ut iussio eius vel monitio sive doctrina fermentum divinae iustitiae in discipulo-

II. Qualis debeat esse abbas

[1] Abbas qui praeesse dignus est monasterio semper meminere debet quod dicitur et nomen maioris factis implere. [2] Christi enim agere vices in monasterio creditur, quando ipsius vocatur pronomine, [3] dicente apostolo: *Accepistis spiritum adoptionis filiorum, in quo clamamus: abba, pater.* [4] Ideoque abbas nihil extra praeceptum Domini quod sit debet aut docere aut constituere vel iubere, [5] sed iussio eius vel doctrina fermentum divinae iustitiae in discipulorum mentibus conspargatur,

rum mentibus conspargatur. ⁶ Memor semper abbas quia doctrinae suae vel discipulorum oboedientiae, ambarum rerum in tremendo iudicio Domini facienda erit discussio. ⁷ Et sciat abbas culpae pastoris incumbere, quicquid in ovibus paterfamilias utilitatis minus potuerit invenire. ⁸ Tantundem iterum erit, ut, si inquieto vel inoboedienti gregi pastoris fuerit omnis diligentia attributa et morbidis earum actibus universa fuerit cura exhibita, ⁹ pastor eorum in iudicio Domini absolutus dicat cum propheta Domino: *Non abscondi in corde meo veritatem tuam et salutare tuum dixi. Ipsi autem* contemnentes *spreverunt me.* ¹⁰ Et tunc demum inoboedientibus curae suae ovibus poena sit eis praevalens ipse mortis morbus.

¹¹ Ergo cum aliquis suscipit nomen abbatis, duplici debet doctrina suis praeesse discipulis, ¹² id est omnia bona et sancta factis amplius quam verbis ostendere. Quomodo? Intellegentibus discipulis mandata Domini verbis proponere, duris corde vero et simplicibus factis suis divina praecepta monstrare. ¹³ Omnia vero quae discipulis docuerit esse contraria, in se factis indicet non agenda, *ne aliis praedicans ipse reprobus inveniatur,* ¹⁴ ne quando illi *dicat Deus peccanti: Quare vero tu enarrasti iustitias meas et sumpsisti testamentum meum per os tuum? Tu vero odisti disciplinam.* ¹⁵ Et: *Qui in fratris tui oculo festucam videbas, in tuo trabem non vidisti.*

¹⁶ Non ab eo persona in monasterio discernatur. ¹⁷ Non unus plus ametur quam alius, nisi quem in bonis actibus invenerit meliorem. ¹⁸ Non convertenti servo pro merito nationis praeponatur ingenuus.

⁶ memor semper abbas quia doctrinae suae vel discipulorum oboedientiae, utrarumque rerum, in tremendo iudicio Dei facienda erit discussio. ⁷ Sciatque abbas culpae pastoris incumbere quicquid in ovibus paterfamilias utilitatis minus potuerit invenire. ⁸ Tantundem iterum erit ut, si inquieto vel inoboedienti gregi pastoris fuerit omnis diligentia attributa et morbidis earum actibus universa fuerit cura exhibita, ⁹ pastor eorum in iudicio Domini absolutus dicat cum propheta Domino: *Iustitiam tuam non abscondi in corde meo, veritatem tuam et salutare tuum dixi; ipsi autem* contemnentes *spreverunt me,* ¹⁰ et tunc demum inoboedientibus curae suae ovibus poena sit eis praevalens ipsa mors.

¹¹ Ergo, cum aliquis suscipit nomen abbatis, duplici debet doctrina suis praeesse discipulis, ¹² id est omnia bona et sancta factis amplius quam verbis ostendat, ut capacibus discipulis mandata Domini verbis proponere, duris corde vero et simplicioribus factis suis divina praecepta monstrare. ¹³ Omnia vero quae discipulis docuerit esse contraria in suis factis indicet non agenda, *ne aliis praedicans ipse reprobus inveniatur,* ¹⁴ ne quando illi *dicat Deus peccanti: Quare tu enarras iustitias meas et assumis testamentum meum per os tuum? Tu vero odisti disciplinam et proiecisti sermones meos post te,* ¹⁵ et: *Qui in fratris tui oculo festucam videbas, in tuo trabem non vidisti.*

¹⁶ Non ab eo persona in monasterio discernatur. ¹⁷ Non unus plus ametur quam alius, nisi quem in bonis actibus aut oboedientia invenerit meliorem. ¹⁸ Non convertenti ex servitio praeponatur ingenuus, nisi alia rationabilis causa exsistat. ¹⁹ Quod si ita, iustitia dictante, abbati visum fuerit, et de cuiuslibet ordine id faciet. Sin alias, propria teneant loca,

[19] Quare? Quare? Quia *servus sive liber, omnes Christo unum sumus* et sub uno Domino aequalem servitii militiam baiulamus, quia *non est apud Deum personarum acceptio.* [20] Solummodo in hac parte apud Deum discernimur, si ab aliis meliores factis inveniamur. [21] Et tamen, ut ostendat Deus circa omnes pietatis suae clementiam pariter, iubet *elementa* vel terram *iustis* vel peccatoribus *famulari aequaliter.* [22] Ergo aequalis sit ab eo ab omnibus caritas, una praebeatur in omnibus disciplina.

[23] In doctrina sua namque abbas apostolicam debet illam semper formam servare, in qua dicit: *Argue, obsecra, increpa*, [24] id est, miscens temporibus tempora, terroribus blandimenta, dirum magistri, pium patris ostendat affectum, [25] id est, indisciplinatos debet et inquietos arguere, oboedientes, mites et patientissimos ut in melius proficiant obsecrare, neglegentes et contemnentes ut increpet admonemus.

[26] Humilitatis vero talem in se eis formam debet ostendere, qualem Dominus contendentibus de gradu fortiori apostolis demonstravit, [27] id est, cum *apprehensa* manu *infantem in medio eorum deduxisset, dixit:* [28] *Qui vult esse inter vos fortior*, sit talis. [29] Ideoque quicquid abbas discipulis pro Deo agendum iniunxerit, inchoet factis, et tradens omnia ordinationis suae protelo sequantur membra, qua duxerit caput.

[30] Caritatem vero vel gratiam talem debet circa omnes fratres habere, ut nullum alio praeferens omnibus discipulis vel filiis suis amborum parentum in se nomen exhibeat, [31] matrem eis suam praebens aequaliter caritatem, patrem se eis mensurata pietate ostendat.

[20] quia sive *servus, sive liber, omnes in Christo unum sumus* et *sub uno Domino aequalem* servitutis militiam baiulamus, quia *non est apud Deum personarum acceptio.*

21 Solummodo in hac parte apud ipsum discernimur, si meliores ab aliis in operibus bonis et humiles inveniamur.

[22] Ergo aequalis sit ab eo omnibus caritas, una praebeatur in omnibus secundum merita disciplina.

[23] In doctrina sua namque abbas apostolicam debet illam semper formam servare in qua dicit: *Argue, obsecra, increpa*, [24] id est, miscens temporibus tempora, terroribus blandimenta, dirum magistri, pium patris ostendat affectum, [25] id est, indisciplinatos et inquietos debet durius arguere, oboedientes autem et mites et patientes ut in melius proficiant obsecrare, neglegentes et contemnentes ut increpat et corripiat admonemus.

[26] Neque dissimulet peccata delinquentium; sed et mox ut coeperint

32 Meminere debet abbas semper quod est, meminere quod dicitur, et scire quia *cui plus creditur, plus ab eo exigitur.*

33 Et sciat quia qui suscipit animas regendas, paret se ad rationes reddendas. 34 Et quantum sub sua cura fratrum se habere scierit numerum, agnoscat pro certo quia in die iudicii ipsarum omnium animarum tantas est red-

oriri radicitus ea ut praevalet amputet, memor periculi Heli sacerdotis de Silo. 27 Et honestiores quidem atque intellegibiles animos prima vel secunda admonitione verbis corripiat, 28 improbos autem et duros ac superbos vel inoboedientes verberum vel corporis castigatio in ipso initio peccati coerceat, sciens scriptum: *Stultus verbis non corrigitur,* 29 et iterum: *Percute filium tuum virga et liberabis animam eius a morte.*

30 Meminere debet semper abbas quod est, meminere quod dicitur, et scire quia *cui plus committitur, plus ab eo exigitur.*

31 Sciatque quam difficilem et arduam rem suscipit regere animas et multorum servire moribus, et alium quidem blandimentis, alium vero increpationibus, alium suasionibus; 32 et secundum uniuscuiusque qualitatem vel intellegentiam, ita se omnibus conformet et aptet ut non solum detrimenta gregis sibi commissi non patiatur, verum in augmentatione boni gregis gaudeat. 33 Ante omnia, ne dissimulans aut parvipendens salutem animarum sibi commissarum, ne plus gerat sollicitudinem de rebus transitoriis et terrenis atque caducis, 34 sed semper cogitet quia animas suscepit regendas, de quibus et rationem redditurus est. 35 Et ne causetur de minori forte substantia, meminerit scriptum: *Primum quaerite regnum Dei et iustitiam eius, et haec omnia adicientur vobis,* 35 et iterum: *Nihil deest timentibus eum.*

37 Sciatque quia qui suscipit animas regendas paret se ad rationem reddendam, 38 et quantum sub cura sua fratrum se habere scierit numerum, agnoscat pro certo quia in die iudicii ipsarum omnium animarum est redditurus

diturus Domino rationes, sine dubio addita et sua, [35] quia ut fratres in monasterio propriam non agerent voluntatem, huius semper iussionibus omni oboedientia militarunt, [36] quia cum discussi fuerint de omnibus actibus suis, dicturi sunt in iudicio Domino omnia facta sua per oboedientiam a iussione impleta esse magistri. [37] Ideoque debet semper cautus esse magister, [38] ut omnia quae imperat, omnia quae docet, omnia quae emendat, de praeceptis Dei iustitia dictante monstretur, quod futuro iudicio non condemnetur. [39] Timens semper futuram discussionem pastoris de creditis ovibus, quia et cum de alienis ratiociniis cavet, redditur de suis sollicitus, [40] et cum de monitionibus suis emendationes aliis sumministrat, ipse efficitur a vitiis emendatus.

Domino rationem, sine dubio addita et suae animae.

[39] Et ita, timens semper futuram discussionem pastoris de creditis ovibus, cum de alienis ratiociniis cavet, redditur de suis sollicitus, [40] et cum de monitionibus suis emendationem aliis sumministrat ipse efficitur a vitiis emendatus.

III. De abhibendis ad consilium fratribus

[41] Quicquid vero abbas pro utilitate monasterii agere aut facere voluerit, cum consilio fratrum agat [42] et convocatis omnibus fratribus de utilitate monasterii tractetur communiter. [43] Ita tamen, non libero ausu fratres aut invito suae potestatis arbitrio, sed iussione et imperio abbatis eligendis forte consiliis applicentur. [44] Nam ideo omnium quaeratur consilium, quia *quot homines, tot* sunt pro diversitate interdum *sententiae*, — [45] ne forte a quo non speratur, melius subito detur consilium et communi utilitati hoc magis proficiat, — [46] et de multis consiliis quod eligatur facile invenitur. [47] Quod si de omnibus nullus aptum potuerit dare consilium, tunc abbas reddita ratione consilii sui constituat quod vult, et iustum est ut membra caput sequantur. [48] Ideo

[1] Quotiens aliqua praecipua agenda sunt in monasterio, convocet abbas omnem congregationem et dicat ipse unde agitur, [2] et audiens consilium fratrum tractet apud se et quod utilius iudicaverit faciat. [3] Ideo autem omnes ad consilium vocari diximus quia saepe iuniori Dominus revelat quod melius est. [4] Sic autem dent fratres consilium cum omni humilitatis subiectione, et non praesumant procaciter defendere quod eis visum fuerit, [5] et magis in abbatis pendat arbitrio, ut quod salubrius esse iudicaverit ei cuncti oboediant. [6] Sed sicut discipulos convenit oboedire magistro, ita et ipsum provide et iuste condecet cuncta disponere.

[7] In omnibus igitur omnes magistram sequantur regulam, neque ab

omnes fratres diximus ad consilium debere vocari, secundum sententiam monasterii, quod res monasterii omnium est et nullius est. [49] Ideo omnium, quia proficiendo successionem quandoque in monasterio vicibus de se fratres exspectant, [50] ideo nullius, quia nihil in monasterio aliquid sibi a fratribus peculiariter vindicatur et nullus suo aliquid constituit aut facit arbitrio, sed omnes sub imperio degunt abbatis.

[51] Qui ergo abbas sanctae huius artis sit artifex, non sibi ipsius artis, sed Domino assignans ministerium, cuius in nobis gratia fabricatur, quicquid a nobis sancte perficitur. [52] Quae ars doceri et disci debet in monasterii officina et exerceri potest cum spiritalibus ferramentis.

ea temere declinetur a quoquam. [8] Nullus in monasterio proprii sequatur cordis voluntatem, [9] neque praesumat quisquam cum abbate suo proterve aut foris monasterium contendere. [10] Quod si praesumpserit, regulari disciplinae subiaceat. [11] Ipse tamen abbas cum timore Dei et observatione regulae omnia faciat, sciens se procul dubio de omnibus iudiciis suis aequissimo iudici Deo rationem redditurum.

[12] Si qua vero minora agenda sunt in monasterii utilitatibus, seniorum tantum utatur consilio, [13] sicut scriptum est: *Omnia fac cum consilio et post factum non paeniteberis.*

Part Four

CLASSIFIED REFERENCE RESOURCES

Guides to Investigation

A SELECTED LATIN CONCORDANCE

INTRODUCTION

This Concordance furnishes the Latin student of the Rule of St. Benedict with a means for independent study and a basis for amplifying the content of the Thematic Index. Readers will find that it provides a conspectus of St. Benedict's vocabulary and a ready reference to ideas and subjects in connection with the Thematic Index. Basic words of the Rule are listed, but minor, less significant words are omitted. Most words are given in context with chapter and verse indicated — **acceptio**: 2.20 personarum acceptio. Others are noted with only chapter and verse — **advenire**: 4.50; 7.44. Some entries indicate only the number of times a word is used — **ad** (116). Complete Latin concordances may be found in de Vogüé 2 and Hanslik, *Benedicti Regula*, whose "Index Verborum" was, in the main, the basis for the entries in this Selected Latin Concordance.

A

a, ab (146)
abbas:
    1.2; 2.t,1,3,4,6,7,11,19,23,30; 3.1,5,9,11; 4.61; 5.12; 7.44; 9.5; 11.6,7,8,9,10; 21.2,3; 22.2; 24.2; 25.5; 26.1; 27.t,1,5; 28.2,6; 31.4,12,15; 32.1,3; 33.2,5; 36.6,10; 39.6; 41.4; 42.10; 43.5,11; 44.3,4,5,6,8,9; 46.3,5; 47.1,2,4; 48.25; 49.8,10; 50.2; 51.2; 53.12,13,16; 54.1,2,3; 55.3,8,16,17,18,20,21; 56.t,1; 57.1,3; 58.19,29; 60.4; 61.4,11,12,13; 62.1,3,6; 63.1,2,7,13; 64.t,1,4,7; 65.2, 3,5,6,8,11,12,14,15,16,22; 67.1,7; 70.2, 6; 71.1,3,6; 72.10
abesse:
  4.61   'si . . . aliter quod absit agat'
  11.12 nisi . . . quod absit tardius surgant
  28.2   si . . . quod absit in superbia elatus
  34.2   ut personarum quod absit acceptio sit
  48.19 talis si quod absit repertus fuerit
  58.28 ut egrediatur . . . quod absit
  59.6   perire possit quod absit
  64.3   vitiis suis quod quidem absit
  67.2   commemoratio . . . absentum

abiectio: 7.52
abire: 27.8
ablactatus: 7.4
abnegare: 4.10
abominabilis: 7.22
abrenuntiare: Prol. 3
abscisio: 28.6
abscondere: 2.9
absconsus: 7.44
absolvere: 2.9
absorbere: 27.3
absque: (5)
abstinentia:
  40.4   donat Deus tolerantiam abstinentiae
  49.4   abstinentiae operam damus
  49.5   potus abstinentiam
abstinere:
  36.9   a carnibus . . . abstineant
  39.11 carnium . . . abstineatur comestio
absurdus: 65.4
abundare: 27.3
ac: (9)
accedere:
  28.1   acrior ei accedat correptio
  42.5   mox accedant ad lectionem

43.13   omnes accedant ad mensam
63.4   sic accedant ad pacem
acceptabilis:
5.14   oboedientia ... acceptabilis
erit
acceptio:
2.20   'personarum acceptio'
34.2   personarum ... acceptio
accipere:
Prol. 27; 2.3; 5.18; 22.2; 24.5; 33.2; 34.t;
35.12,17,18; 38.4,10; 43.19; 48.15; 54.1;
55.9,12,13,14,17; 66.1,2,5
accommodare: 53.20
acediosus:
48.18   frater acediosus
acer: 28.1; 30.3; 69.4
acies: 1.5   fraterna ex acie
acquirere:
31.8   'gradum bonum sibi acquirit'
35.2   caritas acquiritur
36.5   copiosior mercis acquiritur
actus:
Prol. 5   de malis actibus ... contristari
Prol. 21   observantia bonorum actuum
Prol. 22   nisi ... actibus curritur
2.8   morbidis ... actibus
2.17   in bonis actibus ... meliorem
4.20   saeculi actibus ... alienum
4.48   actus vitae ... custodire
7.6   actibus nostris ascendentibus
55.20   sententia Actuum Apostolorum
acus: 55.19
ad: (116)
addere: 2.38; 39.3
adducere: Prol. 37
adesse: Prol. 18
adhibere:
3.t   de adhibendis ... fratribus
28.4   adhibeat etiam ... orationem
36.1   infirmorum cura ... adhibenda
est
62.9   episcopus adhibeatur in testimonio
65.19   adhibeatur ei correptio
adhortatio:
28.3   si unguenta adhortationum
adhuc: (5)
adicere: 2.35
adimplere:
4.63   praecepta Dei ... adimplere
4.76   fuerint ... incessabiliter adimpleta
7.42   praeceptum ... adimplentes
aditus: 29.3
adiungere: 58.22

adiutorium:
Prol. 41   adiutorium ministrare
17.3; 18.1; 35.17 'Deus in adiutorium'
68.5   confidens de adiutorio Dei
adiuvare:
1.13   adiuvante Domino
18.1; 35.17 'Domine ad adiuvandum
me'
31.17   a quibus adiutus
35.16   'Deus qui adiuvasti me'
73.8   adiuvante Christo
administrare:
53.18   solacia administrentur
53.22   sapienter administretur
admonere:
Prol. 9   quid nos admonet vox
2.25   ut ... corripiat admonemus
23.2   admoneatur semel et secundo
33.7   admoneatur semel et iterum
40.9   ante omnia admonentes
62.9   saepe admonitus
65.18   admoneatur ... usque quater
admonitio:
Prol. 1   admonitionem ... excipe
2.27   admonitione ... corripiat
adoptio:
2.3   'spiritum adoptionis filiorum'
adorare:
53.7   Christus in eis adoretur
adulari: 65.9
adulescens: 22.7; 30.2; 63.18
adulterare: 4.4
advenire: 4.50; 7.44
adversus: Prol. 27; 7.48
advertere: 65.4
aedificare:
Prol. 33   'aedificavit domum'
38.12   qui aedificant audientes
42.3   quod aedificet audientes
47.3   ut aedificentur audientes
53.9   ut aedificetur
aedificatio:
6.3   de ... aedificationum eloquiis
38.9   nisi ... prior pro aedificatione
voluerit ... dicere
aegritudo:
35.1   nullus excusetur ... nisi aut
aegritudo
aegrotus:
39.11   praeter ... debiles aegrotos
aequalis: 2.20,22; 11.11; 18.20; 34.t
aequitas: Prol. 47
aequus: 3.11; 31.17
aer: 55.1
aerugo: 64.12
aestas: 10.t; 11.11; 40.5; 41.2,4; 55.5
aestimare:
7.13   aestimet se homo ... respici

7.38 'aestimati sumus ut oves'
7.64 reum se ... aestimans
7.64 se ... iudicio repraesentari
aestimet
65.2 aestimantes se secundos esse
abbates
aetas: (12)
aeternus:
4.46 vitam aeternam ... desiderare
5.3 gloriam vitae aeternae
5.10 ad vitam aeternam gradiendi
6.8 aeterna clausura
7.11 vita aeterna ... praeparata est
72.2 ducit ... ad vitam aeternam
72.12 ad vitam aeternam perducat
affectus:
2.24 patris ostendat affectum
7.51 cordis credat affectu
20.4 affectu inspirationis
afficere: 7.38
affligere: 30.3
ager:
7.63 in agro vel ubicumque sedens
41.2 si labores agrorum non habent
41.4 si operis in agris habuerint
agere:
Prol. 4,26,44; 2.2,13; 3.1,12; 4.61; 5.8;
7.55; 8.4; 10.t; 11.t; 12.t; 13.t,1,12,14;
14.t,1; 16.t; 34.3; 41.8; 48.4,6,11; 49.10;
50.3,4; 63.13; 64.12; 65.16
agnoscere: 2.38
ait: (9)
alias: 2.19; 60.5
alibi: 6.5
alienus: 2.39; 4.20; 5.12; 46.6
alimenta: 37.2
aliquando: (8)
aliquantulum: 57.8
aliquantum: 55.14; 61.11
aliquatenus: 64.4; 70.6; 73.1
aliquis(-qui): (50)
aliunde: 38.8
alius: (51)
alleluia: 9.9; 11.6; 12.2; 15.t,1,3,4
allidere:
Prol. 28 cogitatos ... 'allisit ad Christum'
4.50 cogitationes ... ad Christum
allidere
altare: 31.10; 58.20,29; 59.2; 62.6
alter: (6)
altus: 63.7
amare:
2.17 non unus plus ametur
4.13 ieiunium amare
4.52 loqui non amare
4.54 risum ... non amare
4.64 castitatem amare

4.68 contentionem non amare
7.31 si propriam ... non amans voluntatem
64.15 studeat plus amari
amaritudo:
72.1 zelus amaritudinis
ambo: 5.9
ambrosianum: 9.4; 12.4; 13.11; 17.8
ambulare:
5.12 ambulantes alieno iudicio
7.3 'neque ambulavi in magnis'
7.63 sedens ambulans
64.18 'plus in ambulando ... laborare
Amen: Prol. 50; 11.10; 64.22; 73.9
amicus: 60.3
amor:
4.21 nihil amori Christi praeponere
4.72 in Christi amore pro inimicis
orare
5.10 ad vitam aeternam gradiendi
amor incumbit
7.34 pro Dei amore ... oboedientia
se subdat maiori
7.69 amore Christi et consuetudine
63.13 sed ... amore Christi
72.3 zelum ferventissimo amore
exerceant
72.9 amore Deum timeant
amplecti:
4.12 delicias non amplecti
7.35 patientiam amplectatur
amplius: 2.12; 8.2; 40.5; 55.2
amputare:
2.26 radicitus ea ... amputet
33.1 hoc vitium ... amputandum est
55.11 superfluum est amputari debet
55.18 vitium ... radicitus amputetur
64.14 cum caritate ea amputet
anachorita: 1.3
analogium: 9.5
Ananias: 57.5
angariare: 7.42
angelus: (5)
angustus:
Prol. 48 angusto initio incipienda
5.11 angustam viam arripiunt
5.11 'angusta via est'
anima:
2.29 'liberabis animam'
2.31 regere animas
2.33 parvipendens salutem animarum
2.34 animas suscepit regendas
2.37 qui suscipit animas
2.38 omnium animarum ... rationem
2.38 addita et suae animae
4.1 'diligere ... tota anima'
7.4 'si exaltavi animam meam'

60.7 illum locum attendat
62.5 locum . . . attendat
attingere:
7.5 humilitatis . . . culmen attingere
attonitus:
Prol. 9 attonitis auribus
attribuere: 2.8
auctor: 65.10
auctoritas:
9.8 codices . . . divinae auctoritatis
37.1 regulae auctoritas eis prospiciat
73.3 qui sermo divinae auctoritatis
audire: (23)
auditus: 67.4
auferre: 7.42; 28.6; 55.19
augere:
39.6 si expediat aliquid augere
49.5 augeamus . . . aliquid solito pensu
augmentatio: 2.32
auris:
Prol. 1 inclina aurem cordis tui
Prol. 9 attonitis auribus audiamus
Prol. 11 'qui habet aures audiendi'
Prol. 18 'aures meas ad preces vestras'
4.77 'nec auris audivit'
5.5 'obauditu auris oboedivit'
aurum: 1.6
aut: (85)
aut(=et): (12)
autem: (85)
auxiliari:
1.5 Deo auxiliante
avaritia:
31.12 neque avaritiae studeat
57.7 non surripiat avaritiae malum
avertere:
7.19 'a voluntatibus tuis avertere'
38.2 ut avertat . . . Deus spiritum elationis

B

baiulare:
2.20 militiam baiulamus
balneae: 36.8
Basilius: 73.5
benedicere: (10)
benedictio: (9)
biber: 35.12
bibere: 38.6; 40.6
bibliotheca:
48.15 accipiant . . . codices de bibliotheca
bini: 1.8; 18.5
blandimentum: 2.24,31
bonus: (39)
brachium: 1.5

bracile: 55.19
breviare: 11.12; 20.5
brevis: 10.2; 20.4; 32.3; 38.9
brevitas: 10.2

C

cadere: Prol. 34
caducus: 2.33
caedere: 70.t,2
caelestis:
7.5 ad exaltationem . . . caelestem
73.8 ad patriam caelestem festinas
caelum:
7.8 vita . . . erigatur ad caelum
7.13 de caelis a Deo . . . respici
7.27 'Dominus de caelo . . . respicit'
7.65 'levare oculos . . . ad caelos'
calamus: 64.13
calciarium: 55.t
calidus: 55.2
caliga: 55.6,19
candela: 22.4
canere:
9.9 sex psalmi . . . canendi
17.t psalmi . . . canendi sunt
18.12 vespera . . . quattuor psalmorum modulatione canatur
canonicus:
37.3 praeveniant horas canonicas
67.3 per . . . canonicas horas . . . petant orationem
cantare:
9.5 tria responsoria cantentur
9.6 qui cantat dicat gloriam
11.3 dicatur a cantante gloria
38.12 non per ordinem . . . cantent
47.3 cantare . . . non praesumat
canticum: (9)
cantor: 9.7
capax: 2.12
capitale: 55.15
capitulum: 18.2,3,7
caput:
7.41,63; 15.2; 18.23; 41.6; 44.2; 48.10, 16; 53.7; 65.10
caritas:
Prol. 47 conservationem caritatis
2.22 aequalis sit . . . caritas
4.26 caritatem non derelinquere
7.67 'ad caritatem' Dei perveniet
27.4 'confirmetur in eo caritas'
35.2 merces et caritas acquiritur
35.6 sibi sub caritate . . . serviant
53.3 occurratur . . . cum omni officio caritatis
61.4 si . . . cum humilitate caritatis reprehendit

73.8 adiuvante Christo
cibus: (9)
cingulum: 22.5
circa: 7.18; 27.t,1; 28.5
circuitus: 58.12
circulus: 18.24; 58.9
circumire: 48.17
citius: 5.9; 60.1
clamare:
Prol. 9 cotidie clamans . . . vox
Prol. 14 quaerens . . . cui haec clamat operarium
2.3 'spiritum . . . in quo clamamus'
7.1 clamat . . . scriptura
66.3 ut . . . pauper clamaverit
clamosus:
7.60 non sit clamosus in voce
52.4 oret non in clamosa voce
clarescere:
62.10 clarescentibus culpis
64.4 vitia ipsa . . . ad abbates . . . claruerint
claustrum:
4.78 officina . . . claustra sunt monasterii
67.7 claustra monasterii egredi
clausura: 6.8
clericus: 60.8; 61.12
codex:
9.5 legantur . . . in codice . . . lectiones
9.8 codices . . . legantur in vigiliis
10.2 lectiones in codice . . . legantur
11.2 legantur in codice . . . lectiones
33.3 habere proprium . . . neque codicem neque tabulas
38.1 qui arripuerit codicem
48.15 accipiant . . . codices de bibliotheca
48.16 codices in caput quadragesimae dandi sunt
coenobita:
1.2 primum [genus est] coenobitarum
1.13 coenobitarum . . . genus disponendum
coenobium:
5.12 in coenobiis degentes
coepisse: 2.26
coercere:
2.28 castigatio in . . . initio peccati coerceat
30.3 verberibus coerceantur
69.4 acrius coerceatur
cogitare:
2.34 semper cogitet quia . . . suscepit
55.22 Dei retributionem cogitet

63.3 cogitet semper quia . . . redditurus est
63.14 cogitet et sic se exhibeat ut
64.7 cogitet . . . quale onus suscepit
64.18 cogitans discretionem
65.22 cogitet . . . abbas se . . . reddere rationem
cogitatio:
1.5 vitia . . . cogitationum
4.50 cogitationes malas . . . allidere
7.12 custodiens se . . . a peccatis . . . cogitationum
7.14 in cogitationibus . . . Deum . . . praesentem ostendit
7.15 'Dominus novit cogitationes hominum'
7.16 'intellexisti cogitationes meas'
7.17 'cogitatio hominis confitebitur'
7.18 sollicitus sit circa cogitationes
7.44 si . . . cogitationes malas . . . non celaverit
65.5 ei suggeritur a cogitationibus
cogitatus:
Prol. 28 'parvulos' cogitatos . . . 'tenuit'
cognoscere:
7.47 'delictum . . . cognitum tibi feci'
46.4 dum per alium cognitum fuerit
cohortari:
7.55 maiorum cohortantur exempla
22.8 invicem se moderate cohortentur
collatio:
42.3 legat unus Collationes
42.5 accedant ad lectionem Collationum
73.5 Collationes Patrum . . . quid . . . sunt
collocare: 60.8
colloqui:
53.23 hospitibus . . . neque colloquatur
53.24 colloqui cum hospite
colloquium:
25.2 in nullo iungatur . . . colloquio
collum: 58.16
color: 55.7
comedere: 38.6
comestio: 39.11
commemorare: 73.9
commemoratio: 67.2
commendare: 67.1
commendaticius: 61.13
comminatio: 27.7
committere:
2.30,32,33; 4.41; 7.44; 31.17; 42.7; 63.2; 65.13
commonere: 18.22
commotio: 71.8

commovere: 71.7
communio:
38.2   post missas et communionem
38.10   propter communionem sanctam
63.4   accedant . . . ad communionem
communis:
5.9   res communiter citius explicantur
7.55   communis monasterii regula
33.6   omnium 'sint communia'
43.15   mensae communis participa-
tioner₁
comparare: 55.7
compati:
27.9   infirmitati . . . compassus est
competere:
25.5   hora qua praeviderit abbas ei
competere
31.18   horis competentibus
47.1   omnia horis competentibus compleantur
50.1   occurrere hora competenti
complere:
Prol. 1   admonitionem . . . efficaciter
comple
Prol. 35   haec complens Dominus
Prol. 39   si compleamus habitatoris officium
12.4; 13.11   litania et completum est
42.8   in unum positi compleant
43.6   completo opere Dei
47.1   horis competentibus compleantur
completorius: 16.2,5; 17.9; 18.19; 42.t,8
comprehendere: Prol.13
comprobare:
29.2   ut . . . humilitas comprobetur
65.18   contemptor . . . fuerit comprobatus
compunctio:
20.3   compunctione lacrimarum
49.4   compunctioni cordis . . . operam
damus
computare: Prol. 5
concedere: 6.3; 36.8,9; 60.4,7
concordare:
19.7   mens nostra concordet voci nostrae
concors: 64.1
concupiscentia:
4.46   omni concupiscentia spiritali
desiderare
7.25   'post concupiscentias . . . non
eas'
concupiscere:
4.6   'non concupiscere'
condecere:
3.6   condecet . . . disponere

6.6   docere magistrum condecet
condere: 52.1
conferre:
57.2   aliquid conferre monasterio
58.24   res . . . conferat monasterio
confessio:
7.44   commissa per humilem confessionem . . . non celaverit
confidere:
68.5   confidens de adiutorio Dei
confirmare:
27.4   'confirmetur in eo caritas'
confiteri:
4.57   mala . . . Deo confiteri
7.17   'cogitatio hominis confitebitur
tibi'
7.46   'confitemini Domino'
16.4   'surgebam ad confitendum tibi'
16.5   'surgamus ad confitendum' ei
conformare: 2.32
confortare: 7.37
confundere: 7.53; 58.21
confusio: 73.7
congregatio:
3.1; 4.78; 17.6; 21.1; 31.1,2,17; 35.4,5;
46.3; 53.13; 58.14,22,23; 61.8; 62.6;
63.t; 64.1,2,3; 65.2,14,21; 66.8
congruus:
24.7   satisfactione congrua veniam
consequatur
43.19   nihil percipiat usque ad emendationem congruam
53.2   omnibus congruus honor exhibeatur
coniungere: 18.17
consanguinitas: 69.2
conscientia:
7.35   conscientia patientiam amplectatur
consedere: 63.16
consensus:
61.13   sine consensu abbatis eius
64.5   prohibeant pravorum praevalere
consensum
consentire:
40.6   saltem vel hoc consentiamus
58.28   si . . . diabolo consenserit
64.3   vitiis suis . . . consentientem
personam
consequi:
5.19   nullam consequitur gratiam
24.7   veniam consequatur
63.18   ordines suos consequantur
64.10   ut idem ipse consequatur
conservare:
58.27   vestimenta . . . in vestiario conservanda
63.1   ordines . . . ita conservent

conservata:
63.9 pueris . . . disciplina conservata
64.20 regulam . . . conservet

conservatio:
Prol. 47 conservationem caritatis

conservus:
64.21 erogavit triticum conservis suis

considerare:
19.6 consideremus qualiter oporteat
36.4 infirmi considerent . . . sibi servire
37.2 consideretur semper in eis imbecillitas
40.5 considerans in omnibus ne surrepat
48.25 imbecillitas ab abbate consideranda est
55.20 consideretur illa sententia
55.21 abbas consideret infirmitates
64.1 consideretur ratio
64.17 providus et consideratus

consideratio:
8.1 iuxta considerationem rationis
34.2 infirmitatum consideratio
37.3 sit in eis pia consideratio
53.19 sit consideratio ut . . . solacia accommodentur
55.3 haec . . . consideratio penes abbatem est

consignare:
32.2 singula . . . consignet custodienda
35.11 item intranti consignet

consilium:
3.t de adhibendis ad consilium fratribus
3.2 audiens consilium fratrum
3.3 ad consilium vocari
3.4 dent fratres consilium
3.12 seniorum . . . utatur consilio
3.13 'omnia fac cum consilio'
63.7 quos . . . altiori consilio . . . praetulerit
64.1 saniore consilio elegerit
64.3 pari consilio elegerit
65.15 elegerit . . . cum consilio fratrum

consistere:
40.5 in arbitrio prioris consistat

consolari:
4.19 dolentem consolari
27.3 qui . . . consolentur fratrem
27.3 'consolentur' eum
35.16 'consolatus es me'

consolatio:
1.5 sine consolatione alterius

consors:
Prol. 50 regno eius . . . consortes

consortium:
24.4 privati . . . a mensae consortio

25.2 in nullo iungatur consortio
43.16 sequestratus a consortio

conspargere:
2.5 doctrina . . . in . . . mentibus conspargatur

conspectus:
Prol. 28 a conspectibus cordis
19.5 'in conspectu angelorum'
19.6 in conspectu divinitatis

conspicere:
31.10 vasa sacrata conspiciat

constituere:
Prol. 45 constituenda est . . . schola servitii
Prol. 46 nos constituturos speramus
2.4 abbas . . . debet . . . constituere
18.21 psalmi . . . per unamquamque constituens noctem
21.1 et constituantur decani
21.7 de praeposito eadem constituimus
31.16 fratribus constitutam annonam
40.2 mensura victus . . . constituitur
43.5 loco quem . . . constituerit abbas
50.4 non eos praetereant horae constitutae
58.15 lege regulae constitutum
61.11 in superiori . . . constituere loco
62.7 regulam . . . praepositis constitutam
63.1 utque abbas constituerit
63.4 secundum ordines quos constituerit
64.1 hic constituatur quem
64.5 constituant dispensatorem
64.22 'super omnia . . . constituit eum'
66.6 monasterium . . . ita debet constitui
70.2 constituimus ut nulli liceat
71.3 qui ab eo constituuntur
73.t observatio in hac sit regula constituta

consuetudinarius:
18.24 cum canticis consuetudinariis

consuetudo:
7.68 ex consuetudine incipiet custodire
7.69 consuetudine ipsa bona
13.3 psalmi dicantur secundum consuetudinem
53.11 consuetudines ieiuniorum prosequantur

61.2   contentus est consuetudinem
       loci
consummare: 41.8
contagiare: 28.8
contemnere:
2.9   'contemnentes spreverunt me'
2.25   contemnentes ut increpat
7.11   contemnentes Deum gehenna
       ... incendat
71.9   qui contempserit facere
contemptor:
23.1   seniorum suorum contemptor
       repertus
65.18   contemptor sanctae regulae
contendere:
3.9   cum abbate ... contendere
contentio:
4.68   contentionem non amare
contentiosus:
71.5   si quis contentiosus reperitur
contentus:
7.49   si ... extremitate contentus sit
61.2   contentus est consuetudinem
61.3   contentus est quod invenerit
conterere:
64.13   'calamum ... non conterendum'
contingere:
11.13   quod si contigerit ... satisfaciat
65.1   contigit ut ... oriantur
continuare: 41.4
continuo: 46.3
contra: 1.4,5; 65.16; 71.7
contradicere:
68.3   resistendo vel contradicendo
contrarius:
2.13   quae ... docuerit esse contraria
7.35   duris et contrariis rebus
7.38   universa ... contraria sustinere
23.1   contrarius exsistens ... regulae
39.8   contrarium est omni christiano
65.8   dum contraria sibi ... sentiunt
contristare:
Prol. 5   de malis actibus ... contristari
31.6   fratres non contristet
31.7   non ... eum contristet
31.19   nemo ... contristetur
34.3   qui minus indiget ... non
       contristetur
36.4   non ... contristent fratres
48.7   non contristentur
54.4   non contristetur frater
contueri: 40.3
contumacia:
62.11   si ... talis fuerit ... contumacia
contumax:
23.1   si quis ... contumax ... repertus
       fuerit
71.9   si contumax fuerit ... expellatur

conturbare:
63.2   abbas non conturbet gregem
convenire:
3.6   discipulos convenit oboedire
       magistro
5.2   haec convenit his
6.6   audire discipulum convenit
13.13   ut conventi ... purgent se
conventus:
20.5   in conventu ... brevietur oratio
conversatio:
Prol. 49   processu ... conversationis
1.3   conversationis fervore novicio
1.12   de ... miserrima conversa-
       tione
21.1   fratres ... sanctae conversa-
       tionis
22.2   pro modo conversationis ...
       accipiant
58.1   veniens quis ad conversati-
       onem
58.17   promittat de ... conversati-
       one morum suorum
63.1   ut conversationis tempus ...
       discernit
73.1   initium conversationis ... ha-
       bere
73.2   ad perfectionem conver-
       sationis qui festinat
convertere:
Prol. 38   'sed convertatur et vivat'
2.18   convertenti ex servitio
7.30   exspectat nos converti in me-
       lius
63.7   ut convertuntur ita sint
convocare: 3.1
copiosus: 36.5
coquere: 39.1,3
coquina: (8)
cor:
Prol. 1   aurem cordis
Prol. 10   'nolite obdurare corda'
Prol. 26   'loquitur veritatem in corde
       suo'
Prol. 28   a conspectibus cordis sui
Prol. 40   praeparanda sunt corda
Prol. 49   dilatato corde ... curritur
2.9   'non abscondi in corde meo'
2.12   duris corde
3.8   proprii ... cordis voluntatem
4.1   'diligere ex toto corde'
4.24   dolum in corde non tenere
4.28   veritatem ex corde ... pro-
       ferre
4.50; 7.44   cogitationes malas cordi
       suo advenientes
5.17   in corde si murmuraverit
5.18   cor ... respicit murmurantem

7.3 'non est exaltatum cor meum'
7.8 humiliato corde ... erigatur
7.14 'scrutans corda et renes'
7.18 dicat ... utilis frater in corde suo
7.37 'confortetur cor tuum'
7.48 'remisisti impietatem cordis mei'
7.51 intimo cordis credat affectu
7.62 si non solum corde monachus ... indicet
7.65 dicens sibi in corde
9.10 lectio ... ex corde recitanda
12.4 lectionem ... una ex corde
20.3 in puritate cordis ... exaudiri
39.9 'ne graventur corda vestra'
49.4 compunctioni cordis ... operam damus
52.4 in lacrimis et intentione cordis

coram: (8)
corona: 7.33
corporalis:
23.5 vindictae corporali subdatur
71.9 corporali vindictae subiaceat
corpus:
Prol. 40 praeparanda sunt corda et corpora
Prol. 43 dum ... in hoc corpore sumus
2.28 corporis castigatio ... coerceat
4.11 'corpus castigare'
7.9 latera ... scalae ... esse corpus et animam
7.62 corpore humilitatem ... indicet
33.4 nec corpora sua nec voluntates ... habere in propria voluntate
49.7 subtrahat corpori suo de cibo
53.7 prostrato omni corpore
57.5 mortem quam ... in corpore pertulerunt
58.25 nec ... corporis potestatem se habiturum
61.6 sociari corpori monasterii
72.5 infirmitates ... sive corporum sive morum

correptio:
28.1 acrior ei accedat correptio
33.8 correptioni subiaceat
48.20 correptioni regulari subiaceat
64.12 in ... correptione prudenter agat
65.19 adhibeatur ei correptio disciplinae regularis
corrigere:
2.28 'stultus ... non corrigitur'
23.4 si ... neque sic correxerit ... excommunicationi subiaceat

28.2 si nec ita correxerit
45.2 noluit humilitate corrigere
62.9 si non correxerit ... episcopus adhibeatur
65.20 si neque sic correxerit ... deiciatur de ordine praepositurae
corripere:
2.25 increpat et corripiat
2.27 verbis corripiat
21.5 correptus semel et iterum
28.t saepius correpti
28.1 frequenter correptus
30.t qualiter corripiantur
32.4 si quis ... tractaverit corripiatur
43.14 pro hoc corripiatur
48.19 corripiatur semel et secundo
71.5 contentiosus ... corripiatur
71.6 a quocumque priore suo corripitur
corrumpere: 7.22
cotidianus: 39.1; 48.t
cotidie: (8)
crapula: 39.7,8,9
crassus: 27.7
creator:
16.5 referamus laudes creatori nostro
73.4 perveniamus ad creatorem nostrum
credere:
2.2 Christi ... agere vices ... creditur
2.39 discussionem ... de creditis ovibus
7.23 Deum credamus ... praesentem
7.51 cordis credat affectu
19.1 credimus divinam esse praesentiam
19.2 maxime ... credamus cum ... assistimus
27.5 de ovibus sibi creditis
39.1 sufficere credimus ad refectionem
40.3 credimus heminam vini ... sufficere
48.2 ac dispositione credimus utraque ... ordinari
55.4 sufficere credimus monachis
63.13 vices Christi creditur agere
cuculla: (5)
culmen:
7.5 humilitatis ... culmen attingere
73.9 ad maiora ... culmina ... pervenies
culpa:
2.7 culpae pastoris incumbere
23.t de excommunicatione culparum
24.1 secundum modum culpae
24.2 culparum modus

24.3   si . . . in levioribus culpis invenitur

25.t   de gravioribus culpis

25.1   qui gravioris culpae noxa tenetur

28.1   correptus pro qualibet culpa

44.1   qui pro gravibus culpis . . . excommunicantur

44.9   qui . . . pro levibus culpis excommunicantur

45.3   infantes . . . pro tali culpa vapulent

62.10   clarescentibus culpis

cultellus: 22.5; 55.19

cum (praep.): (81)

cum (coni.): (16)

cuncti: (8)

cupere: Prol.15; 61.3; 64.12,19

cura:

2.8   universa . . . cura exhibita

2.10   inoboedientibus curae suae ovibus

2.38   sub cura sua . . . habere

27.1   curam gerat abbas circa delinquentes

27.6   infirmarum curam suscepisse animarum

31.3   curam gerat de omnibus

31.9   curam gerat sciens

31.15   habeat sub cura sua

36.1   infirmorum cura . . . adhibenda est

36.6   cura maxima sit abbati

36.10   curam . . . maximam habeat

47.1   sit cura abbatis

47.1   fratri iniungat . . . curam

53.15   susceptioni cura . . . exhibeatur

curare:

46.6   qui sciat curare . . . vulnera

curiosus: 58.6

currere:

Prol. 13   'currite dum lumen vitae habetis'

Prol. 22   nisi illuc bonis actibus curritur

Prol. 44   currendum et agendum est

Prol. 49   curritur via

27.5   industria currere

43.1   cum festinatione curratur

cursus:

73.4   recto cursu perveniamus

curtus: 55.8

custodia:

6.1   'posui ori meo custodiam'

63.19   et custodiam habeant

65.11   propter pacis caritatisque custodiam

70.4   infantum . . . custodia sit

custodire:

4.48   actus . . . custodire

4.51   os suum . . . custodire

6.1   'custodiam vias meas'

7.12   custodiens se . . . a peccatis

7.68   ex consuetudine . . . custodire

31.5   quae iubentur custodiat

31.8   animam suam custodiat

32.2   singula . . . consignet custodienda

49.2   vitam suam custodire

58.14   promiserit se omnia custodire

D

damnare:

6.8   scurrilitates . . . in omnibus locis damnamus

58.18   ab eo se damnandum sciat

Daniel: 63.6

dare: (31)

dator: 5.16

de: (185)

debere: (44)

debilis:

27.7   'quod debile erat'

36.9   infirmis omnino debilibus

39.11   praeter . . . debiles aegrotos

decania: 21.2

decantare: 9.3

decanus: (7)

decere: 11.10

decernere:

44.5   in ordine quo abbas decreverit

decipere: 59.6; 65.18

declinare: 3.7; 7.29

deducere: Prol. 28

deesse:

2.36   'nihil deest timentibus'

38.1   lectio deesse non debet

53.16   qui numquam desunt monasterio

defendere:

3.4   procaciter defendere

28.2   defendere . . . opera sua

69.t   ut . . . non praesumat alter alterum defendere

69.1   alter alium defendere

defigere: 7.63

degere: 5.12; 55.7

degradare: 63.7

deicere:

21.5   si emendare noluerit deiciatur

65.20   deiciatur de ordine praepositurae

deificus:

Prol. 9   ad deificum lumen

deinde: (7)

deiungere: 48.12

delectare:
7.31 desideria sua non delectetur implere
33.7 nequissimo vitio . . . delectari
delectatio:
7.24 secus introitum delectationis
7.69 custodire . . . delectatione virtutum
deliberatio:
58.14 habita . . . deliberatione
58.16 sub tam morosam deliberationem
delicatus:
48.24 fratribus infirmis aut delicatis
deliciae:
4.12 delicias non amplecti
delictum: 7.47; 46.3
delinquere:
2.26 peccata delinquentium
6.1 'non delinquam in lingua mea'
27.1 curam gerat . . . circa delinquentes fratres
30.3 tales dum delinquunt
36.10 quicquid a discipulis delinquitur
45.2 quod neglegentia deliquit
46.t qui in aliis . . . rebus delinquunt
46.1 si quis . . . aliquid deliquerit
demergere: 7.21
demonstrare:
Prol. 20 demonstrat . . . viam
7.14 demonstrans . . . hoc propheta
7.70 dignabitur demonstrare
73.1 initium conversationis nos demonstremus habere
demum: 2.10; 73.9
denegare: 29.3; 31.7
deni: 22.3
denuo: 29.3; 42.8; 43.15; 57.3
deposcere: Prol. 4
deprehendere:
33.7 si . . . vitio deprehensus fuerit delectari
34.7 si deprehensus fuerit
deputare:
7.28 ab angelis nobis deputatis
36.7 cella super se deputata
48.17 deputentur unus aut duo seniores
48.22 variis officiis deputati sunt
49.9 praesumptioni deputabitur
58.6 senior eis . . . deputetur
derelinquere:
4.26 caritatem non derelinquere
descendere:
7.6 'descendentes et ascendentes angeli'
7.7 exaltatione descendere

descensus:
7.7 descensus ille et ascensus
describere:
73.1 regulam . . . hanc descripsimus
73.8 regulam descriptam
deserere:
5.7 voluntatem propriam deserentes
desiderare:
4.46 vitam aeternam . . . desiderare
5.12 abbatem . . . praeesse desiderant
43.19 hora qua desideraverit hoc
desiderium:
1.8 desideriorum voluntas
4.59 'desideria carnis non efficere'
5.12 desideriis suis . . . oboedientes
7.12 custodiens se . . . desideria carnis
7.23 in desideriis vero carnis
7.23 'ante te est omne desiderium meum'
7.24 cavendum . . . malum desiderium
7.31 desideria sua non delectetur implere
49.7 spiritalis desiderii gaudio
60.8 eodem desiderio . . . sociari
desidia: Prol. 2
desidiosus: 48.23; 73.7
desperare: 4.74
destructio: 67.5
desub: 58.16
desuper: 58.29
detegere: 46.6
deterior: 1.11
detractio: 65.7
detractor: 4.40
detrimentum: 2.32
Deus: (99)
Deuteronomium: 13.9
devertere: Prol.17
devotio:
18.24 inertem devotionis . . . servitium ostendunt monachi
20.2 puritatis devotione supplicandum est
diabolicus: 53.5
diabolus: Prol.28; 1.4; 54.4; 58.28
diacon: 62.1
dicere: (144)
dictare:
Prol. 47 dictante . . . ratione
2.19 iustitia dictante
dictio: 17.9
dies: (55)
difficilis:
2.31 difficilem . . . rem
difficultas:
58.3 difficultatem ingressus

63.18 cum disciplina ordines ... consequantur
63.19 et custodiam habeant et disciplinam
65.19 adhibeatur ei correptio disciplinae regularis
70.4 disciplinae diligentia ... sit
70.6 disciplinae regulari subiaceat

discipulus:
2.5 in discipulorum mentibus conspargatur
2.6 discipulorum oboedientiae ... discussio
2.11 praeesse discipulis
2.12 capacibus discipulis
2.13 quae discipulis docuerit esse contraria
3.6 discipulos convenit oboedire
5.9 perfecta discipuli opera
5.16 a discipulis praeberi
5.17 si oboedit discipulus
6.3 discipulis ... rara loquendi concedatur licentia
6.6 audire discipulum convenit
6.8 discipulum aperire os non permittimus
36.10 quicquid a discipulis delinquitur

discordare: 4.73

discretio:
64.18 cogitans discretionem sancti Iacob
64.19 testimonia discretionis matris virtutum
70.6 sine discretione exarserit

discussio:
2.6 in ... iudicio Dei facienda erit discussio
2.39 futuram discussionem ... de ... ovibus

dispensatio:
22.2 secundum dispensationem abbatis sui

dispensator:
64.5 constituant dispensatorem

displicere: 18.22

disponere:
1.13 ad coenobitarum ... genus disponendum
3.6 cuncta disponere
11.2 modulatis ut ... disposuimus
18.20 disposito ordine psalmodiae
41.5 temperet atque disponat
63.2 nec ... iniuste disponat aliquid
65.12 ut ante disposuimus
65.12 prout abbas disposuerit

disposite:
11.2 residentibus cunctis disposite

dispositio:
18.10 versuum dispositionem uniformem
48.2 ac dispositione credimus

dissensio:
65.2 dissensiones in congregationes faciunt
65.7 suscitantur ... dissensiones exordinationes
65.8 sub hanc dissensionem animas periclitari

dissimulare: 2.26,33
distollere: 48.18
distributio: 18.22
districtio: 37.2
districtus:
34.7 districtiori disciplinae
diu: 44.3
diurnus: 16.3; 18.20; 43.10
diuturnus: 1.3
diversus: (6)
dives: 53.15
dividere: 13.9; 18.16,20; 34.1
divinitas:
7.13 ab aspectu divinitatis videri
19.6 in conspectu divinitatis ... esse
divinitus:
5.4 ac si divinitus imperetur
divinus:
Prol. 9 divina ... vox
2.5 fermentum divinae iustitiae
2.12 divina praecepta monstrare
7.1 clamat ... scriptura divina
7.9 evocatio divina ... inseruit
7.39 spe retributionis divinae
8.t de officiis divinis
9.8 codices ... divinae auctoritatis
16.t divina opera per diem agantur
19.1 ubique ... divinam esse praesentiam
19.2 ad opus divinum assistimus
20.4 ex affectu inspirationis divinae gratiae
28.3 medicamina scripturarum divinarum
31.16 memor divini eloquii
43.1 ad horam divini officii
48.1 certis ... horis in lectione divina
50.3 cum tremore divino flectentes genua
53.9 legatur coram hospite lex divina
64.9 doctum lege divina
73.3 qui sermo divinae auctoritatis ... non est ... norma

docere:
Prol. 12 'timorem Domini docebo vos'
1.4 multorum solacio iam docti pugnare
2.4 abbas . . . debet . . . docere
2.13 quae discipulis docuerit esse contraria
6.6 docere magistrum condecet
7.21 docemur . . . non facere voluntatem
64.9 doctum lege divina
doctor: 5.6 dicit doctoribus
doctrina:
Prol. 50 in eius doctrinam . . . perseverantes
2.5 doctrina fermentum . . . conspargatur
2.6 doctrinae . . . facienda erit discussio
2.11 duplici . . . doctrina . . . praeesse
2.23 in doctrina sua . . . abbas . . . debet . . . servare
21.4 eligantur . . . secundum . . . sapientiae doctrinam
64.2 sapientiae doctrina eligatur
73.2 sunt doctrinae sanctorum Patrum
73.9 ad . . . doctrinae . . . culmina . . . pervenies
dolere:
4.19 dolentem consolari
dolus:
Prol. 17 'labia . . . ne loquantur dolum'
Prol. 26 'egit dolum in lingua'
4.24 dolum in corde non tenere
domesticus: 53.2
dominicus: (22)
Dominus: (62)
domus:
Prol. 33 'aedificavit domum'
Prol. 34 'impegerunt in domum'
31.19 contristetur in domo Dei
53.22 domus Dei a sapientibus . . . administretur
64.5 domui Dei . . . constituant dispensatorem
donare: 40.4
donatio:
58.24 facta . . . donatione
59.5 faciant . . . donationem
donum: 40.1
dormire:
22.t quomodo dormiant monachi
22.1 per singula lecta dormiant
22.3 in uno loco dormiant
22.5 vestiti dormiant

22.5 cultellos . . . ad latus . . . non habeant dum dormiunt
22.5 ne . . . vulnerent dormientem
43.8 qui se aut recollocet et dormit
58.5 ubi . . . et dormiant
dorsum: 7.40
dubitatio:
19.2 sine . . . dubitatione credamus
dubium:
2.38 sine dubio addita et suae animae
3.11 procul dubio
5.13 sine dubio . . . imitantur
7.7 sine dubio descensus ille . . . intellegitur
31.9 sciens sine dubio
ducatus:
Prol. 21 per ducatum evangelii pergamus
ducere: 5.11; 31.11; 53.8,11; 72.1,2
dulcedo:
Prol. 49 dilectionis dulcedine
dulcis:
Prol. 19 quid dulcius nobis ab hac voce
5.14 oboedientia . . . dulcis hominibus
dum: (23)
durus:
2.12 duris corde
2.25 durius arguere
2.28 duros . . . castigatio . . . coerceat
7.35 duris et contrariis rebus
58.8 praedicentur ei . . . dura et aspera

E

ebrietas: 40.5
ecce: Prol.18,20; 4.75; 58.10
ecclesia:
Prol. 11 'quid spiritus dicat ecclesiis'
13.10 sicut psallit ecclesia Romana
edax: 4.36; 31.1
edere: 39.2
efferre: (v. **elatus**)
efficax: Prol. 1
efficere: 2.40; 4.59; 5.14
effugare: 48.24
effugere: 6.4; 7.57
ego: (74)
egredi:
29.1 qui proprio vitio egreditur
29.1 pro quo egressus est
35.7 egressurus de septimana
35.9 tam ipse qui egreditur quam
35.16 egrediens . . . de septimana
35.17 accepta benedictione egrediens
58.15 non liceat egredi de monasterio

58.28 ut egrediatur de monasterio
67.7 claustra monasterii egredi
eiusmodi: 25.4
elatio:
4.69 elationem fugere
38.2 avertat ... spiritum elationis
62.2 caveat elationem aut superbiam
65.18 elatione deceptus
elatus:
Prol. 29 non se reddunt elatos
7.3 'elati sunt oculi mei'
28.2 si ... in superbia elatus
31.1 non elatus non turbulentus
electio:
62.6 electio congregationis ... promovere voluerint
eleemosyna: 59.4
eleison: 9.10; 17.4,5,10
eligere:
1.9 quicquid ... elegerint
21.1 eligantur ... fratres boni testimonii
21.3 decani tales eligantur
21.4 non eligantur per ordinem
31.1 cellararius ... eligatur de congregatione
62.1 de suis eligat
64.1 quem ... saniore consilio elegerit
64.2 eligatur qui ordinandus est
64.3 personam pari consilio elegerit
65.15 quemcumque elegerit abbas
eloquium:
4.51 a ... pravo eloquio custodire
6.2 a bonis eloquiis ... tacere
6.3 de ... aedificationum eloquiis ... rara loquendi concedatur licentia
6.8 ad talia eloquia ... aperire os
31.16 memor divini eloquii
58.21 'secundum eloquium tuum'
emendare:
2.40 a vitiis emendatus
4.58 de ... malis ... emendare
5.19 cum satisfactione emendaverit
21.5 si emendare noluerit
23.3 si non emendaverit obiurgetur
28.t qui saepius correpti emendare noluerint
28.1 si ... excommunicatus non emendaverit
32.5; 33.8; 48.20 si non emendaverit ... subiaceat
43.7 pro verecundia sua emendent
43.9 et de reliquo emendent
43.15 si denuo non emendaverit non permittatur

62.10 si nec sic emendaverit ... proiciatur
65.19 si non emendaverit adhibeatur
emendatio:
Prol. 36 propter emendationem malorum
Prol. 47 propter emendationem vitiorum
2.40 emendationem aliis sumministrat
29.1 spondeat ... emendationem
43.16 usque ad ... emendationem
43.19 usque ad emendationem congruam
46.4 maiori subiaceat emendationi
emulatio: 65.7
enarrare: 2.14
enim: (8)
episcopus: 62.9; 64.4
eradere: 64.12
eremita: 1.3
eremus: 1.5
ergo: (40)
erigere:
7.6 scala illa erigenda est
7.8 scala ... ipsa erecta
7.8 vita ... a Domino erigatur ad caelum
57.3 talis erigatur ab ... arte
erogare:
58.24 res ... eroget ... pauperibus
64.21 erogavit triticum conservis
errare: 27.8
erudire: 61.9
esse: (246)
esus: 36.9
et: (381)
et(=etiam): (44)
etiam: (28)
eulogia: 54.1
evangelicus: 7.65
evangelium:
Prol. 21 per ducatum evangelii
Prol. 33 Dominus in evangelio ait
11.9 lectionem de Evangelia
12.4; 13.11; 17.8 canticum de Evangelia
evenire: 11.13
evocatio: 7.9
evolvere: 7.11
ex: (35)
exaltare:
7.1 'qui se exaltat humiliabitur'
7.1 'qui se humiliat exaltabitur'
7.3 'non est exaltatum cor'
7.4 'si exaltavi animam meam'
7.53 'exaltatus sum'
7.59 'stultus ... exaltat vocem suam'

extendere: 24.1
extollere:
34.4   non extollatur pro misericordia
57.2   si ... extollitur pro scientia
extra: 2.4; 15.3
extremitas: 7.49
exuere: 58.26,27,28; 65.5

F

fabula:
43.8   fabulis vacat
48.18   vacat otio aut fabulis
facere: (66)
facilis:
7.59   non sit facilis ... in risu
58.1   non ei facilis tribuatur ingressus
65.4   absurdum facile advertitur
factum:
Prol. 35   monitis factis ... respondere
2.1   nomen maioris factis implere
2.12   bona ... factis ... ostendat
2.12   factis suis divina praecepta monstrare
2.13   in suis factis indicet non agenda
3.13   'post factum non paeniteberis'
4.63   praecepta Dei factis ... adimplere
5.8   iubentis vocem factis sequuntur
5.19   pro tali facto nullam consequitur gratiam
7.13   facta sua ... videri
7.28   factorum nostrorum opera nuntiantur
7.32   vocem ... Domini factis imitetur
fallere: 45.t,1
falsus:
4.7   'non falsum testimonium dicere'
4.25   pacem falsam non dare
7.43   falsos fratres sustinent
femorale: 55.13
feria: (10)
fermentum: 2.5
ferramentum: 32.t,1
ferrum: 28.6
fervere:
72.3   zelum ferventissimo amore exerceant
fervor:
1.3   conversationis fervore novicio
41.4   aestatis fervor nimius fuerit
66.4   responsum ... cum fervore caritatis
festinare:
18.1; 35.17 'ad adiuvandum me festina'

22.6   festinent invicem se praevenire
66.4   reddat responsum festinanter
73.2   ad perfectionem ... qui festinat
73.8   ad patriam caelestem festinas
festinatio:
43.1   summa cum festinatione curratur
festivitas: 14.1
festuca: 2.15
fidelis:
7.38   fidelem pro Domino universa ... sustinere debere
fides:
Prol. 21   succinctis ... fide ... lumbis
Prol. 49   processu ... fidei ... curritur via mandatorum Dei
1.7   servantes saeculo fidem
53.2   'domesticis fidei'
fieri: (22)
figere: 7.65
filius:
Prol. 1   Obsculta o fili
Prol. 5   in filiorum ... numero computare
Prol. 6   ut non ... filios exheredet
Prol. 12   'venite filii'
2.3   'accepistis spiritum adoptionis filiorum'
2.29   'percute filium tuum virga'
7.27   'Dominus ... respicit super filios'
59.t   de filiis nobilium
59.1   si quis ... offerit filium Deo
59.8   cum oblatione offerant filium
finire: 9.11; 35.15
finis: 7.21,36
firmare: 61.5
flamma: 65.22
flare: Prol. 34
flectere: 50.3
fletus:
49.4   orationi cum fletibus
fluctuare: 27.3
flumen: Prol. 34
folium: 42.6
fomentum: 28.3
fomes: 43.2
foris (subst.): 44.1
foris:
3.9; 7.67; 43.8; 51.1; 63.19; 66.7; 67.5
forma: 2.23
formido:
7.68   non sine formidine observabat
fornax: 1.6
forte: (35)
fortis:
Prol. 3   oboedientiae fortissima ... arma

1.13 coenobitarum fortissimum genus
18.16 psalmi . . . qui . . . fortiores inveniuntur
64.19 fortes quod cupiant
70.6 in fortiori aetate
fortuitus: 38.1
fragilitas:
64.13 suamque fragilitatem . . . suspectus sit
frangere:
46.2 si . . . aut fregerit quippiam
53.10 ieiunium . . . frangatur
64.12 ne . . . frangatur vas
frater: (102)
fraternitas:
72.8 caritatem fraternitatis . . . impendant
fraternus:
1.5 fraterna ex acie
fraus: 57.4
frequens:
4.56 orationi frequenter incumbere
28.1 frater frequenter correptus
55.16 lecta frequenter . . . scrutinanda sunt
frigidus: 55.2
frux: 48.7
fugere:
Prol. 42 fugientes gehennae poenas
4.69 elationem fugere
7.10 oblivionem . . . fugiat
fundare: Prol. 34
fungi: 62.1
funis: 22.5
furtum: 4.5
futurus:
2.39 timens . . . futuram discussionem
7.30 ne dicat . . . in futuro

G

gaudere:
2.32 in augmentatione . . . gregis gaudeat
7.39 subsequuntur gaudentes
gaudium:
49.6 'cum gaudio Sancti Spiritus'
49.7 cum spiritalis desiderii gaudio
gehenna:
Prol. 42 fugientes gehennae poenas
4.45 gehennam expavescere
5.3 propter metum gehennae
7.11 contemnentes Deum gehenna . . . incendat
7.69 non iam timore gehennae
gemitus:
4.57 cum . . . gemitu . . . confiteri

genu:
35.15 omnibus genibus provolvantur
50.3 flectentes genua
genus: (8)
gerere:
2.33 ne plus gerat sollicitudinem
21.2 sollicitudinem gerant super decanias
27.1 curam gerat abbas circa . . . fratres
27.5 sollicitudinem gerere
31.3 curam gerat de omnibus
31.9 infirmorum . . . curam gerat
52.1 nec ibi . . . aliud geratur
gloria:
Prol. 7 sequi . . . ad gloriam
Prol. 30 'nomini tuo da gloriam'
5.3 propter . . . gloriam vitae aeternae
9.2; 11.3; 18.1 gloria
9.6 sine gloria dicantur
9.6 dicat gloriam
13.9 dividatur in duas glorias
17.2 non sub una gloria
18.1 'ad adiuvandum me festina,' gloria
43.4 post gloriam psalmi
43.10 post versum et gloriam
49.9 deputabitur . . . vanae gloriae
58.22 adiungentes Gloria Patri
gloriari:
Prol. 32 'qui gloriatur in Domino glorietur'
glorificare:
57.9 'ut in omnibus glorificetur Deus'
gradi: 5.10
gradus: (18)
graphium: 33.3; 55.19
gratia:
Prol. 31 'gratia Dei sum'
Prol. 41 gratiae suae iubeat nobis adiutorium ministrare
5.19 nullam consequitur gratiam
20.4 ex affectu inspirationis divinae gratiae
24.6; 63.8 verbi gratia
34.3 qui minus indiget agat Deo gratias
66.3 Deo gratias respondeat
gravare:
39.9 'ne graventur corda'
gravis:
Prol. 46 nihil grave . . . constituturos
25.t de gravioribus culpis
25.1 qui gravioris culpae noxa tenetur
35.1 in causa gravis utilitatis . . . occupatus

35.13 sine . . . gravi labore serviant
38.10 ne forte grave sit ei ieiunium sustinere
42.9 gravi vindictae subiaceat
44.1 qui pro gravibus culpis . . . excommunicantur
55.17 gravissimae disciplinae subiaceat
65.1 scandala gravia . . . oriantur
68.1 si . . . gravia . . . iniunguntur
69.3 gravissima occasio scandalorum

gravitas:
6.3 propter taciturnitatis gravitatem
7.60 humiliter cum gravitate . . . loquatur
22.6 se praevenire . . . cum . . . gravitate
42.11 cum summa gravitate . . . fiat
43.2 curratur cum gravitate tamen
47.4 cum humilitate et gravitate . . . fiat

grex:
2.8 inoboedienti gregi
2.32 detrimenta gregis . . . non patiatur
2.32 in augmentatione boni gregis gaudeat
27.9 reportare ad gregem
28.8 omnem gregem contagiet
63.2 non conturbet gregem
64.18 'si greges . . . fecero laborare'
grossitudo: 55.7
gula: 1.11
gyrovagus: 1.10

H

habere: (44)
habitare:
Prol. 22 si volumus habitare
Prol. 23 'quis habitabit in tabernaculo'
Prol. 39 habitandi praeceptum
40.8 qui ibi habitant
55.1 secundum locorum qualitatem ubi habitant
60.t in monasterio habitare
61.1 habitare in monasterio
61.13 ad habitandum suscipiat
habitator:
Prol. 39 de habitatore tabernaculi
Prol. 39 habitatoris officium
hebdomada: 18.23; 38.1
hebdomadarius: 10.11; 35.13; 38.t
Heli: 2.26
hemina: 40.3
Heptateuchus: 42.4
hic: (119)
hic (adv.): 6.2

hiems: 8.1; 9.1; 11.1; 55.5
hinc: 65.7
hodie: Prol. 10
homo:
Prol. 15; 4.8; 5.14; 7.13,15,17,21,27,41, 52; 20.1; 25.4; 54.1; 73.2
honestas:
73.1 honestatem morum . . . habere
honestus:
42.11 cum . . . moderatione honestissima fiat
61.7 honestiores . . . admonitione . . . corripiat
honor:
9.7 ob honorem . . . Trinitatis
11.9 legat . . . cum honore et timore
36.4 in honorem Dei sibi servire
53.2 omnibus congruus honor exhibeatur
53.15 divitum terror . . . exigit honorem
63.13 sed honore . . . Christi
63.14 dignus sit tali honore
63.17 'honore . . . praevenientes'
72.4 'honore se . . . praeveniant'
honorare:
4.8 'honorare omnes' homines
63.10 priores suos honorent
hora: (65)
hortari: 7.45
hortus: 7.63; 46.1; 66.6
hospes:
31.9 hospitum pauperumque . . . curam gerat
42.10 si necessitas hospitum supervenerit
53.t de hospitibus suscipiendis
53.1 hospites tamquam Christus suscipiantur
53.1 'hospes fui'
53.3 ut . . . nuntiatus fuerit hospes
53.6 discedentibus hospitibus
53.8 hospites ducantur ad orationem
53.9 legatur coram hospite lex divina
53.10 ieiunium . . . frangatur propter hospitem
53.12 aquam . . . hospitibus det
53.13 pedes hospitibus . . . lavet
53.16 coquina . . . hospitum super se sit
53.16 hospites qui numquam desunt
53.21 cellam hospitum habeat
53.23 hospitibus . . . ullatenus societur
53.24 colloqui cum hospite
56.1 mensa . . . cum hospitibus . . . sit
56.2 minus sunt hospites
58.4 sit in cella hospitum
61.1 si pro hospite voluerit habitare

immo: 5.19
impedimentum: 52.5
impedire:
52.3   non impediatur alterius impro-
        bitate
impendere:
72.6   oboedientiam sibi ... impen-
        dant
72.8   caritatem ... impendant
imperare: 5.4,4; 53.18,20; 58.14
imperfectus:
5.8   quod agebant imperfectum re-
        linquentes
imperium: 5.12; 64.17; 68.1,4; 71.3
impietas:
7.48   'remisisti impietatem cordis
        mei'
impingere: Prol. 34
implere:
Prol. 43   dum ... haec omnia ... vacat
            implere
2.1   nomen maioris factis implere
5.18   etiamsi impleat iussionem
7.31   desideria ... non delectetur
        implere
10.3   reliqua omnia ut dictum est
        impleantur
16.2   septenarius ... numerus ...
        implebitur
18.18   canticum ... impleatur
18.25   uno die hoc ... implesse
31.17   impleat officium
47.3   officium implere
53.17   officium bene impleant
imponere:
7.41   'imposuisti homines super ca-
        pita'
24.4   antiphonam non imponat
27.9   humeris suis ... imponere
44.6   psalmum ... in oratorio impo-
        nere
47.2   quibus iussum fuerit imponant
58.21   quam dum imposuerit
63.4   ad psalmum imponendum
impossibilis:
68.t   si ... impossibilia iniungantur
68.1   si ... impossibilia iniunguntur
impossibilitas:
68.2   impossibilitatis suae causas
improbitas:
52.3   non impediatur alterius impro-
        bitate
improbus:
2.28   improbos ... castigatio coerceat
23.5   sin ... improbus est
imputare: Prol. 31
in (cum acc.): (47)
in (cum abl.): (257)

incendere: 7.11
incertus: 53.16
incessabilis:
4.76   incessabiliter adimpleta
inchoare: Prol. 4
inchoatio: 73.8
incipere:
Prol. 48; 7.68; 8.4; 9.7; 11.3,8,10; 17.3;
18.6,11,13; 38.3,10; 58.21
inclinare:
Prol. 1   inclina aurem cordis
7.63   inclinato sit semper capite
53.7   inclinato capite ... adoretur
includere: 1.8
incompetens: 48.21
increpare:
2.23   'obsecra, increpa'
2.25   increpat et corripiat
increpatio:
2.31   alium ... increpationibus alium
        suasionibus
incumbere:
2.7   culpae pastoris incumbere
4.56   orationi ... incumbere
5.10   amor incumbit
incurrere: 5.19
incurvare: 7.66
inde: (5)
indicare:
2.13   in suis factis indicet non agenda
7.3   cavere propheta indicat
7.62   corpore humilitatem ... indicet
54.2   nisi ... indicatum fuerit abbati
indicere: 49.6
indigere:
8.3   qui ... lectionum aliquid indi-
        gent
34.3   qui minus indiget
34.4   qui ... plus indiget
38.6   nullus indigeat petere aliquid
41.8   ut lumen ... non indigeant
53.18   ut indigent solacia administren-
        tur
53.20   quando indigent solacia ac-
        commodentur eis
55.2   in frigidis ... amplius indigetur
55.21   consideret infirmitates indigen-
        tium
66.5   portarius si indiget solacio
indigeries: 39.7
indignus:
7.49   se malum iudicet et indignum
indisciplinatus:
2.25   indisciplinatos ... arguere
inducere: 7.40
induere: 58.26
indumentum: 55.6

industria:
27.5   sagacitate et industria currere
28.4   nihil suam praevalere industri-
       am
indutiae: Prol. 36
inenarrabilis: Prol. 49
iners: 18.24
infans: (7)
inferior: 7.51
infernum:
7.21   'ad profundum inferni demergit'
72.1   zelus . . . malus qui . . . ducit ad
       infernum
inferre: 58.3
infidelis:
28.7   'infidelis si discedit'
infirmitas:
27.9   infirmitati . . . compassus est
34.2   infirmitatum consideratio
34.4   humilietur pro infirmitate
39.1   propter diversorum infirmita-
       tibus
55.21   abbas consideret infirmitates
       indigentium
72.5   infirmitates suas . . . tolerent
infirmus:
4.16   'infirmum visitare'
27.6   infirmarum curam . . . animarum
28.5   operetur salutem circa infirmum
       fratrem
31.9   infirmorum infantum . . . curam
36.t   de infirmis fratribus
36.1   infirmorum cura . . . adhibenda
       est
36.2   'infirmus fui et visitastis me'
36.4   infirmi considerent . . . sibi ser-
       vire
36.7   fratribus infirmis sit cella
36.8   balnearum usus infirmis . . . of-
       feratur
36.9   carnium esus infirmis . . . con-
       cedatur
36.10   ne . . . neglegantur infirmi
40.3   infirmorum contuentes imbecil-
       litatem
42.4   quia infirmis intellectibus non
       erit utile
48.24   fratribus infirmis aut delicatis
64.19   infirmi non refugiant
inflare:
21.5   decani si . . . quis inflatus super-
       bia repertus fuerit reprehen-
       sibilis
65.2   spiritu superbiae inflati
ingenuus: 2.18
ingredi:
Prol. 25   'qui ingreditur sine macula'

35.17   subsequatur ingrediens
35.18   accepta benedictione ingre-
       diatur
38.1   dominica ingrediatur
38.2   ingrediens post missas . . .
       petat
38.4   ingrediatur ad legendum
43.9   sed ingrediantur intus
53.17   ingrediantur duo fratres
58.10   si potes observare ingredere
58.12   ut sciat ad quod ingreditur
60.7   ingressus est in monasterio
61.12   in maiori quam ingrediuntur
       loco
62.5   locum . . . quod ingressus est
ingressus:
58.1   non ei facilis tribuatur ingressus
58.3   difficultatem ingressus
58.4   annuatur ei ingressus
inimicus:
4.31   'inimicos diligere'
4.72   pro inimicis orare
48.1   otiositas inimica est animae
iniquitas: 7.18
initium: Prol. 43; 2.28; 65.4; 73.1
iniungere:
7.49   ad omnia quae . . . iniunguntur
25.3   ad opus sibi iniunctum
31.15   quae ei iniunxerit abbas
47.1   sollicito fratri iniungat . . . curam
48.11   in opus . . . quod eis iniungitur
48.14   operentur quod eis iniungitur
48.23   iniungatur ei opus
48.24   ars iniungatur
64.17   opera quam iniungit
65.16   quae . . . ei iniuncta fuerint
68.t   si impossibilia iniungantur
68.1   si . . . impossibilia iniunguntur
iniuria:
4.30   iniuriam non facere
7.35   quibuslibet irrogatis iniuriis . . .
       patientiam amplectatur
7.42   in adversis et iniuriis
58.3   illatas sibi iniurias . . . portare
iniuriosus:
31.1   [cellararius] non iniuriosus non
       tardus
iniustitia:
7.47   'iniustitias meas non operui'
7.48   'pronuntiabo . . . iniustitias me-
       as'
iniustus:
63.2   nec . . . iniuste disponat
innotescere:
7.61   sapiens verbis innotescit paucis
inoboediens:
2.8   inoboedienti gregi

2.10 inoboedientibus ... ovibus
2.28 inoboedientes ... castigatio ... coerceat
23.1 si quis ... inoboediens aut superbus ... repertus fuerit
inoboedientia:
Prol. 2 per inoboedientiae desidiam
inordinatio:
65.10 inordinationis ... auctores
inquietare:
48.5 ut alium non inquietet
53.16 non inquietentur fratres
inquietus:
2.8 inquieto ... gregi
2.25 inquietos ... arguere
inquirere:
Prol. 17 'inquire pacem'
inserere: 7.9
inservire:
8.3 meditationi inserviatur
inspiratio:
20.4 nisi ... ex affectu inspirationis ... protendatur
instans:
Prol. 4 instantissima oratione
instituere:
11.6 cantica ... quas instituerit abbas
institutio:
Prol. 46 in qua institutione ... nos constituturos speramus
institutum:
73.5 Instituta et Vitas eorum
instrumentum:
4.t instrumenta bonorum operum
4.75 instrumenta artis spiritalis
73.6 instrumenta virtutum
integer: 18.23,25; 48.15
intellectus:
30.1 omnis aetas vel intellectus
42.4 quia infirmis intellectibus non erit utile
intellegentia:
2.32 secundum ... intellegentiam
intellegere:
7.7 non aliud ... descensus ille et ascensus a nobis intellegitur
7.16 'intellexisti cogitationes meas'
7.27 'ut videat si est intellegens'
23.4 si intellegit qualis poena sit
30.2 qui minus intellegere possunt
63.12 nonnos vocent quod intellegitur paterna reverentia
intellegibilis:
2.27 intellegibiles animos ... corripiat
63.19 ad intellegibilem aetatem perveniant

intendere:
18.1; 35.17 'Deus in adiutorium meum intende'
58.6 super eos ... curiose intendat
intentio:
52.4 oret ... in ... intentione cordis
intentus:
48.18 non est intentus lectioni
inter: 9.5; 18.21
interdum: 6.2
interitus: 25.4
intermissio: 15.1
interrogare:
Prol. 23 interrogemus ... Dominum
Prol. 39 cum ... interrogassemus Dominum
interrogatio:
Prol. 24 post hanc interrogationem ... audiamus
7.56 usque ad interrogationem non loquatur
intervallum: 8.4; 42.5
intimus: 7.51
intra: 66.6
intrare: 35.9,11,15; 52.4
introitus:
7.24 secus introitum delectationis
intus: 43.9
inutilis:
7.29 'nos ... inutiles factos'
48.18 sibi inutilis est
invenire:
2.7,13,17,21; 18.16; 24.3; 40.8; 42.9; 43.2; 48.18; 55.7,16,17; 61.2,3,6; 66.2
invicem:
22.6 festinent invicem se praevenire
22.8 invicem se moderate cohortentur
35.1 fratres sibi invicem serviant
35.6 ceteri sibi ... invicem serviant
54.1 nec sibi invicem litteras ... accipere
63.17 'honore invicem praevenientes'
71.t oboedientes sibi sint invicem
71.1 sibi invicem ita oboediant
72.4 'honore se invicem praeveniant'
invidere: 55.21
invidia:
4.67 invidiam non exercere
65.7 suscitantur invidiae rixae
65.22 invidiae aut zeli flamma urat animam
invitare: Prol.19
invocare: Prol.18
involvere: 59.2

ipse: (90)
ira:
  4.22 iram non perficere
iracundia:
  4.23 iracundiae tempus non reservare
iratus:
  Prol. 6 iratus pater
  71.7 senserit animos prioris . . . iratos
ire:
  7.25 'post concupiscentias . . . non eas'
  58.8 per quae itur ad Deum
  65.9 eunt in perditione
  67.7 quocumque ire
  71.2 se ituros ad Deum
irrationabilis:
  31.7 si . . . irrationabiliter postulat
irridere: 58.18
irritare:
  Prol. 7 irritatus a malis nostris
irrogare: 7.35
is: (173)
iste: (6)
ita: (32)
itaque: 7.10
item: (17)
iter:
  Prol. 21 pergamus itinera eius
  50.4 qui in itinere directi sunt
iterum: (21)
itidem: 18.10
iubere:
  Prol. 41 gratiae suae iubeat nobis adiutorium ministrare
  2.4 abbas . . . debet . . . iubere
  5.8 iubentis vocem factis sequuntur
  5.14 quod iubetur non trepide . . . efficiatur
  31.5 quae iubentur custodiat
  42.10 si . . . abbas . . . aliquid iusserit
  44.4 iussus ab abbate
  44.5 si iusserit abbas recipiatur
  44.6 nisi iterum abbas iubeat
  44.8 usque dum ei iubeat . . . abbas
  47.2 quibus iussum fuerit imponant
  47.4 cui iusserit abbas
  53.8 aut cui iusserit ipse
  54.3 si iusserit suscipi
  54.3 cui illud iubeat dari
  57.3 nisi . . . abbas iubeat
  60.4 si . . . iusserit ei abbas
  68.1 suscipiat . . . iubentis imperium

iudex:
  3.11 aequissimo iudici Deo rationem redditurum
iudicare:
  3.2 quod utilius iudicaverit
  3.5 quod salubrius esse iudicaverit
  7.49 operarium se malum iudicet
  18.22 si melius aliter iudicaverit
  32.2 ut iudicaverit utile
  43.7 eos . . . iudicavimus debere stare
  44.3 usque dum abbas iudicaverit satisfactum esse
  62.8 rebellio iudicetur
  63.6 presbyteros iudicaverunt
  65.14 et abbas iudicaverit expedire
  72.7 quod sibi utile iudicat
iudicium:
  2.6 in tremendo iudicio Dei
  2.9 in iudicio Domini absolutus
  2.38 in die iudicii . . . redditurus . . . rationem
  3.11 de omnibus iudiciis . . . rationem redditurum
  4.44 diem iudicii timere
  4.76 in die iudicii reconsignata
  5.12 ambulantes alieno iudicio
  7.64 tremendo iudicio repraesentari
  16.5 laudes . . . super iudicia iustitiae suae
  24.2 in abbatis pendet iudicio
  31.9 in die iudicii rationem redditurus est
  55.22 in omnibus . . . iudiciis suis Dei retributionem cogitet
  63.3 de . . . iudiciis . . . redditurus . . . rationem
  64.10 'superexaltet misericordiam iudicio'
  65.22 de omnibus iudiciis . . . reddere rationem
iugiter: 22.4
iugum:
  58.16 collum excutere desub iugo regulae
iumentum: 7.50
iungere:
  25.2 in nullo iungatur consortio
  26.t iungunt se excommunicatis
  26.1 excommunicato . . . se iungere
  48.21 neque frater ad fratrem iungatur
  69.2 etiam si . . . propinquitate iungantur
iunior: (10)
iurare:
  4.27 non iurare
iusiurandum:
  59.3 promittant sub iureiurando

iussio:
2.5 iussio eius . . . conspargatur
5.9 magistri iussio
5.18 etiamsi impleat iussionem
26.t sine iussione iungunt se
26.1 sine iussione . . . excommunicato . . . se iungere
31.4 sine iussione abbatis nihil faciat
31.12 faciat secundum iussionem abbatis
33.2 ne quis praesumat . . . accipere sine iussione abbatis
44.9 usque ad iussionem abbatis
67.7 sine iussione abbatis facere

iustitia:
Prol. 25 'qui . . . operatur iustitiam'
2.5 iussio eius . . . fermentum divinae iustitiae . . . conspargatur
2.9 'iustitiam . . . non abscondi'
2.14 'enarras iustitias meas'
2.19 iustitia dictante
2.35 'quaerite . . . iustitiam eius'
4.33 'persecutionem pro iustitia sustinere'
16.5 laudes . . . super iudicia iustitiae suae
73.t iustitiae observatio

iustus:
3.6 iuste . . . disponere
41.5 absque iusta murmuratione faciant

iuvenis: 36.8
iuxta: 8.1; 22.7; 66.2

K

kalendae: 8.1; 10.1; 48.3,10
Kyrie eleison: 9.10; 17.4,5,10

L

labium: Prol. 17; 9.1; 38.3
labor:
Prol. 2 per oboedientiae laborem
7.68 absque ullo labore . . . custodire
35.13 sine . . . gravi labore serviant
39.6 si labor . . . factus fuerit maior
40.5 vel labor aut ardor . . . poposcerit
41.2 si labores agrorum non habent
46.1 dum in labore quovis . . . laborat
48.1 occupari . . . in labore manuum
48.8 si labore manuum . . . vivunt

48.24 nec violentia laboris opprimantur
50.1 longe sunt in labore

laborare:
46.1 si quis . . . dum laborat
48.3 laborent quod necessarium fuerit
48.11 in opus suum laborent
50.t qui longe . . . laborant
64.18 'si . . . fecero laborare'

lacrima:
4.57 cum lacrimis . . . confiteri
20.3 in . . . compunctione lacrimarum nos exaudiri
52.4 oret . . . in lacrimis

laqueus: 7.40
lassescere: 7.36
latere: 46.5
latus: 7.9; 22.5
laudare:
11.8 'Te Deum laudamus'

laus:
9.1 'os . . . adnuntiabit laudem'
10.t agatur nocturna laus
11.10 'Te decet laus'
12.4 laudes
13.11 sequantur laudes
16.1,3 'septies in die laudem dixi tibi'
16.5 referamus laudes creatori
38.3 'adnuntiabit laudem tuam'

lavare: 35.8,9; 53.13,14; 55.10,13

lectio:
4.55 lectiones sanctas . . . audire
8.3 qui . . . lectionum aliquid indigent
9.5 legantur . . . tres lectiones
9.6 post tertiam . . . lectionem
9.9 post . . . tres lectiones
9.10 lectio apostoli sequatur
10.2 lectiones . . . minime legantur
10.2 pro . . . tribus lectionibus una . . . dicatur
11.2 quattuor lectiones cum responsoriis
11.4 post quibus lectionibus sequantur
11.5 aliae quattuor lectiones
11.7 quattuor lectiones de novo testamento
11.9 legat . . . lectionem de Evangelia
11.12 aliquid de lectionibus breviandum est
12.4 lectionem de Apocalypsis
13.11 lectio una apostoli . . . recitanda
14.2 lectiones ad ipsum diem pertinentes

linguosus:
7.58 'vir linguosus non dirigitur'
linteum: 35.8
litania: 9.10; 12.4; 13.11; 17.8
littera: 54.t,1; 58.20; 61.13
locus: (30)
longe: 7.16; 50.t,1; 51.t
longinquus: 61.1
loquacitas:
49.7 subtrahat . . . de loquacitate
loqui:
Prol. 17 'labia . . . ne loquantur dolum'
Prol. 26 'qui loquitur veritatem'
1.12 melius est silere quam loqui
4.52 multum loqui non amare
4.53 verba vana . . . non loqui
6.3 rara loquendi . . . licentia
6.6 loqui . . . magistrum condecet
7.56 si linguam ad loquendum
prohibeat
7.56 si . . . non loquatur
7.60 cum loquitur monachus
7.60 pauca verba . . . loquatur
26.1 aut loqui cum eo
42.t post completorium nemo loquatur
42.8 nulla sit licentia . . . loqui aliquid
lucerna: 41.8
lucrari: 58.6
luctus: 25.3
lumbus: Prol. 21
lumen:
Prol. 9 apertis oculis . . . ad deificum
lumen
Prol. 13 'dum lumen' vitae 'habetis'
41.8 ut lumen lucernae non indigeant
lux:
Prol. 43 omnia per hanc lucis vitam
vacat implere
8.4 matutini qui incipiente luce
agendi sunt
41.8 luce . . . diei omnia consummentur
41.9 ut luce fiant omnia

M

macula: Prol. 25
magis: (10)
magister:
Prol. 1 Obsculta . . . praecepta magistri
2.24 dirum magistri pium patris
ostendat affectum
3.6 oboedire magistro
5.9 magistri iussio et perfecta discipuli opera . . . explicantur

6.6 docere magistrum condecet
magisterium:
Prol. 50 ab . . . magisterio discedentes
magistra:
1.6 experientia magistra
3.7 magistram sequantur regulam
magnificare:
Prol. 30 Dominum magnificant
magnopere: 27.5
magnus: 7.3
maior: (19)
maledicere:
4.32 maledicentes . . . non remaledicere
7.43 'maledicentes' se 'benedicent'
malignus:
Prol. 28 malignum diabolum . . . respuens
43.8 datur occasio maligno
64.2 maligno spiritu . . . inflati
malum: (14)
malus: (14)
mandatum:
Prol. 49 curritur via mandatorum Dei
2.12 mandata Domini . . . proponere
7.54 'ut discam mandata tua'
21.2 sollicitudinem gerant . . . secundum mandata Dei
26.1 mandatum ei dirigere
manducare: 51.1; 58.5
mane: 22.4; 48.3,14
manifestus: 1.1
mansuetudo:
66.4 mansuetudine timoris Dei reddat responsum
68.1 cum omni mansuetudine
manus: (15)
mappula: 55.19
mater:
7.4 'ablactatum super matrem'
64.19 discretionis matris virtutum
materia: 65.4
matta: 55.15
maturitas: 66.1
maturus: 31.1
matutini: (13)
maxilla: 7.42
maximus: (9)
mediare: 48.6
medicamen:
28.3 si exhibuit . . . medicamina scripturarum
medicus:
27.1 'non est opus sanis medicus'
27.2 ut sapiens medicus immittere
senpectas
28.2 abbas faciat quod . . . medicus
mediocris: 55.4; 60.8

meditare:
48.23   non possit meditare
58.5   ubi meditent
meditatio:
8.3   meditationi inserviatur
medius: 8.2; 16.4; 53.14
melior: (8)
meliorare: 36.9
membrum: 34.5
meminere:
2.1   meminere debet
2.30   meminere debet . . . abbas
2.30   meminere quod dicitur
2.35   meminerit scriptum
64.13   memineritque 'calamum . . . non conterendum'
memor:
2.6   memor semper abbas
2.26   memor periculi Heli
4.61   memores illud dominicum praeceptum
7.11   sit memor omnia quae
19.3   memores simus quod ait
31.8   memor illud . . . apostolicum
31.16   memor divini eloquii
memorare:
57.5   memorentur . . . Ananiae
memoriter:
10.2   pro . . . lectionibus una . . . memoriter dicatur
13.11   lectio . . . memoriter recitanda
mens:
2.5   in discipulorum mentibus conspargatur
19.7   mens nostra concordet voci
mensa: (17)
mensis: 58.9,12,13
mensura:
11.2   teneatur mensura
24.1   disciplinae mensura debet extendi
25.5   mensura vel hora qua praeviderit abbas
30.1   aetas . . . debet habere mensuras
39.t   de mensura cibus
40.t   de mensura potus
40.2   cum . . . scrupulositate . . . mensura victus aliorum constituitur
40.8   ut nec suprascripta mensura inveniri possit
49.6   super mensuram sibi indictam . . . offerat
55.8   abbas de mensura provideat
68.2   virium . . . mensuram . . . excedere
70.5   custodia sit sed . . . cum omni mensura

mensurare:
31.12   omnia mensurate faciat
48.9   omnia . . . mensurate fiant
55.8   vestimenta . . . mensurata
mentiri: 1.7
merces:
4.76   illa merces . . . recompensabitur
35.2   maior merces et caritas acquiritur
36.5   de talibus copiosior merces acquiritur
40.4   propriam se habituros mercedem
49.9   deputabitur . . . vanae gloriae non mercedi
59.4   offerre . . . in eleemosynam . . . pro mercede
64.6   recepturos mercedem bonam
mereri:
Prol. 21   ut mereamur . . . videre
Prol. 50   mereamur esse consortes
31.16   quid mereatur qui scandalizaverit
61.8   qui mereatur proici
meritum:
2.22   una praebeatur . . . secundum merita disciplina
7.21   docemur . . . merito
21.4   eligantur . . . secundum vitae meritum
62.6   pro vitae merito . . . promovere
63.1   ut vitae meritum discernit
64.2   vitae . . . merito . . . eligatur
metuere:
Prol. 7   metuendus Dominus
27.7   metuat prophetae comminationem
metus:
5.3   propter metum gehennae
70.3   'ut . . . metum habeant'
meus: (29)
miliarium: 7.42
militare:
Prol. 3   Christo . . . militaturos
Prol. 40   oboedientiae militanda
1.2   militans sub regula
58.10   lex sub qua militare vis
61.10   uni regi militatur
militia:
2.20   aequalem servitutis militiam baiulamus
minimus: (5)
ministerium:
35.10   vasa ministerii . . . cellarario reconsignet
46.1   in ministerio in pistrino
ministrare:
Prol. 41   adiutorium ministrare

31.8 'qui bene ministraverit'
38.6 sic sibi vicissim ministrent
64.21 dum bene ministraverit
minor: (21)
mirabilis: 7.3
miscere: 2.24
miser: 1.12
miseria:
61.7 ne eius miseria ... vitientur
misericordia:
4.74 de Dei misericordia numquam desperare
7.46 'in saeculum misericordia eius'
34.4 non extollatur pro misericordia
37.1 natura ... trahatur ad misericordiam
53.14 'suscepimus ... misericordiam tuam'
64.10 'superexaltet misericordiam iudicio'
misericors:
64.9 oportet ... eum esse ... misericordem
missa: 17.4,5,8,10; 35.14; 38.2; 60.4
mitis:
2.25 mites ... obsecrare
mittere: 5.13; 7.32,67
mixtum: 38.10
moderatio:
42.11 cum ... moderatione honestissima fiat
moderatus:
22.8 se moderate cohortentur
modestia:
22.6 cum omni gravitate et modestia
modicus: 8.2; 13.2; 55.14; 71.7
modo: Prol. 44
modulare: 11.2
modulatio: 18.12
modus: (13)
molendinum: 66.6
mollire: 1.6
momentum: 5.9
monachus: (42)
monasterialis: 1.2
monasterium:
Prol. 50; 1.3; 2.1,2,16; 3.1,8,9,12; 4.78; 7.55,63; 21.t; 29.t,1; 31.t,1,10,12; 32.t,1, 4; 33.1,5; 48.17; 51.1; 52.t; 53.16,19; 57.t,1,2,6; 58.15,24,26,28,29; 59.1,4, 5; 60.t,1,6,7,8; 61.1,2,6,13; 62.t,5,10; 63.1,8; 65.t,1,11,12,21; 66.t,1,6; 67.5,7; 69.t,1; 70.1; 71.9; 73.1
monitio: 2.40
monitum: Prol. 35
mons:
Prol. 23 'requiescet in monte'
27.8 relictis ... ovibus in montibus

monstrare:
2.12 factis ... praecepta monstrare
7.6 'ascendentes angeli' monstrabantur
7.57 monstrante scriptura
mora:
5.1 primus humilitatis gradus est oboedientia sine mora
5.4 moram pati nesciant
22.6 facto signo absque mora surgentes
31.16 sine ... mora offerat
42.7 per hanc moram lectionis
71.8 sine mora ... prostratus
morbidus:
2.8 morbidis ... actibus universa fuerit cura exhibita
28.8 ne una ovis morbida omnem gregem contagiet
mori: 64.18
morosus: 43.4; 58.16
mors:
Prol. 13 'ne tenebrae mortis ... comprehendant'
Prol. 38 'nolo mortem peccatoris'
Prol. 50 usque ad mortem ... perseverantes
2.10 poena sit ... ipsa mors
2.29 'liberabis animam ... a morte'
4.47 mortem ... suspectam habere
6.5 'mors et vita in manibus linguae'
7.24 mors secus introitum delectationis posita est
7.34 'oboediens usque ad mortem'
7.38 'propter te morte afficimur'
57.5 mortem quam illi ... pertulerunt
mortuus:
4.17 mortuum sepelire
mos:
2.31 multorum servire moribus
31.1 cellararius ... maturis moribus
32.1 de quorum moribus securus sit
36.9 a carnibus more solito ... abstineant
58.17 de ... conversatione morum suorum
72.5 infirmitates ... sive morum
73.1 honestatem morum aut initium conversationis ... habere
movere: 6.8
mox: (17)
multiloquium:
6.4 'in multiloquio non effugies'
7.57 'in multiloquio non effugitur peccatum'

20.3   non in multiloquio sed in puri-
        tate . . . exaudiri

multitudo: Prol. 14; 22.3
multus: (8)
munditia: 35.7
mundus: 7.70; 35.10
munusculum: 54.1
murmurare:
  5.17   in corde si murmuraverit
  5.18   cor . . . respicit murmurantem
  5.19   poenam murmurantium incurrit
  23.1   frater . . . murmurans vel in ali-
        quo contrarius
  40.8   et non murmurent
murmuratio:
  34.6   ne murmurationis malum . . .
        appareat
  35.13   sine murmuratione et gravi la-
        bore serviant
  40.9   ut absque murmurationibus sint
  41.5   absque iusta murmuratione
        faciant
  53.18   absque murmurationem serviant
murmuriosus:
  4.39   non murmuriosum
murmurium:
  5.14   quod iubetur non . . . cum mur-
        murio . . . efficiatur
mussitatio:
  38.5   ut nullius mussitatio . . . audia-
        tur

N

nam: (9)
namque: 2.23
nasci: 39.3
natalicium: 14.t
natura:
  Prol. 41   quod minus habet . . . natura
        possibile
  1.6   in plumbi natura molliti
  8.4   ad necessaria naturae exeant
  37.1   licet . . . natura humana traha-
        tur ad misericordiam
naturalis:
  7.68   velut naturaliter ex consuetu-
        dine . . . custodire
ne: (40)
nec: (30)
necessarius:
  8.4   quo fratres ad necessaria naturae
        exeant
  33.5   necessaria a patre sperare
  34.t   necessaria accipere
  38.6   quae vero necessaria sunt come-
        dentibus
  48.3   laborent quod necessarium
        fuerit

55.18   dentur . . . omnia quae sunt ne-
        cessaria
66.6   ita . . . ut omnia necessaria . . .
        exerceantur
necesse:
  65.8   necesse est sub hanc dissen-
        sionem animas periclitari
necessitas:
  7.33   necessitas parit coronam
  40.5   si aut loci necessitas . . . popo-
        scerit
  40.8   ubi . . . necessitas loci exposcit
  42.10   si necessitas hospitum super-
        venerit
  48.7   si . . . necessitas loci . . . exegerit
  55.19   ut omnis auferatur necessitatis
        excusatio
  66.7   ut non sit necessitas . . . vagandi
necnon: 73.5
neglectus:
  11.13   per cuius evenerit neglectum
neglegentia:
  36.6   ne . . . neglegentiam patiantur
  43.14   qui per neglegentiam suam . . .
        non occurrerit
  45.2   quod neglegentia deliquit
  49.3   neglegentias . . . diluere
neglegere:
  2.25   neglegentes . . . increpat
  7.22   de neglegentibus dictum est
  31.11   nihil ducat neglegendum
  32.4   si . . . neglegenter res . . . trac-
        taverit
  36.10   ne . . . neglegantur infirmi
  43.5   talibus neglegentibus . . . con-
        stituerit
  48.23   ita neglegens et desidiosus
  50.4   pensum non neglegant reddere
  64.6   peccatum si neglegant
  73.7   neglegentibus rubor confusionis
        est
nemo: 31.19; 42.t
neque: (13)
nequissimus: Prol. 7; 33.7
nescire: Prol. 37; 5.24; 7.50
nihil: (21)
nihilominus: 18.10
nimietas: 41.2
nimis: 18.24; 64.12,16
nimius: 30.3; 41.4; 64.16
nisi: (28)
nobilis:
  59.t   de filiis nobilium
  59.1   si quis . . . de nobilibus offerit
        filium
noctu: 4.76; 7.28
nocturnus: (11)
nolle:
  Prol. 7   qui eum sequi noluerint

Prol. 10   'nolite obdurare corda'
Prol. 38   'nolo mortem peccatoris'
1.9   quod noluerint hoc putant non licere
4.61   'quae . . . faciunt facere nolite'
5.14   cum responso nolentis
21.5   si emendare noluerit
28.t   emendare noluerint
45.2   qui noluit humilitate corrigere
59.4   si hoc facere noluerint
62.11   ut . . . oboedire regulae nolit
nomen: Prol. 30; 2.1,11; 58.19; 63.11,12
nominare: 1.10; 9.8
non: (144)
non(=ne): (61)
nonnus:
63.12   priores nonnos vocent
nonus: (16)
norma:
73.3   rectissima norma vitae humanae
noscere:
1.7   mentiri Deo . . . noscuntur
7.15   'Dominus novit cogitationes'
27.6   noverit . . . se . . . curam suscepisse
63.8   iuniorem se noverit
noster: (24)
notitia: 64.4
notus: 61.13
Novembris: 8.1,4; 10.1
novicius: 1.3; 58.5,11,20,21,23
noviter:
58.1   noviter veniens quis ad conversationem
novus: 9.8; 11.7; 55.9,12; 64.9; 73.3
nox:
8.t   de officiis . . . in noctibus
8.1   octava hora noctis surgendum est
8.2   amplius de media nocte pausetur
10.2   propter brevitatem noctium
15.2   omnibus noctibus . . . dicatur
16.4   'media nocte surgebam'
16.5   et 'nocte surgamus'
18.20   dividantur in . . . noctium vigilias
18.21   duodecim [psalmi] per unamquamque . . . noctem
47.1   nuntianda hora . . . dies noctesque sit cura
55.10   duas cucullas habere propter noctes
noxa:
25.1   qui gravioris culpae noxa tenetur
nudus:
4.15   'nudum vestire'

nullatenus (v. **ullatenus**): 54.1
nullus: (15)
numquam: (9)
nunc: Prol. 3; 17.1
nuntiare:
7.28   Domino factorum . . . opera nuntiantur
47.1   nuntianda hora operis Dei
47.1   aut ipse nuntiare
53.3   ut . . . nuntiatus fuerit hospes
nutrire: 64.14; 65.2

O

ob: 9.7
obauditus: 5.5
obdurare: Prol. 10
obiurgare: 23.3
oblatio: 59.1; 59.8
oblivio: 7.10
oblivisci: 62.4
obmutescere: 6.1
oboedientia:
Prol. 2   per oboedientiae laborem
Prol. 3   oboedientiae . . . arma
Prol. 40   praeceptorum oboedientiae
2.6   oboedientiae . . . discussio
2.17   nisi quem . . . oboedientia invenerit meliorem
5.t   de oboedientia
5.1   oboedientia sine mora
5.8   vicino oboedientiae pede
5.14   oboedientia acceptabilis erit
5.15   oboedientia . . . Deo exhibetur
7.34   omni oboedientia se subdat
7.35   si in ipsa oboedientia . . . patientiam amplectatur
58.7   sollicitus . . . ad oboedientiam
58.17   promittat . . . et oboedientiam
62.4   nec . . . obliviscatur regulae oboedientiam
68.1   cum . . . mansuetudine et oboedientia
71.1   oboedientiae bonum . . . exhibendum est
71.2   per . . . oboedientiae viam se ituros
72.6   oboedientiam sibi . . . impendant
oboedire:
2.25   oboedientes . . . obsecrare
3.5   ei cuncti oboediant
3.6   convenit oboedire magistro
4.61   in omnibus oboedire
5.5   'obauditu auris oboedivit'
5.12   voluptatibus oboedientes
5.17   cum malo animo si oboedit discipulus

59.1 si quis . . . offerit filium
59.2 sic eum offerant
59.4 si . . . aliquid offerre volunt
59.8 cum oblatione offerant filium

officina: 4.78

officium:
Prol. 39 sed si compleamus habitatoris officium
8.t de officiis divinis
16.2 nostrae servitutis officia persolvamus
31.17 impleat officium
35.1 nullus excusetur a coquinae officio
43.1 ad horam divini officii mox auditus fuerit signus
47.3 qui potest ipsud officium implere
48.22 qui variis officiis deputati sunt
53.3 occurratur . . . cum omni officio caritatis
53.17 qui ipsud officium bene impleant
53.19 in omnibus officiis monasterii ista sit consideratio
62.6 praeter officium altaris

omittere: 1.13
omnimodis: 18.23
omnimodo: 39.11
omnino: (19)
omnis: (192)

onus:
21.3 in quibus . . . abbas partiat onera sua
64.7 cogitet . . . quale onus suscepit
68.2 pondus oneris excedere

opera:
5.9 perfecta discipuli opera
48.t de opera manuum
48.12 deiungant ab opera sua
48.24 talis opera . . . iniungatur
49.4 abstinentiae operam damus
64.17 opera quam iniungit

operari:
Prol. 25 'qui . . . operatur iustitiam'
Prol. 30 operantem in se Dominum
4.78 diligenter operemur
28.5 ut Dominus . . . operetur salutem
48.6 operentur usque ad vesperam
48.14 operentur quod eis iniungitur
50.3 opus Dei ubi operantur

operarius:
Prol. 14 quaerens . . . operarium
7.49 operarium se malum iudicet
7.70 in operarium suum mundum . . . demonstrare

operire: 7.47
oportere: 5.16; 19.6; 41.t; 64.8,9; 65.17
opportune: 68.2
opprimere: 48.24

opprobrium:
Prol. 27 'opprobrium non accepit'
7.52 'ego . . . opprobrium hominum'
58.7 sollicitus . . . ad opprobria

optimus: 31.14

opus:
1.7 operibus servantes saeculo fidem
2.21 si meliores . . . in operibus bonis . . . inveniamur
4.t instrumenta bonorum operum
7.28 factorum nostrorum opera nuntiantur
16.t qualiter divina opera per diem agantur
19.2 ad opus divinum assistimus
25.3 solus sit ad opus
27.1 'non est opus sanis medicus'
28.2 quod si . . . defendere voluerit opera sua
41.4 si operis . . . habuerint
48.11 in opus suum laborent
48.23 iniungatur ei opus
52.5 qui simile opus non facit
53.18 exeant . . . in opera
55.6 et scapulare propter opera
55.16 propter opus peculiare
57.4 si . . . ex operibus artificum venumdandum est
63.3 de . . . operibus suis redditurus est . . . rationem

opus Dei:
7.63; 22.6,8; 43.t,3,6,10; 44.1,7; 47.t,1; 50.3; 52.2,5; 58.7; 67.2,3

opus esse:
34.1; 55.20 'prout cuique opus erat'
38.7 si quid . . . opus fuerit

orare:
4.72 pro inimicis orare
27.4 oretur pro eo
35.15 postulantes pro se orari
38.2 petat . . . pro se orari
43.13 dicant versu et orent
44.4 ut orent pro ipso
52.3 qui . . . peculiariter vult orare
52.4 secretius orare . . . intret et oret
53.4 primitus orent
58.23 ut orent pro eo

oratio:
Prol. 4 instantissima oratione deposcas
4.56 orationi . . . incumbere
4.57 in oratione Deo confiteri

7.14	Deum ... praesentem ostendit
7.38	ostendens fidelem pro Domino
7.41	ut ostendat sub priore ... nos esse
18.24	inertem ... servitium ostendunt monachi
61.4	si ... reprehendit aut ostendit

ostiarius: 66.t
otiositas: 48.1
otiosus:

6.8	verba otiosa ... damnamus
48.24	ut nec otiosi sint
67.4	otiosi sermonis

otium:

48.18	qui vacat otio

ovile: 1.8
ovis:

2.7	in ovibus ... invenire
2.10	inoboedientibus ... ovibus
2.39	discussionem ... de creditis ovibus
7.38	'ut oves occisionis'
27.5	ne aliquam de ovibus sibi creditis perdat
27.8	relictis ... ovibus in montibus
27.8	unam ovem quae erraverat quaerere
28.8	ne una ovis morbida ... gregem contagiet

P

paene: 48.3
paenitentia:

Prol. 37	'patientia Dei ad paenitentiam te adducit'
25.3	persistens in paenitentiae luctu

paenitere:

3.13	'post factum non paeniteberis'
43.6	publica satisfactione paeniteat

pagina: 73.3
palla: 59.2
pallium: 7.42
panis: 35.12; 39.4
par: 64.3
parare:

2.37	paret se ad rationem reddendam
22.6	parati sint monachi
48.12	et sint parati

parcere: 7.30
parcitas: 39.10
parcus: 40.6
parentes: 54.1,2; 59.1
parere: Prol. 6
parere: 7.33

pariter:

20.5	omnes pariter surgant
49.3	omnes pariter, et neglegentias ... diluere
53.4	primitus orent pariter
72.12	qui nos pariter ad vitam aeternam perducat

pars: 2.21; 13.14; 39.5; 64.1; 65.9
participari:

Prol. 50	passionibus Christi per patientiam participemur

participatio:

24.3	a mensae participatione privetur
43.15	ad mensae ... participationem

partire: 18.5,21; 21.3
parvipendere: 2.33
parvulus: Prol. 28
parvus: (6)
Pascha:

8.1	a kalendas Novembres usque in Pascha
8.4	a Pascha ... usque ad ... Novembres
10.1	a Pascha ... usque ad kalendas Novembres
15.1,4	a Pascha usque Pentecosten
41.1	a sancto Pascha ... reficiant
41.7	in quadragesima ... usque in Pascha
48.3	a Pascha usque kalendas Octobres
49.7	sanctum Pascha exspectet

passim: 70.t
passio:

Prol. 50	passionibus Christi ... participemur

pastor:

1.8	singuli sine pastore
2.7	culpae pastoris incumbere
2.8	pastoris ... diligentia
2.9	pastor eorum ... dicat
2.39	timens ... futuram discussionem pastoris de creditis ovibus
27.8	pastoris ... imitetur exemplum

patefacere:

4.50	seniori ... patefacere
46.5	senioribus patefaciat

pater:

Prol. 1	admonitionem pii patris ... excipe
Prol. 6	ut ... iratus pater suos non aliquando filios exheredet
2.3	'abba pater'
2.24	patris ... ostendat affectum
9.8	expositiones ... quae a ... patribus factae sunt

Pentecoste: 15.1,2,4; 41.1,2
per: (49)
percelebrare: 44.1
percipere: 25.5; 43.19
percomplere: 44.7
percutere: 2.29; 7.42
perdere:
27.5   aliquam de ovibus ... perdat
43.9   ut nec totum perdant
46.2   si quis ... quippiam aut perdi-
        derit
perdicere: 11.9
perditio:
65.9   eunt in perditionem
perducere:
72.12   ad vitam aeternam perducat
73.2   observatio perducat ... ad cel-
        situdinem perfectionis
perdurare: 68.4
peregrinus: 53.2,15; 56.1; 61.t,1
perfectio:
73.2   ad perfectionem ... qui festinat
73.2   perducat hominem ad celsitu-
        dinem perfectionis
perfectus:
5.9   perfecta discipuli opera
6.3   perfectis discipulis ... rara lo-
        quendi concedatur licentia
7.67   'caritatem Dei ... quae perfecta
        foris mittit timorem'
perferre: 57.5
perficere:
Prol. 4 ab eo perfici ... deposcas
4.22   iram non perficere
44.10   hoc perficiant usque dum ...
        dicat
73.8   hanc ... regulam ... perfice
pergere: Prol. 21
periclitari: 65.8
periculum: 2.26; 65.10
perire: 59.6
periurare: 4.27
perlegere: 11.10
permiscere: 22.7
permissio:
49.9   sine permissione patris spiritalis
permittere:
6.8   aperire os non permittimus
33.5   quod abbas non ... permiserit
42.6   lectis ... quantum hora permit-
        tit
43.15   non permittatur ad mensae ...
        participationem
52.5   non permittatur ... remorari in
        oratorio
57.1   faciant ... artes si permiserit ab-
        bas

64.14   non dicimus ut permittat nutriri
        vitia
71.3   cui non permittimus privata im-
        peria praeponi
perpendere: 50.2
perpetuus:
Prol. 7   perpetuam tradat ad poenam
Prol. 17 habere ... perpetuam vitam
Prol. 42 ad vitam ... pervenire perpe-
          tuam
Prol. 44 in perpetuo ... expediat
persecutio:
4.33   'persecutionem ... sustinere'
perseverantia:
58.9   si promiserit de stabilitate sua
        perseverantia
perseverare:
Prol. 50 in monasterio perseverantes
7.36   'qui perseveraverit usque in
        finem'
58.3   si veniens perseveraverit
persistere:
25.3   persistens in paenitentiae luctu
58.3   persistere petitioni
persolvere: 16.2; 18.25
persona:
2.16   non ... persona ... discernatur
2.20   'non est ... personarum accep-
        tio'
7.38   dicit ex persona sufferentium
34.2   ut personarum—quod absit—
        acceptio sit
59.3   per suffectam personam ... dant
64.3   consentientem personam ...
        elegerit
perspicere: 61.11,12
perstare: 60.2
persuadere: 40.6
perterrere: Prol. 48
pertinere: 14.2; 64.4
pertransire: 53.24
perturbare:
31.19   ut nemo perturbetur ... in domo
        Dei
41.2   nimietas aestatis non perturbat
61.2   non ... perturbat monasterium
pervenire:
Prol. 22 nisi ... curritur minime per-
          venitur
Prol. 42 ad vitam ... pervenire per-
          petuam
7.5   ad exaltationem illam caele-
        stem ... pervenire
7.67   'ad caritatem' Dei perveniet
63.19   usque dum ad intellegibilem
        aetatem perveniant
73.4   perveniamus ad creatorem
73.9   ad ... culmina ... pervenies

2.4   extra praeceptum Domini . . .
      docere
2.12 factis . . . praecepta monstrare
4.61 praeceptis abbatis . . . oboedi-
      re
4.61 memores . . . praeceptum
4.63 praecepta Dei . . . adimplere
7.42 praeceptum Domini in adver-
      sis . . . adimplentes
21.2 secundum mandata Dei et
      praecepta abbatis
23.1 praeceptis seniorum . . . con-
      temptor
23.2 secundum Domini . . . prae-
      ceptum admoneatur
54.1 accipere aut dare sine prae-
      cepto abbatis
65.17 observare praecepta regulae
70.6 qui praesumit aliquatenus
      sine praecepto abbatis
praecipere:
7.11 omnia quae praecepit Deus
7.25 scriptura praecipit . . . 'post con-
      cupiscentias . . . non eas'
51.2 nisi . . . ab abbate suo praecipia-
      tur
53.23 hospitibus . . . cui non praecipi-
      tur . . . neque colloquatur
62.3 nisi . . . ab abbate praecipitur
63.16 nisi ei praecipiat senior
praecipuus:
3.1   quotiens . . . praecipua agenda
      sunt
18.22 hoc praecipue commonentes ut
33.1 praecipue hoc vitium . . . ampu-
      tandum est
53.10 nisi . . . praecipuus sit dies ieiu-
      nii
64.20 praecipue . . . regulam . . . con-
      servet
praeclarus: Prol. 3
praedicare: 2.13
praedicatio: Prol. 31
praedicere: 5.9; 58.8
praeesse:
2.1   abbas qui praeesse dignus est
2.11 doctrina . . . praeesse discipulis
5.12 abbatem sibi praeesse deside-
      rant
64.8 prodesse magis quam praeesse
68.2 ei qui sibi praeest
praeferre:
63.7 excepto hos quos . . . abbas prae-
      tulerit
65.17 quantum praelatus est ceteris
praeiudicare: 63.5
praemittere:
53.5 nisi oratione praemissa

71.3 praemisso . . . abbatis . . . impe-
      rio
praeparare:
Prol. 40 praeparanda sunt corda
4.77 'quae praeparavit Deus his'
7.11 vita . . . quae . . . praeparata est
praeponere:
2.18 non . . . praeponatur ingenuus
4.21 nihil amori Christi praeponere
43.3 nihil operi Dei praeponatur
71.3 cui non permittitur privata im-
      peria praeponi
72.11 Christo . . . nihil praeponant
praepositura: 65.20
praepositus:
21.7; 62.7; 65.t,1,3,8,15,16,18; 71.3
praesens:
7.5   per praesentis vitae humilitatem
7.14 Deum semper praesentem
7.23 Deum credamus . . . praesentem
43.17 ad illum versum non fuerit
      praesens
55.9 in praesenti reponenda
58.19 ad nomen . . . abbatis praesentis
59.3 in praesenti petitione promittant
64.20 praesentem regulam . . . conser-
      vet
66.2 venientes . . . praesentem inve-
      niant
praesentia:
19.1 ubique credimus divinam esse
      praesentiam
praesumere:
3.4   non praesumant . . . defendere
3.9   neque praesumat . . . contende-
      re
3.10 quod si praesumpserit
20.1 non praesumimus nisi cum
      humilitate
26.1 si quis . . . praesumpserit . . . ex-
      communicato . . . se iungere
31.15 a quibus eum prohibuerit non
      praesumat
33.2 ne quis praesumat . . . dare
33.6 'ne . . . suum aliquid' . . . praesu-
      mat
38.8 nec praesumat . . . de . . . lec-
      tione . . . requirere
43.11 nec praesumant sociari choro
43.18 ne quis praesumat . . . quicquam
      cibi aut potus praesumere
44.6 psalmum . . . non praesumat in
      oratorio imponere
47.3 legere non praesumat
51.1 non praesumat foris manducare
54.2 non praesumat suscipere
54.5 qui . . . aliter praesumpserit
57.4 ne . . . fraudem praesumant

61.8   qui mereatur proici
62.10   proiciatur de monasterio
prolixus: 18.21
promissio:
58.19   de qua promissione ... faciant petitionem
promittere:
4.76   merces ... quam ... promisit
58.9   si ... promiserit de stabilitate
58.14   si ... promiserit se omnia custodire
58.17   promittat de stabilitate sua
59.3   de rebus ... suis ... promittant
60.9   si promittunt de observatione
promovere: 62.6
promptus: 7.59
pronomen: 2.2
pronuntiare:
7.48   'pronuntiabo adversum me'
7.51   si ... se ... viliorem ... pronuntiet
45.1   dum pronuntiat psalmum
pronus: 44.2
propendere: 39.4
propheta: (19)
propinquitas: 69.2
proponere: 2.12
proprius:
Prol. 3   abrenuntians propriis voluntatibus
1.11   propriis voluntatibus ... servientes
2.19   propria teneant loca
3.8   proprii ... cordis voluntatem
4.60   voluntatem propriam odire
5.7   voluntatem propriam deserentes
7.12   a peccatis ... voluntatis propriae
7.19   voluntatem ... propriam ita facere prohibemur
7.31   si propriam ... non amans voluntatem
29.1   qui proprio vitio egreditur
30.1   omnis aetas ... proprias debet habere mensuras
33.t   si debeant ... proprium habere
33.3   aliquid habere proprium
33.4   habere in propria voluntate
40.1   'proprium habet donum'
40.4   propriam se habituros mercedem
49.6   propria voluntate ... offerat
58.25   nec proprii corporis potestatem ... habiturum
58.26   exuatur rebus propriis

60.9   si ... promittunt ... propriam stabilitatem
propter: (24)
prosequi: 53.11
prospicere: 37.1
prosternere:
44.1   ante fores ... prostratus
53.7   prostrato omni corpore in terra
58.23   novicius prosternatur singulorum pedibus
67.3   prostrati solo
71.8   prostratus in terra
protegere: 73.9
protendere: 20.4
protervus: 3.9
prout: 34.1; 55.20; 65.12
provenire: 11.13
providentia: 41.4
providere: 55.8
providus: 3.6; 64.17
provincia: 1.10; 55.7; 61.1
provocare: 27.3
provolvere: 35.15
proximus: Prol. 27; 4.2
prudens:
61.4   tractet abbas prudenter
64.12   in ... correptione prudenter agat
64.14   prudenter et cum caritate ea amputet
psallere: (12)
psalmodia: 10.1; 17.1; 18.20
psalmus: (103)
psalterium: 8.3,24,32
publicanus: 7.65
publicare: 46.6
publicus: 23.3; 43.6
puer: (10)
pugna:
1.5   bene exstructi ... ad singularem pugnam eremi
pugnare:
1.4   contra diabolum ... pugnare
1.5   contra vitia ... pugnare
pulmentarium: 39.1,3
pulsare:
48.12   dum secundum signum pulsaverit
58.3   si ... perseveraverit pulsans
66.3   mox ut ... pulsaverit
purgare: 13.13
puritas:
20.2   cum ... puritatis devotione supplicandum est
20.3   in puritate cordis ... exaudiri
49.2   omni puritate vitam ... custodire
purus:
20.4   brevis debet esse et pura oratio

recedere: Prol. 2

recipere:

29.t	exeuntes . . . iterum recipi
29.2	in ultimo gradu recipiatur
29.3	tertio ita recipiatur
32.3	ut . . . sciat . . . quid recipit
35.11	ut sciat quod . . . recipit
44.5	si iusserit abbas recipiatur
58.29	petitionem . . . non recipiat
64.6	recepturos mercedem

recitare:

9.10	lectio . . . ex corde recitanda
13.11	lectio . . . memoriter recitanda
17.4	recitetur lectio una
17.8	lectio recitanda est
24.4	neque lectionem recitet

recolligere:

32.2	consignet . . . recolligenda
48.7	ad fruges recolligendas

recollocare: 43.8

recompensare: 4.76

reconsignare:

4.76	in die iudicii reconsignata
35.10	vasa . . . cellarario reconsignet

recreare: 4.14

rectus:

7.21	'viae quae putantur . . . rectae'
73.3	rectissima norma vitae
73.4	ut recto cursu perveniamus

recusare: 43.19

reddere:

Prol. 29	non se reddunt elatos
2.34	de quibus . . . rationem redditurus est
2.37	ad rationem reddendam
2.38	est redditurus . . . rationem
2.39	redditur . . . sollicitus
3.11	Deo rationem redditurum
4.29	'malum . . . non reddere'
31.9	pro his . . . rationem redditurus est
39.5	pars . . . servetur reddenda cenandis
50.4	servitutis pensum non neglegant reddere
55.9	vetera . . . reddant
55.12	quodcumque est vetere reddant
63.3	redditurus est Deo rationem
64.7	cui redditurus est rationem
65.22	Deo reddere rationem
66.1	responsum et reddere
66.4	reddat responsum

redigere: 7.50

redire:

Prol. 2	per . . . laborem redeas
4.73	in pacem redire
67.3	die quo redeunt

refectio: (8)

referre:

16.5	referamus laudes creatori
67.5	referre alio quaecumque . . . viderit

reficere: (10)

refugere: Prol. 48; 64.19

regere:

2.31	regere animas
2.34	animas suscepit regendas
2.37	suscipit animas regendas

regio: 55.2

regnum:

Prol. 21	'vocavit in regnum suum'
Prol. 22	in . . . regni tabernaculo . . . habitare
Prol. 50	regno eius . . . consortes
2.35	'quaerite regnum Dei'

regula:
1.t,2,6; 3.7,11; 7.55; 23.1; 37.1,2; 42.9; 58.9,12,13,15,16; 60.2,9; 62.4,7,11; 64.20; 65.17,18; 66.8; 73.t,1,5,8

regularis:
3.10; 32.5; 48.20; 54.5; 60.5; 62.3; 65.19; 67.6; 70.6

relaxare:

Prol. 36	dies ad indutias relaxantur
60.3	nec aliquid ei relaxabitur

relegere: 58.13

relinquere:

5.7	relinquentes statim . . . sua
5.8	quod agebant imperfectum relinquentes
27.8	relictis . . . ovibus in montibus
43.1	relictis omnibus

reliqui:
9.9; 10.3; 18.3,15,18,20; 41.3; 43.9; 63.7

reliquiae: 58.19

remaledicere: 4.32

remanere: 43.8; 59.6

remissio: 43.11

remittere: 7.48

remorari: 52.5

removere: 39.7

renes: 7.14

renuere: 43.19; 61.5

renuntiare:

7.13	facta . . . ab angelis . . . renuntiari

reparatio:

36.9	carnium esus . . . pro reparatione concedatur

reperire:

21.5	si . . . repertus fuerit reprehensibilis
23.1	seniorum . . . contemptor repertus fuerit
48.19	hic talis si . . . repertus fuerit

7.20   rogamus ... ut fiat illius vo-
       luntas
51.1   etiam si ... rogetur a quovis
58.20 alter ab eo rogatus scribat
60.1   si quis ... se suscipi rogaverit
Romanus: 13.10
rubor: 73.7

S

sabbatum: 13.9; 35.7
sacer: 27.9
sacerdos: 2.26; 60.t,1; 61.12; 62.t,8; 65.3
sacerdotium: 60.7; 62.1,4
sacrare:
16.2   septenarius sacratus numerus
31.10 vasa ... sacrata conspiciat
saecularis: 57.8
saeculum:
1.7   servantes saeculo fidem
4.20   saeculi actibus se facere alie-
       num
7.8   scala ... est vita in saeculo
7.46   'quoniam in saeculum miseri-
       cordia eius'
64.17 sive secundum Deum sive se-
       cundum saeculum sit opera
saepe: 3.3; 28.t; 62.9; 65.1; 66.8
sagacitas: 27.5
sagum: 55.15
saltem: 40.6
salubris:
3.5   quod salubrius esse iudicaverit
salus:
Prol. 48   refugias viam salutis
2.33   parvipendens salutem anima-
       rum
28.5   ut ... operetur salutem
salutare:
55.24 salutatis humiliter
salutaris:
2.9   'salutare ... dixi'
salutatio:
53.6   in ipsa ... salutatione ... exhi-
       beatur humilitas
salvare: 41.5
salvus:
7.36   'hic salvus erit'
25.4   'ut spiritus salvus sit'
Samuel: 63.6
sanare:
28.6   si nec ... sanatus fuerit
30.3   coerceantur ut sanentur
71.8   benedictione sanetur ... com-
       motio
sanctus:
Prol. 23   'in monte sancto tuo'

Prol. 35   suis sanctis monitis
Prol. 40   sanctae ... oboedientiae mili-
           tanda
1.9   hoc dicunt sanctum
2.12   omnia bona et sancta
4.55   lectiones sanctas ... audire
4.62   non velle dici sanctum
5.3   propter servitium sanctum
6.3   de ... sanctis et aedificatio-
       num eloquiis
7.70   Spiritu Sancto ... demon-
       strare
9.7   ob ... reverentiam sanctae
       Trinitatis
14.t   in nataliciis sanctorum
14.1   in sanctorum festivitatibus ...
       ita agatur
15.1   a sanctum Pascha usque Pen-
       tecosten
18.25 sanctos patres nostros uno die
       ... implesse
21.1   fratres ... sanctae conversa-
       tionis
23.1   contrarius ... sanctae regulae
38.10 propter communionem sanc-
       tam
41.1   a sancto Pascha ... reficiant
49.3   neglegentias ... his diebus
       sanctis diluere
49.6   'cum gaudio Sancti Spiritus'
49.7   sanctum Pascha exspectet
58.18 coram Deo et sanctis eius
58.19 petitionem ad nomen sancto-
       rum
64.18 discretionem sancti Iacob
65.18 contemptor sanctae regulae
73.2   doctrinae sanctorum patrum
73.4   quis liber sanctorum ... pa-
       trum
73.5   regula sancti ... Basilii
sane:
18.5; 44.6   ita sane ut
48.17 ante omnia sane deputentur
61.4   si qua sane rationabiliter ... re-
       prehendit
sanus:
27.1   'non est opus sanis medicus'
27.6   super sanas [animas] tyranni-
       dem
35.10 vasa ... sana cellarario consig-
       net
36.8   balnearum usus ... sanis ... et
       ... iuvenibus tardius conce-
       datur
64.1   pars ... saniore consilio elegerit
Saphira: 57.5
sapiens:
Prol. 33   'similabo ... viro sapienti'

7.61	sapiens verbis innotescit paucis
19.4	'psallite sapienter'
27.2	ut sapiens medicus
27.2	seniores sapientes fratres
28.2	faciat quod sapiens medicus
31.1	cellararius . . . eligatur . . . sapiens
40.7	'vinum apostatare facit . . . sapientes'
53.22	domus Dei a sapientibus et sapienter administretur
66.1	ad portam . . . ponatur senex sapiens

sapientia:

21.4	eligantur . . . secundum . . . sapientiae doctrinam
64.2	sapientiae doctrina eligatur

sarabaita: 1.6,11
satietas: 40.5,6
satis: 51.t
satisfacere:

11.13	digne inde satisfaciat Deo
43.12	ut satisfaciat reus
44.t	qui excommunicantur quomodo satisfaciant
44.3	abbas iudicaverit satisfactum esse
44.8	et sic satisfaciat
44.9	in oratorio satisfaciant
46.3	ipse ultro satisfecerit
71.8	iaceat satisfaciens

satisfactio:

5.19	si non cum satisfactione emendaverit
24.4	neque . . . recitet usque ad satisfactionem
24.7	satisfactione congrua veniam consequatur
27.3	provocent ad humilitatis satisfactionem
43.6	publica satisfactione paeniteat
43.11	sociari choro . . . usque ad satisfactionem
43.16	sublata ei portione sua vinum usque ad satisfactionem
44.8	quiescat . . . ab hac satisfactione
45.1	nisi satisfactione ibi . . . humiliatus fuerit

scala: 7.6,8,9
scamnum: 9.5
scandalizare:

31.16	ut non scandalizentur
31.16	'qui scandalizaverit unum de pusillis'

scandalum:

13.12	oratio dicatur . . . propter scandalorum spinas

65.1	scandala gravia . . . oriantur
65.2	scandala nutriunt
69.3	occasio scandalorum oriri potest

scapulare: 55.6
schola:

Prol. 45	constituenda est . . . dominici schola servitii

scientia: 57.2
scilicet: 18.11,21
scire: (32)
scribere: (14)
scriptura:

Prol. 8;	7.1,19,21,25,33,36,40,45,57; 28.3; 42.4

scrupulositas:

40.2	cum aliqua scrupulositate a nobis mensura . . . constituitur

scrutari: 7.14
scrutinare: 55.16
scurrilitas:

6.8	scurrilitates . . . damnamus
43.2	ut non scurrilitas inveniat fomitem
49.7	subtrahat . . . de loquacitate, de scurrilitate

secrete:

23.2	admoneatur . . . secrete
27.3	quasi secrete consolentur fratrem
52.4	secretius orare

secundum: (15)
securus: 1.5; 7.39; 21.3; 32.1
secus: 7.24
sed: (85)
sedere: 7.63; 9.5; 42.3; 43.8; 53.8; 63.16
sedile: 9.7
semel: 21.5; 23.2; 33.7; 48.19
semper: (43)
senex: 37.t,1; 66.1
senior: (13)
senpecta: 27.2
sententia:

5.13	Domini imitantur sententiam
25.3	terribilem apostoli sententiam
55.20	sententia Actuum Apostolorum quia 'dabatur . . .'
68.4	in sua sententia prioris imperium perduraverit

sentire:

7.4	'si non humiliter sentiebam'
65.8	contraria . . . abbas praepositusque sentiunt
71.7	si . . . senserit animos . . . iratos

seorsum: 43.5,7
separare: 72.1,2
sepelire: 4.17
September: 41.6
septenarius: 16.2

septimana: 18.24,25; 35.7,16
septimanarius: 35.t,12
sequestrare:
  18.14 qui ... ex eis sequestrantur
  43.16 sequestratus a consortio
sequi:
  Prol.7,17; 3.7,8; 4.10; 5.8; 9.4,9,10;
  11.4; 13.11; 17.1; 72.7
sera: 41.1
sermo:
  Prol. 3 ad te ... sermo dirigitur
  2.14 'proiecisti sermones meos'
  31.13 sermo responsionis porrigatur
        bonus
  31.14 'sermo bonus super datum op-
        timum'
  67.4 auditus ... otiosi sermonis
  73.3 sermo divinae auctoritatis ...
        est ... norma
servare:
  1.7 servantes saeculo fidem
  2.23 apostolicam ... formam servare
  18.10 dispositionem uniformem ...
        servatam
  39.5 tertia pars a cellarario servetur
  39.10 pueris ... non eadem servetur
        quantitas
  39.10 servata ... parcitate
  58.14 imperata servare
  60.2 se ... disciplinam servaturum
  62.7 regulam ... servare sciat
servire:
  1.11 gulae illecebris servientes
  2.31 multorum servire moribus
  19.3 'servite Domino in timore'
  35.1 fratres sibi ... serviant
  35.6 invicem serviant
  35.13 sine ... gravi labore serviant
  36.1 sicut ... Christo ita eis serviatur
  36.4 in honorem Dei sibi servire
  36.4 fratres suos servientes sibi
  53.18 absque murmuratione serviant
  61.10 uni Domino servitur
servitium:
  Prol. 45 constituenda est ... dominici
        schola servitii
  2.18 convertenti ex servitio
  5.3 haec convenit ... propter ser-
        vitium sanctum
  18.24 devotionis suae servitium
        ostendunt
servitor:
  36.7 quibus fratribus infirmis sit ...
        servitor timens Deum
  36.10 ne ... a servitoribus neglegan-
        tur infirmi
  38.11 cum ... servitoribus reficiat

servitus:
  2.20 servitutis militiam baiulamus
  16.2 nostrae servitutis officia persol-
        vamus
  49.5 augeamus nobis aliquid solito
        pensu servitutis
  50.4 servitutis pensum ... reddere
servus:
  Prol. 7 ut nequissimos servos ... tra-
        dat ad poenam
  2.20 'sive servus sive liber...
        unum sumus'
  64.21 audiat ... quod servus bonus
seu: 5.3; 32.1
si: (146)
si: (interr.): (11)
sibi: (121)
sic: (25)
sicut: (26)
significare: 47.t
significatio: 34.6
signum:
  20.5 facto signo a priore
  22.6 facto signo absque mora surgen-
        tes
  38.7 sonitu ... signi ... petatur
  43.1 mox auditus fuerit signus
  48.12 facto ... primo signo nonae ho-
        rae
  48.12 dum secundum signum pul-
        saverit
  58.20 novicius signum faciat
silentium:
  38.5 summum fiat silentium
  42.1 omni tempore silentium ... stu-
        dere
  48.5 pausent ... cum omni silentio
  52.2 cum summo silentio exeant
silere:
  1.12 melius est silere
  6.1 'silui a bonis'
Silo: 2.26
similare: Prol. 33
similis: 26.2; 43.17; 50.4; 52.5; 59.7; 67.7
simplex: 2.12; 52.4; 59.8; 61.3
simul: 25.1; 43.13
sin: 2.19; 22.3; 23.5; 60.5
sincerus: 72.10
sine: (30)
sinere: 22.3; 66.1
singillatim: 17.2
singularis: 1.5
singuli: (12)
sive: (8)
sobrius:
  31.1 cellararius ... sobrius, non mul-
        tum edax

stramentum: 55.15
strenuus: 18.25
studere:
31.12   neque avaritiae studeat
42.1   silentium debent studere
64.15   studeat plus amari
stultus:
2.28   'stultus . . . non corrigitur'
7.59   'stultus in risu exaltat vocem'
suadere:
Prol. 28   diabolum aliqua suadentem
           sibi
49.2   suademus istis diebus . . . vi-
        tam . . . custodire
58.28   suadenti diabolo consenserit
61.9   suadeatur ut stet
suasio:
Prol. 28   diabolum . . . cum ipsa sua-
           sione sua
2.31   alium . . . suasionibus
sub:
1.2   militans sub regula vel abbate
2.20   sub uno Domino . . . baiulamus
2.38   sub cura sua . . . habere
7.41   sub priore . . . esse
17.2   sub una gloria
31.15   habeat sub cura sua
35.6   sub caritate invicem serviant
43.13   sub uno omnes accedant
58.10   lex sub qua militare vis
58.16   sub tam morosam deliberatio-
        nem . . . excusare
59.3   promittant sub iureiurando
65.8   sub hanc dissensionem peri-
        clitari
65.9   qui sub ipsis sunt
subdere:
7.34   omni oboedientia se subdat
        maiori
23.5   vindictae corporali subdatur
34.7   districtiori disciplinae subdatur
60.5   disciplinae regulari subditum
62.3   disciplinae regulari subdendum
62.11   subdi aut oboedire regulae
subiacere:
3.10   regulari disciplinae . . . subia-
        ceat
23.4   excommunicationi subiaceat
32.5; 54.5; 70.6   disciplinae regulari
        subiaceat
33.8   correptioni subiaceat
42.9   gravi vindictae subiaceat
45.1   maiori vindictae subiaceat
46.4   maiori subiaceat emendationi
48.20   correptioni regulari subiaceat
55.17   gravissimae disciplinae sub-
        iaceat
67.6   vindictae regulari subiaceat

71.9   corporali vindictae subiaceat
subiectio:
3.4   cum omni humilitatis subiec-
        tione
6.7   cum . . . subiectione reverentiae
        requirantur
subiungere: 9.2
subsellium: 11.2
subsequi:
7.39   subsequuntur gaudentes
7.41   subsequitur dicens
8.4   mox matutini . . . subsequantur
10.2   responsorius subsequatur
11.10   subsequatur mox abbas hym-
        num
35.17   subsequatur ingrediens
substantia:
2.35   ne causetur de minori . . . sub-
        stantia
31.10   cunctamque substantiam . . .
        conspiciat
31.12   stirpator substantiae monasterii
31.13   cui substantia non est
32.1   substantia monasterii . . . prae-
        videat abbas fratres
subtrahere:
13.2   dicatur . . . subtrahendo modice
43.4   omnino subtrahendo . . . dici
49.7   subtrahat corpori suo de cibo
subvenire: 4.18
succedere: 32.3
succingere: Prol. 21
sufferre:
4.30   iniuriam . . . patienter sufferre
7.38   dicit ex persona sufferentium
sufficere:
1.5   pugnare sufficiunt
39.1   sufficere . . . ad refectionem
39.3   duo pulmentaria . . . sufficiant
39.4   panis libra . . . sufficiat
40.3   heminam vini per singulos suf-
        ficere
44.10   et dicat: Sufficit
53.22   lecti strati sufficienter
55.4   mediocribus locis sufficere . . .
        cucullam
55.10   sufficit . . . monacho duas tuni-
        cas . . . habere
55.15   sufficiant matta, sagum
59.3   per suffectam personam . . . ali-
        quid dant
suggerere:
20.1   si cum . . . potentibus volumus
        aliqua suggerere
49.8   hoc . . . abbati suo suggerat
65.5   dum ei suggeritur
68.2   opportune suggerat
suggestio: 68.4

sumere: Prol. 3; 64.19

sumministrare: 2.40

summus:
7.5	summae humilitatis . . . culmen attingere
38.5	summum fiat silentium
42.11	cum summa gravitate . . . fiat
43.1	summa cum festinatione curratur
52.2	cum summo silentio exeant

super: (22)

superare: 7.39

superbia:
7.2	exaltationem genus esse superbiae
21.5	decani si . . . quis inflatus superbia repertus fuerit
28.2	in superbia elatus
62.2	caveat . . . superbiam
65.2	spiritu superbiae inflati

superbire:
65.4	materia ei datur superbiendi
65.13	unus non superbiat
65.18	praepositus si repertus fuerit . . . superbire
68.3	suggerat non superbiendo

superbus:
2.28	superbos . . . castigatio . . . coerceat
4.34	'non esse superbum'
23.1	frater . . . aut superbus aut murmurans

superesse: 18.20

superexaltare:
64.10	semper 'superexaltet misericordiam iudicio'

superfluitas:
36.4	non superfluitate sua contristent fratres
61.2	non . . . superfluitate sua perturbat

superfluus:
55.11	quod supra fuerit superfluum est
61.6	si superfluus aut vitiosus inventus fuerit

superior: 61.11

supervenire:
42.10	necessitas hospitum supervenerit
53.1	supervenientes hospites . . . suscipiantur
53.16	supervenientes hospites . . . non inquietentur fratres
61.1	si . . . monachus . . . supervenerit

supplicare:
20.2	cum . . . puritatis devotione supplicandum est

supplicatio:
9.10	supplicatio litaniae
60.2	si . . . perstiterit in hac supplicatione

supra: (10)

supradictus: 8.4; 58.11

suprascriptus:
9.1; 14.2; 18.3,16; 40.8; 61.12

surgere:
Prol. 8	'de somno surgere'
8.1	octava hora . . . surgendum est
8.2	iam digesti surgant
9.7	de sedilia sua surgant
11.1	temperius surgatur
11.2	nisi . . . tardius surgant
11.3	cum reverentia surgant
16.4	'media nocte surgebam'
16.5	et 'nocte surgamus'
20.5	omnes pariter surgant
22.6	surgentes festinent invicem se praevenire
22.8	surgentes . . . ad opus Dei . . . se . . . cohortentur
42.3	mox surrexerint a cena
48.5	surgentes a mensa
63.16	minor surgat

surrepere: 40.5

surripere:
39.7	ut numquam surripiat monacho indigeries
57.7	non surripiat avaritiae malum
67.4	ne . . . surripuerint in via visus

surrogare:
21.6	alter in loco eius . . . surrogetur
65.20	alius . . . in loco eius surrogetur

susceptio:
53.15	maxime susceptioni cura . . . exhibeatur

suscipere:
2.11	cum aliquis suscipit nomen abbatis
2.31	arduam rem suscipit
2.34	animas suscepit regendas
2.37	qui suscipit animas regendas
27.6	curam suscepisse animarum
53.t	de hospitibus suscipiendis
53.1	hospites tamquam Christus suscipiantur
53.1	'suscepistis me'
53.7	Christus . . . adoretur, qui et suscipitur
53.8	suscepti . . . hospites ducantur ad orationem
53.14	'suscepimus Deus misericordiam'
53.15	magis Christus suscipitur
54.t	litteras vel aliquid suscipere
54.2	non praesumat suscipere illud

54.3 si iusserit suscipi
58.t de disciplina suscipiendorum fratrum
58.14 suscipiatur in congregatione
58.16 licuit . . . aut suscipere
58.17 suscipiendus . . . in oratorio
58.21 'suscipe me Domine'
60.1 in monasterio se suscipi
61.t de . . . peregrinis qualiter suscipiantur
61.3 suscipiatur quanto tempore cupit
61.8 si petierit suscipiatur
61.13 ad habitandum suscipiat
64.7 cogitet . . . quale onus suscepit
68.1 suscipiat . . . imperium
suscitare: 65.7
suspendere:
25.1 suspendatur a mensa
suspicere:
4.47 mortem . . . suspectam habere
64.13 suamque fragilitatem . . . suspectus sit
suspicio:
59.6 nulla suspicio remaneat
suspiciosus:
64.16 non sit . . . nimis suspiciosus
sustinere:
4.33 'persecutionem . . . sustinere'
7.36 sustinens non lassescat
7.37 'sustine Dominum'
7.38 contraria sustinere debere
7.43 falsos fratres sustinent
35.14 usque ad missas sustineant
38.10 ne . . . grave sit ei ieiunium sustinere
suus: (125)
synaxis: 17.7

T

tabernaculum:
Prol. 22 in . . . regni tabernaculo . . . habitare
Prol. 23 'habitabit in tabernaculo'
Prol. 24 viam . . . tabernaculi
Prol. 39 de habitatore tabernaculi
tabula: 33.3; 55.19
tacere:
6.2 a bonis eloquiis . . . tacere
6.6 tacere . . . discipulum convenit
7.30 'haec fecisti et tacui'
taciturnitas:
6.t de taciturnitate
6.2 propter taciturnitatem debet taceri
6.3 propter taciturnitatis gravitatem
7.56 taciturnitatem habens

42.9 praevaricare hanc taciturnitatis regulam
tacitus:
7.35 tacite . . . patientiam complectatur
taeter: 1.6
talis: (23)
tam: (8)
tamdiu: 71.8
tamen: (36)
tamquam: 4.2; 53.1
tandem: Prol. 8
tantum: (7)
tantundem: 2.8
tardus:
5.14 non tarde . . . efficiatur
11.12 nisi . . . tardius surgant
31.1 cellararius . . . non tardus, non prodigus
36.8 balnearum usus . . . tardius concedatur
43.t ad mensam tarde occurrunt
taxare: 18.18
temere: 3.7
temperare:
8.4 sic temperetur hora
41.5; 64.19 sic omnia temperet
41.9 sic temperetur ut luce fiant omnia
49.4 si ab . . . vitiis temperamus
64.17 discernat et temperet
temperies: 55.1
temperius: 11.1; 48.6
templum:
53.14 'in medio templi tui'
tempus: (27)
tenebrae: Prol. 13
tenere:
Prol. 28 cogitatos . . . tenuit et allisit
2.19 propria teneant loca
4.24 dolum . . . non tenere
10.1 psalmodiae quantitas teneatur
11.2 in . . . vigiliis teneatur mensura
11.11 qui ordo . . . die dominico teneatur
14.2 modus . . . teneatur
25.1 qui . . . culpae noxa tenetur
32.3 ex quibus abbas brevem teneat
37.2 ullatenus . . . districtio regulae teneatur
60.4 missas tenere
tepidus:
5.14 non tepide . . . efficiatur
18.25 quod nos tepidi . . . persolvamus
tergere: 35.8
terminare: 17.7,9

terra:
7.58 'non dirigitur super terram'
7.63 defixis in terram aspectibus
7.65 fixis in terram oculis
44.2 posito in terra capite
44.7 proiciat se in terra
53.7 prostrato . . . corpore in terra
71.8 prostratus in terra

terrenus:
2.33 sollicitudinem de rebus terrenis

terribilis:
25.3 terribilem apostoli sententiam

terror:
2.24 miscens . . . terroribus blandimenta
53.15 divitum terror . . . exigit honorem

testamentum:
2.14 'assumis testamentum meum per os tuum'
9.8 codices autem legantur . . . veteris testamenti
10.2 una de veteri testamento memoriter dicatur
11.7 legantur . . . lectiones de novo testamento
73.3 sermo divinae auctoritatis veteris ac novi testamenti

testimonium:
4.7 'non falsum testimonium dicere'
21.1 fratres boni testimonii
62.9 episcopus adhibeatur in testimonio
64.19 testimonia discretionis

testis: 59.8

timere:
Prol. 29 timentes Dominum
2.36 'nihil deest timentibus eum'
2.39 timens . . . discussionem
4.44 diem iudicii timere
7.11 vita . . . timentibus Deum praeparata
31.2 cellararius . . . timens Deum
36.7 servitor timens Deum
48.20 ut ceteri timeant
64.15 plus amari quam timeri
65.15 fratrum timentium Deum
72.9 amore Deum timeant

timor:
Prol. 12 'timorem Domini docebo vos'
3.11 cum timore Dei . . . omnia faciat
5.9 in velocitate timoris Dei
7.10 timorem Dei . . . ante oculos . . . ponens
7.67 'foris mittit timorem'
7.69 non iam timore gehennae

11.9 cum honore et timore
19.3 'servite Domino in timore'
53.21 cuius animam timor Dei possidet
64.1 secundum timorem Dei
66.4 mansuetudine timoris Dei

tolerantia:
40.4 quibus . . . donat Deus tolerantiam abstinentiae

tolerare:
72.5 infirmitates tolerent

tonsura:
1.7 mentiri Deo per tonsuram

totus: (18)

trabes: 2.15

tractare:
3.2 tractet apud se
32.4 si . . . neglegenter res monasterii tractaverit
61.4 tractet abbas prudenter

tradere:
Prol. 7 tradet ad poenam
25.4 'traditum eiusmodi hominem in interitum'

trahere:
37.1 licet . . . natura . . . trahatur ad misericordiam

transgredi:
69.4 si . . . haec transgressus fuerit

transigere:
57.4 per quorum manus transigenda sint

transire:
13.12 agenda . . . vespertina non transeat
25.6 nec a quoquam benedicatur transeunte
57.3 per eam non transeat
63.16 transeunte maiore minor surgat

transitorius: 2.33

tremere:
2.6 in tremendo iudicio Dei
7.64 tremendo iudicio Dei repraesentari

tremor:
47.4 cum . . . gravitate et tremore fiat
50.3 cum tremore divino flectentes genua

trepidus: 5.14

tribuere:
31.13 cui substantia non est, quod tribuatur
58.1 non ei facilis tribuatur ingressus
59.3 tribuunt occasionem habendi

tribulatio:
4.18 in tribulatione subvenire
7.40 'posuisti tribulationes in dorso'

Trinitas:
9.7   ob ... reverentiam sanctae Trinitatis
tristitia:
27.3   'ne ... tristitia absorbeatur'
35.3   ut non cum tristitia hoc faciant
triticum: 64.21
tu: (31)
tueri:
69.1   defendere ... aut ... tueri
tunc: (14)
tunica: 7.42; 55.4,10,14,19
turbulentus:
31.1   cellararius ... non elatus non turbulentus
64.16   non sit turbulentus
tuus: (17)
typhus: 31.16
tyrannis:
27.6   suscepisse ... super sanas tyrannidem
65.2   assumentes sibi tyrannidem

U

ubi: (11)
ubicumque: 7.63; 63.15
ubique: 19.1
ubiubi: 46.2; 63.19
ullatenus: 37.2; 53.23; 60.5
ullus: 7.68
ultimus: (9)
ultro: 46.3
unde: (7)
unguentum: 28.3
uniformis: 18.10
universus:
2.8   universa fuerit cura exhibita
7.38   universa etiam contraria sustinere
7.68   universa quae prius ... observabat
20.2   Deo universorum cum omni humilitate ... supplicandum est
unusquisque: (7)
urere: 65.22
usque: (48)
usquequaque: 7.66
ustio: 28.3
usus: 36.8; 59.5
ut (final. et hortat.): (85)
ut (consec.): (43)
ut (modal.): (26)
ut (tempor.): (3)
uterque: 2.6; 48.2
uti: (5)
utilis:
3.2   quod utilius iudicaverit
7.18   dicat ... utilis frater

32.2   ut iudicaverit utile
42.4   non erit utile illa hora ... audire
72.7   quod sibi utile iudicat
utilitas:
2.7   utilitatis minus ... invenire
3.12   si ... minora agenda sunt in monasterii utilitatibus
35.1   in causa gravis utilitatis ... occupatus fuerit
35.5   maioribus utilitatibus occupantur
65.12   ordinetur ... omnis utilitas monasterii
utinam: 18.25

V

vacare:
Prol. 43   dum adhuc vacat
Prol. 43   dum ... vacat implere
43.8   fabulis vacat
48.4,10,22   lectioni vacent
48.13,14   vacent lectionibus suis
48.17   vacant fratres lectioni
48.18   qui vacat otio
48.23   ut non vacet
53.20   quando vacant oboediant
vadere: 7.42
vagari: 66.1,7
vagus: 1.11
vanus:
4.53   verba vana ... non loqui
49.9   deputabitur ... vanae gloriae
vapulare: 45.3
varius: 48.22
vas:
31.10   omnia vasa ... ac si altaris vasa sacrata conspiciat
35.10   vasa ministerii sui ... cellarario reconsignet
64.12   ne ... frangatur vas
vel: (104)
velle: (30)
velocitas: 5.9
velox: 7.5
velut(i): 5.9; 7.49,68
venerare:
4.70   seniores venerare
venia: 24.7
venire:
Prol. 12   'venite filii'
Prol. 34   'venerunt flumina'
1.13   ad coenobitarum ... genus ... veniamus
5.13; 7.32   'non veni facere voluntatem'
18.16   quia minus veniunt tres psalmi
44.4   dum iussus ab abbate venerit

vilis:
7.51 se inferiorem et viliorem ...
      pronuntiet
55.7 quod vilius comparari possit
57.8 vilius detur
vilitas:
7.49 si omni vilitate ... contentus sit
villosus: 55.5
vindicta:
23.5 vindictae corporali subdatur
26.2 sortiatur excommunicationis
      vindictam
28.1 verberum vindicta ... procedant
42.9 gravi vindictae subiaceat
45.1 maiori vindictae subiaceat
67.6 vindictae regulari subiaceat
71.9 corporali vindictae subiaceat
vinolentus: 4.35
vinum: 40.3,6,7; 43.16
violare: 53.10
violentus: 48.24
vir: Prol. 33; 7.58
virga: 2.29; 28.3
virtus:
4.1 'diligere ... tota virtute'
7.69 delectatione virtutum
49.2 paucorum est ista virtus
64.19 discretionis matris virtutum
73.6 instrumenta virtutum
73.9 ad ... doctrinae virtutumque
     culmina ... pervenies
vis: 68.2
visitare:
4.16 'infirmum visitare'
36.2 'et visitastis me'
visus: 67.4
vita:
Prol. 13 'dum lumen' vitae 'habetis'
Prol. 15 'qui vult vitam'
Prol. 17 habere veram et perpetuam
         vitam
Prol. 20 demonstrat ... viam vitae
Prol. 36 vitae dies relaxantur
Prol. 42 ad vitam ... pervenire perpe-
         tuam
Prol. 43 haec omnia per hanc lucis
         vitam vacat implere
1.10 tota vita ... hospitantur
4.46 vitam aeternam ... desiderare
4.48 actus vitae suae ... custodire
5.3 propter ... gloriam vitae ae-
    ternae
5.10 ad vitam aeternam gradiendi
     amor
5.11 'via ... quae ducit ad vitam'
6.5 'mors et vita in manibus lin-
    guae'

7.5 per praesentis vitae humilita-
    tem ascenditur
7.8 scala ... nostra est vita in
    saeculo
7.11 vita aeterna ... animo ...
     evolvat
21.4 eligantur ... secundum vitae
     meritum
32.1 de quorum vita ... securus sit
42.3 legat ... Vitas Patrum
49.1 vita monachi quadragesimae
     debet observationem ha-
     bere
49.2 puritate vitam ... custodire
61.5 potuit eius vita dinosci
61.12 eorum talem ... esse vitam
62.6 pro vitae merito eum promo-
     vere
63.1 ut vitae meritum discernit
64.2 vitae ... merito ... eligatur
72.2 ducit ... ad vitam aeternam
72.12 qui nos ... ad vitam aeternam
      perducat
73.3 norma vitae humanae
73.5 Instituta et Vitas eorum
vitare: 70.1
vitiare: 61.7
vitiosus:
61.6 si superfluus aut vitiosus inven-
     tus fuerit
65.18 praepositus si repertus fuerit vi-
      tiosus
vitium:
Prol. 47 emendationem vitiorum
1.5 contra vitia carnis ... pugnare
2.40 a vitiis emendatus
7.12 custodiens se ... a ... vitiis
7.70 in operarium ... mundum a
     vitiis
13.13 purgent se ab ... vitio
29.1 qui proprio vitio egreditur
33.1 hoc vitium radicitus am-
     putandum est
33.7 huic nequissimo vitio ... de-
     lectari
43.14 qui ... vitio non occurrerit
49.4 si ab omnibus vitiis tem-
     peramus
55.18 ut hoc vitium peculiaris ...
      amputetur
64.3 vitiis suis ... consentientem
     personam
64.4 vitia ... in notitia episcopi ...
     claruerint
64.11 oderit vitia
64.14 nutriri vitia
72.2 zelus ... qui separat a vitia

THEMATIC INDEX

INTRODUCTION

This Index is intended to heighten the reader's awareness of the unifying ideas expressed or implied in the text of the Rule. Although not exhaustive in the selection or analysis of themes, its purpose is to provide a means for discovering the profound spirituality of the Rule. Readers may also find it helpful for personal reflection, exposition in homilies, and more comprehensive thematic study.

Based essentially on the Latin vocabulary of the Rule, this Index lists concepts suggested by language, Scripture passages, allusions, imagery and other literary devices. The aim of each entry is to indicate certain themes in a consistent form while allowing for various types of thematic association, such as direction, indirection and antithesis.

Entries point to thematic patterns in the following ways:

1. Numbers refer to the Rule by chapter and verse: 2.5. Italicized numbers indicate that the entire chapter refers to the theme under consideration: *53*; and "t" refers to the title of a chapter.

2. Dashes with a descriptive phrase offer a possible analysis of a theme: GRACE (**gratia**)—as gift.

3. Latin words in parentheses give the term in which each concept is rooted, thus providing a link with the Latin text and also with the Selected Latin Concordance. Readers unfamiliar with Latin may disregard these and use instead the English analysis and references to locate essential material: GRACE (**gratia**).

4. Scripture citations (*Scrip.cit.*) and allusions (*Scrip.allu.*) point to the biblical references related to an entry: e.g., *Scrip.cit.* (John 6:38) 7.32; *Scrip.allu.* (1 Cor 9:27) 2:13.

5. Images record mental pictures contained in themes: *Image:* Divine light (**lumen**) Prol.9.

6. Embodiment indicates sacramental realization of a theme in monastic life and practice (*Embodied in:*).

7. Actualization of thematic content in monastic ceremonial is noted under the heading: *Monastic ritual.*

8. Relevant Scripture passages that are not directly or indirectly found in the text are indicated by the phrase: *Relate to.*

9. Additional thematic content to be found in other entries is cross-referenced by words in small capitals, which refer to main entries or to headings found under a main entry: e.g., GRACE, as gift.

Some themes may be explored from a fourfold dynamic operative in the text. As the author no doubt read Scripture, internalized its message, changed in accord with it, and lived out the change in his way of life, this process is found in the Rule. It appears in those passages wherein the author cites or alludes to Scripture or uses a biblical image, expresses the same idea in his own statements, finds it focused in liturgical ritual, embodied in a monastic reality, and lived in the daily monastic life.

The following diagram shows this fourfold dynamic for the theme GUESTS:

Scripture:	RB Statement:	Monastic Ritual:	Monastic life:
"I was a stranger and you welcomed me." (Matt 25:35) 53.1	"All guests ... to be welcomed as Christ." 53.1	Guest ceremonial: 53.3-14	(every expression of monastic hospitality)
	"Christ is to be adored because he is indeed welcomed in them." 53.7		
Image: Christ (as guest)	". . . because in them more particularly Christ is received." 53.15		Embodiment: Guest (as Christ)

Because many entries include multiple interrelated concepts, the total number of indexed themes is much larger than the number of entries. Not all of these are cross-referenced. Thoughtful use may reveal interrelationships not specifically noted. An example of this kind of interrelationship can be seen in the following model:

COURAGE: CHRIST, *Images*: Rock; —CONVERSION, **convertere**; —HUMILITY, to be tested; —MEASURE, of personal strength; —MONK, kinds, cenobites; —OBEDIENCE, qualities of, courageous, patient and enduring, sustained by Christ in us, swift, zealous; —PASCHAL MYSTERY, in us; —PRAYER, as conversion and as offering of self; —SERVICE, as spiritual combat; —STABILITY, of heart, always guarded, *Images*; —WILL, self-will, renunciation of; —ZEAL, good.

ABBOT (abbas)
—believed to hold place of Christ in the monastery: (vices) 2.2; 63.13
    Scrip.cit.(Luke 10:16) 5.6
    —at the head of the monastery: (praeesse) 2.1,11; 5.12; 64.8
    —called abbot, father: (abbas; pater) 2.11,24,30; 63.13 *Scrip.cit.*(Rom
        8:15) 2.3 —Lord: (dominus) 63.13 —superior: (maior) 2.1
    —to remember what he is and is called: 2.1,30
—chosen:
    —by entire community or a minority: (eligere) 64.1
    —by local bishop, abbots, Christians: (constituere) 64.3-6
    —possible conspiracy concerning election of: 64.3-6
—directs all affairs of the monastery: (consideratio) 55.3 (consignare)
    32.2 (disponere) 3.6; 65.12 (dispensatio) 22.2 (iniungere) 31.5
    (iussio) 31.4; 33.2 (voluntas) 49.8,10 (omnia facere) 3.11 (ordinatio)
    65.11 (praeesse) 5.12 (praecipere) 51.2; 62.3 (permittere) 57.1
    (providere) 55.8
    —authority of: AUTHORITY
    —chooses all other monastic leaders: (eligere) 21.1,3,4 (ordinatio)
        65.11 (surrogare) 21.6; 65.20 *Implication*: (deputare) 58.6
    —establishes rank in the monastery: 2.19; 44.5; 60.4; 62.6; 63.1,7
    —gives blessings: MONASTIC RITUALS, blessings
    —judges: (iudicare) 32.2; 44.3; 65.14 (iudicium) 3.11; 24.2; 55.22; 63.3;
        65.22 *Implication*: 5.12
        —is to exalt mercy above judgment: *Scrip.cit.*(Jas 2:13) 64.10
    —regulates discipline: 25.5; 26.1; 27; 28.2,6; 43.11; 44; 46.3 *Implica-
        tion*: 64.10-19
        —uniformly for all: 2.16-22 *Scrip.cit.*(Rom 2:11) 2.20
        —DISCIPLINE, embodied in teaching of abbot
    —respects other abbots: *Scrip.cit.*(Tob 4:16) 61.14
    —role in monastic rituals: guest ceremonial: 53.12 profession cere-
        monial: 58.19,29 Work of God: gives blessings (benedicere) 9.5;
        11.7,10 intones: 47.2 *Te Deum*: 11.8 *Te decet laus*: 11.10 reads
        Gospel: 11.9 recites the Lord's Prayer: 13.12 selects canticles:
        11.6
    —seeks counsel: (consilium) 3 —of visiting monks: 61.4
        —of the seniors: 3.12 *Scrip.cit.*(Sir 32:24) 3.13
        —of the whole community: 3.1-11; 65.15
    —teaches: DISCIPLINE, as divine teaching, *Embodied in*: the teaching of
        the abbot
    —to be loved: (amari) 64.15 (caritas) 2.8-10 (diligere) 72.10 *An-
        tithesis*: (spernere) *Scrip.cit.*(Isa 1:2) 2.9
    —also under the Rule: 7.55 (sequatur) 3.7 (observatio) 3.11 (conser-
        vare) 64.20
    —kitchen and table of: 53.16; 56
—qualities:
    —authentic: HUMILITY, as authenticity
    —caring: CARE and CONCERN, of monks: abbot
    —God-fearing: 3.11

—just: (iustitia) 2.9   (iustus) 41.5   (iuste) 3.6   (non iniuste) 63.2
—loving: (amare) 2.17; 64.15   (caritas) 2.22   (diligere) 64.11
  —all equally: 2.16,17,20,22   Scrip.cit.(Eph 6:8; Rom 2:11) 2.20
—moderate and temperate: MEASURE, as quality of the abbot
—sober: 64.9
—wise: (discretio) 64.18,19   (discernere) 63.1; 64.17   (sapiens) 27.2;
  28.2   (sapienter) 53.22   (sagacitas) 27.5
—worthy: (dignus) 2.1
—Images:
  —Father: (pater) 2.24; 33.5   Scrip.cit.(Rom 8:15) 2.3
  —See also: A Selected Latin Concordance: abbas
  —Healer: 64.10-20   (vulnera) 46.6   (de suis sollicitus . . . ipse emen-
    datus) 2.39,40   (suamque fragilitatem semper suspectus) 64.13   (idem
    ipse consequatur) 64.10   Scrip.cit.(Isa 2:13) 64.10   (studeat plus amari
    quam timeri) 64.15   (ipse reprobus) 2.13   Scrip.cit.(Ps 49[50]:16,17)
    2.14   Scrip.allu.(1 Cor 9:27) 2.13   Implication: Monastic ritual:
    Our Father: 13.12
  —Judge: see above: judges
  —Master: (magister) 2.24; 3.6
  —New Moses: Implication: 21.1   Scrip.allu.(Deut 1:13-15; Exod
    18:21-22) 21.1,3
  —Servant: (servire) 2.31   (prodesse magis quam praeesse) 64.8
  —Shepherd: (pastor) 2.7-10,32,39; 27.8,9; 63.2   Implication: 64.18
    —Antithesis: Scrip.cit.(Ezek 34:3,4) 27.7   (Gen 30:13) 64.18
  —Spiritual father: 7.44; 46.5; 49.8-10   (pater spiritalis) 49.9
  —Steward: STEWARD, abbot as
  —Teacher: DISCIPLINE, as divine teaching, Embodied in: teaching of
    the abbot
  —Wise physician: 27.2; 28.2

Adoption, spirit of: GRACE, as spirit of adoption

AUTHORITY (auctoritas)
  —of Scripture: 9.8; 73.3
  —of the abbot: (potestas)
    —not to be unjust: 63.2   (tyrannis) 27.6
    —to intervene against abuse of Rule: 54.3; 70.2
    —to mitigate: 39.6; 56.2
    —to be delegated to other monastic leaders: (committere) 65.13   (prae-
      videre) 32.1
      —cellarer: (cellararius): (committere) 31.17   (iniungere) 31.15   (quae
        iubentur custodiat) 31.5   (prohibuerit) 31.15   (secundum iussionem
        abbatis) 31.12   (sine iussione abbatis nihil faciat) 31.4
      —deans: (decani): (constituere) 21.1   (disponere) 65.12   (eligere) 21.1;
        65.15   (partiat onera sua) 21.3   (secundum praecepta abbatis)
        21.2   Scrip.allu.(Deut 1:13-15; Exod 18:13-27) 21.1,3,4
      —prior: (praepositus): (iniungere) 65.16
        —not to be unjust: (tyrannis) 65.2
      —seniors: (senior): (deputare) 48.17; 58.6   (ponere) 66.1

—sharing all things in common: (**communis**) *Scrip.cit.*(Acts 4:32) 33.6   (**ac-cipere**) 22.2;   34.t;   43.19;   48.15;   54.1;   55.9,12,13,14   (**habere**) 33.t
(**suscipere**) 54.t,2,3
—the substance of the community: (**ferramenta**) 32.t   (**res**) 32.t; 57.6;
58.26   (**substantia**) 31.12; 32.1
—*Antithesis:*
      —avarice: AVARICE
      —personal ownership: *33* (**peculiaris**) 55.16,17-19   (**vitium**) 33.1,7
      (**nec liceat**) 33.5   (**habere**) 59.3   *Scrip.allu.*(Acts 4:32) 33.6   *Im-plication:* 34.3,4; 55.21; 59.3-7
            —to be cut out from the root: (**radicitus amputare**) 33.1; 55.18
—*Images:*
      —Apostolic Church: *Implication: Scrip.cit.*(Acts 4:35) 34.1; 55.20
      Scrip.allu.(Acts 2:42; 4:32) Prol.50; 33.6   (Acts 6:3) 21.1
      —Battleline: (**acies**) 1.5
      —Body: (**corpus**) 61.6
      —Flock: (**grex**) 2.8,32; 27.9; 28.8; 63.2; 64.18   (**ovile**) 1.8
      —House of God: HOUSE OF GOD
      —Israel in desert: *Implication: Scrip.allu.*(Deut 1:13-15) 21.1
      —School: (**schola**) Prol.45   DISCIPLINE, as divine teaching
      —Workshop: (**officina**) 4.78
—*Relate to:* Exod 12:2,6,19,47; 16:1,2,7,10
—STEWARD, *see also:* A Selected Latin Concordance: **congregatio, frater, monasterium**

CONVERSION (**conversatio**)
—conversatio: Prol.49; 1.3,12; 21.1; 22.2; 58.1; 63.1; 73.1,2
      —conversatio morum: *Monastic ritual:* profession ceremonial: 58.17
      —COMMUNITY, perseverance in; LIFE, as journey; STABILITY
—convertere: 2.18; 7.30; 63.7   (**emendare**) Prol.36; 4.58   (**sic correxerit**)
23.4   (**ut convertatur et vivat**) *Scrip.cit.*(Ezek 33:11) Prol.38   (**exspec-tat nos converti**) *Scrip.cit.*(Ps 49[50]:21) 7.30   (**paenitentia**) *Scrip.cit.*
(Rom 2:4) Prol.37
—DISCIPLINE, means include; PASCHAL MYSTERY, in us; WILL, self-will,
renunciation of

Correction, DISCIPLINE, means

Deans, MONASTIC LEADERS

DEATH (**mors**)
—as suffering: *Scrip.cit.*(Rom 8:36; Ps 43[44]:22) 7.38
—of Christ: *Scrip.cit.*(Phil 2:8) 7.34
—of the body: (**corpus**) *Scrip.allu.*(Acts 5:5) 57.5   *Implication:* 2.26
      —to be kept daily before one's eyes: 4.47
—of the soul: 2.10; 7.24   *Scrip.cit.*(Ezek 30:11) Prol.38   (Prov 23:14) 2.29
(Prov 18:21) 6.5
—*Image:* Darkness: (**tenebrae**) *Scrip.cit.*(John 12:35) Prol.13

DISCIPLINE (**disciplina**)
—as divine teaching: (**doctrina**) Prol.50   (**admonitio**) Prol.1   (**iustitia**) 2.5

Scrip.cit.(Ps 49[50]:16) 2.14 (**magisterium**) Prol.50 (**mandatum**) Prol.49; 2.12; 21.2 *Scrip.cit.*(Ps 118[119]:71) 7.54 *Scrip.allu.* (Ps 118[119]:32) Prol.49 (**praeceptum**) 2.4,12; 4.63 (**praecipere**) 7.11 (**sermones; testamentum**) *Scrip.cit.*(Ps 49[50]:16) 2.14 *Image: Scrip.allu.*(Matt 13:33) 2.5

—of Christ: (**monita**) Prol.35 (**praeceptum**) Prol.39,40; 2.4; 4.61; 7.42; 23.2

—of Scripture: (**praecipere**) 7.25 (**lex divina**) 53.9; 64.9

—communicated through the spirit of adoption of sons: *Scrip.cit.*(Rom 8:15) 2.3 (**docere**) (Ps 33[34]:12) Prol.12 *Scrip.allu.*(Rom 5:5) 7.70 **GRACE**

—*Embodied in*:

  —teaching of the abbot: **ABBOT**

    —believed to hold the place of Christ: 2.2; 63.13

    —chosen for wise teaching: (**sapientiae doctrina**) 64.2

    —commands of, received as if divine: 5.4 *Scrip.cit.*(Luke 10:16) 5.6,15

    —learned in divine law: (**doctus**) 64.9 seeks justice (**iustitia**) *Scrip.cit.*(Matt 6:33) 2.35

    —responsible for obedience of his disciples: 2.6; 36.10

    —teaches: (**doctrina**) 2.6,11,23 divine justice (**iustitia**) 2.5 (**veritatem tuam et salutare tuum**) *Scrip.cit.*(Ps 39[40]:11) 2.9

      —by enforcing discipline: *see below*: Correction, Punishment

      —by his example: (**monstrare**) 2.12 (**observatio**) 3.11

      —by his words: (**verbum**) 2.12

      —through command: (**imperium**) 64.17; 71.3 (**iniungere**) 31.15 (**iudicium**) 3.11 (**iussio**) 2.5; 26.1; 31.4,12; 33.2; 44.9; 67.7 (**praeceptum**) 4.61; 21.2; 54.1; 70.6 *Antithesis: Scrip.cit.* (Ps 49[50]:16,17) 2.14

      —*Image*: Leaven: *Scrip.allu.*(Matt 13:33) 2.5

  —teaching of superiors: (**imperare; imperium**) 5.4,12; 68.1-4 *Scrip.cit.*(Luke 10:16) 5.6,15 (Ps 17[18]:45) 5.5 (**iudicium**) 5.12 (**iubere**) 5.14; 47.2; 53.8; 68.1 (**iussio**) 5.9,18

  —found reflected in the teaching of: deans: (**doctrina**) 21.4 —of experience: 1.6 —of the holy Fathers: 73.2 —of the master: Prol.1 —of the Rule: 65.17 *Implication*:73.8 **RULE**

—imparted to disciples: (**discipulus**) 2.5,11,13; 6.3,6,8 —who:

  —attain learning: (**doctrina; doctus**) 1.4; 73.9

  —listen: (**audire**) 6.6 **LISTENING**

  —obey: (**oboedire**) 2.25; 3.6 **OBEDIENCE**

  —*Antithesis*: grumbling: (**murmurium**) 5.14 **GRUMBLING**

—work justice: (**operatur iustitiam**) *Scrip.cit.*(Ps 14[15]:2) Prol. 25 (**bona opera**) 4.t (**ars spiritalis**) 4.75 (**operari**) 4.78

  —*Images*:

    —Workman: (**operarius**) Prol. 14; 7.49,70 **MONK**

    —Tools: (**instrumentum**) 4.t,75; 73.6

—as means to spiritual healing: (**salus; sanare**) 28.5; 30.3 *Antithesis*: 2.33; 28.6 *Scrip.cit.*(1 Cor 5:5) 25.4 (**liberare**) *Scrip.cit.*(Prov 23:14) 2.29

—*Image*: Way of salvation: Prol. 48
—HEALING; PASCHAL MYSTERY; LIFE, as journey
  —means include:
    —amendment: (**emendare**) 4.58; 5.19; 43.7,9 (**emendatio**) Prol.
    36,47; 2.40; 29.1
      —*Antithesis*: (**corrigere**) 23.4; 45.2; 62.9; 65.20 *Scrip.cit.*(Prov
      29:19) 2.28 (**emendare**)23.3; 28.t,1; 32.5; 33.8; 43.15,16,19;
      46.4; 48.20; 62.10; 65.19
    —correction:
      —by the abbot who: admonishes: (**admonere**) 2.25,27 rebukes:
      (**corripere**) 2.25,27; 71.6 entreats: (**obsecrare**) 2.23 per-
      suades: (**suasio**) 2.31 rebukes: (**increpare**) 2.23 reproves:
      (**arguere**) 2.23,25; 70.3 *Scrip.cit.*(2 Tim 4:2) 2.23 *Scrip.allu.*
      (1 Sam 2:11-34; 3:11-14; 4:12-18) 2.26 is to be prudent: (**pru-
      denter**) in correcting: 64.12,14 *Implication*: 64.11-21 CARE
      and CONCERN, of abbot
      —by pilgrim monks: (**reprehendere**) 61.4 —superiors: 23.2
      —of boys: *30*.t (**disciplina**) 63.9,18,19; 70.4 —deans: 21.5
      —priests: 62.9 —the prior: (**admonere**) 65.19 —the conten-
      tious: (**contentiosus**) 71.5 —the undisciplined: (**indisciplinatus**)
      2.25 *Scrip.allu.*(1 Tim 5:20) 2.25
      —of grumbling: 40.9
      —of private ownership: 33.7
—punishment: (**poena**)
  —as discipline of the Rule: RULE, regular discipline
  —as satisfaction: (**satisfacere**)
    —corporal: (**corporis castigatio**) 2.28 (**affligere**) 30.3 (**vindictae cor-
    poris subdi**) 23.5 (**vindictae corporali subiacere**) 71.9 (**vapulare**)
    45.3 (**virga**) *Scrip.cit.*(Prov 23:14) 2.29
    —due to disobedience, grumbling and pride: 2.8-10,28; 7.33; *23*
    Scrip.allu.(1 Cor 10:10) 5.19 (1 Tim 5:20) 23.3
    —faults: *see also*: A Selected Latin Concordance: **culpa, iniquitas,
    malum, peccatum, vitium**
    —the wicked: (**nequissimi**) Prol.7.
    —for any fault: 46.3 lie prostrate (**iacere**) 71.8
    —for excommunication from table and oratory: 24.4,7 lie prostrate:
    44.1,2 (see **proicere**) 44.7,8,9
    —for grumbling: 5.19
    —for mistakes in the oratory: 45.1
    —limit of: 44.3 —judgment of abbot: 44.3 —(**congruus**) 24.7 —un-
    til blessing (**benedicere**) 44.10; 71.8 —until it is enough (**sufficere**)
    44.10
—everlasting: (**perpetua**) Prol. 7
—excommunication: (**excommunicatio**)
  —from God:
    —*Images*:
      —Father disinheriting children: Prol. 7
      —Weaned child: *Scrip.cit.*(Ps 130[131]:2) 7.4

—*Monastic ritual*:
  —Guest ceremonial: *Scrip.cit.*(Ps 47[48]:10) 53.14
  —Profession ceremonial: *Implication: Scrip.cit.*(Ps 118[119]:116,
    58.21
  —Servers' blessing: (adiuvare; consolari) *Scrip.cit.*(Dan 3:52; Ps
    85[86]:17) 35.16
  —Work of God: (Kyrie eleison) 9.10; 12.4; 13.11; 17.4,5,8,10
—*Image*: Good Shepherd: CHRIST, *Images*
—condescension of: (dignari) Prol.5; 7.70 *Scrip.cit.*(Luke 15:5) 27.9
  —*Monastic ritual*: Work of God: (intendere) *Scrip.cit.*(Ps 69[70]:1)
    18.1
—creator: (creator) 16.5; 73.4 *see also, below*: universality of
—forgiveness of: FORGIVENESS, divine
—glory of: (laus) *Scrip.cit.*(Ps 118[119]:164) 16.3 (confiteri) 16.4 (gloria)
    Scrip.cit.(Ps 114[115]:1) Prol. 30 (1 Pet 4:11) 57.9
  —*Monastic ritual*: Work of God: *Gloria*: 9.2,6; 11.3; 13.9; 17.2; 18.1;
    43.4,10; 58.22 *Te decet laus*: *Scrip.cit.*(Ps 64[65]:2) 11.10 *Te
    Deum*: 11.8
—goodness of: (bonus) *Scrip.cit.*(Ps 105[106]:1; Ps 117[118]:1) 7.46
—judgment of: (iudicium) 2.6,9; 7.64
—justice of: (iustitia) 2.5 *Scrip.cit.*(Ps 39[40]:11) 2.9 (Matt 6:33) 2.35
    Scrip.allu.(Ps 118[119]:164) 16.5
  —*Image*: Judge: (iudex) 3.11
—law of: (lex divina) 53.9; 64.9
—love of: (amor) 7.34 (diligere) 4.1 *Scrip.cit.*(2 Cor 9:7) 5.16 (caritas)
    Scrip.allu.(1 John 4:18) 7.67
—name of: (nomen) *Scrip.cit.*(Ps 113[114]:9) Prol.30
—patience of: (patientia) *Scrip.cit.*(Rom 2:4) Prol.37 *Implication: Scrip.
    cit.*(Ps 49[50]:21) 7.30
—power of:
  —omnipotence: (qui omnia potest) 28.5
  —in us: GRACE
—presence of: (ecce adsum) *Scrip.cit.*(Ps 33[34]:15) Prol.18 (praesentia)
    7.14; 19.1 (scrutans) (Ps 7:10) 7.14 (novit cogitationes) (Ps 93[94]:11)
    7.15 (Ps 138[139]:3) 7.16 (ante te) (Ps 37[38]:10) 7.23 (respicere)
    Scrip.allu.(Ps 13[14]:2) 4.49; 7.13,27 (aspicere) 7.29 GRACE
  —*Images*:
    —Divine light: (lumen) *Scrip.cit.*(John 12:35) Prol.13
    —Ear of God: (auris) *Scrip.allu.*(Isa 58:9; 65:24) Prol.18
    —Eye of God: (oculus) *Scrip.cit.*(Prov 15:3) 7.26; 19.1
    —House of God: HOUSE OF GOD
    —Voice: WORD OF GOD, *Images*
—protection of: (Deo protegente) 73.9 (quod absit) 4.61; 11.12; 28.2; 34.2;
    48.19; 58.28; 59.6; 64.3
—silence of: (tacere) *Scrip.cit.*(Ps 49[50]:21) 7.30
—teaching of: DISCIPLINE, as divine teaching
—Trinity: (Trinitas) 9.7
  —*Monastic ritual*: Work of God: *Gloria*: 9.2,6; 11.3; 13.9; 17.2; 18.1;

43.4,10; 58.22   *Te decet laus: Scrip.cit.*(Ps 64[65]:2) 11.10   *Te Deum*: 11.8
—universality of: (**universus**) 20.2
—will of: 7.20
—word of: WORD OF GOD
—wrath of: (**irritatus**) Prol.7   (**retributio**) 55.22   *Scrip.cit.*(Ps 130[131]:2) 7.4
  —*Images*:
    —Angry father: (**iratus**) Prol.6
    —Dread lord: (**metuendus**) Prol.7
—*Images*:
  —Loving father: (**pius**) 7.30
  —Nursing mother: *Scrip.cit.*(Ps 130[131]:2) 7.4

GRACE (**gratia**)
—as divine power working in us: (**inspirare**) 20.4   (**operari**) Prol.30; 28.5
    Scrip.cit.(1 Cor 15:10) Prol.31   (2 Cor 10:17) Prol.32   *Scrip.cit.*
    (Ps 136[137]:9) Prol.28
—as gift: (**donum**) *Scrip.cit.*(1 Cor 7:7) 40.1   (**bonum**) Prol.6
—as help of Christ: (**adiuvare**) 73.8
—as help of God: (**gratia; adiuvare; auxiliari; adiutorium**) Prol.41; 1.5,13;
    5.19; 17.3; 20.4; 68.5   *Scrip.cit.*(1 Cor 15:10) Prol. 31   (Ps 69[70]:2)
    18.1; 35.17
—as spirit of adoption: *Scrip.cit.*(Rom 8:15) 2.3   (Ps 33[34]:12) Prol.12
    Scrip.allu.(Rom 5:5) 7.70
—*Embodied in*:
  —commands: (**imperare**) 5.4
  —teaching: *Scrip.cit.*(Ps 17[18]:45) 5.5   (**doctor**) (Luke 10:16) 5.6
—*Images*:
  —Divine light: (**lumen**) Prol. 9
  —Guidance of the Gospel: (**per ducatum**) Prol.21
  —Medicine of holy Scripture: (**medicamen**) 28.3
—*Monastic Ritual*:
  —Reader's blessing: *Scrip.cit.*(Ps 50[51]:17) 38.3
  —Servers' blessing: (**adiuvare; consolari**)   *Scrip.cit.*(Dan 3:26,52; Ps
    85[86]:17) 35.16   (Ps 69[70]:1) 35.17
  —Work of God: (**adiutorium**) *Scrip.cit.*(Ps 69[70]:1) 17.3; 18.1
—DISCIPLINE, as divine teaching; GOD, presence of

Grief, JOY, *Antithesis*, not to be in monastery

Growth, LIFE, as journey

GRUMBLING (**murmurare; murmuratio**)
—admonition against: 5.14; 34.6; 40.8,9   (**murmuriosus**) *Scrip.allu.*(Wis
    1:11) 4.39   *Relate to*: Matt 21:29
—in one's heart: 5.17,18
—justifiable: 41.5   *Implication*: 35.13; 53.18
—punishment due to: 23.1   *Scrip.allu.*(1 Cor 10:10) 5.19   (Matt 18:17) 23.3
—*Relate to*: Exod 16:2-12; Num 14:27,36; John 6:41-43

GUESTS (hospites)
—are welcomed as Christ: (suscipere) 53.1,7,15 (occurrere) 53.3
   Scrip.cit.(Matt 25:35) 53.1
   —with gentleness: (mansuetudo) 66.4 —honor: (honor) 53.2 —courtesy: (humanitas) 53.9 —love: (caritas) 53.3; 66.4
   —with greater care: (cura; sollicitudo) —for Christians: *Scrip. cit.* (Gal
   6:10) 53.2 —pilgrims: (peregrinus) 53.2,15; 56.1 —visiting monks:
   61 —poor people: (pauperes) 31.9; 53.15; 66.3 (recreare) 4.14
—arrive at irregular hours: 53.16 *Implication*: 42.10
—community not to be disturbed by: 53.16
—concern of monastic leaders for: 31.9; 53.8,10,12; 56.1
—housing for: (cella hospitum) 53.16,21; 58.4 —porter: (ostiarius) 66.1-5
—*Monastic ritual*:
   —Greeting by porter: 66.3
   —Guest ceremonial:
      —context: Christ's presence: 53.7 —courtesy: 53.3-14 *Scrip.cit.*
      (Ps 47[48]:10) 53.14 —meal: 53.10 —reverence: 53.7
      —elements:
         —announcement: 53.3
         —greeting of abbot and community: 53.3
         —kiss of peace: 53.4,5
         —prayer: 53.3,4,8
         —Scripture reading: 53.9
         —washing of feet: 53.13 *Relate to*: John 12:1-8; 13:4,5; Luke 7:36-
         50
—*Image*: Christ as guest: 53.1,7,15 *Scrip.cit.*(Matt 25:35) 53.1

HEALING (salus)
—as power to heal:
   —divine: (salus) 28.5 (salutare) *Scrip.cit.*(Isa 1:2) 2.9 (liberare)
   Scrip.cit.(Matt 6:13) 13.14 *Implication*: (salvus) *Scrip.cit.*(1 Cor 5:5)
   25.4 (Matt 24:13) 7.36 (parcere) 7.30
   —of the abbot: (salvare) 41.5 (salus) 2.33
      —*Images*: ABBOT, *Images*: Healer, Wise physician
   —of the seniors: MONASTIC LEADERS, seniors, *Image*: Healer
   —of Scripture: *Image*: Medicine of holy Scripture: (medicamen) 28.3
—of monks: (cura) 27.6 (sanare) 71.8 (liberare) *Scrip.cit.*(Prov 23:14) 2.29
   Implication: (diluere) 49.3
—of poor people: (recreare) 4.14
—wholesome counsel: (sanus) 64.1
—*Image*: Way of salvation: (via salutis): Prol. 48

HOUSE OF GOD (domus Dei)
—(domus Dei) 31.19; 53.22; 64.5 tent: (tabernaculum) Prol.22,24,39 *Scrip.
   cit.*(Ps 14[15]:1) Prol.23 temple: (templum) *Scrip.cit.*(Ps 47[48]:10)
   53.14 (Deo protegente) 73.9
—*Embodied in*:
   —monastery: (monasterium) and oratory: (oratorium; domus Dei) 31.19;

53.22; 64.5 (cella) 1.10 (coenobium) 5.12 (monasterium) 1.3; 2.2,16; 3.1,8; 7.55; 21.t; 29.t,1; 33.1,6; 53.16,19; 57.t,2,6; 58.15,24,26,28; 59.1,4,5; 60.t,1,6; 61.13; 62.t,5,10; 63.1,8; 65.t,1,11,12,21; 69.t,1; 70.1; 71.9; 73.1

—substance of, regarded as sacred vessels of the altar: (substantia; altaris vasa sacrata) 31.10   oratory: 7.63; 11.13; 24.4; 25.1; 35.15; 38.3; 43.8; 44.1,2,6,9; 45.t; 50.t; 52; 58.17,26; 63.18; 67.3

—*Images*:

—House of God: 31.19; 53.22; 64.5 COMMUNITY, *Images*

—Sheepfold: (ovile) 1.8

—Workshop: (officina) 4.78

—*Relate to*: Gen 28:17; 25:17; Ps 21[22]:8; Ps 26[27]:4

HUMILITY (humilitas)

—as authenticity: (meminere . . . quod dicitur; nomen . . . factis implere) 2.1 (dolum in corde non tenere) 4.24   (pacem falsam non dare) 4.25   (veritatem ex corde et ore) 4.28 (non velle dici sanctum) 4.62 (intimo cordis credat affectu) 7.51 (sincerus) 72.10 (humilitatem corde et corpore) 7.62,63 Scrip.cit.(Ps 130[131]:1) 7.3 Implication: 6.5

—*Antithesis*: (mentiri Deo) 1.7 (numquam stabilis) 1.11

—as quality of monks: (humiliare) 34.4 (humilis) 2.21 (humilitatis subiectio) 3.4 (humilitatis culmen) 7.5 (non elatus) Prol. 29 (elationem fugere) 4.69 (non superbus) 4.34

—abbot: (fragilitatem . . . suspectus sit) 64.13 ABBOT, as healer

—artisans: (humilitas) 57.1

—cellarer: (humilitas) 31.7,13

—priests: (humilitas) 62.3 (caveat elationem aut superbiam) 62.2

—reader: (humilitas) 47.4 (avertat . . . spiritum elationis) 38.2

—*Monastic ritual*: Reader's blessing: Scrip.cit.(Ps 50[51]:17) 38.2,3

—visiting priests: (humilitas) 60.5

—whole community: (humilitas) 65.14

—steps of: (gradus)

— 1. awe (timor Dei) 7.10 PRAYER, as awe

—obedience: (oboedientia) 5.1

— 2. not to love one's own will: 7.31-33 WILL, renunciation of

— 3. subject self to a superior: 7.34 OBEDIENCE

— 4. hold fast to patience in obedience: 7.49-50; 68 PASCHAL MYS-TERY, in us, as patience

— 5. confess evil thoughts: 7.44-48 FORGIVENESS, aspect of confession

— 6. be content with the lowest: (contentus sit) 7.49,50 Scrip.cit.(Ps 72[73]:22,23) 7.50

— 7. believe oneself inferior to others: (inferior) 7.51 (intimo cordis affectu credat) 7.51-53 (bona non a se) Prol. 29 (minus habet in nos) Prol. 41 Scrip.cit.(1 Cor 15:10) Prol. 31 (2 Cor 10:17) Prol. 32 (Ps 113[114]:9) Prol. 30 (Ps 21[22]:7) 7.52 (Ps 87[88]:16) 7.53 (Ps 118[119]:71) 7.54

— 8. follow common rule and example of superiors: 7.55

— 9. be silent: (taciturnitatem habens) 7.56-58 SILENCE
—10. be not prompt to laugh: (risus) 6.8; 7.59 (scurrilitas) 6.8
—11. speak humbly: (humiliter) 7.60-61
—12. be humble in heart and manifest it: (semper indicat) 7.62-65
   (non sum dignus) Scrip.cit.(Ps 118[119]:107) 7.66 Scrip.allu.(Luke
   18:13) 7.65
—effect of: exaltation: (exaltare) Scrip.cit.(Luke 14:11; 18:14) 7.1
—extent of: (semper) 7.18,62,63,65 Scrip.cit.(Ps 37[38]:9) 7.66
—goal of: perfect love that casts out fear: Scrip.allu.(1 John 4:18) 7.67
—in making satisfaction: (humiliari) 45.1; 57.3 (humilitas) 45.2
—in prayer: (humilitas) 20.1,2 (Domine non sum dignus) Scrip.cit.(Ps
   118[119]:71) 7.54 Scrip.allu.(Luke 18:13; Matt 8:8) 7.65 PRAYER,
   as compunction
—toward:
   —abbot: (humilis) 72.10
   —guests: (humilitas) 53.6 (humiliter) 53.24
   —men of rank: 20.1
—to be tested: (probare) 58.11 Scrip.cit.(Ps 65[66]:10,11) 7.40 (1 John
   4:1) 58.2 (Ps 118[119]:71) 7.54 (Ps 130[131]:1,2) 7.4 (Luke 14:11)
   7.1
—Antithesis: (exaltatio) 7.1,2,7 Scrip.cit.(Luke 14:11) 7.1 (Ps 130[131]:
   1,2) 7.4 (Ps 87[88]:16) 7.53
   —Image: Weaned child: Scrip.cit.(Ps 130[131]:2) 7.4 PRIDE
—Image: Ascend ladder: (scala) 7.6,8

JOY (gaudium)
—as delight in virtue: (dilectio) Prol.49 (delectatio) 7.69 (amor) 72.3,9
   (hilaris) Scrip.cit.(2 Cor 9:7) 5.16
—at increase of worthy flock: (gaudere) 2.32
—in the Paschal Mystery: (spiritalis desiderii gaudium) 49.7
   —in us: (gaudere) 7.39 Scrip.cit.(Rom 8:36) 7.39 (inenarrabili dilectionis dulcedine) Prol. 49
—of the Holy Spirit: (gaudium) Scrip.allu.(1 Thess 1:6) 49.6
—Antithesis: grief: (tristitia)
   —consolation of:
      —by God: Monastic ritual: Scrip.cit.(Dan 3:52; Ps 85[86]:17) 35.16
      —by monks: 4.19; 27.3
   —not to be in the monastery: (contristare) 31.6,7,19; 34.3; 36.4; 48.7;
      54.4 (tristitia) 35.3 Scrip.cit.(2 Cor 2:7) 27.3
   —of Christ: (contristare) Prol. 5
   —PRAYER, compunction
—Image: Enlarged heart: (dilatato corde) Scrip.allu.(Ps 118[119]:32) Prol. 49

JUSTICE (iustitia)
—divine: GOD, judgment of, justice of, law of
—in the monastery:
      —abbot: ABBOT, judges, just; MEASURE, as quality of the abbot
      —others: (iustitia) Scrip.cit.(Ps 14[15]:1) Prol.25 (iustus) 41.5 Impli-

cation: leaven: (**fermentum**) 2.5 (**non abscondi**) *Scrip.cit.*(Ps 39[40]: 11) 2.9

—suffer persecution for: *Scrip.cit.*(Matt 5:10) 4.33 *Relate to*: 1 Cor 4:12; 1 Pet 3:14

—whole observance of, not in the Rule: 73.t

—RULE

Lectio divina, SCRIPTURE, to be read

LIFE (**vita**)

—as journey: (**ambulare**) 5.12 (**currere**) Prol. 22,44 *Scrip.cit.*(John 12:35) Prol.13 *Scrip.allu.*(John 12:35; 1 Cor 9:24) Prol.44 (**festinare**) 73.2 (**ingredi**) Prol.25 (**moram pati nesciant**) 5.4 (**perducere**) 73.2 (**pervenire**) Prol.22,42; 7.5,67; 73.4 (**processus**) Prol.49 (**proficere**) 2.25 (**inquire pacem**) *Scrip.cit.*(Ps 33[34]:15) Prol.17 (**venire**) 1.13 *Scrip.cit.*(Ps 33[34]:12) Prol.12 (**gradi**) 5.10 *Implication*: (**initium**) 2.28; 65.4; 73.1 *Scrip.allu.*(Matt 7:14) Prol.48

—following Christ: (**qui nos perducat**) 72.12 *Relate to*: Matt 16:24; Luke 9:23 (**pergere iter**) Prol.21 (**sequi**) 4.10 *Implication: Scrip. cit.*(Ps 33[34]:13) Prol.15 *Antithesis*: (**sequi nolle**) Prol.7 (**discedere**) 7.36

—in obedience: (**vicino . . . pede**) *Scrip.allu.*(Matt 4:22) 5.8 (**via mandatorum Dei**) *Scrip.allu.*(Ps 118[119]:32) Prol.49

—*Image*: Christ as light: (**lumen**) *Scrip.cit.*(John 12:35) Prol.13

—to heaven: (**ascendere; regni tabernaculo**) Prol.22; 7.5-9,67 (**attingere**) 7.5 (**ducit; vita aeterna**) 4.46; 5.3; 72.2 (**gradus**) 5.10 (**ducere**) 5.11 (**erigere**) 7.6,8 (**pervenire**) 7.5

—to God: (**ducere**) 72.2 (**ire ad Deum**) 58.8; 71.2 (**proficere**) 62.4 (**recto cursu ad creatorem**) 73.4 PRAYER, as desire for God

—*Image*: Way: (**ire; cursus**) 58.8; 71.2; 73.4 (**iter**) Prol.21 (**via**) Prol. 20,24,48,49; 5.11; 71.2 *Scrip.cit.*(Matt 7:14) 5.11 (Ps 36[37]:5) 7.45 *Scrip.allu.*(Ps 15[16]:10) Prol. 20

—*Relate to*: 1 Sam 12:23; 2 Sam 12:31; Ps 100[101]:2,6

—The two ways: *Implication*: 1.1-5 contrasted: Prol.6,7,42; 1.6-11 *Scrip.cit.*(Matt 7:14) 5.11 (Prov 16:25) 7.21 *Relate to*: Prol.42; Jer 21:8

—*Images*:

—Light and darkness: *Scrip.cit.*(John 12:35) Prol.13

—Life and death: *Scrip.cit.*(Ezek 33:11) Prol.38 (Prov 10:19; 18:21) 6.4,5

—Good and evil: 7.26 *Scrip.cit.*(Ps 33[34]:14-15) Prol.17 (**zelus**) 72.1,2

—*Relate to*: Ps 1:6; Prov 4:18; 12:28

—earthly: Prol. 36,43; 1.10; 4.48 (**praesens**) 7.5 (**in saeculo**) 7.8

—eternal: (**aeternus**) 5.3,10; 7.11 (**perpetuus**) Prol. 42 *Implication*: 72.2

—lives of Fathers: 42.3; 73.5

—merit of: (**mores**) 32.1 (**dinoscere**) 61.5 (**meritum**) 21.4; 62.6; 63.1; 64.2 (**puritas**) 49.2

—rule of: 73.3

LISTENING (audire)
—of abbot to community: (audire) 3.2   Scrip.cit.(Sir 32:24) 3.13
—of disciples: 6.6   Scrip.cit.(Ps 17[18]:45; Luke 10:16) 5.6,15   (obauditus)
    5.5
—on journeys: (auditus malae rei) 67.4,5
—to the divine voice: (audire) Prol.9,16,24,39; 64.21   Scrip.cit.(Luke 10:16)
    5.6,15   (Ps 94[95]:8) Prol.10   (Rev 2:7) Prol.11   (Ps 33[34]:12)
    Prol.12   (Matt 7:24) Prol.33
—to the master: (obscultare) Prol.1
—to holy reading: 4.55; 38.5
    —edification in: (aedificare audientes) 38.12; 47.3
    —times for: 38.1; 42.3
    —of the Fathers: (Collationes vel Vitae Patrum) 42.3-5   Implication:
    73.4
    —of Scripture: SCRIPTURE, reading
    —of the Rule: Implication: 58.9,12,13; 66.3
—Monastic ritual: Work of God: to the Lord's Prayer: 13.12
—Image: Ear of heart: Prol.1
—OBEDIENCE, of monks

LOVE (amor)
    —for Christ: (amor) 4.21,72; 7.69; 63.13   (carius) 5.2   (nihil praeponere)
    4.21; 72.11
    —for God: (amor) 7.34   (diligere) Scrip.cit.(1 Cor 2:9) 4.77   (Luke 10:27)
    4.1   (caritas) (1 John 4:18) 7.67
    —motive for obedience: (caritas) 68.5
    —mutual: (amor) 4.72; 72.9   (carissimi) Prol. 19   (caritate) 72.10   (diligere)
    4.71; 63.10; 64.11   (caritatem fraternitatis) Scrip.allu.(Rom 12:10)
    72.8 Implication: 27; 72
        —expressed in mutual service: (caritas) 35.2,6; 61.4
        —of abbot for monks: (amare) 2.17; 64.14   (caritas) 2.22   (diligere)
        64.11
        —of monks for abbot: (caritate diligere) 72.10
    —of Christ for us: (diligere) Scrip.cit.(Rom 8:37) 7.39
    —of God for us: (diligere) Scrip.cit.(2 Cor 9:7) 5.16
    —of enemies: Scrip.cit.(Matt 5:44; Luke 6:27) 4.31
    —of virtues: (amor) 4.13; 5.10; 72.3   Scrip.allu.(Jdt 15:11) 4.64   Implica-
    tion: (amare) 4.52,54; 7.31   Scrip.allu.(Jas 3:14,15) 4.68

MASS (missa)
    —(missa) 35.14; 38.2
    —(communio) 38.2,10; 63.4
        —Implication: (altare) 58.20,29; 59.2; 62.6
        —Monastic ritual:
            —Kiss of peace: 53.5; 63.4
            —Oblation of children: 59.2-7
            —Profession ceremonial: 58.20-27

MEASURE (mensura)
—as balance in:
  —feeling: (aequo animo) 31.17
  —reason: (ratio) Prol. 47
  —receiving necessities: 34.t
—as equality of service: (aequalis) 2.20
—as quality of the abbot: (discretio) 64.17-20   (temperare) 2.24; 41.5;
    64.17-19 (mensura) 24.1 (prudenter) 61.4; 64.12,14 (providus)
    64.17 Scrip.cit.(Gen 33:13) 64.18   (Isa 42:3) 64.13
—in all things: (mensurate) 31.12; 48.9
—in daily schedule: (horarium; consideratio rationis) 8.1   (temperare) 8.4;
    41.9
—in food: (mensura) 25.5; 39.t —clothes: 55.8 —drink: 40.t,2,8 —all
    needs: 49.6
—in personal service: (temperare) 49.4
—in psalm arrangement: 11.11; 18.20
—in punishment: (mensura) 30.1; 70.5
  —excommunication: (mensura) 24.1   (modus) 24.t,2
—in speech: (moderatio) 42.11
—of displeasure: (modus) 71.7
—of personal strength: (mensura) 68.2

Moderation, MEASURE

MONASTIC LEADERS
—abbot: ABBOT
—to administer wisely: (administrare sapienter) 53.22
—to be chosen by the abbot: (eligere) 65.15   (praevidere) 32.1
—to share abbot's responsibility: (committere) 65.13   (onera partire) 21.3
—cellarer: (cellararius) 31
  —qualities: (qualis) 31.t
    —care and concern: (curam gerat) 31.3   (sollicitudine curam gerat)
      31.9 (non contristet) 31.6,19   —for aged and children; guests:
      31.9 —for sick: 31.9; 36.10
    —God-fearing: (timens Deum) 31.2
    —humble: (humilitas) 31.7,13
    —kind in speech: (sermo bonus) Scrip.cit.(Sir 18:17) 31.14
    —mature: (maturus) 31.1
    —peaceful: (aequo animo) 31.17
    —sober: (sobrius) 31.1 Scrip.allu.(1 Tim 3:2) 31.1
    —to know he must give an account: (scire rationem reddere) 31.9
      —Antithesis: an excessive eater: (multum edax)   proud: (elatus)   of-
        fensive: (iniuriosus)   dilatory: (tardus) 31.1   conceited: (sine typho)
        31.16   greedy: (avaritia) 31.12   negligent: (neglegere) 31.11
        leading astray: (scandalizare) Scrip.cit.(Matt 18:6) 31.16
    —Images:
      —Father to whole community: 31.2
      —Steward: STEWARD, cellarer as

—deans: (decani) *21*
> —chosen for: holy life: (**boni testimonii; sanctae conversationis**) wise
> teaching: (**sapientiae doctrina**) *Scrip.allu.*(Deut 1:13-15; Acts 6:3)
> 21.1-4
> —keep the Rule: (**servare regulam**) 62.7
> —order affairs of the monastery under the abbot: (**ordinare**) 65.12
> (**praecepta abbatis**) 21.2
> —share abbot's burden: (**onus**) *Scrip.allu.*(Deut 1:13-15; Exod 18:13-
> 27) 21.3
> —to be corrected when irresponsible: (**reprehensibilis; corripere**) and
> deposed: (**deicere**) 21.5

—prior: (**praepositus**) *65*
> —appointed:
>> —risk of dissension: (**dissensio**) 65.1-10 *Scrip.allu.*(2 Cor 12:20; Gal
>> 5:20,21) 65.7
>> —to be chosen by the abbot: (**eligere**) 65.15 (**surrogare**) 65.20
> —duties designated by the abbot: (**iniungere**) 65.16
> —is to observe the Rule: 65.17
> —*Antithesis*: (**contemptor**) 65.18 (**elatio**) 65.18 (**superbire**) 65.4,18
> —to be disciplined: admonition: (**admonere**) punishment: (**corripere**)
> deposition: (**deicere**) 21.5,6 expulsion: (**pellere**) 65.19-21

—seniors: (**senior**)
> —appointed to watch over new members: (**deputare; curiose intendat**)
> 58.6
> —appointed porter: (**ponere; senex sapiens**) 66.1
> —counsel abbot: (**consilium**) 3.12
> —supervise: dormitories: 22.3,7 —reading: 48.17 —discipline in
> abbot's absence: 56.3 *Implication*: 63.19
> —to be reverenced: (**venerare**) 4.70
> —*Images*:
>> —Spiritual father: (**seniori spiritali patefacere**) 4.50; 46.5 (**admoneatur**
>> **secrete**) 23.2; 46.6 (**ad lucrandas animas**) 58.6
>> —Healer: (**vulnera**) 46.6 (**senpectae**) 27.2

—*see also*: A Selected Latin Concordance: **maior, prior**

MONASTIC RITUALS
> —blessings: (**benedicere**) 9.5; 11.7; 44.10; 66.3 *Scrip.cit.*(Luke 6:28)
> 4.32 (**oratio**) 49.8
>> —at meals: 43.13 —no blessing for the excommunicated: 25.6
>> —for weekly reader: 38.2-5 *Scrip.cit.*(Ps 50[51]:17) 38.3
>> —for weekly table servers: 35.15-18 *Scrip.cit.*(Dan 3:52; Ps 85[86]:17)
>> 35.16 (Ps 69[70]:2) 35.17
>> —for those traveling: 67.1-4
>> —of guests: 53.24
>> —porter's greeting: 66.3,4
>> —priest's: 60.4
> —guest ceremonial: 53.3-15 GUESTS
> —Mass: (**missa**) MASS

—profession ceremonial: 58.17-26   (suscipe) *Scrip.cit.*(Ps 118[119]:116)
    58.21 PRAYER, as offering
—Work of God: chapters *8–19*   *see also*: A Selected Latin Concordance:
    divina opera, opus Dei
—nothing to be preferred to: 43.3

MONK (monachus)
—kinds: (genera)
    —anchorites: (anachoritae) 1.3-5
       —former cenobites: 1.4,5   —live alone: 1.5   —not in first fervor: 1.3
    —gyrovagues: (gyrovagi) 1.10-12
       —always wander: (vagus) 1.11   —never stable: (numquam stabilis) 1.11
         —serve self-will: (propriae voluntates) —gluttonous: (gula) 1.11
    —sarabaites: (sarabaitae) 1.6,9
       —are untested by rule or experience: 1.6
       —live in twos, threes or alone: 1.8
       —serve the world: (saeculum) 1.7
       —their rule (lex) is desire for pleasure: (desideriorum voluntas) 1.8
    —cenobites: (cenobitae) 1.2,13
       —the strong kind (fortissimum) 1.13   —live in a monastery under rule
         and abbot: 1.2
       —rule provides for: (disponere) 1.13
       —social differentiation:
         —age: children: (infantes) 31.9; 37; 45.3   boys, minors (pueri; mi-
           nore aetate) 30.t,2; 39.10; 59.1,2,6; 63.9,18   (minores) 63.10,16
           (iuniores) 3.3; 4.71; 63.8-16; 66.5; 68.4; 71.4   (adulescentiores)
           22.7; 30.2; 63.18   (seniores) 3.12; 4.50,70; 22.3,7   old men (senes)
           37.t; 66.1
       —ecclesiastical status: cleric: (clericus) 60.8; 61.12
         —deacon: (diacon) 62.1
         —priest: (presbyter) 62.1   (sacerdos) 60.t,1; 61.12; *62*
           —chosen from monastery by abbot: (eligere) 62.1
           —received as new members: (suscipere) *60*.t,1
              —not to be easily admitted: 60.1
              —to promise obedience to the rule and stability: 60.9
           —to be:
              —humble: (humilitas) 60.5   —*Antithesis*: pride (elatio;
              superbia) 62.2
              —obedient: (oboediens) 60.9; 62.4
                 —subject to the regular discipline: 60.2,5; 62.3,4,8
                 —to observe regulations for deans and prior: 62.7
                 —*Antithesis*: stubbornness: (contumacia; subdi aut oboe-
                 dire regulae nolit) 62.10,11   (oblivisci regulae oboedien-
                 tiam et disciplinam) 62.4   —*Image*: Rebel: (rebellio) 62.8
           —worthy: (dignus) 62.1   (meritum) 62.6
           —to offer Mass: 60.4; 62.6   MONASTIC RITUALS, blessings
         —to receive regular rank: 60.7; 62.5   —special rank: 60.4;
           62.6   (clericus) 60.8

—when rebellious to be dismissed: (**proicere**) 62.10
—intelligent: quick-witted: (**capaces**) 2.12 (**intellegibiles**) 2.27 wise: (**sapientes**) 27.2; 31.1; 53.22; 66.1 mentally slow, simple: (**simpliciores**) 2.12 (**improbus**) 23.5 (**infirmis intellectibus**) 42.4
—social status: freemen: (**ingenuus**) 2.18 (**liber**) 2.20 nobles: (**nobiles**) 59.t,1 poor men: (**pauperes**) 59.t,1,7 former slaves: (**ex servitio**) 2.18 (**servus**) 2.20 artisans: (**artifices**) 57
—variety of character:
    —amenable: (**mitis**) 2.25 good, upright: (**honestiores**) 2.27
    —*Antithesis*: arrogant, callous, opinionated, disdainful: (**durus corde**) 2.12,28 (**contemnens**) 2.25; 7.11; 71.9 (**contemptor**) 23.1; 65.18 (**superbus**) 2.28; 21.5; 23.1; 28.2 rebellious, stubborn: (**inoboediens**) 2.8,10,28; 23.1 (**contumax**) 23.1; 62.11; 71.9 (**contrarius**) 23.1 (**improbus**) 2.28; 23.5 (**malo animo**) 5.17 (**murmurare**) 5.17,18,19
    —dutiful, upright; (**oboediens**) 2.25 (**honestior**) 2.27 (**utilis frater**) 7.18
    HUMILITY; as quality of monks
    —*Antithesis*: indolent, negligent: (**desidiosus**) 48.23; 73.7 (**otiosus**) 48.24 (**acediosus**) 48.18 (**somnulentus**) 22.8 (**neglegens**) 2.25; 7.22; 43.5; 48.23; 73.7
    —patient, strong: (**patiens**) 2.25 (**fortis**) 64.19
    —*Antithesis*: moody, discontented: (**indisciplinatus; inquietus**) 2.25 wayward, wavering, weak: (**delinquens**) 27.1; 30.3 (**fluctuans**) 27.3 (**infirmarum animarum**) 27.6 (**pusillanimis**) 48.9

—*Images*:
    —Brother: *see*: A Selected Latin Concordance: frater
    —Disciple: (**discipulus**) 2.5,6,11,12,13; 3.6; 5.9,16,17; 6.3,6,8; 36.10
    DISCIPLINE, as divine teaching, imparted to disciples
    —Servant-soldier: (**militare**) SERVICE, as spiritual combat
    —Sheep: (**ovis**) 2.7,10,39; 27.8,9; 28.8
    —Son: (**filius**) Prol. 1,5,6 *Scrip.cit.*(Rom 8:15) 2.3 (Ps 33[34]:12) Prol. 12 (Ps 13[14]:23) 7.27
    —Workman: (**operarius**) Prol.14; 7.49,70
    —*see also*: A Selected Latin Concordance: monachus

Murmuring, GRUMBLING

OBEDIENCE (**oboedientia**)
—as renunciation of self-will: WILL, self-will, renunciation of
    —motives for:
    —fear of the Lord: (**timor Dei**) 5.9
    —fear of hell: (**gehenna**) 5.3
    —glory of life everlasting: (**gloria**) 5.3,10
    —holy service professed: (**servitium sanctum**) 5.3
    —imitation of Christ: (**imitari**) 5.13; 7.32,34
    —love: (**caritas**) 68.5 (**dilatato corde**) Prol.49
        —of Christ: (**amor**) 7.69
        —of God: (**amor**) 7.34 (**caritas**) 7.67

—persevering even to death: Prol.50   *Scrip.cit.*(Phil 2:8) 7.34 (Matt 10:22) 7.36   (Ps 26[27]:14) 7.37   PASCHAL MYSTERY, as patience
—sustained by Christ in us: *Scrip.cit.*(Rom 8:37) 7.39   GRACE
—swift: 5.7-10; 43.1
—total: monks not to have wills or bodies at their own disposal: 33.4
—trusting: (**confidere**) 68.5
—zealous: (**sollicitus**) 58.7
   —*Antithesis*: 1.8-11 (**inoboedientes**) Prol.2; 2.8,10,28; 23.1 (**oboediens non fuerit**) 65.21 (**cum malo animo oboedire**) 5.17 (**tyrannis**) 65.2   GRUMBLING *Image*: Sloth of disobedience: Prol.2
—*Monastic ritual*: Profession ceremonial: 58.17
—*Images*:
   —Labor of obedience: (**labor**) Prol.2
   —Spiritual combat: SERVICE, as spiritual combat
   —Swift step: (**vicino oboedientiae pede**) 5.8
   —Way of God's commandments: (**via mandatorum Dei**) Prol.49 LIFE, as journey
   —Weapons of obedience: (**arma**) Prol.3
—MONK, *Images*: Disciple, Servant-soldier, Sheep, Workman

PASCHAL MYSTERY (**Pascha**)
—Christ: *Scrip.cit.*(Phil 2:8) 7.34   *Scrip.allu.*(Rom 8:17; 1 Pet 4:13) Prol.50
   —*Monastic ritual*:
      —Easter celebration: (**Pascha**) 8.1,4; 10.1; 15.1,4; 41.1,7; 48.3; 49.7
      —Lenten observance: (**quadragesima**) 15.2,3; 41.6,7; 48.10,14-16; 49.t,1,2
      —Work of God: (**Alleluia**) 9.9; 11.6; 12.2; 15.t,1,3,4
—in us: (**imitans Dominum**) 7.34 (**propter te; propter eum**) 7.38,39 (**abnegare semetipsum sibi ut sequatur Christum**) 4.10 (**participari**) Prol. 50 *Implication: Monastic ritual*: (**suscipe**) *Scrip.cit.*(Ps 118 [119]:116) 58.21 —*Antithesis*: (**noluerint . . . gloriam**) Prol.7
   —through patience: (**patiens; patienter**) 2.25; 7.35,42; 36.5; 58.3; 68.2; 72.5 (**tacite**) 7.35   *Scrip.allu.*(1 Pet 3:9) 4.30 (1 Pet 4:13) Prol.50 (2 Tim 4:2) 58.11
   —as endurance: (**sustinere**) 4.33; 7.36,38   *Scrip.allu.*(1 Cor 4:12; 1 Pet 3:9) 4.32; 7.43 (**tolerare**) 72.5 *Implication*: 7.35-43 (**examinare**) *Scrip.cit.*(Ps 65[66]:10,11) 7.40 (**sufferre**) 4.30; 7.38 (Ps 43[44]:22; Rom 8:36) 7.38,39   *Scrip.allu.*(1 Pet 3:9) 4.32
   —as perseverance: (**perseverantia**) 58.3,9   *Scrip.cit.*(Matt 10:22) 7.36 (**persistere**) 25.3; 58.3 (**sustinere**) 4.33; 7.36
   —as waiting: (**sustinere Dominum**) *Scrip.cit.*(Ps 26[27]:14) 7.37 (**Pascha exspectare**) 49.7
      —*Monastic ritual*: Work of God: Vigils: 8.3,4; 9.8,11; 10.3; 11.t,1,2,11; 14.t; 16.4; 18.6,20,23; 43.4
   —as victory: (**superare**) *Scrip.cit.*(Rom 8:37) 7.39
   —*Images*:
      —Arise from sleep: (**surgere**) *Scrip.cit.*(Rom 13:11) Prol.8

—Jacob's ladder: (**ascendere; erigere; exaltatio**) *Scrip.allu.*(Gen 28:12) 7.6-9

—Narrow way to life: *Implication: Scrip.cit.*(Matt 7:14) Prol.48; 5.11

—Silver refined in fire: *Scrip.cit.*(Ps 65[66]:10) 7.40

—JOY; MASS

Patience, PASCHAL MYSTERY, in us, through patience

PEACE (**pax**)

—as goal: *Scrip.cit.*(Ps 33[34]:14) Prol.17   (**requiescere**) (Ps 14[15]:1) Prol. 23

—as quiet mind: (**tacite**) 7.35   (**aequo animo**) 31.17

—as reconciliation: *Scrip.allu.*(Eph 4:26) 4.73

—in community: 34.5 *Implication:* 65.22

   —with guests: 53.4

—*Monastic ritual:*

   —Public recitation of the Lord's Prayer: 13.12,13

   —Kiss of peace: 53.5; 63.4

—*Antithesis:* (**pacem falsam**) 4.25   (**numquam requiescit**) 64.16

   —anxiety: (**anxius**) 64.16

   —disturbances: (**conturbare**) 63.2   (**exordinationes**) 65.7   (**inquietare**) 48.5; 53.16   (**perturbare**) 31.19; 61.2   (**turbulentus**) 31.1; 64.16

   —idleness: (**otiositas**) 48.1

   —quarreling: factions: (**discordare**) 4.73   (**dissensiones**) 65.2,7,8   (**rixa**) 65.7

   —rebel: (**rebellio**) 62.8

Perseverance, PASCHAL MYSTERY, in us, patience as perseverance; STABILITY, of heart

Poverty, COMMUNITY, sharing all things in common

PRAYER (**oratio**)

—as:

   —adoration: 53.7

   —awe: fear of the Lord: (**timere**) Prol.29; 7.11; 31.2; 36.7; 64.15; 65.15; 72.9   (**timor**) Prol.12; 3.11; 5.9; 7.10; 11.9; 53.21; 64.1; 66.4 *Implication:* 19.6   *Scrip.cit.*(Ps 33[34]:10) 2.36   (Ps 2:11) 19.3

     —reverence: (**reverentia**) 20.t,1; 9.7; 11.3; 52.2   (**adorare**) 53.7   (**honor**) 9.7; 36.4; 63.13

     —*Antithesis:* (**irridere**) 58.18   (**non facere**) 52.5   (**improbitas**) 52.3

—call-response: (**evocare**) 7.9   (**vox invitans**) Prol.19   (**respondere**) Prol. 35   (**interrogare**) Prol.23,39   (**interrogatio**)Prol.24   (**vocare**) Prol.21

—compunction: (**compunctio**) 20.3; 49.4   (**fletus**) 49.4   (**lacrimae**) 4.57; 52.4   (**diluere**) 49.3   (**gemitus**) 4.57 *Antithesis:* JOY

—confession: FORGIVENESS, aspect of confession, to God

—conversion: (**convertere**) 2.18; 7.30; 63.7   *Scrip.cit.*(Ezek 33:11) Prol.38 (Ps 49[50]:21) 7.30   (**paenitentia**)*Scrip.cit.*(Rom 2:4) Prol.37   (**emendare**) Prol.36; 4.58   (**redire**) Prol.2

   —CONVERSION, **convertere**; DISCIPLINE, means, amendment

—desire for God: (**desiderare**) 4.46   (**desiderium**) 7.23; 49.7 *Scrip.cit.*(Ps

37[38]:10) 7.23   love of eternal life: (amor) 5.10   (cupere) *Scrip.cit.*
(Ps 33[34]:13) Prol.15   LIFE, as journey to God
—hope: (spes) 4.41; 7.39
—seeking God: (quaerere) Prol.14; 58.7   (regnum Dei) *Scrip.cit.*(Matt
    6:33) 2.35
—waiting for God: (exspectare) 49.7   (exspectatio) *Scrip.cit.*(Ps 118
    [119]:116) 58.21   (sustinere) *Scrip.cit.*(Ps 26[27]:14) 7.37   *Implication*: 7.38
—experience of God: (ecce adsum) *Scrip.cit.*(Ps 33[34]:16) Prol.17   (Isa
    58:9; 65:24) Prol.18   *Scrip.allu.*(Ps 15[16]:11) Prol.20   (caritas perfecta foris mittit timorem) (1 John 4:18) 7.67
—offering: 49.6
    —of sons: (filius) 59.t,1,2,4,8
    —of self: (suscipere) *Scrip.cit.*(Ps 118[119]:116) 58.21   (promittere)
        58.14,17,19   (petitio) 58.19,20,29
—praise: (confiteri) 4.57; 7.46; 16.5   (laudare) 11.8   (laus) 10.t; 11.10; 16.5
    Scrip.cit.(Ps 75[76]:11) 7.17   (Ps 105[106]:1; Ps 117[118]:1) 7.46
    (Ps 118[119]:164) 16.1,3   (Ps 50[51]:17) 9.1; 38.3   (Ps 118[119]:62)
    16.4   (gloria) *Scrip.cit.*(Ps 113[114]:9) Prol.30   (gloriari) *Scrip.cit.*(1
    Cor 10:17) Prol.32   (glorificare) 57.9   GOD, Trinity
—petition: Prol.4   (invocare) Prol.18   (rogare) Prol.41; 7.20   (supplicare) 20.2   (preces) Prol.18
—union and mutual communion: (pariter) 53.4; 72.12   (unum) 2.20;
    61.10   *Scrip.cit.*(Eph 6:8) 2.20   *Scrip.allu.*(Gal 3:28) 2.20   (visitare)
    Scrip.cit.(Matt 25:36,40) 36.2
—attitudes:
    —fervor: (instantissima oratio) Prol. 4   (intentio cordis) 52.4   (incumbere)
        4.56   *Implication*: 18.23; 20.3   *Antithesis*: (tepidus) 18.24,25
    —humility: (humilitas) 20.1,2   (humiliasti me) *Scrip.cit.*(Ps 118[119]:71)
        7.54   (Luke 18:13) 7.65
    —purity: (purus) 20.4   (puritatis devotione) 20.2   (puritas cordis)
        20.3   (omni puritate vitam custodire) 49.2   (immaculatus coram te)
        Scrip.cit.(Ps 17[18]:24) 7.18   LIFE, as journey
    —sincerity: 19.7; 20.3; 52.4
—duration:
    —brief: (brevis) 20.4,5
    —continual: (semper) 7.11,14,65   (omni hora) 7.13,29
    —frequent: (frequenter) 4.56   (cotidie) 4.57   more frequent in Lent:
        49.5
    —prolonged: (protendere) 20.4
—kinds:
    —alone: (secrete) 52.4   (peculiaris) 49.5; 52.3
    —corporate: (in conventu) 20.5   (chorus) 43.4,11; 44.5; 63.4
        —for delinquent monks: 27.4; 28.4; 44.4
        —for absent monks: 67.2
        —for new members: 58.23
        —monastic rituals: MONASTIC RITUALS

PRIDE (superbia)
—cautioned against in:
—leaders: abbot: (obstinatus) 64.16 —cellarer: (elatus) 31.1 (typho)
31.16 (spernere) 31.7 *Implication*: (praesumere) 31.15 —deans:
21.5 —prior: (superbia; elatus) 65.2,18 (tyrannis) 65.2 (maligno
spiritu superbiae) 65.2 (contemptor) 65.18 —priests: 62.2 (contumacia) 62.11 (praesumere) 62.8 (rebellio) 62.8 —reader: 38.2
—monks: 4.34,69 (spernere) Prol.29; 2.9; 7.2; 68.3 *Scrip.cit.*(Ps
130[131]:1,2) 7.3,4
—defined as self-exaltation: (exaltatio) 7.2,7 *Scrip.cit.*(Luke 14:11; 18:14)
7.1 (Ps 130[131]:1,2) 7.3,4 (Ps 87[88]:16) 7.53
—fault of monks: (durus; inoboedientes) 2.12,28 (superbus) 23.1 (contumax)
23.1; 71.9
—means to avoid: 38.2; 65.13
—punishment of: 2.28; 21.5,6,7; 23.4,5; 28.6; 62.8,9; 64.4,5; 65.19,21
Scrip.cit.(Ps 29[30]:12) 2.28 (Prov 23:14) 2.29 (1 Cor 5:13; 7:15)
28.6,7
—*Monastic ritual*: MONASTIC RITUALS, for weekly reader
—*Images*:
—Hard-hearted: (durus corde) 2.12,28
—Puffed-up person: (inflatus) 21.5; 65.2
—OBEDIENCE, *Antithesis*
Prior, MONASTIC LEADERS
Punishment, DISCIPLINE, means
Reading, LISTENING, to holy reading; SCRIPTURE, to be read
RULE (regula)
—all observance of justice not in: (iustitia) 73.t,1 —for beginners: 73.8
—authority of: (auctoritas) 37.1
—basis for monastic promise: 60.9 *Implication*: 58.14
—law of: (lex) 58.10,15
—observance of: (observare) —by abbot: 3.11; 64.20 *Implication*:
3.7 —monks: 3.7; 7.55 *Antithesis*: 1.6; 23.1 —priests: 60.2,9;
62.4,11 —deans: 62.7 *Antithesis*: 62.11 —prior: 65.17 *Antithesis*: 65.18
—read aloud: —to novice: 58.9,12,13 —to all: 66.8
—regular discipline: (regulari disciplinae subiaceat) 3.10; 32.5; 48.20; 54.5;
60.5; 62.3; 65.19; 67.6; 70.6
—sadness, JOY, *Antithesis*, not to be in monastery
—Scripture as rule of life: (norma) 73.3 (lex divina) 53.9; 64.9
—spiritual combat under: 1.2; 58.10,16 SERVICE, as spiritual combat
—strictness of, not applied to children or elderly: 37
—unlawful monastic actions: (non licere) 54.1; 58.15,16; 63.11 (non permittere) 43.15; 52.5
—*Images*:
—Master: (magister) Prol.1
—Yoke: (iugum) 58.16
—OBEDIENCE, to the Rule

Sadness, JOY, *Antithesis*, not to be in monastery

SCRIPTURE (scriptura)
  —as divine law: (lex divina) 53.9; 64.9
  —as rule of life: (norma) 73.3
  —authority of: (auctoritas) 9.8; 73.3
  —personification of: (apostolus) Prol.31,37; 2.3; 25.3; 27.4; 28.6; 58.2
      —Gospel as guide: Prol.21
      —Psalmist as prophet: Prol.23,30; 6.1,2; 7.3,14,23,29,47,50,52,66;
        16.1,4; 19.3
  —to be heard: LISTEN
  —to be read: (legere)
      —lectio: (lectio divina) 48.1 (lectio) 48.4,5,10,13,14,22; 49.4 (lectioni-
        bus) 48.13,14
      —to edify: (aedificare) 38.12; 42.3; 47.3; 53.9
      —weekly reader: 38 MONASTIC RITUALS, for weekly reader
      —*Monastic ritual*:
          —Guest ceremonial: (lex divina) 53.9
          —Work of God: liturgical reading: (lectiones) 9.5,9,10; 11.2,4,5,9,12;
            13.11; 14.2; 17.4,5,8; 18.10,18; 42.5,7
  —to be reflected on: (meditare) 48.23; 58.5
  —*Images*:
      —Medicine: (medicamen) 28.3
      —Word: (verba) *Scrip.cit.*(Matt 7:24) Prol. 33 (sermones) *Scrip.cit.*(Ps
        49[50]:17) 2.14

Seniors, MONASTIC LEADERS

SERVICE (servire)
  —as spiritual combat: (militare)
      —under Christ, King: (rex) Prol.3,40 *Scrip.allu.*(Eph 6:13-16; 2 Tim
        2.3,4) Prol.3 (servitus) 2.20; 61.10 (indutiae) Prol.36
      —under a rule and abbot: 1.2; 58.10 (pugnare) 1.5
          —against the devil: (diabolus) 1.4
          —against vices: (vitium) 1.5
      —with weapons of obedience: (arma) Prol.3
      —within fraternal army: (acies) 1.5 (militia) 2.20
  —mutual: (servire) 35.1,6,13 (servitor) 38.11 (ministerium) 35.10; 46.1
    (ministrare) 38.6
  —of abbot: 2.31 (ministrare) 64.21
  —of Christ: (ministrare) Prol.41
  —of cellarer: (ministrare) *Scrip.cit.*(1 Tim 3:13) 31.8
  —professed: (servitium) 5.3
      —measure of: 49.5; 50.4 *Implication*: 16.2
  —school for the Lord's: Prol.45
  —to guests: 53.18 GUESTS
  —to the sick: 36.1-4 (servitor) 36.7,10
  —*Image: Antithesis*: Wicked servants: Prol.7
  —CARE and CONCERN; STEWARDSHIP

Shepherd, ABBOT, *Images*; CHRIST, *Images*

SILENCE (silentium)
—as inner stillness: (silentium) 42.1   (cum summo silentio) 52.2   (tacere) 7.35
   Implication: (mansuetudo) 66.4; 68.1   (patienter) 68.2   (cum gravitate) 43.2   —*Antithesis*: (inquietos) 2.8,25   (quietus non fuerit) 65.21
   GRUMBLING; PEACE
—as discipline in speech: 7.56   (multum loqui non amare) 4.52   (verba non
   loqui) 4.53   (silui a bonis) *Scrip.cit.*(Ps 38[39]:3) 6.1   (scurrilitates
   vero vel verba otiosa . . . damnamus) 6.8   (aut fabulis) 48.18   (non sit
   clamosus) 7.60   *Scrip.cit.*(Ps 139[140]:12) 7.58   *Scrip.allu.*(Ps
   33[34]:14) 7.56
—motives for:
     —fear of sin: 6.2,3   (taciturnitas) 7.56   *Scrip.cit.*(Prov 10:19) 6.4;
        7.57   (Prov 18:21) 6.5   (Ps 14[15]:2,3) Prol.25,26   (Ps 38[39]:2)
        6.1   (Ps 33[34]:14-15) Prol.17
     —to foster listening: (tacere et audire) 6.6   (summum fiat silentium)
        38.5   LISTENING
     —value of silence itself: (taciturnitas; tacere) 6.2   (propter taciturnitatis
        gravitatem) 6.3
—of disciples: 6.6
—of God: (tacere) *Scrip.cit.*(Ps 49[50]:21) 7.30
—of the wise man: 7.61
—times of:
     —at all times: 42.1
     —at night: 42.1
     —during Lent: (subtrahat corpori . . . de loquacitate) 49.7
     —during meals: 38.8
     —during times of reading: 38.8; 48.5   *Implication*: 48.17,18
     —during siesta: (cum omni silentio) 48.5
     —during the Work of God: *Implication*: (fabulis vacet) 43.8
     —in the oratory: (cum summo silentio) 52.2
     —with the excommunicated: (nec in colloquio) 25.2   (aut loqui cum eo)
        26.1
     —with guests: (neque colloquatur) 53.23   (non licere colloqui) 53.24
     —after a journey: (nec . . . referre alio . . . viderit aut audierit) 67.5
—*Antithesis*: (clamosus) 52.4
     —*Image*: Talkative man: *Scrip.cit.*(Ps 139[140]:12) 7.58

Sincerity, HUMILITY, as authenticity

Spiritual combat, SERVICE

STABILITY (stabilitas)
—of heart: (dicat semper in corde) 7.18,65   (puritas) 20.3   (purus) 20.4   (vita)
   49.2
—always guarded: (custodiens se omni hora) 7.12   (cavere) 7.29   (semper; memor) 2.1,6,30,34; 7.10,11,18; 19.3; 31.8   (semper) 2.23,39;
   7.63,64; 31.8; 55.20; 63.3; 64.1,7,10,13   (incessabiliter) 4.76
—as remaining: (stare) 61.9   *Scrip.allu.*(2 Tim 4:2) 58.11,13

—as being content: (contentus) 7.49; 61.2,3 (tacite) 7.35 (aequo animo) 31.17

—in community: (congregatio) stability: (stabilitas) 4.78; 61.5 (habitare) 40.8; 55.1; 60.t; 61.1,13 (stare) 61.9 *Implication*: 66.6,7

—purpose, motive, goal: desire to dwell in the tent of his kingdom: (habitare) Prol.22,23,39 *Scrip.cit.*(Ps 14[15]:1-3) Prol.23-27

—promise of: (stabilitas) 58.9,17; 60.9 (firmare) 61.5

—*Antithesis*: never stable: (vagus) 1.11 (vagari) 66.7

—*Images*:
    —House on rock: (aedificare domum suam super petram) *Scrip.cit.*(Matt 7:24,25) Prol.33,35
    —Rock: (Christus) dash evil thoughts against: CHRIST, *Image*, Rock

—PASCHAL MYSTERY, as perseverance; LIFE, as journey, *Image*, Way

STEWARDSHIP (vilicatio)
    —of abbot: (vilicatio) *Scrip.cit.*(Luke 16:2) 64.7 (dispensator; dignus) *Scrip.allu.*(Ps 104[105]:21; Luke 12:42) 64.5 (servus bonus) *Scrip.cit.*(Matt 24:47) 64.22 (committere) *Scrip.allu.*(Luke 12:48) 2.30 (ministrare) *Scrip.allu.*(Matt 24:45) 64.21 (servire) 2.31 *Scrip.allu.*(Matt 13:52; 1 Tim 3:2) 64.9

    —over the House of God: 64.5
        —its members: (anima; committere) 2.30,31-33 (suscipere) 2.37 (regere; servire) 2.31,34,37 (dispensatio) 22.2 (disponere) 3.6
        —its substance: (substantia) 2.35 (necessaria) 33.5; 55.18 (utilitas) 65.12 (res) 2.33 (consignet recolligenda) 32.2 (sciat quid dat aut quid recipit) 32.3 *Scrip.cit.*(Acts 4:35) 55.20 (iniungere) 31.15 (iubere) 31.5; 54.3 (iussio) 31.4,12; 33.2 (permittere) 33.5 (sine praecepto) 54.1 (ab abbate non accepit) 55.17 —clothing: (consideratio) 55.3 (providere) 55.8

    —is not to have greater solicitude for things than for souls: 2.33 *Scrip.cit.*(Matt 6:33) 2.35 (Ps 33[34]:10) 2.36

    —is to know (scire) he must render an account: (rationem redditurus) 3.11 (memor) 2.6,7 (timere discussionem) 2.39
        —of his judgments: (iudicium) 3.11; 63.3; 65.22
        —of his works: (opera) 63.3
        —of souls: (anima) 2.34,37,38

—of the cellarer: (ministrare) *Scrip.cit.*(1 Tim 3:13) 31.8 (curam gerat) 31.3
    —under abbot: (committere) 31.17 (iubere) 31.5 (iussio) 31.4,12 (iniungere) 31.15
    —over substance of the monastery: (substantia) 31.10,12 (vasa) as vessels of the altar: *Scrip.allu.*(Zech 14:20) 31.10 —food: 31.16; 37.5
    —is to know (scire) he must give an account: (rationem redditurus) 31.9

—of monks: (consignet custodienda atque recolligenda) 32.2 (res) 32.4 (fregerit quippiam aut perdiderit) 46.2 (revertentes restituant) 55.13,14

—ABBOT, *Image*, Shepherd; MONASTIC LEADERS, cellarer

Teaching, DISCIPLINE, as divine teaching

Two ways, LIFE, as journey, *Image*, Way

Way, LIFE, as journey, *Image*, Way

WILL (**voluntas**)
—divine: 7.20
—human:
  —desire: (**desiderium**) 49.7; 60.8   (**cupere**) 61.3; 64.12,19 *Scrip.cit.*(Ps 33[34]:13) Prol.15   (Ps 37[38]:10) 7.23
  —personal choice: (**propria voluntas**) 49.6   (**voluntas**) 49.8,10; 62.6   (**eligere**) 1.9; 21.1,3,4; 31.1; 62.1,2,3; 65.15
—self-will: (**propria voluntas**) 4.60; 5.7; 7.19,31; 33.4
  —renunciation of:
    —in Christ: *Scrip.cit.*(John 6:38) 5.13; 7.32
    —in monks:
      —guard against: (**custodiens**) 7.12   (**cavere**) 7.3,21,24,29; 62.2 *Scrip.cit.*(Sir 18:30) 7.25
      —hate: (**odire**) 4.60   —not to love: 7.31
      —imitate Christ in: (**imitari**) *Scrip.cit.*(John 6:38) 5.13; 7.32
      —learn not to do: 7.21   *Scrip.cit.*(Prov 16:25) 7.21   (Ps 13[14]:1) 7.22
      —not to follow: 3.8   —not to fulfill: *Scrip.allu.*(Gal 5:16) 4.59
      —not to have at one's disposal: 33.4
      —turn from: (**abrenuntiare**) Prol.3   (**averti**) *Scrip.cit.*(Sir 18:30) 7.19   (**deserere; exoccupatis manibus relinquere**) 5.7,8   (**fugere**) 4.69 CONVERSION, **convertere**
      —*Antithesis*: desire for pleasure: (**malum desiderium**) 7.24   (**desideriorum voluntas**) 1.8   (**desideria carnis**) 4.59; 7.12; 60.8   (**voluntatibus**) *Scrip.cit.*(Ps 37[38]:10) 7.22 *Implication*: (**sequi noluerint**) Prol.7
        —*Image*: Soft as lead: 1.6
      —GRUMBLING; PRIDE

WORD OF GOD (**eloquium; sermo**)
—(**eloquium**) *Scrip.cit.*(Ps 118[119]:116) 58.21   (**sermo**) *Scrip.cit.*(Ps 49[50]:16) 2.14
—as call: (**clamare**) Prol.9,14   (**evocare**) 7.9   (**invitare**) Prol.19   (**vocare**) Prol.21
—*Embodied in*: Scripture reading: SCRIPTURE, to be read; Voice of Teacher: DISCIPLINE, as divine teaching
—*Images*:
  —Voice of God: (**vox**) Prol.9 *Scrip.cit.*(Ps 94[95]:8) Prol.10 *Scrip.cit.*(Rev 2:7) Prol.11   (**dicere**) Prol.12,14,16,18,25   (**respondere**) Prol.24
  —Voice of Christ: (**eloquium**) 31.16   (**verbum**) *Scrip.cit.*(Matt 7:24) Prol.33   (**vox**) Prol.19; 7.32   (**ait**) Prol.33   (**dicere**) 5.5,6,11,15 *Scrip.cit.*(Matt 24:47) 64.22 *Implication*: (**audire**) *Scrip.cit.*(Luke 10:16) 5.6,15 LISTEN, to divine voice

ZEAL (**zelus**)
—for God: 64.6
—for trials, obedience, Work of God: (**sollicitus**) 58.7

INDEXES OF SCRIPTURE IN RB

In the Scriptural Indexes that follow, boldface type indicates direct scriptural citations, quoted word for word or even only one word; loci in parentheses identify indirect citations where Scripture is quoting Scripture, or alternate locations of the same text. Loci in roman type are allusions to scriptural passages, either certain or possible. In some instances allusion is made to a unique locus in Scripture: e.g., the Good Shepherd, Matt 18:12–RB 27.8.

SCRIPTURE TO RB

Gen 28:12	7.6	Ps 13(14):3	7.29
Gen 33:13	64.18	Ps 14(15):1	Prol.23
		Ps 14(15):2-3	Prol.25-27
Exod 8:21-22	21.1-3	Ps 14(15):4	Prol.28-30
(Exod 20:13-17)	4.3-7	Ps 15(16):10	Prol.20
Lev 19:17	4.65	Ps 17(18):24	7.18
(Lev 19:18)	4.2	Ps 17(18):45	5.5
Lev 19:32	63.16	Ps 21(22):7	7.52
Deut 1:13-15	21.1-4	Ps 26(27):14	7.37
(Deut 5:17-21)	4.3-7	Ps 27(28):3	4.25
(Deut 6:5)	4.1	Ps 31(32):5	7.47-48
1 Sam 2:11-34	2.26	Ps 33(34):10	2.36
1 Sam 3:1-21	62.1	Ps 33(34):12	Prol.12
1 Sam 3:11-14	2.26	Ps 33(34):13	Prol.15
1 Sam 4:12-18	2.26	Ps 33(34):14	4.51
		Ps 33(34):14-15	Prol.17
Isa 1:2	2.9	Ps 33(34):14	7.56
Isa 1:17	4.18	Ps 35(36):2	7.10
Isa 42:3	64.13	Ps 36(37):5	7.45
Isa 58:9	Prol.18	Ps 37(38):7-9	7.66
		Ps 37(38):10	7.23
Jer 9:8	4.25	Ps 38(39):2-3	6.1
Ezek 20:27	2.9	Ps 39(40):11	2.9
Ezek 33:11	Prol.38	(Ps 43[44]:22)	7.38
Ezek 34:3-4	27.7	Ps 46(47):8	19.4
		Ps 47(48):10	53.14
Zech 14:20	31.10-11	Ps 49(50):16-17	2.14
Ps 2:11	19.3	Ps 49(50):21	7.30
Ps 7:10	7.14	Ps 50(51):17	9.1
Ps 13(14):1	7.22	Ps 50(51):17	38.3
Ps 13(14):2	4.49	Ps 65(66):10-11	7.40
Ps 13(14):2	7.13	Ps 65(66):12	7.41
Ps 13(14):2	7.27	Ps 69(70):2	17.3

SS	RB	SS	RB
Ps 69(70):2	18.1	Jdt 15:11	4.64
Ps 69(70):2	35.17	(Sir 2:5)	1.6
Ps 72(73):22-23	7.50	Sir 6:37	4.63
Ps 72(73):28	4.41	Sir 18:17	31.14
Ps 75(76):11	7.17	Sir 18:30	4.60
Ps 77(78):7	4.41	Sir 18:30	7.19
Ps 85(86):17	35.16	Sir 18:30	7.25
Ps 87(88):16	7.53	Sir 19:2	40.7
Ps 93(94):11	7.15	Sir 21:23	7.59
Ps 94(95):8	Prol.10	Sir 32:24	3.13
Ps 104(105):21	64.5	Sir 35:10-11	5.16
Ps 105(106):1	7.46	Sir 37:10	4.36
Ps 113:9(Ps 115:1)	Prol.30	Sir 42:7	32.3
Ps 117(118):1	7.46	Sir 45:19	62.1
Ps 118(119):32	Prol.49	Tob 1:17-18	4.17
Ps 118(119):62	16.4-5	Tob 4:16	4.9
Ps 118(119):71	7.54	Tob 4:16	61.14
Ps 118(119):73	7.54	Tob 4:16	70.7
Ps 118(119):107	7.66	Wis 1:11	4.39-40
Ps 118(119):116	58.21	(Wis 3:6)	1.6
Ps 118(119):164	16.1	Matt 3:15	73.t
Ps 118(119):164	16.3	Matt 4:22	5.7-8
Ps 118(119):164	16.5	Matt 5:7	64.10
Ps 127(128):2	48.8	Matt 5:10	4.33
Ps 128(129):8	25.6	Matt 5:22	4.22
Ps 130(131):1	7.3	Matt 5:33-37	4.27
Ps 130(131):2	7.4	Matt 5:39-41	7.42
Ps 136(137):9	Prol.28	Matt 5:44	4.31
Ps 136(137):9	4.50	Matt 5:44	4.72
Ps 137(138):1	19.5	Matt 6:7	20.3-4
Ps 138(139):3	7.16	Matt 6:10	7.20
Ps 139(140):12	7.58	Matt 6:12	13.13
Prov 1:8	Prol.1	Matt 6:13	13.14
Prov 4:20	Prol.1	Matt 6:33	2.35
Prov 6:20	Prol.1	Matt 7:3	2.15
Prov 10:19	6.4	Matt 7:12	4.9
Prov 10:19	7.57	Matt 7:12	61.14
Prov 12:20	4.24	Matt 7:12	70.7
Prov 14:12	7.21	Matt 7:13-14	72.1-2
Prov 15:3	4.49	Matt 7:14	Prol.48
Prov 15:3	7.26	Matt 7:14	5.11
Prov 15:3	19.1	Matt 7:24-25	Prol.33-34
Prov 16:25	7.21	Matt 8:8	7.65
Prov 18:21	6.5	Matt 9:12	27.1
Prov 20:13	4.37	Matt 10:22	7.36
Prov 23:14	2.29	Matt 11:15	Prol.11
Prov 27:21	1.6	Matt 11:25	3.3
Prov 29:19	2.28	Matt 12:20	64.13
Dan 3:52	35.16	Matt 13:33	2.5
Dan 13:44-62	63.6		

SS	RB	SS	RB
Gal 3:28	2.20	2 Tim 2:2-4	Prol.3
Gal 4:17-18	72.1-2	2 Tim 4:2	2.23
Gal 5:16	4.59	2 Tim 4:2	58.11
Gal 5:20-21	65.7	Titus 1:7	4.34-35
Gal 6:7	58.18	Titus 1:7-9	64.9
Gal 6:10	53.2	Titus 2:2-5	64.9
Eph 4:26	4.73		
Eph 4:27	38.8	Heb 4:11	73.8
Eph 4:27	43.8	Heb 4:15	27.9
Eph 4:27	54.4	Heb 11:14-15	73.8
Eph 6:8	2.20	Heb 13:1	72.8
Eph 6:10-17	Prol.3	Heb 13:17	2.38
Eph 6:14-15	Prol.21	Jas 1:27	4.20
Phil 2:4	72.7	Jas 2:13	64.10
Phil 2:8	7.34	Jas 3:14	4.66
Phil 2:13	Prol.29	Jas 3:14	4.68
		Jas 3:14	72.1
1 Thess 1:6	49.6	1 Pet 1:22	72.8
1 Thess 2:12	Prol.21	1 Pet 2:17	4.8
1 Thess 4:9	72.8	1 Pet 2:17	72.9
1 Thess 5:15	4.29	1 Pet 3:9	4.29
1 Thess 5:17	4.56	1 Pet 3:9	4.32
2 Thess 3:10-12	48.8	1 Pet 3:10-11	Prol.15-17
1 Tim 3:2-4	31.1	1 Pet 4:8	4.26
1 Tim 3:2-4	64.9	1 Pet 4:11	57.9
1 Tim 3:3	4.35	1 Pet 4:13	Prol.50
1 Tim 3:13	31.8	1 John 4:1	58.2
1 Tim 5:14	38.8	1 John 4:18	7.67
1 Tim 5:14	43.8		
1 Tim 5:14	54.4	2 John 9	Prol.50
1 Tim 5:20	23.3	Jude:16	5.12
1 Tim 5:20	48.20		
1 Tim 5:20	70.3	Rev 2:7	Prol.11

RB TO SCRIPTURE

Prol.1	Prov 1:8	Prol.15-17	1 Pet 3:10-11
	Prov 4:20	Prol.17	Ps 33(34):14-15
	Prov 6:20	Prol.18	Isa 58.9
Prol.3	Eph 6:10-17	Prol.20	Ps 15(16):10
	2 Tim 2:2-4	Prol.21	Eph 6:14-15
Prol.8	Rom 13:11		1 Thess 2:12
Prol.10	Ps 94(95):8	Prol.23	Ps 14(15):1
Prol.11	Matt 11:15	Prol.25-27	Ps 14(15):2-3
	Rev 2:7	Prol.28	Ps 14(15):4
Prol.12	Ps 33(34):12		Ps 136(137):9
Prol.13	John 12:35		1 Cor 10:14
Prol.15	Ps 33(34):13	Prol.29	Phil 2:13

RB	SS	RB	SS
4.65	Lev 19:17	7.41	Ps 65(66):12
4.66	Jas 3:14	7.42	Matt 5:39-41
4.68	Jas 3:14		Luke 6:29
4.72	Matt 5:44	7.43	2 Cor 11:26
4.73	Eph 4:26		1 Cor 4:12
4.77	1 Cor 2:9	7.45	Ps 36(37):5
5.5	Ps 17(18):45	7.46	Ps 105(106):1
5.6	Luke 10:16		Ps 117(118):1
5.7-8	Matt 4:22	7.47-48	Ps 31(32):5
5.11	Matt 7:14	7.50	Ps 72(73):22-23
5.12	Jude 16	7.52	Ps 21(22):7
5.13	John 6:38	7.53	Ps 87(88):16
5.15	Luke 10:16	7.54	Ps 118(119):71,73
5.16	Sir 35:10-11	7.56	Ps 33(34):14
	2 Cor 9:7	7.57	Prov 10:19
5.19	1 Cor 10:10	7.58	Ps 139(140):12
6.1	Ps 38(39):2-3	7.59	Sir 21:23
6.4	Prov 10:19	7.65	Matt 8:8
6.5	Prov 18:21		Luke 18:13
7.1	Matt 23:12	7.66	Ps 37(38):7-9
	Luke 14:11		Ps 118(119):107
	Luke 18:14	7.67	1 John 4:18
7.3	Ps 130(131):1	9.1	Ps 50(51):17
7.4	Ps 130(131):2	13.13	Matt 6:12
7.6	Gen 28:12	13.14	Matt 6:13
7.10	Ps 35(36):2	16.1	Ps 118(119):164
7.13	Ps 13(14):2	16.3	Ps 118(119):164
7.14	Ps 7:10	16.4	Ps 118(119):62
7.15	Ps 93(94):11	16.5	Ps 118(119):164
7.16	Ps 138(139):3		Ps 118(119):62
7.17	Ps 75(76):11	17.3	Ps 69(70):2
7.18	Ps 17(18):24	18.1	Ps 69(70):2
7.19	Sir 18:30	19.1	Prov 15:3
7.20	Matt 6:10	19.3	Ps 2:11
7.21	Prov 14:12	19.4	Ps 46(47):8
	Prov 16:25	19.5	Ps 137(138):1
7.22	Ps 13(14):1	20.3-4	Matt 6:7
7.23	Ps 37(38):10	21.1	Acts 6:3
7.25	Sir 18:30	21.1-3	Exod 18:21-22
7.26	Prov 15:3	21.1-4	Deut 1:13-15
7.27	Ps 13(14):2	23.2	Matt 18:15-16
7.29	Ps 13(14):3	23.3	Matt 18:17
7.30	Ps 49(50):21		1 Tim 5:20
7.32	John 6:38	25.4	1 Cor 5.5
7.34	Phil 2:8	25.6	Ps 128(129):8
7.36	Matt 10:22	27.1	Matt 9:12
7.37	Ps 26(27):14	27.3	2 Cor 2:7
7.38	Rom 8:36 (Ps 43[44]:22)	27.4	2 Cor 2:8
7.39	Rom 8:37	27.7	Ezek 34:3-4
7.40	Ps 65(66):10-11	27.8	Matt 18:12

INDEXES OF PATRISTIC AND
ANCIENT WORKS IN RB

Numbers in boldface refer to passages that may be considered quotations from Patristic and Ancient sources, although this does not necessarily imply that St. Benedict was directly citing the work in question. All other loci indicate possible sources and allusions that illustrate the cultural and linguistic background, even though they may not be immediate sources. For complete bibliographical information, see pp. xxi–xxxi.

PATRISTIC AND ANCIENT WORKS TO RB

Act. Anastasiae
  17:7.33
Act.S.Sebast.
  4,14:7.24
Ambr. apol.Dav.
  51:2.30
Ambr. epist.
  63,85:2.20
Ambr. exhort.virg.
  74:4.27
Ambr. explan.ps.
  1,18:7.6-9
Ambr. expos. de psalm.
  18,10:72.1,9
  18,11:72.1,7-8; 73.7
  18,12:72.1
  18,13:72.1; 73.7
  18,14:72.3
  18,17:72.1; 73.6
  18,18:73.6
Ambr. off.
  2,107:53.7
  2,135:28.3-6
Ambr. paenit.
  2,96-97:4.10
  2,106:Prol.28
Ambr. virg.
  3,17:49.5
Aug. civ.
  11,28:Prol.2

13,20:71.1
14,6:64.11
19,19:64.8
22,2:2.33
Aug. conf.
  8,12,28:Prol.28
Aug. cons.evang.
  1,13:5.14
Aug. c.Cresc.
  4,37:1.9
Aug. c.Faust.
  25,56:64.8
Aug. c.Parm.
  2,13,31:1.9
Aug. de mend.
  15,28:4.27
Aug. epist.
  22,6:31.16
  48,3:19.7
  130,20:20.3-4
  157,40:4.27
  211,5:33.6; 34.1; 55.20
  211,6:57.2
  211,7:19.7; 52.1-3
  211,9:34.3-4
  211,11:28.8; 46.3-4; 54.1; 64.11
  211,12:54.2-3
  211,13:35.13
  211,15:2.34; 64.7; 64.15

13,6:62.4
14,2:38.6; 53.15; 55.1-2
15,2:59.6
16,3:3.11
38,2:4.55-56; 48.1
55,15-16:27.5-9; 28.2-3
55,21:63.2-3
57,1-3:Prol.50; 1.1-8
57,4:2.38-39
58,11:7.10-11
59,13:4.25
59,15:28.8
60,5:4.55-56
63,1:5.14; 31.4-5
65,1:4.55-56
65,5:Prol.2
65,10:Prol.49-50
67,2:7.10-11
67,2-3:64.1-5
68,4:27.1-9
72,1:4.61
76,7:7.13-14; 72.11-12
Cypr. *hab.virg.*
  3:Prol.3
  17:28.6,8
  21:Prol.50; 58.8
Cypr. *quod idola*
  11:72.11-12
Cypr. *testim.*
  prol.:Prol.20
  3:4.21,27; 40.8; 48.1; 63.16-17
  12:4.27
  13-14:4.32
  14:40.8
  18:4.21
  19:4.60
  22:4.30
  23:4.29
  39:7.43
  41:4.53
  49:4.31
  85:63.16-17
  103:4.52
  106:4.30
  109:4.16
  120:4.56
Cypr. *zel. et liv.*
  6:65.1-2,15-22
  10:4.66-67
  10-11:72.1
  12:2.1-2,12-13,30
  16:4.55-56; 48.1

18:4.49; 7.13-14
Didache
  2,7:4.65
Evagr. *sent.mon.*
  1,55:4.50
Fulg.Rusp. *epist.*
  17,47:Prol.41
Hier. *epist.*
  2,1:28.8
  14,9:2.30
  16,1:28.8
  22,1:Prol.1
  22,6:Prol.28
  22,15:Prol.3
  22,34:1.1-8
  22,35:1.13; 21.1; 35.1; 37.2; 48.22
  58,1:63.6
  58,5:4.55
  58,6:4.56
  58,8:1.12
  60,7:64.12
  60,10:4.55
  77,17:1.12
  79,9:4.22
  81,1:4.29
  98,3:7.6-9
  108,20:64.12
  117,6:63.12
  125,9:1.3-5
  130,11:64.12
  130,13:4.22
  130,19:28.8
Hier. *in Ezech.*
  16,52:72.1
Hier. *in psalm.*
  130,8:Prol.28
Hil. *in psalm.*
  136,14:Prol.28
Hist.mon.
  1:20.4; 48.8
  1-2:53.1-13
  2:66.7
  3:38.5
  7:1.12; **53.3-13**
  9:Prol.48; 4.17; 53.1-13
  17:53.3-13; 66.1,6-7
  21:53.1-13
  31:Prol.3; 4.10; 7.5,31-32; 73.1
Iren. *demonstr.apost.praedic.*
  1:72.1
Leo.M. *tract.*
  2,2,3:49.3

30-31:33.2
31:67.7
32:23.2-4; 24.2,4; 25.1-2
33:26.1-2
35:28.8; 62.10
Vita Anton.
  14:4.21
  25:48.8
Vita Macar. Rom.
  2:58.16
Vita Pachom.
  25:58.6
  28:33.3
Vitae patr., Verb.senior.
  3,6:18.25
  3,170:31.6
  3,196:4.47
  3,206:7.51
  5,1,9:Prol.3
  5,1,16:48.8

5,3,5:4.47
5,4,25:4.50; 7.44; 46.5
5,4,31:40.6
5,4,57:18.25
5,5,3:46.5
5,5,4:27.2; 28.2-3
5,6,21:48.3
5,7,18:Prol.4
5,10,85:27.2; 28.2-3
5,10,98:57.9
5,11,29:Prol.48-49; 73.1,8
5,13,13:27.4; 58.23
5,14,10:1.11
5,14,13:9.8
5,14,15:Prol.2
5,15,59:67.5
7,32,3:7.56
7,35,1:4.47
11,29:Prol.4

ANCIENT WORKS

Concil.Agathense a. 506
  38:28.1
Concil.Gerund. a. 517
  10:13.12
Decret.Gelasianum
  21:58.14
Digesta
  41,2,20:2.18
Orat.Manassae
  9:7.65
Porphyr. ad Marcell.
  12:4.42-43
Sacr.Gelasianum
  3:Prol.49
  25:Prol.49
  37:16.2
  38:2.32; 53.7

41:35.15
55:49.7
66:53.7
1322:Prol.49
Sacr.Leon.
  30,1104:72.9
Sext.Pythag. enchirid.
  113-114:4.42-43
  145:7.61
Stob. flor.
  3,1,173:4.70
Ter. Andr.
  I,i,34:64.12
Visio Pauli
  7:7.13,28
  10:7.28

RB TO PATRISTIC AND ANCIENT WORKS

Prol.1	Basil. ad fil. 1; Hier. epist. 22,1	Prol.2	Leo.M. tract. 90,2
		Prol.3	Basil. ad fil. 1
Prol.2	Aug. civ. 11,28; Vitae patr., Verb.senior. 5, 14,15; Aug. nat. et grat. 20,22; Cypr. epist. 65,5	Prol.3	Hier. epist. 22,15; Vitae patr., Verb.senior. 5,1,9; Hist.mon. 31; Cypr. hab.virg. 3

53.21-24	*Reg. iv patr.* 2,37-38; 2,40
53.23-24	Basil. *reg.fus.* 32-33; Pachom. *reg.* 50
54.1	Aug. *epist.* **211**,11; Pachom. *reg.* 106; Caes. Arel. *reg.mon.* 15; Caes.Arel. *reg.virg.* 23; Cassian. *inst.* 4,16
54.2-3	Aug. *epist.* **211**,12; Caes.Arel. *reg.mon.* 1; Caes.Arel. *reg.virg.* 40; Pachom. *reg.* 52
54.4	Cypr. *epist.* **4,2**
55.1	Cassian. *inst.* 1,10
55.1-2	Cypr. *epist.* 14,2
55.7	Basil. *reg.* **9**
55.7-11	Cassian. *inst.* 1,3
55.9	Caes.Arel. *reg.virg.* 40
55.10	Orsiesii *lib.* 22
55.11	Pachom. *reg.* 81
55.16	Cassian. *inst.* 4,14; 4,16,3; 7,7
55.17-18	Cypr. *epist.* 2,2
55.20	Aug. *epist.* 211,5; Basil. *reg.* 94
56.1	*Reg. iv patr.* 2,41
57.2	Aug. *epist.* 211,6
57.4-7	Aug. *ord.mon.* 8
57.5-6	Cassian. *inst.* 7,25,1
57.9	*Vitae patr., Verb.senior.* 5,10,98
58.1	Pachom. *reg.* 49
58.1-4	Caes.Arel. *reg.mon.* 1; Caes.Arel. *recapit.* 8; Cassian. *conl.* 20,1; Cassian. *inst.* 4,3
58.3	*Reg. iv patr.* 2,27
58.6	*Vita Pachom.* **25**; Cassian. *inst.* 4,7
58.7	Basil. *reg.* 6
58.8	Cassian. *conl.* 24,25, 2; *Reg. iv patr.* 2,26; Cypr. *hab.virg.* 21
58.9	Caes.Arel. *reg.virg.* 58
58.9-14	Caes.Arel. *recapit.* 8; Ps-Macar. *reg.* 23; *Decret.Gelasianum* 21
58.16	*Vita Macar. Rom.* 2
58.17	Cassian. *inst.* 7,9
58.18	Cassian. *inst.* 4,36,2
58.23	*Vitae patr., Verb.senior.* 5,13,13
58.24-25	Ps-Macar. *reg.* **24** Caes. Arel. *reg.mon.* 1
58.25	Cassian. *inst.* 2,3,1; 4,20; Cassian. *conl.* 24,23; Basil. *reg.* 106
58.26	Cassian. *inst.* **4,5-6**; Pachom. *reg.* 49
59.6	Cypr. *epist.* 15,2
59.8	Basil. *reg.* 7
61.13	*Reg. iv patr.* 4,3-8
62.4	Cypr. *epist.* 13,16
62.10	Vigil. *reg.(orient.)* 35
63.2-3	Cypr. *epist.* 55,21
63.4	Pachom. *reg.* praef. 3
63.6	Hier. *epist.* 58,1
63.7	Sulpic.Sever. *dial.* 1, 10,1
63.12	Hier. *epist.* 117,6
63.16-17	Cypr. *testim.* 3,85
64.1-5	Cypr. *epist.* 67,2-3; Cypr. *domin.orat.* 23
64.7	Aug. *epist.* 211,15
64.8	Aug. *serm.* 340,1; Aug. *civ.* 19,19; Aug. *c. Faust.* 25, 56
64.11	Aug. *serm.* **49,5**; Aug. *civ.* 14,6; Aug. *epist.* 211,11; Caes.Arel. *reg.virg.* 22
64.12	Ter. *Andr.* I,i,34; Hier. *epist.* 60,7; 108,20; 130,11; Aug. *in psalm.* 118,4,1
64.15	Aug. *epist.* **211,15**
64.19	Cassian. *conl.* 2,4,4; Cassian. *inst.* 2,12,2
65.t	Caes.Arel. *reg.virg.* 16; Ps-Macar. *reg.* 27
65.1-2	Cypr. *eccl.unit.* 10; Cypr. *zel. et liv.* 6
65.11	Cypr. *domin.orat.* 23
65.12	Cypr. *eccl.unit.* 10; Cassian. *inst.* 7,9
65.15-22	Cypr. *zel. et liv.* 6
65.16	Pachom. *reg.* 158
66.1	Cassian. *inst.* 4,7; *Hist. mon.* 17
66.6-7	*Hist.mon.* **17**
66.7	*Hist.mon.* **2**
67.5	*Vitae patr., Verb.se-*

BENEDICTINE MONKS AND NUNS
OF NORTH AMERICA

North American houses of Benedictine men and women are listed below, with affiliation to the several federations/congregations, and the European origins noted. In the main, the federations tend to represent the same European origin, though there are a few exceptions. The different indentations in the listing are meant to indicate the "generation" or stage of removal from the European source. The only published history of a federation is that of R. Baska, *The Benedictine Congregation of St. Scholastica: Its Foundation and Development (1852–1930)* (Washington, D.C.: Catholic Univ. Press 1935).

AMERICAN BENEDICTINE MONKS

The American Cassinese Federation

METTEN

St. Vincent (1846) Latrobe, Pennsylvania
    St. John's (1856) Collegeville, Minnesota
        St. Martin's (1895) Lacey, Washington
        Tepeyac (1946) Tlalnepantla, Mexico
        St. Maur Priory (1947) Indianapolis, Indiana
        St. Augustine Priory (1947) Nassau, Bahamas
    St. Benedict's (1857) Atchison, Kansas
    St. Mary's (1857) Morristown, New Jersey
        St. Anselm's (1889) Manchester, New Hampshire
  Newark Abbey (1857) Newark, New Jersey
Belmont Abbey (1876) Belmont, North Carolina
    St. Leo (1889) St. Leo, Florida
St. Procopius (1885) Lisle, Illinois
    St. Andrew's (1922) Cleveland, Ohio
    Holy Trinity Priory (1948) Butler, Pennsylvania
Holy Cross (1886) Canon City, Colorado

St. Bernard (1891) St. Bernard, Alabama

St. Bede (1891) Peru, Illinois

St. Peter (1892) Muenster, Saskatchewan

St. Gregory's (1875 PIERRE-QUI-VIRE) Shawnee, Oklahoma

Assumption (1893 EINSIEDELN) Richardton, North Dakota

The Swiss-American Federation

EINSIEDELN

St. Meinrad (1854) St. Meinrad, Indiana

　New Subiaco (1878) Subiaco, Arkansas

　　　Corpus Christi (1927) Corpus Christi, Texas

　St. Joseph (1890) St. Benedict, Louisiana

　Marmion (1933) Aurora, Illinois

　Blue Cloud (1950) Marvin, South Dakota

　St. Charles Priory (1958) Oceanside, California

ENGELBERG

Conception (1873) Conception, Missouri

　St. Benedict's (1945) Benet Lake, Wisconsin

　　　Glastonbury (1954) Hingham, Massachusetts

　　　Guadalupe (1955) Pecos, New Mexico

　Pius X (1951) Pevely, Missouri

　Mount Michael (1956) Elkhorn, Nebraska

Mount Angel (1882) St. Benedict, Oregon

　Westminster (1939) Mission, B.C., Canada

Other Affiliations

Solesmes: Abbaye Saint-Benoît (1912) Saint Benoît-du-Lac, Quebec

English: St. Gregory's (1918) Portsmouth, Rhode Island

　St. Anselm's (1924) Washington, D.C.

　St. Louis (1955) St. Louis, Missouri

Ottilien: St. Paul's (1924) Newton, New Jersey

Independent: Mount Saviour (1950) Pine City, New York

　Weston Priory (1952) Weston, Vermont

Annunciation: St. Andrew's (1955) Valyermo, California

Camaldolese: Immaculate Heart (1958) Big Sur, California

Sylvestrine: St. Benedict (1960) Oxford, Michigan

AMERICAN BENEDICTINE NUNS

The Federation of St. Scholastica

EICHSTÄTT

St. Joseph's (1852) St. Mary's, Pennsylvania
    Mount St. Benedict (1856) Erie, Pennsylvania
        St. Walburga's (1859) Covington, Kentucky
            St. Scholastica (1870) Covington, Louisiana
                Sacred Heart (1902) Cullman, Alabama*
        St. Scholastica (1861) Chicago, Illinois
    St. Gertrude's (1857) Ridgely, Maryland
    (*St. Benedict's [1857] St. Joseph, Minnesota*)
        Mount St. Scholastica (1863) Atchison, Kansas
            St. Benedict (1950) Mexico City, Mexico
            St. Lucy's (1952) Glendora, California
            Benet Hill (1965) Colorado Springs, Colorado
    St. Walburga's (1868) Elizabeth, New Jersey
        Emmanuel (1971) Severn, Maryland
    Mount St. Mary's (1870) Pittsburgh, Pennsylvania
        St. Joseph (1879) Tulsa, Oklahoma
            Holy Family (1947) Benet Lake, Wisconsin
            Red Plains (1968) Oklahoma City, Oklahoma
        Holy Name (1889) St. Leo, Florida
            Sacred Heart (1902) Cullman, Alabama*
        Sacred Heart (1895) Lisle, Illinois
            Our Lady of Sorrows (1951) Oak Forest, Illinois
            Queen of Heaven (1969) Warren, Ohio
        St. Scholastica (1911) Boerne, Texas
    St. Benedict (1874) Bristow, Virginia

The Federation of St. Benedict

EICHSTÄTT

(*St. Joseph's [1852] St. Mary's, Pennsylvania*)
    St. Benedict's (1857) St. Joseph, Minnesota
        St. Scholastica (1892) Duluth, Minnesota
        Annunciation (1947) Bismarck, North Dakota
        St. Bede (1948) Eau Claire, Wisconsin

St. Paul (1948) St. Paul, Minnesota

St. Placid (1952) Olympia, Washington

(*St. Scholastica [1861] Chicago, Illinois*)

St. Mary (1874) Nauvoo, Illinois

The Federation of St. Gertrude the Great

EICHSTÄTT

(*St. Walburga's [1859] Covington, Kentucky*)

Immaculate Conception (1867) Ferdinand, Indiana

St. Scholastica (1879) Fort Smith, Arkansas

Our Lady of Peace (1969) Columbia, Missouri

Our Lady of Grace (1957) Beech Grove, Indiana

Queen of Peace (1963) Belcourt, North Dakota

Holy Spirit (1966) Sunnymead, California

(*St. Scholastica [1892] Duluth, Minnesota*)

St. Benedict's (1912) Winnipeg, Manitoba

Mount St. Benedict (1919) Crookston, Minnesota

(*St. Joseph's [1852] St. Mary's, Pennsylvania*)

Sacred Heart (1919) Richardton, North Dakota

MARIA RICKENBACH

Sacred Heart (1880) Yankton, South Dakota

Mother of God (1961) Watertown, South Dakota

Queen of Angels (1882) Mount Angel, Oregon

St. Benedict's (1897) Madison, Wisconsin

SARNEN

St. Gertrude's (1882) Cottonwood, Idaho

MELCHTHAL

St. Martin's (1889) Rapid City, South Dakota

Congregation of the Benedictine Sisters of Perpetual Adoration

MARIA RICKENBACH

St. Scholastica (1874) Clyde, Missouri

Christ the King (1935) Tucson, Arizona

Holy Spirit (1943) Kansas City, Missouri
St. Pius X (1954) San Diego, California
Divine Heart (1966) St. Louis, Missouri

Other Affiliations

Diocesan: Holy Angels (1887) Jonesboro, Arkansas
Tutzing: Immaculata (1923) Norfolk, Nebraska
Solesmes: Abbaye Sainte-Marie (1936) Sainte-Marthe-sur-le-Lac, Quebec
Jouarre: Regina Laudis (1948) Bethlehem, Connecticut
Eichstätt: St. Walburga's (1951) Boulder, Colorado
    St. Emma's (1953) Greensburg, Pennsylvania

GENERAL INDEX

NAME INDEX

SUBJECT INDEX

Numbers in italics refer to the text of the Rule.

abbot, as father *175, 231*; as physician *223, 225*; as shepherd *173*; as steward *283*; as teacher *173*; announces the Work of God *249*; represents Christ *173, 279*; discretion of *261*; election of *281–285*; power of *275, 277, 279*; qualities of *171–179, 283–285*; according to St. Benedict 346–354; as spiritual father 92, 93, 376; as teacher 364–367, 447; defined by relationship 355; discretion of 91; election of 371–378; in tradition 145; represents Christ 356, 378; 557, 558, 572

Abbot Primate 136

aged, consideration of *235–237*; 27

Ambrosian hymn *203, 207, 213*; 400, 401

amendment, of faults *179*; satisfaction and *245*; 435

anchorite *169*; 17, 18, 20, 26, 46, 54, 58, 62, 67, 68, 302, 303, 310, 313, 314, 317, 318, 319

anthropomorphism 41

antiphon (*See* refrain)

apatheia 39, 361

Apophthegmata Patrum 12, 129, 323, 332, 336, 464, 467

Arian heresy 30–31, 45, 63, 66, 362

artisan, in monastery *265–267*

asceticism, tradition of 4, 9, 43, 49, 52, 55, 114, 123, 303, 314, 316, 318, 333, 415; in Ambrose 45; in Basil 31, 32, 34, 343, 344; in Benedict 92–95, 418; in Cassian 58–59; in Jerome 44–50

Asceticon, of Basil 13, 32, 34, 50, 67, 344, 450

authority *237, 239, 291*; of abbot 558; of Scripture 558; source of 349, 378

avarice *267*; 559 (*See* private ownership)

baptism, and monastic profession 15, 441, 456; and penance 415, 428

bishop, as having jurisdiction *277, 281, 285*; role in installation of abbot 371–378

blessing, by abbot *205, 207, 213, 293*; by guests *259*; by priests *273*; by seniors *279, 293*; by visitors *289*; for kitchen servers *235*; for reader *237*

books, in Lent *251*; 29

canticle, Gospel *207, 213*; of Deuteronomy *209*; of Prophets *207, 209*; of the Three Young Men 403–404

care and concern, of abbot, for excommunicated *223*; for sick *225*; of cellarer, for sick, children, guests and poor *229*; for poor and pilgrims *259*; 559

Carthusians 127, 128

celibacy 4, 306, 308, 309, 310, 315, 317

cellarer, qualities of *227–229*; special care of sick, children, guests and poor *229*; responsible for tools, etc. *233*; excused from kitchen service *233*; 370; 559, 572

cenobite, strong kind of monks *169, 171*; contrasted with anchorite 30, 67, 68; Augustine on 62; Cassian as 58; in monastic tradition 301, 303, 308, 313–319; in Egyptian tradition 337–343; obedience for 448

chapter, as monastic assembly 82; General Chapter 133

charism 74, 77, 342

chastity *185*, 310

children (*See* young)

Christ, follow *183*; love of *183, 187, 203*; help of *297*; king *157*; rock *163*; pray for enemies for sake of *185*; serve sick as *235*; welcome guests as *255, 257*; abbot holds place of *173*; prefer nothing to *295*; abbot holds place of 370, 378; oneness in 367; covenant with 424, 452; conversion to 428; as rock 475; as

621